terra australis 41

Terra Australis reports the results of archaeological and related research within the south and east of Asia, though mainly Australia, New Guinea and island Melanesia — lands that remained terra australis incognita to generations of prehistorians. Its subject is the settlement of the diverse environments in this isolated quarter of the globe by peoples who have maintained their discrete and traditional ways of life into the recent recorded or remembered past and at times into the observable present.

List of volumes in Terra Australis

Volume 1: Burrill Lake and Currarong: Coastal Sites in Southern New South Wales. R.J. Lampert (1971)

Volume 2: Ol Tumbuna: Archaeological Excavations in the Eastern Central Highlands, Papua New Guinea. J.P. White (1972)

Volume 3: New Guinea Stone Age Trade: The Geography and Ecology of Traffic in the Interior. I. Hughes (1977)

Volume 4: Recent Prehistory in Southeast Papua. B. Egloff (1979)

Volume 5: The Great Kartan Mystery. R. Lampert (1981)

Volume 6: Early Man in North Queensland: Art and Archaeology in the Laura Area. A. Rosenfeld, D. Horton and J. Winter (1981)

Volume 7: The Alligator Rivers: Prehistory and Ecology in Western Arnhem Land. C. Schrire (1982)

Volume 8: Hunter Hill, Hunter Island: Archaeological Investigations of a Prehistoric Tasmanian Site. S. Bowdler (1984)

Volume 9: Coastal South-West Tasmania: The Prehistory of Louisa Bay and Maatsuyker Island. R. Vanderwal and D. Horton (1984)

Volume 10: The Emergence of Mailu. G. Irwin (1985)

Volume 11: Archaeology in Eastern Timor, 1966–67. I. Glover (1986)

Volume 12: Early Tongan Prehistory: The Lapita Period on Tongatapu and its Relationships. J. Poulsen (1987)

Volume 13: Coobool Creek. P. Brown (1989)

Volume 14: 30,000 Years of Aboriginal Occupation: Kimberley, North-West Australia. S. O'Connor (1999)

Volume 15: Lapita Interaction. G. Summerhayes (2000)

Volume 16: The Prehistory of Buka: A Stepping Stone Island in the Northern Solomons. S. Wickler (2001)

Volume 17: The Archaeology of Lapita Dispersal in Oceania. G.R. Clark, A.J. Anderson and T. Vunidilo (2001)

Volume 18: An Archaeology of West Polynesian Prehistory. A. Smith (2002)

Volume 19: Phytolith and Starch Research in the Australian-Pacific-Asian Regions: The State of the Art. D. Hart and L. Wallis (2003)

Volume 20: The Sea People: Late-Holocene Maritime Specialisation in the Whitsunday Islands, Central Queensland. B. Barker (2004)

Volume 21: What's Changing: Population Size or Land-Use Patterns? The Archaeology of Upper Mangrove Creek, Sydney Basin. V. Attenbrow (2004)

Volume 22: The Archaeology of the Aru Islands, Eastern Indonesia. S. O'Connor, M. Spriggs and P. Veth (2005)

Volume 23: Pieces of the Vanuatu Puzzle: Archaeology of the North, South and Centre. S. Bedford (2006)

Volume 24: Coastal Themes: An Archaeology of the Southern Curtis Coast, Queensland. S. Ulm (2006)

Volume 25: Lithics in the Land of the Lightning Brothers: The Archaeology of Wardaman Country, Northern Territory. C. Clarkson (2007)

Volume 26: Oceanic Explorations: Lapita and Western Pacific Settlement. S. Bedford, C. Sand and S. P. Connaughton (2007)

Volume 27: Dreamtime Superhighway: Sydney Basin Rock Art and Prehistoric Information Exchange. J. McDonald (2008)

Volume 28: New Directions in Archaeological Science. A. Fairbairn, S. O'Connor and B. Marwick (2008)

Volume 29: Islands of Inquiry: Colonisation, Seafaring and the Archaeology of Maritime Landscapes. G. Clark, F. Leach and S. O'Connor (2008)

Volume 30: Archaeological Science Under a Microscope: Studies in Residue and Ancient DNA Analysis in Honour of Thomas H. Loy. M. Haslam, G. Robertson, A. Crowther, S. Nugent and L. Kirkwood (2009)

Volume 31: The Early Prehistory of Fiji. G. Clark and A. Anderson (2009)

Volume 32: Altered Ecologies: Fire, Climate and Human Influence on Terrestrial Landscapes. S. Haberle, J. Stevenson and M. Prebble (2010)

Volume 33: Man Bac: The Excavation of a Neolithic Site in Northern Vietnam: The Biology. M. Oxenham, H. Matsumura and N. Kim Dung (2011)

Volume 34: Peopled Landscapes: Archaeological and Biogeographic Approaches to Landscapes. S. Haberle and B. David.

Volume 35: Pacific Island Heritage: Archaeology, Identity & Community. Jolie Liston, Geoffrey Clark and Dwight Alexander (2011)

Volume 36: Transcending the Culture–Nature Divide in Cultural Heritage: Views from the Asia-Pacific. Sally Brockwell, Sue O'Connor and Denis Byrne (2013)

Volume 37: Taking the High Ground: The archaeology of Rapa, a fortified island in remote East Polynesia. Atholl Anderson and Douglas J. Kennett (2012)

Volume 38: Life on the Margins: An Archaeological Investigation of Late Holocene Economic Variability, Blue Mud Bay, Northern Australia. Patrick Faulkner (2013)

Volume 39: Prehistoric Marine Resource Use in the Indo-Pacific Regions. Rintaro Ono, David Addison, Alex Morrison (eds) (2013)

Volume 40: 4000 Years of Migration and Cultural Exchange: The Archaeology of the Batanes Islands, Northern Philippines. Peter Bellwood and Eusebio Dizon (eds) (2013) terra australis 41

Degei's Descendants

Spirits, Place and People in Pre-Cession Fiji

Aubrey Parke

Edited by

Matthew Spriggs and Deryck Scarr

Australian National University

PRESS

ANU PRESS

© 2014 ANU Press

Published by ANU Press
The Australian National University
Canberra ACT 0200 Australia
Email: anupress@anu.edu.au
Web: http://press.anu.edu.au

National Library of Australia Cataloguing-in-Publication entry

Author: Parke, Aubrey L., author.

Title: Degei's descendants : spirits, place and people in pre-cession Fiji / Aubrey Parke

                edited by Matthew Spriggs and Deryck Scarr.

ISBN: 9781925021813 (paperback); 9781925021844 (ebook)

Series: Terra Australis ; 41.

Subjects: Parke, Aubrey L.

                Mythology, Fijian.

                Fiji--Civilization.

                Fiji--History.

                Fiji--Social life and customs.

Other Authors/Contributors:

                Spriggs, Matthew, 1954- editor.

                Scarr, Deryck, editor.

Dewey Number: 996.11

The cover photograph is of Navatu Crag or Uluinavatu, Ra, northern Viti Levu. It is a very taboo area associated with the myths of origin of the people of that region and with the immediate descendants of the culture hero Degei. Photograph by Matthew Spriggs, November 2013.

Cover design by Nic Welbourn and layout by ANU Press

Contents

Aubrey Parke: An Enthusiastic Amateur in Fiji?

Matthew Spriggs

Over the next 16 years [after Gifford's 1947 project] the only archaeological work was carried out by enthusiastic amateurs. One of these was Aubrey Parke... (Best 1993:396)

Background and Career

Aubrey Laurence Parke was born on 11 November 1925, the son of Laurence Stanley Parke (1890–1940) and Mildred Frances Parke. He was born some two years after his father participated in the Dorset Minor Counties Cricket Championship team. Aubrey—no mean hand with the bat himself—came from a long line of cricketers, his grandfather Laurence P. Parke (1860–1929) having participated in the same Counties championship in 1902. Aubrey's father was the only one of three cricketing brothers to have survived the Great War, and Aubrey was presumably named after one of the two that didn't return, John Aubrey Parke (1892–1915). The third brother was Walter Evelyn Parke (1891–1914), who merited an obituary in *Wisden* such was his prowess on the pitch as a left-handed batsman. The family had a military and legal background, which included service in places such as the Crimea, Jamaica and even a diplomatic posting in Mexico.[1]

Aubrey was born in Moreton, Dorset, while the previous few generations hailed from Henbury House in Sturminster Marshall parish, near Wimborne. Henbury House had been bought in 1847 by his great-great-grandfather Charles (born Jamaica 1791). The family are traceable back to Whitbeck Hall in Cumberland in the 1620s. His father Laurence Stanley Parke took up the position of Commissioner of Police in Aden, then a British colony, leaving the family, including a younger sister Bridget, to be raised by relatives. The father died in Aden in 1940. Bridget recalled Aubrey's interest in archaeology from a very young age, with many surface-collecting expeditions across the Downs near their home at Sixpenny Handley. His collections from that time can now apparently be seen in the Dorchester Museum. He participated in Mortimer Wheeler's classic excavation at Maiden Castle Iron Age hillfort at the age of about 12. His Aunt Merry, who lived nearby, recalled that although very young, he was trusted as an active participant because of his clear understanding of archaeological technique.[2]

Aubrey spent 1939–1941 living with his great-uncle Colonel Henry Aubrey Cartwright (born c.1858 in London) at Upwood, just outside the village of Sixpenny Handley. It seems to have been there that he developed an interest in local myths and legends, which he collected assiduously at that time and later published in *Folklore* (Parke 1963). His uncle and aunt Mildred (née Parke,

---

1   Information here on Aubrey's family comes, perhaps most appropriately, in part from a cricketing website (cricketarchive.com/Archive/Players), consulted July 29 2012, augmented by information from his son John (personal communication, July 2012) and from the eulogy presented at his funeral service on 26 February 2007 by his daughter Fiona Parke; I have drawn freely on this latter source throughout the paper. Wider details of his family come from Burke (1912), and from census information presented at (www.opcdorset.org/Sturminster/SturminsterMarshall), again consulted July 19 2012.

2   Information from the eulogy presented at his 2007 funeral service by Fiona Parke, and from my own conversations with Aubrey over the years.

born c.1859), the latter a noted cat breeder, were both donors to Pitt Rivers' second collection after 1880, which became the basis for the Pitt Rivers Museum in Oxford, so a continuing interest in archaeology may well have been fostered by them.[3]

Aubrey was educated at Hordle House and Winchester schools. Upon leaving Winchester in 1942, he joined the Royal Air Force as a navigator/bomb aimer and saw active service. Like so many, he never talked about it much afterwards. One thing he did talk about was an excavation of Bokerley Dyke adjacent to one of the airfields he was based at in 1942–43. A later publication on this earthwork noted that his work was carried out under 'difficult wartime conditions' (Bowen 1990:21). When I asked him what these were, he told me that German planes were machine-gunning the field at the time, but he felt quite safe as his excavation pit was rather deep. After the War he read Greats—Greek and Latin—at Lincoln College, Oxford, and participated in the Oxford Scientific Expedition to Tunisia in 1950 in search of a unique hot water shrimp, *Thermosbaena mirabilis*. The shrimp was finally located in the women's baths at El Hamma, necessitating special permission from the Caliph and a police escort to investigate. The report of this discovery in the *Illustrated London News* mentioned that 'Aubrey Parke, archaeologist...was able to examine some of the prolific Roman and megalithic remains in the area'.[4] Upon leaving Oxford he spent a year based in London preparing for overseas service in the British Colonial Service, and attending lectures at the Institute of Archaeology and the School of Oriental and African Studies (SOAS). He claimed such luminaries as archaeologist Stuart Piggott, anthropologist Raymond Firth and linguist George Milner as mentors at this time. He also found time to excavate a bell barrow on Oakley Down, Dorset in what must have been a busy year (Parke 1951, 1952, 1954a). It was the first excavation at the site since Pitt Rivers himself had dug there in 1898.

In 1951 he was posted to Fiji and worked there for 20 years, initially in the Western District, and during the 1950s and 1960s collected much of the information presented in his 2006 thesis and here in slightly revised form. He held various official positions as discussed in his Preface including: District Officer for Ra, for Lautoka, Nadi and the Yasawa Group (twice), for Suva, for Navua, and during a period in 1964 for the island of Rotuma, as Deputy Secretary for Fijian Affairs, and as Commissioner for the Northern Division. These various positions, not an exhaustive list, allowed him to travel widely in the Colony, particular on Viti Levu, Vanua Levu, the Yasawas and of course Rotuma. He was also a Trustee of the Fiji Museum and its archaeological adviser.

In 1955, after four years' service he went home to England on leave. He seems to have got right back into the swing of Dorset archaeology during this 'time off', directing excavations at Greyhound Yard/St Rowland's Chapel Site in Dorchester over two seasons 1955–56. Remains of Roman and medieval buildings were recovered (reported in Farrar 1957, Draper 1981). The excavation archive is in the Dorset County Museum. He also found time to meet his wife of 50 years, Tamaris, at the time a cordon bleu chef, and after a whirlwind romance of 6 weeks they married and she relocated to Fiji 4 months after his return in 1956, the plane journey at the time taking 5 days from London.[5] In his Preface he describes her, one hopes somewhat tongue-in-cheek as his "long-suffering research assistant", acknowledging that she was 'a marvel with the trowel, the camera and the measuring tape'.

After Fiji became independent on 10 October 1970 Aubrey soon moved on, doubtless feeling he had accomplished a job well done. He settled in Canberra taking up an invitation to become

---

3   Information from the Pitt Rivers Museum website (web.prm.ox.ac.uk/rpr/attachments/), "Donors to Pitt Rivers Second Collection", accessed 29 July 2012.

4   Illustrated London News, December 2 1950: 917.

5   I am again indebted to the eulogy by Fiona Parke for this information.

Administrative Officer for the recently established Canberra College of Advanced Education, now the University of Canberra. He restarted his academic career at this time, obtaining an MA at the Australian National University in 1981 for his thesis *Clause Structure in Fijian* (Parke 1981). A B Litt in Fijian archaeology followed, and then in 1992, after having retired in 1990, he embarked on full-time study for a PhD. It was a very rough road over the next 14 years and relied tremendously on the support of his wife, Tamaris. Patrick Guinness recounts that his medical problems were such that in 2002, he had medical certificates covering 10 of the 12 months of study. He bore his afflictions with quiet determination, a determination that paid off in October 2006 when in a formal academic ceremony at his hospital bedside he was awarded his degree, the second oldest student, at very nearly 81, ever to receive a PhD from The Australian National University. Patrick Guinness recounts that soon afterwards he was summoned to Aubrey's bedside for a consultation on publication plans for the thesis, and for four further papers that he wanted to work on. Sadly, these were not to be and he died on 20 February 2007, in his 82nd year.[6]

Although I had seen Aubrey around ANU, I had no real idea who he was until I joined the then-Department (now School) of Archaeology and Anthropology as a Professor in 1997 and soon after took over as Head of Department. I must admit I found his old-school courtesy, indeed deference, to the Head somewhat unnerving; being of a later generation I suspected there must be irony involved, but I don't think there was. I also saw first hand the tremendous determination that he had both to finish his thesis and to return the results of his wider research to the host communities concerned. Given his deteriorating health he realised that he might not have much time to reach his goals. Over the 11 years from 1993 to 2003, after which his health curtailed much of his writing, he produced two substantial monographs on Rotuma and a further nine papers that I know of, six of them in internationally refereed journals. Apart from one paper that completed his Rotuman work, the rest concentrated on aspects of the history and archaeology of the two main islands of Viti Levu and Vanua Levu and their satellite islands. This book, based on his thesis, is his major contribution in this regard.

He definitely had much more to contribute, not least on the linguistic study of the various communalects of Fijian spoken on Viti Levu. The linguist Alfred Schütz, working in Fiji in 1962, had noted that: 'At the time of the writer's own survey Aubrey Parke was completing a grammar and a word list of the Navatu dialect in Ra; material for a study of Navatu kinship terms; and word lists for certain Ra and Ba dialects. He was also beginning to collect word lists from the Sigatoka area, planning eventually to produce a grammar of that dialect' (Schütz 1963:259). He produced a 146-page report on the Navatu dialect, undated but possibly in 1954 (Parke 1954b), and drew upon his linguistic researches both in his MA thesis (Parke 1981) and throughout the current book. Professor R.M.W. Dixon acknowledges Aubrey in his *Grammar of Boumaa Fijian* (1988), noting that he 'speaks the language fluently; we had four or five long sessions together, in Canberra, in which he went through the grammar, chapter by chapter, helping me to amend and improve it' (Dixon 1988:xii). But much remained to be done. Very sadly, his extensive archive was destroyed in the inevitable downsizing of belongings that follows a death.

An Enthusiastic Amateur?

The quotation that begins this appreciation suggests merely a very minor contribution to scholarship. In defence of the author of it, the date of composition must be mentioned—1993 was just on the verge of Aubrey's amazingly productive period of publication. He had previously only published five papers on his Fijian and Rotuman studies, two of them in the limited-circulation proceedings of the Fiji Society, and a short linguistic monograph on Rotuman—see

---

6   Much of this information comes from Patrick Guinness' eulogy given at the funeral.

the bibliography of this book for references. His last publication had been more than a decade earlier. His work was barely mentioned in the only reasonably up-to-date summary of Fijian archaeology at the time (Frost 1979). It is fair to say that Aubrey had, in effect, been hiding his light under a bushel.

I have to admit that until I came to prepare this piece, I too was almost completely ignorant of his contribution. I had never read his seminal paper, delivered to the Fiji Society, on 11 April 1960 that constitutes a masterly overview of what was and wasn't known at the time about 'Archaeology in Fiji'. It was eventually published in 1965, a victim of 'Pacific Time' clearly (Parke 1965)! By then Bruce Palmer had taken over the Directorship of the Fiji Museum and had begun an aggressive program of archaeological survey and engagement with overseas scholars in Auckland and elsewhere to open up Fiji to outside archaeological interest. Aubrey's earlier contribution was thus overshadowed, and he was too modest to push forward his continuing claims to archaeological expertise.

In part this was because his particular interest was in what he called protohistoric studies, the melding of oral tradition, recorded in his case in the vernacular, and its materialization in archaeological and 'natural' sacred sites relating to the recent Pre-European past. The push in Fiji and elsewhere among most other archaeologists was to find the earliest sites of human occupation in the islands and to build a chronological framework through sequencing of pottery styles linked to radiocarbon dating (Frost 1979). His own interests may have seemed quaint and 'non-scientific', hence amateur.

But let us go back to the beginning of his time in Fiji, and this evaluation appears seriously flawed. When Aubrey arrived in Fiji in 1951 he would have been the most highly-trained archaeologist living and working in the Western Pacific, having absorbed the classic British prehistoric site excavation techniques of Wheeler and Piggott. Jack Golson, coming from the same archaeological background, was not to arrive in Auckland to take up the first Australasian academic post dedicated to regional prehistory for another three years.

Aubrey's problem was that he had no institutional support to conduct serious excavations in Fiji, and indeed was employed to do something quite different; to assist in administering a British colony. While he could doubtless argue that a knowledge of the customs and traditions of the Fijians was a valuable skill in dealing with land and other administrative issues, the same could not have been argued at the time for his archaeological interests, which would have had to be largely confined to weekend excursions. Nevertheless he was able to take advantage of the clearly-comprehensive libraries of the Colonial Secretary and Dr H.S. Evans in Fiji, and was familiar with Alphonse Riesenfeld's magisterial compilation of 'pre-modern' sources for knowledge of Western Pacific archaeology, *The Megalithic Culture of Melanesia*; he cites Riesenfeld (1950) in his 1960 paper (Parke 1965).

The 'modern' era of archaeology in Fiji had been ushered in only a few years before his arrival, when Berkeley professor E.W. Gifford had conducted surveys and excavations on Viti Levu, the results of which were published in 1951 in a major archaeological monograph and an article on 'Fijian Mythology, Legends and Archaeology' (Gifford 1951a, b), and in a much lesser-known monograph *Tribes of Viti Levu and their Origin Places* in the following year (Gifford 1952). Radiocarbon dating was invented by Willard Libby in 1949 and Gifford was quick to take up Libby's offer to date samples (Gifford 1955). Aubrey immediately got in contact with Gifford upon his arrival in Fiji and in his 1960 paper quotes from a 1953 letter he received revealing details of the first radiocarbon dates from Fijian sites that Gifford had received from the laboratory:

The carbon-14 date is 1000 A.D. and is based on an ample sample of charcoal from a hearth that lay on sterile soil, 30 inches deep in the rock shelter at Navatu. With this age for 30 inches deep, I anticipate that the bottom of the deposit outside the rock shelter must be much older. It goes down ten feet as you will see in consulting my paper. At location B the deposit goes down to twelve feet. I recently submitted a sample from 96 inches deep at Location B, Navatu, but it was too small, only 3 grams. Unfortunately I did not get sufficient charcoal from the deeper parts of the Navatu and Vuda sites. It is too bad, because an adequate sample would give us the approximate date of the founding of the settlements. My guess would not be later than the time of Christ. I recently obtained a date for a New Caledonian sample I dug last year at 78–84 inches. The date is 73 A.D. (Parke 1965:36).

Thus Aubrey was one of the first to hear of the Fijian dates two years ahead of publication and of the exciting dates Gifford was also receiving from his 1952 excavations in New Caledonia, including at the eponymous site of Lapita. In 1953 Aubrey was truly at the heart of Western Pacific archaeology; recall Jack Golson hadn't yet packed his bags for the journey out! As recognised by Best (1993), Aubrey's 1960 paper included the first classification of Fijian archaeological site types and it began the systematisation of Fijian archaeology, taken over in the 1960s by Bruce Palmer, Roger Green and others.

Aubrey realised what the problems were for a clear understanding of Fijian prehistory, the most pressing being chronology and sequence building. He had a very British scepticism of the—at the time very new—technique of radiocarbon dating, presumably communicated to him by Stuart Piggott among others. He wrote: 'Even when sufficient carbon is available the resulting date is not necessarily reliable. Certainly British archaeologists do not generally pin such faith in this method of dating as apparently do their confreres across the Atlantic' (1965:11). This attitude lingered a long time in Britain; dying echoes of it were still voiced when I began my own undergraduate training there in 1973. So Aubrey was thrown back upon relative dating of artefacts linked to genealogical dating by number of generations, the pre-radiocarbon staple of much of Polynesian archaeology. This necessitated linking sites mentioned in myths and legends to such genealogies, very much the method employed in this book. Aubrey's long-standing interest in legends and oral traditions, the pertinence of them in this case to issues of land ownership and traditional governance, and Gifford's published but largely unrecognised attempts in this regard combined with British scepticism of radiocarbon dating to drive his own archaeological agenda, both in Fiji and in 1964 on Rotuma.

In the 1960s and later Aubrey's type of approach appeared somewhat old-fashioned to the newly 'tech-savvy' archaeologists of the Australasian centres. Important too was a growing scepticism of the value of oral traditions as history, and an unmasking of those in New Zealand of 'The Great Fleet' as being an illegitimate melding of disparate traditions to create a seemingly unified history (Simmons 1969, 1976; Sorrenson 1979). French scholars were much more open to the kind of approach that Aubrey was perfecting in Fiji, and José Garanger's stunning results in the then New Hebrides in relation to archaeology and traditions of Roi Mata and of the Kuwae eruption of the AD 1450s (Garanger 1972) provided a resounding confirmation of the value of combining oral traditions and archaeology. Garanger's work was recognised among Anglophone scholars, but largely ignored in their own practice for many years after. Pat Kirch and Doug Yen's work on Tikopia, which clearly drew inspiration from it, is one honourable exception (Kirch and Yen 1982). Much of what today passes for landscape archaeology or cultural geography in the wider region is largely a development from the kind of research Aubrey undertook in Fiji and Rotuma; ironic, as these are claimed to be very much 'post-modern' theoretical pursuits.

When he could, Aubrey did also excavate—although the records of most of his efforts in this regard are lost, preventing an evaluation. The necessity of rebuilding the Council House on the ceremonial mound of Navatanitawake on the island of Bau, led to an early Western Pacific example of salvage archaeology in 1970, albeit much constrained by the sacredness of the site. It was also an early example of multidisciplinary field investigation of a burial site, otherwise a feature mainly of new millennium practice:

> Members of the project team included Mr. W. Bullock, a Government surgeon with experience in osteometrics, who came to Bau and measured bones and made comments on their characteristics; Mr. M. Maberly and Mr. Titus, two Government dentists, who spent some time on the island in order to study the teeth and jaws and to make plaster casts; and Mr. Les Thompson, a Government surveyor, who prepared survey plans…officers of the Fiji Departments of Geology and Forestry who commented on the stones and charcoal (Parke 1998; cf. Parke 1993).

In his writing up of this work more than two decades after the excavation, Aubrey also drew on bioanthropological opinion from Prof. Colin Groves and fellow-student Peter Dowling, the study of animal bones by Dr Wilfred Shawcross, also of ANU, and comments on his paper by Professors Marshall Sahlins of Chicago, and Dave Burley of Simon Fraser University in Canada (Parke 1998). Another 1970 study was carried out in association with anthropologists Ron Crocombe and Asesela Ravuvu of the University of the South Pacific in Suva (Parke 1997).

Even in 1960, the signs that the cultural heritage of Fiji was fast disappearing because of economic development, particularly of the sugar industry, were also apparent to Aubrey. His suggestion was eminently practical, if also showing his colours as a budget-conscious functionary of the Empire:

> I suggest that an archaeologist be invited to visit the Colony, at no expense to Government, and to carry out a proper survey of the ancient sites, and after consultation with the owners, to recommend to the Board of Trustees of the Museum, and thence to Government, which objects, if any, should be declared to be monuments under the ordinance. This would serve the purpose of providing a schedule of ancient monuments in the Colony, which would thereby be afforded official recognition because of their importance (Parke 1965:36–7).

One wonders to what extent this suggestion led indirectly or directly to the 1963 appointment of Bruce Palmer to the Directorship of the Fiji Museum and the renaissance in archaeological research into Fiji's early prehistory that followed?

Aubrey's own renewed vigour in archaeological pursuits at this time came as a result of his posting to Rotuma for a period of four months in 1964 as District Officer. In this isolated outpost of the Colony he could clearly do pretty much as he pleased with his time, and he devoted an amazing energy to research on the 'Legends, Language and Archaeology of Rotuma' (Parke 1969), which ultimately led to three monographs and three other academic papers on these subjects—all listed in his bibliography. They all give generous acknowledgement to previous studies of the island and are meticulous bibliographically. Notable is Aubrey's acknowledgement of the immediately preceding work of anthropologist Alan Howard, later a distinguished Professor at the University of Hawaii and a colleague of mine there in the 1980s.

One of Aubrey's Rotuma books is subtitled 'Traditions of Rotuma and its Dependencies, with excerpts from an archaeologist's field notebook' (Parke 2001). To my shame I had never heard of this work until now, although I suspect I must also blame Aubrey's extreme modesty for never bringing it to my attention. In my own recent research I have been trying to construct an archaeology that is sensitive to indigenous interests and places importance on the kinds of sites that people locally in Vanuatu find significant, and which records for the future traditions and places that may be lost otherwise. In looking at *Seksek e Hatana/Strolling in Hatana* (Parke 2001) I realise that Aubrey was there long before me, in what I was imagining was a rather innovative approach in the region.

All those who have conducted research in relatively remote areas of the Pacific can recall times when it all seems to go so well—the findings are significant, the field experiences overwhelmingly pleasant, the landowners interested and cooperative. Clearly on Rotuma in 1964 it all came together for Aubrey. We also all have those moments when we are tempted to undertake actions that could potentially be disastrous. I loved Aubrey's own laconic description of one such moment, when visiting some Rotuman cave sites 'would have entailed the erection of a winch to enable me to go up and down the 80 foot pit (there was no other way up or down the sheer walls). But pressure was put on me to desist—and I regret to say that I gave way to pressure and so I cannot record a first hand account of the depths and caves of Mamfiri. The last man to try apparently passed out from lack of oxygen' (Parke 1969:112–3).

Aubrey Parke was no amateur. In terms of those living and working in the Western Pacific in the early 1950s before Jack Golson's arrival, he was without doubt the most highly trained. He was in touch with those, such as Professor E.W. Gifford, who were kick-starting archaeology in the region after World War II, and he was among the pioneers of an archaeology informed by oral traditions that is only now really coming back into its own, after a period when such oral sources were largely disparaged. He operated entirely in local languages wherever he worked, and was evidently a gifted linguist as well as archaeologist. He has been largely ignored in the history of archaeology in the region because the vast majority of his publications came long after he had left Fiji, in the years between 1993 and 2003 and culminating in his 2006 thesis, which will constitute his final work. The publication of his very important stock-take and summary of what was then known in Fijian archaeology in 1960 was delayed for five years as well as being inaccessible to most scholars outside Fiji (Parke 1965). Another important paper on his Rotuma work written in 1965 also had a delayed publication in the same journal (Parke 1969). Apart from these two papers and a two-page summary of his Rotuman research published in the *Journal of the Polynesian Society* (Parke 1964), he had no further archaeology-related works published until after he had left Fiji.

With the loss of his archive, the opportunity to evaluate his contribution fully has gone. But enough remains to make it clear that although he was an extremely unassuming man he was a uniquely significant figure in the development of Pacific archaeology. It is indeed sad that the discipline did not at all realise this until after his death and that he did not receive the recognition he deserved.

Aubrey Parke at his PhD graduation ceremony at the age of nearly 81 in hospital in Canberra on 21st October 2006. His award represented a lifetime's dedication to anthropology, archaeology and linguistics, particularly in Fiji.

Photo: John Parke

References

Best, S. 1993. In the halls of the mountain king. Fijian and Samoan fortifications: Comparison and analysis. *Journal of the Polynesian Society* 102(4):385–448.

Bowen, H.C. (ed. B.N. Eagles) 1990. *The Archaeology of Bokerley Dyke*. HMSO, London.

Burke, B. 1912. A *Genealogical and Heraldic History of the Landed Gentry of Great Britain and Ireland*, 2 vols (revised by A.C. Fox-Davies). Harrison, London.

Dixon, R.M.W. 1988. *A Grammar of Boumaa Fijian*. University of Chicago Press, Chicago.

Draper, J. 1981. St Rowald's Chapel, South Street, Dorchester. *Proceedings of the Dorset Natural History and Archaeology Society* 102:112–114.

Farrar, R.A.H. 1957. Archaeological fieldwork in Dorset 1956. *Proceedings of the Dorset Natural History and Archaeology Society* 78:73–92.

Frost, E.L. 1979. Fiji. In J.D. Jennings (ed.) *The Prehistory of Polynesia*, pp. 61–81. ANU Press, Canberra.

Garanger, J. 1972. *Archéologie des Nouvelles-Hébrides*. ORSTOM, Paris.

Gifford, E.W. 1951a. *Archaeological Excavations in Fiji. Anthropological Records* 13(3). University of California Press, Berkeley.

Gifford, E.W. 1951b. Fijian Mythology, Legends and Archaeology. In W.J. Fischel (ed.) *Semitic and Oriental Studies: A volume presented to William Popper, Professor of Semitic languages, Emeritus, on the occasion of his 75th birthday, October 29 1949*, pp. 167–177. *University of California, Publications in Semitic Philology 11*. University of California Press, Berkeley.

Gifford, E.W. 1952. *Tribes of Viti Levu and their Origin Places, Anthropological Records* 13(5). University of California Press, Berkeley.

Gifford, E.W. 1955. Six Fijian radiocarbon dates. *Journal of the Polynesian Society*, 64:240.

Kirch, P.V. and D.E. Yen. 1982. *Tikopia: Prehistory and Ecology of a Polynesian Outlier. Bernice P. Bishop Museum Bulletin* 238. Bishop Museum Press, Honolulu.

Parke, A.L. 1951. Barrows on Oakley Down, Wimborne St Giles. *Proceedings of the Dorset Natural History and Archaeology Society* 72:91–2.

Parke, A.L. 1952. The excavation of a bell barrow on Oakley Down, Wimborne St Giles. *Proceedings of the Dorset Natural History and Archaeology Society* 73:103–4.

Parke, A.L. 1954a. The excavation of a bell barrow, Oakley Down, Wimborne St Giles. *Proceedings of the Dorset Natural History and Archaeology Society* 75:36–44.

Parke, A.L. 1954b. *The Navatu Dialect of Fijian*. Manuscript 146 pp.

Parke, A.L. 1963. The folklore of Sixpenny Handley, Dorset, Part I. *Folklore* 74(3):481–7.

Parke, A.L. 1964. Rotuma: a brief anthropological survey. *Journal of the Polynesian Society* 73(4):436–7.

Parke, A.L. 1965. Archaeology in Fiji. *Transactions and Proceedings of the Fiji Society* 8 (for 1960–61):10–42.

Parke, A. L. 1969. Legends, language and archaeology of Rotuma. *Transactions and Proceedings of the Fiji Society for the Year 1964 and 1965*:97–115.

Parke, A.L. 1981. Clause Structure in Fijian. Unpublished M.A. Thesis, The Australian National University.

Parke, A.L. 1993. Investigations at Vatanitawake: a ceremonial mound on the island of Bau, Fiji. *Bulletin of the Indo-Pacific Prehistory Association* 13:94–115.

Parke, A.L. 1997. The Waimaro Carved Human Figures: Various Aspects of Symbolism of Unity and Identification of Fijian Polities. *Journal of Pacific History*, 32(2):209–216.

Parke, A.L. 1998. Navatanitawake Ceremonial Burial Mound, Bau, Fiji: Some results of 1970 investigations. *Archaeology in Oceania* 33(1):20–27.

Parke, A.L. 2001. *Seksek e Hatana/ Strolling on Hatana: Traditions of Rotuma and its dependencies, with examples from an archaeologist's field notebook.* Suva: Institute of Pacific Studies, University of the South Pacific.

Riesenfeld, A. 1950. *The Megalithic Culture of Melanesia*. Brill, Leiden.

Schütz, A. 1963. Survey for the study of Fijian dialects. *Journal of the Polynesian Society* 72(3):254–60.

Simmons, D.R. 1969. A New Zealand myth: Kupe, Toi and the "Fleet". *New Zealand Journal of History* 3(1):14–31.

Simmons, D.R. 1976. *The Great New Zealand Myth. A study of the discovery and origin traditions of the Maori.* Reid, Wellington.

Sorrenson, M.P.K. 1979. *Maori Origins and Migrations. The genesis of some Pakeha myths and legends.* Auckland University Press, Auckland.

Acknowledgements

Aubrey Parke

I am grateful for having been granted a Postgraduate Research award by The Australian National University, and an ANUTECH scholarship.

I must record the inspiration given to me, before I went to Fiji in 1951, by George Milner (Linguistics), Stuart Piggott (Archaeology), and Raymond Firth (Anthropology). On my arrival in Fiji, I was given great encouragement by G.K. Roth, R.S. Derrick, the Reverend C.M. Churchward, Ulaiasi Vosabalavu, the Reverend Kolinio Saukuru, C.H. Nott, and the Reverend A. Tippett.

In the course of my research I was assisted considerably by officers and members of the Native Lands Commission and Native Lands Trust Board; and especially by officers and members of the Fijian Affairs Office and the offices of the Roko Tui of Provinces and the Buli of the Tikina—not only in my immediate research area but also in carrying out comparative research in all parts of Fiji. I was fortunate to have close, often personal, and official connections with them over the years. Also I worked in close liaison with the Government Archivist and staff, and the Director of the Fiji Museum of which I was a member of the Board of Trustees and Archaeological Advisor.

At the beginning of my final research, I was encouraged and assisted by Ron Crocombe, Deryck Scarr, Paul Geraghty, Professor Asesela Ravuvu and his colleagues in the Centre for Pacific Studies. Outside Fiji I received the same encouragement from David Burley, Marshall Sahlins, and Richard Shutler. I must also thank the Managers and Staff of the Rakiraki Hotel, the Nadi Bay Motel and the Sheraton at Denarau, where I was welcomed and well looked after during my many visits.

I especially acknowledge with heartfelt thanks the assistance and encouragement I received from Ian Farrington and Peter Bellwood (my appointed Supervisors); Andy Pawley and Patrick Guinness (my ever-patient Advisors); Nicolas Peterson and Ian Keen (who ever encouraged me in preparing my thesis); and Kathy Callen who was always a wonderful source of strength, good cheer, knowledge and expertise in the protocol of Postgraduate Studies in the University. To Patrick Guinness I give particular thanks for his friendship, enthusiasm, assistance and advice.

These acknowledgements would not be complete without a record of appreciation of discussions and arguments with my Postgraduate Student colleagues in and around LG23 where I was formally established for some 10 years. Without their cheerful banter and occasional drinks, I doubt if I could have survived. Thanks especially to Peter Dowling, Keiko Tamura, Tom Knight and Bec Parkes.

I also acknowledge my thanks to all the traditional Turaga/Momo (Chiefs), Bete (Priests), and Mata ni Vanua (Ceremonial Officials) and other members of the 87 *Yavusa* (Socio-Political Units), most of whom, in the course of my research over the years, spent many hours discussing their respective Units, and helped me to identify many archaeological sites. It would be most invidious to name even a few of these people.

The traditional Chiefs of *Vanua* (Socio-Political Federations), and of *Matanitū* (the most extensive and powerful confederations) were always willing to help me, not only in my research area but also through out the rest of Fiji, especially the Vunivalu of Bau, the Roko Tui Dreketi of Rewa, the Tui Cakau of Cakaudrove, and Bulou Eta (the Kwa Levu of Nadroga).

I must mention the following individuals who took a great interest in my research, discussing socio-political affairs and walking with me, often for a considerable distance, to visit archaeological sites:-

Solomone of Lomolomo; Jale Silimaibau; Tanoa of Rakiraki; Apakuki Tuitavua; Emosi Tavai; Kolinio Qoro; Jotame (Matanivanua of Naivuvuni); the Momo Levu of Saunaka; the Bete of Limasa (War spirit of the Nakovaki); the Turaga ni Koro of Narewa; and the Bete of Betoraurau, Sabeto.

Finally, to Liz Walters, Sue Fraser, Marian Robson, Virginia Woodland and Karuna Honer, in partnership with my daughter Fiona Parke, who did so much in the last stages of preparing my thesis.

It would be very ungracious and ungrateful if I did not acknowledge the help from my long-suffering research assistant, Tamaris Parke, who accompanied me to many archaeological sites, often difficult to access. Together we went uphill and down the valleys, in mangrove swamps, and through mud. She was a marvel with the trowel, the camera and the measuring tape, and without her assistance my final work would surely have taken more than 14 years! Vinaka Vakalevu.

Additional Acknowledgements from the Editors

Matthew Spriggs and Deryck Scarr

The editors were originally approached by John Parke as to how Aubrey's PhD thesis could be produced as a book and circulated to interested scholars. His family was persuaded that it was of sufficient interest to be published as a refereed academic monograph and we thank Aubrey's widow Tamaris, and his children John and Fiona for their constant support and patience during its production. The text was lightly edited by us with the early copy-editing assistance of Gillian Scott, and the bibliography underwent major surgery before submission to the *Terra Australis* monograph series. We particularly thank the TA reviewers David Burley and Geoffrey Clark, and the series editors Sally Brockwell and Sue O'Connor for their agreement to publish the monograph. The Australian National Univerisity generously supported production of the volume through a publication subsidy to Matthew Spriggs, awarded in 2013. The original rather cumbersome title of the PhD was *Traditional Society in North West Fiji and its Political Development: constructing a history through the use of oral and written accounts, archaeological and linguistic evidence.* We sought to construct a more succinct title appropriate for a published work, and *Degei's Descendants* is the result. The cover photograph of Navatu Crag, central in some of the oral traditions collected by Aubrey, was taken by Matthew Spriggs during an exciting dash in Ravindra Sewak's taxi from Lautoka during a short cruise ship stopover in November 2013. Mr Sewak is commended for his safe, reliable and courteous driving.

28th December 2013

Preface

The first aim of my research is to determine, from oral accounts I recorded over a period of some fifty years, how Fijians especially in western areas of Fiji currently understand and explain (a) the origins, characteristics, development and interactions of the social and political divisions of late pre-Colonial traditional Fijian society, and (b) the general principles of traditional land tenure. The second aim is to assess the reasoning, consistency and, where possible, the historical accuracy of such understandings.

The period on which the research concentrates is the two centuries or so immediately prior to Cession. Under the Deed of Cession a number of the major chiefs of Fiji had offered to cede Fiji to Queen Victoria; and after the offer had been accepted, Fiji became a British Crown Colony on 10th October 1874. The traditional Fijian society and system of land tenure with which the project is particularly concerned are referred to in this work as 'pre-Colonial' or 'pre-Cession' Fijian society. For the sake of chronological convenience, pre-Colonial Fijian society has been divided into 'late prehistoric' and 'proto-historic' periods. 'Proto-historic' refers to the century ending at Cession in 1874 and beginning with the arrival of the first outsiders to have significant interaction with Fijians.

Other studies of Fijian traditional social structure have generally concentrated on areas in the eastern parts of Viti Levu and in other parts of Fiji to the east of the main island (the so-called Na Tu i Cake). Partly for this reason and partly because I have been familiar with the area since 1951, my investigations have concentrated on the relatively little known west (the Yasayasa vakaRa). It is hoped that the outcome of my research will now enable people to endorse more easily the line with which I introduce Chapter 1, 'But westward look, the land is bright.'

Research into pre-Colonial Fijian society began incidentally when I was an officer of the Colonial Service in the Fiji District Administration and in the Fijian Administration in the 1950s and 1960s. My experience and general investigations while a member of these two Administrations served as a background to my later formal research conducted directly in relation to this project. When I returned to carry out the latter research in the 1990s, I endeavoured to operate through both these Administrations as well as through the currently recognised socio-political units or polities.

My personal involvement in Fiji

As a member of the British Colonial Service (later Her Majesty's Overseas Civil Service), I served from 1951 to 1971 in the Fiji Civil Service, as a member of the Fiji Administrative Service. As was the usual practice, I spent part of my time as a member of the District Administration and part of the time in the Secretariat. I was also fortunate to spend some time in the Fijian Affairs Office, working with the fourteen provinces of the Fijian Administration which ran parallel with the District Administration.

I lived for a year in what is now the township of Vaileka, in the area of Rakiraki, when I was the District Officer, Ra, in the early 1950s; and my administrative duties took me to every village in the province of Ra at least once. I was also able to pay visits to archaeological and other sites, including those of special spiritual importance on the top of the Nakauvadra Range, and to hold many discussions about archaeological and socio-political matters and about local communalects.

I was District Officer for Lautoka, Nadi and the Yasawa Group for two periods in the early 1950s, and visited every village at least once and usually at least twice. During the next 17 years, I was at various times District Officer for Rotuma, for Suva and for Navua covering Namosi and Serua.

Later I held the post of Deputy Secretary for Fijian Affairs and Local Government (DSFALG), and in the course of my duties I visited all the main parts of Fiji except for the Lau Archipelago. Later I was appointed to be the Commissioner of the Northern Division which comprised the three Provinces of Bua, Cakaudrove and Macuata; and I visited all the villages in these three Provinces.

In the 1990s, during the period of my postgraduate research, many months were spent in Rakiraki and Vuda/Nadi/Nawaka. Return to the Yasawa Group was practicable only once in the 1990s, because of difficulties of transport and shortage of time. The data obtained from the earlier investigations were duly integrated with the information gained from the research undertaken in the 1990s.

It has been of assistance to me that, apart from some fluency in Standard Fijian, I have been able to achieve a sufficient working knowledge of the Rakiraki/Navatu communalects and of the western communalects, so that I was able to understand and carry on a reasonable level of conversation in either these local communalects or in Standard Fijian. During discussions with Fijians, the medium of conversation was, as far as possible, that with which the Fijians were most comfortable.

Aubrey Parke

Maps

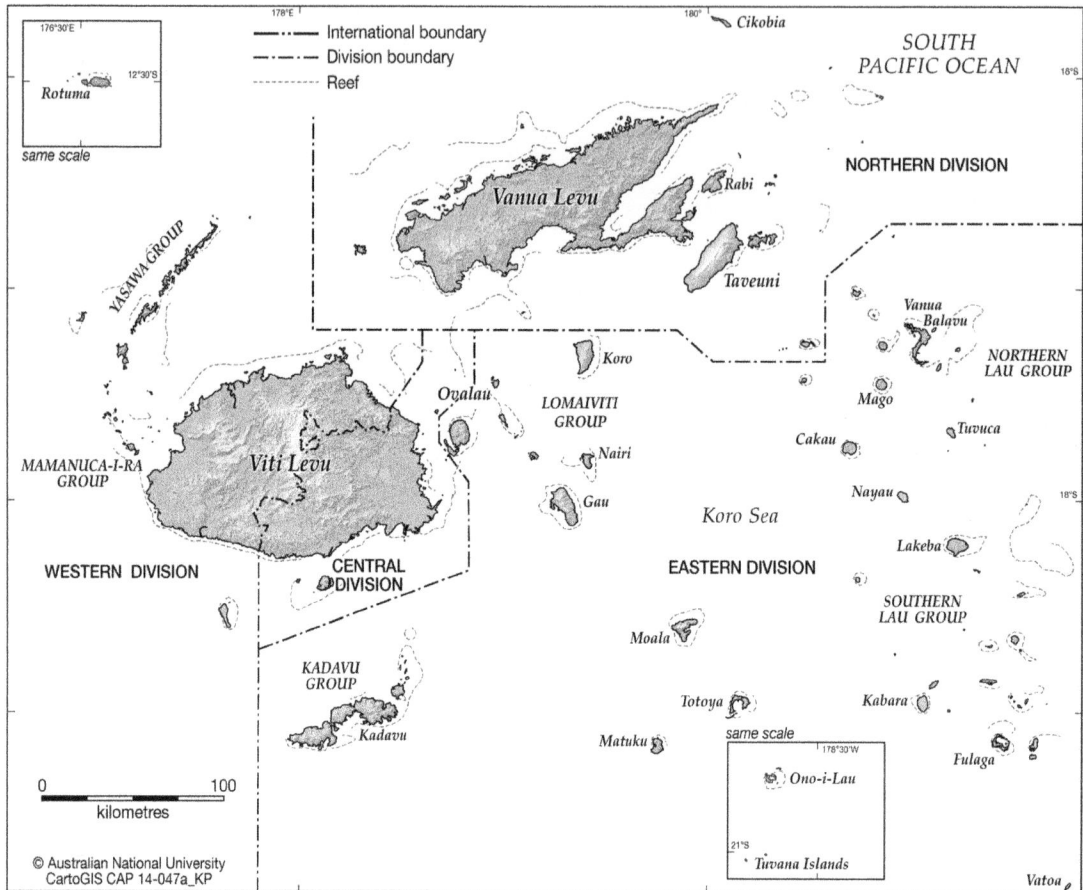

Map I The Fijian Islands

Source: ANU Carto-GIS.

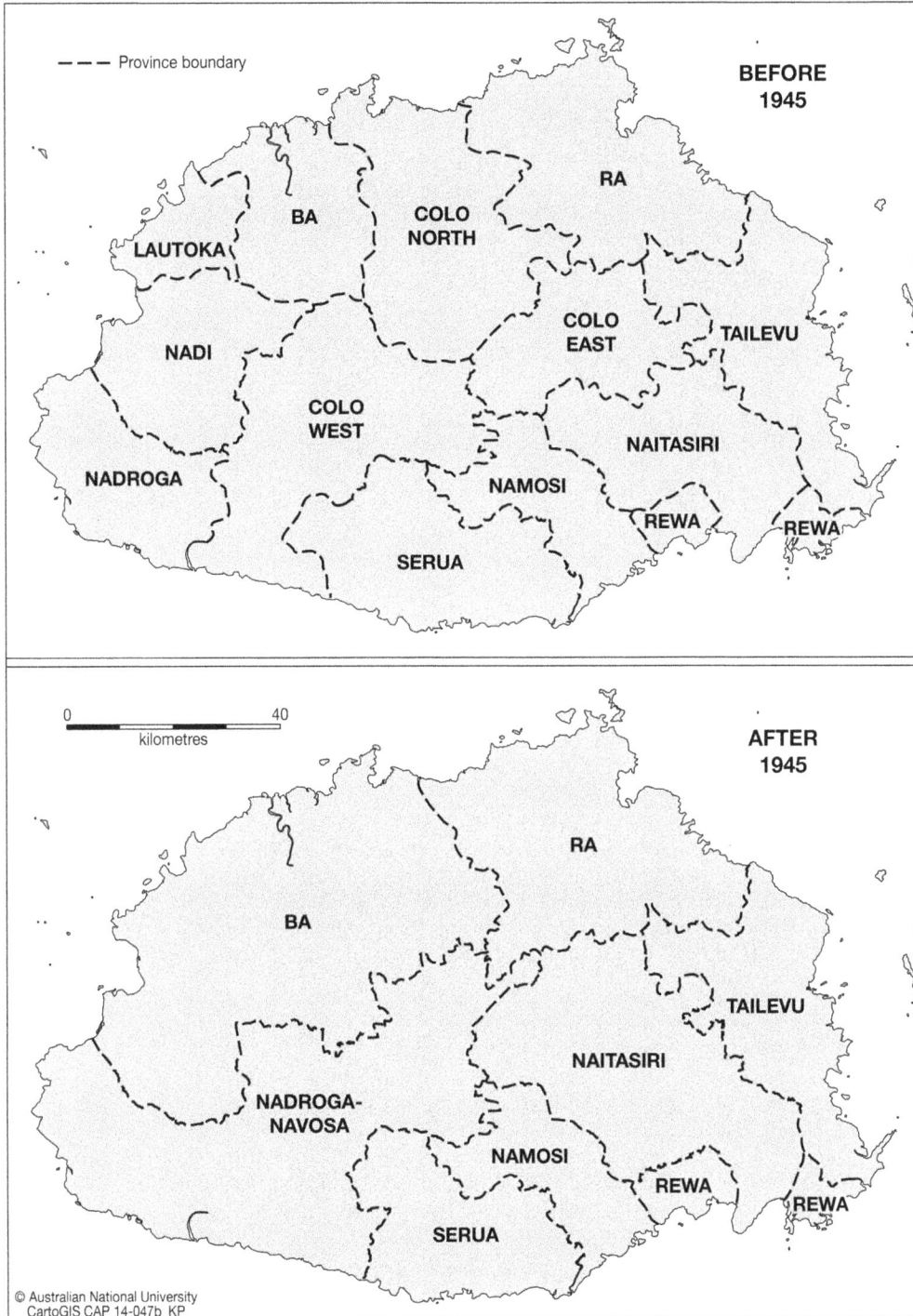

Map II The Provinces of Viti Levu before and after 1945

Source: After Derrick 1951: Figure 85, redrawn by ANU Carto-GIS.

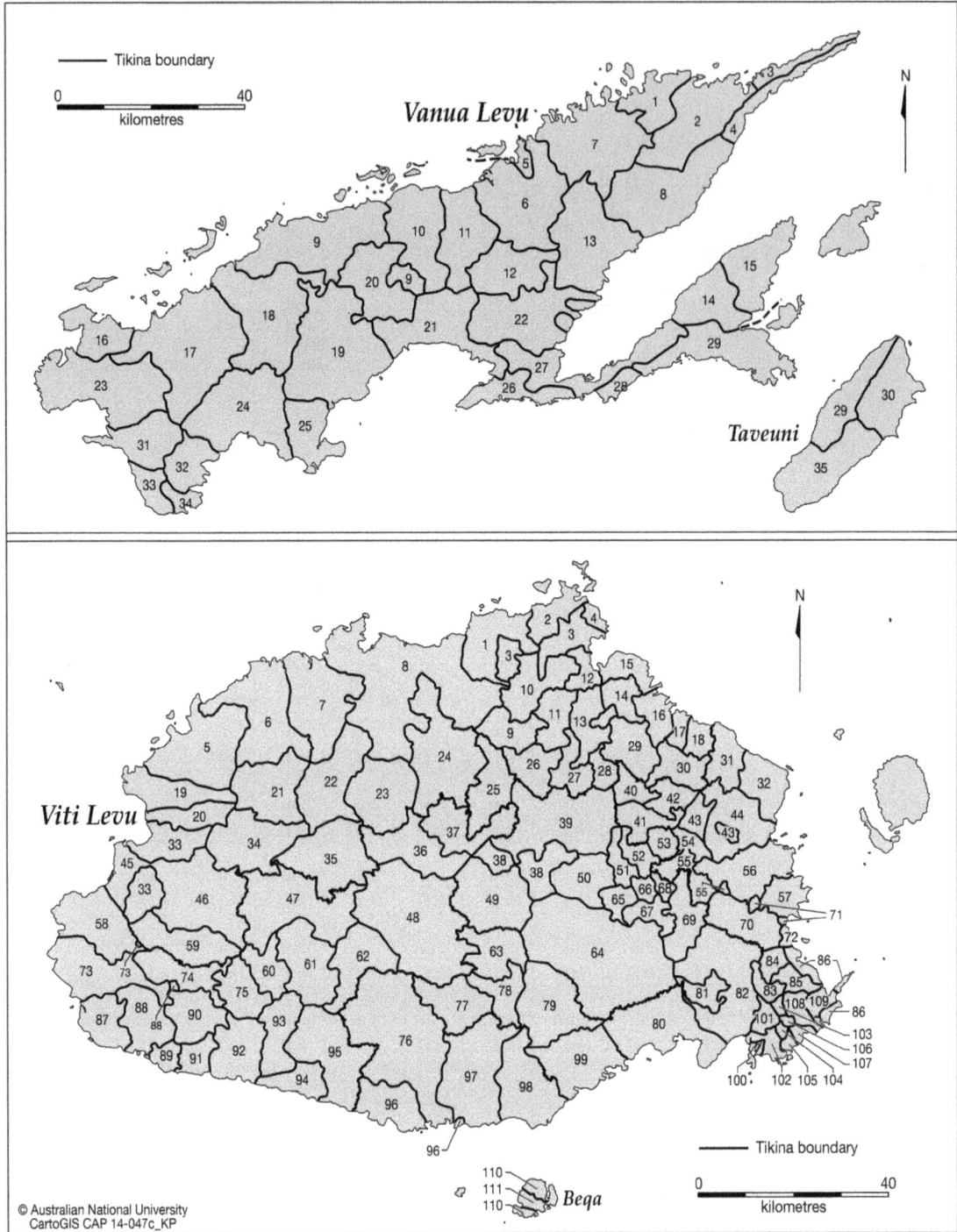

Map III The Location of the Old *Tikina* in Viti Levu and Vanua Levu

Source: After Ward 1965: Figure 02, redrawn by ANU Carto-GIS.

Key to Map III The Location of the Old *Tikina* in Viti Levu and Vanua Levu

Vanua Levu Alphabetical List

Bua	23	Namuka	1	Tumaloa	15
Cakaudrove	29	Nadi	32	Udu	3
Dama	31	Nasavusavu	26	Vaturova	13
Dogotuki	2	Natewa	14	Vuna	35
Dreketi	18	Navakasiga	16	Vuya	33
Koroalau	22	Navatu	27	Wailevu	11
Kubulau	25	Naweni	28	Wailevu East	21
Labasa	6	Saqani	8	Wailevu West	19
Lekutu	17	Sasa	10	Wainikeli	30
Macuata	9	Seaqaqa	20	Wainunu	24
Mali	5	Solevu	34	Wairiki	12
Nadogo	7	Tawaki	4		

Viti Levu Alphabetical List

Batiwai	97	Naitasiri	82	Raviravi (Beqa)	110
Bau	86	Nakelo	108	Raviravi (Ra)	1
Bemana	61	Nakorotubu	16	Rewa	102
Bulu	7	Nakuailava	29	Rukuruku	59
Burebasaga	104	Nalaba	11	Sabeto	20
Bureivanua	30	Nalawa	13	Saivou	12
Bureiwai	18	Nalotawa	21	Savatu	24
Buretu	109	Naloto (Ba)	22	Sawakasa	44
Conoa	92	Naloto (Tailevu)	43	Sawau	111
Cuvu	89	Namalata	56	Serua	96
Dawasamu	31	Namara	72	Sigatoka	91
Deuba	98	Namata	84	Sikituru	45
Dravo	85	Namataku	47	Soloira	65
Dreketi	105	Namena	32	Suva	80
Kavula	17	Namosi	79	Tai	71
Komave	95	Naqarawai	63	Taivugalei	55
Koroinasau	93	Naroko	3	Tavua	8
Korolevuiwai	94	Nasau	26	Toga	101
Lawaki	27	Nasautoko	41	Tokaimalo	10
Lutu	53	Nasikawa	62	Tokatoka	106
Magodro	35	Nausori	83	Tuva	88
Malomalo	87	Navatusila	36	Vaturu	34
Matailobau	51	Navitilevu	15	Veinuqa	77
Mataso	14	Navolau	4	Veivatuloa	99
Mavua	75	Navuakece	67	Verata	57
Momi	58	Nawaka	46	Viria	69
Muaira	38	Nayavu	42	Vitogo	5
Nababa	28	Noco	107	Vuda	19
Nabaitavu	68	Noikoro	48	Vugalei	70
Naboubuco	25	Noimalu	49	Vuna	81
Nadaravakawalu	50	Nokonoko	90	Vutia	100
Nadi	33	Nuku (Serua)	76	Wai	73
Nadrau	37	Nuku (Tailevu)	103	Waicoba	74
Nagonenicolo	39	Qalimare	60	Waidina	64
Nailaga	6	Qaliyalatina	23	Waima	52
Nailega	40	Rakiraki	2	Wainikoroiluva	78
Nailuva	9	Rara	66	Wailotua	54

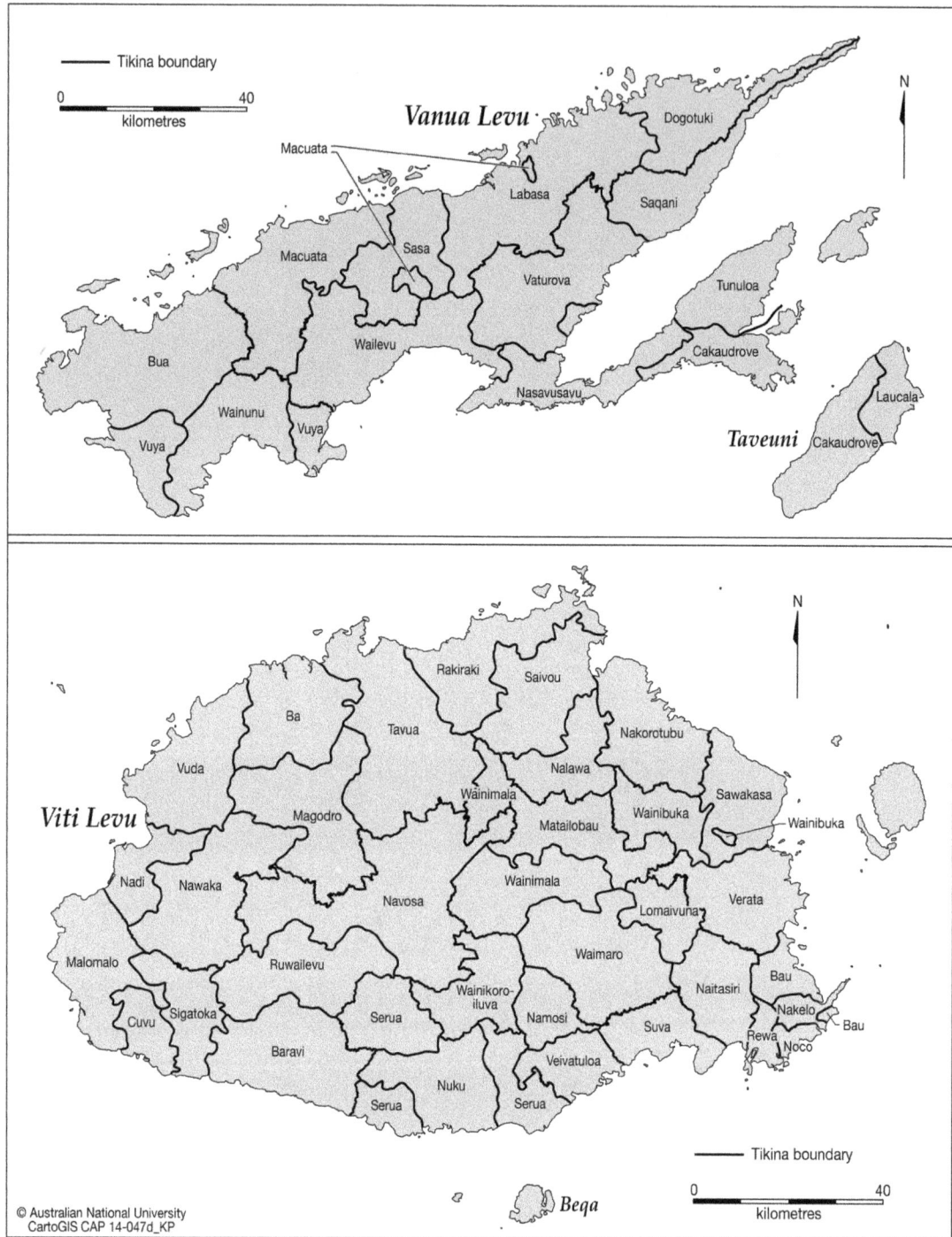

Map IV The Location of the New *Tikina* in Viti Levu and Vanua Levu

Source: After Ward 1965: Figure 03, redrawn by ANU Carto-GIS.

SOUTH
PACIFIC OCEAN

Round

Yawini

Yawa

Yasawa

Nanuya
Sawa-i-lau

Yaromo

Nacula

Tavewa

Matacawalevu

Nanuyalailai

Nanuyalevu

Devuilau

Kubulau

Yaqeta

YASAWA
GROUP

Viwa

Naviti

Drawaqa

Naukucavu

Nanuyabalavu

Narara

N

0   20
kilometres

Waya

Wayasewa

Kuata

Eori

Vanualailai

Navadra

Vanualevu

Kadomo

Vomo

MAMANUCA
GROUP

Yanuya

Tokoriki

Monu

Monuriki

Tavua

Nautanivono

Matamanoa

Iai

Levuka

Kadavu

Mana

Viti Levu

Nadi
Bay

Gualito

Malolo

Malololailai

Namotu

Tavarua

© Australian National University
CartoGIS CAP 14-047e_KP

Map V The Western Islands off Viti Levu

Source: After Derrick 1951: Figure 86, redrawn by ANU Carto-GIS.

Map VI The Northern Islands of the Yasawa Group

Source: After Derrick 1951: Figure 89, redrawn by ANU Carto-GIS.

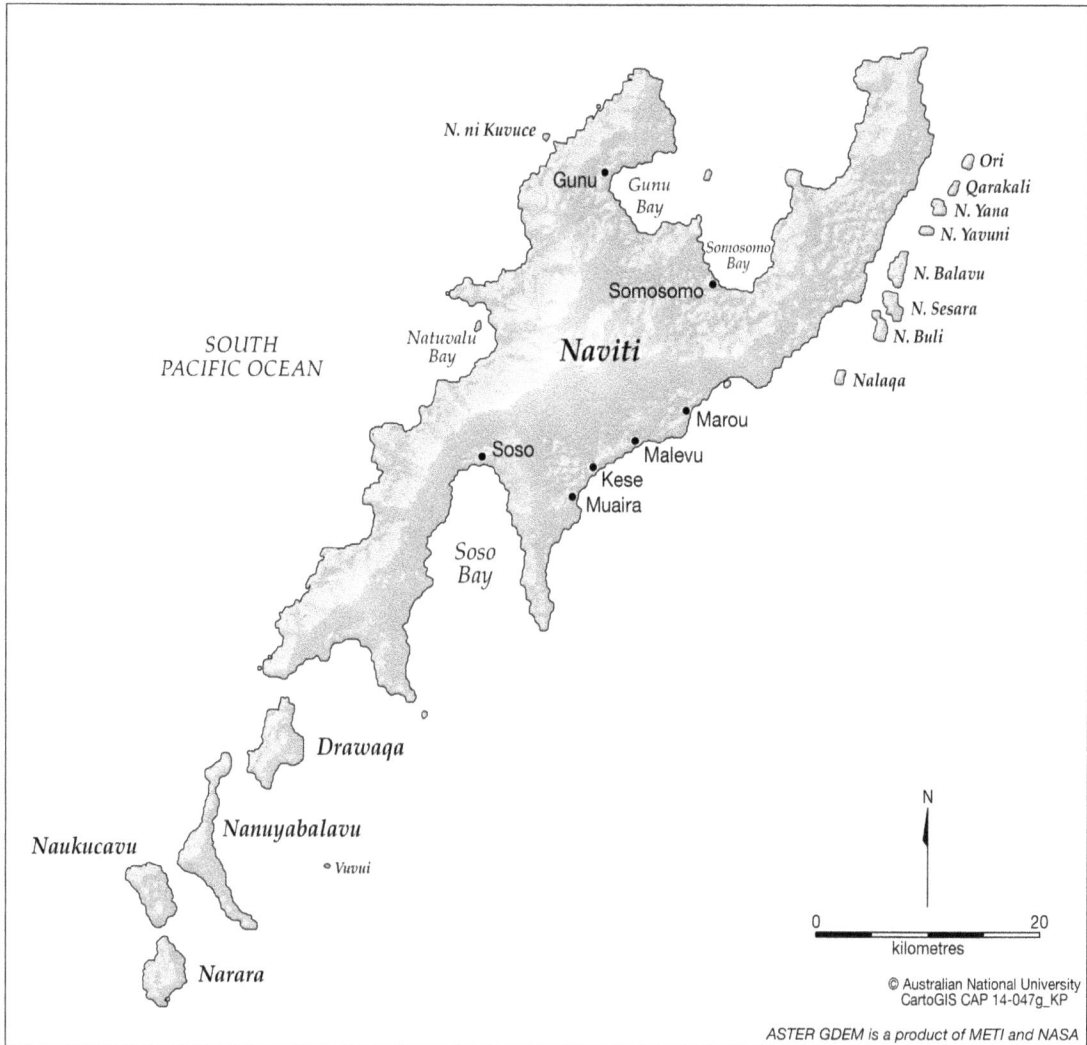

Map VII The Central Islands of the Yasawa Group

Source: After Derrick 1951: Figure 88, redrawn by ANU Carto-GIS.

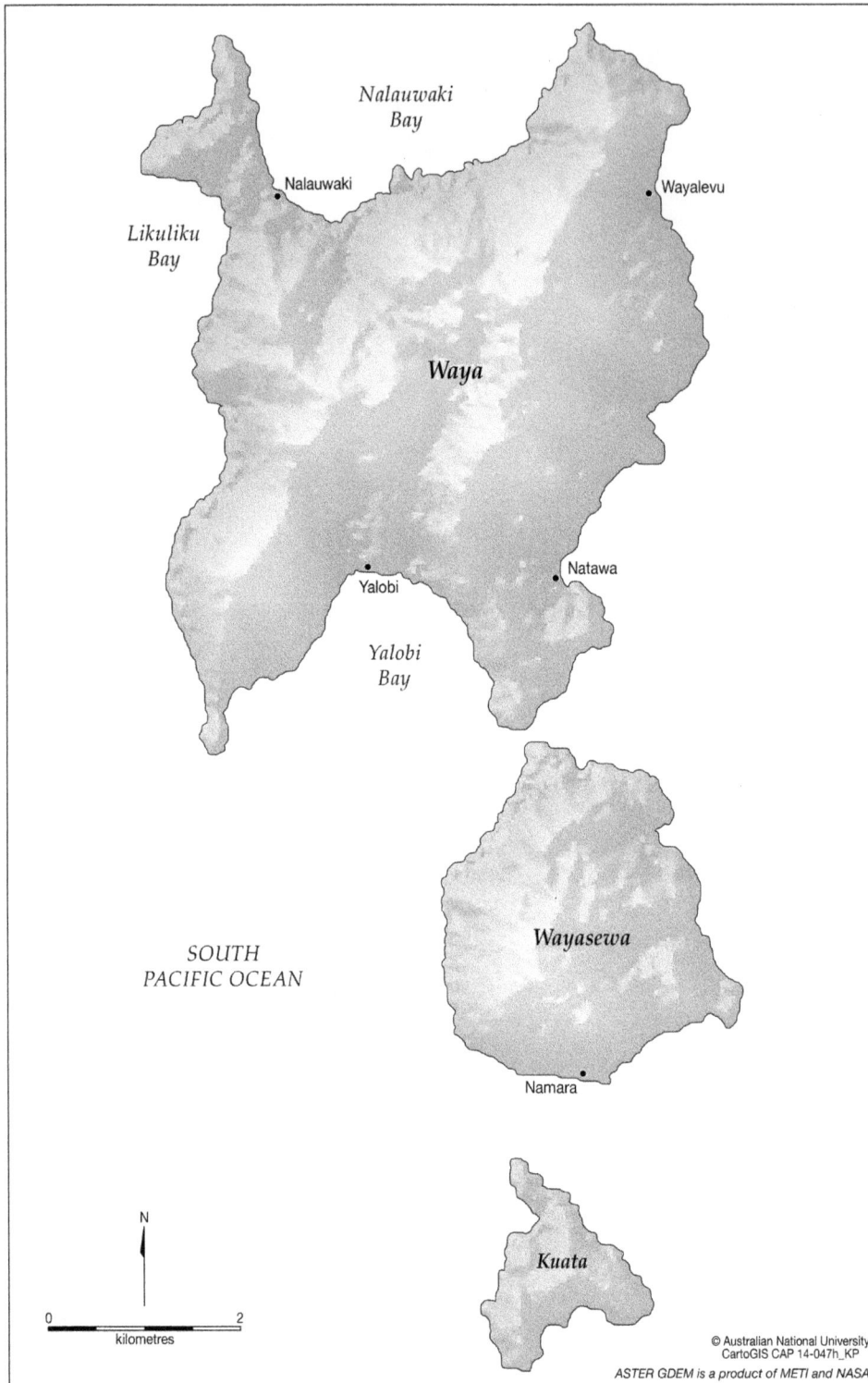

Map VIII The Southern Islands of the Yasawa Group

Source: After Derrick 1951: Figure 87, redrawn by ANU Carto-GIS.

1

Fijian Society: The Islands of Fiji (General)

But westward look, the Land is Bright

Fiji, a general geographical setting

Fiji and its neighbours

The islands of Fiji, Rotuma, Samoa and Tonga define an oceanic geographical quadrilateral in which Fiji has the largest landmass and the greatest diversity of climate and topography. Among these four regions, traditional Fijian society shows much the greatest variety in patterns of language and socio-political structure.

What is Fiji?

When investigations leading to this project began tentatively in 1951, Fiji (Viti in Fijian) was a British Crown Colony, after Ratu Seru Cakobau, Vunivalu of Bau, and twelve other high chiefs had ceded the 'Islands of Fiji' to Queen Victoria under the Deed of Cession dated 10th October 1874. The Colony was extended in 1881 when the chiefs of Rotuma ceded 'Rotuma and its dependencies' to Queen Victoria under the Deed of Cession dated 13th May 1881 and the British Government combined Rotuma with Fiji for administrative convenience. It was extended further in the 1960s when a small unowned reef to the southeast of the main group was annexed.

Ratu Seru Apenisa Cakobau had been installed in the position of Vunivalu of Bau and paramount of the *matanitū* of Kubuna (Bau) in the first half of the 19th century. In 1867, an allegedly pan-Fiji government with Cakobau as the head was established with the backing of some politically ambitious Europeans in the east. Cakobau was made King of Bau; and his self-adopted title of Tui Viti or King of Fiji was recognised by those who found it suited their political purposes to do so when the 1871 Government was established with Cakobau as the head.

On 10th October 1970 this overall area became the independent Dominion of Fiji, with a Governor-General who represented The Queen. Fiji ceased to be a member of the British Commonwealth on 7 October 1987, and became the Republic of Fiji with a President. It was temporarily readmitted to the Commonwealth in 1997 and became the Republic of the Fiji Islands with a President.

The term 'Fiji' today embraces a wider area than that which was originally covered by the term in 1874. The territory and society explored in my project are, however, restricted to those of 'the whole of the group of islands in the South Pacific Ocean known as the Fijis' lying within the area delineated in paragraph 1 of the 1874 Deed of Cession (Derrick 1950:252) and comprising the original Colony of Fiji.

The islands of Fiji

The Crown Colony as defined in the Deed of Cession has a total area of about 400,000 square km, of which the land area is about 11,288 square km. The largest island, Viti Levu, comprises 6418 square km; and to the north-east the second largest island, Vanua Levu, comprises 3419 square km. These two islands make up more than 85 per cent of the total land mass, the next largest, Taveuni, being only 272 square km. About 100 of the more than 300 islands in the Fiji group are inhabited. Many of the smaller islands are unsuitable for permanent habitation but are visited by the Fijian owners for fishing or to cut copra. Some islets, such as Narokorokoyawa in the Mamanuca group are of particular importance to Fijians because of their association with the Fijian spirit world, and are only visited for communication with the spirits.

To the northwest of Viti Levu lies the Yasawa Group, comprising seven main islands (including the outlier of Viwa), and many small islets, with a total landmass of 83 square km. To the south-east of Vanua Levu lies the Lau Group, an archipelago of twenty-nine main islands, some of which are closer to Tonga than to Viti Levu.

The island of Viti Levu

Excluding the continental remnants of New Guinea, the North and South Islands of New Zealand, and the *Grande Terre* of New Caledonia, and after the island of Hawai'i, Viti Levu is the largest island in Oceania. It is roughly oval in shape, about 144 km long from east to west and 104 km wide from north to south.

Some geological characteristics of Viti Levu

The structure of the island is mainly volcanic in origin, with volcanic flows and agglomerations near vents. The steep-sided, crested ridges are natural locations for defended sites. Outcrops of limestone occur, and caves and crevices provide a number of archaeological as well as natural sites that have come to be associated with the spirit world.

The dividing range

The main dividing range runs roughly north to south down the centre of the island and includes a number of peaks over 900 m in height. The highest, 1315 m, is Tomaniivi or Mount Victoria which lies towards the north end of the range. From Nadarivatu, to the east of Tomaniivi, the main range stretches towards the northeast, developing into the Nakauvadra range, the highest peak of which is Uluda, 861 m high. The terminal peak of the east of the range is Supani, 536 m high.

The dividing range lies across the path of the prevailing south-east trade winds; and the consequent patterns of orographic precipitation result in a basic climatic division of Viti Levu, with a wet zone in the south-east and a dry zone in the north-west. The annual rainfall in the wet zone may be as high as 5000 mm a year, and in the dry zone as low as 1375mm.

To the windward, wet side of the range, the rain forest is generally heavy and dense. To the leeward, dry side, in places where any forest remains, it is generally lighter and more open. Most of the leeward side is covered by open land with grass, ferns and reeds, with a few clumps of stunted casuarina trees in the gullies and along the banks of streams. Much of the land has been burned off by people searching for wild yams; without cover, the soil has become leached and will support little except tough bracken. Such land is referred to as *talasiga* or sun-scorched.

The broken highlands

On both sides of the main dividing ranges are tracts of broken highlands, mostly hemmed in by ranges of hills. On the seaward side of these hills, precipitous escarpments or steep slopes fall down to the lowlands facing the coast.

Forming a north-west spur to the west of the main central range, the Conua range (referred to as the Tualeita or Spirit Path) dominates the west-north-western side of Viti Levu. Starting some 15 km inland, the range runs westwards from its highest point at Mount Evans (Koroiyanitu or Peak of the Spirits, 997 m above sea level) nearly to the sea at Edronu. Its northern side rises abruptly from the southern piedmont lands of Vuda, and its southern side from the Sabeto valley. The Sabeto valley is overshadowed to the east by the Nausori highlands of which the highest point is Koroba (Mount Pickering, 1069 m).

The coastal lowlands

The coastal lowlands around the interior system of highlands mainly comprise rolling hills with a strip of flat land along the coast. This piedmont is generally 4 to 8 km wide. When, as in the Navua lowlands, the flat land is wider, it may be broken in places

The rivers

Viti Levu has an extensive series of river systems associated with the mountain ranges and the rainfall, some flowing south, others north and west.

Of those flowing south, the Rewa and the Sigatoka River systems are the most extensive. The former flows southwards for some 144 km (of which 64 km are navigable), and enters the sea at the south-east corner of Viti Levu, passing through an elaborate delta system with mangrove swamps. The latter flows southwards from near Nadarivatu for about 120 km through pockets of flat land hemmed in by hills, to the sea at the south-western corner of Viti Levu. The Navua River flows south for about 64 km through narrow gorges to flatlands and finally a delta of mangrove swamps into the sea, in the centre of the south coast of Viti Levu.

Of those flowing north, the Ba River goes through about 64 km into a mangrove-covered delta in the centre of the north coast of Viti Levu. The Penang River passing through my north-eastern focal area of research (see below), has three main tributaries, the Nakauvadra (developing into the Wailevu), the Vatudamu and the Dranayavutia (developed from the Naqorokawa). These rise from the northern slopes of the Nakauvadra range and its extension towards Supani peak. The Penang River passes through a wide valley and enters the sea amid the mangrove swamps to the west of the Rakiraki village complex.

Of those flowing west, the Sabeto and Nadi rivers pass through my western project area. The former rises in the slopes to the south-west of Mount Evans, runs parallel with the south side of the Conua range along the broad Sabeto valley, and empties into Nadi Bay through a maze of mangrove swamps. The latter has three principal tributaries, the Malakua, the Nawaka and the Namosi, which rise on the slopes of the Nausori highlands and Koroba peak. It flows through undulating countryside and mangrove swamp (now largely reclaimed) into Nadi Bay.

The Yasawa Group

Most of the Yasawa group of islands, known as Natu Yasawa, form an almost straight line in a north-north-east direction for a distance of more than 80 km from a point 40 km west-north-west of the north-west corner of Viti Levu. The main islands in this chain are, from north to south, Yasawa, Nacula, Matacawalevu, Yaqeta, Naviti and Waya, being mainly volcanic in origin. The exception is the limestone islet of Sawa-i-lau at the south end of Yasawa, with its system of caves and well known for its petroglyphs.

These main islands are relatively high. The summits range from 568 m and 497 m on Waya, to about 227 m on Yasawa. The islands are generally long and narrow, ranging from Yasawa which is about 17.5 km long and up to 1.6 km wide, to Matacawalevu which is 4.8 km long and between 1.2 km to 2.4 km wide. Waya is about 6.4 km long and 4.8 km wide, with high ridges parallel to the east and west coasts, and a transverse ridge between them to the centre.

The main ridges of the long, narrow islands have steep slopes to the western faces, drained by short watercourses flowing into steep valleys. The eastern, gentler slopes have larger streams which flow into lagoons or mangrove swamps.

The peaks and high ridges are wooded, especially on the western slopes; but the slopes are generally grassy with few trees, perhaps because of shifting cultivation and fires.

Barrier reefs occur between the islands and the open sea to the west, and isolated patches of coral are plentiful near to the islands, but reefs fringing the coasts are scanty.

The Yasawa group includes Viwa, the most westerly of the islands of Fiji, which lies about 32 km west-north-west from Waya. An isolated cay of coral sand, some 80 ha in extent, its highest point is only about 7 m above sea level. No natural source of fresh water exists on the island, although there is a fresh water spring in the sea in the southern bay.

Post-Cession Fijian society, land tenure and administration

Sir Arthur Gordon (later Lord Stanmore), the first substantive Governor of Fiji, was a son of former Prime Minister Lord Aberdeen and a 'protégé of Mr Gladstone and Lord Selborne, who could write confidentially, confidently, to Secretaries of State and permanent officials at the Colonial Office' (Scarr 1980:10). He took up his appointment in 1875, and his instructions, largely drafted by Gordon himself as Scarr has suggested in conversation, were that the Fijians should be governed 'in accordance with native usage and customs' (Carnarvon to Gordon, 4 March 1875, Fiji Archives), and that a system of land administration should be devised 'with a view to disturbing as little as possible existing tenures'.

Gordon was faced with an evident dilemma. He had, first, to follow these instructions. Secondly, he had to take into account the demands by an increasing number of European settlers and traders for safety and security of tenure. Thirdly, he was faced with the need for an efficient and economic form of administration which would at the same time take account of the sort of colony he felt it appropriate to establish.

So, while developing Fiji along the lines of the classic pattern of a British colony with a Governor answerable to the British Colonial Office, a Colonial Secretary with overall executive responsibilities, and other Colonial officials such as European magistrates, Gordon proceeded to establish and develop a system of local government with jurisdiction over Fijians. This system, the Fijian Administration, was intended from the start to be based on what were understood to be customary Fijian forms of government and land administration.

Invaluable sources of material for my studies of pre-Colonial Fijian society are the detailed accounts and reports of a long-drawn-out series of official investigations into these matters. Also valuable is a study of the systems of Fijian administration and the administration of Fijian-owned land, adopted and developed by Gordon and his successors. These systems were based not only on the findings of these accounts and reports, but also on the widespread, continual and often contradictory discussions which took place before and after the submission of such reports.

Fijian administration

The establishment of a system of Fijian administration to accord with the instructions by the British Government would have required a detailed knowledge of the generally accepted principles of traditional Fijian society. Gordon may not have had such detailed knowledge but he had advisers such as J.B. Thurston who had first come to Fiji in 1863. Thurston had acquired a wide first-hand knowledge of Fijian society; he had held cabinet rank in the 1871 supposedly pan-Fiji Cakobau Government of the Kingdom of Fiji (see below) and played a major part in events leading up to Cession. He was Acting Colonial Secretary of the Interim Government established immediately after Cession, and later held the substantive posts of Auditor General, Colonial Secretary, Administrator, Lieutenant Governor and finally Governor until his death in 1897 (Scarr 1984:83). He was aware of the reality of the diversity of traditional Fijian society and also, when land legislation was considered, of the principles of Fijian land tenure.

Gordon followed the guidance of Sir Henry Maine that a local community's usages and institutions should be retained in the face of conflicting demands by outside settlers until 'new social wants have taught new practices', and had his own preconceptions of the importance of initially adhering to 'native usage and customs'. An aristocrat, he recognised aristocracy when he saw it in the course of his encounters, both ceremonial and *en famille*, with the Fijian high chiefs such as Cakobau. Thurston, after years of experience in Fiji, had similar views of social change. In spite of much discussion, disagreement and misunderstanding in the course of consultations with Fijians (as well as old-timers), Gordon generally adopted the views of Thurston, and proceeded to determine the form of Fijian Administration. Generally he took advantage of Thurston's extensive knowledge about the nature of traditional pre-Colonial Fijian society. He also took into account the system of administration of the 1871 Kingdom of Fiji which had been divided into geographical areas known as *yasana* or provinces ruled by governors. These *yasana* had been established to correspond with traditional *matanitū* or major socio-political confederations, where they occurred.

So it was decided that the major administrative unit of the Colonial system of Fijian Administration should be the *yasana* or province, based on the *yasana* of the Cakobau Government. A *yasana* was divided into a number of *tikina* or districts (a term apparently invented for the purpose and presumably associated with the word *tiki-na*, a part of) based on traditional *vanua* or minor socio-political federations. Each *tikina* included a number of officially recognised *koro* or villages (*koro* was the eastern pre-Colonial term for a village, whereas the western word was usually *rara*).

After it had been decided that the *yasana* should be equated with the Cakobau Government *yasana* and as far as possible with the traditional *matanitū*, and the *tikina* with the *vanua*, Gordon and the Colonial government had to decide on titles for the official heads of provinces and districts (*yasana* and *tikina*). A problem arose because of the diversity of customary titles of heads of traditional *matanitū* and *vanua*, and the need for uniformity of official titles. The title of Roko, chosen as that of the administrative head of a province, originated from the traditional title of the spiritual paramount chief of certain major polities or *matanitū*, such as Roko Tui Bau of Bau, and Roko Tui Dreketi of Rewa. In the same way, the title of Buli which was selected as the official title for the head of a *tikina*, originated from the traditional title of the head of certain federations or *vanua* such as Buli Nadi of the *vanua* of Nadi in south western Vanua Levu. Such decisions at first caused a certain amount of confusion among those who had no understanding of the significance of these new titles, and especially among those in the west whose chiefly title was generally Momo.

The chiefs had ceded Fiji not to the British Government but to Queen Victoria, who thereby became recognised as the paramount chief of Fiji. Gordon considered that as Governor and The Queen's representative he had assumed, by acting on behalf of The Queen, the duties and responsibilities of the position of paramount chief of Fiji. So he personally was the only one appropriate to appoint heads of *yasana*. The person to be appointed was almost invariably the senior member of the principal polity of the *yasana*. Then, in the course of what Sir Arthur regarded to be an appropriate form of ceremony, he would hand the newly installed Roko a staff of office and charge him to look after his *yasana*. This procedure was a departure from 'native usages and customs', but was apparently accepted by the rather bemused or perhaps amused chiefs and people.

At the beginning the greater part of the Colony was divided into 12 *yasana*, and the Roko was the Governor's deputy in his own *yasana*. These *yasana* were in turn subdivided into a total of 86 *tikina*, each with a Buli responsible to the Roko. According to the 1881 census these *tikina* included about 1400 villages, each one of which had an officially recognised Turaga ni Koro or Village Headman answerable to the Buli. Most of the 115,000 Fijians recorded at the time of the census lived in a village with which they had traditional connections. Each administrative unit of the Fijian Administration therefore had an appointed Fijian official administratively responsible for the unit, and there was a chain of responsibility from the lowest official to the highest and eventually (later, through the District Commissioner as Deputy Secretary for Fijian Affairs) to the Governor.

Schematically, the Colonial system of Fijian Administration may be illustrated as follows:

AREA	OFFICIAL IN CHARGE
YASANA or PROVINCE	ROKO
TIKINA or DISTRICT	BULI
KORO or VILLAGE	TURAGA NI KORO

Immediately following Cession, parts of the mountainous interior of Viti Levu were still politically unstable because local independent chiefs had not been formally consulted and did not recognise Cession. This mountainous interior, known as Na Colo, was placed directly under officials of the Central Administration until the Government considered that it had become sufficiently stable for it to come under the Fijian Administration. Part of this stabilisation process involved what is referred to as Gordon's Little War in 1876, in which coastal Fijians under the general direction of the Governor attacked and overcame the independent dissidents in the hills, many of whom happened to be their traditional enemies. Sir Arthur wanted to gain the confidence of the hill folk in the newly established Colonial Government. As a first step, he was determined to cause as few casualties as possible and therefore he kept fire-eaters like Colonel Pratt, a Royal Engineer, out of the campaign. The latter had for public works purposes been appointed the British Military Commander but he was also keen to demonstrate his military prowess in the field.

The final pacification of Na Colo resulted in, first, the alteration of the boundaries of some already established *yasana* and, secondly, the creation of two new *yasana* based on traditional relationships and administrative convenience, each under a Roko. Since then the number of provinces has remained at fourteen.

Some individual officials such as Thurston were aware of the diversity of pre-Colonial Fijian society and land tenure. Only later, however, did the Government generally accept that the principles of socio-politics and land tenure were not so uniform as was originally thought to be the case and that there was greater diversity than was at first realised in these aspects of 'native usages and customs'.

As time went by, much more information (some correct, some misleading, some dubious) about traditional Fijian society became available to the Colonial administration as the result of the investigations and findings of Lands Claims Commissions appointed under the Lands Claims Ordinance of 1879 and Native Land Commissioners appointed under the Native Lands Ordinance of 1880. There was perhaps a growing realisation that local sensitivities and rivalries had not been given the recognition that was necessary if the new administration was to receive general acceptability. As a result, principally of having to meet the demands of local sentiment and local rivalries, and partly of having to extend the *tikina* system to the now pacified Na Colo, there had been a substantial increase in the number of *tikina* from 86 to 184 by 1945. Of these, there were no fewer than 109 in Viti Levu and even two in the associated offshore island of Beqa (part of the Viti Levu province of Rewa).

In course of time, it came to be realised that this increasingly widespread proliferation of Fijian Administration administrative units and officials, and the need to take into account local sensitivities and rivalry had to be balanced against what were seen to be the benefits of improved socio-political and economic conditions to be gained from a tighter and more efficient form of Fijian Administration. The Government accordingly reviewed the Fijian Administration. As a result, the Fijian Affairs Ordinance was enacted in 1945, whereby, *inter alia*, agreement was given, perhaps grudgingly, that the number of *tikina* should decrease. It is nowadays customary to refer to those original *tikina* as 'Old *Tikina*', in contrast to those recognised after the review, which were referred to as 'New *Tikina*'.

When I began my investigations of the development of Fijian society in late prehistoric and proto-historic times, I studied the origins and development of Old *tikina* and *yasana* of the Colonial Fijian administration. I assumed that a study of the identity of *tikina*, being ideally based on *vanua* or pre-Colonial socio-political federations of *yavusa* or descent groups, would give clues to the final stages of the development of pre-Colonial Fijian society. The variations in the number of *tikina* and of their boundaries should provide evidence for the principles basic to the structure and development of such Fijian society and for the diversity within such principles acceptable to Fijian society. At a higher level, the same assumptions were applied to a study of Colonial *yasana* based immediately on those Cakobau Government *yasana* which in turn were generally based on *matanitū* or pre-Colonial major socio-political confederations. Similar studies to which I refer below have concentrated on Eastern Fiji (Na Tu i Cake), and so I focused my investigations on the following three western areas with which I had been officially familiar since 1951.

The three focal areas (see Maps I to VIII)

The north-east focal area is about 32 km by 8 km on the coastal piedmont to the north of the Nakauvadra range and the east of the Supani Peak, together with several off-shore islands including Malake, Nanuya i Ra and Nanuya i Cake. It is based on the present *tikina* of Rakiraki (in the *yasana* of Ra), which comprised before 1945 the Old *tikina* of Navolau, Rakiraki and Raviravi. Three peripheral villages in the project area which after 1945 were included in the present *tikina* of Saivou, had previously been included in the Old *tikina* of Naroko. Naroko now forms part of the present *tikina* of Saivou.

The western area is about 32 km by 10 km on the coastal lowlands to the west of the Nausori highlands, and is divided into two by the Conua range from Koroiyanitu peak to Edronu near the coast. It includes the island of Waya Sewa at the south end of the Yasawa group, because this island is socio-politically and administratively part of Vuda *tikina* on the mainland. It is part of the present *yasana* of Ba, and is based on the three present *tikina* of Nawaka, Nadi and part of Vuda. Before 1945 Nawaka comprised the Old *tikina* of Rukuruku, Nawaka and Vaturu; Nadi comprised the Old *tikina* of Sikituru and of Nadi which by then had absorbed a previous *tikina* known as Buduka; and Vuda included Sabeto, Vuda and Vitogo (of which I concerned myself mainly with the western part).

The western insular area is the main Yasawa group, also in the present *yasana* of Ba, which is based on the two present *tikina* of Naviti and Yasawa. Before 1945 Naviti comprised the two Old *tikina* of Waya (which included the islands of Waya and Viwa), and Naviti (based on the island of Naviti). Yasawa comprised the two Old *tikina* of Nacula which included the islands of Yaq(w)eta and Matacawalevu, and Yasawa (based on the island of Yasawa).

All three areas are included in that western part of Fiji known as the Yasayasa vakaRa.

Fijian land tenure

So far in this discussion, the term '*vanua*' has referred to a minor socio-political federation. *Vanua* is also a term for the social concept of traditional Fijian society in which the elements of people, spirits and places run through and unite the society. Because of this inextricable association between people, their associated spirits and their lands, the governance of the Fijians 'in accordance with native usages and customs' required not only the provision of a system of administration of the people in accordance with such instructions. It also needed an understanding of the traditional system for the administration of land held by Fijians under customary tenure, and the recognition of such a system in Colonial native land legislation.

Customary land tenure

Investigations relevant to native land tenure were carried out by the Lands Claims Commission (LCC) and the Native Lands Commission (NLC) (see references under Native Lands Commission). Records of discussions between traditional landowners and the LCC, and of investigations by successive NLCs, as well as reports of discussions held by the Council of Chiefs formed the basis of the official Colonial understanding of the building blocks of traditional Fijian society. These records and reports included evidence, the critical study of which provided a useful basis for previous studies, especially those by Peter France (1969). They also formed the basis for my own investigations of the structure and development of pre-Colonial Fijian society and the principles of native land tenure.

The Deed of Cession made provision for categories of land not to be regarded as native land. These were land 'deemed necessary for public purposes,' (Crown Land Schedule A); land vacant at the time of Cession, (Crown Land B); and 'lands shown to the satisfaction of the LCC, (see below) to be alienated so as to have become bona fide the property of Europeans or other foreigners'. Before areas of native land could be officially recognised and the officially accepted principles of native land tenure could be determined and secured by appropriate legislation, it had first to be decided which lands were 'shown to be alienated'.

Under the provisions of the Deed of Cession, some 12,500 ha were set aside as Crown Land 'deemed necessary for public purposes'. After investigations, the LCC set up under the provisions of the Lands Claims Ordinance of 1879 were satisfied that of 1335 claims made by 'Europeans and other foreigners', 517 claims to freehold title over more than 166,500 ha should be upheld and approved by the Governor in Council. The remaining 83 per cent of the land (about 1,625,000 ha) was regarded as held under 'native customary tenure', and was designated as native land (Roth 1953:88; Burns 1960:105–107).

The NLC, established under the Native Lands Ordinance 1882, investigated the principles of traditional Fijian land ownership and of Fijian society. Earlier efforts on the part of Governor Gordon to understand such matters were hindered partly by his inability to speak Fijian and his dependence on interpreters, and partly by the diverse views and misunderstandings of the Fijians whose traditional rights were being investigated. Nevertheless, the Council of Chiefs, after a most confused discussion in 1878, was reported by David Wilkinson, the interpreter, as having agreed that land ownership was communally based on a descent group generally known as a *mataqali*. Gordon accepted this report and proceeded with the enactment of the Native Lands Ordinance of 1882. The preamble to the Ordinance said that careful inquiry had revealed that such lands were held mostly by *mataqali* or family communities as the proprietary unit according to native custom. Section 2 of the Ordinance provided that 'The tenure of lands belonging to the native Fijians as derived from their ancestors and evidenced by tradition and use shall be the legal tenure thereof'.

Gordon's views prevailed until Sir Everard im Thurn was appointed Governor in 1904. With the evidence of several investigations and Commissioners before him but with no previous knowledge of Fiji or previous experience as a Governor, im Thurn argued that registration of Fijian land and land owners by *mataqali* was not based on the principles of traditional ownership. He believed that the Fijians, a dying race, should not monopolise most of the land, and that his duties lay rather to the white settlers. In 1905, he made native land alienable and, by 1908, over 40,470 ha of fertile Fijian land had been sold. After considerable debate in the House of Lords, initiated by Stanmore in 1907, a decision by the House was relayed by order from the Colonial Office, and this practice was stopped by the incoming Governor Sir Henry May who initiated further investigations by the NLC into the increasingly uncertain nature of the principles of customary social units and traditional land tenure (see France 1969 for details).

A spate of activity followed on the part of the NLC, and in 1912 Commissioner Maxwell tabled before the Legislative Council a report on Fijian social structure. He gave distinctive names to the various social units, and set out definitively their relationships to each other. The findings became the generally accepted model of Fijian society, and were set out in Council Paper No. 27 of 1914. These findings, doubtless influenced in the first place by Ratu Sukuna (an influential authority on such matters in spite of his relative youth), were later endorsed by the NLC under the Chairmanship of Ratu Lala Sukuna in Council Paper No. 94 of 1927[1] (see references under NLC).

Fijian society: official colonial model

The following diagram represents schematically the official Colonial model of the polities of traditional Fijian society, based on that set out by Maxwell in Council Paper No. 27 of 1914, and endorsed in Council Paper No. 94 of 1927.

	(a) Socio-political Constructs
MATANITŪ	Confederation
VANUA	Federation
	(b) Descent Groups
YAVUSA	Major descent group
MATAQALI	Intermediate descent group
TOKATOKA	Minor descent group

1   Ratu, later Sir, Lala Sukuna (of aristocratic lineage, Foreign Legionnaire and holder of the *Medaille Militaire*, barrister), was from early on a highly respected member of the Administrative Service of Fiji and a leading adviser to the Government on Fijian matters. Later, he was Chairman of the Native Lands Commission, Secretary of Fijian Affairs and Speaker of the Legislative Council.

This diagram indicates the socio-political constructs and descent groups that comprise the two main categories of polities forming the building blocks of Fijian society.

The polities in the model

Discussion of official accounts of the principles on which the model was based will be clearer if I first consider the descent groups (the *yavusa*, the *mataqali* and the *itokatoka*), and then the socio-political constructs (the *matanitū* and the *vanua*). The model did not include reference to the *vūvale* (household or family unit), one or more of which may have comprised an *itokatoka*.[2]

The descent groups

Maxwell (see above) explained that: 'A *yavusa* consists of the direct agnate descendants of a single *kalou vu* or ancestor god, whose sons became the founders of component *mataqali*. As the population increased, the sons of the founders of the *mataqali* founded the various *tokatoka* which constituted the lowest order of subdivision exercising rights to land'.

Some current myths of origin recorded by me in Ra and in Vuda related that sometimes the original ancestor of a *yavusa* was a spirit who came directly or indirectly from the Nakauvadra Range (see Gifford 1951a:167), the home of Degei, or were descended from such a spirit. In other myths, the original ancestor was descended, directly or indirectly, from other mythical heroes who remained at Vuda having arrived there in the first canoe, the *Kaunitoni*.[3]

Each *yavusa* had a name, usually derived from the name of some natural feature near to the *yavutū* or of the *yavutū* itself. This term may be preceded by a word for 'people of' or 'inhabitants of', such as Kai, Noi or Lewe i. Thus a *yavusa* whose *yavutū* was known as Nasaumatua became known as the Kai Nasaumatua or Noi Nasaumatua or Lewe i Nasaumatua (Council Paper No. 94 of 1927). The head of a *yavusa* is recognised in the model as the senior member of the senior *mataqali*, and may or may not have a traditional title. For instance, the head of the Tububere, the second senior *yavusa* in the *vanua* of Vuda, has the title of iTaukei Sawaieke, meaning 'the owner of the chiefly *yavu* called Sawaieke'. Among the Rakiraki heads of *yavusa*, the head of Navuavua was the Tu Navua, and of Natiliva was Lei Natiliva. Because of this diversity of traditional titles, the Colonial Government created the official title of Turaga ni Qali for a person holding the position of senior member of a *yavusa*. This title is non-traditional but presumably was derived from the word *qali*, a polity subject to the authority of another polity.

---

2   Unless there is some special reason not to do so, I use Bauan terms in this thesis to refer to features of social organisation that are generally pan-Fijian in substance but not necessarily in name.

3   Sometimes sundry relatives accompanied an original ancestor, and current accounts usually include details of his wanderings. The place where he finally settled down and, if unmarried, took a woman usually of a neighbouring group and founded a family, was known as the *yavu tu*. On his death, his agnatic descendants who formed the *yavusa* would treat him as their *kalou vu* or ancestral spirit. The shrine or spirit house associated with a *kalou vu* was known as the bure kalou, or *beto/bito* in the west. *Kaunitoni* is the name of the vessel as used in current versions of the legend. The antiquity of the legend been queried *in toto* by Peter France (1966) who cautioned that it is but a missionary/anthropologist invention. Paul Geraghty (1977) has also queried the authenticity of the name on linguistic grounds. He pointed out that the western communalect equivalent for *kau* (tree) is *kai*. I might point out that the name Nakauvadra (currently translated as screwpine tree) contains the same word *kau*, whereas the Rakiraki word for tree is also *kai*. Even in 1952, I never heard the speakers of the broadest form of communalect use the words Nakaivadra or Kainitoni, and the use of such names was vigorously denied as not just inappropriate but incorrect and unauthentic. It is possible that the archaic pronunciation was *kau* in proto-western speech but changed in present everyday speech to *kai* in the west, though it survived in proper names. Similarly we find *anuya* in names of islands, from the old Fijian *(a)nuya*), though 'island' is now '*yanuyanu*'.

Under the NLC model, as the descendants of an original ancestor increased in numbers the resulting *yavusa* evolved into a number of *mataqali*, membership of which was based on common agnatic descent from one of the sons of the original ancestor.

Each *mataqali* had a distinctive name, and was ranked hierarchically within the *yavusa*, the senior one comprising the descendants of the eldest son of the original ancestor. Every *mataqali* had specific hereditary functions within the overall structure of the *yavusa*, and was categorised accordingly. In Council Paper No. 94 of 1927, Ratu Sukuna, leading expert on traditional Fijian society and Chairman of the NLC, explained that the functions of the various *mataqali* in a model *yavusa* were in order of seniority as follows:

(i)   *Turaga*; including the person who was acknowledged as the traditional leader of the *yavusa*, as well as others of chiefly status at a *yavusa*-wide level;

(ii)   *Sauturaga*, being the immediate henchmen and executive officers of the chief;

(iii)   *Matanivanua*, being the chiefs' heralds and masters of ceremonies;

(iv)   *Bete*, being the priests into whose bodies the spirit of the original ancestor was supposed to enter from time to time and to issue advice to the chief and the *yavusa*;

(v)   *Bati*, being the warriors.

This model was duly accepted by the Colonial Government and the British Government. Further the *mataqali*, again on the advice of Ratu Sukuna, was accepted as being the main communal land-owning unit suitable for the purposes of the official registration of recognised native land and of the names of landowners. The Colonial Government also accepted that the person holding the position of senior member of a *mataqali* should have the official title of Turaga ni Mataqali. The territory of a *yavusa* may then be regarded as the totality of the land owned by the component *mataqali*.

As the descendants of the sons of the original ancestor of a *yavusa* increased in numbers, the resulting *mataqali* evolved according to the model into a series of *itokatoka* based on common agnatic descent from one of the sons of the sons of the original ancestor. Although the official term *itokatoka*[4] was recognised as traditional in some eastern parts of Fiji, the equivalent term was different in other parts.[5]

This tripartite division of categories of descent groups represents the Colonial model of Fijian society as a hierarchy based on recursive birth-order. The following diagram illustrates schematically the official Colonial model of those polities of Fijian society claimed as descent groups:

GROUP	OFFICIAL TITLE OF HEAD
YAVUSA	TURAGA NI QALI
MATAQALI	TURAGA NI MATAQALI
TOKATOKA	No recognised title

The model accords with the underlying principle of unity running through the formal structure of Fijian society, at any rate at the level of the descent groups. It also determines the ranking not only of groups and sub-groups but also of individuals. The titles show that the question of 'who

---

4   *itokatoka* is used in eastern Viti Levu and in Standard or 'Bauan' Fijian. Although the model refers to 'tokatoka', the present generally accepted form of '*itokatoka*' is used in the body of this thesis. Different terms for this sub-division, a pan-Fiji socio-political feature, are used in other parts of Fiji. For instance, in Lau, the term used is *bati ni lovo*; *kausivi* occurs in the Yasawas, *kete* in Waya, *ma'anibure* in Ra, *beto* in Vuda and Nadi, *bito* in Nadroga and part of Nawaka.

5   Whatever the name for it, this minor social grouping was recognised as a reality in traditional Fijian society. Under the model, each *itokatoka* had a distinctive name, and was ranked hierarchically within the *mataqali*. The senior *itokatoka* represented the descendants of the eldest son of a son of the original ancestor. The senior member had no traditional or official title.

is the *turaga* or head or chief?' has no absolute answer. A person may be head of his *vūvale*, or household, which is included in an *itokatoka* of which he is not necessarily the head. Similarly a person may be the head not only of his *vūvale* but also of his *itokatoka* which is included in a *mataqali* of which he is not necessarily the head. Finally a person may be head of his *vūvale*, *itokatoka*, and *mataqali*, but not necessarily of his *yavusa*. In each grouping of which he is head, he could be regarded as having the status of *turaga* or chief. Further, all members of the senior *mataqali* are regarded by virtue of such membership as having the status of *Turaga* or *Marama* (if female) and may take a traditional honorific pre-nomen such as Ratu (m), Adi (f), Ro (m or f), Bulou (f) or Lo(f).

The person regarded as the head of the *yavusa* is *turaga* over all members of the groupings subsumed within the *yavusa*. As such he has traditionally recognised socio-political responsibilities and privileges in relation to the *yavusa* as well as to land associated with the *yavusa*. Such responsibilities and privileges were recognised by the NLC, the person was accorded the official title of Turaga ni Qali and was allocated a small percentage of any rent money received from lessees of land associated with the *yavusa*.

Descent groups: the reality

Successive NLCs continued their investigations for many years. They recorded detailed traditional accounts of the origins and development of descent groups as explained under oath and sometimes unwillingly by Fijian landowners; and determined at least to their own satisfaction the identity of social units holding land at the times of the investigations. The boundaries of the lands held by each unit were surveyed and plotted, and the NLC registered the names of the units, their relative seniority and their associated land. These units, their relative seniority and their associated land then became the official basis of Colonial Fijian society, land ownership, social ranking and leadership.

A woman was registered as a member of the descent group of her father (or mother, if illegitimate), and remained a member after marriage. Women often married for political reasons out of their descent group in order to create alliances or seal relationships between polities, especially *vanua* or *matanitū*. Much of the power of pre-Colonial federations resulted from such marriages, and chiefs practised a system of polygamy developed for such socio-political reasons. However, no instance is known to me of polyandry in the case of a female chief. Marriages were generally virilocal.

Descent was customarily patrilineal, except in certain parts of Vanua Levu where it was matrilineal, and this pre-Colonial principle was adopted by the Colonial Government for the purposes of registration. There was, however, a custom, referred to by Roth (1953:72), known as *ilakovi* (the nominalisation of a form of *lakova*, meaning 'to go to'), whereby a person could be transferred from the father's to the mother's descent grouping or vice versa, but to no other grouping. Such a transfer severed all interest in the land of the previous grouping.

The rigid situation embodied in legislation has resulted in departures from accepted practice in pre-Colonial times. In reality, a particular *yavusa* may have split over leadership problems or some insult or disagreement; and some of the component *mataqali* may have remained loyal to their parent *yavusa*, while others transferred their loyalty to another *yavusa*.

By establishing a standard form of Fijian administration and land tenure throughout the Colony, the Colonial Government did not provide in the legislation for certain customary practices prevailing in pre-Colonial times. For instance, pre-Cession Fijian society accepted the practice of including in a *yavusa* a *mataqali* which, typically following a dispute, wished to transfer its collective allegiance from its own *yavusa* of origin to another *yavusa*. Further, before the system imposed by the Administration, the practice prevailed of establishing a new and separate *yavusa* comprising one or more *mataqali* which might have decided to leave their *yavusa* of origin, following some internal split, perhaps over problems of leadership or as the result of some insult or breach of protocol.

The Colonial Government deemed that succession to leadership in traditional Fijian society should be based on the principle of *veitarataravi vakaveitacini* (seniority of descent), and this may have been the ideal in pre-Colonial times. In practice, if there was a disagreement about the leadership in pre-Colonial times, the matter was decided by formal discussion or, if unresolvable, by the war club. Dominant status and leadership mainly depended on achievement rather than on birth, reflecting individual ambition, internal rivalry and success in war. The possibility of usurpation was ever present, especially because of rivalry between members of the senior group. In the case of Bau, the Vunivalu or war chief usurped the position of the Roko Tui Bau, or spiritual chief, having attacked and burned the chiefly village, killed many of the inhabitants and driven away the paramount chief, the Roko Tui Bau. The incessant warring in the Nadi area resulted in the constant reshuffling of the loyalty of groups who left the district, sought refuge among more powerful neighbours or submitted to superior conquerors. 'Stranger kings' (Sahlins 1981) from other polities may have achieved chiefly status in a polity in the course of war either through conquest or by way of gratitude for assistance in war, or simply in recognition of the stranger's particular qualities of strength or leadership. In one case, according to tradition, when the people could not agree on who should be successor to the title of Kwa Levu of Nadroga, a shipwrecked Tongan chanced to be washed up on the beach and was found by women who were fishing. Wakanimolikula was installed as Kwa Levu, so the story goes, on the basis of his good looks and personality.

Such divergent pre-Colonial practices could not prevail under the system of Fijian administration, leadership and land legislation established under the Colonial Government. Such a system had to satisfy the instructions of the British Government that the Fijians should be governed in accordance with 'native usages and customs' and the claims of the Fijians. It also had to meet the needs of the increasingly vociferous members of other races who had settled in Fiji. They had been critical, though barely heeded, about what they considered to be, first, official disregard for their own safety and, secondly, the heavily Fijian-favoured land tenure situation, not only before Cession but increasingly so since then.

The general principles of the resulting officially-recognised systems of Fijian society, administration, land tenure and communal ownership may have been in general accord with the ideals of 'native usages and customs'. These officially recognised systems based on the need for unification and simplification, could not, however, take fully into account the fact that traditional systems were, in practice, subject to widespread and significant diversity.

The model: the socio-political constructs

The vanua

The NLC determined that frequently throughout Fiji several *yavusa* had combined temporarily or more permanently to comprise a *vanua* or federation. For instance, in times of war, a number of *yavusa* might form a military alliance for mutual protection and military assistance, not only in the face of threats of assault by neighbours but also when Western Fiji was threatened by the Vunivalu of Bau, Ratu Seru Cakobau, or when Fiji was threatened by expansionist Tongans. *Yavusa* involved would then agree among themselves to *vakarorogo* or heed the paramount authority of the head of the strongest of the participating *yavusa* and accept his leadership. Such a resulting *vanua* might continue until the easing of the situation which had brought about the federation. Participating *yavusa* might then revert to an independent status (*tu vakai koya*). Alternatively, the participating *yavusa* might see some mutual advantage in forming a more permanent form of federation in times of peace (*sautu*) for the purpose of ensuring continuing access to goods and assistance or for the gaining of prestige through association with a *yavusa* with a forceful and powerful leader. An able and ambitious head of *yavusa* might seek to demonstrate his power and forward his ambitions by extending his sphere of influence through some form of alliance or through conquest.

Some *yavusa* combined to form a *vanua* on the basis of kinship relationships, either mythical, genealogical or matrimonial. Other factors leading to the formation of *vanua* included geographical convenience based on territorial proximity, or a mutual need for access to resources both natural and human. The NLC claimed to have found that such federations were of general occurrence and a feature of pre-Colonial Fijian society throughout Fiji. The territory of a *vanua* may be regarded as the totality of the territory of the various component *yavusa*. The membership of a *vanua* may be regarded as the totality of the membership of the component *yavusa*.

The Government decided that such *vanua* were appropriate forms of socio-political constructs in pre-Colonial Fijian society to serve as the basis for *tikina* or subdivisions of provinces in the Colonial Fijian Administration.

The matanitū

The NLC also found that in some parts of Fiji, several *vanua* might sometimes combine voluntarily from time to time under a powerful chief for purposes of mutual convenience or for protection in times of war. *Vanua* might also have been united forcefully, when an ambitious, able and powerful chief wanted to extend his area of authority and also to have access to natural resources or to military assistance. Such combinations of *vanua* might develop by consolidating to form relatively stable *matanitū* or confederations under a paramount chief, as in such cases as Verata (under the Ratu mai Verata), Bau (under the Vunivalu) and Rewa (the Roko Tui Dreketi). The traditional title varied but was recognised by the Government and retained for ceremonial purposes. Since the Government did not consider that this category of chief had traditional privileges over land sufficiently strong to justify a share of rent money, there was no need to create an official title. The NLC used the term *matanitū* to refer to such confederations of *vanua*. The Government accepted that such *matanitū* were recognised elements in pre-Colonial Fijian society and had formed the basis of *yasana* in the 1871 Cakobau Government for the Kingdom of Fiji. Accordingly it was agreed that *matanitū* should become the basis of what were termed *yasana* or provinces in the Colonial system of Fijian administration.

The socio-political constructs and administrative areas: general

The following diagram shows the equation of Fijian socio-political constructs and officially recognised titles of heads, with Fijian Administration areas and official titles of administrators in charge:

CONSTRUCT	OFFICIAL HEAD	ADMIN: AREA	ADMIN: HEAD
MATANITŪ	no official title	YASANA	ROKO
VANUA	TURAGA iTAUKEI	TIKINA	BULI

The Vanua and the Tikina

Vanua, being federations of *yavusa*, were recognised by the NLC as a widespread form of polity in pre-Colonial Fijian society. Names and boundaries of the *tikina* of the Colonial Fijian administration were ideally equated with those of the pre-Colonial *vanua*. These were duly prescribed under Colonial legislation and so given legal status for the purposes of the Fijian Administration. As far as land legislation was concerned, the traditional privileges of the paramount of the *vanua* were recognised. For instance, when land owned by a *mataqali* of a *yavusa* forming part of a *vanua* was leased, a specific percentage of the rent money was assigned to the paramount chief in recognition of his or her traditional privileges and responsibilities as paramount. In my time, I have known female paramounts in Vuda, Nadroga, Ba and Rewa. The occupant of such a paramount position would have continued after Cession to hold the traditional title associated with such a position. Such a title varied considerably over different parts of Fiji. For instance, the head of the *vanua* of Nawaka was the Momo i Nawaka; and the head of Natokea, Rakiraki, was the Ra'u (two long vowels) ni Na'okea.

The paramount of a *vanua* also holds the official title of Turaga i Taukei as selected by the Colonial Government, in the context of land legislation. The origin of this Government title is obscure, though it appears in the west of Fiji. For instance, the iTaukei Nakelo was head of part of Sabutoyatoya, the leading *yavusa* in Vuda. Nakelo was the name of a chiefly *yavu*. The holder of this title of Momo (Turaga) iTaukei, or owner of, Nakelo, had important ceremonial and advisory/executive duties in respect of or on behalf of, the Momo Levu i Vuda, or paramount chief of Vuda. The head of the Naua *vanua* (composed of a single independent *yavusa*) was before formal installation titled iTaukei Sawaieke or Owner of Sawaieke, the chiefly *yavu* of Naua. After installation he was given the title of Momo i Naua or paramount of Naua. Sawaieke is also the name of the chiefly *yavu* of of the *yavusa* of Tububere, Vuda, and the title of the head of the *yavusa* is iTaukei Sawaieke. In neither case could I find any agreed explanation of the origin of the name. Sawaieke does, however, also occur as the name of an area in the Lomaiviti island of Gau, and may reflect connections by marriage or that Gau was a place prisoners were sent by Cakobau in the aftermath of wars involving Naua and Vuda referred to later.

The matanitū and the province

In accordance with the model, traditional *matanitū* where they occurred formed the basis of Colonial *yasana*. For instance, at one time probably the most powerful *matanitū* in eastern Viti Levu was Verata, whose paramount held the title of Ratu mai Verata (see Appendix A). However, in 1829 Verata's powers had been finally eclipsed by the *matanitū* of Bau of which the leading *yavusa* was Kubuna. The paramount chief was the Vunivalu or war chief who had earlier deposed the spiritual paramount, the Roko Tui Bau. Another powerful *matanitū* was that of neighbouring and rival Rewa based on the *yavusa* of Burebasaga of which the spiritual paramount was the Roko Tui Dreketi and the second highest chief was the Vunivalu or war chief. A third major *matanitū*, that of Cakaudrove (commonly referred to nowadays as the Tovata), was led by the AiSokula polity of which the paramount was the Tui Cakau. These duly became the *yasana* of Tailevu, Rewa and Cakaudrove respectively.

It is interesting to explore how the Colonial Government established provinces in those areas where there was no recognised *matanitū*. For instance, there were *vanua* in Nadi, Nawaka, Vuda, the Yasawa Group and Rakiraki, but no recognised confederation of a higher order, in spite of kinship and marital ties between leading chiefly families. However, the provinces of Ba and Ra were created on the basis of such ties as the Government could identify from advice and investigations but also on contiguity of large geographical areas and administrative convenience. On the island of Kadavu, fifteen *vanua* were recorded, though only six were recognised in a pan-Kadavu ceremonial context. There has been no confederation of these *vanua*, and the ultra-independence of Kadavu polities is recognised in the well-known saying '*Manu dui tagi*', roughly equivalent to 'Every man is cock of his own dung-heap'. The province of Kadavu corresponded to the geographical bounds of the island and its associated offshore islets.

Two others were based eventually on what, at the time of Cession and for a while afterwards, had been areas of continuing political instability in the mountainous interior (Na Colo) of Viti Levu, where people claimed not to have been consulted about, or to have agreed to Cession (see above).

The constructs and reality

In exploring pre-Cession customary Fijian society, it is fortunate that the Colonial form of Fijian administration established immediately after Cession was intended to be based on what the Colonial government understood to be such customary society. Further, NLCs were set up to investigate land-owning units, land boundaries and the justification for these landowning units to own the lands which they claimed. A tremendous wealth of information was recorded and has been used by France (1969), Macnaught (1971, 1982) and Scarr (1980), and it is these records which form one of the main sources of information which I used in preparing for this project. It is these records which I have since used to check the accuracy and reasonableness of the oral accounts of the current Fijian understanding and explanation of the origins and development of their polities. It can, however, reasonably be pointed out that first, the NLC accounts and reports were biased, being based on evidence given, albeit under oath, by landowners who may have misunderstood the interrogations or more likely preferred to give only such evidence as would justify their claims to traditional rights over their lands. Secondly, such accounts were biased towards giving support for the NLC views that the principles of Fijian society and land tenure were (or should be) the same throughout the Colony. Thirdly, the accounts may have been incomplete or inaccurate, though given in good faith. Fourthly, Ratu Sir Lala Sukuna did pretty well as he pleased in the activities of the NLC, in order to ensure the acceptance by the Colonial Government of those principles of traditional society and land tenure which would be most advantageous to the Fijian people when Colonial legislation was being drafted. Indeed it may have to be admitted that neither the NLC accounts nor my oral accounts will ever be accepted as being historically accurate. The results of archaeological field surveys and linguistic investigations, however, should provide data from these other disciplines which throw light on the question of the accuracy or reasonableness of the recorded and oral accounts.

Records of discussions of the Council of Chiefs at meetings following Cession and during the 1880s determined the contemporary structure of the descent groups (the *yavusa*, the *mataqali* and the *itokatoka* or its equivalent) and the socio-political constructs (the *vanua* and the *matanitū*). These were then recognised officially and prevailed throughout Fiji. This official structure did not, however, by any means always accord with the customary principles of Fijian society found to prevail in many parts of Fiji. Some of the terms and groups of the model may not have applied in the west before they were imposed by the Government. For instance, there were apparently special western groups remembered as *kete* and *lewe*.[6] Further, I quite often heard in some areas in the west that certain socio-political groups had been subdivided by the NLCs and re-created into separate groups in order to solve local disagreements. Some of this may well be regarded as parochial grumbling, but its nature, basis and significance should be taken into account.

This chapter, then, emphasises that a detailed study of pre-Colonial traditional Fijian society, especially in the west, surely begins with an understanding and appreciation of how the Colonial Government worked to form an effective and economic form of Government. The Government strove to combine what was understood to constitute 'native usages and customs', together with the needs and demands of the significant expatriate and part-European population. A close study of the records of the LCC, the successive NLCs and early meetings of the Council of Chiefs did indeed provide useful information to stimulate my own studies. This complemented

---

6   An informant told the NLC at the turn of the last century that in Nadi *kete* was equated with *mataqali* and *lewe* with *itokatoka*. Their actual meaning is now obscure, though the terms appear in present western polity names such as Ketenitukani and Leweiwavuwavu.

information I obtained from oral traditions, archaeological surveys and linguistic discussions in the course of my own investigations. It was self-evident that in using oral traditions as a basis for my investigations, the problems were, first, to assess the accuracy and reasonableness of those oral accounts I recorded as to how Fijians currently understand and explain pre-Colonial Fijian society; and secondly, to attempt to elucidate how and why such accounts may differ from time to time and from person to person. The next chapter gives a general introduction to my project.

2

Overview of Project

The first aim of this research is to determine from present-day oral accounts how Fijians, especially in western areas from 1951 to date, understand and explain, first, the origins, characteristics, development and interactions of the social and political divisions of late pre-Colonial Fijian society; and secondly, the general principles of traditional land tenure. The second aim is to assess the reasoning and accuracy of such understandings by taking into account anthropological, archaeological, historical and linguistic evidence based on my own investigations and on the records of others, especially the Native Lands Commission (NLC). The constant question with which my research was concerned was how and why oral accounts differed. Investigations of the understandings of these aspects of traditional Fijian society, including leadership, during the last 200 years or so of pre-Colonial Fijian society focused on the two areas of Rakiraki on the north-east and Vuda/Nadi/Nawaka on the west of the main island of Viti Levu, and on a third area comprising the western archipelago of the Yasawa group.

Scope of the project

The research explores:

- secular and spiritual factors relating to the unity, identification, leadership and the dynamics of fusion and fission of polities, including their social and political relationships both internal or external to the polities;
- what factors, internal or external, might have led to the development of polities of different degrees of complexity and stability at different times and in different parts of Fiji; and
- certain aspects of Fijian cosmology, especially those features of the spirit world and the relationship between the realm of the supernatural and the realm of people which form the ideological basis for polities.

Areas of research

The three field areas on which this project focuses are:

- the present district of Rakiraki in the province of Ra, on the north-east corner of Viti Levu;
- the present adjacent districts of Vuda/Nadi/Nawaka in the province of Ba, on the west side of Viti Levu; and
- the islands of the western archipelago known as Natu Yasawa or Yasawa Group, which comprise the present districts of Naviti and Yasawa.

These three areas were chosen because, first, they had attracted relatively little attention from prehistorians, though a modest amount of excavation work had been undertaken in each of them (see below); and secondly, field work based on the piedmont of the mountainous centre of Viti Levu and on the more easily accessible offshore islands was within the physical capability of my research assistant, my wife Tamaris, and myself.

Areas on Viti Levu

The two areas of Rakiraki and Vuda/Nadi/Nawaka have the following features:

- Each is a piedmont area about 35 km by 5 km bounded by the sea on one side and by mountains on the other.

- Each area is closely associated with sites connected with widely-known origin myths of the present inhabitants of Vuda and Rakiraki. These are sites in Vuda of the mythical first landing and the first settlements of the original ancestors who are said to have come by vessel from the west. A site overlooking Rakiraki is that of the mythical centre for a number of those who came on from Vuda and settled on the mountain range of Nakauvadra to the south of Rakiraki.

- Each area has polities the social structures of which are generally different in complexity from those of the powerful and well-developed Eastern polities such as those based on Verata, Bau, Rewa and Cakaudrove (Appendix A).

- Vuda/Nadi/Nawaka include a number of independent individual *yavusa* (descent groups) or small, independent politico-territorial federations, whereas in Rakiraki one descent group at present claims general paramountcy over a number of the polities. Some polities, however, including the Nakauvadra-hallowed federation of Navatu strongly maintain their independence.

- Neither area has been the subject of detailed accounts by visitors, settlers or missionaries to the extent that the Eastern areas have been, although some Europeans had settled in both areas in pre-Colonial times.

- Each area has one site excavated in depth by Professor E. Gifford (1951b) in the late 1940s. These are Korovatu in the Vuda area, and Navatu in the Rakiraki area. Navatu has more recently been re-excavated by Geoffrey Clark (Clark and Anderson 2001).

- No detailed linguistic studies have been published in respect of either area, though a descriptive grammar of the Navatu communalect, in the Rakiraki area, has been completed (Parke n.d.- a).

The Yasawa Group

The islands of the Yasawa Group, including the western outlier of Viwa have the following features:

- The Yasawa group is a chain of relatively small volcanic islands stretching in a north-north-easterly direction for a distance of 80 km from the south side of Waya to the north tip of Yasawa. This group, which has a total land area of 135 square km, lies between Bligh Waters to the east and the Ethel Reefs to the west. The greatest distance between islands is 5 km, between Waya and Naviti.

- The longest island, Yasawa, is 17.5 km long; and the shortest of the inhabited islands is 5 km long. The greatest width in the chain is 5 km. Each island has a mountainous central ridge, with steeper slopes to leeward (west) and flatter land lying to windward (east). The highest peak (on Waya) is 568 m above sea level.

- The sand cay of Viwa lies about 32 km north-west of Waya, and is about 80 ha in extent.

- Each island including Viwa has a number of small, independent polities, comprised often of aggregations of small groups coming from Viti Levu as refugees or adventurers.

- Perhaps reflecting this immigrant element of the population, the myths of origin are diffuse. Indeed, some islands such as Waya claim an autochthonous guardian spirit.

- The islanders of Waya claim some early association with Samoans; and most of the islands except Viwa have had some association with the major eastern polities of Bau and Bua. The northern islands, especially Yasawa, were subject at one stage to Buan and Tongan influence. Vakawaletabua, Tui Bua, had family connections with Yasawa and his mother was Tongan. Some Europeans had also settled in various parts of the group in pre-Colonial times.

- None of these islands has been described in any detail by early visitors or missionaries. However, a number of references to them had been made by early explorers and surveyors such as Wilkes in

1840, or by people concerned with politico-religious troubles involving Bua, Bau and Tonga, or by those concerned with the investigation of murders of Europeans and with retributive action.

- Some excavation work has been undertaken by Terry Hunt on the island of Waya (personal communication).

- Linguistic research has been undertaken on Yasawa by Raven-Hart (1953); and on Waya and Viwa by Andrew Pawley and Timoci Sayaba (1971 and the Wayan dictionary in press). Triffitt (2000) also recorded notes on Yasawa communalects.

Nature of data used

I now briefly describe the sources of data used in the project, and I will comment on the value of oral accounts and on the procedures used in assessing such accounts.

Sources of data

The various sources of data include:

- oral accounts of the origins, structure, leadership and dynamics of polities from mythological times, generally based on the major descent group known nowadays as the *yavusa*. These accounts of 123 *yavusa* were written down by me and were based on personal interviews conducted in the early 1950s and during the 1990s;

- written accounts into the circumstances under which land had been sold in pre-Colonial times, and who had approved such sales. These accounts were recorded by the Land Claims Commission (LCC) after Cession in the course of their enquiries into claims by Europeans to freehold title in respect of land allegedly sold to them by Fijian owners;

- written accounts of the origins and histories of units of landowners and of boundaries of land, recorded by the NLC in the late 19th century and at the beginning of the 20th century, in the course of their enquiries into land ownership;

- a few written accounts of polities recorded by leaders of these polities for posterity for their own people and for the Colonial Government's education;

- contemporary accounts of experiences in the research areas by European missionaries, visitors and settlers during the 19th century;

- accounts of visits by me accompanied by representatives of the polities concerned, to over 200 archaeological and mythological/natural sites associated with the people and spirits of the polities in the research areas; together with some survey work, and limited excavation carried out by me in the Nadi area;

- a basic 250-word glossary for eleven communalects recognised in the research areas, as recorded by me and taking into account the earliest form of the words as remembered; together with a supplementary 250-word glossary of one typical communalect each from the areas of Rakiraki and Nawaka. I have completed a descriptive grammar of the Navatu (Rakiraki) communalect (Parke n.d.- a), and George Milner and I are combining our resources to prepare a sketch of the Nawaka communalect.[1] Andrew Pawley (Waya) and Raven-Hart (Yasawa) have recorded communalects for the north and south of the Yasawa group (for references, see above);

- About 300 pages of texts of *sere* (songs) and *meke* (chants), including *meke ni yaqona* and *meke ni tū yaqona*, being chants used when preparing or serving *yaqona* in the course of ceremonies.

---

1 (Editors' note) Sadly George Milner (1918–2012) has now passed away as well and it appears that this linguistic work was never completed.

On the appropriateness of using oral accounts

One of the prime sources of data for this research is the corpus of oral accounts of the *yavusa* recorded in the three research areas. These accounts essentially record how current members of *yavusa*:

- understand the origins, structure, development and interactions of their *yavusa* in the pre-Colonial period;
- explain and evaluate their pre-Colonial inter- and intra-polity relationships; and
- appreciate what influences (both internal and external) brought about such relationships at the *yavusa* and *vanua* levels and, so far as they apply, in a pan-Fiji context.

A decision on the appropriateness of using oral traditions as a primary source for my research first necessitates a general consideration of the pros and cons of the use of such accounts. On the one hand, current oral accounts, as recorded, may be regarded as being subject to memory loss about incidents experienced, or as being subject to faulty transmission from earlier times. Further, bias to promote one's own good or the good of one's polity is a constant factor when assessing the appropriateness of using oral accounts. Such accounts may, thus, be criticised as simply records of folklore which have no substantial backing and provide no basis for serious discussion, analysis or explanation of pre-Colonial Fijian society. In short, it may be claimed that 'palaeoethnography' or folklore should have no place in a prehistorian's attempt to explore such a society.

Oral accounts may also be criticised as being chronologically inaccurate. No attempt has, however, been made to determine the absolute chronology and dating of events recorded in these accounts, although if the absolute date for an event can be determined from other sources, it is recorded. I record the relative chronology of what the narrators considered to be those events and features significant in the development of a *yavusa* and its relationship with other *yavusa*. Absolute dating is not, however, considered crucial for the purposes of this research.

On the other hand, this research suggests that these claims should be regarded as reflecting a narrow-minded, somewhat purist and old-fashioned point of view. My questions are rather 'What is the significance of these oral traditions?' and 'For what explanations or interpretations can they be useful?' A distinction is seen between myths of origin and oral histories. The former are regarded by narrators as their explanations of their spiritual and mythical origins. As such, they may be of interest to the ethnologist, but they have a much more significant aspect from the point of view of this work. They may be regarded as one of the symbols of unity and identification of a *yavusa* and one of the traditional grounds for bonding between *yavusa*.

The oral history of just a single *yavusa* in an area may be criticised, first as liable to bias towards the triumphs of that *yavusa*'s development in relation to its neighbours; and secondly as atypical of *yavusa* generally in an area. It should, however, be emphasised first of all that the oral accounts record not only triumphs but also disasters; and secondly that the accounts are not simply those of a few selected samples of the *yavusa*. To avoid criticism of inadequate or atypical sampling, accounts of all the 123 *yavusa* in my three field areas were recorded as fully and carefully as the time available for the recording and the level of understanding of the narrators allowed.

An oral history may, indeed, be subject to faulty memory or to faulty transmission of handed-down accounts, or to deliberate alteration over a period of time, or to disagreement between the narrator and the rest of the *yavusa*. The version of the account recorded would be that given by the person who was regarded by the members of the *yavusa* as the most reliable 'guardian of the lore', of whom there was usually one such person. Such a person was usually, but not necessarily, the oldest or one of the most-high ranking members of the *yavusa* available, or the *bete* or priest, or the *mata ni vanua* or official spokesman and master of ceremony. Attempts were made to record in the presence of the head of the *yavusa* or nominee and as many of the members of the *yavusa* who wished to attend. The investigations involved, at this stage, simply the recording of how current members of a *yavusa* understood its origins and development, not an assessment of the reliability and accuracy of the accounts nor an external reconstruction of the history of pre-Cession society.

In recording such current accounts, it was sometimes clear that:

- once evidence became available from other sources, the chosen narrator who was the oldest or the most high-ranking or the recognised 'guardian of the lore' may not necessarily have given the most reasonable account; or

- two different oral accounts had been given by different contemporary narrators, perhaps reflecting bias, current internal conflicts or self-aggrandisement. In such a case, both the 'authorised' version and the other version would be recorded. In particular, it was appreciated that bias to promote one's own group is a constant factor over time. Attempts are made to assess and evaluate which account was the most reasonable one. The oral accounts of individual *yavusa* should not however, be regarded in isolation nor as being of little interest save to the folklorist or to the members of those *yavusa*.

Questions about the reliability and reasonableness of the oral accounts of current understanding of what took place in pre-Colonial times and, ultimately, about the value and use of such accounts are crucial for this research. These are considered from the point of view of a 'palaeo-ethnographer', whilst paying due homage to the archaeologist, anthropologist, historian and linguist. As stated earlier, the constant question before me was how and why accounts from different narrators or evidence from other sources of information may have varied.

Evaluating the oral accounts

My project therefore aims, first, to evaluate the individual accounts recorded in the three research areas by setting them in a multi-disciplinary environment, and secondly, to place them within a pan-Fijian context.

In assessing the reasonableness and consistency of individual oral accounts of the current understandings of the origins, structure and dynamics of polities in pre-Colonial times, the research takes into account the totality of these accounts as well as other sources of evidence from archaeology, linguistics, and accounts written by early Commissions, visitors and early settlers, as follows:

- individual *yavusa* accounts were compared and contrasted for consistency when more than one account referred to the same event;

- written accounts by early European missionaries, visitors and settlers, records of enquiries by the LCC of the early 1880s, and by the NLC during the early part of the 20th century, archaeological and natural sites, linguistic evidence, and texts of *meke* (chants) were explored for any information relevant for comparative and integrative purposes;

- these other sources of information were considered together with the oral accounts, in order to test to what extent they could be reasonably, reliably and significantly integrated and correlated;

- the polities and associated sites, spirits and communalects in the three research areas were then considered in the general context of Fijian polities, sites, spirits and communalects, especially those in Eastern Viti Levu and Eastern Fiji.

Field surveys in the three areas and elsewhere indicate that there is an extensive amount of archaeological evidence available for the period covered by this project (Gifford 1951b, Frost 1979, Best 1984, Palmer 1969, Clark 2000). Even if archaeological evidence is not at present particularly intensive or extensive qualitatively or quantitatively, the potential is such that eventually archaeological research will provide a reliable and extensive source of evidence to be compared satisfactorily with that of the current oral accounts and linguistics. The evidence of archaeology, linguistics or early writers or Commissions alone is, however, inadequate for the aims of this project. A coordinated multi-disciplinary approach is the most satisfactory methodology to adopt in order to assess the significance of Fijians' current understandings and explanations of the origins, structure and dynamics of pre-Colonial Fijian polities in a pan-Fijian context.

Vanua 1 and *vanua* 2

In Chapter 1, the main polities or building blocks of traditional Fijian society were categorised broadly as descent groups termed *yavusa*, and socio-political constructs termed *vanua* or *matanitū*. *Yavusa* and *vanua* (federations of *yavusa*) were categories of polities recognised in many parts of Fiji, though perhaps less so in the west in pre-Colonial times. The *matanitū* or confederation of *vanua* was a category of the most complex form of polity which developed in the east and was more generally recognised at the time of Cession. After Cession, these terms were officially recognised as those for polities in traditional Fijian society for all parts of the Colony. At this stage, I should draw attention to the polysemous nature of the term *vanua*.

The term 'vanua' is used not only to refer to a certain category of Fijian polity of traditional Fijian society, with the meaning of a federation of *yavusa*. 'Vanua' was also used in pre-Colonial times, and is still used, as a complex and comprehensive term which formed, and still forms, the ideological basis of identity in traditional Fijian society. This second meaning of *vanua* had and still has social, spiritual and physical dimensions inextricably interrelated. The integration of these three dimensions within this meaning of *vanua* is the ideological basis of the nature and cosmology of pre-Colonial traditional Fijian society generally. Pawley and Sayaba in their dictionary (in press) distinguish in detail, as did Capell (1941) but more superficially, between *vanua* as 'land, district, region, territory, country' and *vanua* as 'community, the people living in the community'. To distinguish between the semantics of the term *vanua*, I refer to the overall concept of Fijian society as *vanua* 1, and to the polity or federation of *yavusa* as *vanua* 2.[2]

Post-Cession Fijian society

The forms of post-Cession Fijian society and the systems of land tenure officially recognised by the British Government for the purposes of administration and legislation were intended, as explained earlier, to be 'in accordance with native usages and customs', following Colonial Office instructions to this effect. So, in setting the scene for this project, a brief account of those principles of traditional Fijian polities and land tenure which were adopted and the background to their adoption will be useful.

Post-Cession officially recognised traditional Fijian society is based on polities, as follows:

- a series of registered descent groups known as *yavusa*, with sub-groups known as *mataqali* which in turn are divided into *itokatoka* (sometimes referred to simply as *tokatoka)*;
- a number of socio-political constructs known as *vanua* (that is *vanua* 2) or federations of *yavusa*, and *matanitū* or confederations of *vanua*; and

---

2   *Vanua* has cognates in other Austronesian languages, such as *hanua* (Rotuman), *fanua* (Samoan), *honua* (Tongan), *benua* (Malay) and *whenua* (Maori). Blust (1987) as well as Green and Pawley (1999) explore the etymology and polysemy of this term and its varieties. Single glosses given in bilingual dictionaries should not be regarded as accurate descriptions of their meanings but only as shorthand designed to fit the categories of the target language. I will use the simple expression 'traditional society' as referring to, but not accurately describing, the meaning of the complex term *vanua* 1 in Fijian. Some of the senses in various Austronesian languages do not involve all the dimensions and may be regarded as discrete. In the situation in Fiji, the two senses are doubtless related but the basic issue is whether they are discrete or not. I do not propose to pursue this argument here.

- traditional leadership based on seniority of descent in the male line.

It was also officially determined that generally traditional land-tenure should be based on the precept that the land-owning unit is the *mataqali*.

Such a basis for Fijian society was adopted by the Colonial Government, following long-drawn-out investigations and often fiercely argued findings by the NLC, established under the Native Lands Ordinance 1880. After consultation with the Council of Chiefs and in the face of considerable debate, the British Colonial Government (Council Paper No. 94 of 1927) eventually endorsed these findings as authoritative and acceptable for official purposes of government. France (1969) has drawn attention to the controversial nature of the Commission's findings and their stormy passage over a period of thirty years, discussed in more detail later on.

Post-Cession society appears as a rather static form of society. It is, however, evident from the arguments that took place especially in meetings of the Council of Chiefs, that pre-Colonial traditional Fijian society in reality enjoyed a much more flexible and fluid socio-political way of life.

Post-Cession Fijian land tenure

Under the circumstances previously explained, Sir Arthur Gordon received instructions from the Secretary of State for the Colonies to devise a system of land administration 'with a view to disturbing as little as possible existing tenures' (Carnarvon to Gordon, 4 March 1875, Fiji Archives). Such instructions were in accordance with Gordon's somewhat fraternal philosophy in dealing with the relationships between the rights of local inhabitants at a certain level of social advancement whilst taking into account the needs and some of the demands of expatriate settlers.

Gordon had arrived in June 1875, and the next year he asked the newly created Council of Chiefs to outline the traditional rights to land so that legislation could be framed to provide for a system of land registration which would embody such rights. This involved the recording of boundaries of recognised blocks of land and the recognised basis of the ownership of such blocks. Considerable argument followed about the terminology for polities. Further, some said that the land-owning unit was the *itokatoka*, others said the *mataqali*, others simply did not, purposely or otherwise, seem to understand the question. The record of the Council indicates that, at one stage, the Council came to agree that the *mataqali* was the landowning unit throughout Fiji. It is not, however, clear whether this surprising unanimity of opinion resulted from frustration or pressure from European 'experts'; or whether, as was apparently the view of Ratu Sukuna, the Council record had been, perhaps deliberately, over-simplified by the recorder.

On the basis of this agreement, the Native Lands Ordinance was enacted in 1880, providing for the appointment of a Commissioner to investigate the system. Neither the councils set up in respect of each Fijian province nor the overriding Council of Chiefs nor the various successive Commissioners could however, agree on the basis of such a system.

Years of disagreement, changes of Commissioner, amendments of the Ordinance in 1892, opposition by Fijians and Europeans, and frustration were to follow. Eventually G.W. Maxwell, a Fiji Government administrative officer, was appointed Commissioner. He produced an analysis of the Fijian social system which served as the basis for all subsequent investigations of the NLC, and which was duly accepted by the Legislative Council (Council Paper No. 27 of 1914). The Secretary of State saw the necessity for the Commission to 'secure some practical result at the earliest possible time' and thought it best for land ownership on a *mataqali* basis to be settled, at any rate in the first instance. Maxwell objected that this was against the principles of traditional land administration, which were much more fluid, and pointed out that Fijians would not or could not mould their society into the form required by the Commission. Opposition mounted too among the Europeans who saw the NLC as a mechanism for frustrating the ambitions of planters to acquire land on terms of tenure which they understood and which were to their advantage. The climax came when the Europeans in Legislative Council criticised the NLC as a waste of time and public funds, 'for which this colony gets no benefit, and never will' (Fiji Legislative Council Debates, 1917:176). It was finally agreed in 1927, doubtless with the agreement and probably on the initiative of Ratu Sukuna, that for the sake of expediency the *mataqali* should be accepted as the land owning unit. The NLC would now cease to try to discover the varied traditional systems of land tenure in Fiji, and would confine its activities to recording *mataqali* boundaries.

Ratu Sukuna accepted the pragmatic approach of adopting a simple and homogeneous basis for land tenure even if such basis was not strictly in accordance with the principles of traditional land administration. He surely realised that the adoption of such a position was more important from the point of view of the traditional landowners than a fruitless, long-drawn-out continuation of hitherto unsuccessful attempts to determine the elusive and bewilderingly varied local principles of land tenure. Otherwise, ultra-conscientious Commissioners acting as amateur anthropologists would have continued to pursue the matter without practical solution, yea, to the very end of the rainbow. As a practical administrator with a great love for his own people, he accepted that it would be best for Fijians as traditional landowners if the question of land ownership was settled once and for all. Otherwise, it could well have been taken out of the hands of the NLC, and the administration of Fijian-owned land could have been undertaken directly by the Colonial Government. Indeed, following the investigations by O.H.K. Spate into the economic problems and prospects of the Fijian people (Spate 1959, Fiji Legislative Council Paper No.13 of 1959), the Council of Chiefs was forcefully opposed to the suggested land reforms. The Council was 'of the unanimous opinion that the "Mataqali" should continue to be the landowning social unit… It is recommended that the present system of Fijian land tenure, ownership, administration, and reservation be rigidly maintained' (Fiji Legislative Council Paper No. 29 of 1959:5).

So, somewhat paradoxically, the *mataqali* was accepted, and has been confirmed during the time of my investigations, as the social unit of ownership of Fijian land; even though the principles on which the NLC worked and continues to work may not wholly accord with the instructions of the Secretary of State for the Colonies.

3

The Ideological Sense of *Vanua*

This chapter addresses the ideological sense of *vanua* (that is, *vanua* 1) as the basis of pre-Colonial traditional Fijian society. Such a sense can best be considered in the light of the three elements of spirits, places, and humans. This view is based on my investigations of current Fijian understandings, in various parts of Fiji but particularly in Rakiraki, Vuda/Nadi/Nawaka and the Yasawas, and in this respect, I find compelling the views of Professor Asesela Ravuvu (1983:70) who defined the *vanua* in this sense as a complex term which has physical, social and cultural dimensions inextricably interrelated.

These three elements of the *vanua* were the source of security, both physical and spiritual, for members of the group or *yavusa*. The ideological sense of *vanua* was the basis of their sense of belonging and identity, symbolised by the founding ancestor and his *yavutū* or site first settled by the founding ancestor. A person felt confident when they understood that they belonged to a particular *yavusa*; that they were associated with the territory in which the *yavusa's* roots were established; and that they were protected by the spirits associated with that *yavusa*.

Vanua and spirits

An investigation of the present understanding of the pre-Colonial Fijian spirit world was a major objective of this project, in so far as it was relevant to the overall aim of determining how Fijians at present understand the origins, development and structure of polities. After several years of discussions about this somewhat arcane subject, I found that there was considerable unanimity on current Fijian understanding of beliefs and postulates relevant to my investigations of pre-Colonial Fijian cosmology. Seymour-Smith (1986:55) defined cosmology as 'The theory of, or sets of belief concerning, the nature of the universe or cosmos. These beliefs may include postulates of the structure, organisation and functioning of the supernatural, natural and social worlds.'

The spiritual dimension was an essential part of the systems of beliefs and values of the people forming the group, and of the various relationships between spirits and spirits, humans and humans, humans and spirits, and between humans and spirits and the environment. These factors largely determined what people thought and what they did.

The concept of *vanua* with its three dimensions of spirits, places and people will now be considered in the context of pre-Colonial Fijian cosmology, particularly:

- the characteristics, roles and powers of spirits in the spirit world relevant to the origins, unity and development of an individual polity, relationships between particular polities; and the validation of *kaukauwa* or secular power;
- the importance of the part the spirits played and the influence they had in the socio-politics of pre-Colonial Fijian society generally;
- the relationship between the realm of the supernatural and the realm of people; and

- the relationship between *mana* or spiritual power derived from a *kalou* or spirit (discussed understandingly by Katz 1993:20–22) and *kaukauwa* or secular power based on political and military strength; or, as it was conceived in the west of Fiji, between spiritual power or *sau* derived from a *(y)anitu* or spirit, and secular power or *qwāqwā* based on the *malumu*, or warclub.[1]

The Fijian spirit world was concerned with a great variety of supernatural spirits. Essentially benevolent spirits included the *kalou ni valu* (war spirits); protecting spirits; spirits of prosperity, sometimes referred to as *digiwai*; and spirits concerned with social conduct, sometimes referred to as *turaga ni ovisa* (policemen). There were also essentially malevolent spirits, covered by the present term of *tevoro*; and a number of supernatural phenomena, including the little folk known as *leka*, gnome-like figures known as *veli*, and such cult spirits as the *luve ni wai* and *kalou rērē*.

From the point of view of this research, some of the most significant myths especially in the west are those connected with spirits, especially the *(y)anitu /kalou vu* (founding ancestral spirits), associated with the arrival, dispersal and settlement of the first Fijians. In the Yasawa Group, however, where many groups were refugees or adventurers from Viti Levu, a particular category of spirit referred to as the *itaukei du* (true owner) was recognised by the newcomers but was not regarded as their ancestral spirit.

The following account is based largely on information from my three main study areas in *ihe yasayasa vakara* or the west. In particular, the Vuda and Rakiraki areas were closely connected with some of the best-known myths of the first arrivals and settlements of the Fijians and with many of the myths relating to the dispersal of founding ancestral spirits of *yavusa* or descent groups.

This account is well known at present especially in the three areas where it is currently respected as an integral part of Fijian cosmology. I copied it from a written account in Fijian by Ratu Vuki, the late iTaukei Nakelo, who was the recognised guardian of the lore at Vuda. I was also able to discuss it with him, and the myth was essentially the same as the one I recorded in Rakiraki.

A vessel, now known as the *Kaunitoni*, brought the first of the ancestors from the west. It arrived in the western reefs of Viti Levu and, having been holed, ended up on the beach just to the north of the present village of Viseisei between Nadi and Lautoka. The crew, including women, divided up and some remained near the first landing under the leadership of the culture hero Lutunasobasoba. The *Kaunitoni* then sailed eastwards along the north coast of Viti Levu under the leadership of the culture hero Degei. Degei and his companions landed in Rakiraki and went up to the Nakauvadra Mountains, which form the backdrop of Rakiraki and which are still regarded by Fijians generally as *tabu sara* (very sacred).

A second party led by Lutunasobasoba followed an inland route to the mountains. Others remained behind and settled in the Vuda area. In course of time, quarrels occurred among those on the Nakauvadra Mountains, including one arising from the killing of the dove Turukawa,

---

1   The term *(y)anitu* or *nitju* occurs generally in north-western, western and south western Viti Levu, from Ba to Vuda/Nadi to Nadroga and even to Serua (as in the toponym Waiyanitu). It also occurs in the Yasawa group. It refers to ancestral spirits and a variety of other spirits discussed in the monograph. East of these areas the term *kalou* is found with the same general meaning. I am, however, unable to determine the provenance of this word which appears to be a neologism restricted to these eastern areas of Fiji.

(Y)anitu was probably part of a language brought to Fiji by Austronesian speakers who came from the west and who spoke the language from which the present-day Fijian communalects are descended. With the 'n' retained, the term appears with similar meanings in many Austronesian languages throughout the islands of Southeast Asia and Oceania, as reflexes of proto-Austronesian 'qanitu'. In contrast, the occurrence in Rotuman of the n-less reflex *aitu* (with a glottal stop at the beginning of the word, and with a dot under the first a—see Churchward (1940:13) is a borrowing, not a direct retention by Rotuman, from Samoan where a similar term occurs or from Tongan where the form *oitu* is found. There are two linguistic grounds why it can be affirmed that Rotuman *aitu* is a Polynesian borrowing. First, the Proto-Malayo-Polynesian *n is lost. Secondly, because in Rotuman, the consonant t in otherwise similar Austronesian words normally occurs as f (e.g. *vatu* in Fijian, *hofu* in Rotuman; stone). This interpretation is supported by tradition (see Parke 2001), and the discovery in Rotuma by the author of adzes which have been tentatively identified as of Samoan or Uvean origin.

which had been brought from Tonga and which used to wake Degei in the morning with its cooing. So a number of those on the mountains dispersed around the islands, and the belief is still widespread that the founding ancestors of many of the present descent groups throughout Fiji came from the Nakauvadra Mountains.

Peter France (1969) may well disparage this myth as having been largely missionary-and anthropologist-influenced. However, there could well be an original kernel, even if overlaid by accretions since the 1890s which have come about thanks partly to the enthusiasms of European amateur ethnographers and linguists. These claim to trace the origins of the *Kaunitoni* (or whatever the first vessel might have been called) to Tanganyika on the basis of pseudo-cognates in East African and Fijian. Further, as Fijians became aware of their place in a wider world, accounts have also been given by Fijians of their supposed mythical connections with Germany, Egypt and other exotic places.

The original founding spiritual ancestors of *yavusa* are generally referred to as *kalou vu*. Each such original founding ancestor of a descent group has a recognised site, often a mound, as his or her *yavutū*. The spirit of that ancestor continues to be associated with that site, which is regarded as *tabu sara*, and especially difficult of access except by certain people such as the official *bete* (priest) who might communicate there with the spirit.

Each original ancestral spirit has a name and is associated with a particular species of object such as a bird, fish or insect, or with a pseudo-animate object such as a whirlwind. Such an object is known as the *waqawaqa* or *ivakatakilakila* (spirit's manifestation). The term *tolatola* is also used in the west. If such an object is seen, heard or smelt, especially by a member of the *yavusa* descended from that spirit, it is believed that the spirit is at hand and has a message to pass to the living, typically of the forthcoming death of a person.

The ancestral spirit is concerned primarily with the prosperity and continuity of the *yavusa* or group of descendants. Relationships between the living and the ancestral spirits are reciprocal; and the living are expected to present *isevu* (first-fruits) to the ancestral spirits and to maintain respect for them and their associated sites by keeping at a distance from the sites.

For instance, Erovu was the founding ancestor of the *yavusa* known as the Kai Vuda who live in the village of Lauwaki near to the first landing place of the *Kaunitoni*. He settled on top of the rocky crag inland from Viseisei, known as Korovatu. To this day, several earth/stone mounds lie on the top, to which access is physically very difficult. One of these is pointed out as the housemound of Erovu. Erovu's manifestation is a *vevewa* or owl, and, if people see an owl, they know that Erovu has a message for them. Erovu looks after the welfare of the Vuda people.

It was generally agreed in the areas where my enquiries were being made that when a person dies the *yalo* (spirit) leaves the body and goes to a cliff, waterfall or other high natural feature regarded as the *icibaciba* or *ivilavila ni yalo* (jumping-off place of the spirit) associated with its *yavusa*. From there it jumps into the sea or a pool. Such places often face the west, and by jumping towards the west the spirits may be said to be returning to the direction from whence their ancestors had come. Some told me that the *yalo* then goes first to the *yavutū* or to the Nakauvadra Mountains and then heads west. Others said that the *yalo* goes eventually to Bulu, the spirit world which is located under the Earth's surface. Burotu Kula was also described to me as a spiritual place where the living may go and stay for a while in circumstances similar to those assumed for paradise. No one ever claimed to have seen Bulu, but as recently as 1995 people of Rakiraki had seen Burotu Kula, shimmering on the horizon of the sea. They told me that they heard the spirits talking to each other, in what was referred to as the *dali/vosa vakaNiulala* (Niulala speech). In the 1950s, I met people in Rakiraki who claimed to be able to understand this speech, but in the 1990s, this facility was not ascribed to any living person. Paul Geraghty (1983a:343–384) investigated in considerable detail the possible historical origin of the mythical Polynesian homeland, Pulotu, as being in eastern Fiji. The occurrence of a site in Moala, Nadi, in the very west of Fiji is worth further investigation in connection with the overall distribution of the name. Could this reflect the origin myths of the first arrival of Austronesians from the west, their landing in Vuda (not far from Moala) and their later spread across Fiji to Polynesia? I suggest that this is a reasonable alternative to it being but a mythical echo of Polynesians returning to Fiji, especially Lau, and then to the west of Fiji.

As well as *kalou vu* there are also *kalou ni valu* responsible for the protection of the founding ancestral spirits and their descendants against some threat or impending disaster such as an imminent attack. For instance, in the general Nadi area, the war spirit Limasa is associated with the original inhabitants, the Kovacaki. He appears as an owl by day and as a *kitou* or honeyeater by night. His abode is at Naviqwa west of Nadi, and comprises an earthen mound in a grove of trees. The site where the *bete* communicates with him is at Nasavusavu on the edge of the town of Nadi. It comprises a dolmen-like structure, being a capstone with petroglyphs and collapsed uprights, and some nearby earthen mounds. A large brown spirit dog is said to guard the site.

Communication between the living and the *kalou vu* or *kalou ni valu* would normally be through the *bete* of the group associated with that spirit. This would involve the presentation of *yaqona* (*kava*) to the *bete*, and the pouring of a libation onto the ground for the spirit. The priest would either go into a trance or receive a message from the spirit in a dream. Other people find in a dream or in a trance that they have a certain power to communicate with spirits, which they would do again through the medium of the *yaqona* ceremony. Such unofficial seers are known by such terms as *daurairai*, *dautadra* or *daunivucu*. This communication is two-way, and the living might approach the spirit, or the spirit might approach the living in a dream or in a trance. As well as ancestral spirits responsible for the prosperity and continuity of a descent group, and spirits of war responsible for defence against and assistance in combating threats and disasters, other protective spirits aim to ensure that such disasters do not occur at all. In the Nadi/Vuda area, they were referred to as *tuwawa*, a word which is sometimes translated as 'giant'. In Rakiraki they were referred to as (*sasa*)*bai* or *ba*, literally a physical defence work such as a bank, fence or wall, but in the case of the spirits, the word is used figuratively as a spiritual defence or deterrent.

A *tuwawa* named Bituwewe is said to dwell on top of the Tualeita, the mountain range overlooking the Sabeto Valley just north of Nadi. He appears as an *ecola balavu* (tall man). Although he has no apparent ancestral connections with the Betoraurau people living in the valley, he is regarded by them as the defender of the valley and was in times of war the spiritual deterrent against attack by the Vuda people on the other side of the range. A rock formation on top of the range is pointed out as his head (towards the sea), his stomach, his legs and his feet.

The spirit of the *kalou vu* is responsible for the general prosperity of the *yavusa* of which it is progenitor, and in some areas there are also spirits regarded as being responsible for prosperity in spheres of activity such as agriculture, fishing or hunting. Nawaka, a federation of *yavusa* just inland from Nadi, recognised not only ancestral spirits and war spirits but also a number of so-called *digiwai* spirits—one responsible for successful food crops, another for success in hunting, and a third for fishing. These spirits could in turn expect to be respected and looked after by the living, by suitable presentations of food and *yaqona*. Failure on the part of the living to fulfill their reciprocal obligations could result in drought or in a person being bitten by a wild pig or by a shark.

Spirits are not only concerned with the way that mortals treat them. Some spirits are primarily concerned with the way mortals behave towards each other in their *yavusa*. Social offences include, at any rate nowadays (perhaps under missionary influence), the wearing of inadequate clothing in public (especially by women), yelling, laughing unduly in the middle of the village, or wearing a head cover in the village. These spirits watch out for such breaches of customary codes of conduct, propriety and behaviour in relation to their fellow mortals, and are liable to appear before the offenders and cause them to be very frightened or to suffer some spiritual punishment such as sickness or worse. An offender was formerly also liable to be beaten or fined on the instructions of the local chief.

Near Vunitogoloa to the west of Rakiraki, a low mound under some trees is said to be the abode of Losausauega, a female spirit who, if there is too much noise in the village, appears as a spider. In the local communalect, *sausauega* means 'spider' and *lo* is an honorific female prefix. Similarly, in Vitawa in the *vanua* of Navatu to the west of Rakiraki, the male spirit 'Abumasi appears without his clothes to shame persons who make an unseemly noise in or near the Sue Levu, the house of 'U Nava'u, head of the Navatu group.

Spirits referred to so far have been fundamentally benevolent, but they might become malevolent if not properly respected or treated, or if accepted codes of conduct of mortals are abused or disregarded. Other spirits appear to be innately malevolent, though they could be induced to be benevolent. Lewatumomo, a female spirit, has as her abode a large rock at Koronubu south of Ba between Rakiraki and Lautoka. She was recently seen riding a bicycle, appearing as a half-woman, half-*veli* or gnome. If she wishes to cause a woman's death, she would appear as a handsome young man and seduce the woman who would duly die. She appears as a girl if her intended victim is a man. However, those who wish to seek her protection, especially those connected with her, may do so after presenting her with *yaqona*.

The capacity to change sex to achieve death by seduction was fairly common among malevolent individual and basically female spirits. It occurred in cases involving pairs of female spirits—one regarded as benevolent and one regarded as malevolent—who were recorded in both Vuda/Nadi and in Rakiraki, usually associated with rocks and mounds. The malevolent one of the pair had the capacity to change sex. For instance, two such female spirits known as the Lewasasa dwell at Nalala near the present village of Saunaka near Nadi. A similar pair of female spirits referred to as Na Drua, the twins, are associated with a stone mound on AiSokula land at Namolausiga, east of Rakiraki.

Among other well-known spirits are the *leka* (dwarfs) reported in coastal areas and the interior. They appeared to humans, and seemed to be generally benevolent. *Veli* (gnomes) occurred mainly in the interior, and seemed to be disinterested in humans and human behaviour. *Luve ni vai* (water elfs), and *kalou rērē* (with long vowels, so Capell 1941 who called them 'timid spirits' is probably wrong) appear to be spirits associated with specific cults. *Luve ni vai* were evidently the object of attention of youth groups, and *kalou rērē* were apparently invoked in cults concerned with immortality. *Kalou vatu* (stone spirits) were apparently carried into battle. Unfortunately there is little information about these other supernatural spirits, and nowadays their significance and powers are generally not understood.

Vanua and places

Place, the second of the three elements of *vanua* 1, includes agricultural land, forest land and fishing areas owned communally by people descended, ideally, unilineally from a recognised common ancestor. Especially, for the purpose of this research, it includes sites associated with the original and other spirits as well as sites associated with people.

Sites associated with the spirits may be broadly divided into archaeological sites, being mortal-made or developed, and natural sites. Not all sites can however be fitted exactly into one or other of these categories. One of the best-known sites associated with the spirits is the Nakauvadra

Mountains from which so many of the founding ancestors of descent groups were believed to have originated. The mountains are steeply sloped and, rising to nearly 870 m, literally and spiritually dominate the Rakiraki area, for which they provide a dramatic and fascinating backdrop. On the mountain tops and slopes, many sites, both archaeological and natural, are associated with such creatures as the culture hero Degei; original spirits known in Rakiraki as O Kora na 'U Matu'a (the old folk); Na Drua (the twins); a spirit drum known as Rogorogo i Vuda (Sounding to Vuda); Degei's cave (really a crevice in a rock); Turukawa, a dove from Tonga as well as Bilovesi, a girl from Tonga; and the *vugayali*, a tree the roots of which are associated with spirit paths. These various myths may be regarded as separate myths of different origins diachronically or synchronically; or they may represent a series of separate myths integrated into what is now regarded as one overall myth.

In the course of the research, visits were made to over 200 archaeological and natural sites, and it soon appeared that almost any Fijian archaeological site was regarded as having some general connection with the spirit world. Such sites would include those of habitation, defence, ceremony or burial. In addition, a large number of sites are regarded as having a particular association with the spirit world and with individual spirits. A brief description of such archaeological and natural sites follows, together with accounts of protocol to be followed in connection with visits to sites and of consequences to breaches of protocol.

Koro makawa (old habitation sites) are generally manifested by *yavu*, usually being rectangular mounds of earth, sometimes surrounded by *lauvatu* (stone walling). Defended sites fall broadly into two categories. The ring-ditch or oval site, typically including a number of mounds surrounded by a bank and ditch with four causeways, is usually found on flat land. The hill fort with walls of stone or earth banks and terracing is usually found on hilltops or sides. Some natural caves had been developed for defensive purposes by the addition of stone walling.

Burial sites include *sautabu* (chiefly burial grounds sometimes represented by long rectangular earth mounds with the graves marked with stones); burials in old habitation or ceremonial sites such as the main ceremonial mound on the chiefly island of Bau known as Navatanitawake; or burials in caves with either single or multiple burials present.

A common feature of the archaeological landscape is the monolith, either standing on the level or on a mound. They include monoliths associated with particular spirits, *vatu ni veibuli* or installation stones for chiefs, *vatu ni bokola* or braining stones for cannibal rites, and boulders with petroglyphs.

Many archaeological sites have a particular association with the ancestors and spirits, and are regarded as *tabu* or very difficult of access. Such sites include mounds regarded as *yavutū* (sites first settled by the founding ancestor; mounds for the presentation of goods including *isevu* (first fruits) to the ancestral spirits; mounds for the *veibuli* (installation) of chiefs; mounds usually circular and high for the house where the ancestral spirits were consulted, known as *bure kalou* or, in the Vuda/Nadi area, *beto* or *bito*; linear banks of stone or earth with associated mounds and monoliths, connected either with the performance of *solevu* (ceremonial exchange of goods between groups) or, in certain areas where they are known as *naga*, with the enactment of initiation ceremonies.

The *yavutū* especially is regarded as imbued with *mana* (supernatural power) through its association with the founding ancestor and his or her *mana*. Thus emotional feeling and psychological attachment to the *yavutū* are strong among members of the *yavusa* or group descended from that founding ancestor. It is generally believed that disturbance of the *yavutū* by any persons irrespective of group would cause the ancestors through their *mana* to bring about death, sickness or misfortune to the transgressors or to their relations or to members of the group or their descendants. The *mana* associated with the *yavutū* and the ancestors was believed to enhance the productivity of the natural resources of the associated land and the sea, to ensure the continuity of the *yavusa*. Thus the *mana* of the *yavutū* and the associated spirits could result in good or evil, depending on how people practise, or fail to practise, customarily acceptable behaviour in regard to the site and the associated spirits.

Some of these sites particularly associated with the spirit world include multiple stone settings, sometimes being dolmen-like structures with capstone and stone uprights but more commonly a number of stones set on a mound. Most common are monoliths set up on a mound or apparently standing by themselves, sometimes marked with petroglyphs. Basalt hexagonal columns seem to have been of special significance—those beside Navatanitawake (the main spirit mound on Bau); and those beside the church at Lomanikoro, Rewa, were brought traditionally from Kadavu.

Natural sites associated with spirits are usually isolated rocks or rock faces, with or without petroglyphs; or pools, being either springs or pools in a stream or pools in the sea. Other such sites include hilltops or isolated islands. A special category of natural sites is the jumping-off place of the spirits of the dead, one of which is usually associated with a particular *yavusa* or several closely associated *yavusa*. Such sites are often cliff faces, waterfalls or hillsides, beside a stream or the sea. When a person dies, the spirit is believed to go to such a site and jump into the water, often onto a rock or *yamotu* (isolated reef) sometimes identified as a vessel in which the spirit sails off to the spirit world. In many cases the spirit is said to jump in a westerly direction, the direction from which the progenitors of the Fijians are said, according to the *Kaunitoni* myth, to have come. It is also the direction of the setting sun, which is associated with the death of a chiefly person, as in the expression 'Sa dromu na mata ni siga' (the sun has set).

One could generally see how a particular mound associated with, for instance, a deceased paramount chief came to be regarded with fear and respect. On the other hand, an innocuous-looking rock or an insignificant pool was often regarded as *tabu* because it was believed to be associated with some spirit. For instance, on the island of Malake, there is a rock with a mark recognised as resembling a vagina, and this is pointed out as the abode of a female spirit. It is, however, often problematic as to how a featureless natural site initially came to be associated with a spirit and hence became regarded as *tabu*, whereas another apparently similar pool or rock was said to have no such association and was not regarded as *tabu*. Such connection may have originated from an experience in a dream or trance, as I have been told.

Such is the great variety of sites that can be found in Fiji, both man-made and natural, including rocks inscribed with petroglyphs, which are associated with the spirits and the spirit world. These archaeological and natural sites associated with the supernatural represent an important element of the physical dimensions of the *vanua* and are collectively referred to as *vanua tabu* (tabu sites). *Vanua tabu* have a supernatural importance for a polity, being the physical focus points of beliefs in supernatural spirits, including ancestral spirits or other categories of spirits associated with a *vanua* which are also feared and respected.

The spirits are usually benevolent provided that due respect and attention is paid to them by the living. The relationship between humans, spirits and places was and is such that Fijians are anxious not to offend spirits or to place themselves in a position where the spirits might be able to exercise their malevolence. *Rere* (with short vowels) or fear of and respect for the spirits is expressed by taking appropriate measures not to disturb the sites and the spirits and by maintaining distance from the sites. This meant that traditionally people did not visit these sites, except for some particular ceremonial purpose such as interceding with the spirits. If a Fijian *tabu* site is to be visited for any particular purpose, a ceremonial request through the presentation of *yaqona* should first be made to the landowners. The request is then transmitted by the landowners usually through the *bete* to the spirits associated with the site.

If customary procedures such as those referred to above are not followed, the spirits can be malevolent. Cases of disrespect may be followed by sickness or death; and the anger of the spirits may continue to affect relations of the transgressor or other people involved in the disturbance and their descendants until ceremonies of apology have been performed and a peaceful relationship between the spirits and the living has been resumed. Offended spirits may show offence by entering the body of the transgressor and causing sickness or death. Such offence may be alleviated by the presentation of *yaqona* in a ceremony of *soro* (apology) known as *ibulubulu* or burial.

Fijians are especially anxious that other people do not offend the spirits, particularly by not disturbing the sites with which they are associated. Disturbances to a site could be taken to include simple visits to the site or some more physical form of disturbance such as by excavation, or even by photography or surveying. These sites are feared and respected because the associated spirits are feared and respected. They are *tabu*, because of the *mana* or *sau* of the spirits who watch over, guide and control people's activities and who have the power to do good or to harm, depending on how they and their sites are treated.

As far as my investigations are concerned, many archaeological or natural sites associated with particular spirits were identified in the Vuda/Nadi and Rakiraki areas. To avoid disturbing or offending the spirits in the course of a visit to the *yavutū* or indeed to any *tabu* site, certain recognised customary procedures were followed in order to establish a working relationship with the site owners and the spirits of the place. Such procedures involved the presentation of *yaqona* on two occasions. Before visiting a site, the first ceremony that would be performed is the *isevusevu* (a request to be allowed to visit the site and an assurance to the owners and the spirits that no undue disturbance to the site or to the spirits would result). After a visit, the ceremony to be performed was the *madrali*. This represents an expression of thanks to the owners and the spirits and a procedure to *vakasavasavataka* (to clean up) everything with a request that, if there has been some error of omission or commission on the part of the visitor, this should be excused. The spirit is asked that no misfortune or sickness should result as a consequence of the error.

Over the past few decades or so the spread of urbanisation and cash-crop agriculture had resulted in the disturbance of a number of traditional *tabu* sites. Cane farmers, especially Indians, have disturbed or levelled several sites, particularly those of *yavu* associated with the spirits of the founding ancestors. Fijian landowners often referred to the death of some of those involved in such disturbances. Not long ago, in Vatukacevaceva to the south of Rakiraki, the mound of the traditional *bure kalou* (spirit house) where the priest communicated with the ancestral spirits had been levelled and a large wooden house had been built on the site. The person for whom the house was built died almost immediately after occupying the house. Banyan trees (*vu ni baka*) were regarded as spirit places. A low rectangular mound at Vaileka, Rakiraki and some nearby *baka* or banyan trees were closely associated with Leka, the founding original ancestor of one local *yavusa*. During a hurricane in the early 1950s, one *baka* tree was badly damaged and in order to tidy up the tree some of the branches were lopped off. Leka expressed his annoyance at this additional damage to his tree by appearing as a short person (his name means short) in the middle of the night at a nearby house. Next day some of Leka's present descendants performed ceremonies of apology by first presenting dried *yaqona* and then by pouring a libation made from the *yaqona* onto the mound. Leka did not re-appear, at any rate not on this occasion.

From this it is apparent that Fijian spirits generally were, and still are, greatly respected and there is a close interrelationship between them and their human descendants. Spirits could be dangerous, especially if offended by disturbance or neglect. They could, however, be approached and appeased by ceremonial presentations of *yaqona* (*kava*) or food. Such spirits could communicate through dreams or trance, and could make their presence known by the appearance of an animate object of a certain category with which they were particularly associated. Fijian beliefs were and still are tied up intimately with sites associated closely with the ancestors in accordance with the concept of *vanua*.

The spirit world had and still has a vital part to play in the origins, unification and relationships between polities, and in validating and legitimising certain ceremonial activities such as the installation of a chief. It also had a vital role to play in the economic, social and ceremonial life of a polity, and in the behaviour of members to each other and to others. Even when reality suggests that secular power was more important in the development of a polity than spiritual power, the wielder of secular power would still seek spiritual support and legitimisation for his military and political activities.

This chapter emphasises that running through this work there is a theme to the effect that the notional basis of pre-Colonial Fijian polities was the ideological concept *vanua* 1 (as the encompassing term for traditional Fijian society), the three elements or dimensions of which were spirits, places and people. One of the most striking things about Fijian cosmology was that there was no disjunction between the realm of people and the realm of spirits. Spirits and people shared a common world, of which the geographical component included places with which both people and spirits were closely and directly associated.

Vanua and people

I now turn to a discussion of 'people' being the third dimension of *vanua* 1—that is, people, in terms of the building blocks of traditional Fijian society identified as *yavusa*, *vanua* (being *vanua* 2) and *matanitū*—concentrating on the period from the 18th century until Cession in 1874.

The human element of the ideological concept of *vanua* 1 is exemplified by that polity or group of people now referred to as a *yavusa* who trace their ancestry usually along the male line from a common founding ancestor associated with the *yavutū*. The founding ancestor was the source of *mana* which was passed down the line from father to son. Ideologically the greatest amount of *mana* was considered to have passed to the eldest son and to his eldest son, so that the group leader was ideally the eldest of the patrilineal descendants of the eldest son of the founding ancestor. It was he who was regarded as the person endowed with the greatest *mana* and on that account was ideally the person most respected and feared. If he is offended, it is as if the founding ancestor was offended and it was the *mana* of the founding ancestor which would bring retribution to the offender.

When discussing people as an element in the concept of *vanua* 1, it is appropriate to consider them in terms of polities, especially in the context of factors relating to the unity, identification, structure, dynamics and leadership of polities, be they *yavusa*, *vanua* (that is, *vanua* 2) or *matanitū*. Some factors are common to all forms of polity whether single independent *yavusa* or federations of *yavusa* forming *vanua* or confederations of *vanua* forming *matanitū*.

The yavusa

The symbols of unity and identification of a *yavusa* include:

- a common name;
- a common origin myth and a common founding ancestor; a particular form of manifestation of the spirit of this progenitor, usually an animal; a recognised place of 'residence' of the spirit, being

usually a natural feature or a mound; and a recognised place where presentations would be made to the spirit and where the bete or priest would communicate with the spirit;

- a common, usually tripartite, series of 'totemic' features, comprising a particular kind of tree and two other features, being animal or vegetable, and regarded as *tabu*;
- a common jumping-off place of the spirits of the dead; and, usually,
- a communalect, perhaps shared with other related polities.

In addition, a *yavusa* has the following features:

- it contains a number of named *mataqali* or sub-groups, and named *itokatoka* or sub-divisions within the *mataqali*. The term for such a subdivision varied in different parts of Fiji;
- it has a pattern of social stratification and traditional roles for *mataqali* and *itokatoka* within the *yavusa*. This provides a framework within which members relate to each other;
- it has recognised bases of appointment and validation of leaders. It recognises certain manifestations of social stratification and leadership. These may be sociological, such as the seating arrangements at feasts or meetings, the order of drinking *yaqona*, and the form of address. Others may be archaeologically recognisable, such as the height of a housemound, the amount of high-status pottery found in or near a mound, or the discovery of chiefly articles such as whale tooth necklaces;
- certain factors may affect the origins of, and changes to, the pattern of social stratification and the basis of leadership.

The vanua and the matanitū

Various factors may have affected the creation and organisation of named *vanua* or socio-political federations of *yavusa*, and of named *matanitū* or confederations of *vanua*; and the nature of socio-political relationships between component polities of a *vanua* or *matanitū*. They may also have affected the recognised basis of paramount leadership of a *vanua* or *matanitū*, and procedures for the appointment and validation of appointment of such a paramount. Particular spirits in the spirit world have characteristics, roles and powers relevant to the origins and unification and interrelationships of polities and the validation of appointments to chiefly office. Indeed, spirits played an important and influential part in the socio-politics of pre-Colonial Fijian society generally. However, the crucial consideration is, in reality, the interrelationship between *sau* or *mana* (spiritual power) derived from a *nitu/kalou* or spirit, and *qwaqwa* or *kaukauwa* (secular power) based on political and military strength as symbolised by the *malumu* or *iwau* (warclub).

In the case of *yavusa*, *vanua* and *matanitū*, *sema* or links, and *vau* or bonds, may have been within and between individual *yavusa* or within and between *vanua* or groups of *yavusa*, so linked and bonded. These links and bonds may have been of a mythical, genealogical, or marital nature; or have resulted from alliances of mutual socio-political advantage; military alliances; and 'tributary' relationships. My investigations consider especially how and why such links and bonds were formed, how they were maintained, and how they were discontinued. Equally important are the recognised formal and informal channels of communication within and between *yavusa*, and within and between *vanua* and *matanitū*, as well as between polities not formally federated or confederated. Various factors to be discussed later indicate how and why such channels of communication came to be established, maintained and discontinued.

4

Understanding Traditional Fijian Society

This monograph is particularly concerned with variation between polities, as following a general geographical pattern. This pattern represents a broad continuum of polities of degrees of complexity, with the simplest in the western areas of Fiji, and the most complex in the east. Previous studies (Schütz 1962, Pawley and Sayaba 1971, Geraghty 1983a, 1983b) have contrasted the east and the west in terms of history, linguistics and mutual intelligibility of communalects. They have indicated a broad dichotomy between an eastern group of communalects and a western group, whilst pointing out that within each group there is a chain of communalects of differing degrees of mutual intelligibility. Pawley and Sayaba (1971) proposed a geographical and demographic explanation which explains a considerable amount, and Pawley (1981) added some social features. This study puts forward a proposal for a pan-Fiji continuum of differing degrees of complexity and stability of polities, taking into account the various internal and external factors already referred to as well as the patterning of communalects.

These factors affected different polities to different degrees at different times depending on local circumstances which were liable to vary. Such differences can sometimes be explained by recourse to the current oral accounts; whereas other differences, especially those involving outside pressures such as those from Tonga, could be explained by recourse to sources other than the current accounts and by taking into account the proximity of the polity to the source of the pressure.

Current understanding

The first aim of my investigations is to determine how Fijians currently understand and explain the origins, development and interaction of their various polities in pre-Colonial times.

To this end, current oral accounts were recorded in the course of discussions with representatives of all the polities in the three field areas comprising Rakiraki in North-eastern Viti Levu; Nadi/Nawaka/Vuda in Western Viti Levu; and the western archipelago of the Yasawa Group. For comparative purposes, the project took into account, first, polities in areas other than the study areas; and, secondly, inter alia, the *itukutuku raraba*, being the narratives of origins and movements of polities as recorded by the Native Lands Commission (NLC) at the turn of the 19th/20th centuries. This will be discussed further in this chapter. In the course of the research, a record was made of the current oral accounts of Fijian myths, traditions, histories and symbols associated with eighty-seven *yavusa* in the Nadi/Nawaka/Vuda and Yasawa areas, and with thirty-six *yavusa* in the Rakiraki area. These were recorded by myself first when District Officer in the areas in the early 1950s and later as a researcher at ANU in the 1990s. In compiling my own accounts, I was constantly referring to the *itukutuku raraba* (traditional accounts) of the NLC (n.d).

Common features and themes for polities

The term 'polity' refers to both *yavusa* or descent groups, and socio-political constructs or (con) federations, known as *vanua* (in the sense of *vanua* 2) and *matanitū*. An analysis of the oral accounts recorded indicates how those Fijians with whom the matters were discussed, currently understand and explain:

- the origins, structure and dynamics of polities in pre-Colonial times;
- the basis of pre-Colonial socio-political and military leadership;
- pre-Colonial intra- and inter-*yavusa* relationships; and
- the internal and external influences that brought about and affected such relationships.

From these accounts and from accounts of polities in other parts of Fiji, a number of features and themes emerged as common to the pre-Colonial polities studied. They flow throughout the monograph, and form the nerves and muscles of the discussions and arguments.

Common features

Several common features of polities emerged from the accounts of pre-Colonial polities both in the study areas and in other parts of Fiji. These accounts indicate that generally:

- each *yavusa* had myths of origin and ancestral spirits;
- each *yavusa* exhibited certain symbols of group unity and identification;
- each *yavusa* had a pattern of social hierarchy, and a recognised basis for leadership;
- a number of *yavusa* often joined together wholly or partly, and formed a socio-political federation referred to as a *vanua*;
- a number of *vanua* sometimes joined together and formed a socio-political confederation referred to as a *matanitū*;
- there were patterns of linkage and bonding between polities at all levels;
- there were recognised channels of communication between certain polities at *yavusa*, *vanua* or *matanitū* level; and
- the spirit world of ancestral and other spirits, such as war spirits and defending spirits, was important in:
    - achieving and maintaining unity and 'proper behaviour';
    - ensuring prosperity and continuity;
    - validating group activities and appointments to chiefly office of leadership; and
    - maintaining some degree of stability in a society faced with outside influences such as Tonga, Christianity, and European visitors and settlers.

Common themes

Two common themes emerge from the accounts of pre-Colonial polities in the study areas. They are the following contrasting sets of ideologies and realities:

(a)
    (i)   the ideology of social unity and integrity; and

    (ii) the realities of social fusion and fission;

(b)
    (i)   the ideology of allocation of power based on the concept of inherited *sau* or *mana* (spiritual power); and

    (ii) the reality of achieved *kaukauwa* or *qwāqwā* (secular power) based on the war club and the spear, leadership disputes and external leadership.

A key focus of the research has been to assess the linking of, and synthesis between, these two contrasting sets of ideologies and realities.

Social unity, fusion and fission

The current oral accounts may reflect an ideology of social unity and integrity at *yavusa* level, but they also indicate how a *yavusa* was seen to develop not only on the basis of natural increase but also through the realities of social fusion and fission. The latter came about not only internally through factors of ambition and jealousy, but also on the development of good and bad relationships with other polities. Current accounts of the past are also important to a *yavusa* as symbols of its unity and identification. They recount its supposed victories and successes which are a matter of pride, and its supposed defeats. The victories and successes are recounted in order to explain how a *yavusa* became the paramount of a federation of polities consisting of a number of *yavusa*. This could have been either by defeating its neighbours or by associating with weaker *yavusa* which came to it for protection or by forming military alliances with other *yavusa*. The defeats could have been included as an explanation for the *yavusa*'s formal association with the strong, respected polity which defeated it and brought it under its authority. Currently the *yavusa* may well take pride in this association, however it may have developed in reality. In this way, the accounts can turn successes and defeats to the advantage of a *yavusa* in its position in current Fijian society.

Spiritual and secular power

The current accounts also indicate an underlying ideology of allocation of power based on the concept of maximum *mana* inherited through the most direct male line of descent from the original ancestral spirit. They also indicate how leadership may have been based not only on inherited *mana* and descent but also on the realities of internal leadership changes or disputes, as well as the acceptance (forced or voluntary) of external leaders. Such themes are relevant to the understanding of Fijian society past and present, and also, to a limited extent, to an exploration of Fijian society in the wider context of neighbouring Tonga, Rotuma and even Samoa as forming a quadrilateral interaction zone in late prehistoric and proto-historic times. There is archaeological evidence of such interaction before the period covered by this monograph. The forms of structure and leadership of Fijian polities are considered in the general perspective of neighbouring Oceanic polities. The project is also placed in the context of relevant literature and comparable accounts such as those recorded by the NLC, relating to Fijian polities, places and spirits.

Factors affecting variation in polities

By the period immediately preceding Cession in 1874, the polities in the Yasawa Group, the west and northeast of Viti Levu, and eastern Fiji, especially Bau, Rewa and Cakaudrove, had developed to different degrees of socio-political complexity. Of these, the simplest were generally in the west and the most complex were in the east. It is easier to understand any particular polity in relation to a continuum rather than a dichotomy of complexity.

The simplest form of polity was an independent *yavusa*, a group who claimed descent from a single original ancestor in spirit form (*kalou vu*) or in human form (simply *vu*); and who maintained its internal unity and its independence from any external authority. The most complex form of major polity was a *matanitū* or confederation of several *vanua*, or federations of *yavusa*, with a recognised leading *yavusa* and an accepted paramount chief. Such a confederation included a number of *bati* or military allies, and of *qali* or tributaries, being minor federations of *yavusa* (or *vanua*), or single *yavusa*. Such allies or tributaries might have been conquered or have sought protection from hostile neighbours or have simply recognised the socio-political advantages of a formal association with a strong and respected leading group and a powerful and generous paramount chief.

In between these extremes, investigation shows that there were forms of polity which manifested varying quantitative degrees of complexity of federation of *yavusa* or parts of *yavusa* or of groups of *yavusa*, and which experienced varying qualitative degrees of stability.

An analysis of available evidence based on current accounts has indicated that during the earliest period to which these accounts relate, the simplest form of polity, the independent *yavusa*, or descent group, was, generally, the earliest form of polity recognised. More complex forms, such as *vanua* based on a federation of *yavusa*, were usually a later development. However polities developed in the pre-Colonial period, they retained certain common features and themes as already described. In spite of these common themes and features, it is highly unlikely that there had ever been a golden age of homogeneity. Indeed, an analysis of current Fijian understandings of the structure and dynamics of pre-Colonial polities indicates a considerable variation in the degree of complexity of these polities. Variation was manifested in such factors as socio-political unity, and structure and dynamics including leadership especially as socio-political federations developed, at any rate towards the end of the pre-Colonial period. An analysis of the factors affecting the variation between polities can be undertaken from the point of view of whether they were internal or external to the system of polities being studied. Internal factors are those which can be considered within the parameters of the three elements of the ideological concept of *vanua* (in the sense of *vanua* 1); that is, spirits, places and people. These elements of *vanua* 1 permeated all forms of polity, including the *yavusa* or descent group and such socio-political constructs or federations referred to as *vanua* (in the sense of *vanua* 2) or as *matanitū*.

Internal factors: spirits, places and people

Variations in pre-Colonial socio-political unity and structure, in fusion and fission, and in federation and confederation, may have been due in part to factors internal to the polities. Such factors might have been ease of geographical access between polities, availability of planting land in the areas involved, insults and quarrels, and the expansive careers of ambitious and able leaders with military and naval powers, such as Cakobau, Vunivalu of Bau.

Another significant factor affecting the variations in the unity, structure and dynamics of polities is the extent to which they were connected with important centres of the spirit world, often based on dramatic natural features. For instance, the settlements of the various *yavusa* of the polities in the Rakiraki area lie just below the glowering Nakauvadra range and one of the most respected of Fijian spirit centres at the peak of Uluda. Many of the *yavusa* of the polities in the Vuda area were adjacent to the spirit path along the dramatic Tualeita Range and a respected spirit centre based on caves at Edronu at the west end of the Range. Uluda is associated with the spirit Degei and the other spirits who settled there with him and later spread throughout Fiji as progenitors of many *yavusa*. Edronu is associated with the first mythical arrivals in Fiji, many of whom went on and settled on the Nakauvadra range. The Rakiraki and Vuda *yavusa* have close traditional connections with these places. They gained considerable spiritual and political prestige from their close association with these spirit centres and from their spiritual connections with other *yavusa* whose progenitors had spread from these centres to other parts of Fiji.

Oft-recurring internal factors in the emergence of differences between polities as they developed are:

* local ambitions and quarrels within a *yavusa* leading to fission and fusion with other *yavusa* or to the establishment of a separate *yavusa*; and quarrels and rivalries;

- recognition by a *yavusa* that another *yavusa* was particularly strong and worthy of respect and subservience; and
- regional pressures from other *yavusa* with ambitious leaders wishing to expand their sphere of influence through the development of socio-political relationships or through warfare.

External factors

Variation between polities may also have been due once again to factors external to the polities being studied, such as:

- the influence of Tonga;
- the introduction of Christianity;
- the demands of European settlers and traders for land and security; and
- the need for the Cakobau Government to assert its authority outside Cakobau's traditional areas of authority especially in the independent west.

Oft recurring external factors in the emergence of differences between polities as they developed are:

- external pressures from expansionist Tongans; Christianity and overseas missionaries; Cakobau, first as Vunivalu of Bau and then in 1867 as European-crowned King of Bau, and later in June 1871 as proclaimed King of Fiji; and the Cakobau Government of Fiji established at the same time with the backing of some European settlers;
- the ideology of Tongan paramount authority and eventual monarchy, of which ambitious Eastern chiefs, especially of Bau, had had first hand experience during visits to Tonga;
- proximity to spiritual central places such as Uluda and the Nakauvadra Mountains or the cave complex of Edronu at the west end of the Tualeita Range, and the interplay between the spiritual unifying force derived from a common place of origin of ancestral spirits, and the secular sense of security derived from association with a strong and protective paramount;
- the degree of availability, strength and loyalty of allied military and naval forces which could enable an ambitious leader to expand his traditional sphere of influence and to maintain his position of paramountcy in the face of internal dissidence and external hostility; and
- the realities of *kaukauwa* or secular power as symbolised by the war club and the spear, and the ideology of *sau* or *mana* or spiritual power as a legitimising force.

As far as the east is concerned one of the most significant factors in the dynamics of polities was the highly ambitious and remarkably able chiefs and the military and naval forces at their command. A second was a series of external factors, namely the external influences of Tongan ideology of paramountcy; Tongan military power and expansion ambition; and the acceptance of Christianity, perhaps often largely in return for Tongan military assistance.

As far as the central regions are concerned the most important factors were the proximity to the main spiritual centre of the Nakauvadra as a unifying force; warfare to the south of Nakauvadra resulting in people being forced over the range to take refuge with the polities on the north side; and quarrels between ambitious leaders who gathered people together to assist them in their warfare.

As far as the western area and the islands were concerned the polities were noteworthy for the spirit of independence and local pride which prevailed, especially as regards the east. This spirit was symbolised by the myths of origin of several groups which relate not to the Nakauvadra but to the central spirit place at Edronu near the traditional first landing, where those who did not go on up to the Nakauvadra remained. Edronu was regarded in Vuda as more important than the Nakauvadra because it was an earlier and therefore more respected site. The external factors listed had a minimum effect on the west until the time of Cakobau and the sometimes-forced introduction of Christianity which was regarded as a political device of Cakobau and of the eastern polities. These outside influences were regarded with grave suspicion in the west as being likely to affect their independence, except perhaps in those areas in Vuda. Traditions of a very early arrival of Christians in Vuda and the apparently supporting evidence of ancient buttons carefully preserved in Viseisei Church cause the Vuda people to believe that they had become Christianised before the east.

Assessment of current accounts

Sources of data

The second aim of this research is to assess the reasonableness and accuracy of the recorded oral accounts of current Fijian understanding of the origins, and structure and dynamics, including leadership, of late pre-Colonial *yavusa* and the more complex forms of polity.

These accounts may be assessed by taking into account:

- evidence for internal and external consistency and inconsistency;
- early written records;
- limited archaeological evidence resulting from surface (and somewhat superficial) surveys; and
- linguistic information obtained from speakers of local communalects.

This is the basis of the evaluation in this research of the current oral accounts of the *yavusa* in the three geographical areas in the northeast and west of Viti Levu and in the Yasawa group. This evaluation focuses on questions such as whether the accounts have some absolute chronological and historical basis; or whether they are merely myths of origin and tales of half-remembered, half-fictional military and political successes aimed at validating current attempts at self-aggrandisement. In the assessment of the reasonableness and accuracy of current Fijian understanding, account is given of the consistency or inconsistency between accounts by different *yavusa* when referring to the same event. The following sources of data are also used:

- accounts recorded by the Lands Claims Commission (LCC) between 1875 and 1882; by the NLC at the turn of the 19th/20th centuries; and by written accounts by early visitors, missionaries and settlers as well as occasional personal accounts written by members of some *yavusa* and preserved in villages;
- information about the locations and features of about 200 archaeological and natural sites associated with these *yavusa* and their associated spirits as recorded in the course of my explorations; and
- basic linguistic information I recorded in the 1950s and the 1990s, in respect of eleven communalects recognised by the polities in the two mainland study areas, as well as data collected by me from various parts of the Yasawa group. The main sources of information about Yasawa communalects are from the work of Raven Hart on the island of Yasawa and of Andrew Pawley on the island of Waya.

Particular attention is paid to inconsistencies as well as consistencies arising from this use of data other than current oral accounts. Attempts are made to explain such inconsistencies, especially in regard to the extent to which current accounts either deliberately follow the NLC records or deliberately contradict them. Generally, even the earliest places mentioned in the oral accounts have been found by exploration to exist in the archaeological landscape. A comparison between features of such sites, such as the size and nature of spirit mounds, can be used to show a correlation between the importance of such a site according to the oral account and the characteristics of such features on the ground. People currently regard their communalect as a symbol of unity and identification. Investigations support the reasonableness of a communalect as such a symbol, and patterns revealed by the distribution of the communalects seem to show a parallel with the nature and patterning, either geographical or social, of Fijian society as revealed in the oral accounts.

An analysis of these sets of data reveals links between the spirit world, archaeological and natural sites, people and communalects. These sets of data can be integrated in ways relevant to a favourable assessment of the reasonableness and accuracy of current accounts of how Fijian society understands and explains the origins and the structure and dynamics, including leadership, of late prehistoric and proto-historic Fijian society.

Integrating the data

The multi-disciplinary and integrative methodologies used in this monograph are able to:

- use oral traditions to help to locate archaeological and natural sites;
- use the archaeological evidence of located sites to complement, and help to assess and evaluate the reasonableness of such oral traditions;
- compare the patterns, both social and geographical, of communalects and socio-political groups; and
- elucidate what are currently claimed to be the myths of origin of specific *yavusa*, integrating these myths with the evidence of oral history, archaeology and such symbols of identification and unification as ancestral and other spirits and their associated sites and manifestations, as well as particular totem-like categories of tree, living creature or food, and the jumping-off places of spirits of the dead.

The value of such an analysis of integrated data from several study areas is that the project is not dependent on simply one set of data, but on a series of integrated sets of data involving various disciplines. Such an interdisciplinary approach has been helpful in the final analysis of the information, not only from the point of view of those immediately concerned (that is, the living members of the groups subject to the investigation), but also from the point of view of the investigator as a sympathetic but critical outsider concerned with analysing the data from the various sources in order to assess the reasonableness and accuracy of current oral accounts.

When sources appeared to differ in explanation or in a material degree, such differences were first referred to informants, and the reasonableness of the varying accounts and the circumstances in which they were obtained were discussed. Where the accounts differed and the matter could not be resolved satisfactorily, both accounts were recorded with some argument for the preferred version, taking into account all the evidence available, even if such an account was to the disadvantage of the informants. For instance, Cakaudrove chiefs told me that they were descended from Tongans. The NLC records, Sayes' (1982) doctoral research and my own investigations in Ra and southern Vanua Levu suggest otherwise. It is almost certain that the Tui Cakau and other leading Cakaudrove chiefs were in fact descended from some Rakiraki people who came to Cakaudrove and were singularly successful in helping those already there in their local quarrels. The locals, out of gratitude and recognising the strength of these Rakiraki people, made them paramount. Such an origin from a place of scant repute as far as the east is concerned would quite understandably be unacceptable, indeed insulting, to the proud Kings of the Reef.

Polity dynamics: general comments

My research concentrates on exploring those factors, both local and external, which generally affected the origins, development, structure and interaction of pre-Colonial forms of polities such as the *yavusa* or descent groups, and *vanua* 2 or socio-political federations, as well as the dynamics of their restructuring by fusion and fission. It investigates how pre-Colonial Fijian society, the geographical landscape and the Fijian spirit world were intermeshed. It identifies internal factors which created unity at the *yavusa* level and led to relationships of varying degrees of complexity between *yavusa*. The concepts of unity, identification and the sense of belonging; hierarchy, leadership based on descent, and reciprocal obligations; and spiritual support and sanctions are seen to be golden threads running through Fijian society. These threads were strengthened, tarnished, weakened or disentangled because of a variety of circumstances arising from time to time and from area to area. These circumstances often led to situations in which the protagonists involved needed to take measures for self-preservation and mutual protection. Such situations might have arisen out of a variety of circumstances. Investigations have focused on, first, breaches of propriety and failure to meet obligations; secondly, personal ambition and arrogance; thirdly, leadership based on factors other than descent, such as personal suitability; fourthly, military or political expansion based on secular force; and, fifthly, on the influences of external economic, military, political, spiritual and religious ideologies and forces.

The degree of interplay of these concepts in differing circumstances and situations shows variations in the complexity of socio-political structure. These variations were manifestations of a flexibility characterising, in reality, the structure and dynamics of pre-Colonial Fijian society. Whatever varieties might, however, have occurred in particular polities in Fijian society, there were also common features which formed the basis of such a society. These features are the spiritual, social and physical dimensions of the ideological concept of *vanua* 1.

The results of explorations of the oral accounts of the origins and development of *yavusa* recorded in the course of this project in the three main study areas indicate that there were general ideal principles and concepts underlying Fijian society before the Lands Commissioners made their investigations and pronouncements. Further, the basis of pre-Colonial Fijian leadership, at any rate during the two centuries or so before Cession was as much dependent on circumstances and achievement as it was on descent. In practice, the interpretation of, and degree of adherence to, such principles was varied and pragmatic. It emerges that the dynamics of late pre-Colonial Fijian society were, not unexpectedly, much more fluid and flexible than those of its Colonial period successor, the structure of the polities of which had been regularised by the NLC and the Colonial Government, and regulated by Colonial legislation.

5

Factors Affecting Development and Interaction

This chapter discusses factors that might have, first, led to the development of differing degrees of complexity and stability in polities in different parts of Fiji; and secondly, resulted in various forms of interaction between polities and between polities and external influences.

General background

Socio-political, historical, archaeological and linguistic information, as gathered from other sources as well as my own enquiries, indicate that southeastern and eastern polities outside the areas directly covered by my research project included highly complex, relatively stable, socio-political confederations or *matanitū,* such as those of Bau, Cakaudrove, Rewa and Verata (see Appendix A).

Research in the field revealed first, a proliferation of small, independent social polities (usually identified as *yavusa,* or descent groups) or simple, generally unstable socio-political federations (sometimes identified as *vanua)* found in western areas in Vuda, Nadi and Nawaka, and in the Yasawa Group; and, secondly, the development of relatively complex and stable socio-political federations or *vanua* found in Rakiraki in the northeast of Viti Levu.

The exploration of factors, internal and external, relating to the unity, identification, structure, dynamics and leadership of polities throughout Fiji indicates that polities in different areas tended to develop to different degrees of complexity and to manifest different degrees of stability (cf. Sahlins1963).

Internal factors

Variations in the socio-political unity and structure of pre-Colonial polities generally may have resulted from fusion and fission within and between polities, or through federation and confederation. These variations might have been due in part to factors internal to a particular region, such as:

- ease of geographical access between polities;
- availability of planting land in the areas involved;
- access to natural resources;
- or internal to a particular polity, such as:
- insults and quarrels;
- the need for mutual assistance between polities, especially in times of assault by neighbouring polities; and

- the expansive careers of ambitious and able leaders such as Cakobau of Bau, with supporting military and naval power.

External factors

Variations may also have been due to external factors outlined already, such as:

(a)   the multiple settlements of Fiji in earliest times, from the west and from the east;

(b)   the impact of Tongan monarchical ideology and expansionist ambitions;

(c)   the arrival of European visitors, settlers and traders;

(d)   the introduction of Christianity and the arrival of overseas missionaries; and

(e)   the degree of influence of Cakobau and the Cakobau Governments of 1867 and 1871.

These factors affected the development and interaction of pre-Colonial Fijian polities to a greater or less degree in different parts at different times, but especially in the west during the somewhat novel circumstances of the 19th century. To make them more readily understandable and to emphasise their significance, I will discuss the backgrounds to, effects from, and reactions in traditional Fijian polities to each of these factors.

Discussion on external factors

(a) The multiple settlements of Fiji in earliest times

Except for a single 'palaeolith'—and that of dubious provenance—held in the Fiji Museum, no evidence is currently available that Fiji was settled in pre-Lapita times. The first arrival in Fiji, presumably from the west, of people associated with the Lapita culture was about 2900 BP (Anderson et al. 2001:7). Geoff Clark (2000:253), studying the 1500 years after the end of the Fiji Lapita period in about 2650 BP, was primarily concerned with socio-political divergence in Fiji, and especially when it 'first began, and the rate, timing and cause of culture change in the archipelago', whereas this monograph is more concerned with interaction between Tonga and Fiji during this period, especially during late prehistoric and proto-historic times involving Tongan ambitions to dominate Fiji.

Interaction between Tonga and Fiji had long been military, socio-political and marital. The earliest archaeological evidence for Tongan ambitions to impose their authority in Fiji may be the massive defended site at Ulunikoro, Lakeba, dated to about 1000 BP (Best 1984:658). Best suggested that Tongans built this fortress to serve as a base from which they could assert their power initially over the Lau group before extending westwards. Later, Tongans began to move to other parts of Fiji. Fortifications were constructed on Taveuni by 800 BP. Though Frost (1974:118) explained them as defences against migration from the west, they could equally have been erected in anticipation of Tongan aggression from the east.

(b) The impact of Tongan expansionist ambitions and monarchic ideology

The impact of Tongan political ambitions on the polities of Fiji was plainly manifested in the Tongan settlement of Lau during the 19th century. As for the west, traditions tell of a Tongan, known in Fiji as Wakanimolikina, who became stranded on the island of Yanuca near Cuvu, Nadroga. Because of his fair skin and good looks, he was chosen to be the chief of the Nadroga people. Other Tongans are said to have landed on the island of Vatulele south of Nadroga, and on Viwa, the furthest west in the Yasawa group. In Nadroga, members of the *yavusa* of Noi Toga claimed (Gifford 1951b:254; and I have checked with Fijians in the area) to be descendants of Finau Maile Latumai, a chief of Tongatapu who with a number of Tongans was banished from

Tonga. They sailed first to the island of Serua and then to the southern coast of Nadroga where they settled. Later they moved inland to the magnificent hill fort of Tavuni on the Sigatoka River. Maile is buried on the hill of Serua where he had lived, and present descendants live below Tavuni at Narara and the nearby villages of Malevu and Nawamagi. The Tongan population in Lau increased considerably during the 19th century with the arrival of disaffected chiefs, restless warriors and adventurers.

In later prehistoric times, considerable social intercourse had persisted between Fijian chiefs and Tongans, and the former were fully aware of Tongan expansionist ambitions. These were reflected in the patterns of political, military and religious rivalries.

In proto-historic times, Tongan impact and influence affected the stability of, and interaction between pre-Colonial Fijian polities in two ways. First, the Tongan political ideology of, and ambitions for high chieftainship and, from 1845, knowledge of Tongan monarchy spread to eastern Fiji through marriage and the exchange of visits with Tonga. For many years, considerable social intercourse persisted between Fijian chiefs and Tongans, and the former were fully aware of the Tongan ideology of paramountcy and ambitions for eventual monarchy. Paramountcy was a factor of the patterns of political, military and religious rivalries between the major groups in Tonga; and monarchic ambitions were realised in 1845 in the union of Tonga under the strongest paramount, Tui Kanakopolu, whose baptismal name was Kini Jioji (King George) Taufa'ahau. He became Tupou I, the first King of Tonga. The Tongan political ideology of paramountcy and achievement of monarchy fired the ambitions of the able eastern Fijian chiefs such as Cakobau. Cakobau, as Vunivalu or war chief of Bau had risen to the position of paramountcy in the major *matanitū* of Bau by forcefully subordinating and expelling the spiritual chief, Roko Tui Bau.

Secondly, the political Tongans living in far-eastern Fiji proceeded to obtrude themselves significantly into Fijian affairs, challenging the chiefs and imposing on the people. This obtrusion developed into an expansionist policy of Tonga to control all Fiji, affected partly under the guise of imposing the Tongan Wesleyan religion, and partly though the sheer military and naval might and resources of Tongans living in Fiji. With the blessings of King Tupou I who was glad to get rid of his troublesome young kinsman, Enele Ma'afu'otu'itonga came to Lau in 1848 and after some years proceeded to organise and lead the Tongans there. At the same time Tongan teachers came to spread Christianity. Ma'afu, by intervening in local quarrels, working through the teachers and extending the new faith, proceeded to control the Lomaiviti islands. Then, by assisting Vakawaletabua, Tui Bua, whose mother was Tongan and whose authority was being challenged in Bua, he extended his authority by military might over much of Macuata and Bua on the island of Vanua Levu. He later sent parties of warriors to occupy Beqa and Kadavu. Tui Bua in return assisted in imposing the Tongan Church on the island of Yasawa, where he had traditional connections.

A skilled warrior, statesman, diplomat and administrator, Ma'afu posed as protector of the missionaries, patron of the traders and friend of Cakobau. Nevertheless, he still maintained and extended the areas where he could impose his authority, if necessary by force. He had two lieutenants, Wainiqolo or Vainikoro, and Semisi Fifita. They terrorised those in the Yasawa Group who opposed the Tongan Church (referred to as the *lotu lasu* or false Christianity by Fijians whom the Wesleyan missionaries had converted). They even interfered in leadership quarrels in Rakiraki.[1]

(c) Interaction with European visitors, settlers, planters, traders and representatives

The first recorded appearances of Europeans in Fiji were by Tasman in 1643, Cook in 1774 and Bligh in the ship's launch after the *Bounty* mutiny in 1789. These appearances resulted in no

---

1   Derrick (1946) provides a useful background to such interaction between Fijians and Tongans.

direct contact, although Bligh recorded in his log on 7th May, that he had discovered islands in Fiji and 'was chased by two large canoes', probably in the north Yasawa group. In 1794, Captain Wilson in the *Arthur* on her way from Port Jackson to America was attacked and two crew members were wounded by arrows off the western coast of Viti Levu.

Early European visitors had no social contact with Fijians, except for members of the crew of the *Pandora*'s tender in 1791. They were looking for the crew of the *Bounty*, and spent five weeks on an island, perhaps Ono-i-Lau or Matuku, where they were hospitably received by the locals. They were probably the first Europeans to have such close contact with Fijians.

Among the first to settle in Fiji were those who survived shipwrecks or deserted visiting trading vessels; and a number of these became integrated into Fijian society. The first record of Europeans living among the Fijians for any length of time was probably in or about 1800. The United States schooner *Argo* was wrecked on the Bukatatanoa Reef near Lakeba in the Lau group, and one or two of the crew survived slaughter and cannibalism, and remained in Fiji. One of these was Oliver Slater, who first reported the existence in western Vanua Levu of sandalwood, a commodity much sought after in China, and thereby brought Fiji to the attention of international traders. These traders brought disastrous epidemics of new diseases against which the Fijians had no natural resistance. Tradition refers to the *lila balavu* or wasting sickness which extended as far west as Rakiraki.

More significant contact began in the 19th century when visiting European vessels sought Fijian help to collect sandalwood or *bêche-de-mer*, and in return assisted one polity against its rivals. Later to settle were planters, traders and missionaries. They came in close contact with Fijian society, but generally had no intention of forming an integral part of it. Interaction with the Fijians differed greatly, but whether relationships were murderous, disastrous, sexual, or tolerant, these *Vavalagi* (foreigners) inevitably had an impact on the dynamics of, and interaction between Fijian polities. They were a source of exotic ideas and goods including firearms and metal axes. These could be useful to Fijians, without destroying those elements of pre-contact society which were considered to be vital for maintaining their traditional way of life. Demand for firearms increased, partly as symbols of prestige. At first, the importance of firearms in warfare was exaggerated because Fijians without the help of friendly *Vavalagi* did not know how to operate them effectively. The noise of a musket discharging could, however, have a devastating effect especially on those who were unaware of their existence. When Nadroga attacked their traditional enemies in Nadi, the attack was preceded by the firing of muskets. The noise was considered by the Nadi people to be that of *anitu* (supernatural spirits), and they fled from their attackers. On the other hand, Fijians came to realise that these visitors with superior weapons and large vessels could be useful in times of inter-polity war.

The next stage in the development of interaction between *Vavalagi* and Fijians was when foreign government vessels started to visit the islands for the purposes of exploration and surveying, or to enquire into alleged offences by the Fijians against nationals. In the west, Wilkes, commander of the United States Exploring Expedition, carried out extensive surveys in Fijian waters in 1840. In the Yasawa group, survey work was completed without any clash with the people, although Wilkes remarked (1845) that the endeavours of his surveyors were sometimes watched with not very friendly appearances. This indicated a degree of mutual tolerance singularly absent when survey work was started on the island of Malolo. A boat went ashore and a hostage was taken while members of the crew tried to purchase supplies. The hostage tried to escape and a shot was fired over his head to deter him. The Malolo people thought he had been killed and they retaliated by killing two of the ship's officers including Wilkes' nephew. To avenge their deaths and to teach the Fijians a lesson, a party of sixty or seventy was sent ashore to attack and burn the villages. Fifty-seven Fijians were killed, the crops were destroyed and the chiefs and people made an abject surrender. In 1853, the *Wave*, a cutter from Levuka, became becalmed off the island of Malake, Rakiraki, and the islanders captured it and the crew. An expedition of European traders from Levuka went to Malake with the object of making a demonstration of strength to deter the islanders from repeating such an incident. Tui Levuka, who had an old grudge against the islanders, joined the expedition and a group of his warriors turned the demonstration into a massacre. Fourteen islanders were killed and thirteen were captured.

After Christian missions had been established in Fiji, Wesleyan in 1835 and Roman Catholic in 1844, warships of different nationalities, mostly British or French, began to visit Fiji irregularly. For instance, in 1855, fifty men from the USS *Vandalia* stormed a village on the island of Waya. This was a reprisal for the killing and eating of the crew, including an American, of a boat belonging to the mission teacher and trader, John Binner. This resulted, according to one account, in the killing of twenty defenders.

The arrival of an increasing number of permanent settlers, both planters and traders, resulted in a change to the basic interaction between *Vavalagi* and Fijians. Instead of living alongside their hosts, some Europeans, with their Fijian or island families, started to form their own communities, such as the little settlement of Levuka on Ovalau, which developed into the first capital of Fiji. These European settlers and traders wanted not only access to land on terms of freehold with which they were familiar but also security of tenure and security to trade, in the face of what they saw to be a lawless and often hostile local population.

Foreign countries started to take a political interest in Fiji. The first representative of any foreign government to be appointed to Fiji was John Brown Williams of Salem who, in 1840, became the United States Commercial Agent in Fiji. His houses on the island of Nukuku and at Laucala, Rewa, were burned, probably accidentally, but some of his property was carried off by Fijians. The American Government began to press Cakobau for compensation, arguing that these houses were on territory under his alleged authority.

The first British Consul, T.W. Pritchard, was appointed to Fiji in 1857 and arrived in 1858 (Pritchard 1866). Owing partly to Pritchard's energetic efforts to encourage immigration to Fiji and partly to favourable reports by Dr Seemann (1862) that the islands were suitable for the growing of cotton, an ever-increasing number of people came from Australia and New Zealand. The former had found that anticipated fortunes in the Australian gold fields were often illusory. The latter wished to escape from the trauma of the Maori Wars. They came, seeking land on which to cultivate cotton or raise sheep. Some were disappointed and left because they found that Pritchard's promises of favourable conditions for settlement were exaggerated. Those who remained settled at first on land along the coast of southeast Viti Levu and in the eastern islands which they understood were under the authority and protection of such powerful paramounts as Cakobau of Bau and Tui Cakau of Cakaudrove; as well as Ma'afu in the Lau group. Cakobau, under an agreement signed by him in 1868, transferred some 200,000 acres of land to the Polynesian Company in Melbourne in payment of compensation for the destruction of Williams' property (France 1969:81). However experience showed that in spite of his claims to the contrary his traditional authority and powers of protection did not cover much of this land, especially up the Rewa River.

Land became scarcer and more expensive in the relatively safe eastern islands and the east of Viti Levu. So some who found themselves forced off their properties up the Rewa River, as well as newcomers who had come to plant and trade, had to look to the north, south-west and west of

Viti Levu. Land was opened up in Rakiraki and its offshore islands, in the river valleys of Nadroga and Ba, and in the plains and deltas of Vuda, Nadi and Nawaka. Some settled in some of the Yasawa islands such as Naviti, and planted cotton or traded.

These western Fijians had had little early experience of or interaction with Europeans, and what they had was scarcely auspicious for the easy development of good neighbourly relationships. Unlike those in the east, they had not come into early contact or interacted with European sandalwood and *bêche-de-mer* traders or with shipwrecked sailors or deserters from vessels. European missionaries had scarcely penetrated so far from their centres in the east, except the unfortunate Reverend Thomas Baker, of whom more later. They may well have been suspicious or hostile in the face of the arrival of these European settlers and traders even though they were but few in numbers in those early days.

In contrast to planters and traders in the east, these first settlers in the west were well outside the traditional spheres of influence of powerful paramounts such as Cakobau in Bau, or Tui Cakau or Ma'afu in the east. Local chiefs had comparatively restricted spheres of influence or powers to mediate in the event of quarrels between traditional landowners and *Vavalagi* settlers. The latter often found themselves in precarious situations involving misunderstandings and disputes. For instance, the first Europeans to settle in the Nadi area were Messrs A. Campbell and C.H.H. Irvine (formerly a planter in Ceylon) who came from New Zealand in 1866 and bought land for thirty muskets, five barrels of gunpowder and six kegs of lead. They found themselves in the midst of a war between three neighbouring villages, and left their land to seek safety. On their return, they found that their house had been damaged and property had been stolen. In 1869 they sold part of their property to the Muir brothers, originally from Scotland but more immediately from Otago, New Zealand. Relations with their Fijian neighbours were reasonably good at first. Then, in 1872, their house was burned by an inland man, apparently because he had been placed on a horse by one of the brothers and had fallen off and injured himself but was not given compensation. It later emerged that he had burned the house on the instructions of a chief who was upset because the Muirs had ploughed up an old village site on what they regarded as their land.

In the same year, the Miller brothers bought some Vuda land from a Sabeto chief whose mother came from Vuda (and therefore he claimed to have rights to the land in question). The Vuda chief sent his son with eleven others to *buturaki* (stamp on) one of the Millers for wrongfully obtaining the land. News of the *buturaki* reached other Nadi settlers, and a number of them, with their islander labourers, moved off to Vuda in military array. They surrounded the chief of Vuda, and took the eleven involved in the *buturaki* to the top of a nearby hill. They flogged them in full view of the villagers, and lectured the chiefs on the enormity of laying hands on a white man. One of the first to settle in the Sigatoka area was an American, G.R. Burt, who was exceptionally unpleasant to his labourers. He was attacked in 1869, and was *buturaki*, only just escaping with his life. Cakobau and J.B. Thurston, the Acting British Consul, later charged him with nine murders.

The supposedly pan-Fiji Government headed by Cakobau who had been crowned and given the dubious title of King of Bau, was established in 1867 and based in Levuka, with the backing of a number of influential and ambitious local Europeans. It soon became apparent that it had little authority outside the traditional areas of authority of Cakobau, as Vunivalu of Bau.

Living in an area of marginal security, far from likely protection by Cakobau or the Cakobau Government, the Nadi community of fifteen or twenty Europeans developed a spirit of self-sufficiency, symbolised by their uniform of Tokelau hats and Turkey puggarees and by adopting the soubriquet of the Nadi Swells. In 1869, they formed the Nadi Bay Planters Association, and held regular meetings to promote self-reliance and mutual protection. For instance, they aimed to prevent guns being given to the local Fijian landowners, by preventing further newcomers from purchasing land. On one occasion, they sent the obnoxious Mr Burt back to Sigatoka. One member of this colourful community was George H. Worsley Markham who lived in the area from 1869, having come from Christchurch, New Zealand, though originating in Ulster. One interesting source of information about pre-Colonial Fiji is the Markham diary (1869–1874), though sadly only part of it relating to his time in the west survives. By 1871, those who had settled in the west had so little faith in, or respect for, the far-away Cakobau Government that they either ignored it or actively opposed it.

Such attitudes about the 1867 Government were expressed not only by Europeans living in the west; a general feeling of physical insecurity and danger also prevailed among settlers and traders throughout Viti Levu. The Reverend Thomas Baker was clubbed and eaten in 1867 at Nagagadelavatu in the hills of Navosa. Rewa settlers were driven from their properties up the Rewa River. In August 1871, two European planters on the Ba River were murdered by local Fijians. Government punitive expeditions, if they were undertaken, were unsuccessful, and it was generally realised that the 1867 Government was ineffective and inadequately representative. Settlers and traders, especially in the west, increasingly sought some form of stable government, provision for negotiable land titles and security of land tenure.

This situation was due largely to a quite understandable lack of awareness on the part of settlers about traditional land tenure and the right of chiefs to dispose of land. The most common motive for Fijians to dispose of land was the need to obtain firearms, especially as the ability of Fijians to use muskets improved. To the local chiefs the appearance of new settlers must have appeared as a godsend. Disputes resulted, however, between chiefs or between a chief and his people about the right to sell land owned by polities under his traditional authority.

It was disputed whether a chief had any right to sell the lands of those under his authority or even land of which he was one of the traditional owners. It was also disputed whether he had any traditional authority to sell the land of those whom he had conquered in war. Whatever the ideal principles of land tenure and ignoring whether or not they had any recognised traditional right to sell land, be it their own or of those under their authority or the lands of the conquered, it is evident that chiefs assumed such rights. By virtue of the chiefs' actual political power over their people or their achieved power over the people they had conquered, the traditional landowners were in no position to disagree. Such situations prevailed not only in the powerful paramountcy in the east but also in the west. Tui Ba for instance sold vast areas of land belonging to people over whom he had some degree of traditional authority. He did so not only as a means of obtaining firearms but also of creating a buffer between his area of authority and those in the interior who were independent of his authority and were ever liable to descend and harass him. In these cases the traditional landowners did not play any part in the negotiations for the sale of their lands and, in reality, the power of the paramount could not be gainsaid.

Those *Vavalagi* who settled in this buffer zone found that they were in a precarious position. The reality of the situation in Ba soon became clear, when, first, James Macintosh and John Spiers were murdered in 1871, and in 1873 after being continually attacked, the Burns family were speared and clubbed together with twenty of their foreign labourers.

It had already become apparent that the 1867 government was powerless and ineffective, and after meetings of, and discussions by, a wide selection of delegates including those from the west, a new constitution was agreed to. The Constitution Act of Fiji received Royal Assent on 18 August 1871, and the first meeting of the new Legislative Assembly was held in November 1871. The European proponents of Cakobau's Government had not fully taken into account, first, the limited extent of Cakobau's traditional authority especially in the west; secondly and perhaps more importantly, the strength and determination of the independent west and interior of Viti Levu to resist the Government, Cakobau and Christianity; and thirdly, the misunderstandings and disputes about the sale of land and security of tenure. Nevertheless, the European community, in contrast to the European and other legislators, had a significant impact and influence on the Fijian population. In the country areas, they were a source of goods, including arms, which the Fijians wanted; they employed labour, when it was available; many were educated and experienced in trades and professions potentially useful to Fijians; and they could participate directly or indirectly in wars and rivalries between polities. They were, at any rate during the decade immediately prior to Cession in 1874, a factor with differing degrees of influence in the development of and interaction between polities in different parts of Fiji, especially in the West.

(d) The introduction of Christianity into Fiji

Rivalries developed between different proponents of the Gospel, as they sought (and sometimes fought) for political support and for converts, and this rivalry impacted on and influenced the Fijian community by splitting it. The first European Wesleyan missionaries arrived from Tonga at Lakeba in October 1835 and the Roman Catholics in 1844. The Tongan settlers came from a Wesleyan background and brought their own brand of Christianity, the *Lotu Tonga* as it is called in Fiji. The first Tongan attempts to spread Christianity to the west from Lau were doubtless perceived, at any rate in Bau, as a guise for the spreading of Tongan political and military influence.

For instance, the Tongans tried to establish a foothold on the island of Yasawa, partly as a base for their expansionist ambitions in Fiji, and partly because Yasawa was a main source of sail mats. They left a teacher there, to spread the beliefs of the *Lotu Tonga*. Not all Fijians accepted the Tongan brand of Christianity, nor the political influence of the Tongans; and some accepted Roman Catholicism perhaps as a gesture of opposition to the Tongans. The Tongans hastened to squash such opposition to their plans to expand their authority over Fiji; and Fifita, to whom reference has already been made, severely ill-treated the Catholics, flogging, kicking and hitting them. This came to the attention of Father Bréhéret, who complained to the captain of a visiting French warship (Pritchard 1866:300). Fifita was tried on board the *Cornelie* and was deported to New Caledonia.

Wesleyan missionaries had first settled in the east, associating themselves with such paramounts as Tui Nayau in Lau and after some opposition with Cakobau who adopted Christianity as a matter of necessity. The expansion of the Wesleyan Church from duly Christianised Bau outside Cakobau's traditional areas of authority was regarded with suspicion and hostility as covertly spreading the authority of the Vunivalu, whose religion it had become and whose traditional authority was not recognised in those independent areas. Here the spread of Christianity often led to local warfare, especially in the west. On the one side were those polities which refused to abandon their own spirits and political independence and which therefore would not accept Christianity or Cakobau. On the other side were those who saw some material or spiritual benefit in accepting the new religion or who were too weak militarily to refuse it and thereby face the might of Cakobau and his allies. In the West especially, it was seen as Cakobau's religion and any early attempts by missionaries at proselytising outside Cakobau's traditional areas of authority were foolhardy. The Reverend Thomas Baker went into the pagan interior of western Viti Levu in 1867 and was killed and eaten 'boots and all', according to a song, in the village of Nagagadelavatu in Navosa. One popular but unlikely account suggests that his death was due to an indiscretion of Baker in insulting a chief by removing his (Baker's) comb from the chief's head. A more prosaic account is that the people accepted a *tabua* or whale tooth, originating from enemies of Cakobau and Christianity in the east, which accompanied a request that Baker be killed. As Christianity gradually spread westwards, it led to warfare within and between polities. In the western areas of the Nadi and Nawaka polities, some polities fought in the first instance to maintain their political independence, especially from Cakobau whom they saw as an eastern mountebank. Secondly they resisted Christianity as undermining their spirit world which they saw as essential to their wellbeing and from which they feared dreadful revenge if the spirits were spurned through missionary activities. It could be argued that such fighting also reflected old rivalries.

Christianity propounded a form of spiritual paramountcy running contrary to the principles of the spiritual element of the ideological concept of *vanua* 1. In so far as they understood them, the missionaries, especially the Wesleyans, denigrated beliefs and sites associated with the Fijian spirit world. They did this verbally, or by having groves desecrated, monoliths broken or buried, or churches constructed on the mounds of the *bure kalou* (*beto* or *bito* in the west) or spirit houses where the spirits were consulted (Parke 2000). They challenged the spiritual basis of chiefly leadership and the spiritual powers or *mana* which validated and supported the chiefs. In so doing, they challenged the very validity of those spirits which, first, provided an ideological basis for the unity of a polity; secondly, ensured the continuing prosperity of the polity and of its natural food sources based on agriculture, hunting and fishing; and, thirdly, provided a control over unacceptable social behaviour and dissent within a polity as well as a spiritual backing to defence against outside attack. They associated the spirit world with what they regarded as devils or demons (the missionary words for Fijian spirits were *tevoro* or *timoni)* and the horrors of cannibalism, wife-strangling and polygamy. In trying to impose Christianity in place of the Fijian spirit world, and to stamp out practices such as those referred to, the missionaries were striking at important elements at the very basis of traditional politico-spiritual Fijian society

Missionaries aimed to associate with chiefs, realising that if a paramount chief converted to Christianity, his people would be likely to follow. Such tactics sometimes resulted in fusion and fission, especially in complex federated polities such as Nawaka. In some cases the chiefs of some of the polities involved might accept Christianity while other chiefs might refuse to do so. In other cases, as in Yasawa, some accepted Wesleyanism and others accepted Catholicism. Such developments resulting from the influence of Christianity in its various forms sometimes took advantage of old rivalries, and exacerbated them.

It is evident that, in pre-Colonial times, the Wesleyan Mission, the Roman Catholic Mission and the *Lotu Tonga* in different ways and to different degrees, played increasingly significant roles in influencing the spiritual beliefs and the socio-political dynamics of Fijian polities, albeit with varying degrees of effectiveness especially in the West.

(e) The impact of Cakobau and the Cakobau Government on the west

Cakobau and the eastern-based Cakobau Governments, particularly the 1871 Government, were factors having differing degrees of impact on the dynamics of, and interaction between, polities in the west. Cakobau needed to justify the title of Tui Viti or paramount chief of Fiji, by extending his authority outside his traditional realms. Taking advantage of his position as head of the Government and with the excuse that he was spreading Christianity, Cakobau attempted to extend his personal authority from those areas over which he had traditional or recognised authority and to impose it over other areas of Fiji. The initiative to do so was not only his, because Cakobau was often pushed into it by his European Ministers and by the needs of the planters. In Rakiraki and the West, some adopted Christianity because they saw material advantage in doing so, or because they feared the military wrath of the Cakobau Government. Others who considered that they were strong enough to maintain their traditional independence from Cakobau refused to accept Christianity, because they saw such a step as tantamount to accepting the religion and the governance of Cakobau. They would have feared the reaction of their ancestral and other spirits if they were to reject their own spirits and accept a new spirit with whom they had no traditional associations. Polities in the west especially in Nadi and Nawaka would sometimes combine to oppose these external factors.

The powers of Cakobau often but not invariably proved to be ineffective in these western areas, and the dubious authority of the 1867 government had already suffered a real test in 1868 when Cakobau suffered a major set-back. After the murder of the Reverend Thomas Baker at Nagagadelavatu, Namosi, the Acting British Consul, J.B. Thurston, demanded that Cakobau as head of the 1867 government should arrest the murderers. Cakobau was very hesitant to commit himself or his troops to military action so far from his traditional areas of authority, but Thurston repeated his demands. Eventually, Cakobau was persuaded by the British warship, HMS *Brisk* to avenge the murder. He sent in two columns of troops, one of which he led himself. One column was, however, ambushed and thirteen influential chiefs were killed by the independent hill folk who had no intention of allowing easterners to interfere in their affairs. The other column was forced to retire, having lost sixty-one dead and fifteen wounded. Generally Cakobau doubted whether his authority could be enforced in distant areas such as Nadi, Ba, and Sigatoka or even in the upper Rewa River where his navy could not go. The situation came to a head in July 1868, when eighty-five well-armed marines from the H.M.S *Challenger* went up the Rewa River to help sort out a problem between local landowners and settlers, but having suffered casualties were driven back by gunfire from the Fijians. Such military setbacks emphasised how precarious and ephemeral was the authority of Cakobau in the hills and in the west.

In Levuka, after the 1867 Government proved to be ineffective, the new constitution introduced in 1871 involved Ba, Nadroga, Nadi, the Yasawa group, and Rakiraki/Tavua as well as eastern Fiji. Many of the leading chiefs including Ma'afu had tendered their allegiance to the new government members. Ma'afu may have hoped that the government would fail and that he would be asked to take over the administration of all Fiji. This apparent consensus boded well for the new government in 1871, and Cakobau was proclaimed King of Fiji. Thereby he achieved his ambition, driven by a desire to emulate his Tongan neighbour, King Tupou I, to be recognised as paramount over all Fiji. These machinations might be claimed by some cynics to have culminated in the issue of government postage stamps bearing the symbol of C.R. However, in reality, such recognition was nominal and still had no firm basis in the west at any rate, with little traditional validity there, inadequate military power or legal backing, and no enthusiastic recognition beyond a limited circle of supporters, Fijian or European. Even with government troops at his disposal, Cakobau still faced opposition not only from Fijians but also from those Europeans in the west who were more concerned with their own security than with the maintenance of what they regarded as a far-away form of government without legitimacy or adequate power to enforce law and order in their area.

Cakobau and the new government was almost immediately in trouble when the people of the interior of Ba murdered James Macintosh and John Spiers on the Ba River. The victims were hardly blameless; the diarist Markham (1869–74) recorded that the murder was in revenge against 'those white men who went about with revolvers popping off at Fijians'. The Cakobau government did not attempt to undertake a punitive expedition. Local European planters, acting on their own initiative, did, however, form a force of volunteers including some Fijians provided by the chief of Ba and some imported labourers. They advanced into the hills, attacked the wrong village, skirmished with the wrong people, and retired without achieving the revenge which they had set out to wreak. In this as in the following case, the Cakobau Government forces were slow to take action because Cakobau did not consider that he was in a position of sufficient strength to undertake a punitive expedition into the hostile mountainous interior.

In 1873, the Burns family and some imported island labourers were murdered on their property at Vunisamaloa about 20 km inland from the mouth of the Ba River. This followed the shooting by Burns' men of two mountain women who had come down to the Ba River to gather *kaikoso/tuace* (fresh mussels), as was their wont. A government force was sent from Levuka under European officers, but on reaching Ba found that an avenging local European force had already gathered there. Having no faith in the government, these westerners refused to allow the force to proceed. To avoid a bloody confrontation, the government force returned eastward to Rakiraki. Here they learnt of the murder of a Lasakau man from Bau who had been recruiting labour in the interior of Ra. The people of Korowaiwai had apparently killed him because he was a man from Christian Bau and as such was anathema to these independent people. Cakobau's government approved the immediate assault and destruction of Korowaiwai and the capture of its inhabitants as 'rebels-in-arms against the king's throne and person' (Markham 1869–1874), and required the prisoners to be sent to Levuka, presumably to be made available as labour for plantations and so act as revenue earners for the government. However, what followed was a massacre of some 300 inhabitants, mainly by auxiliaries who attacked alongside the government troops.

After the Korowaiwai massacre, the government troops went back to Ba and faced the hostile planters still anxious to avenge the murders by themselves and insisting that the government forces should leave the matter in their capable hands. H.M.S. *Dido* arrived, and Captain Chapman was able to mediate between the planters and the government. The government troops proceeded to attack the offending village of Karawa which they captured, although the inhabitants fled. A message was received that the people of Nubutautau, Magodro, had met with the people of Sabeto and Vaturu, Nawaka, and had bound themselves to resist any encroachment by the government. The troops divided into two, no longer as a punitive force but as one aiming to bring the mountain people under the authority of government. One part attacked from Ba and the other from Sabeto in Vuda district. They went to Sabeto, as it was known to be in league with the enemy, and here twenty-three men of the district were arrested and the old chief, Mataitoga, was executed by shooting, in the presence of the awestruck villagers. This time the Government succeeded in imposing its authority. There followed a long, bloody and bitter campaign in the course of which about 1000 prisoners were taken and several executions took place in public. Many of the prisoners had had nothing to do with the murder, but Cakobau may have wanted by avenging the Burns murders to convince Europeans to support the Government of which he was head by demonstrating that it could assert its authority over wrongdoers. Perhaps more to the point however, Cakobau may have wanted, after avenging the murders, to continue into the Colo country in the central mountains of Viti Levu and forcefully demonstrate his own power of authority over the independent hill folk there.

The campaign continued until the government forces reached the offending village of Nubutautau. Against orders, some undisciplined troops burned it in a manner the diarist said 'marred the success of our final action in the Ba expedition of our labours of seven months' (Markham 1869–1874). Many prisoners were shipped off to Levuka, the Sabeto people ending up on the island of Koro. The methodical devastation of the villages and gardens and the removal of considerable numbers of people as prisoners may, however, have resulted in the longer term in a bitter peace and the hardening of the attitude of many westerners and hill folk against Cakobau, his government and perhaps Christianity.

A significant feature of this period just before Cession in 1874 was the degree to which some small independent polities joined together or opposed each other, as in the cases of some polities in Nadi and Nawaka. They joined to provide mutual assistance against, or support for, the inroads of Christianity, Cakobau and the Cakobau Government. Some accepted Christianity and the Cakobau Government, and others were forced into accepting eastern hegemony or saw it to their advantage to do so. On the other hand, other independent western polities opposed this acceptance by their neighbours because they objected to heeding the authority of an outsider, an easterner, especially if he was the head of a Fiji-wide Government to the establishment of which they claimed not to have given their assent. This feeling of independence from Government and its manifestations, some bloody, continued until after Cession in 1874 and thus beyond the parameters of this present work.

6

The *Yavusa*: The Ideal and the Reality

The basic Fijian polity or *yavusa* is ideally taken to be a group of people (both male and female) claiming descent usually in the male line from a common mythological ancestral spirit, and associated with commonly held land. To the extent that a person can ideally belong to only one *yavusa,* the *yavusa* is exclusive and members are referred to as *itaukei* in contrast to non-members who are referred to as *vulagi.*

The yavusa ideally comprises sub-descent groups, referred to currently as *mataqali* in all recognised communalects of which I am aware. These have a recognised order of seniority based ideally on the mythical birth order of sons of the common ancestor. Each *mataqali* comprises a number of sub-divisions having an order of seniority again based ideally on the mythical birth order of grandsons of the common ancestor and usually referred to as *itokatoka*. To this extent, the *yavusa* is socio-politically hierarchical. This summary of the structure of Fijian polities is based on what has become an idealised model for Fijian socio-political structure, as described by Roth (1953:58), France (1969:166), Nayacakalou (1975:16) and Ravuvu (1987:16).

Identity of *yavusa*

To maintain the characteristic of exclusiveness, each *yavusa* has a number of features of identity which distinguish it from other *yavusa*. They reflect the three crucial and interacting elements of the ideological concept of traditional Fijian society (*vanua* 1). These elements are spirits, people and land, and they form the basis for investigating, understanding and analysing Fijian socio-political groups.

Spirits

Original ancestral spirits

Each *yavusa* recognises a common original ancestral spirit (*kalou vu* in the East; *nitu* in the West), as well as other spirits. Such an ancestral spirit usually has the following features of identification, although some features may now be forgotten:

* name;
* place of origin and place(s) of settlement;
* place where presentations are made to the spirit;
* place of communication between the spirit and the living;
* *waqawaqa* or object (usually animal) of manifestation (not embodiment);
* name and place of origin of spouse;

In Rakiraki, Drilo Dadavanua was the ancestral spirit of the Malake *yavusa*. He came on the instructions of the culture hero Degei from the Nakauvadra Mountains to Navatu where he married Likumasei, a woman from the offshore Navatu islet of Cubu. They moved to Malake

Island in order to supply *seka* or crabs to Degei. Later the Malake people became the turtle fishers for Degei. Dadavanua and Likumasei settled on the hilltop at Uluidrilo (the site is marked by a ring of stones) before moving to the coast to the swampy area of Lomalake. Here they settled at Navuniviavia, marked by a rectangular earth mound for the house where the *bete* would communicate with Dadavanua. Near the mound is a flat area where presentations were made to Dadavanua. Dadavanua's *waqawaqa* is a *gata* or snake living in a *werewere* tree at Navuniviavia.

Other spirits associated with a yavusa

- Spirits of war or *kalou ni valu* (*nitu ni valu* in the West)

  Limasa is the *nitu ni valu* of the Kovacaki people of Nadi. His manifestation is an owl. His place is at Naviqwa, marked by an earth mound in a grove of trees. He has a holiday place nearby, identified by two earth mounds. Presentations were made to him at Nasavusavu, where a dolmen-like stone structure comprising a rectangular capstone and supporting uprights is surrounded by low earth mounds in a grove. The site, currently fenced and kept meticulously clean, is protected by the spirit of a brown dog. The present *bete* lived in a modest Fijian-style house, the only one in the village of Navoci, near Namotomoto, beside the main road into Nadi town. During my visit in 2003, this house was being dismantled after a fire, and a decision had not yet been taken about its replacement. The building where the *bete* used to communicate with Limasa was destroyed when the main road was widened.

- Spirits associated with prosperity

  The Vunatoto people of Nawaka respect a series of spirits known as *digiwai*. These include the Digiwai ni Marawa or spirit of the gardens, and the Digiwai ni Ika and the Digiwai ni Manumanu responsible respectively for success in fishing or hunting. *Qeti* or presentations were made to the *digiwai* through the *bete* in the *beto*. If they were not made correctly, the gardens would suffer, or when people went fishing or hunting, a fisherman was liable to be bitten by an eel or shark; or a hunter might either fail to catch a pig, or be bitten by one.

- Spirit defenders (*ba* or *sasabai*) with associated places and manifestations

  Bituwewe was the *ba*, the *tuwawa* or defending champion of the Leweiwavuwavu, the first *yavusa* to settle in the Sabeto valley south of the Tualeita range. He was a tall man whose head was at Unuineivua, his stomach at Neisauniwaqa, his legs at Nasaqa and his feet at Conua where they may still be seen as rock formations on top of the Tualeita. His manifestation was a *ga ni vatu* or falcon named Voili.

- Spirits ensuring good behaviour of members of a polity

  Losausauega was a female spirit (her name includes the female honorary prefix *lo-*) whose place was on the right bank of the river flowing past Vunitogoloa, village of the Naqilaqila *yavusa*. If any one living there misbehaves, she appears in the form of a spider (*suasauega* means 'spider' in the Rakiraki communalect). A female spirit, LoRubaroba, associated with the Nairara people of Nakorokula, has a place at Vunitawa. Her face and body are swollen up. If anyone misbehaves, she will appear and spit at the person, whose face and body then become covered in spots.

- Cult spirits, such as *rere* (land spirits) and *luve ni wai* (water spirits)

  The young men of the inland village of Nawaka saw a spirit in places around the village and set up a cult based on this spirit which was known to be a *rere* (with two long vowels). Because they ministered to this *rere*, the people of Nawaka had successes in war. A man of Ba living on the island of Nananu i cake off Rakiraki told me how he was approached by *luve ni wai* from a nearby islet with offers of assistance if required. He already had his own spirit from Ba, called Lewatumomo, who would come to his assistance if required. He rejected the offer from the *luve ni wai*, because he feared that if he were to accept their offer, he would then be in a position of obligation to the spirits. This he did not want. It is difficult to obtain detailed information nowadays about the *rere* or the *luve ni wai*.

People

Each *yavusa* has a name. Each *mataqali* has a name; and each *mataqali* has a socio-political status identified by such a term as *turaga* or chief; *mata ni vanua* or ceremonial official; or *bete* or communicator with the ancestral spirit. Each *itokatoka* has a name.

A *yavusa* usually had features of identification such as:

- the title of the paramount 'chief', such as Tu Navitilevu in Rakiraki, or Momo Levu in Vuda;
- a housemound *(yavu)* for the 'chief', with a title such as Erenavula for the Momo of Sabeto, or Supani for the Ratu ni Natokea (Rakiraki);
- a mound for the building for communication with the ancestral spirit *(bure kalou or beto/bito)* Such a mound has a name. A permanent building on a low mound known as Nukuwasiga in Namotomoto village, Nadi, is still used by the *bete* of the Kovacaki people for communication with the ancestral spirit, Tutuvanua. The *bete* lives nearby in a fine modern-style house. He comes from the *bete* group known as the Naobekwa. A well-known mound (outside my main study areas, but where I have carried out excavations: see Parke n.d.- b, 1993, 1998) is Navatanitawake for the Kubuna people on the island of Bau. This had been the *bure kalou* of the original ancestral spirit, Ratu mai Bulu, whose place was on the mainland. After a military coup in the early part of the 19th century, the war chief or Vunivalu deposed and expelled the traditional paramount chief or Roko Tui Bau. Navatanitawake was then considerably heightened and developed and became the *bure kalou* of Cagawalu, the war spirit of the Kubuna people and particularly associated with the Vunivalu;
- 'Totemic' features, usually three, referred to as *vutiyaca* in the West or *icavuti* in the East. One such feature often represents the male genital organs; and another, the female organs. For instance, among the Navatu people near Vaileka, the *deiro* or sandfish represents the male genitals, and the *boro* or kind of mussel represents the female genitals. One may represent both. For instance, in the village of Korobebe up the Sabeto valley, three socio-politically associated *yavusa* have *vutiyaca* as follows:

Yavusa	kai	magiti	kea ilava
Ne	vesi	vutuna	qo
	hard wood	kind of yam	pig
Leweidrasa	vesi	vutuna	qo
Leweikoro	kavika	botia	volo (two long vowels)
	Malay apple	wild yam	kind of fish

They are all very *tabu,* and the mere mention of them can be disastrous unless ceremonies of apology are made immediately. I could not discover any convincing explanation for their origins or for the association between a particular set of such features and a particular *yavusa*. The only explanation suggested to me was that the original ancestral spirit brought them down from the Nakauvadra Mountains. In the West, such features usually include a type of tree, a root vegetable, and an edible creature of the land or sea, referred to in the western dialects as *kai* (tree), *magiti* (vegetable) and *kea ilava* or food concomitant with the vegetable.

In Rakiraki the classification *of icavuti* is less straightforward. In the Namotutu *yavusa*, this chiefly *yavusa* has four such 'totems'—a *kai* (tree), being the *vesi*; a *manumanu* (animal), being the *kula* or parakeet; an *ika* (fish), being the *vonu* or turtle; and a *vivili* (shell fish), being the *kusau* or small cockle which represents the genitals of both males and females. I was told that the *icavuti* also included the *vara* (a shooting coconut) and the *kuka* (a small red land crab). To confuse the issue even more, the Rakiraki *bete* told me that each *mataqali* of the Namotutu *yavusa* had its own *icavuti* as follows:

mataqali	plant	fish	food
Tunavitilevu	bu'a		vudi
	a sugarcane	none	cooking banana
Vosatabua	sinu	yawa	vudi
	a tree	sea fish	
Tuinamo	yasi	kusau	vudi
	sandalwood	shellfish	
Tuicakau and Vuninokonoko	nokonoko	sulua	vudi
	ironwood	octopus	

It will be noted that the *vudi* is a common *icavuti* of all the *mataqali* in the Namotutu *yavusa*. This could be the unifying feature of a *yavusa* comprised of groups from other *yavusa*.

On enquiry, a greater number of *icavuti* may be given for any particular *yavusa*. This may be due to ignorance or confusion on the part of informants, or it may show that the original *yavusa* or group claiming descent from a single ancestral spirit now includes part or parts of another or other *yavusa* which brought with them one or more of its or their own *icavuti*. Further enquiries may reveal the origins of any such external groups. Thus, the reality of the composition of a particular current *yavusa* may be different from that of the ideal *yavusa* representing common descent from a common mythical ancestral spirit.

- A jumping-off place (*na icibaciba* in Rakiraki; *ne ivilavila ni yalo* in Western Viti Levu and the islands) for the *yalo* or spirits of the newly dead

Each place, often a cliff, would have a name and usually an associated pool in the sea or river into which spirits would jump. Some places have a rock in the pool or sea, which represents a vessel (*vatu waqa* or stone canoe) in which the spirit would sail away to join the ancestors. The spirits of the dead of the Malake *yavusa* go to the little broken cliff at Namuremure at the western end of the island of Malake. They jump into the sea. To the west of the cliff is a rock called Muadua. It is shaped like a vessel, and if someone sleeps on the rock they dream of it as a large vessel. The spirit boards the vessel and sails round the island to see the villages for the last time. Then the vessel heads to mangrove swamps at Rukuvakadua where the spirit disembarks, and the vessel returns to Namuremure.

A rock may have some other part to play in the journey of the spirit. The spirits of Namotutu, Rakiraki, jump from a beach at Navolivoli into the sea where there is an isolated coral rock on which the spirit is injured as it jumps. The spirit then limps ashore with the aid of a walking stick until it reaches another rock a short distance inland. Having recovered from its injuries, the spirit plunges its walking stick into the rock which may itself testify to this because it is covered with small round holes. The spirit then departs to join its ancestors. The spirits of Navunatoto, Nawaka which is beside a river, jump from the bank into a river pool at Nawakalevu and return to the land to a big *baka* or fig tree. A *baka* tree is generally associated with spirits.

The *ivilavila ni yalo* of the Yaukuve people on the island of Waya is at Nacilau near Nalauwaki. The spirit of the dead person flies around the island and then goes off to Nacilau with its *iyaya* or belongings. It throws its *iyaya* ahead of it down the cliff at Nacilau and then it jumps or *vila* into a pool beside a large flat rock known as Waqa ni Senio. The rock represents a vessel (*waqa*). The people of Waya hear two thuds representing the sound of the *iyaya* and of the spirit falling into the pool. The spirit goes aboard the vessel, and sails off into the West together with its *iyaya*.

- Other *vanua tabu*

  Apart from the original ancestral spirit and *vanua tabu* ('sacred' places) associated with that spirit, other spirits connected generally with a *yavusa* have *vanua tabu* associated with them. The headland above the cave at Sawailau off Yasawa Island is regarded as the *vanua tabu* of the famous spirit Lewaqoroqoro associated with the Natubasa people of Nabukeru village, who appeared as a female person. She was carried off to Malolo Island by Tutusilo, the main spirit on the island, at the end of his penis which had erected when he smelt her urinating on Sawailau.

- Personal names

  Certain personal names may be especially connected with a particular *yavusa,* such as 'Bolobolo' with the Namotutu *yavusa* of Rakiraki; and 'Dawai' with the Navatulevu *yavusa* of Nadi.

Land

Nowadays, land is generally communally owned by a sub-division of the *yavusa*. In some areas, the land-owning unit was traditionally the *mataqali,* in others it was the *itokatoka* or equivalent. Andrew Pawley (personal communication) told me that on Waya, the unit was the *yavu* or housemound. This situation can occur sometimes on Rotuma in the case of *hanua ne fuag ri* or land associated with a particular housemound. I know of no example in my research areas where the *yavusa* owned land. The traditional *iyalayala* or boundaries of such areas were recognised, although the precise boundaries may have been vague. Nowadays land boundaries are fixed by legislation. Each area of land has a name. Land (*qele*) may be divided into three categories: village sites, *iteitei* or gardens, and *veikau* or bushland. On such land there would be a number of *vanua tabu* or 'sacred' sites associated with an ancestral spirit or other spirit.

Village sites

Each *yavusa* occupies one or more villages *(koro,* or *rārā* in the West), which it may share with one or more neighbouring or related polities or parts of polities. Usually it would be situated on land owned by one or more of the occupying *mataqali* or *itokatoka* whichever was the land-owning unit. In the district of Rakiraki, the *yavusa* of AiSokula is the only *yavusa* based on the village of Nakorokula. To the west lie the immediately adjacent villages of Navuavua and Navutulevu, commonly referred to together as the village of Rakiraki. The original owners were the *yavusa* of Namotutu who were later joined by four stranger *yavusa,* the Navuavua, Natiliva, Cakova and Wailevu, who originated from the other side of the Nakauvadra Mountains. The inhabitants of the Nadi village of Sikituru belong to the *yavusa* of Saunivalu. Following what they regarded as the wrongful distribution of a ceremonially presented pig, they had split from the Saunivalu *yavusa* who live in the present village of Keiyasi, far up the Sigatoka River, and they now form an independent unit. They assisted the Nadi people against the Sabeto people in battle, including the great battle of Vauroka. Out of gratitude, the Saunivalu were given land by the two *yavusa* of Kai Loa and Vucunisai, who agreed that the leader of the Saunivalu should be recognised as *Momo* or paramount of the three *yavusa*. In 1993, they were finally reconciled with the Saunivalu of Keiyasi in the course of a tearful ceremony, with pigs being presented in the correct manner.

Features of a village

Each village would have a name, and would be divided socio-politically, ideally round a central unoccupied ceremonial area (*rara,* or *darata* in the West). Each *mataqali* or *itokatoka* would have a recognised area in the village. At one end of the ceremonial area might be the chief's house referred to by such terms as *Vale Levu, Sue Levu* or *Were Levu*. At the other end might be the building where the *bete* communicates with the ancestral spirit or where socio-political ceremonies take place. Nowadays this may have been replaced by the church or the ceremonial meeting house. The village plan of Bulia, Kadavu, follows exactly this model. The chief's house is at one end of the *rara,* and the church at the other. At Lalati, Beqa, the chief's house is at one end, the community hall at the other, and the church is halfway between, on the edge of the *rara.*

Gardens and bush

Some garden sites may be close to the village, particularly those used by the women. Other sites may be some distance from the village, but seldom so far that a gardener cannot get home at night though he may have a garden house. The bush is mainly useful for gathering firewood, house posts, wild yams, and for hunting wild pigs. Some areas are cut down for garden sites in the process of shifting agriculture.

The spirit world and associated geographical features

The areas of Rakiraki and of Nadi/Vuda/Nawaka in my study areas have mountainous backgrounds behind the coastal plains. Most of the Yasawa islands have a mountainous centre, except for the isolated sandy cay of Viwa, lying far westward of the other islands. The mainland areas have hilly piedmonts with rocky outcrops and isolated errant boulders. The coastal areas are relatively flat but otherwise characterised by cliffs, streams, rivers and deltas often associated with mangrove swamps. Where the rivers flow from the mountainous interior, waterfalls often occur. With such a varied and dramatic terrain, it is not surprising that many features, natural, humanly made or natural but humanly modified, abound in association with the spirit world of the polities in these areas.

Such features generally fall into the following categories:

Subterranean or sub-surface features

- Pools in the sea

  Waicacavori is a spirit associated with the AiSokula people of Nakorokula, Rakiraki. His place is at Sogoi, a pool in the sea to the west of Ellington wharf. His *waqawaqa* is a big *vai* or ray often seen jumping out of the water in the bay. If someone in the bay is in trouble, a *vai* will appear and push a log or something else in order to save him.

- Pools in the mangrove swamps

  Namo (meaning a pool full of fish) is a pool on the edge of mangroves to the west of the village of Namuaimada, Rakiraki. It is the place of a female spirit called Vai'eka, associated with the local Natokea people. Passers-by are very frightened of her, and she would ill-treat those who fail to pay her due respect. Natokea people wishing to fish can, with suitable ceremony and presentations, seek Vai'eka's permission to fish at Namo.

- Pools created by subterranean water seepage

  Naqali is a small pool of fresh water seeping from the hillside near the village of Korokula. It is the *vanua tabu* of Varoi, a male spirit associated with the Naisokula *yavusa*. His *waqawaqa* is a *duna* or eel. If someone comes with a container to get water from the pool, an eel's tail may be seen to wave and splash water into the container.

- Pools in rivers or streams

  A Tongan woman called Bilovesi while visiting the Nakauvadra Mountains became pregnant by Degei who sent her to give birth at Navatu. Degei's *waqawaqa* is a *gata* or snake, and he is known as Gata i vanua (snake on land). When he heard of his son's birth, Degei decided that the son should be called Gata i wai (snake in the water). Gata i wai's place is a pool in the stream near the present village of Narewa, beside a rock called Vatudamu. His *waqawaqa* is also a *gata,* and his descendants are the people of Naivuvuni who are regarded by their neighbours as having a Tongan look.

- Caves

  In the Rakiraki area, Salusalumatana is a spirit associated with the Natokea people. His place is at Naqaraituruturu, near the village of Navolau. It is a shallow cave in a big rock, which had a coconut palm on top in my time. The place of Degei is described in legend as a cave at the peak of Uluda, on top of the Nakauvadra Mountains. I have been shown a rock with a modest crevice, said to be the cave, where I made suitable presentations. This reality contrasts with legends which refer to a deep cave, where people are said to have entered and seen marvelous things, including Degei, as a snake or as a half man/half snake. Williams (1858:217) referred to a 'gloomy cavern— the hollow of an inland rock'. Joske (later Brewster) in 1885 actually visited and described the cave. He is cited by Kaplan (1988:152) as saying that 'Degei the Kalouvu or Fijian Creator lived in a cavern at Na Kauvadra. He was a gigantic serpent but, at such times as he willed, assumed the human form'. I was told in Rakiraki that within living memory two men from the village went into the cave and were allowed by Degei to take some *buli tabua* (white cowry) back to Rakiraki where they were placed at the end of the *balabala* (tree fern) ridge poles of Tu Navitilevu's house. They were shown to me on his house in 1952.

  At the northern base of the Tualeita Range about 3 km from the western end at Edromu there is an impressive rock formation, with a cave and a pool. This is the place of Sadidi, female ancestral spirit of people living at the present village of Lomolomo, and the pool is her bathing place. Her manifestation is a *duluduluwai* or dragon fly. Nearby is an earth mound where presentations are made to her. To the west, at Edronu at the base of the end of the Tualeita, there are two caves. At the western cave, known as Qwara ni Masumasu, supplications for support were made to the local spirit, Balawakula, whose place is inside the cave. The eastern cave, known as Qwara ni iYau, is the place of the spirit Sagavulunavuda, son of Lutunasobasoba. Persons wanting *sau* or supernatural power for war clubs for use against the enemy, or for a *meke* to be performed by the supplicants would place the clubs inside the cave for four nights. The *bete* would communicate with Sagavulunavuda and request the help being sought. Such presentations were made when the Fijian Military Force's troops departed for the Solomons Campaign in 1943.

  The impressive and well-known cave on the island of Sawailau, south of Yasawa island, has a pool where two fishes are said to be the *waqawaqa* or manifestations of spirits associated with the people of the village of Nabukeru. One wall has a series of petroglyphs associated, according to some I met, with the spirit Lewaqoroqoro. However, most people denied any such association. Steps cut in the wall of the cave lead up to an alcove described as the seat for the *bete* when communicating with the spirits.

Superficial features, natural and man-made

- Rocks, naturally static or errant

  These may be found on land, in a river or in the sea. Some rocks may show no obvious feature to merit choice among otherwise similar rocks as being spirit-associated. At the edge of the village of Namuaimada beside the main road, a large but otherwise unremarkable rock called Tadili was said to be the place of Qelo, the club-footed ancestral spirit of the Navolau *yavusa*. When I called there in 2001, the road had been widened and the surrounds of Tadili had been disturbed. Qelo is a violent spirit if disturbed, and I asked the people living beside the rock if anything unfortunate had happened. They said that Qelo had simply gone away from Tadili.

  In the area known generally as Korotabu near the village of Vatutu, Nadi, is the place of Raituvulaki, ancestral spirit of the Vunataqwa *yavusa*. A feature of this site is an otherwise unremarkable rock identified as the seat of Raituvulaki. On one occasion, he sat here with a local female spirit, Lewatu. He had an erection and entered her, and his penis so extended that it carried her as far as the black sand beach at Wailoaloa. It was suggested to me that this was the origin of the name Utiloaloa (black penis) which refers collectively to Vunataqwa and other associated *yavusa*.

- Other rocks with a natural feature

  A rock on the north coast island of Malake has a cone-shaped hollow, described to me as resembling a vagina, and associated with the female spirit Bilovesi. A rock I saw at Edronu with markings described as resembling male genitals was associated with a male spirit, Sagavulunavuda, being either Balawakula referred to above, or Lutunasobasoba, a culture hero who came with Degei aboard the *Kaunitoni*.

- Rocks modified by human activity

  Some rocks may be inscribed with petroglyphs, such as those near to the caves at Edronu; or at Natuvi, the rocky hilltop of the ancestral spirit, Raituvulaki. Others may be shaped to resemble a shark, such as the rock known as Nadakuvatu sited beside the *yavu* of Sayake in the village of Tavakubu, near to Lautoka. Others may be ground to form a either a round hollow (for pounding *yaqona*) as on several boulders beside the burial mound Kawalevu, to the north side of the Navatu acropolis in Rakiraki; or to more elongated hollows suitable for sharpening adze blades, of which there are many on the rocks near Edronu referred to earlier.

- Rocks associated with a pool

  These may represent the place of a spirit or where it bathes. To the northern side of the Tualeita up not far up the valley from Lomolomo is the pool shaded by trees beside rocks, identified as the place of Sadidi, the ancestral spirit referred to earlier. Twin spirits, known as the Ciri, associated with legends of Degei, have a place at Nukunitabua to the north side of the Nakauvadra Mountains. It is a mound with a megalithic complex on top. Below it a stream runs between rocks, in which is the bathing pool for the Ciri.

- Rocks carried from an earlier site

  These may be erected in a new settlement, perhaps on the ceremonial site for communication with the spirit. In the *naga*-like ceremonial site at Wasavulu, Labasa, on the north side of the central mountain range on Vanua Levu, there now stands a massive monolith, possibly the tallest in Fiji. I was told that the Labasa people carried it over the range from their antecedent site at Nukubola when they came over from the southern side of the range to settle on the north side. With it came their ancestral spirit.

- Rocks hallowed in connection with the installation (*veibuli*) of a new paramount chief

  For the installation of the Momo Levu of Sabeto, two round stones are used. Momo Levu sits on one and holds the other. They are kept in the house on the ceremonial mound of Erenavula in Koroiaca village. For the installation of Tu Navitilevu of Rakiraki, the chief leans against a monolith, which at present stands beside the church. It was brought from the *yavu tabu* of Yavunuku in the original settlement of the Namotutu people, where it stood on top of the mound and was associated with the ancestral spirit of the Namotutu *yavusa.*

- Rocks used in connection with cannibal activities (*vatu ni bokola*) usually found at *vanua tabu*

  Standing beside Navatanitawake, the main *bure kalou* on the island of Bau, was a monolith used for the killing of people to be presented as *bokola* or bodies to the spirit of the 'temple'. The stone was later moved to the newly built church, and was used as the font when I saw it.

- Earthen mounds, which may have a monolith on top

  Such mounds may be places where the spirit stays, or where presentations are made to the spirit, or where the *bete* communicates with the spirit. They are usually man-made. They may be rectangular or round, terraced, and flanked by natural or carved stones; and are generally higher than other mounds in the village, or in their the vicinity. On Bau, the *bure kalou* of Navatanitawake is rectangular, terraced, flanked by carved and natural stones, and is higher than any other mound on the island. In Rakiraki, the *yavu tabu* of Yavunuku at Namotutu is almost round, unterraced, with no flanking features. It had a monolith on top until the Namotutu people moved to the present combined village of Rakiraki, and took the monolith with them and re-erected it beside the church. In the old village of Saravi, Nadi, one high rectangular mound had been surmounted by a monolith. This stone had been taken down, deliberately broken up and the pieces had been buried in the mound. Nearby, a simple circular mound was pointed out to me as being associated with the presentation of gifts to the spirit of the place.

  Height above ground is an important element in the symbolism of Fijian socio-politics and the spirit world; and in this connection, comparative height is an important feature in the construction of man-made mounds. The higher the housemound, the higher is the social status of the owner, and the closer is the owner connected with the original ancestral spirit. The highest mounds in a village are usually those connected with the paramount chief and the ancestral spirit. Vunisei, the house mound of the Momo Levu of Vuda, is high and impressive in comparison with the other mounds in Viseisei village. Excellent examples of high and impressive spirit mounds are Navatanitawake (Bau), Natavasara (Taveuni) and at Tokatoka (Rewa).

Features rising significantly above the land or sea

- Cliffs

  Cliffs are often associated with jumping-off places for the spirits of the newly-dead. The cliffs at Nacilau, Waya Island, and Namuremure on the island of Malake are places from which spirits jump into the sea where there were rocks. A cliff at Ucunivanua, Nakelo, is the end of a spirit path connecting Nakelo with the spirit centre at Uluda on the Nakauvadra Mountains. This path is symbolised by the roots of a tree which grew on the Mountains. It is referred to as the *wakanivugayali* or the roots of a large tree of the myrtle variety. I have been shown what are purported to be the roots sticking out of the cliff at Ucunivanua.

- Waterfalls

  Vaikitu is a *bara ni sava* or waterfall above the present village of Nayaulevu on the south side of the Nakauvadra. This is the settlement of Kitu, the original ancestral spirit of the Nacolo people now living at Vatukacevaceva on the north side of Nakauvadra. Kitu's *waqawaqa* is an *ula,* a kind of frog, which stays in a *qila* or crevice in the waterfall. If it appears in his house, the *bete* will speak to it *vakaula* or in frog's talk which no one else understands. If there is trouble, the *bete* prepares *yaqona* and presents it to Kitu at Vaikitu.

- Islets, with or without man-made features, caves or pools

The islet of Cubu, offshore from Navatu, has a small cave associated with the female spirit Bilovesi. The islet of Narokorokoyawa in the Northern Mamanucas has a number of features associated with the ancestral spirit Tuirevurevu. These include caves, a pool, man-made structures and monoliths; and a more recent stone complex where visitors now make presentations to Tuirevurevu. Tuirevurevu's place called Rukurukulevu is regarded as very *tabu*, greatly feared and respected.

- Mountain tops, on which may be natural features such as rocks and caves

The Nakauvadra Mountains dramatically overshadow the Rakiraki area. Features include, first, the main spirit centre at Uluda symbolised by the cave of Degei in a rock; secondly, an impressive rock known as Rogorogo i Vuda, representing a *lali* or drum for passing messages to the other main spirit centre at Vuda; and thirdly, the site of the *vugayali* or myrtle tree, the roots of which symbolise the spirit paths (see under 'trees'). Further research may determine whether these elements represent more than one original cult even if present tradition weaves them into one. On the top of the Tualeita mountain range above the spirit centre of Edronu with associated caves and petroglyph-covered boulders, a tree-covered rocky eminence represents the *ivilavila ni yalo* were spirits who have followed the Tualeita spirit path jump into the sea and head west. On the island of Waya, the southern peak of Ulu i Tunaiau (about 550 m above sea-level) is the place of the autochthonous ancestral spirit Tunaiau. He is regarded as the *ivakatawa* or guardian, and the *itaukei du* or true owner of Waya. He went to Samoa and brought back his wife and other Samoans who settled on Waya. The Wayans still recognise what they regard as their Samoan connections.

- Natural hillocks, on which may be natural features such as rocks or caves, or man-made features such as mounds

These include the two hill-top sites of Navatu (Rakiraki), and Korovatu (Vuda). The former was first settled by Waqabalabala, the original ancestral spirit of the Navatu people, and then by his two sons, all three of whom have a particular rocky peak. Among other spirits associated with Navatu is Coci, who has a harelip, and occupies a cave on the south side. Korovatu was first occupied by Lutunasobasoba who came to Fiji from the west in the vessel *Kaunitoni*. When he left to travel overland towards the Nakauvadra, his eldest son, Sagavulunavuda remained on Korovatu. A number of *yavu* or housemounds can be seen on top of the hill, and one is regarded as that of Sagavulunavuda, and others those of his *bete* and household. Even in my time, people still approached him on top of Korovatu, for assistance. There is supposed to be a cave beneath the hill where lives a spirit who is part of the defence apparatus against those who try to attack Korovatu.

Trees (being partly subterranean, partly surficial and partly rising towards the sky)

- Certain species of tree such as *baka* or fig trees, being either the places of the spirits, or closely associated with them

These trees are regarded as *tabu;* and if they are cut down or damaged on purpose some disaster will befall the perpetrator unless appropriate ceremonies of apology are performed. After the 1952 hurricane destroyed much of Rakiraki, a *baka* tree near the mound of Leka, the ancestral spirit of the Cakova *yavusa,* was badly damaged and several of the branches had to be cut off. Leka took great offence and appeared in the form of a short man (*leka* means short). Ceremonies of apology were performed on his mound, and all was well.

- Particular mythical trees

  Certain trees may have special connections with the passage of the spirits of the dead. The mythical *vugayali* on the Nakauvadra above Rakiraki has roots (the *wakanivugayali*) branching out to a number of places in Fiji including Edronu (Vuda), Ucunivanua (Nakelo), Waya and Ucunivanua (Bua). These roots symbolise spirit paths between the spirit centre on Nakauvadra and these other places. A particular *balawa* or pandanus lies on a spirit path running along the North coastal region of Vanua Levu. It is referred to as *na balawa viriki* (the pandanus tree which has something thrown at it). When the spirit of a recently dead person reaches this tree, it must throw at it a stone known as a *vatu ni balawa* or stone for the pandanus. If it hits, the spirit proceeds on its journey. If it misses, it remains there. I have been shown the place near Udu Point.

- Living trees

  Some living trees, either particular individual trees or trees of a particular species, are regarded as having spirit-derived properties. There is a particular tree in the old village of Nawaka Makawa, near the present village of Nawaka. If a mother is short of milk, she may go to this tree, and slash it. As the resin runs out, so will her milk supply miraculously increase.

- Trees as symbols of identification

  A most important aspect of the spiritual and socio-political aspect of trees is the almost general reference to a particular type of *kau* or *kai* tree among the *icavuti* or *vutiyaca* ('totems') of a particular *yavusa*. As such, the tree is one of the symbols of identification of the *yavusa*. Its exact significance is nowadays not at all clear, though it is often associated with the male genital organs. Any insult to it such as a derogatory reference can still lead to most unfortunate results for the offender unless ceremonial apologies are hastily performed.

Orientation, horizontal and vertical

Myths abound about spirits from the east travelling westward along the appropriate spirit path to the central spirit place on the Nakauvadra. Others tell how spirits go either directly from the *icibaciba* or jumping-place or *via* the Nakauvadra and the western spirit-path, to Edronu and thence head west. I am aware of little evidence for the significance of horizontal orientation in such tasks as the siting and design of a village.

Similarly, I have scant evidence for vertical orientation in the spirit world. Some myths refer to a spiritual settlement known variously as Burotu Kula, Vanua Kula or Purotu, (see Geraghty 1983a:343–384), described to me as floating in the sky, as it was recently seen in Rakiraki. Other myths refer to the underworld of Bulu, and the original ancestor of the Bauan paramount polity is known as Ratu mai Bulu. His place is on the Viti Levu mainland whereas his present mound of communication is Navatanitawake on the island of Bau (see Parke n.d.- b, 1993, 1998). Similarly there are myths regarding Lagi, the sky, and of spirits or spirit places floating in Lagi. There is an expression 'ki Bulu, ki Lagi' or 'to Bulu, to Lagi' used in ceremonial speeches, which connect the underworld with the spirit world. These questions of horizontal or vertical orientation in the spirit or the socio-political worlds of Fijian society need further consideration. There is little evidence of which I am aware in the current literature. It is therefore important to carry out further investigations in the field before relevant myths are forgotten.

The centre, the outside and the threshold

A *yavusa* is described earlier as ideally being socio-politically exclusive and hierarchical, but these ideal characteristics can be looked at from another angle too.

The paramount chief is the socio-political centre of the *yavusa* just as the original ancestral spirit is the centre of the *yavusa*'s spirit world. The two worlds merge in the person of the paramount chief when his installation has been validated by installation ceremonies. These include invoking the ancestral spirit, and may involve the use of installation stones associated with the spirit. Nowadays installation is formalised by the drinking of *yaqona*. I was told that in the west *tovu* or sugar cane was once used in the place of *yaqona*. *Yaqona* or *tovu* may be the medium for transferring *mana* or spiritual power from the spirit to the paramount.

Because of this association between spirit and installed chief, the installed chief becomes *tabu* or *dredre* (difficult to approach). Similarly, the paramount's housemound is *tabu*, just as the sites associated with the ancestral spirit such as the spirit house are *tabu*. It is regarded as *dredre sara*, or very difficult, to approach the house mound or enter the house of the paramount chief, just as it is *dredre sara* to approach a *tabu* site associated with the ancestral or indeed any other spirit. To put this in another way, the chief's house may be regarded as the socio-political, physical centre of the village; and it is *dredre sara* to go from the outside (*tuba*) of the house across the threshold (*tabailago*) to the inside (*loma*). Similarly at the village level, it is difficult for a stranger casually to cross the boundary (*iyalayald*) of a village from outside (*tuba*) of the village into the inside (*loma ni koro*). Once inside the village, it is difficult for the stranger casually to enter the inside of a house, with the household of which he or she has no socio-political or spiritual connection. It is certainly very difficult indeed to approach the chief, or to enter his house or the ceremonial house. To cross such thresholds or boundaries, ceremonies of request and appeasement of the spirits must be conducted in the appropriate manner, to the appropriate person or persons, and in the appropriate order, depending on the nature of the centre to be reached, be it socio-political or spiritual. In theory and practice this comes down to the same thing.

It is similarly extremely disrespectful for any one casually to cross or wander about on the ceremonial central area (*rara*, or *darata* in the west) in the middle of the village. Nowadays it may be used for a cricket pitch, and this may be an indication of the attitude of the traditional chief of the village to cricket.

The yavusa in reality: fusion, fission and movement

The ideal *yavusa* appears to be exclusive, hierarchical, static, independent (*tu vakaikoya*) and socio-separate from other *yavusa*. In reality, socio-political internal fusion and fission as well as geographical movement and interaction with other *yavusa* and with external forces such as Tongan and European visitors, settlers and missionaries, were features in the development of most *yavusa*, but this raises the issue of how a social unit becomes a *yavusa* in the first place. Ideally again, a *yavusa* is the descent group of a particular ancestral spirit. In reality if a group from an established *yavusa* arrived in a new place they would probably not regard themselves as of separate *yavusa* status unless invited by the host *yavusa* to do so, or until they become sufficiently numerous to justify doing so without appearing to the *itaukei* to be *viavialevu*. This means having ideas above their station without physical or spiritual justification to maintain their new status—a deadly socio-political sin.

Fusion and fission

One of the most interesting features in a *yavusa* development is the degree of socio-political and socio-economic connections with other *yavusa* through fusion and fission. Fusion and fission within a *yavusa* may have come about through:

- disagreements and insults between one *mataqali* or *itokatoka* and another.

  These could result in the disaffected group leaving the rest of the *yavusa* unless ceremonies of reconciliation were performed successfully.

- an increase in numbers in the *yavusa*.

  This could lead to insufficient space in the village site, or inadequate planting land close at hand, or an inadequate water supply. This could result in an amicable polity-wide decision to split and form another village with adequate facilities, either on land owned by the splitting group or on land requested by the group from a neighbouring *yavusa*.

- a request from outsiders to join the *yavusa*, perhaps after an unreconciled quarrel.

  Members of a *mataqali* or *itokatoka* of another *yavusa* could approach the *yavusa* in question with a request to join them and settle on their land. Similarly, a *yavusa* could invite members of another *yavusa* to join them, perhaps for reasons of prestige. In either case the approach would be made formally through the ceremony of *ilakovi*. The *vulagi* would then be accepted as *itaukei* for all intents and purposes, although if they tried to override the real *itaukei* in important traditional discussions they could be reminded of their origins.

Change in social structure of a yavusa

The social structure of the hierarchy recognised by the status of the different *mataqali* comprising a *yavusa* or the ranking of individuals within a *mataqali* might change because of:

- internal quarrels, including fighting, within a *yavusa*

  This could lead to a *mataqali* lower in the hierarchy forcefully replacing a more senior or the most senior *mataqali*.

- refusal to accept responsibility

  The most senior member of the chiefly *mataqali* may not wish to accept the responsibilities of installation to paramountcy.

- unsuitability for office

  Members of the various *mataqali*, especially the senior *mataqali*, may not consider the most senior member to be worthy of installation and a person whom they regard as more suitable may be installed instead. Alternatively, no-one may be installed as paramount. This may be a face-saving temporary alternative for the most senior member or for *the yavusa* as a whole. However, sooner or later, the socio-political situation of the *yavusa* may result in internal instability, or in political machinations or misunderstandings on the part of other *yavusa* in the course of their relations with the *yavusa* concerned.

Geographical movement

The first settlement

Parallel with the realities of socio-political fusion and fission within *a yavusa*, my investigations show or confirm that, in reality, the *yavusa's* village site was not static but usually changed on several occasions from the traditional first settlement (*yavutū*) of the *yavusa*. According to local myth, the site for such a settlement may have been the same place as where the original ancestral spirit finally settled, having wandered about looking for a suitable and vacant site.

Many myths have it that the original ancestral spirit may have come down either from the spirit centre on Nakauvadra, or from the mythological first landing of the first craft in the Vuda area. Alternatively, the son of the original ancestor may have been born a spirit at the final settlement of the original ancestor and turned into a human who remained in the spirit settlement of his father and grandfather. Finally, the first human settlement may have been near that of the final settlement of the original ancestor.

The descendants increase in number

Whatever the nature of the first human settlement, it was here according to the model that the human descendants of the ancestral spirit increased in numbers. In course of time these descendants divided up and comprised recognised groups which are now referred to as *mataqali*, the hereditary status of which was based on the mythological order of birth of the sons of the original ancestor. Eventually these *mataqali* divided into what are now referred to as *itokatoka* or some equivalent term depending on the dialect and geographical area, the seniority of which within the *mataqali* was based mythologically on the order of birth of the grandsons of the original ancestor. Whatever the reality of the situation in prehistoric times, this was the socio-political situation allegedly derived from mythological origins as accepted by the Native Lands Commission (NLC) and the Colonial Government for practical purposes and for the ease of Fijian land administration. The question may well be raised as to whether the first split was not rather into *itokatoka* which later united with related *itokatoka* and created a *mataqali*. It is probably too late to try to determine this matter and beyond the main purposes of this project. In course of time, whatever its precise pattern of development, the *yavusa* may have moved from the first settlement *in toto* or may have split up and settled in various settlements, or it may have been joined by members of other *yavusa*.

Later settlements

In any case, parts or the whole of the *yavusa* moved to new village sites, settling either by themselves or together as a *yavusa,* or joining other *yavusa* and sharing a village site. The new site(s) may have been chosen for better access to gardening land, water supplies, or fishing or hunting areas, or as being more easily defended in the course of inter- or intra-polity quarrels or warfare. Sometimes a new village was sited to be near a place of spiritual significance. Sometimes it was situated deliberately far away from the earlier site, especially if the new settlement had arisen from a split in the *yavusa* as the result of internal quarrels and insults. Sometimes the change in village site resulted from an invitation from another *yavusa* to settle with it for the purposes of mutual protection. In other cases the new settlement may have resulted from a powerful *yavusa* wanting to settle trusted people in a newly conquered area. A new village site may have taken with it the name of a previous settlement or it may have been given a name based on a local feature, geographical or spiritual.

Symbolic connections with older sites

If a polity or part of a polity moved to a new site, the new site would retain some features from the previous site, especially those connected with the spirits, and it would do so in spite of any realities of socio-political fusion and fission. The polity might take with it a monolith representing the original ancestor, or the installation stone for the paramount and associated with the spirits. It would construct special mounds for the house of the paramount or for the building where the *bete* communicates with the ancestral spirit, perhaps taking the names of the similar mounds at the previous village site. The names of some of the other housemounds might also be taken from those in the old village site.

Networks and inclusiveness

A feature of the ideal *yavusa* is its exclusiveness, but my investigations indicate that, in reality, some of the most significant factors in the development of Fijian society were the socio-political and socio-spiritual connections existing or created between one *yavusa* and one or more other *yavusa*. Such connections may have arisen through myth or by custom; they may have developed voluntarily between *yavusa;* they may have been forced by factors outside a *yavusa*'s control, but brought about by other *yavusa*; or a grouping of *yavusa* may have developed because of external factors outside Fijian society. Sometimes the formally acknowledged membership of a *yavusa*, based on direct descent from the original ancestral spirit usually along the male line, may have been extended by the inclusion through custom and due ceremony of persons who would not otherwise have been recognised as members of the ideally constituted *yavusa*.

To this extent, the realities of fusion and fission indicate that a *yavusa* may be characterised as being potentially inclusive. An analysis of the development of a particular *yavusa* should examine the extent of exclusiveness and inclusiveness in its composition both synchronically and diachronically. I will now consider some recognised mechanisms for establishing networks between *yavusa*.

(a) Myth or custom

Connections may have been established by myth or custom through:

- *veitauvū*

  Veitauvū is a relationship between the ancestral spirit of a particular *yavusa* and one or more ancestral spirits of one or more other *yavusa*. Such relationship may have been based on sibling spirits, or on an ancestral spirit who married the sibling of the ancestral spirit of another *yavusa*.

- *Vasu*

  Vasu is a relationship arising from marriage between members, especially high-ranking members, of different *yavusa*. The children of the brother of the female spouse had a special relationship with the members of the *yavusa* of which the uncle was a member. Requests by the former from the latter were difficult to refuse.

(b) Voluntary associations

Associations may have been voluntary and based on such factors as:

- mutual convenience

  Hill-folk and sea-folk might agree to exchange root crops and *yaqona* for salt and fish.

- mutual assistance in times of trouble or war.

- an ineffective *yavusa* without adequate martial or natural facilities for survival in times of war or peace. Such a *yavusa* may voluntarily approach a powerful and rich *yavusa* seeking to come under its protection and authority. This dependence is called *tiko vakararavi* in Bauan.

- association between a politically powerful *yavusa* and a warrior *yavusa*,

  A politically powerful *yavusa* may have established a relationship which enabled it to call upon a warrior *yavusa* for assistance in times of war. The relationship would continue until the powerful polity failed to provide the expected goods in exchange for the military services provided by the warriors, or until another powerful *yavusa* seduced the warrior *yavusa* by agreeing to provide more attractive goods in exchange for services. The warrior *yavusa* in such a relationship is known as *bati* (literally 'tooth' or 'border') and may break the relationship (known as *veibati*) under the circumstances described.

(c) Involuntary associations

Associations may have been involuntary on the part of one or more of the polities involved, due to such situations as when a powerful polity may compel, by force or threat, a weaker polity to come under its sway. This relationship is known as *veiqali*. The weaker *yavusa* is referred to *qali* (literally 'twisted' as a coil of rope). Rather than being available on request to provide assistance, as in the case of the *bati,* the *qali* is essentially subject to the demands of the more powerful *yavusa.* The *qali* may attempt to revolt from the relationship and may be severely punished, even by death. Alternatively it may successfully escape the relationship and become recognised as the *qali* of another more powerful *yavusa.* This may well lead to war between the two powerful *yavusa.*

(d) Influence of outside circumstances

As discussed in detail earlier, polities may combine for mutual convenience and protection due to factors outside Fijian society such as the Tongans' monarchical ideology and their ambitions to expand and impose their authority over Fijian territory; the arrival of European settlers and traders; and the arrival of missionaries who wanted Christianity to supersede the traditional Fijian socio-spiritual world. In trying to impose Christianity in the place of the Fijian spirit world, and to stamp out practices such as those referred to earlier, the missionaries were striking against important elements at the very basis of traditional politico-spiritual Fijian society.

Spirit and socio-political networking

Networks were facilitated or symbolised by:

- spirit paths—*sala ni yalo* in the east, or *calevu ni (y)anitu* in the west.

  Some spirit paths may be followed by the spirits of the newly dead travelling from an *icibaciba* or *ivilavila* (jumping off place of their particular *yavusa)* to the spirit centre of Uluda on the top of the Nakauvadra Mountains. Other spirits may go by one of the main spirit paths of the *wakanivuniyali* to the central spirit place of the *vugayali* on the Nakauvadra. In either case, Uluda and the *vugayali* and associated spirit paths to Nakauvadra represent communication systems of spiritual unity symbolic of the inclusiveness of Fijian society. Another such system is based on the main spirit centre at Edronu and the spirit path represented by the *wakanivugali* stretching from Nakauvadra along the mountain ridges of the Tualeita and ending at Edronu.

  These paths to Nakauvadra lead not only to the *vugayali* but also to the mighty peak of Uluda where dwelt the major culture hero Degei who himself may be regarded as a spiritual symbol of unification of Fijian society. The myths about the *vugayali* and its roots, and about Degei at Uluda are nowadays usually interconnected by a single myth. As suggested earlier, it is possible that these two myths were diachronically or even synchronically separate at some earlier period. From Edronu, the spirits of the dead head off to the west. Other spirits may go off to the west direct from their *i cibaciba* which often itself faces west. The tendency for spirits of the recently dead is to go west towards the setting of the sun and the mythical area from which the original ancestors are said to have come in the *Kaunitoni.* This mythical connection with the west could be regarded as a spiritual symbol for the recognition by traditional Fijian society that it had some connection with the outside world—in other words, for the inclusiveness of Fijian society.

- paths of socio-political communication—*sala* in the east or *calevu ni matamataraki* in the west.

  Such paths may be associated with the bringing of tribute from *qali* or *yavusa* subject to a paramount polity; or the sending of messages from the paramount to subject *qali,* demanding goods or services, or to allied *bati,* requesting assistance in war; or for sending messages of request (*kerekere*) or invitations (*veisureti*) from the paramount of one *yavusa* to that of another.

- the development of a system of representatives of *a yavusa* being sent to live with an associated *yavusa.*

This may be based on an exchange of 'diplomatic postings' between associated polities, especially when geographically far apart. Such a posting is referred to as a *mata ki*. It may also be based on a system of posting representatives of a powerful *yavusa* to another *yavusa* under its sway to make sure that such a polity, especially if recently defeated or if likely to revolt, toes the party line.

- a system of ceremonial officers (*mata ni vanua*) symbolising the threshold between one *yavusa* and another.

  A ceremonial approach to a chief would be made by first approaching the chief's *mata ni vanua* who is in a traditional position to open the door and escort the visitor across the threshold into the chief's house. The arrival of such a visitor would be announced from the outside by calling out the *tama*. This varies from place. In Rakiraki, the announcement of a male visitor would be '*Dua! Dua! Dua!*' and of a female '*Mai na vaka dua!*' In each case the reply from inside the house would be '*Oi dua!*' followed by an expression such as '*Mai*' (here), '*Vano mai*' (come) or '*Ruku mai*' (enter).

Emerging geographical patterns of complexity

Having identified various factors, both internal and external, which may have affected the development of *yavusa* both diachronically and synchronically, I now proceed to an introductory study of how *yavusa* variously developed at the period before Cession in 1874. This attempts to indicate whether geographical patterns of complexity in traditional Fijian society generally can be recognised to have emerged by that time.

7

The Diversity of Fijian Polities

An overall discussion of the general diversity of traditional pan-Fijian polities immediately prior to Cession in 1874 will set a wider perspective for the results of my own explorations into the origins, development, structure and leadership of the *yavusa* in my three field areas, and the identification of different patterning of interrelationships between *yavusa*. The diversity of pan-Fijian polities can be most usefully considered as a continuum from the simplest to the most complex levels of structured types of polity, with a tentative geographical distribution from simple in the west to extremely complex in the east.

Obviously I am by no means the first to draw attention to the diversity of these polities and to point out that there are considerable differences in the principles of structure, ranking and leadership between the *yavusa* and the *vanua* which I have investigated and those accepted by the government as the model. G.K. Roth (1953:58–61), not unexpectedly as Deputy Secretary of Fijian Affairs under Ratu Sir Lala Sukuna, tended to accord with the public views of his mentor; although he did point out that 'The number of communities found in a federation was not the same in all parts of Fiji'. Rusiate Nayacakalou who carried out his research in 1954, observed (1978: xi) that 'there are some variations in the traditional structure from one village to another'. Ratu Sukuna died in 1958, and it may be coincidental that thereafter researchers paid more emphasis to the differences I referred to. Isireli Lasaqa who was Secretary to Cabinet and Fijian Affairs was primarily concerned with political and other changes in the years before and after independence in 1970. He also discussed critically (Lasaqa 1984: 19 *et seq.*) the views of O.H.K. Spate (1959) about Fijian society, as implying 'a thoroughly conservative social order'. He investigated the situation in the case of the *vanua* of Dawasama, Tailevu and determined that 'the authoritarian and rigid traditional structure was not always adhered to, particularly by the younger generation to whom this traditional structure was fast becoming obscure, if not obsolete'. He did not specifically explore pre-Cession society, but he told me (personal communication) that he equally considered that the reality did not accord with the model. In the case of a *matanitū*, I am generally in accord with Sayes (1982) who entitled her thesis 'Cakaudrove: Ideology and Reality in a Fijian Confederation' about a major complex polity with which I am familiar as former District Commissioner for the area. Nicholas Thomas, no respecter of graven images, claimed (1986:6, 65) that 'From the late 1840s, various major social and cultural changes became apparent' and that 'Investigations of the nature of factional conflict involved posing the question of the extent to which Fijian leadership and succession was ascribed or achieved'. David Routledge (1985:27–30) presented what he described as a schematic representation of a theoretical abstraction of the social structure of Fijian society and said that 'Quarrels…particularly over ceremonial matters, resulted in the break-up of *yavusa* and the fortunes of war caused them to be conquered and dismembered'. Asesela Ravuvu, former Director of the Institute of Pacific Studies at the University of the South Pacific, was to my knowledge the first (Ravuvu 1983:14) to differentiate the two meanings on *vanua* on the lines on which I have based my research: *vanua* 1 covering traditional society, with the three elements of spirits, places and people; and contrasting with *vanua* 2 having the more familiar meaning of a socio-political federation of *yavusa*. Christina Toren was, however, the first to discuss (1995:163–183) the concepts of spirits, places and people in the context of the village of Sawaieke, Gau where she stayed for twenty months from 1981–1983. I believe that I am the first to pursue these two meanings of *vanua*, and the three elements of *vanua* 1 in exploring the realities of traditional Fijian society.

With simple polities tending to be found towards the west and the most highly complex polities generally found towards the east, Marshall Sahlins (1963, 1968) discussed political types in Melanesia and Polynesia with a cultural intergrading in and around Fiji. Melanesian society is described as typically segmental, consisting of many autonomous kinship-residential groups, each being economically self-governing and the equal of the others in political status. Leadership is based on power, and the so-called big-men do not succeed to office but attain status by a series of acts which attract the loyalty of lesser men. Such local independent groups appear in Polynesia as subdivisions of an inclusive political body which is described as 'pyramidal', and 'an enclaving chiefdom-at-large' (Sahlins 1968:31, 65). As Sahlins put it: 'Polynesian chiefs did not make their positions in society—they were installed in societal positions' (1968:90). Sahlins did not see a dichotomy between Melanesian and Polynesian societies. Rather he saw the overall situation as a continuum. Linguists in the past tended to interpret the linguistic scene in Fiji as a dichotomy between east and west but have now determined that there is an element of continuum within and between the two divisions. I have gone one step further, and I believe that I am the first to interpret the overall socio-political situation as a continuum as well. This follows synchronic and diachronic as well as geographical studies of the *yavusa* and *vanua* and (where relevant) *matanitū*.

Synchronically, Fijian polities can be classified socio-organisationally, not absolutely but relatively in relation to a continuum based on levels of hierarchical complexity of the individual polities. At one end of the continuum would be the simple, independent descent group. At the other would be the highly complex socio-political confederation, involving lesser federations and descent groups bonded in several hierarchical levels of authority, culminating in a top level of independent paramountcy. In between would be many varieties of lesser socio-political federations and of associations of descent groups.

Diachronically, Fijian polities can be classified in accordance with the same criteria. The simple, independent descent group would have been the oldest form of polity, and the stable and highly complex socio-political confederation of federations and associations of descent groups would have been the most recent form.

Geographically, Fijian polities in the west tended to be single *yavusa* or simple groupings of descent groups and minor socio-political federations with limited spheres of influence. In the east, Fijian polities tended to be most highly complex confederations with wide spheres of influence. This was especially the case, first, where the chiefs were able and ambitious but perhaps more importantly had the most powerful military and naval facilities at their disposal; and, secondly, where the ideological and military influences of eventually-monarchical Tonga were strongest.

This chapter discusses the general patterning of pan-Fijian polities of differing degrees of socio-political complexity of structure, bearing in mind the synchronic, diachronic and geographical implications of such patterning. I have based the degree of complexity of an individual polity not so much on some absolute scale of criteria but rather on a tendency towards a continuum of complexity of hierarchical levels within a polity. At one extreme of the continuum would be the *yavusa* as a simple independent descent group. At the other extreme would be the *matanitū* or highly complex multi-level confederation, comprised of a number of dependent *vanua* or groups of *yavusa*, each at various levels of hierarchy and complexity with their own chiefly authorities but culminating at the highest level in the person of a paramount chief to whom all the lesser chiefs acknowledge authority. In between would be *vanua* or less complex federations of individual *yavusa* or groups of *yavusa* each acknowledging their own chiefs but accepting the authority of a paramount chief.

A continuum of socio-politically structured polities

The basis of the idea of a continuum is the premise that the complexity of a polity depends on the number of levels of hierarchy in which the leaders of each sub-polity at one level *vakarorogo* or heed the authority of the leader of a higher level of sub-polity or to the paramount leader of the polity. The paramount who does *vakarorogo* to no one is independent of any higher authority (*tu vakai koya*). The continuum is illustrated by the following examples:

(a) The simplest structure: the independent yavusa

At one end of the socio-organisational continuum of late Fijian social polities is the independent, single social group or *yavusa*. An independent *yavusa*, with its internal structure of *mataqali* and *itokatoka* had its own overall chief (*na kena turaga*) who *tu vakaikoya* and *vakarorogo* to no other person. The sub-groups may all claim descent from a common original ancestor or ancestral spirit (*vu* or *kalou vu*). On the other hand, some sub-groups may not claim descent from this ancestor but may have become included in the *yavusa* for reasons already discussed.

Na kena turaga may be either a descendant from the original ancestor or a *vulagi* or *kai tani*, a stranger who has been invited to become leader. In some cases, a female may be appointed (as in cases I have been familiar with in Nadroga, Vuda, Ba and Rewa). The person to be leader may or may not be formally installed at a ceremony of *veibuli* or installation at which he will be given a *yaca buli* or title. If a stranger who does not claim descent from the original ancestral spirit of the *yavusa* is invited to be leader, it is likely that he or she will be formally installed and given a title (*yaca buli*), and at ceremonies be *vagunuvi* (presented with the first ceremonial bowl of *yaqona* to drink). The essential part of the *veibuli* is *the yaqona ni veibuli* or *yaqona* ceremony for installation, at which *yaqona* is prepared in a *tanoa* or *yaqona* mixing-bowl. A *bilo* or half coconut shell is filled with *yaqona* and is presented first to the person to be installed, by the *tu yaqona* on behalf of the *yavusa* to the accompaniment of *cobo* or ceremonial clapping. This procedure is regarded as the essence of the transfer of *mana* or *sau* (spiritual power) from the *kalou vu* to the person being installed as the spiritual leader of the *yavusa*. Katz (1993: 47, 57) described *yaqona* presented in ceremonial circumstances as 'a spiritual messenger' and 'a channel for *mana*'.

If the new leader of a *yavusa* is a descendent of the original ancestor, and if the *yavusa* is composed of sub-groups, all of which claim descent from the same original ancestor, the eldest member of the senior division of the senior sub-group of the *yavusa* would ideally be recognised as the leader. However, even if the appointment of the new leader of a *yavusa* is made in accordance with this ideal basis of *veitarataravi vakaveitacini* or descent from elder brother to younger brother and then from eldest son of eldest brother to younger brother, the appointment could well be disputed, especially if the candidate is weak or unsuitable or if the *yavusa* includes members not descended from the original ancestor. It is plainly politic, in practice, to make quite clear who the candidate is to be.

The overt presentation of the first *bilo* to the person to be installed clearly indicated the choice of the new chief to the assembled participants. Similarly, when the *yaqona* is about to be presented to the person to be installed, the *wā* or coir rope attached to the *tanoa* is stretched out in the direction of that person. This aspect of the *yaqona ni veibuli* presumably derives from similar Tongan ceremonial with which such Fijian visitors to Tonga would have become familiar. The end of the *wā* facing the person is often adorned with one or two *buli tabua* or white chiefly cowry shells which have been described to me as the eyes of the snake—perhaps associating the *mana* of the ceremony with Degei, and thereby combining the validating traditions of Tonga with those associated with the myths of the Nakauvadra Mountains. The ceremony in the context of leadership of a political federation is discussed later.

The new head of a *yavusa* may be recognised but not formally installed, at least not initially. In this case he may hold a title relating to the chiefly *yavu* of the *yavusa*. In the case of the independent *yavusa* of Naua in the *tikina* of Nadi, the recognised but not yet installed leader held the title of iTaukei Sawaieke (owner of Sawaieke, the chiefly *yavu*). After a considerable period of time he was formally installed with the title of Momo i Naua (Chief of Naua) in the presence of a number of dignitaries from other connected polities.

The following two examples illustrating the characteristics of independent *yavusa* are both in the Yasawa group. Ketekete is a simple descent group associated with the village of Vuake on the island of Matacawalevu, being part of the Old *tikina* of Nacula in the New *tikina* of Yasawa. Kai Kese is a simple political group or construct associated with the village of Kese on the island of Naviti, being part of the Old *tikina* of Naviti in the New *tikina* of Naviti.

(i) Ketekete: a simple descent group

The Ketekete at Vuake are nowadays recognised as a *yavusa*, divided into two related *mataqali*; and each *mataqali* is divided into several related *tokatoka*, as follows:

Mataqali	iTokatoka
Nasivitu	Nasivitu
	Taganikula
	Bau
Ketekete	Ketekete
	Sava
	Davekadra Tabale

A member of the Nasivitu is installed as the Momo or iTeiteimata (chief or leader) of the Ketekete *yavusa*, with the title of Rātū. He is independent of any higher authority. The original ancestral spirit (*anitu*, in the local communalect) is Ravokavoka. He came from the Nakauvadra Mountains to the island of Matacawalevu where he settled at Ketekete at the place regarded and respected as the original spiritual settlement (*yavutū*) of the Ketekete. His patrilineal descendants comprise collectively the Ketekete *yavusa*. He had two children, Baba and Loaloa, whose descendants stayed together in the original settlement. The descendants of Baba, the elder son, became known collectively as the Nasivitu *mataqali*, and the descendants of his sons became known as the Nasivitu (the chiefly *itokatoka*), Taganikula and Bau respectively. The descendants of Loa, the younger son, comprise collectively the Ketekete *mataqali*, and the descendants of his sons became the *itokatoka* of Ketekete, Sava, Davekadra and Tabale. When the water supply at Ketekete became inadequate, the descendants of Ravokavoka moved and settled together at Vuake where they have remained ever since.

I recorded from present members of the Ketekete this account of the *yavusa*, and their current understandings accord with the investigations of the Native Lands Commission (NLC). Membership, including leadership, is based on patrilineal descent from a common ancestral spirit. The *iteiteimata* of the *yavusa* is appointed from the *tokatoka* comprised of descendents of the eldest son of the eldest son of the original ancestral spirit. Ketekete therefore exemplifies the model of a simple independent descent group having a hierarchical structure at three levels, being at one extreme of the posited continuum of structural complexity of socio-political groups and constructs spanning the overall structure of later Fijian traditional society.

(ii) Kai Kese: a simple political group or construct

The Kai Kese at Kese are nowadays recognised as a single *yavusa*, divided into two *mataqali*; and each *mataqali* is divided into several *tokatoka*, as follows:

Mataqali	iTokatoka
Luvuka	Nasukamoce
	Luvuka
	Ko
	Vunatagia
	Nacova
	Savusavuwa
Leweivawa	Nabouvatu
	Nasolo
	Lasawa Naqeleravu Nadonia
	Vite (or Vile?)

A member of the Nasukamoce is installed as the leader of the Kai Kese *yavusa*, with the title of Rokotakala. He is independent of any higher authority.

The Kai Kese are constructed of three socio-political elements. The first, the majority of the Kai Luvuka, are the descendants of Botabota, the original ancestral spirit, who settled at Kese. The second, the Kai Nasukamoce, came from Marou, Naviti, but originally from Votua, Ba. The third, the Leweivawa, originally from Vitogo, Vuda, are the descendants of a number of persons who split from of the Leweivawa *yavusa* of Muaira on the island of Naviti and joined the Kai Luvuka.

As for the Kai Luvuka, the origin myth tells how Botabota came from the Nakauvadra Mountains to the island of Naviti, and settled at Vanua in the middle (*luvuka*, in the local communalect) of the island. Vanua is regarded and respected as the *yavutū* or original spiritual settlement of the Luvuka *mataqali*. Botabota's patrilineal descendants comprise collectively the Luvuka *mataqali*. He had six children, the eldest of whom was Matatini, whose *yavu* or housemound was called Luvuka, and whose descendants comprise respectively six of the seven *tokatoka* of the *mataqali* of Luvuka—one of them is now extinct. Each was named after the respective *yavu* of the six children.

The Nasukamoce, the senior *itokatoka* of the Luvuka *mataqali* are descended not from Botabota, but from persons who had split from the Kai Koro of Marou, Naviti. The latter had come to the island of Naviti following a quarrel at Votua, Ba. They were settled at Marou by the leading Naviti group, the Suelevu, who decided that, because of their strength and abilities, one of the Kai Koro chiefs should be installed as paramount for the adjacent villages of Marou and Malevu. The person chosen was not the first-born but a younger brother. This upset the Kai Koro, who split up, and many left Marou among whom were the group who went to Kese and were invited to settle with the Luvuka original landowners. The Luvuka were so impressed with the qualities of these *vulagi* that they decided to make them a part of the Luvuka and to install the Kai Koro leader as leader of the Luvuka, with the title of Rokotakala. Those of the Kai Koro who came to Kese were known as the Nasukamoce, after the name of the land given to them by the Luvuka landowners.

As for the origins and development of the third element, the Leweivawa, oral tradition states that a group of people came from Vitogo, just east of Lautoka, to the island of Naviti and was settled by the Kai Suelevu at Muaira on land called Vawa. Hence they were known as the Leweivawa or People of Vawa. With the permission of their hosts, the Leweivawa accepted an invitation (*veilakovi*) from the Luvuka to go and join them at Kese. So the Leweivawa moved from Vawa and settled on Luvuka land at Nabouvatu.

The Leweivawa heeding the authority of the Luvuka as their landowners had not been long at Nabouvatu when they decided to install the elder of two brothers formally as leader and to give him the title of Ratu. They may have taken this formal step because of a split brought about through ill feelings by the younger brother against his elder brother, spurred on by his ambitions to take over the position of leader himself.

The resulting political construct was comprised of the Luvuka (as original landowners) and the Nasukamoce (as invited leaders, originally from Votua) forming one *mataqali,* the Luvuka; and the Leweivawa (originally from Vitogo) forming another *mataqali,* the Leweivawa.

The *yavusa* Kai Kese, because of its composition, is not in accord with the official model. The construction of the composite *mataqali* and *itokatoka* of this *yavusa* is based on principles different from those of descent from a common original spiritual ancestor. Similarly its leadership is noteworthy because over the course of time the leader has not been the senior patrilineal descendant of the original ancestor whose position would normally be legitimised on the basis of 'divine right'. Indeed, the leader does not claim any form of descent from the original ancestor of the first settlers. He is a 'stranger king', after the Sahlins (1981) model, selected for leadership on the basis of personal qualities by the *itaukei* (literally, the persons owned by the land) and installed by them. Leadership is legitimised first by his being presented with *yaqona* which will pass the *mana* of the original spirit of the landowners to the stranger, and secondly by his being given the title of Rokotakala which would normally be given to a Luvuka person. The original landowners retain their prestige by becoming masters of ceremonial (*mata ni vanua*) and by retaining their right to install the stranger as the leader of their choice.

Further consideration as to why the Luvuka voluntarily handed over the leadership to the Kai Koro can be productive, bearing in mind that an important element of Fijian traditional society is the ideology of *vanua* with its three dimensions of people, lands and spirits. A clue may lie in the position of *bete* or priest for the *yavusa* curiously resting with the Lasawa division of the Leweivawa. Although the Luvuka, the Kai Koro and the Leweivawa each recognised their own *anitu*, the *anitu* which the Leweivawa brought over with them from Vitogo in the powerful Ba mainland territory may have been accepted as much more powerful than the local spirits. To expand this theme, mainland coastal Ba may have been considered to be a place of both spiritual and secular prestige and power, and the Yasawa islanders may have welcomed the mainlanders and their spirits as useful and prestigious additions to their local cosmology and polities.

(b) Intermediate structures: formative and expansionist federations

I have so far discussed the characteristics of the independent single *yavusa* as the simplest form of polity which *tu vakaikoya* and *vakarorogo* to no higher authority. It lies at one extreme of the structural continuum of polities of differing degrees of complexity which comprise the totality of traditional Fijian society. At the other extreme lies the *matanitū* or confederation that will be discussed later. Between these extremes investigations reveal a bewildering variety of ephemeral or opportunist associations of *yavusa,* parts of *yavusa* or groups of *yavusa,* as well as formative, expansionist and more stable federations. These intermediate structures represent *vanua* or federations at different levels of political complexity, and studies show how the process of federation is subject to varying degrees of fusion and fission, development and decline.

A *vanua* is a socio-political federation comprising polities at two or more socio-political levels of hierarchy. Such a hierarchy is one of social and political status, as demonstrated on ritual and ceremonial occasions and in making decisions on the extent of participation of the *vanua* in activities, be they social, political or military. These may be co-operative efforts such as fish-drives or building a house for the paramount chief; matters of mutual interest with other *vanua* such as alliances or the exchange of goods (perhaps salt and fish from a maritime *vanua*, and *yaqona* and root-crops from an inland vanua); or actual military assistance in times of war. The leader of the most senior *yavusa* among *yavusa*, by virtue of power in war or as a protector of weaker *yavusa*, or through prestige both political and spiritual, would be recognised as the paramount chief of the *vanua*. Such a leader would be independent and heed no higher authority, except when a *vanua* forms part of a *matanitū*, in which case the head of the *vanua* would heed the authority of the paramount of the *matanitū*. Studies show that there is a variety of ways that seniority and ranking are recognised in the development of social structure including leadership of a *vanua*. I will now discuss how a *yavusa* comes to be the senior *yavusa*, and an individual person becomes the leader of the *vanua*.

In a more complex polity, the component *yavusa* or part-*yavusa* at any level of hierarchy within the complex may be descent groups or socio-political constructs or both. The groups of *yavusa* may be bonded by myth, blood or marriage, or they may be socio-politically bonded. This bond or *ivau* may have arisen or been created in various ways described in more detail later. Perhaps the strongest is the *Veitauvū* or spiritual relationship between original ancestral spirits. More mundane but equally binding are bonds created typically by common agreement for mutual protection and assistance; or on the basis of obligations of conquered or subservient groups (*qali*) to heed the demands by the paramount for food, goods and services (*vakatadumata*); or on the basis of military assistance provided, when the occasion demands, by sympathetic neighbours at the request of the paramount; or by groups in the more formal relationship of *bati* or military alliance with the paramount. Such demands or requests would usually be conveyed formally by the presentation of a *tabua* or whale tooth.

In the case of a more complex polity in which the member *yavusa* are bonded socio-politically, political dominance determines the ranking and principles of leadership. So long as a *yavusa* remains an independent polity (*tu vakaikoya*), leadership is ideally based on inheritance in accordance with the principles of *veitarataravi vakaveitacini*. The assumption of these principles is that the person recognised to be the most senior in descent from the original spiritual ancestor is the person most closely associated with the spirit and thereby having the greatest amount of *mana* or spiritual power, and is the person most qualified to be leader.

Once a polity becomes more complex and members are bonded according to socio-political principles other than seniority of descent from a common ancestor, leadership becomes based schematically on a hierarchy of leaders, graded in relation to each other according to their relative secular power (*kaukauwa*). The leader of the dominant group would become the leader of the complex polity by virtue of his superior *kaukauwa*. In effect, succession to the leadership of a political complex generally depends on a person's ability to demonstrate and maintain secular power over rivals, by political or military dominance. Leadership is no longer a divine right but an institution. Installation (*veibuli*) is a ceremony for the general recognition of the new occupier of the office of leader, after his selection by groups within the polity. Such ceremonies involve especially the presentation of *yaqona* for the leader to drink and thereby acquire the *mana* which provides a spiritual legitimisation to his secular power. The overt aspects of these ceremonies emphasise the institutional nature of leadership. The *yaqona* is prepared publicly in a wooden *tanoa*, from which a rope of sinnet is attached. This rope is stretched to point to the leader. The first bowl of *yaqona* is offered to the leader. Once the leader and his *mata ni vanua* or ceremonial officer have drunk, the *tanoa* is declared empty. No one else partakes of this first round of drinking. In such ways the difference between the new leader and his possible rivals is emphasised. The people participate in these ceremonies by clapping and chanting together. This manifests a feeling of unity between the people and the leader and confirms their support and allegiance as well as their acknowledgement of his paramount authority. The appointment is also regarded as having been legitimatised spiritually through the *yaqona* ceremony.

In some cases, the paramountcy of a socio-political hierarchy may take account of what is recognised as the relative power of the spirits of those in a complex polity. For instance, Limasa, the war spirit of the Nakovacaki people of Nadi, was regarded as very strong. When the Navatulevu people came down from the hills and settled in Nadi, they were regarded as very powerful militarily and took over the leadership of Nadi from the Nakovacaki. To validate their superior position spiritually as well as militarily and politically, they asked the Nakovacaki for Limasa to be their war spirit. Later the neighbouring Navo people asked if Namama, Limasa's son, could be provided as their war spirit. This created a bond between the polities, and was one of the elements on the basis of which the Navo felt respect towards the Navatulevu.

Once the position of secular leader becomes more institutionalised and succession depends on military and political dominance and mutual acceptability rather than on the closeness of descent to an original ancestral spirit and the amount of *mana* thus acquired, the accepted principles of leadership become more flexible. Not only is the choice of leader potentially much wider, but also a selected leader can be the more readily toppled either by ambitious or jealous rivals who consider that they have the greater political and military support, or because the paramount has shown undue arrogance or failed to meet his reciprocal obligations to those *qali* or *bati* who have provided him with food, goods and military assistance. To topple a spiritual leader is a matter of grave concern because it would almost certainly be followed by spiritual retribution through the ancestral spirit, probably involving the death or serious sickness of the perpetrator and perhaps his descendants, until such time as ceremonies of apology and contrition (*isoro*) are performed to the offended ancestral spirit. To topple a secular leader may not be a matter of such concern to the perpetrator unless he has misjudged the extent of his support, in which case apologies would usually have little effect and physical retribution would normally follow. Even so, the new leader would normally still not only demonstrate overtly his position socio-politically but would also legitimise it spiritually through the *yaqona* ceremony.

So far I have discussed the first level of hierarchy of a *vanua*, and have shown how a particular *yavusa* comes to be ranked as the senior *yavusa*, and how a paramount achieves or acquires that position. The second level of hierarchy would comprise one or more individual *yavusa* or groups of *yavusa* which in turn may be termed *vanua*, and be referred to in this description as subsidiary *vanua*. In the case of one or more individual second-level *yavusa*, members of each *yavusa* would heed the authority of the head of their own *yavusa*, and the senior member of each *yavusa* would heed the authority of the paramount of the first-level *yavusa*. In the case of a group of *yavusa* which includes one or more subsidiary third-level *yavusa* and comprises a subsidiary *vanua*, the head of each subsidiary *yavusa* at the third level would acknowledge the head of the senior *yavusa* of the group at the second level. The head of the senior *yavusa* of the group would, on behalf of the other *yavusa* in the group, acknowledge the overall authority of the paramount of the *vanua*. The heads of these third-level subsidiary *yavusa*, together with the head of any other *yavusa* that may itself be the head of a group forming a third-level subsidiary *vanua* would acknowledge the authority of the head of the second-level subsidiary *vanua*. The same principles apply if there is a lower socio-political level of hierarchy.

These principles are illustrated in the following diagram:

	YAVUSA A	FIRST LEVEL
YAVUSA B	*YAVUSA A(i) YAVUSA A(ii)*	SECOND LEVEL
YAVUSA B(i) YAVUSA B(ii)		THIRD LEVEL

Yavusa A is the senior *yavusa* of the *vanua*, and their head is the paramount. *Yavusa* A(i) and *Yavusa* A(ii) are individual single *yavusa,* the heads of which heed the authority of the paramount. *Yavusa* B is the most senior of a group of *yavusa,* the subsidiaries of which are *Yavusa* B(i) and *Yavusa* B(ii). The heads of these subsidiary *yavusa* heed the authority of the head of *Yavusa* B, who in turn heeds the authority of the paramount.

In reality, in groupings and federations of *yavusa* it may well occur that not all the component *mataqali* of a *yavusa* heed the authority of the leader of that *yavusa* or the overall authority of the leader of a group of *yavusa* at the same level of hierarchy, or indeed the authority of the paramount of the federation. Characteristic of the development of polities is the fission of a part of a *yavusa* from the parent *yavusa* and consequent fusion with a different *yavusa.* The case of the Kai Kese *yavusa* already discussed was that of a typical simple political construct, with which there might or might not have been some previous connection, by blood, marriage or *veitauvū* (relationship between original ancestral spirits).

The following examples from the Navua area of the southern coast of Viti Levu illustrate the working of the principles and mechanics of fusion and fission which may be regarded as characteristic of the creation and development of formative socio-political federations or *vanua.* I choose this area which comprises the *yasana* of Namosi and Serua partly because it is some distance east of the major socio-political complexes of Bau and Rewa and is away from the traditional areas of influence of these two *matanitū*; and partly because, although these *yasana* are not included in my specific field areas, I am familiar with the polities in the area and visited all their villages at least once at the time I was District Officer Suva/Navua.

In the Navua area there are three *vanua* with associated spheres of influence. The *vanua* of Namosi is based on the chiefly *yavusa* of Nabukebuke, and its sphere of influence lies generally to the east of Navua and up the Navua River to the mountainous main village known as Namosi. The *vanua* of Serua is based on the chiefly *yavusa* of Korolevu, and its sphere of influence lies to the west of Navua along the coast of Viti Levu. It includes the island of Yanuca and the main village on the offshore island of Serua, and inland towards the mountain range peaked by Tikituru. The *vanua* of Dravuni is geographically between those of Namosi and Serua, but confined to the coastal area around the mouth of the Navua River.

The *vanua* of Dravuni comprises two *yavusa*. One *yavusa,* the Deuba, includes the original people at the mouth of the river who were fishermen of unknown origin or interrelationship. The other, the Dravuni, is a construct of various groups of people who came down from the mountainous interior of Viti Levu at different times. As these groups arrived, they each in turn agreed to join together as one *yavusa* under the leadership of the first group to arrive. Through marriage, a group of the Dravuni joined the Korolevu at Serua. Meanwhile the fisherfolk had settled on land and formed the *yavusa* Deuba, and had federated with the remaining groups of the Dravuni.

The *vanua* of Namosi was based on a descent group with nine sub-groups, living in the north-eastern interior of Viti Levu. Following attack by a neighbour, they split up. One group went south and ended up in Namosi. Here the son of the leader quarrelled with his father about some coconuts, and ceremonially burned Namosi village, after telling his father to evacuate. This is known as *buka vakaturaga* or chiefly burning without bloodshed. Some of the father's followers were recalled to build Namosi, while others went and joined the Dravuni people at Navua by the sea. There were continual family quarrels about the leadership, and another group from Namosi settled near Navua, but inland from the coast. Another group joined the Korolevu people at Serua where they were given land.

The *vanua* of Serua was based on the Korolevu *yavusa*, formed of Noi Koro people who had come down from the interior of Viti Levu from the upper reaches of the Sigatoka River. They settled on the coast, basing themselves on the island of Serua. They were attacked continually by their neighbours, and were allowed by the Dravuni people to go to Navua and settle there in peace, provided that they acted as labourers for the Dravuni. The Korolevu became so dominant towards their hosts that the Dravuni people left and went to the Namosi people to ask for help against the Korolevu. The Namosi drove the Korolevu back to Serua, and the Dravuni returned to Navua. The Dravuni people thanked the Namosi people ceremonially for their services, but the Namosi people proceeded to demand that the Dravuni paid them regular tribute, eventually including women. At this stage the Dravuni became resentful and sought the help of the Korolevu people to drive the Namosi away. By now the Namosi had become so powerful that they threatened to dominate not only the Dravuni but also the Korolevu. Fighting then broke out and the Namosi attacked not only the Dravuni but also the Korolevu at Serua. The war lasted for some years until the Namosi were finally driven back to their own territory (for details see Appendix B).

This account illustrates the procedures for the creation and dissolution of alliances in a situation such as when two relatively small but powerful polities, Namosi and Serua, have spheres of influence bordering on a weaker polity, the Dravuni, living between them. Each powerful polity in turn gives the appearance of helping the weaker polity against the excessive demands of the other powerful polity. In doing so, each powerful polity takes advantage of the situation to extend its own sphere of influence over the weaker in the first instance but eventually over the other powerful polity as well. It also raises the question of the real reason for family quarrels leading to splits in polities, a situation frequently met in those accounts of polities which I have recorded. Excuses such as a quarrel over coconuts or, as I have noted, receiving the wrong piece of a pig or a fish, probably conceals an ongoing and smouldering political ambition and jealousy on the part of a son or a half-brother against a father or more favoured half-brother.

Even at a high level of development, the basic concept of *vanua* with its elements of persons, place and spirits remains crucial. Important considerations in respect of these higher levels of complexity of development and structure concern how the principles of unification and integration of a polity were developed and maintained in practice. These considerations concern not only the extent to which the principles of hierarchy of sub-groups within a descent group and of seniority of birth within a sub-group were adhered to in practice; but also to the degree of flexibility within these principles. In particular, such considerations concern, first, those cases of divergence from such principles which occurred by general consensus. For instance, an elder brother might voluntarily pass the position of leadership to a younger brother, or a respected or related outsider might be preferred by all. Secondly, and perhaps even more importantly in relation to the circumstances of warfare and socio-political expansion prevailing before Cession, these considerations concern cases of divergence from these principles which occurred on the basis of the realities of political expediency or of superior secular and perhaps spiritual force.

(c) The most complex structure: the matanitū

In contrast to the independent, simple social group or *yavusa*, and at the other end of the socio-organisational continuum of late Fijian social polities stands the highly complex socio-political confederation or *matanitū*.

The most complex form of socio-organisational confederation is found in the eastern parts of Fiji, especially in areas which have come into close contact with influences and ideologies originating from outside Fiji, particularly those of monarchical or near-monarchical Tonga and perhaps also the highly stratified and status-differentiating Samoa. Such a confederation may be expected to remain in power, provided that it can resist the ambitions of a more powerful rival *matanitū* or of an external power such as Tonga, or can enlist the assistance of friendly *matanitū*, or turn to its own advantage the forces of an external power such as Tonga.

Tabular outlines of the main elements making up the highly-complex socio-political confederations or *matanitū* of Bau and Rewa will serve to illustrate the general character of this apical institution in comparison with the other side of Viti Levu. The crucial problem for the paramount of each of these polities was how to control a wide-flung sphere of influence by means of diplomatic and administrative arrangements backed up by easily transportable military might, and by judicious use, when appropriate, of spiritual legitimisation of leadership and decision-making (for details see Appendix A(i) and (ii)). The terms *bati* and *qali* used in these tables and elsewhere will be discussed in some detail later in this chapter.

Tables of structure of Bau and Rewa confederations

(i) The Polity of Bau

The Chiefly Core (Kubuna) and Officials

Vunivalu (war-chief)

Roko Tui Bau (spiritual chief)

Masau (Paramount's personal herald)

Tunitoga (*Kubuna* herald)

Takala (law and order)

Vusaradave (bodyguard of *Vunivalu*)

Bouta (personal servants of *Vunivalu*)

Core craftsmen

Lasakau (fishers)

Soso (carpenters)

Peripheral specialists

Matainoco (craftsmen)

Waikete (potters)

Daku (priests)

Kai Kaba (maintain canoe fleet)

Bati

Namata (north)

Namuka (north)

Viwa (eastern island)

Waimaro (highlands)

Navuloa (base of Kaba peninsula)

Eastern Ra—

    Gonesau

    Natauya

    Nasese

Qali

Lomaiviti (part)

Cautata

Buretu

Namena

Kaba

Macuata (part)

Cakaudrove (part)

Each element cited above *vakarorogo* or heeds the authority directly or indirectly of the Vunivalu or war chief of Kubuna, being at Cession the paramount of the polity of Bau. It will be recalled that the Vunivalu had earlier deposed the Roko Tui Bau or spiritual chief as paramount. Most of these elements, especially the core and peripheral craftsmen, are themselves complex polities with a leading chief, a leading *yavusa* and several other *yavusa*, the leaders of which in turn heed the authority of the overall leader of the complex polity. I have not included a number of elements of the Rewa polity, which, after the 19th century wars between Bau and Rewa came, as the result of Rewa's defeat, to be part of the Bau polity. This included some of the *bati* such as the Nakelo, the Tokatoka and the Waikete who changed sides when they saw how the wars were going to favour Bau.

(ii) The Polity of Rewa

The Core (Burebasaga)

Roko Tui Dreketi (spiritual chief of Narusa)

Vunivalu (war chief of Nukunitabua)

Sauturaga (6 groups of landowners, who led the army and acted as heralds)

The *Qase* or 'old men' (special supporters of chiefs)

The *Kaso* (descendants of young chiefs), including the Kai Nalea, who were priests)

Qalitabu (no duties to chiefs), responsible for installing the paramount. They may have been earlier settler chiefs or a senior branch of present chiefs but had lost paramount position during internal upheavals.

Core craftsmen

Nukui and *Naselai* (fishermen)

Nadorokavu (carpenters)

Vutia (potters)

Nabua, Sigatoka (Tongan sailors)

Bati

Nakelo (12 villages), with Kuku and others subservient to Nakelo

Noco, with Tui Noco and several villages

Tokatoka (7 villages)

Waikete

Qali

Beqa Island, including Raviravi (4 *yavusa)* under Tui Raviravi;

Sawau (6 *yavusa)* under Tui Sawau: and Rukua (1 *yavusa).*

Kadavu Island (parts)

Other groups

Kai Batikeri (comprising Kai Nadoi and villagers of 3 villages, Nakuru, Drekena and Veiniu)

Muainasau

Qalivakawai (comprising 3 groups of Kai Narocivo, Kai Tavuya and Kai Nateni, living in the mangrove swamps)

Kai Lokia

Kai Nadoria

Each element cited above *vakarorogo* or heeds the authority directly or indirectly of the Roko Tui Dreketi of Narusa, Burebasaga, being the paramount of the polity of Rewa. Most of these elements, especially the core and peripheral craftsmen, are themselves complex polities with a leading chief, a leading *yavusa* and several other *yavusa,* the leaders of which in turn heed the authority of the overall leader of the complex polity. As mentioned above, a number of elements of the Rewa polity came to be part of the Bau polity as the result of Rewa's defeat at the end of the 19th century wars between Bau and Rewa. This included some of the *bati* such as the Nakelo, the Tokatoka and the Waikete which changed sides when they saw how the wars were going to favour Bau. The inclusion of Tongan sailors is noteworthy with regard to the question of the extent of the importance of Tongan influence in eastern Fiji through ideology, military power or, in the case of Rewa, through naval assistance. Bau had the final advantage over Rewa because of the size and strength of its naval fleet, but Rewa made good use of its fleet (including its Tongan sailors) when keeping its island *qali* of Beqa and part of Kadavu under control.

The main conclusions to be drawn from these two accounts are that in reality:

- simple local polities in the east developed into major polities which became widespread geographically, and highly complex socio-politically, with varying levels of groups associated with the paramount group through an system of alliances and tributaries, resulting from conquest and from voluntary association based on judicious marriage, common origins both ancestral and mythical, mutual aid and protection;

- able and ambitious leaders, through judicious marriages, military (including naval) power backed by spiritual power, and a competent system of socio-political communication, could expand and maintain their sphere of influence geographically and politically;

- the personal position of the paramount could become dangerously precarious either if they were too arrogant and tyrannical, or if there was internal treachery among relations, especially half-brothers, who considered that they should hold the position of paramount. Continuing potential tension between loyalty and expediency on the part of allies, and between loyalty and rivalry on the part of relations, could affect the stability of the polities; and

• the indirect and direct influence of Tongan political ideology and military and technical assistance could be of particular importance in the development of major polities. Ambitious paramounts, through visits to Tonga or through visits to them by Tongans to whom they might be related by blood, had become aware of socio-political developments and ideologies in Tonga, and might well seek to emulate the semi-monarchical position of Tonga. They could also seek to obtain assistance from Tongans, either as craftsmen or sailors or warriors.

Waxing and waning within a complex polity: *Na iVau kei na kena iSereki*

The fortunes of the complex polities in Fiji which I have described would have waxed and waned from time to time as I have indicated. Nevertheless each of these polities and especially the *matanitū* managed to maintain, at least for a while, a certain level of stability even in times of trouble. This level of stability may have enabled a polity on the wane to survive and re-assert itself as a power or at least to command respect from its neighbours, respect based perhaps on memories of its former glories and wider powers. Stability would depend on the bond between the component polities and between their respective leaders. Emphasis was and is still placed on the importance of the bond (*na ivau*) in the course of ceremonies involving the presentation of *tabua* and *yaqona*. *Mata ni vanua* while accepting the presentation would often use the expression '*Me tu dei tiko ga na kena ivau*' or 'May the bond between the donors and the recipients be always maintained'. In smaller polities the bond may be that of blood (*dra*). In descent groups, the theoretical bond is by definition that of common blood, and the bond is referred to as '*dra vata*' or common blood. Members who are *dra vata* claim to be descended from a common original ancestor, usually along the male line. In some parts of Vanua Levu, the basis of common descent is along the female line. An extension of the concept of a bond based on *dra vata* is the concept of a bond of relationship based on common spiritual blood. Such a bond is based on a spiritual kinship relationship between two original ancestral spirits. The basis of the bond may have been two brothers who came to be regarded as the original ancestors of two separate descent groups of the nature of *yavusa*; or a brother and sister, in which case one may have been an original ancestral spirit and the other the spouse of another original ancestral spirit. A relationship based on descent from two such related ancestral spirits is referred to as *veitauvū*, and people in such a relationship address each other as '*Tau*'. A bond created by the relationship of *veitauvū* is considered to be very strong.

An interesting question concerns the nature of bonding when the basis of the bond is less straightforward than that of descent from a common original ancestor or related original ancestral spirits. In such case, the bond must become more a socio-political matter than a family issue. The creation and maintenance of the bond was especially important in such highly complex polities as Bau, Rewa, Cakaudrove and Verata (see Appendix A(iii) and (iv) for the latter two) which had not confined their spheres of influence to areas that were geographically contiguous.

For example, according to Sayes (1982), Cakaudrove's first power base was at Wainimosoi on the banks of the Waikavu River on south central Vanua Levu, and here the first Tui Cakau was installed as paramount chief of a motley construct of locals and visitors. Following a split, the leading chiefs went to Taveuni and the others followed in about 1820. The influence of the *matanitū* of Cakaudrove then extended from its new power base on the island of Taveuni along the south coast of Vanua Levu and to the islands to the east of Taveuni. Similarly, Rewa spread to the island of Beqa and part of the island of Kadavu, while Bau spread to Lomaiviti and to Vanua Levu.

Any discussion of the development and structure of these great socio-political complexes of the east must inevitably involve some consideration of devices developed and introduced in order to maintain their stability or, as the above-quoted ceremonial expression goes, '*me tu dei tiko ga na kena ivau*'.

As these complex polities expanded, the position of the *mata ni vanua* in his formal role as master of ceremony and mouthpiece of the paramount became increasingly important. In these complex polities, the *mata ni vanua* was installed at a ceremony and given a title: at Bau, Tu ni Toga, Naitaka, Mataisau; and in Cakaudrove, Ko Mai Kavula, Ko Mai Nanukurua and Ko Mai Naitala. Equally important were his more informal duties of guarding against breaches of protocol which might have led to offence, and of keeping himself and so his master aware of grumblings (*kudrukudru i Ra Mo* or grumblings by people dissatisfied with the orders of the chief, but who heeded them in silence in his presence) which might have led to plotting (*vere*) and instability within the polity. Similarly, the role *of mata ki* or ambassador was created to enable the paramount to maintain close contact with the far-away periphery of his sphere of influence. Such a person might have been a relation of the paramount and certainly would have been a person of his choice and worthy of his trust. He would act particularly as the representative of the paramount for the purposes of passing on demands for goods and services, and of ensuring that such demands were met. He was also expected to act as the ears of the paramount, and to anticipate any plotting or signs of disobedience or treachery. The bond was also maintained by the judicious use of political marriage. Either the paramount would provide a bride for the local chief, or the local chief would provide a bride for the polygamous paramount. The resulting *vasu* relationship has been discussed above. The paramount was also liable to go and pay visits to his periphery, sometimes to remind a wavering group of his military strength, sometimes to gather tribute from recalcitrant tributaries, or sometimes simply to ensure that good relations were maintained.

As socio-political complexes, both *vanua* and *matanitū* developed with increasing levels of hierarchy and, as they expanded geographically, more formal, more lasting and stronger bonds were developed for administrative necessity and for the purposes of maintaining stability. In this way certain recognised categories of relationship developed between the paramount and the associated polities. The Fijians describe the basic relationship neatly by referring to a paramount as one who *tu vakaikoya* (or stands by himself) and to the associated polities as those which *vakarorogo* or heed the authority of the paramount. In considering the polities associated particularly with Bau and Rewa, the relationship between these and the paramount is distinguished between those referred to as the *bati* and those referred to as the *qali*. The relationships are termed *veibati* and *veiqali* respectively.

The *bati* are referred to as the 'borderers' by Capell (1941:6), and this is probably as good a descriptive term for them as any. The term is used when alluding to a form of relatively stable relationship based on military alliance that developed between paramount and powerful neighbouring polities which were recognised as *bati*. Before the Bau/Rewa wars, the most powerful *bati* associated with Rewa were the Tokatoka and the Nakelo who controlled the major waterways in the Rewa delta. The Bau *bati* included the Namaka, Namuka, Dravuni and Navuloa who were scattered strategically around the Bau heartland. During the Bau/Rewa wars, Tokatoka and Nakelo were excellent examples of how *bati* were liable to change sides, according to what they saw to be to their best advantage, and depending especially on how they were treated by Bau and Rewa respectively. The *bati* lived by their weapons. When the Roko Tui Dreketi of Rewa sought their assistance in war, he would send a message to them and give them presents and request their help. He could not simply order them to fight. In return for what they considered to be adequate respect and presents of food or goods, they would offer their services to fight for him. If not so respected or properly presented with gifts, the *bati* were liable to change their loyalties.

Nakelo was a *bati* of Rewa until Cakobau, the Vunivalu of Bau, induced the Tui Nakelo to change sides, by promising him his half-sister in marriage. Cakobau then found that he needed the girl to give to Gavidi, the chief of the Lasakau who lived on Bau, in order to keep him loyal and firmly in support. So Nakelo changed sides once again, and at one stage compelled the Bau army to retreat (Waterhouse 1866:149). *Bati* were not subservient to the paramount, and did not pay tribute. They were essentially warrior allies, and the bond between *bati* and paramount remained so long as the *bati* were well-treated (Williams 1858:20). The term *bati* is found in accounts of western polities, but does not refer to semi-independent allies but rather, as in the case of the Yasawa, to a specialised warrior sub-group within a descent group. Ratu Sukuna in his model of Fijian polities does include a *mataqali bati* in his model *yavusa*. It may be that in his model he acknowledged the general significance of the term *bati* by using it as that for a particular category of *mataqali*; whereas the reality in the east was that it was a term rather for the relationship between a paramount and his military allies.

The *qali* was described by Capell (1941:189) as 'a province or town subject to another'. Williams (1858:20) who may well have been the authority for Capell's description said that the *qali* 'represents an area or settlement which is subject or tributary to a chief town'. Koto (n.d.) added that a chief town was that to whose chief the *qali vakarorogo* (or heeds its authority). Jackson *alias* Diaper (1853:451) was more explicit when, presumably from his own observations, he stated that *qali* were obliged to pay tribute (*isoro*) periodically. The relationship of *qali* was created by conquest or by fear of conquest. In the case of fear of conquest, the *qali* may have sought this relationship either out of fear of attack by the paramount or out of fear of attack by another power. There are for instance certain areas in Lomaiviti which are described nowadays as *qali vakaBau* or subject to Bau. During the period before 1874, such people would have been obliged to provide goods and food on demand to the Vunivalu of Bau as paramount as recognition of his authority. Failure to do so would have resulted in punitive measures being taken against the disobedient *qali*, some of whom could well have ended up in the cannibal ovens of Bau. In the case of Rewa, the island of Beqa fell to the status of *qali* and was required to pay tribute to Rewa because on one occasion Beqa people ate some Rewan castaways and the island was besieged successfully by the Rewans and reduced to *qali* status out of revenge. In Cakaudrove, the Natewa people had been associated with Cakaudrove; but after transferring their association to Bau thanks to Bauan cunning and trickery (hence the expression *vere vakaBau* or trickery as in the Bauan style) surrendered themselves back to the ambitious Tui Cakau after a long drawn out defence and so fell to a *qali* relationship with Cakaudrove, paying tribute with canoes, barkcloth and coconut sinnet cord. Tribute was sometimes brought by the tributary to the paramount, as in the case of Tui Nayau of the Lau group who brought a double canoe, ten *tabua*, and fifteen rolls of sinnet to Bau in 1843 (Williams 1872:41[1]). Sometimes, the paramount would collect the tribute when on tour of his sphere of influence. Tanoa of Bau spent three years in Somosomo, Cakaudrove, collecting tribute from dependants in Lau (Derrick 1946:80); and Jackson (1853:443) described a visit to Bouma, northern Taveuni, when he went there with the Tui Cakau in order to collect tribute. In the case of Verata and its wide-flung sphere of influence beyond the seas, tribute from Vanua Levu was assembled at collecting points on the island before being transferred to Verata. A situation might have arisen where a paramount considered that a polity was a *qali* to him but the other polity did not consider that it was so obligated. The Vunivalu of Bau thought that Macuata was a *qali* and obliged to provide tribute on demand, whereas Macuata was prepared to acknowledge the power of Bau by presenting goods (*iyau*) on a friendly basis (*solevu*, see below) when it thought appropriate. In 1841, Macuata refused the demands of Bau for tribute, and Bau

---

1   (Editors' note) We have not been able to find this exact reference in Williams' writings. It may represent a later edition of Williams (1858).

sent its ally, Viwa, to attack. The Viwa chiefs prevailed on Macuata to surrender, and Ritova, future paramount of Macuata, paid frequent visits to Bau, bringing gifts. Nevertheless, the formal status of the relationship remained ambivalent.

The bond between two polities depended on the basis on which the lesser polity *vakarorogo* (heeded the authority) of the major polity. It may have been one of military assistance on request and in return for presentations (*veibati*), or of tribute on demand and punishment for failure to comply (*veiqali*). In a highly developed socio-political complex such as Bau, a paramount had to be in a position to obtain sufficient goods (*iyau*) and food from his tributaries for presentation to his *bati*. It was through this regular presentation of food and goods that groups publicly acknowledged the authority of the paramount, and the paramount gave an outward and visible sign of his authority over the tributaries by ceremonially accepting the *isoro*. In the same way, a paramount could give an outward and visible sign of his respect for, and appreciation of, the *bati* for their continuing loyal military assistance by public presentations of goods and food. For their part, the *bati* could make known to all their *kaukaua* or secular strength by performing before the paramount the ceremonial *bolebole*, a fearsome demonstration of their powers to challenge all comers. Alternatively, before a battle, they could assemble and perform the *taqa* or display of their military might. Ostensibly this was to assure the paramount of their loyalty and their ability to meet their military obligations to him in return for his presentations to them. It was also an opportunity for the *bati* subtly to remind the paramount that they were indeed a military power to be reckoned with and not to be underestimated in the event of the paramount's failing to fulfill his obligations towards them.

Groups also established socio-political relations with powerful polities by the ceremonial presentation of *iyau* and food, accompanied by requests for assistance. It is doubtful whether these groups could be described as *qali* or their presentations as *isoro*. For instance, in 1846, the chiefs of the Cakaudrove polity went to Bau to seek military aid. They presented vast numbers of yams, a high wall of *yaqona* and bales of barkcloth, and then a demonstration of several thousand warriors. Thus they planned to show the Bauans how helpful they could be in the wars with Rewa, and how much produce they could make available to Bau in return for a common bond of understanding and mutual assistance in times of war. This situation and relationship was not one of *vakarorogo*, of Cakaudrove heeding the authority of Bau. It was one of mutual assistance and socio-political cooperation in times of need. It was a relationship that would have been confirmed from time to time by the performance of *solevu*, the ceremonial exchange of goods and food recognised as a visible symbol of the maintenance of a bond created or existing between two polities. The presentation of goods and food as *isoro* or tribute by *qali* reflected a relationship based on demands by a polity of superior strength to which a subservient polity refused to accede at its peril. The exchange of food and goods at a *solevu* reflected a relationship of mutual assistance based on good will. All these relationships, be they based on *bati*, *qali*, or *solevu* exchanges, reflect an awareness of the need to stabilise socio-political relationships in highly complex polities.

Paramounts must have been only too aware of factors likely to affect the stability of their positions, such as the political ambitions and plots of rivals within the polity, the military powers and diplomatic abilities of rivals on their borders, and the increasing expansionist ambitions of their Tongan neighbours whom they both admired and feared. Those, especially in the west, who traditionally recognised the authority of neither Cakobau nor Christianity were faced with what they regarded as the insidious spread of Christianity, which they coupled with an extension of Cakobau's sphere of influence. They were forced to determine how to accommodate the *mana* or spiritual power of the Nakauvadra and the *bete* or priests who mediated with the ancestral spirits, with the power of the church militant (the so-called *Lotu* of Tonga) and its incomprehensible priesthood, and the fierce Tongan warriors who were forcefully spreading the *Lotu* around the

Lau group in the east and thence northward to Bua and westward to Cakaudrove and Bau and neighbouring polities, and finally as far west as the island of Yasawa. Any one or any combination of these factors could cause developments in these polities whereby the bonds so forcefully or diplomatically forged were loosened or broken. As in the case of Verata (Appendix A(iv)), a highly developed socio-political complex can become unstable and virtually disintegrate to a much more modest form of polity, albeit still highly respected for its past glories.

The fascination of exploring the development of, and interrelationship between traditional Fijian polities prior to Cession (1874) lies in the great variety of socio-political structures at the time; the factors both internal and external leading to such structural variety; the situations involved in the hierarchical ranking of sub-groups in groups at all levels; and the principles and practices related to the acquisition or achievement of leadership. Equally fascinating is the investigation of the symbols of identity of a group; the nature of bonds created between groups of the same level of structure and between those of different levels; the factors leading to the breaking of such bonds; the ceremonies, both spiritual and socio-political, recognised and accepted as invalidating the installation of a leader at all levels; and the ideals and realities for procedures for a change of leader or for his disposal. I have discussed these points in relation to the three levels of polity described earlier—the *yavusa*, the *vanua* (that is, *vanua* 2) and the *matanitū*. I have taken into account the three elements of the concept of the term *vanua* 1 (discussed earlier) which run through traditional Fijian society at all levels—spirits, places and people. The three following Fijian expressions reflect the very heart of my discussions in this chapter, and summarise the nature of polities, relationships, ranking and leadership.

'*Me tu dei tiko ga na kena ivau*' or 'May the bond between us last for ever' is the customary culmination of a ceremonial speech for the presentation of *yaqona* by one polity to another, giving assurances of a continuing association of friendship or loyalty. The *yaqona* represents the spiritual element, and *na ivau* refers to the people involved.

'*Me cecere tu ga o* Uluda *se* Vunisei' or 'May the chiefly *yavu* or housemound named Uluda or Vunisei remain for ever high' is an example of a recognised culmination of a speech of presentation of *yaqona*, seeking spiritual assurance for the stability of the current paramountcy. Uluda is the name of the *yavu* of Tu Navitilevu, paramount of Rakiraki; and Vunisei is that of the *yavu* of Momo i Vuda, paramount of Vuda. The *yaqona* again represents the spiritual element. The chiefly *yavu* symbolises collectively the people of the polity, and the superior height of the *yavu* symbolises the paramountcy of the chief whose place it is by virtue of his paramountcy.

'*Na ivau kei na kena isereki*' or 'The bond and its becoming untied' is a perhaps wistful expression to signify an acceptance of the often harsh realities of fusion and particularly fission in polities, in contrast to an idealised stable traditional Fijian society with recognised principles of hierarchy, leadership and authority based on primogeniture and seniority of descent.

Overview of Chapters 8–10
Fijian Polities in Three Areas in the Yasayasa Vakara

In previous chapters I have discussed how and why the fortunes of four *matanitū* or highly developed socio-political complexes which typified polities in eastern Fiji in the late period leading up to Cession waxed and waned from time to time. Each one of them maintained a certain level of stability even in times of trouble; and this level of stability enabled a polity even on the wane to survive and usually to re-assert itself as a major power or at least to command a degree of respect from its neighbours. The actual degree of stability would depend on the nature and strength of the bond (*na ivau*) between the component polities, which in turn would often depend on the nature and closeness of the personal relationship between their respective leaders. In the case of the major polities in the east, as these major socio-political complexes developed with increasing levels of hierarchy and expanded geographically, the situation required that more formal and lasting kinds of bonds had to be developed for administrative necessity and for stability.

Among the polities with which the paramount had relationships sealed by such bonds, were those known as the *bati* (military allies) and the *qali* (tributaries). Equally important were the bonds created by mutual respect and the continuing needs for mutual protection against a common enemy or for goods and food generally not otherwise available. The acknowledgement of such bonds was manifested by the ceremonial exchanges known as *solevu*. I also discussed three polities geographically between the east and the west, which are in intermediate positions in a continuum of polities of differing degrees of socio-political complexity.

Against the background typified by these four hierarchically complex polities of the east and the three intermediate polities, I turn now to that major part of my project which relates to polities in the three field areas in the northeast and west of Viti Levu and the Yasawa archipelago with a detailed exposition of the development and structure of the polities of the present six *tikina* of Rakiraki, Nawaka/Nadi/Vuda, and Naviti/Yasawa. In Chapter 8, I discuss the forms of polity in the north-east corner of Viti Levu. In Chapters 9–13, I consider the forms of polity in the far west of Viti Levu and the western archipelago of the Yasawas, where it will be seen that the influence of Tonga was not generally of particular significance and the people were strong, independent and proud. Here the polities tended to be of relatively simple structure, even when ambitious (and sometimes rival) chiefs demonstrated, not always particularly successfully, their schemes to expand their spheres of influence or to attain paramountcy at the expense of those who already were recognised as paramounts.

The traditional accounts detailed in Chapters 8–13 and Appendices A and B show that the polities of the west are generally less highly stratified, less formal and, at any rate until the findings of the Native Lands Commission and the consequent legislation formalised the situation, less stable. The further west one goes from the highly developed eastern polities, the less evident will be the tendency for stable forms of federation and political hierarchy. What emerges is a continuum of complexity of socio-political structures ranging from the generally highly complex confederations of the east, through federations of generally intermediate complexity and hierarchy in Rakiraki, to less formal federations in Nadi, Nawaka and Vuda, to descent groups in the Yasawas which, when and if they associate, do so on the basis of interdependence rather than hierarchical degrees of subservience. The simplest form of polity as found in the west is the oldest form of polity in late Fijian society, and the most complex is the most recent to develop. Indeed, the case studies of all polities I have undertaken indicate a widespread tendency to start as a polity based on a simple descent group. Such a descent group in most cases might develop into an element, either leading or subsidiary, in a more complex federation of two or more levels of hierarchy, and then in the east come to develop into an element of an even more complex confederation of three or more levels of hierarchy. As in the case of Verata in the east, some polities in the west developed over the years into more complex and then subsequently degenerated into less complex ones. In a later chapter I consider why and how the eastern polities became so much more complex than the ones in the west. In particular, I suggest that the eastern polities were strongly influenced both ideologically and militarily by the neighbouring highly complex polities of Tonga (later to become developed into a unified kingdom) with which the eastern Fijian polities and their ambitious paramounts had been in social intercourse for centuries. Not only ideas and military assistance but also spouses were exchanged. One result of the latter is the important high-ranking, mixed-blood group in Tonga known as the *Fale Fiti* or Fiji House.

In these chapters I consider how and why western polities developed, and whether, and if so why, some did not develop beyond the stage of a descent group or *yavusa*. Such a *yavusa* may in reality have included sub-groups of people who are not descended from the original ancestor of the *yavusa* but nevertheless (and contrary to the principles of the Government model) are regarded as members and generally treated as such.

I also consider whether, and if so how, the nature of the bond differed in the east and in the west. I suggest that the bond between polities in the west depended not so much on such administrative formalities, formal military alliances and hierarchical relationships based on brute strength (*kaukaua*) as manifested in the *bati* and *qali* of the east. Rather it depended on such factors as common blood (*dra vata*) based on descent from a common ancestor, real or mythical; or on some common relationship, traditional or mythical, between recognised original ancestors; or on marriage; or on an acknowledged socio-political relationship based on mutual protection or benefit. In the latter case, the bond may have lasted as long as the need for mutual protection prevailed, or the relationship was found to be appropriate or convenient.

In smaller polities, the bond may be that of blood (*dra*). In descent groups, the theoretical bond is by definition that of common blood and the bond is accordingly referred to as '*dra vata*'. Members who are *dra vata* claim to be descended from a common original ancestor, usually along the male line. On a much broader scale is the mythical bond ideally created between all those Fijians who claim their original ancestors came from the Nakauvadra Mountains and who depend on such a descent as a basis for the position of their descent group in wider Fijian society. Not all Fijian groups claim ancestry based originally on the 'U Ma'ua, as the Rakiraki people call those culture heroes such as Degei who in mythical times came on the first vessel, the *Kaunitoni* and went to dwell on the Nakauvadra Mountains. In the western areas, at any rate, some groups claim descent from original spirits who remained in the west, never going on to the Nakauvadra. Indeed at least one group claims to be autochthonous. Others associate themselves with a Tongan ancestor but keep the Nakauvadra connection by saying that the Tongan was made pregnant by Nakauvadra culture hero Degei. I discuss the implications of this emphasis on a mythical Nakauvadra origin, and of other origin myths and of Tongan (and Samoan) connections, both mythical and supposedly historical, in the west.

An extension of the concept of a bond based on *dra vata* is the concept of a bond of relationship based on a spiritual brother–brother or brother–sister relationship between two ancestral spirits. These two spirits came to be regarded as the original ancestors (or spouses of original ancestors) of two separate descent groups or *yavusa*. A relationship based on descent from two such related ancestral spirits is referred to as *veitauvū*. A bond created by the relationship of *veitauvū* is considered to be very strong. As well as bonds created by blood relationship or by spiritual relationship, I also consider how and why other kinds of bonds may have been created in the west, and how and why they may have been maintained. I will explore not only the questions of how and why polities developed and how and why bonds were created in the west, but will also discuss the questions of how a polity identified itself and regarded itself as a unity, and the nature of the symbols of identification and unification recognised by Fijian society. In particular, I identify not only common features but also explore and attempt to explain the anomalies and exceptions as they are found to occur across the three field areas in the west.

I examine the social structure of late western Fijian society in my three study areas, one at a time, in the east/west order of Rakiraki *tikina* and its periphery (Chapter 8); Vuda (Chapter 9); Nadi (Chapter 10), and the three adjoining *tikina* of Nawaka (Chapter 11); and the two *tikina* of Naviti (Chapter 12) and Yawasa (Chapter 13) comprising generally the Natu Yasawa or Yasawa Group.

8

Polities of Rakiraki *Tikina*

General background

There is a certain magic about Rakiraki which is so clearly an area where associated spirits, people and land reflect quite dramatically the three features of Fijian society which are the crucial elements of the ideology of *vanua* 1 underlying and pervading Fijian socio-political groups. Rakiraki is directly overlooked by the often cloud-topped peaks of the Nakauvadra Range which add a mysterious dimension to the Range as a spirit centre for many of the culture heroes of Fijian mythology. This spirit centre is well known and respected throughout Fiji. Rakiraki is itself an area where the people recognise, fear or revere many natural features such as crags, rocks, caves, pools and other physical places associated directly with ancestral and other spirits. Many *yavusa* in Rakiraki claim their original ancestral spirits came down from Nakauvadra and settled on land and in specific places with which the people and the spirits are still intimately associated. People still maintain communication with the spirits through *bete* or priests; and take great care that neither they themselves nor visiting archaeologists should offend the spirits by breaching accepted protocol or by disturbing their places. This involves first obtaining spiritual and socio-political permission to visit sites and afterwards requesting spiritual cleansing, through appropriate *yaqona* ceremonies.

The present Fijian Administration district or *tikina* of Rakiraki (see note at end about Rakiraki) is part of the province or *yasana* of Ra. The other *tikina* are Saivou (to the south of the Nakauvadra), Nakorotubu (on the eastern coast) and Nalawa (in the mountainous interior to the south of Saivou and the west of Nakorotubu). Rakiraki lies in the north-eastern corner of the island of Viti Levu, bordering Navitilevu Bay to the south-east, the Nakauvadra Range to the south, and the *tikina* of Tavua in the *yasana* of Ba, to the west. It includes the island of Malake and other islets in that part of the sea forming its northern boundary. Associated with Rakiraki are thirty-eight *yavusa*, the origins, development and grouping of which will be discussed in this chapter.

These *yavusa* of Rakiraki and its periphery are important because of their particular socio-political, geographical and spiritual features and inter-*yavusa* relationships which distinguish them in significant ways from the major socio-political groups of the east which I have already described and the relatively simple polities which generally characterise the west.

Other factors affecting the correlation between the degree of complexity of a polity in the continuum and its position in the east–west geographical alignment of Fiji could include the terrain. In Rakiraki, where the terrain lies generally between the Nakauvadra Mountains and the sea, inter-polity communication is not particularly difficult. In the west, the terrain in the hill-country of Nawaka and of parts of Vuda *is* difficult and intercommunication away from the rivers is not easy. In the Yasawas, communication is not particularly difficult by land or along the coastal fringe and is relatively easy by sea. The islands themselves are not extensive in area and those of any size are hilly. In the east, the terrain of Rewa is mainly mangrove swamp, and the Kubuna territory on Viti Levu and the Cakaudrove territory on Vanua Levu are hilly, while the island of Taveuni has a mountainous spine and only the west side is occupied. Accordingly I do not consider that difficult terrain is an over-riding factor in curtailing the development of polities anywhere, especially those with a maritime seaboard or with river access; nor do I think that direct Tongan influence was the only factor affecting the development of complex polities. I consider that other important factors were the ability, talents and ambitions of the eastern paramounts whose expansive aims had as a model the monarchical tendencies of Tonga. These monarchic tendencies became well known to the eastern paramounts who either visited Tonga or had considerable dealings, social or military, with Tongans who came to Fiji. They also and more importantly had access to military and naval might which accumulated through *bati* alliances and through *qali* subservience and conquest, and in the case of Bau through Tongan assistance in exchange for the acceptance of Christianity. Some polities accepted or came under Tongan influence for whatever reason, symbolic, social or military, whereas others rejected it.

Bau's traditional sphere of influence through Roko Tui Viwa stretched up to eastern parts of the province of Ra. Away from the direct influence of the Tongans and outside the traditional area of authority of Bau, the independent polities of Rakiraki looked with grave suspicion on any attempts on the part of Cakobau and the eastern polities to extend their sphere of influence to Rakiraki. They were proud of their independence, and had no traditional or socio-political inducement to bow to the monarchical tendencies of Bau.

The polities of Rakiraki generally developed well beyond the form of a single, simple independent *yavusa*, but never attained the extreme complexity and geographical expansion of the major eastern polities. In the context of the posited continuum of forms of complexity of Fijian polities in late prehistoric and early historic times, Rakiraki is important, socially and geographically, in illustrating the obvious point that the further west one goes from the highly developed socio-political complexes of the east, the tendency is away from complex forms of confederation and political hierarchy; whereas the closer one gets to the eastern polities, the tendency is towards the complex forms of the east. Rakiraki lies geographically on the borders of the complex eastern polities, but still some distance from the simple and the less complex forms of polities found in the far west. In brief, Rakiraki lay outside the borders of Bau's traditional sphere of influence during the earlier part of the general period of my project and may show how these differences come about.

Rakiraki, however, did become absorbed into Bau's sphere of influence administratively when Ra (of which Rakiraki was a part) became a province under the Cakobau Government before Cession. The Roko Tui Viwa, who at the time heeded the traditional authority of the Vunivalu of Bau, was appointed by Cakobau to be governor of the province of Ra. So, both administratively and traditionally, the paramounts of the socio-political complexes of Rakiraki were then expected to heed the authority of Cakobau, as head of the Government, through his representative, the governor who happened to be Roko Tui Viwa. They were also expected to heed Cakobau's traditional authority, as Vunivalu of Bau, through the Roko Tui Viwa.

Rakiraki is important linguistically, because not only is it a border area politically and geographically, it is also a border area where the chain of communalects to the southeast of Rakiraki and the chain to the west of Rakiraki show significant changes. The very name of the province, Ra, means 'western'. It is noteworthy that Rakiraki communalects tend to be grammatically more in character with those of eastern polities than with those of the west but to have many characteristics of western communalects which only start geographically at the borders of Tavua. The linguistic factor is important because a communalect was often regarded as a symbol of unification and identification in a polity. Most of the Rakiraki communalects are characterised by the *gato* or glottal stop in the place of the unvoiced apical stop /t/. This linguistic feature is recognised outside Ra with perhaps some amusement as the shibboleth of the Rakiraki and neighbouring Ra communalects.

Rakiraki is important spiritually because of the origin myths about the arrival and activities of those of the culture heroes who are associated with its northern coastal border, the island of Malake and the Nakauvadra Range glowering over its southern border. As we have seen, the origin myth current in the west of Fiji related to these culture heroes arriving from the west in the vessel *Kaunitoni* in the Vuda area, where some remained, while some went by boat to the north coast of Rakiraki and then to the Nakauvadra where they stayed (see also Chapter 9). Others travelled by land across Viti Levu and eventually settled on the Nakauvadra too. One of the leaders was the main culture hero, Degei; and the people of Malake are the traditional turtle fishers of Degei, just as the Rakiraki people are the traditional providers of his root and plantain crops. It was from Nakauvadra that many of the original ancestors of Fijian polities had their mythical origin. These spiritual factors are important in consideration of the origins and development of a *yavusa* which represents a kinship group descended from a common spiritual ancestor. They are also important as a basis for *yavusa* to federate because, according to myth, their respective original ancestral spirits had been related. This important relationship between members of two *yavusa* claiming to have a common ancestor or related ancestors, was known as *veitauvū* which empowered those involved to take what goods they wanted from their *tau*.

The Nakauvadra Range is therefore important as a basis of the spiritual unification of Fijian society. The literal meaning of the word in the Rakiraki communalect is 'fallow yam garden', and relates to the traditional responsibilities of those living in the area to provide yams and other root crops for presentation to Degei. The significance of this will become apparent when I discuss the spiritual interrelationship between my project area and the Nakauvadra in more detail. The Nakauvadra Range itself falls geographically outside the New Rakiraki *tikina*. Because, however, it is intimately associated spiritually and traditionally with Rakiraki, the area for present purposes includes not only Rakiraki *tikina*, but also the peripheral area situated north of the Nakauvadra range. This peripheral area which has been included for administrative purposes within the New *tikina* of Saivou, can usefully be referred to as the Rakiraki periphery. Although it falls outside the administrative boundaries of the New *tikina* of Rakiraki, nevertheless the people now living in the villages on the north slopes of the Range heed the traditional authority of the paramount chief of the Rakiraki polity and may therefore be considered to be part of the structure of that polity.

In conclusion, Rakiraki should be regarded as a border polity, geographically, socio-politically, and linguistically, between the major eastern polities and the relatively simple western polities. This will be demonstrated in the exploration of the polities to which I now turn.[1]

---

1   Rakiraki is a name with several referents, such as:

- before Cession, the area in the north-east corner of Viti Levu island, stretching from Viti Levu Bay (to the south) to Tavua (to the west);
- after Cession, the old Fijian Administration *tikina* comprising the area between the Old *tikina* of Natokea (to the east); Naroko (to the south); Raviravi (to the west); the island of Malake (currently inhabited by Fijians); and the freehold islands of Nananu i Ra and Nananu i Cake (or, in the local communalect, Ya'a);
- after the enactment of the 1945 Fijian Affairs Ordinance, the new Fijian Administration *tikina* comprising the Old *tikina* of Raviravi, Rakiraki and Navolau/Natokea;
- nowadays, commonly used to refer to the main socio-political complex, otherwise referred to as Namotutu, after the name of the leading *yavusa*;
- nowadays used commonly to refer to the two adjoining but separate villages of Navuavua and Navutulevu, being the present heartland of the Namotutu socio-political complex, near the Rakiraki Hotel;
- nowadays used to refer generally to the overall urban area of Vaileka, the residential and industrial area around Penang sugar mill, and the residential and commercial area round the Rakiraki Hotel.
- in this monograph Rakiraki refers, unless otherwise stated, to the New *tikina* of Rakiraki.

The main polities: Rakiraki *tikina* and periphery—a geographical snapshot

Rakiraki New *tikina* comprises the Old *tikina* of Rakiraki, Navolau and Raviravi; and the periphery represents parts of Naroko Old *tikina* on the north slopes of the Nakauvadra Range. My research covered these geographical areas.

The main *vanua* 2 and *yavusa* based on these areas were, at the time of Cession, and are still recognised as follows:

Name of *vanua*	Leading *yavusa*	Title of paramount	No. of *yavusa*	No. of levels	No. of villages
Rakiraki Old *Tikina*					
Rakiraki	Namotutu	Tu Navitilevu	6	2	4
Navolau Old *Tikina*					
Natokea	Natokea	Ratu ni Natokea	5	2	3
Raviravi Old *Tikina*					
Navatu	Naisogoliku	Tu Navatu	9	3	4
Vatukaloko	Nasi	Tui Vatu	3	2	1
Parts of Naroko Old *Tikina* on North Slopes of Nakauvadra					
Nacolo	Vaikitu	Leweivaikitu	6	2	1
Navisama	Navisama	Tui Navisama	1	1	1
Naroko (part)	Navatudamu	Leweinavatudamu	4	2	1

Some other *yavusa* based in Rakiraki New *tikina* need special mention:

(i)   The AiSokula *yavusa* based on the village of Nakorokula, formerly associated with the Namotutu *yavusa* and living on Namotutu land; but later living on Natokea land and associated with the Natokea *vanua*.

(ii)   The Namacuku *yavusa* based on the village of Togovere, though independent, have myths of common origin with the Vatukaloko polity.

(iii)   The Mali *yavusa* and the Nakorosaga *yavusa* based in the Raviravi villages of Naseyani and Nananu respectively, on the boundaries of Raviravi Old *tikina* and Tavua. They are two of the Twelve *Yavusa*, a complex and geographically dispersed socio-political complex, the sphere of influence of which includes the Vatukaloko polity (referred to above) and extends widely across the south side of the Nakauvadra Range, outside the area of this research.

Rakiraki *tikina* and periphery: a snapshot of structure of the main polities

The main federations (*vanua* 2) and independent *yavusa* based in Rakiraki New *tikina* and the periphery were comprised of the following social groups and related to the following geographical areas:

(a)   The Complex Socio-Political Federation of Rakiraki, which comprised:

(i)   The six *yavusa* of the Rakiraki *vanua* (2), in the Old *tikina* of Rakiraki.

(ii)   The five *yavusa* of the Natokea *vanua*, in the Old *tikina* of Navolau.

(iii)   The six *yavusa* of the Nacolo *vanua*, at Vatukacevaceva in the Old *tikina* of Naroko.

(iv)   The Navisama *yavusa*, at Narara in the Old *tikina* of Naroko.

(b)   Part of the Socio-Political Federation of Naroko, which comprised:

(i)   Four *yavusa* of the Naroko *vanua*, at Rewasa in the Old *tikina* of Naroko.

(ii)   Two other *yavusa* of this *vanua* living outside my study area.

(c)   The Anomalous *Yavusa* of AiSokula, at Nakorokula in the Old *tikina* of Navolau.

(d)   The Socio-Political Federation of Navatu, which comprised:

(i) Nine *yavusa* (including Wailevu of the Twelve *Yavusa*) and

(ii) Two other groups of the Navatu *vanua*, in the Old *tikina* of Raviravi.

(e) Part of the Socio-Political Federation of the Twelve *Yavusa*, which comprised:

(i) Three *yavusa* of the Vatukaloko *vanua*, at Drauniivi.

(ii) Two *yavusa* at Naseyani and Nananu, which lie in that part of the Old *tikina* of Raviravi known as Na iYalayala.

(iii) Seven other *yavusa* of the Twelve *Yavusa* which lie outside my study area.

(f) The Independent *Yavusa* of Namacuku, at Togovere in the Old *tikina* of Raviravi.

The main polities: Rakiraki *tikina* and periphery—details of structure

The main polities in the area of my research project in Rakiraki New *tikina* and the periphery were, at the time of Cession, and are still recognised as follows:

(a) *The Complex Socio-Political Federation of Rakiraki, which comprises the following vanua and yavusa:*

Name of *vanua*	Leading *yavusa*	Title of paramount	No. of *yavusa*	No. of levels	No. of villages
The Rakiraki Polity					
Rakiraki	Namotutu	Tu Navitilevu	6	2	4

The six *yavusa* included the chiefly *yavusa*, Namotutu, four spiritually interrelated and apparently settler *yavusa*, Navuavua, Cakova, Natiliva and Wailevu, and the nearby island *yavusa* of Malake. All were based on what was to become the Old *tikina* of Rakiraki. The first five comprised the heartland *yavusa* of the complex socio-political federation of Rakiraki, of which the Tu Navitilevu of Namotutu was paramount. The Malake were fisherfolk, and were responsible to the Tu Navitilevu for providing turtle for presentation to the main culture hero, Degei, at Uluda on the Nakauvadra. They were also responsible for providing turtle and fish for the Tu Navitilevu. Others grew plantains and yams for presentation to Degei.

(i) *The Namotutu yavusa*

Myths of origin

In describing the myths of origin of the Namotutu *yavusa*, Esira Nawaqalevu, the Tu Navitilevu of the Tunavitilevu *mataqali*, said that:

> the original ancestral spirit of the Namotutu was Tunakauvadra, the son of Degei. He had five children, whose descendants comprised the five *mataqali* of the Namotutu *yavusa*, including the chiefly *mataqali* of Tunavitilevu of whom the chief held the title of Tu Navitilevu, the Tuinamo, the Vusatabua and the Tuicakau/Vuninokonoko. Their first settlement when they came down from the Nakauvadra Range was at Namotutu. They later split up and settled in individual settlements near to the chiefly centre at Namotutu.

> The ceremonial spokesman of the present Tu Navitilevu told me that Tunakauvadra came down from the Nakauvadra and settled to the west of Namotutu. He had a son, Naisemaninavitilevu, who settled nearby and it was he who had sons who became the founders of the various *mataqali* of the Namotutu.

On the other hand, Tanoa of the Tuinamo *mataqali*, whom Tu Navitilevu commended to me as the most knowledgeable of the Namotutu people, explained to me that:

the original ancestral spirit who came down from Nakauvadra was named Kalitabua or Tunakauvadra. He settled at Namotutu and had three sons, whose descendants were the Tuinamo *mataqali*, the Vusatabua *mataqali* and the Tuicakau/Vuninokonoko *mataqali*. The senior group was the Tuinamo *mataqali*. The Tunavitilevu *mataqali* were not descended from the original progenitor but were later arrivals (as will be explained below).

Early splits in the Namotutu *yavusa*

The Native Lands Commission (NLC) recorded that:

> there was a quarrel and fighting between Naereere of the Tuinamo *mataqali* on the one side, and the Namotutu chiefs and Kelei of the Vosatabua *mataqali* on the other side. Each collected an army and prepared to fight.

Since this quarrel seemed to me to be an important element in the development of the Namotutu *yavusa* and its relations with its associated *yavusa*, I tried, but without success, to find out from various Namotutu representatives what they saw to have been its basis.

However, the Tu Navua (head of the Navuavua *yavusa*) with whom I discussed the matter closely, said that:

> the quarrel originated from the occasion of a *veitiqa* or dart-hurling contest with the Navuavua people competing against the Namotutu chiefs and the Vusatabua *mataqali*. At the time an old man of Saivou (from where the Navuavua originated) was staying as a *vulagi* or guest with Vutoni, the head of the Navuavua, and when he went to the *veitiqa* contest he was killed by one of the Namotutu. Vutoni was very upset, and at first the two groups would not talk to each other (*veigaluvi*), and then they started to fight. Naereere of the Tuinamo came to the assistance of Vutoni against the Namotutu chiefs and the Vusatabua. The villages of the latter were destroyed and the people scattered to their strongholds. The Namotutu killed Vutoni's brother, when he was caught spying out their stronghold. This enraged Vutoni, and led to widespread fighting, involving military aid from far and wide.

The NLC recorded that:

> Naereere went with his group to the island of Malake, whence he sought military assistance by sending *tabua* or whales teeth to [those with whom he had marriage or spiritual relationships at] Nakorotubu, Namena and Ovalau. Vutoni [the leader of the Navuavua] went to the war village at Draqara [on Wailevu land on the northern slopes of the Nakauvadra], where he stayed and gathered an army, sending *tabua* to Nalawa, Saivou and Naroko.

The Navuavua had connections with these areas through their original ancestral spirit who came from Karoka, Saivou. Also the Navuavua had previously lived in Naroko.

> When Naereere and Vutoni had collected their armies, they attacked the Tunavitilevu chiefs at Namotutu and the settlement of Kelei at nearby Toga. The people there scattered to various areas with which they were connected, abandoning Udreudre, the chief of the Namotutu. Those of the Namotutu and Toga people who did not have family or marital connections on the other side of the Nakauvadra Range could not flee across the Range because the Saivou and the Nalawa people were hostile. So they often scattered to people living in Bua with whom they were related.

Because Vutoni's brother, Bolobolo, had been married to Udreudre's sister, Udreudre himself was not killed. He was eventually given refuge by the Cakova whose particular traditional responsibility was to protect the paramount of the Namotutu. Udreudre settled on their land and when peace was restored he was returned to the paramountcy by Naereere.

Tanoa went on to tell me that at first Naereere was winning, but then the Cakova people came to the assistance of Kelei of the Vusatabua and defeated Naereere. This could explain what was recorded next in the NLC accounts. On the other hand, Naereere may simply have wished to indicate how he had proved by military might that he had the *kaukauwa* or physical power to be the *qaqa* or strong man of Namotutu. Through *kaukauwa*, he had achieved military supremacy and political leadership. Now it was necessary for him to avoid the wrath of Degei and his fellow spirits of the nearby Nakauvadra by returning the leadership to the spiritual chief whose position was legitimised by *mana* or spiritual power.

The NLC went on to record that:

> Naereere went to Bua and then returned and having made the appropriate formal approach (*tadu*), stayed with the Natiliva people at Navutulevu. The chiefs of the Tunavitilevu group and the Navuavua came to Naereere and asked that the troubles could be 'buried' (*bulubulu*). Naereere returned to Bua to collect some *tabua* and other valuables (*iyau*) which he brought back to Navutulevu.

Meanwhile Udreudre, having been abandoned at Namotutu, went to his *vasu* relations, the Vatukaloko people—see below—at Vugala near Drauniivi, and then to the Cakova people who agreed to shelter him at their village of the same name. He was given land there, and his compound is said to have been near his well-marked and famous grave (one of Rakiraki's main tourist attractions) by the roadside near the present Wairuku School. The Cakova may have thought that they would thereby gain favour and some socio-political advantage from the Namotutu paramount. He may have gone to shelter with the Cakova, until the Rakiraki wars were over, because there had been close connections between the Namotutu and the settler *yavusa*, the Navuavua and the Cakova, based on the relationship between the host landlord and the strangers who had been favoured with land on which to settle. The Navuavua had been given their land by the Namotutu, with whom they became closely connected. The village of Navuavua was near the mangroves behind Rakiraki Hotel. When the Cakova had first arrived in the area they were given land by the Navuavua; and relations between the two groups were therefore very close. The village of Cakova was just west of the present villages of Navuavua/Navutulevu. So it was that Udreudre was settled on Cakova land, when Naereere returned from Bua. The NLC accounts recorded how the Tunavitilevu chiefs were returned to the status of leaders of Namotutu and of the associated socio-political complex as it developed.

> Naereere then called together the chiefs from all the villages of Rakiraki, and presented to them first some of the *tabua* and *iyau* as an *ibulu ni dra*, a peace offering for the bad blood that had flowed between them all and as an *isoro* or apology for the warfare; and secondly other *tabua* and *iyau* which he presented as symbolising the return to the Rakiraki chiefs of the position of leadership which he had achieved when he had earlier destroyed Rakiraki and driven away the spiritual chiefs.

At one level, it may be satisfactory to explain how the killing of the old man of Saivou at a *veitiqa* contest led to fighting between Naereere of Tuinamo and Vutoni of Navuavua on one side, and the Navitilevu chiefs and Kelei of the Vusatabua on the other. On the other hand, the incident may rather have been the excuse for which an ambitious Naereere had been looking to align himself with Vutoni and the Navuavua people, to demonstrate his *kaukauwa* or physical power, and to enable the Tuinamo to take over by force the leadership of the Namotutu from the Navitilevu chiefs. This parallels the situation in the major eastern polity of Bau, when the Vunivalu, the ambitious war chief, drove away the Roko Tui Bau, the spiritual chief. The difference was that having won the leadership by force, Naereere feared the wrath of Degei and the ancestral spirits of the Nakauvadra and returned the leadership to the spiritual chiefs.

Be that as it may, the polity returned to a state of peace and prosperity (*sautu*); and the Tunavitilevu acquired once more the leadership of Rakiraki. It will be remembered that Isera Nawaqalevu, the then Tu Navitilevu, had told the NLC that the Navitilevu had from the beginning of the development of the Namotutu *yavusa* been leaders of the *yavusa* on the basis of the primogeniture of their original ancestral spirit at the time that he and his brothers had come down from the Nakauvadra with their father, Tunakauvadra. This represents the Navitilevu explanation of the origins of that *mataqali* and of how the Tu Navitilevu became paramount.

On the other hand, Tanoa, head of the Tuinamo, told me that:

> the Tuinamo were the senior group of the descendants of the original ancestral spirit from Nakauvadra. However, when Naereere was the head of the Tuinamo, he was very tyrannical (*yalo kaukauwa*) and there was much quarrelling between the Namotutu groups and Naereere told the Vusatabua under Kelei to go away. Because of Naereere's behaviour, the people would not install him as paramount chief.

> At this stage, a group of people from Navitilevu, on the Nakorotubu coast, came for a visit and anchored off Rakiraki. The leader was afraid to go ashore. However they came and stayed with the Cakova people, and the chief and his people were seen to be gentle and thoughtful. Naereere realised that he was too strong in his decisions and noted that the Navitilevu people were really chiefly in their bearing and behaviour. They were also reputed to be very strong people. So he went to Bua and to Ovalau to ask for some *tabua*; and on his return, he called together the Namotutu including those whom he had chased away. He firstly presented the *tabua* from Ovalau and asked that Namotutu should be re-united as a *yavusa*. Then, because the Namotutu would not remain united under him, he asked the Navitilevu people for a chief to form a chiefly *mataqali*, Tunavitilevu. The name of the overall ancestral spirit at Namotutu was then Naisemaninavitilevu (The Link between the Navitilevu).

Thus the Navitilevu became paramount in Rakiraki, but the Tuinamo retained their right to choose a paramount for installation. Tanoa explained that there are still close links between the Navitilevu of Namotutu and the Navitilevu of Nakorotubu, maintained by exchanges of formal *lakovi* or visits. Also when either paramount was to be installed either at Yavunuku (for the Tu Navitilevu of Namotutu) or (for the Tui Navitilevu of Nakorotubu), at Naisemasema, Verata opposite the islet of Vatu Turaga, the other paramount had a special place at the installation ceremonies. This reflected these close social links between the two polities.

Nowadays it is probably not possible to reconcile the two accounts of the origins of the Tunavitilevu *mataqali*—that is, the *mataqali* of the Tu Navitilevu or paramount of the Namotutu—and of the origins and possible changes in the basis of the leadership of the Namotutu people. Perhaps somewhat naturally the Tuinamo account is to the effect that the leadership used to be and would perhaps still be with the Tuinamo but for the tyrannical behaviour of Naereere. The Tu Navitilevu originated as an outsider who happened to be in the right place at the right time to solve the leadership problems of the Namotutu. The name of the ancestral spirit was claimed to be Naisemaninavitilevu (The linking of Navitilevu). His name could be explained (*ex post facto*) as that of a spirit who linked the Navitilevu (who came from Nakorotubu) with the original Namotutu people who adopted a Navitilevu person as their chief, when Naereere of the Tuinamo (the traditional leading *mataqali*) was too tyrannical.

The Tunavitilevu account equally naturally aims to validate the position of Tu Navitilevu as based, first, on primogeniture among the grandsons of Degei, the leading culture hero of the Nakauvadra, who sent his son to settle at Namotutu; and secondly, on *mana* derived from the purest spiritual origins of Uluda, the home of Degei. Indeed, the Tu Navitilevu continues to emphasise the intimate connection between the Tunavitilevu *mataqali* and Degei by retaining the name of Uluda as that of the chiefly *yavu* or housemound in 'Rakiraki' village. In this case the explanation of the name Naisemaninavitilevu was that the spirit symbolised a more recent link created between the Navitilevu of Namotutu and the Navitilevu of Nakorotubu.

Some further evidence may provide light for considering these conflicting views and for exploring a possible resolution to these problems of origin. To my knowledge, all are agreed that the first to be titled Tu Navitilevu was Naduva, younger son of Udreudre. Udreudre's eldest son was Nawaqalevu. He evidently thought that as the eldest son he should have been made the leader of the Namotutu on the death of Udreudre. Instead another son, Naduva, was apparently chosen by the Tuinamo 'kingmakers' and some claim that he was installed on Vatu Turaga, a rock islet in Navitilevu Bay, on the south-eastern boundary of Rakiraki territory. If the installation took place here and not at Namotutu, as others have said, this may have been for practical reasons, in order to have the ceremony carried out as far from possible from likely interference by the supporters of the passed-over Nawaqalevu.

> Naduva was taken from Vatu Turaga to bathe in the sacred pool of Viyagoiratu in the mangroves just to the east of Tavua village, at the western boundary of what was then Rakiraki territory. He sailed back to Rakiraki, where he anchored, but he remained on board for several nights because he feared for his life. Indeed Nawaqalevu in his anger for being supplanted by Naduva, would not let him be brought ashore. However Mulase of the Vusatabua group brought him ashore.

Nawaqalevu may have been annoyed that his younger brother was made leader instead of himself; and the incident led to a violent quarrel between Nawaqalevu and Mulase who supported Naduva's leadership. In the quarrels between Naereere of Tuinamo and Kelei of the Vusatabua, the latter had sided with the chiefs. In the Nawaqalevu/Naduva dispute, the Vusatabua had sided with the younger brother, who was the recognised leader. So they consistently sided with the leader. In the latter dispute, the Tuinamo do not appear to have played a part, though they seem to have sided against anyone whom they regarded as the upstart chief. As a result, Mulase took his Vusatabua supporters and went to his mother's relations at Navatu. Here he settled and pursued his quarrels with Nawaqalevu. The latter, assisted by an army from Nalawa, attacked Mulase who was assisted by the Navatu people. The Rakiraki army was repelled, and 'Eki, the strong man of Nalawa, was killed. On the basis of this victory, the Navatu people claimed independence from the authority of the Tu Navitilevu—a claim that the Namotutu still do not accept.

The installation at Vatu Turaga, if it took place, may equally be seen as having taken place there for symbolic reasons. The islet may have had some particularly strong *mana* associated with those Navitilevu people of Nakorotubu from whom, according to the Tuinamo account, a leader for the Namotutu was chosen, when Naereere of Tuinamo was proving to be unacceptable. It was for similar symbolic reasons that some people claimed to me that the installation stone used in connection with installation ceremonies for later Tu Navitilevu may have been brought from this islet to the chiefly *yavu* at Yavunuku. It is generally agreed in Rakiraki that Yavunuku was the provenance for the installation stone which at present stands beside the church in 'Rakiraki' village, but it must be emphasised that there is no such agreement as to whether the chiefly group of the Namotutu came originally from Navitilevu, Nakorotubu, or whether the installation stone came originally from Vatu Turaga.

Others, including Sakeasi, the recent but now-deceased leading *bete* or priest of the Namotutu from the Vuninokonoko *mataqali* already referred to, did not accept the installation of Naduva at Vatu Turaga. They told me that the stone came from the spiritually important mound of Yavunuku at Namotutu where it had acquired particularly strong *mana* from the son of Degei when he had been sent down by Degei to go from Nakauvadra to Namotutu. It had been brought there from Wailevu, where there are still some powerful spiritual places connected with Leka, and where there is a leading *vuniwai* or healer who told me that he had obtained his powers from the Nakauvadra spirits. This claim about the installation stone was made especially by those who did not like to think that the Namotutu paramounts came originally from Navitilevu, Nakorotubu. They agreed, however, that there is a Navitilevu connection, but said that it was only later than the Namotutu people established a social relationship with the Nakorotubu people.

I have to confess that I am unable to reconcile these various opposing views, and if I put the view of one side to the other side, it is simply denied. On balance, there is tempting evidence to support the idea that the Navitilevu of Namotutu did in fact come from Navitilevu Bay, although it is but human for the Tu Navitilevu to see himself as the direct descendant of Degei rather than as the descendant of a member of a wandering band fairly remotely connected with the culture heroes of the Nakauvadra. Historically, the truth may never be known. Politically it may not matter, as at Cession and the NLC, the Navitilevu were recognised as the leaders and the Tuinamo as the 'kingmakers', and this was officially confirmed under Fijian Affairs legislation. Unofficially, the Tuinamo may well be said to be the power behind the throne.

This situation is typical of other polities, and to a certain extent soothes the relationship between elements in Namotutu. The Tu Navitilevu is the spiritual chief, takes the first bowl of *yaqona* at a ceremony, and is the figurehead of traditional life in the Rakiraki socio-political complex. When some particular internal or external problem affecting the polity occurs, it is most likely that the head of the Tuinamo would be accepted as the power behind the scene to advise the Tu Navitilevu. The Tu Navitilevu would then take a decision, taking into account this advice. He may well be influenced by communications from Degei and the spirits relayed to him through the *bete* or priest, being either the Bete Levu of Navatu who lives at Naivuvuni, or the *bete* of the Namotutu who lives behind the Rakiraki Hotel. The head of the Tuinamo would then be responsible for seeing that the decision was implemented in a practical and political manner.

Nevertheless, one can sense some gentle grumblings especially by the Tuinamo about the leadership. Referred to in the proverb *kudrukudru i Ra Mo* or The Gruntings of Mr Pig, such grumblings can no longer be settled by the club or spear but only by reference in the last resort to the NLC. The NLC is legally empowered to arbitrate on matters of leadership, using as an authoritative basis those NLC records with which there is not always general agreement, especially on the part of the unsuccessful grumblers.

The four settler *yavusa*

The four settler *yavusa* of Natiliva, Cakova, Wailevu and Navuavua heed the authority of the paramount of the Namotutu *yavusa*, and form the chief supporters of the Namotutu and the heartland of the Rakiraki polity. The following are brief accounts of their myths of origin, followed by more general accounts concentrating on the interrelationship between the four *yavusa*, and between the four *yavusa* and the Namotutu *yavusa*. These five *yavusa* together with the Malake *yavusa* form the nucleus of the socio-political complex of Rakiraki. This *vanua* of Rakiraki on the north side of the Nakauvadra developed through force, mutual convenience and mutual advantage, with *kaukauwa* or physical power being legitimised and strengthened by the *mana* or spiritual power of Degei and the culture heroes of Uluda and the Nakauvadra Range. Rakiraki is indeed a *vanua rerevaki* or fearsome place, thanks to the ever-present and powerful spirits whose places were on the mountaintops, in the flatlands and even in the sea.

Myths of origin

The myths of origin of the four settler *yavusa*, Natiliva, Cakova, Wailevu and Navuavua, centre round the family of the famous dwarf spirit, Leka, who had come down from the Nakauvadra and settled on the south side at Karoka between Balabala and Vunisea in the inland area of UluiSaivou. One account I recorded claims that Leka married Turoko and had several children including two females, Lovai and Roko Loma. Roko Loma married Kanailagi at Karoka. Another account claims that Leka's wife was Lovai, and they had two children, Cokonawai and Dokidoki.

The NLC recorded Turoko as a male who came down from the Nakauvadra and married a woman on Natiliva. Their descendants were the Viti *yavusa* whose leader held the title of Tui Viti. This is now regarded as an invention. At the time of the NLC, Cakobau and his descendants claimed to hold the title of Tui Viti—implying he was paramount chief of all Fiji, a title to which he was traditionally not entitled since it did not exist until it was invented with the encouragement of some Europeans. These Europeans wanted to have some overall authority in Fiji to whom they could lay complaints especially about what they regarded as their rights over land which they thought they had obtained from local chiefs. The title of Tui Viti was certainly denied by those living outside the traditional sphere of authority of Cakobau, including the Rakiraki people. The extent of such rights as claimed was frequently disputed both by customary landowners and by the chiefs themselves. When the NLC came to Rakiraki, a Rakiraki chief allegedly said that Cakobau might claim to be Tui Viti e Cake (Paramount of eastern Fiji), but he, the Rakiraki chief, was Tui Viti e Ra (Paramount of western Fiji). He named his polity as Viti after a little stream running through the mangroves on the Volivoli peninsular to the east of 'Rakiraki' village. The NLC duly, but evidently wrongly registered a *yavusa* of Viti.

I recorded that Leka and his family came over the Nakauvadra Range from Karoka, together with Taginadula (the ancestral spirit of the Naroko people, see below); and Leka settled at Vaileka [where his place survived as a mound just below the District Officer's house]. He remained at Vaileka, and sent his daughter (or wife), Lovai, to go and settle at Navutulevu in the field and mangroves behind Rakiraki Hotel, and her descendants were the Natiliva *yavusa*.

He sent his son, Cokonawai, to Cakova west of the present Rakiraki village complex of Navuavua/Navutulevu, and his descendants were the Cakova *yavusa*. He sent his son, Dokidoki, to Dakudaku, the site of the mighty war village above Vatuseikiyasawa, and his descendants are the Wailevu *yavusa*.

Kanailagi and Leka's daughter, Roko Loma (who is also described as a woman of Natiliva), had also come over from Karoko and settled at Dranayavutia where the Naroko (descendants of Taganidula from Karoka) also settled. Then the children of Kanailagi and Roko Loma went to Navuavua and their descendants became the Navuavua *yavusa*.

The settlers settle down

The Navuavua, while living near Nayaulevu, to the south of the Nakauvadra Range, used to come across the range to the coast in order to cut *dogo* or mangroves for their digging sticks. The chief of the Namotutu saw them and told them that they could settle at a place near the mangroves, and the Cakova agreed that the Navuavua should join them. Where they settled was swampy land (*na vuavua*, in the local communalect).

The Tu Navua heeded the authority of the Tu Navitilevu, and the particular responsibilities of the Navuavua were to *taqomaka* (or protect) and *dau vakasala* (or advise) the paramount chief personally. The Navuavua were at ease with the Namotutu, except during the Rakiraki wars referred to earlier, and there was considerable mixing of blood, especially with the Tunavitilevu chiefly group. For instance, Bolobolo, one of the two strong brothers of Navuavua, married the daughter of the paramount of Namotutu, Udreudre, and this created a special relationship between the two *yavusa*. This is why the Navuavua under Kelei and the Vusatabua under Naereere did not kill Udreudre when they attacked and destroyed Namotutu in the course of the Rakiraki wars.

> The Cakova were once settled on the southern slopes of the Nakauvadra, and they then came and settled with the so-called '*itaukei makawa*' or 'old owners' near the Rakiraki coast at Cakova. At that time the Tuinamo and the Vusatabua were at Namotutu. It is not known who the 'old owners' were or what happened to them. The Tui Cakova heeded the authority of the Tu Navitilevu, and the Cakova became the *qaqa* or strong protectors of the Namotutu chiefs.

Because of this particular relationship with the chiefs of the Namotutu, the Cakova were bound to protect Udreudre after he had been abandoned during the Rakiraki wars. After he left Namotutu to escape from the Rakiraki wars, Udreudre went first to his relations at Vugala, where he appears to have been betrayed. So he was brought to live with the Cakova as his *qaqa*. He lived and was buried on Cakova land.

> The Wailevu comprised three groups. The Wailevu settled first at Wailevu, inland from the 'Rakiraki' village. They then invited the Draqara to come from the slopes of the Nakauvadra and settle at Wailevu. Finally because of marriage connections, they invited the Dewala of Nabukadra, Nakorotubu, to join them. There were also spiritual connections, in that Leka and the original ancestral spirit of the Gonesau of Nabukadra were so related that the Wailevu and the Gonesau could claim to be related spiritually as *veitauvū* . These three groups moved to the fortress of Dakudaku during the Rakiraki wars, and then settled at Vatuseikiyasawa *makawa*. After the measles epidemic of 1875, they moved to their original site of Wailevu, but renamed it Vatuseikiyasawa, after their previous settlement. They heeded the authority of the Namotutu.

According to Tanoa:

> the Natiliva who came originally from Tiliva on the Bua mainland, arrived directly from the Bua island of Yadua. They were related to the Rakiraki people and were given land by Naereere of the Tuinamo group.

The Natiliva account, as given to me by a 76-year-old woman and a man of high rank in the Natiliva, claimed that:

> the Natiliva came from the other side of the Nakauvadra Range in order to plant foodcrops for Degei. When the chiefs of Namotutu arrived, the Natiliva prepared a settlement for them, planting gardens and making houses. Their chief, LeiNatiliva, heeds the authority of the Tu Navitilevu, and the Natiliva became the *dau visusu* or house people for the Namotutu chiefs. On one occasion, Qarau, chief of the Natiliva, went on a visit to Bua and established there the village of Tiliva. From here, some Natiliva people went to the island of Yadua. During the Rakiraki wars, the Natiliva scattered to Yadua, where some remained after peace resumed. Nowadays, the Natiliva at Rakiraki and those on Yadua still exchange visits. However, the links with the Bua mainland are no longer maintained.

Perforce, these are but potted accounts of the four settler *yavusa*, and especially their myths of origin, their settlement in Rakiraki territory, their involvement in internal and external warfare and consequent fusion and fission, spiritual connections, and socio-political connections with the paramount Namotutu *yavusa*. The evidence is not conclusive and at this stage may never be recoverable from oral tradition or archaeology. Nevertheless, it does seem that all four *yavusa* had origins, in whole or in part, from the south side of the Nakauvadra, and that they came over the range to settle on Rakiraki territory. It may well be that they came seeking sea-produce especially salt (which they would exchange for *yaqona*, yams and *dalo*, none of which grew particularly well in Rakiraki) or wood for digging sticks (mangrove wood was particularly suitable). In the Ba oral traditions, there are accounts of how the hill-folk came down for the same purposes and eventually settled on the coast. They then heeded the authority of the Tui Ba, in the same way that the four settler *yavusa* in Rakiraki heeded the authority of their host *yavusa*. Indeed, the Cakova, Navua and Natiliva had special responsibilities in connection with the Namotutu chiefs.

These three *yavusa* together with the Wailevu came to be regarded as the special supporters of the Namotutu *yavusa;* and they formed the united heartland of the Rakiraki socio-political complex. Perhaps *ex post facto* in order to symbolise this unity, the myths of origin were created to show how all four supporting *yavusa* were closely related spiritually through Leka. This well-known dwarf spirit came from the other side of the Nakauvadra and settled at Vaileka, meaning according to some, 'give respect to Leka'. In the local communalect, 'to a (person named)' is '*vai*'. Equally the name could reflect the names of Leka and his daughter (or wife) Lovai- '*lo*' being the honorific female prefix or particle before a personal name.

Apart from creating a spiritual unity between the four settler *yavusa*, the myths claim no spiritual connection with the main culture hero Degei. This may be significant in that the Namotutu, whose paramountcy is spiritually legitimised through descent from Tunakauvadra, the son of Degei, would hardly want those under their authority to have the same high-ranking spiritual origins. To symbolise unity within the polity, it would suit the Namotutu to posit Leka as a unifying spiritual force for the heartland supporters, whilst recognising that Leka had not the same degree of *mana* as Degei.

The Malake *yavusa*—the fisherfolk

Myths of origin recorded by me on Malake Island on several occasions claim that:

> the original ancestral spirit of the Malake *yavusa* was Drilo Dadavanua who was the younger brother of Degei, the main culture hero of the Nakauvadra spiritual centre. Degei sent him down from the Nakauvadra, telling him to go and be his turtle fisherman. He went first to Navatu to join the ancestral spirits known as Waqabalabala whose descendants were the Navatu people, and Bakadroti, Degei's *bete* or priest, whose descendants were the Naqilaqila people. Here Drilo Dadavanua first settled and married a woman of Navatu. He got tired of the sound of the women beating clay for pots, and so he and his family sailed over to the island of Malake. His descendants were the Malake *yavusa*, the turtle fishers of Degei.

He settled in a swampy area on the north side of the island where his site is marked by a rectangular housemound, sheltered by trees. His sons went to live on the heights in the middle of the island, where their sites are marked by rings of stones. I am not sure whether these stone features are ancient, or whether they date from the mid-19th century when a European ran sheep on the island, and the Malake put up these structures to protect the sites from the sheep. The Malake people nowadays give the former explanation.

> When Degei on Nakauvadra required turtle and plantains (*vudi*), he would make his requirements known to his *bete*, Bakadroti, whom he had sent down to Navatu, to be with Waqabalabala. Bakadroti would communicate spiritually with the head of the Qilaqila people, who held the title of Bete Levu or chief priest of Degei. The Bete Levu would then advise the Tu Navitilevu accordingly. When it was known that the plantains planted for Degei at Namotutu were nearly ripe, the Tu Navitilevu would give orders to the

Malake people to go turtle fishing. When the turtle had been caught, he would co-ordinate the ceremonial presentation of the turtle and plantains at the ceremonial mound at Yavunuku, Namotutu.

In this way, close spiritual and ritual connections developed between the Namotutu, the Navatu and the Malake people; and the Malake people heeded the authority of the Tu Navitilevu.

> In the course of the Namotutu quarrels between Nawaqalevu of the Tunavitilevu and Mulase of the Vusamalua groups, Mulase, whose mother came from Navatu, had gone there as a base from which to pursue his quarrels with Nawaqalevu.

> At the same time, the *yavusa* of Malake was split in two through quarrels between two brothers on the island. The Malake had a close spiritual relationship with the Navatu, through Dadavanua's marriage with a woman of Navatu. So most of the Malake went to Navatu and joined with Mulase. On the other hand, Malake had strong traditional associations with the Namotutu, and so a group sided with Nawaqalevu, remaining on the island. Afterwards the Malake people on Malake killed a supporter of Nawaqalevu and Nawaqalevu was very angry. Those at Navatu then sent a message to those remaining on Malake, to come to Navatu and bring the body of the person whom they had killed. So the Malake joined up together again at Navatu and the island was left vacant.

While the Malake were with Mulase at Navatu, the relationship between them became so close that it became the practice for a chief of Mulase's people, the Vusatabua, to be given the title of the Tu Malake or high chief of the Malake. The head of the Malake *yavusa* was known instead simply by the descriptive term of Ai'Eimada ni *Yavusa* o Malake or Leader of Malake *Yavusa*.

Apart from the Malake at Navatu, some went to the Qilaqila at Vunitogoloa, some to Cobea in the Yasawas, and some to Bua. Nawaqalevu sold Malake Island to a European for some guns. This upset the Malake who, when peace had been restored, went first to Nawaqalevu and then to Cakobau at the seat of his Government at Levuka and asked that the European should be told to leave and that the island be returned to them. This was agreed to. However, the Malake did not return to their island until after Cession. Those at Bua were asked to return but those in the Yasawas were not invited to do so—I could not find out the reason for this.

The origins and development of the Malake *yavusa* provide a wonderful example of how the three elements in the ideological concept of *vanua* 1—that is, spirits, people and land or sea—interact in order to reify not only the *yavusa* of Malake but also its relationships with neighbouring polities and indeed with the major spirits of Degei and Bakadroti. On a more political level, Malake illustrates the fission and fusion that characterises Fijian polities generally, and especially the fraternal quarrels that occur and the disastrous effects they can have. It also provides an interesting example of how a person acquired the paramount title of a *yavusa* although not a member of the *yavusa*—for Tu Malake was *de jure* a 'stranger king'.

(ii) The Natokea vanua

Name of vanua	Leading yavusa	Title of paramount	No. of yavusa	No. of levels	No. of villages
Natokea	Natokea	Ratu ni Natokea	5	2	3

Five *yavusa* comprising the chiefly *yavusa*, Natokea, the three related *yavusa*, Burenitu, Nairara and Rara, and the settler *yavusa*, Navolau, are based on what was to become the Old *tikina* of Navolau in the villages of Namuaimada and Navolau (which during my time split into Navolau No. 1 and Navolau No. 2, due to overcrowding). These five *yavusa* comprise the minor socio-political federation or *vanua* 2 of Natokea, the head of which is the Ratu ni Natokea. He heeds the authority of the Tu Navitilevu, as paramount of the complex socio-political federation of Rakiraki, of which Natokea forms a part. Within the Natokea, there were two levels of hierarchy.

Myths of origin recorded by me relate how:

> Rogata, an original ancestral spirit came down from Nakauvadra and settled below the peak of Supani. He had several children, including Likubale (female), Betenaulia (probably the ancestor of the Burenitu), and Kumivula (the ancestor of the Rara, who may alternatively have been the brother of Rogata), as well as Qelo (the club-footed ancestor of the Nairara, who may alternatively have come separately from Nakauvadra). Likubale was called up to the Nakauvadra where she was made pregnant by Degei, the leading culture hero of the Nakauvadra, and duly gave birth to Rasuaki, the original ancestral spirit of the Natokea (formerly known as Natoka). Because Degei could not stand Rasuaki's crying, mother and son were sent down to Supani, but were looked after by Degei and the other children of Rogata living in the area.

These myths suggest a close kinship relationship between ancestral spirits, which created a spiritual basis for the socio-political unity of four of the *yavusa* of a federation later known as the *vanua* of Natokea. This claimed relationship between the four spiritual ancestors is, however, perhaps an *ex post facto* explanation aiming to validate what the Natokea polity wanted to be seen as the closeness of the relationship between the *yavusa*. Such a suggestion is made especially in regard to the case of Qelo and the Nairara. The accounts are agreed that Qelo came from the Nakauvadra and was going to Verata (a polity discussed above) when his club-foot made him so tired that he settled at Namuaimada. His rock, Tadili, may still be seen beside the roadside at the edge of the village. However, not all are agreed that his descendants, the Nairara, had settled originally at Namuaimada. One account given to me was that the Nairara were from Navatu. The mother of the Natokea leader was from Navatu, and a group was invited to come to Natokea to look after her. The Nairara people indicated to me that Qelo came from Nakauvadra quite separately from Rogata and his relations. Also another group joined the Nairara later, on the basis that they were also from Navatu. One final feature to take into account when considering the claimed spiritual association of these four *yavusa* is their respective *ivilavila ni yalo* or jumping-off place of the spirits of the dead. The spirits of the dead of the Natokea, Burenitu and Rara jump from the same isolated reef of Vunidilo in the sea opposite Navolau. The spirits of the dead of the Nairara on the other hand go to the reef at Vudebawa opposite Namuaimada where Qelo settled. On balance, the Nairara account may be historically correct, but the myths of common origin may be more correct socio-politically. These accounts are of interest as having more than one possible interpretation, the choice for which would probably depend on socio-political rather than historical reasoning.

The accounts are also interesting as illustrating arguments regarding hierarchy in Fijian society. The Burenitu people regarded themselves as the senior *yavusa* through direct descent from Rogata along the male line. The Natokea *yavusa*, however, was generally regarded as the senior, partly because they were descended from the eldest child of Rogata, albeit a daughter, but perhaps especially because the blood of Degei, their male spiritual progenitor, ran through their veins. This argument is maintained in subdued fashion, though outwardly the paramount is accepted as the Ratu ni Natokea from the Natokea *yavusa*. This is typical of the arguments regarding leadership occurring in so many accounts of socio-political development.

> After the descendants of Rogata had been settled for some time in what was to become the Old *tikina* of Navolau, war broke out in Rakiraki. The Namotutu chiefly *yavusa* were divided because of quarrels between the heads of two leading *mataqali*. One faction left Rakiraki and called for help from the people of Saivou and Nalawa, living to the south of the Nakauvadra Range. They came and destroyed the villages

not only of the Rakiraki but also of their confederates, the Natokea and the Burenitu. These two *yavusa* split up and dispersed, some *mataqali* of each *yavusa* going to Bua (Vanua Levu), and some to Koro (Lomaiviti). The latter fared so badly there that they went and joined the others in Bua. The Rara went to join the Cakova, a *yavusa* in Rakiraki. Later, the Rakiraki people brought the Natokea people and the Burenitu people back from Bua, and the Rara people back from Cakova, and re-settled them on their own lands. Their period of refuge in Bua had created such good socio-political relationships with their hosts that there developed close social intercourse between Natokea, Burenitu and Bua, and many Bua people came and settled on Natokea land.

When the Rakiraki villages were being destroyed in the course of the inter-*mataqali* wars referred to above, one group of the Namotutu *yavusa* scattered to the Nagilogilo people of Nakorotubu where they assisted their hosts in fighting the neighbours. After spending a long time there, they decided to return, accompanied by the son of the Ratu ni Natokea. On their way back to Rakiraki, they anchored off Natokea territory and reported to the Ratu that his son had returned. The Ratu thereupon invited the Namotutu group to come ashore and settle with the Burenitu people. This they did, and later they split up, some living inland and some on the coast where they had ready access to their vessels. Later they joined together again and established their own village of Navolau where the mosquitoes were less troublesome than at the coastal village.

The Nairara do not seem to have been involved in this diaspora. Indeed, they may not have settled in Natokea territory until after the return from Bua and Cakova, but before Christianity arrived. When Christianity came to Ra, the first Christian compound was on Nairara land, as they proudly point out nowadays. The Natokea seem to have accepted Christianity, perhaps associating it with the envied goods and services which they hoped the missionaries would provide. The Navatu to the west of Rakiraki territory seem also to have accepted Christianity readily, perhaps for the same reasons, whereas the Namotutu and especially their infamous man-eating chief, Udreudre, realised that the missionaries would frown on their cannibal activities.

(iii) The Nacolo vanua

Name of vanua	Leading yavusa	Title of paramount	No. of levels	No. of villages
Nacolo	Vaikitu	Leweivaikitu	6	2

The leading *yavusa* was the Vaikitu, and the other five were the Nabaqatai, the Vitautau, the Namasasa, the Namoliki (not Namoliti, as recorded by the NLC) and the Natolevu (sometimes referred to as the Naitavu). These six *yavusa* originally came from the south piedmont of the Nakauvadra Range and were later based on the village of Vatukacevaceva lying just below the northern slopes of the Range. They comprised the minor socio-political *vanua* of Nacolo, the head of which was the Leweivaikitu (nowadays referred to by the eastern term of Tui Nacolo). He heeded the authority of the Tu Navitilevu, as paramount of the complex socio-political federation of Rakiraki of which Nacolo formed a part. Within the Nacolo, there were two levels of hierarchy.

All recorded myths of origin said that the original ancestral spirit of the Nacolo people was Botitu whose place was at Nakasekula at Uluda, the highest peak of the Nakauvadra Range.

The NLC recorded that:

Botitu came down to the south slopes of the Range and settled at Vaikitu, above the present village of Nayaulevu. He married a woman of Nukunitabua, and they had a son, Tui Nacolo. Tui Nacolo had a son, Naulumatua, who had six children. All six were born in Vaikitu, and they later married and, when their families increased in number, they split up and settled in six small settlements along the south slopes of the Nakauvadra, above Nayaulevu. Their descendants formed the six *yavusa* of Nacolo *vanua*, each named after their first settlement. The Vaikitu *yavusa* were descended from the first-born son of Naulumatua; the Nabaqatai from the second son.

In 1953, I recorded from Akeni Selavo, head of the Nacolo, that:

> Botitu came down and settled at Drata, above Vaikitu. He was married to another spirit and they had two sons, Kitu and Qilai. Kitu was the original ancestral spirit of the Vaikitu *yavusa*, and Qilai was the spirit of the Nabaqatai *yavusa*. The head of the Vitautau *yavusa* was no relation of Kitu or Qilai.

In the 1990s, I recorded from Semesa, son of Akeni, that:

> Botitu settled at Vaikitu and married a woman of Vaikitu. The Nabaqatai *yavusa* claimed Botitu as their original ancestral spirit, and there was a close relationship between the Nabaqatai and the Vaikitu, based on the spiritual marriage. (Semesa agreed that their son was Tui Nacolo).

> These six groups then decided to cross over the Nakauvadra Range, and they settled in the small settlements of Nasanimai, Takina, Navono and Dakunivatu along the northern slopes of the Nakauvadra and in the piedmont at Buka and Bokulu, near the present village of Narara. Although their southern neighbours, the Saivou people, were warlike, the Nacolo people had crossed over not to escape from attack nor because their numbers had increased but because they wanted to be nearer to the sea and to have ready access to salt-making facilities.

> After the chief of the Nabaqatai had married a woman of the Navatu *yavusa* of Naisogoliku, there was a general movement on the part of the Nacolo people to leave the mountain settlements and to join their *vasu* relations and they stayed at the Navatu settlement of Nasava near Naivuvuni. This was much more convenient for access to the sea and saltpans. Those in the easier terrain of the piedmont remained there. Later a woman of Namoliki married a chief of Naroko, and those at Nasava moved to Naroko, to Dranayavutia.

> Then because the Rakiraki wars of the rival chiefs, Mulase and Nawaqalevu, threatened Dranayavutia, they returned at Nasava. During the war, the Nabaqatai sided with Mulase who was with the Navatu people, and the Vaikitu sided with Nawaqalevu. After the wars which were times of *na vakadavedra* or bloodshed, the Nacolo people asked the Rakiraki chiefs to be allowed to return to below the Nakauvadra where the land was unoccupied. They went and established a settlement at Naibulunidra (the burying of the blood shed during the war), but they did not like this name and so they changed it to Vatukacevaceva.

Vatukacevaceva means either 'the piled up rocks' or 'the place where there are lots of rocks' or 'there is a rock and the prevailing wind is from the south-east'. The name also refers in particular to a big rock in the men's swimming pool near the village. Nowadays people say that the village was named after the rock, and they may well be right. The village and the Nacolo people are closely associated both geographically and spiritually with the main cult centre based on the Nakauvadra Range, and with the highest peak of Uluda and the main culture hero, Degei, whose place is a crevice in a rock at Uluda. Access to Uluda is through the *bete* or priest who lives in the village at the beginning of the path to the peak. The village even now is considered to be the *koro rerevaki duadua* or most revered village in Fiji, and football teams and senior politicians as well as other people of all races visit the village and may seek permission to climb to Uluda. This I have witnessed myself on several occasions, and indeed I have participated in the necessary ceremonies before I made the ascent myself, and also at the cave at Uluda, and finally again after I made the descent.

The myths of origin of the Nacolo vary in detail but generally present an overall picture which can be interpreted as a socio-political explanation, perhaps *ex post facto*, of the interrelationship of the six *yavusa* at the time of Cession in 1874, and of their development into a federation during the years following the crossing to the north side of Nakauvadra Range but before Cession. Some variation in the myths may be explained in terms of a certain rivalry between the Vaikitu and the Nabaqatai about the position of leadership of the Nacolo *vanua*.

(iv) The Navisama yavusa

The single settler *yavusa* of Navisama, the head of which was the Le Navisama (now known by the eastern title of Tui Navisama), came originally from the Old *tikina* of Nalawa well to the south of Nakauvadra Range. The Navisama people later crossed to the northern piedmont of the range and finally established the village of Narara, in what became the Old *tikina* of Naroko. Le Navisama heeded the authority of the Tu Navitilevu, as paramount of the complex socio-political federation of Rakiraki, of which Navisama formed a part.

The NLC recorded that:

> the original ancestor, Silitabua, came from inland Saivou and went to settle closer to the coast at Tarisi, where he married a woman of Dewala. The descendants spent a long time here, and then moved to a place (of uncertain location) known as Naqorokawa. They were known as the Navisama.

Sevuloni, aged 89, and his grandson who had a developed interest in the history of the Navisama, told me that:

> the Navisama came originally from the mountain village of Nubumakita, in the remote southwest corner of the *tikina* of Nalawa, a place with which they retained, and still retain, their traditional connections. After moving from there, they eventually settled at Vunisea on the south side of the Nakauvadra. When at Vunisea, the Navisama used to plant *dalo* to take to the Rakiraki chiefs in return for permission to make salt or to fish in Rakiraki waters. This social obligation became so burdensome for the Navisama that the Rakiraki chiefs arranged for them to come and settle on vacant land at Buka on the north side of the range. This land was owned by the Draqara people who were then living with the Wailevu people at Vatuei'iyasawa, heeding the authority of the Tu Navitilevu of Rakiraki. Here they continued to plant for the Rakiraki chiefs, and were permitted, in return, to continue to fish or make salt. Some of the Navisama continued to live in Vunisea, and traditional links with Vunisea were, and still are, retained.

There is no evidence as to how they fared in the wars of Rakiraki, but they apparently moved to the war village of Draqara on the north Nakauvadra slopes. After peace had resumed, the Navisama were at Buka until Cession. When the measles epidemic of 1875 struck immediately after Cession, the Navisama were affected and there is a cemetery for victims beside the old village site. The survivors moved to the present village of Narara, but they no longer planted *dalo* for the Rakiraki chiefs. Though considerably independent, the Le Navisama nevertheless still heeded the authority of the Tu Navitilevu of Rakiraki; and the settler *yavusa* of Navisama continued to be part of the complex socio-political federation of their later hosts, the Rakiraki, whilst retaining links with their forebears and previous hosts. It is noteworthy that the spirits of the dead only go as far as a rock beside a pool in the river near Vunisea. From the rock, they jump into the pool and here they stay. It is surprising that they do not go to a jumping-off place at the original settlement at Nubumakita, in order to rest in peace in the land associated with their earliest known ancestors.

The Rakiraki socio-political complex in retrospect

The Rakiraki socio-political complex comprises the eighteen *yavusa* identified in paragraphs (i) to (iv). These include the seven *yavusa* identified in paragraphs (iii) and (iv) which were associated with territory peripheral to Rakiraki, lying on the Northern slopes of the Nakauvadra Range in what was to become the Old *tikina* of Naroko. These were united to form a complex socio-political federation with a three level hierarchy, including two federations of *yavusa* which in turn had at least two levels of hierarchy. The leading *yavusa* was Namotutu.

Quarrels and internal fighting characterised the development of the Namotutu *yavusa*, and on the face of it the disputed origins of the leading Tunavitilevu *mataqali* were central to the situation. However, underlying these quarrels was a fierce spirit of ambition for leadership. It was this spirit of ambition and the military power of the leaders and their allies which eventually enabled the Namotutu *yavusa* to create and dominate the overall Rakiraki socio-political complex, as described and analysed in paragraphs (i) to (iv). In reality, these factors associated with *kaukauwa* or physical power of the leaders created and maintained a unity within the *yavusa* and between the *yavusa* and its relatively widespread neighbours who heeded its authority. Ideologically, there were also the ever-present spiritual powers of ancestral spirits of the various leading *yavusa* who were descended closely from Degei and the culture heroes of the Nakauvadra Range which dominated the Rakiraki countryside. These interrelated spirits and their associated *mana* created a spiritual basis for the socio-political unity of Rakiraki, legitimising the activities of its leaders and providing a spiritual backing to their *kaukauwa*.

Rakiraki was dominated by the Nakauvadra-based spiritual powers creating a unifying force for the eighteen *yavusa* forming the socio-political complex. This *mana* gave spiritual legitimisation to the military and political activities of Namotutu and her ambitious and forceful leaders; and these leaders knew how to seek military aid from those with whom they had traditional connections on the other side of the Nakauvadra by diplomatic channels using the *tabua* (whale's tooth).

(b) The yavusa of AiSokula

The *yavusa* of AiSokula, based on the village of Nakorokula in what was the Old *tikina* of Navolau, was once associated with the Namotutu *yavusa* and its members lived on Namotutu land. Later they moved onto Natokea land and the *yavusa* developed affiliations with the Natokea polity. The precise nature of the AiSokula's continuing socio-political associations, if any, with the Namotutu and their present affiliations with, and obligations to, the Tu Navatu (see below) and the Ratu ni Natokea are uncertain.

Ratu Tevita Iliavi, spokesman of the AiSokula, told me the origin myth of the AiSokula *yavusa*. He said that:

> the original ancestral spirit of the AiSokula, Lavaira, was the last of the original ancestors to come down from Nakauvadra to Namotutu, having been sent down by the culture hero, Degei. Having travelled underground, Lavaira settled at the northern base of the Range at Matavotu, near Namotutu. He had one eye in the middle of his forehead, and his *waqawaqa* or manifestation was a *kula* or red parakeet. His son, half-man and half-*veli* (a hairy land-sprite), went to Namotutu where he married a woman of Vatukaloko (see below). One grandson went and settled at Vanuakula (the Place of the Red Parakeets) near the present Rakiraki rubbish dump, where he married a woman of Rewasa, Naroko (see below). The rest of Lavaira's family moved to Namotutu, whence one of them went to settle at Navatu where he married a woman of Navatu. These were the progenitors of the AiSokula (meaning Flight of Red Parakeets).

Iliavi referred to the accounts recorded by the NLC in which it was claimed that the original ancestor of the AiSokula was the same as the ancestor of the Tunavitilevu *mataqali*, and that the AiSokula were part of the Namotutu *yavusa*. A careful study of the records indicates that the Fijian witnesses before the NLC were at best muddled and contradicted each other. It may have been that they simply wanted to seize the chance to increase by official recognition the extent of the socio-political federation of the Namotutu by including another group with which they, in fact, had no descent or traditional connections. However, the *mata ni vanua* or ceremonial head for the Tu Navitilevu told me that the AiSokula were not spiritually related to the Namotutu, having different original ancestral spirits, but that they were closely connected with Namotutu because their respective spirits lived next to each other at Namotutu. The spirit of AiSokula had come down from Nakauvadra after the ancestral spirit of the Namotutu and heeded his authority. This was reflected in the socio-political relationship between the AiSokula and the Namotutu. A recurring factor in considering the significance of these oral accounts is the need to take into account the likelihood of *ex post facto* explanations.

The myths of origin, as told to me by Iliavi, went on to say that:

> the rest of the AiSokula moved east from Namotutu, settling at Narukusara, inland from the peninsula of Volivoli. Among those at Narukusara were three brothers, the youngest of whom was called Dakuwaqa who was described to me as '*kata i wai, kata i vanua*' (biting at sea, biting on land). He was very strong and arrogant towards his elder brothers who told him to go away. So he went to Cakaudrove where he became the original ancestor of the AiSokula, the chiefly family of Cakaudrove.

> Apart from the two remaining brothers, two female spirits, the Drua Marama (or the Twin Ladies), came and settled at Narukusara. There was later a quarrel and the two female spirits left and stayed at Namolausiga from where they found it easier to go fishing. They appear here nowadays as two Fijian women dressed in modern dress.

> A fifth cult figure at Narukusara was a wandering male spirit who came from Nakauvadra and based himself at Narukusara. His manifestation was a grunting pig which used to appear in the village of Nakorokula when the AiSokula went to settle there.

> These five spirits at Narukusara were regarded as the defenders of Rakiraki and of Lavaira who was himself described as the defending spirit of Rakiraki. Narukusara became in course of time a *vanua rerevaki* or much feared place, where until recently ceremonial presentations of *yaqona* were made to the spirits of Nakauvadra.

> The AiSokula developed into a simple descent group at Namotutu, where they were until the Rakiraki wars. When Namotutu was destroyed, the AiSokula scattered up into the hills to the Rakiraki stronghold of Koroqoia.

> After peace was restored, some of the AiSokula went to join the Tui Cakau/Vuninokonoko sub-groups of the Namotutu *yavusa* and settled with them in the village of Navutulevu. Their descendants formed the branch of the AiSokula known as the Nasinukalala who settled eventually at Naivuvuni, a Navatu village to the west of Navatu crag. Here they remained up to the present time.

It is clear from Iliavi's account which was supported by others of the AiSokula with whom I discussed such matters, that the spiritual element was highly important to the AiSokula when they considered the three elements of the ideology of the *vanua*, spirits, people and land. They saw themselves as the *bai* or defence of the Rakiraki heartland, not only physically in their war settlements (Nairaborabo and Nagaga) but also spiritually with the spirits mentioned above as well as a bewildering variety of other spirits which they referred to as *ofisa* or policemen or *bai*. These *ofisa* might pass warnings about impending attacks to the AiSokula. They would also strengthen the physical powers of the AiSokula, and improve especially their expertise with the sling or *irabo*, after which their fortress Nairaborabo was named, meaning The Sling Place.

After the wars, quarrelling broke out among the Navatu people, and Tu Navatu sought the protection (*vakarurugu*) of the Tu Navitilevu of Rakiraki, offering him some land at Nasava. On the basis of this request for protection rested largely the case of the Namotutu that the Navatu people should heed the authority of Tu Navitilevu—a claim that the Navatu repudiate (see the discussion under the Malake accounts above). Tu Navitilevu sent some of the AiSokula to go and settle on this land. Their descendants formed a branch of the AiSokula known as the Nasinukalala who settled eventually at Naivuvuni, a Navatu village to the west of Navatu crag. Here they remained up to the present time.

Others of the AiSokula were sent by the Rakiraki chiefs to settle on Rakiraki lands at Nairaborabo, Volivoli, to the east of Rakiraki Hotel. Here they stayed for a long time, protected by a number of powerful spirits, until the Rakiraki (perhaps thinking that the AiSokula were getting too powerful) came and fought them and took their land and sold it to a European. The latter wanted to use the land and asked the Rakiraki chiefs to move the AiSokula away. The Rakiraki chiefs agreed to move the AiSokula to their village of Navuavua.

Perhaps smarting over their recent defeat in the hands of the Rakiraki, the AiSokula did not want to go to the Rakiraki village, and sent a request to the Ratu ni Natokea, asking if they could settle in Natokea territory. This was agreed to and the AiSokula moved to Nakorokula (the Red Parakeet Village), together with some people from Rewasa to whom they were related by the marriage referred to earlier.

The AiSokula were in a somewhat anomalous position, because although they owed traditional allegiance to the Tu Navitilevu they had now acquired some customary obligations towards the Ratu ni Natokea.

The emphasis by the AiSokula on the spiritual powers characterising their people and territory, and their reliance upon their physical ability especially with the sling, are factors of particular interest. Perhaps through an appreciation by other polities of the development of these spiritual and physical powers, the AiSokula gained a reputation worthy of great respect. They are proud of their past. They are particularly proud, but diffidently so, that they are the progenitors of the great eastern polity of Cakaudrove. The AiSokula chiefly family of Cakaudrove may disclaim what they would regard to be such a humble beginning and prefer the tradition that their progenitors were mighty Tongans of high rank. The AiSokula rest their case, considering their spirits and their military abilities to be every bit as powerful and worthy of respect as the Tongans, irrespective of the latter's political cohesion, ambitions and military might.

(c) The complex socio-political federation of Navatu, which comprised the following yavusa

(i)   The two *yavusa* of Naisogoliku and Daunavatu, being the descendants of the two sons of Waqabalabala, the original ancestral spirit of Navatu. These two *yavusa* formed the heart of the Navatu *vanua*, of which the paramount was the Tu Navatu, chief of the Naisogoliku *yavusa*. The Dawadigo group, being a part-Tongan group descended from Bilovesi, a Tongan woman made pregnant by Degei and sent by him to live with the Navatu progenitors; included by the NLC as a *mataqali* of the Daunavatu *yavusa*.

(ii) The *yavusa* of Qilaqila, having close spiritual connections with the Navatu progenitors. The leader was the Bete Levu or Chief Priest of Waqabalabala. This *yavusa* lived with the Raviravi *yavusa* on the western boundary of Navatu territory.

(iii) Three settler *yavusa*, Burelevu, Bua and Naikoro, from south of the Nakauvadra.

(iv) The Namotutu *yavusa* of Navatu, being representatives of the Vusatabua *mataqali* of the Namotutu *yavusa* of Rakiraki. Their leader was the Tu Malake.

(v)   The Rokotakala group, being representatives of the Tuinamo *mataqali* of the Namotutu *yavusa* of Rakiraki, and now included as part of the Namotutu *yavusa* of Navatu. The seven *yavusa* and two groups identified in paragraphs (ii) to (iv) all heed the authority of the Tu Navatu. The two groups are considered separately in my discussion, though, as noted, they have been included as part of two of the *yavusa* cited above.

(vi)   The Raviravi and the Wailevu, being two *yavusa* which were settled together at the western boundary of the Navatu territory, the Raviravi living on their own land, and the Wailevu being a settler *yavusa* from the Vatukaloko socio-political complex. The Tui Raviravi heeded the authority of the leader of the settlers, the Tui Wailevu, who in turn heeded the authority of the Tu Navatu.

The nine *yavusa* and two groups, as identified in paragraphs (i) to (vi), were all based in what was to become the Old *tikina* of Raviravi. They were united to form a fairly complex socio-political federation with a three level hierarchy, including one combination of *yavusa* which in turn had two levels of hierarchy.

The polity can be summarised as follows:

Name of *vanua*	Leading *yavusa*	Title of paramount	No. of *yavusa*	No. of levels	No. of villages
Navatu	Naisogoliku	Tu Navatu	3	4	9

This polity is of particular interest from three points of view. First, its emphasis on the spirit world and the Nakauvadra Range serves to illustrate the importance of the spiritual element in what I have posited as the trilogy of elements in the concept of *vanua*—people, land and spirits. Secondly, its degree of socio-political complexity provides support for my basic theme that there was a continuum of degrees of socio-political complexity in Fijian late prehistoric polities, as seen on a west-east politico-geographical axis with simple polities tending to be in the west and major confederations tending to be in the east. This does not mean that individual polities in the west did not develop in complexity, or individual polities in the east did not decline. Thirdly, it illustrates some of the features of symbolism of unification and identification of a polity which were characteristic of Fijian late prehistoric polities generally.

(i) The original inhabitants of Navatu

Myths of origin

Tu Navatu's account recorded by me was that:

> Waqabalabala, the original ancestral spirit of the Navatu, and Bakadroti, the original ancestral spirit of the Naqilaqila (see below), came down together from the Nakauvadra Range, having been sent there by Degei. Waqabalabala married Losavisi, known as the *itaukei ni cubu ni wai mei Bakadroti*, or "owner of the crevice where Bakadroti got his drinking water". This is a rocky islet known now simply as Cubu, just off Navatu.

The Bete Levu of Naqilaqila, however, said that Waqabalabala married Naivilawasa from Nakauvadra Range. This was denied by Tu Navatu, and there is no way to resolve the two accounts.

Tu Navatu went on to say that:

> Waqabalabala had two sons, Niudamu and Niumarawa.

> At first, he and his family stayed at Nauluvatu (the highest peak of Navatu crag), and Bakadroti stayed at another peak called Naqilaqila.

> Waqabalabala then left Navatu and went to stay at what is referred to as his resting place at Nacilau, a point

to the west of Navatu. Nacilau is the jumping-off place of the spirits of the Navatu dead. Losavisi returned to Cubu, for some reason not now known. One account said that Bakadroti himself went to the western boundary of Rakiraki territory and stayed at first at Na iTavutavu ni Ciwa near a pool in the mangrove swamp just to the east of Tavua. This became the pool of Viyagoiratu where the Tu Navitilevu washed after his installation, and where he was later massaged by the Tavua people to whom he was related. Later, Bakadroti wanted to be closer to Waqabalabala and so he moved east to Nawailo near the present village of Vunitogoloa. Another account said that he moved directly from Navatu to Nawailo and that it was the Naqilaqila descendants who went to Tavua (see below).

The two brothers, the sons of Waqabalabala, moved down to the southeast side of Navatu crag to settle at Naisogoliku. From there Niumarawa moved to the southwest side of the crag, to Nasakurawa. Between these two sites there is a cave called Naqaqa occupied by Coci, a hare-lipped spirit who came down from Nakauvadra as part of Waqabalabala's retinue. Coci's duties were to teach *meke* or action chants to the Navatu people.

The descendants of Niudamu, Niumarawa and Coci

Niudamu's descendants at Naisogoliku were the Naisogoliku sub-group of the Navatu people.

Niumarawa's descendants at Nasakurawa were the Daunavatu, the turtle fishers for Degei before the Malake (see above).

Coci's descendants were the Naqaqa, later known as the Vunivau, who joined the Naqilaqila at Vunitogoloa, but were still regarded as part of the Daunavatu *yavusa*.

The Dawadigo Group

While Niumarawa was at Nasakurawa the pregnant Bilovesi arrived from Nakauvadra. Bilovesi came originally from Tonga as a *vulagi ki Nakauvadra* or visitor to the Nakauvadra, where Degei invited her to be his personal guest. He made her pregnant and sent her to Nasakurawa to wait there until she had given birth. Bakadroti, however, said that she should go to him at Nawailo and be looked after by Mokomoko, a male spirit of the place whose place was the site of the present village of Vunitogoloa and who is still referred to as *i vakatawa ni koro* or guardian of the village. Just before she gave birth, Bakadroti sent her back to Nasakurawa where she gave birth to a boy. The news reached Degei, whose manifestation was a snake, and he said that he was Ga'a i Vanua (snake of the land), and that his son should be called Ga'a i Wai (snake of the water). He sent a mosquito net (*lawalawa*) to be hung up in Bilovesi's house, and the name of Nasakurawa was changed to Navalelawa (mosquito net house).

Gataiwai went to a pool in a stream to the northwest of Navatu crag; and Bilovesi may have gone to Malake Island (according to the Malake people, she married Dadavanua, their ancestral spirit), where there is a rock shaped like a vagina and known as Bilovesi.

Bilovesi/Gataiwai: descendants

Bilovesi's descendants were the Dawadigo, who were formerly regarded as a separate group but were later included in the Daunavatu *yavusa* because of land at Visoto which Niumarawa had given to Gataiwai. Indeed they were regarded at first as the leaders of the Navatu people on the grounds that they were direct descendants of Degei through Bilovesi, whereas the Naisogoliku were descended from Waqabalabala, who was only an emissary of Degei. Later the leadership was given to the Naisogoliku as the senior group of the Navatu people who, at Degei's request, had looked after Bilovesi during her pregnancy.

(ii) The Naqilaqila yavusa

The Naqilaqila *yavusa* were the descendants of Bakadroti whom Degei had sent down from the Nakauvadra to be the *bete* or priest of Waqabalabala.

After Waqabalabala had settled at Nacilau, Bakadroti had gone to be near him and settled at Nawailo where his mound was called Nailuva. Bakadroti's descendants first settled at Na iTavutavu ni Ciwa, near Tavua, and then at Nawailo.

The Navatu people (the Naisogoliku, the Daunavatu and the Naqilaqila) did not claim descent from Degei, the main culture hero of the Nakauvadra Range, and in this way they were different from the Namotutu people of Rakiraki who claimed descent from Tu Nakauvadra, the son of Degei. On the basis of these myths of origin, the Navatu may be signalling that they were spiritually lower down the hierarchy than the Namotutu people. Nevertheless, they were proud to be descended from the direct emissaries of Degei, Waqabalabala and the priest, Bakadroti. This mythological origin not only gives the Navatu a sense of security and a pride of place in the region. It also provides a sense of unity and identification for the polity, and a spiritual validation for Tu Navatu being the paramount of the Navatu federation.

The Dawadigo are of interest, claiming descent from Bilovesi, a Tongan visitor to Nakauvadra, whom Degei had made pregnant. First, there is mythological connection between Tonga and the Nakauvadra, based not only on Bilovesi's visit but also on the arrival of Degei's favourite dove, Turukawa, said to have come from Tonga. However both visitors may be seen to have suffered. The dove was shot by the Ciri, the Twins, who were not supportive of Degei, and Bilovesi was made pregnant. Instead of her descendants being honoured as part-Tongan as they would have been in the east where Cakaudrove paramounts proudly but probably falsely claim original descent from Tongans, the Dawadigo nowadays are diffident about their Tongan blood and seem to wish to conceal it. In Navatu, the blood of Degei overrides the blood of Tongan ancestors.

Turtle fishing and the Daunavatu diaspora

When Degei's *vudi* or plantains which the Rakiraki people had planted at Waisa were ripe, the Daunavatu would take a certain stone endowed with special *mana* or *sau* and go fishing for turtle. They would be expected to take their catch to the Naqilaqila people, whose head was the Bete Levu or Chief Priest of Degei. It was the responsibility of the Naqilaqila to take the turtle for presentation to Degei, together with the *vudi*.

On one occasion, the Daunavatu caught turtle but only presented the small ones for Degei, keeping the big ones to eat. Degei found out about this transgression and sent down upon the Daunavatu the so-called *lila balavu* or wasting disease. The Daunavatu scattered, fleeing from the disease and the wrath of Degei. They went to Navatusila (in the centre of Viti Levu); Nakorotubu; Dawasama (Tailevu); Bua; the Yasawas; Nadroga (the Navatu people claim that the Kwa Levu or paramount of Nadroga is of Navatu origin); the island of Vatulele—so called because the Navatu poled (*lele*) over to there; and even to the island of Kadavu.

The Bete Levu, head of the Naqilaqila, explained to me that the Naqilaqila had gone to settle near Tavua after the *lila balavu* in order to get as far away as possible from Navatu and still remain on Rakiraki land. The Tu Navatu said that they went to Tavua and then to Nawailo before the *lila balavu*. It might be considered that the Bete Levu's explanation is *ex post facto*, but at least he did provide an explanation, whereas the Tu Navatu could offer no other explanation as to why the Naqilaqila had gone so far from Navatu. At least it makes sense that the Naqilaqila should want to go as far as possible away from the place where the Daunavatu turtle fishers had insulted Bakadroti by eating his turtle. Be that as it may, Bakadroti later called them back from Na iTuvatuva i Ciwa (see above), so that they could settle at Nawailo and be in close association with him at his mound of Nailuva. This was just to the west of the present village of Vunitogoloa.

The NLC were told that ceremonies of *isoro* or atonement were performed to appease the wrath of Bakadroti, and the *lila balavu* ceased. Either because of this atonement or because they were not directly affected by the sacrilegious actions of the Daunavatu, the Naisogoliku people were not affected by the *lila balavu*, and they remained at Naisogoliku. However, it was emphasised to me in the 1950s and in the 1990s that such atonement ceremonies had not been performed. Because traditional lines of communication were not recognised or were difficult to develop and maintain, there was no practice of *veilakovi* or ceremonial exchanges of visits between Navatu and the faraway places of refuge to which the Daunavatu had fled.

Nevertheless I consider that it would be unthinkable that ceremonies of atonement were not performed to Bakadroti by the Naisogoliku chiefs in order to *vakasavasavataka* or clean up the *ivalavala ca* or bad behaviour of their relations. Although it was the Daunavatu who had been in the wrong, the remaining Navatu had to live in peaceful unity with the Naqilaqila descendants (who through the Bete Levu were the means of communication with Degei and the Nakauvadra spirit heroes). It was these heroes who would provide the spiritual power to validate and consolidate the unity of the complex socio-political federation of Navatu. This Nakauvadra-based spiritual validation and consolidation would become increasingly important as the federation developed. The diaspora after the *lila balavu* is still talked about with awe, as an interesting and severe object lesson of what happens to people who do not fulfil their customary obligations. Local spirits are watching closely for transgressions, and over all the Nakauvadra Range looms physically and spiritually. Spirits of both provenances are benevolent if respected; but the spirit world can be equally malevolent and menacing. It is this spiritual element in the concept of *vanua* which plays the role of a policeman who can be friendly but who is particularly responsible for maintaining order. Rakiraki has many spirits in addition to the ancestral spirits who are seen as maintaining order and punishing the transgressions of the people against the spirit world or the polity.

The Naqilaqila later moved from Nawailo to the village of Vunitogoloa *makawa*, an easily defended site in the mangroves near the present village of Vunitogoloa. The spirit house of Bakadroti remained at Nawailo, and old Milika (aged about 90) of Vunitogoloa told me that she remembered seeing the high earthen mound surrounded by stones, with a tall stone on top. The *bete* lived nearby. I could find no trace of the stone, which could have been moved elsewhere or buried for preservation or simply destroyed under the influence of Christianity.

At Vunitogoloa *makawa* the Naqilaqila were joined by a number of people from the inland village of Naseyani (see below) who came either on invitation or through marriage or blood ties with the Naqilaqila and comprised the Raviravi and Wailevu *yavusa* (see below). From there they moved to the present site of Vunitogoloa. Here were settled the Naqilaqila, the Raviravi, the Wailevu, the Vunivau (descendants of Coci from Navatu, see above), the Naikoro from Navatu (originally from south of the Nakauvadra, see above) and representatives of the Vusatabua of Namotutu (see below).

The Naqilaqila lost much of their land to Europeans, and became so short of planting land that they resented the continuing presence of the stranger Wailevu and Raviravi. Much of the Wailevu land had also been sold, and attempts are still being made for some of the Yaqara Estate to be freed from the supervision of a company and returned for the use of the Wailevu. This would release for the Naqilaqila some of their land currently being used by the Wailevu and Raviravi.

(iii) Arrival of the Burelevu, Bua and Naikoro, the settler yavusa

I was told by the 80-year-old head of the Burelevu, the 84-year-old head of the Bua and by a gathering of people at Vitawa in 1996 that:

> the forebears of these three settler *yavusa* came originally from Nabaibai (the Burelevu), Namasaga (the Bua) and Munusavu (the Naikoro) on the south slopes of the Nakauvadra near the present Saivou village of Vunisea. They were among the groups who scattered before the attacks of Yaqayaqa, the *qaqa* or strong man of Saivou in the course of fierce fighting in the interior of Saivou. All three groups left together, crossed the Nakauvadra Range and settled on the north slopes at settlements which still bear their names and can still be identified as archaeological sites with *yavu* or house mounds and ditches.

> When the Daunavatu scattered from Navatu as the result of the *lila balavu*, the Tu Navatu invited the Burelevu, Bua and Naikoro as well as some Nabaqatai from Nacolo (see above) to come and settle as *vulagi* or visitors on the vacated Navatu land. In times of war they helped the Tu Navatu who then gave them land for themselves. The Tui Burelevu, the Ratu ni Bua and the head of the Naikoro heeded the authority of the Tu Navatu. Most of these settlers remained at Naisogoliku and then moved to the present village of Vitawa. Some, however, joined the Naqilaqila at Vunitogoloa.

Apart from their socio-political connections with their Navatu hosts and the Tu Navatu, the Burelevu maintained social connections with their previous co-settlers, the Nabaqatai, who returned to the Nacolo at Vatukacevaceva. All three maintained their blood links with their relations still at Vunisea on the south side of the Nakauvadra, especially when there was a death or marriage. Their links with the other side of the Nakauvadra are also retained spiritually, because the spirits of the dead return to their *yavutū* or places of origin. In the case of Bua, the spirits jump from a rock into a deep pool in the river near Vunisea.

The arrival of these three settler *yavusa* and their consequent activities illustrate well the mechanics of how a complex federation developed from a polity based on spiritual descent and relationships to one which included *vulagi* or strangers. The latter came to *vakarorogo* or heed the authority of the paramount not on the basis of relational hierarchy (either sanguineal or spiritual). They did so as *tiko vakararavi* or people who had fled from their own lands for social, political or war-based reasons and were given shelter and protection by their hosts. In return for such protection they were given the use of land for settlement and for planting, but their relationship with this land was different from that of people who were *itaukei* or members of the recognised land-owning group. This, in fact, is a misnomer, because *itaukei* though usually translated as 'landowner', is the 'passive' form of the word '*tauke-na*' or 'possess' and means 'the owned'. It is not so much that the people own the land as that the land owns the people, symbolising a spiritual connection between the land, the living and the ancestors. The *vulagi*, by definition, do not have that spiritual connection with the land they are allowed to use, and so they can never be true *itaukei*. In the case of the three settler *yavusa* to Navatu, they had been dispossessed, through warfare, of their land on the other side of the Nakauvadra, and had been invited to settle on Navatu land evidently vacated by those who had fled from spiritual wrath. The NLC later officially confirmed their rights to this land but these settler *yavusa* were still regarded traditionally, as they are nowadays, as *vulagi*.

Another interesting point about these settler Navatu people is that they retained their relational and spiritual ties with the other side of the Nakauvadra, even to the extent of the spirits of their dead returning to *icibaciba* or jumping off places near their original settlements south of the Nakauvadra.

(iv) The Namotutu yavusa: representatives in Navatu

Vusatabua

At the time of the Rakiraki wars between Naereere of the Tuinamo *mataqali* of Namotutu *yavusa* on the one side, and Kelei of the Vusatabua *mataqali* of the Namotutu *yavusa* and the Navuavua *yavusa* on the other, some of the Vusatabua sought refuge with the Naisogoliku of Navatu. Some Vusatabua went to Malake and later went with the Malake to Navatu, some joining the other Vusatabua at Naisogoliku and finally settling at Naicuvacuva. Among these, one held the title of Tu Malake or Mata ki Malake, whose responsibility it was to bring the message from the Tu Navitilevu to the Malake people to say that the plantains were ripe for presentation to Degei, and that they should proceed with turtle fishing for Degei. Others went and settled with the Wailevu and the Naqilaqila at Vunitogoloa, which was part of the Navatu territory.

Later, the quarrels arose between the Namotutu chiefs, Mulase of Vusatabua and Nawaqalevu of Navitilevu, due to the appointment of Naduva as Tu Navitilevu (see under the Namotutu account). Mulase went to his *vasu*, the Naisogiliku *yavusa* who were his mother's people, and settled at Naicuvacuva with the rest of the Vusatabua who had gone there earlier. When the rest of the Namotutu proceeded to attack Navatu Mulase helped the Navatu people against the Namotutu and their allies, the Nalawa and the Navatu with Mulase's help killed 'Eki, the *qaqa* or strong man of Nalawa, and chased away the Namotutu. As a result, the Navatu claim that their original obligations to Namotutu on the basis of which the Namotutu claimed that the Navatu owed them allegiance (see below) were wiped out and the Navatu were now independent. The matter is still debated but without resolution.

Rokotakala

Sometime later Navatu was split with internal quarrels; *draunikau* or sorcery was rife, and the polity had a fearsome reputation for strange powers. For instance, if someone wanted to kill an enemy in the Yasawa or elsewhere in Ba, that person had the power to do so by throwing a *tiqa* or dart, or a stone in the direction of that person. The situation became so chaotic that Tu Navatu gave some land to Tu Navitilevu and asked for help. As a result, the Rokotakala group descended from Kanabaya of the Tuinamo *mataqali* were sent by Tu Navitilevu to keep the peace. They settled at Naicuvacuva and later split, some remaining at Naicuvacuva with the rest of the Namotutu representatives, the Vusatabua, and others going to Naisogoliku to be with Tu Navatu. On the basis of this assistance the Namotutu claim that the Navatu thereby put themselves in a position of dependence on the Namotutu which resulted in them having to heed the authority of the Tu Navitilevu. The Namotutu people say that the AiSokula were descended from one of the sons of Kanabaya and were originally part of the Rokotakala. The AiSokula strongly deny this and claim descent from Lavaira, the spirit sent down from Nakauvadra by Degei, and are therefore quite separate from the Namotutu. It is not possible to determine which of these accounts, presumably biased towards the narrator, is historically correct (see the account of the AiSokula above); but for the main purposes of this research this quandary is not unduly significant.

When the development of a complex socio-political federation is being analysed and the component elements have been isolated, it is apparent that in some cases, as in the case of the three settler *yavusa* discussed above, groups of people who were duly recognised as complete *yavusa* or descent groups moved from their own lands to those of a host polity which became their paramount. In the case of the two groups just described, fission took place in the parent *yavusa*, the Namotutu. Fission was not simply on an inter-*mataqali* but rather on an intra-*mataqali* basis. In the cases of the Tuinamo and the Vusatabua *mataqali*, they were split and some of each went to settle in Navatu. The reasons for such fission in the cases described may have reflected internal dynastic quarrels among the Namotutu, or may have been at the request of the host for assistance from a powerful neighbour in order to settle internal Navatu problems. The latter is reminiscent of the phenomenon of the 'stranger king', as Sahlins had claimed for Fiji. There is a third possibility. A paramount such as the Tu Navitilevu may have sent a group of his own people to live among the neighbours such as among the Navatu at Navatu crag, at Vunitogoloa among the Naqilaqila and among the Natokea—see the discussion on the Navolau people of Namotutu origin who settled among the Natokea people. This may have been in the form of a semi-diplomatic/semi-intelligence mission because the paramount concerned wanted to keep in favour with, or maintain a watch over his possibly troublesome neighbours. It may reflect an era, hinted at in the oral traditions, when Rakiraki's sphere of influence really did extend from Navitilevu Bay to Tavua. Certainly, the chiefs of Namotutu nowadays, when discussing the matter with me refer to the *yavusa balavu* or extended *yavusa* of Namotutu, with its influence stretching through its representatives to Vunitogoloa, to Navatu crag and to Natokea, and even, albeit with a wistful smile, to Cakaudrove through the AiSokula people. It is at this stage impossible to tell what is merely wishful thinking on the part of the Namotutu. Suffice it to say that that is what they claim nowadays, and they cite the descent from Degei to validate their claims. This also reflects the continuing argument of the relationship between Namotutu and Navatu as to whether or not the Navatu should heed the authority of Namotutu. The Navatu certainly do not think so. The argument is fairly typical of similar situations elsewhere in Fiji where ambitious leaders seek to justify an extension of their currently recognised spheres of traditional influence, or to escape from the paramountcy of another polity which they say was wrongly claimed and wrongly officially recognised at the time of the NLC.

(v) The Raviravi and Wailevu yavusa

According to the NLC records the original ancestral spirit of these two *yavusa* came down from Nakauvadra and settled at Wailevu, inland from the present villages of Drauniivi and Vunitogoloa. They had two children, the elder of whom was the progenitor of the Wailevu, and the younger that of the Raviravi who went and settled at the mountain fortress of Vugala in the Sawakasa Range.

I was told that:

> because of marriage ties and other social links, these two *yavusa* used to come down to Vunitogoloa *makawa* at the invitation of the Naqilaqila and make salt in the mangroves. They were later given planting land by the Naqilaqila and duly settled with the Naqilaqila at Vunitogoloa. The Tui Raviravi (descended from the younger of the brothers) heeded the authority of the Tui Wailevu (of the line of the elder brother) who heeded the authority of the Tu Navatu, as paramount of the Navatu federation which included the Naqilaqila. The Naqilaqila and the Wailevu are now short of land because much of their land had been sold to Europeans before Cession. The Naqilaqila are still trying to get the Wailevu to leave the Naqilaqila land which the Wailevu claim to be theirs on the basis of the earlier gift from the Naqilaqila. The Naqilaqila claim that they only gave right of use to the Wailevu. So there is still friction in Vunitogoloa between the two *yavusa*.

If the NLC account is accepted, the Raviravi and Wailevu *yavusa* may be categorised simply as settler *yavusa*, and there seems to be no doubt but that the Wailevu people are part of the Twelve *Yavusa* (see below). However, although their origin myths as recorded by the Lands Commission indicate that they were of a common origin, I was told in Vunitogoloa that the original inhabitants of the land where the village is now situated were the Raviravi. The Raviravi must indeed have been people of consequence at some period, because the Old *tikina* of Raviravi was named after them, according to what I was told in Vunitogoloa.

> When the Naqilaqila came from Navatu crag, they were considered by the Raviravi to be powerful people, because of their spiritual connection with Bakadroti, Degei's priest sent down to settle with Waqabalabala.

So the Naqilaqila were given the leadership over the Raviravi. The Naqilaqila invited the Wailevu to come and use some of the land, the control of which the Raviravi had given to the Naqilaqila. This may have been because the Naqilaqila wanted to associate themselves with the Twelve *Yavusa*. The Wailevu as part of the Twelve *Yavusa* were accepted as senior to the Raviravi who heeded their authority; but they heeded the authority of the Naqilaqila first as landlords and secondly because of the spiritual power of their leader, the Bete Levu, who was descended from Bakadroti.

These two *yavusa* are therefore of interest as illustrating how stranger groups came to be included in a complex socio-political polity, and how the hierarchy of *yavusa* within a polity could change, depending on the recognised relative spiritual or secular power of the stranger *yavusa* or the host *yavusa*.

(d) Part of the Socio-Political Federation of Naroko, comprised of the following elements

(i)   The leading *yavusa* of Navatudamu, whose head was the LeweiNavatudamu.

(ii)   The two *yavusa* of Natunu and Kasia whose heads, the Tui Natunu and the Tui Vatuvula respectively, heeded the authority of the LeweiNavatudamu.

(iii)   The settler *yavusa* of Navitini, whose head was the Masibuli who heeded the authority of the Tui Vatuvula of Kasia.

These four *yavusa* were based in the village of Rewasa on what was once Rakiraki land which became a part of the Old *tikina* of Naroko. Lying to the north of the Nakauvadra Range, the village is included in my study area.

(iv)   The *yavusa* of Nawaqavesi, whose head was the LeweiNacokula.

(v)   The *yavusa* of Navudrau, whose head was the Tu Navudrau. He heeded the authority of the LeweiNacokula, when the Nawaqavesi came and settled with the Navudrau and were accepted as leaders.

These two *yavusa* were based in villages south of my study area and I will only discuss them peripherally.

According to the myths of origin told to me at Rewasa by the head of the Navatudamu/Kasia people, an ex-commando from the Second World War Solomons campaign:

> the original ancestral spirit of the Naroko people, Taginadula, and his wife, Souvau, came from over the Nakauvadra Range, from the Karoka region in the interior of Saivou. His actual place was called Nawaqavesi. He had two sons, one of whom was the original ancestral spirit of the Nawaqavesi *yavusa*. He came, together with Leka (the ancestral spirit of the Cakova, see above) and his family, and whilst Leka moved on to Vaileka, Taginadula remained further inland. His manifestation was described to me as a small snake that has two feet like a duck.

Curiously there is another spirit in Naroko which has the same manifestation. It is not unusual to find that original ancestral spirits had remarkable and strange features. Coci had a hare-lip; Qelo had a limp; Lavaira had one eye in the middle of his forehead; Tunabaqa (who does not appear elsewhere in this monograph) had an enormous penis; and Leka was remarkable for his small size. However, these are the only instances I have come across, of a manifestation in the form of a remarkable or strange composite creature, the significance of which could not be explained by those with whom I discussed the matter. The only hint I could find was that the Vatudamu/Kasia have as a harbinger of an imminent death, a *wacori* or kind of duck. Such a harbinger is generally regarded as the manifestation of an ancestral spirit. I suggest that the snake with duck's feet may in some way represent the unification of the manifestations of the ancestral spirits of two descent groups (or perhaps the process of transformation of one manifestation to another) and hence symbolise the unification of two descent groups who have come to regard themselves as one such group, or perhaps the process of transformation of spiritual (and physical power) from one group to another. This could be seen reflected in the fraternal quarrels, to which I will refer below, leading to the creation of the Navatudamu *yavusa*. Either the Naroko wanted to maintain a symbolism of unity between the Navatudamu and the Nawaqavesi, or they wanted to symbolise a transfer of power from the descendants of the elder brother to those of the younger brother. The Navatudamu were the descendants of the younger brother, and the head was regarded as the paramount of the Naroko people. The position of the head of the Navatudamu as paramount of the Naroko was confirmed by the NLC, but this was and still is sharply disputed by the descendants of the elder brother, the Nawaqavesi. The latter claimed that the confirmed leaders of the Naroko were very weak and ineffectual because they were not the traditional leaders who should be those descended from the elder brother, the Nawaqavesi. This dispute continues to the present.

The head of the *yavusa* went on to explain that:

> the descendants of Taginadula first lived at Nawaqavesi in the interior of Saivou on the south side of the Nakauvadra. Nawaqavesi is regarded as the original settlement of the people of the polity of Naroko, which comprised the groups which became known as the Nawaqavesi (who took their name from the original settlement), Navudrau, Navatudamu, Natunu and Kasia. It was these people who gave their collective name to the Old *tikina* of Naroko.

> Two of the progenitors of the Nawaqavesi *yavusa* at Nawaqavesi were brothers. The younger brother refused to pay respect to his elder brother and wanted to go off on his own, so he left Nawaqavesi.

> Those remaining at Nawaqavesi formed the Nawaqavesi *yavusa*. They left Nawaqavesi and went to the Navudrau whose original settlement was near a large rock overlooking the present village of Vaidoko on the Saivou coast. These two groups fled together after being attacked by the Rakiraki people. They now live in the villages of Nokonoko and Vaidoko. The head of the Nawaqavesi has the title of Komainacokula who later heeded the authority of the head of the Naivilaca people of Saivou. The head of the Navudrau was the Tu Navudrau who heeded the authority of the Komainacokula. These two *yavusa* are on the south side of the Nakauvadra, and are only relevant to this research to the extent that they were of the stock from which the Naroko of Rewasa were derived.

> Having left Nawaqavesi, the younger brother went to Kasia, still on the south of Nakauvadra. Here his party split, one part remaining at Kasia and forming the Kasia *yavusa*, while the rest went on north to Navatudamu near the present village of Rewasa. Here they split again, and one group went to nearby Natunu and formed the Natunu *yavusa*. The rest remained at Navatudamu and formed the Vatudamu *yavusa*, of whom the leader had the title of LeiNavatudamu. Meanwhile, the Kasia were joined by the Navitini *yavusa* who were also from the interior of Saivou, where they had been attacked by the neighbouring Naliwani.

> The Masibuli, head of the Navitini, heeded the authority of the Tui Vatuvula. The Tui Vatuvula (head of the Kasia) and the Tui Natunu (head of the Natunu) acknowledged the authority of the Leinavatudamu, who presumably at an earlier time had heeded the authority of his hosts, the Rakiraki chiefs, but was later regarded as independent. These four *yavusa* are now all associated with the village of Rewasa on the edge of, and once part of Rakiraki territory. They were evidently invited by the Rakiraki chiefs to settle there, but they are nowadays independent from the Tu Navitilevu of Namotutu.

These four *yavusa* forming part of the independent socio-political complex of Naroko, are relevant to this research because they later came to live on Rakiraki land. They must therefore, at one stage, have owed allegiance to the Namotutu chiefs and heeded the authority of the paramount, Tu Navitilevu, although they claim to have become independent later. I suggest that they could be regarded as having once been a settler polity seeking land and perhaps refuge from the attacks of Saivou which then became part of the protective, socio-political complex of Rakiraki. Later, for reasons not apparent, they ceased to be regarded as a formal part of this complex polity. Fusion and fission are as much evident in the development of the Rakiraki polities as they are a feature of the major polities of the east and the minor polities of the west. They simply manifest themselves on a much greater socio-political and geographical scale in the east and on a much smaller scale in the west.

(e) Part of the Socio-Political Federation or Vanua of Vatukaloko, generally referred to as the Twelve Yavusa

The Twelve *Yavusa* comprise the following elements:

(i)   The three *yavusa* of Nasi, Wakalou and Nakubuti, comprising a federation known as Vatukaloko, the head of which is the Tui Vatu, based on the village of Drauniivi.

(ii)   The *yavusa* of Mali, of which the head is the Ratu ni Mali, based on the village of Naseyani.

(iii)   The *yavusa* of Nakorosago, based on the village of Nananu. The villages of Naseyani and Nananu were originally in the Tavua area immediately to the west of the Raviravi area, but the boundaries were altered in Colonial times and Drauniivi, Naseyani and Nananu were included in Raviravi *tikina*. This general area was known as Na iYalayala or 'The Boundary', and the traditional affiliations with Tavua and Raviravi are still a matter of discussion and controversy. I have included these villages in my study area, albeit peripherally.

(iv)   The *yavusa* of Wailevu, later based on the Navatu village of Vunitogoloa and included in the polity of Navatu—see Navatu account.

These six *yavusa* (including Wailevu) were based on villages lying to the north of the Nakauvadra Range and fell within my study area of Rakiraki and the periphery.

(v)   The six *yavusa* of Nakoromatua, Naluani, Neitoa, Korosovoulevu, Wacunu and Nasoqo, based in villages in areas lying to the south of the Nakauvadra Range which became part of the New *tikina* of Saivou.

These six *yavusa* were associated with areas near the traditional original settlements of Navatunigauna and Vatukaloko from which developed the Twelve *Yavusa*. The federation of Vatukaloko takes its name from this original settlement. These areas were outside my study area and the six *yavusa* involved will not be referred to further, except in connection with the other six of the Twelve *Yavusa* identified in paragraphs (i) to (iv).

I had many discussions with the chiefs and spokesmen of Drauniivi, including the (now late) Tui Vatu, and also visited Nananu and Naseyani both in the 1950s and the 1990s. The Ratu ni Mali was very helpful and interested in the affairs of the Twelve *Yavusa*, especially Mali and Nakorosago. This account is based generally on those discussions and on the findings of Rosenthal (Rosenthal 1991; cf. Kaplan and Rosenthal 1993).

The Twelve *Yavusa* formed overall a complex socio-political federation scattered over a wide geographical area on both sides of the Nakauvadra Range towards the west end of the range. I discuss this overall federation only briefly because the territories of so many of its *yavusa* fall outside my study area. A spiritual unification of the Twelve *Yavusa* is based upon relationship with the original ancestral spirit, Nasarilevu. He came down from the Nakauvadra with his wife,

Naikavatu, and they settled at Vatunigauna and then at nearby Vatukaloko. At Vatukaloko there is a pool and a rock said to be covered with figures (hence the rock is called Clock Rock, a nice *ex post facto* explanation). Their descendants comprised the Twelve *Yavusa*.

Their region was at first included in the *tikina* of Tavua in the province of Ba. It was not included by the Fijian Administration of the Colonial Government in the Old *tikina* of Raviravi which now forms part of the area included in the New *tikina* of Rakiraki in the province of Ra. Later there was a controversial boundary shift by the Administration and that part of the region of the Twelve *Yavusa* occupied by the six *yavusa* who moved north of the Nakauvadra Range and which is commonly known as Na iYalayala ('The Boundary') was included in the New *tikina* of Rakiraki. I have therefore included in my explorations of Rakiraki the six *yavusa* associated with Na i Yalayala. They are of interest from two aspects.

First, these six *yavusa* are part of a federation of considerable socio-political complexity, paralleling first, that of the Rakiraki polity headed by the *yavusa* of Namotutu and the Tu Navitilevu; and secondly, that of Navatu headed by the *yavusa* of Naisogoliku and the Tu Navatu. The Twelve *Yavusa* were known generally as the Vatukaloko, after their early settlement, although later this name was used to refer particularly to the three *yavusa* living at Drauniivi.

The Twelve *Yavusa* claim common spiritual origins from the sons and relations of Nasarilevu, an ancestral spirit who came down from Nakauvadra and settled first at Navatunigauna and then moved to nearby Vatukaloko towards the slopes of the western end of the Nakauvadra. From here six *yavusa* spread south of the range outside my area, and the other six with whom I am concerned spread north to Vugala, Nananu, Naseyani and Drauniivi. They established the defended site at Vugala to which Udreudre of Rakiraki later fled. There were close links between the Tunavitilevu *mataqali* of the Namotutu and those Vatukaloko who were living at Vugala. Udreudre's mother came from the Vatukaloko People. Because of these links, Udreudre, chief of the Navitilevu of Namotutu, was able to seek refuge with his *vasu* at Vugala after he had been abandoned at Namotutu during the Rakiraki wars of Naereere against Kelei and the Navuavua *yavusa*. After the wars, the Vatukaloko took Udreudre back to the Namotutu boundary, but the Namotutu had by this time accepted Christianity and were not prepared to welcome back their paramount who was a notorious cannibal. So he remained with his old friends, the Cakova, and lived and died with them. It does seem that at some time the Rakiraki polity's sphere of influence extended as far as just east of Tavua. Here was the pool where the Tu Navitilevu bathed after installation. On the reefs off here was the boundary of the turtle fishing activities of the Malake fishers of the Tu Navitilevu. Here the Naqilaqila settled as far as possible from the sacrilege caused by the Daunavatu who ate turtle meant for Degei and the consequent *lila balavu* which smote the Navatu, at a time when the Navatu were possibly part of the Rakiraki polity. This may well account for the initial fixing of the Raviravi boundary to include the region known as Na iYalayala which stretched almost as far as Tavua.

Secondly, the Twelve *Yavusa* were involved in activities to which the Cakobau Government and later the Colonial Government took exception. In the first instance, a Lasakau (Bau) man called Koroikoya came recruiting Ra labour for European plantations in the east. This was seen first, as a case of a stranger (who happened to be a hated Bauan) taunting the traditional authorities of the area by recruiting Ra labour without first seeking the approval of those authorities; and secondly, as a case of an unwelcome infiltration of the Cakobau Government outside Cakobau's traditional area of authority. Koroikoya was killed by the Nakorosago *yavusa* of the Twelve *Yavusa*. Cakobau's troops who happened to be in the area on other matters were ordered to avenge the death of Koroikoya and attacked the assembled warriors of the Twelve *Yavusa* who had assembled within the defence works of Korowaiwai, inland from Drauniivi. The ramifications of Koroikoya's activities involved the Cakobau Government and ended in the Battle of Korowaiwai in 1873. In the course of this successful attack, 157 (according to the *Fiji Times*; Georgius Wright, an eyewitness, later gave the figure as 300) of Vatukaloko warriors were killed in their defended area on the banks of which sat the *bete*, Sadiri, facing the guns of Cakobau's troops in traditional manner by waving a fan defiantly but unsuccessfully. On this occasion, the *kaukauwa* or physical power of firearms used to effect by the military of the Cakobau Government proved to be too strong for the *mana* or spiritual power provided for the Twelve *Yavusa* by their ancestors through their priest. Even with the introduction of Christianity the old beliefs of the Twelve *Yavusa* remained strong and provided a fertile background to the activities of a man of Drauniivi, Dugumoi, also known as Navosavakadua, who was of the *bete* line of the Vatukaloko. Dugumoi was a seer and spiritual activist whose best-remembered deed was to revive a man baked in an earth oven. He had a extensive following throughout the region of the Twelve *Yavusa* who saw in him an embodiment of their past spiritual glories and power. Because of what were interpreted by the Colonial Government to be his anti-government activities, Dugumoi was arrested in 1883 and deported to Rotuma for ten years. Although he never returned to Drauniivi, the Vatukaloko people there persisted and in 1891 they were deported to Kadavu, seen as a Christian and pro-government area. After some years on Kadavu, the Colonial Government thought that the Drauniivi people had learnt their lesson to heed the Government, to accept Christianity and to abandon their old beliefs and ways. They were later allowed to return to the present site of Drauniivi following a probationary period with the Roko Tui Ra at Kadavulailai near the provincial headquarters at Nanukuloa.

A strong fascination with Navosavakadua remains still not only in the Drauniivi area but also more widely throughout many parts of Fiji. A respect for the strong spiritual powers of the Twelve *Yavusa* and particularly for the Drauniivi people manifests itself not only among Fijians but also among Indians. The latter are equally fascinated in, and respectful of the spiritual powers of Uluda and Degei, as may be witnessed by the number of Indians who still visit both Vatukacevaceva and Drauniivi with appropriate offerings.

As I said in my introduction to this chapter, Rakiraki is a magical place.

(f) The yavusa of Namacuku

The *yavusa* of Namacuku, based on the village of Togovere in the Old *tikina* of Raviravi, had myths of common origin with the Vatukaloko polity, but appeared to be an independent group.

The NLC claimed that the ancestral spirit of the Namacuku was a son of Rasare (or -i) levu, the original ancestor of the Kalokolevu Twelve *Yavusa*. I was told differently by Penaia, the presently recognised expert in Namacuku affairs and *dau ni vucu* or chant specialist. He said that the ancestral spirit was Boginiyali, whose connection with Rasarilevu was not clear, although he did not deny it.

> The first settlement was inland from the present village of Togovere, but the Namacuku fled from there during the Rakiraki wars and took shelter with the Navatu people and were settled at Togovere.

> Togovere is closely associated with the Ciri, the Twins, whose place was at Nukutabua on the slopes of the Nakauvadra below Uluda. According to myth they shot Degei's favourite dove, Turukawa, who would wake him up in the morning. The Twins used to go to Togovere to cut mangrove branches for their bows and arrows in the swamps between the village and the sea. Various stones in and around the village and the swamp are shown as places where the Ciri cut the wood, where they sharpened their arrows, where they trod on their way back to the Nakauvadra and where they duly shot Turukawa. This shooting naturally infuriated Degei and led to wars.

I suggest that around the territory of Degei's emissaries and relatives in the Rakiraki and Navatu polities the unifying spiritual force was that of Degei and his associates. To the east, the Twelve *Yavusa* and Namacuku may not have respected Degei to the same extent, and did not need his unifying power. They were sufficiently self-supporting to rely on their own spiritual powers and were keen to show their independence from Degei and his associates. This was mythologically symbolised in the assistance provided by them to the Ciri when they came to seek wood for their bows and arrows to be used to shoot Turukawa and thus to show their lack of respect for Degei. The Namacuku were most likely associated ultimately with the spiritual centre of Navatunigauna/Vatukaloko rather than with Uluda, home of Degei.

9

Polities of West Vuda *Tikina*

The main polities: Vuda *tikina* (western part)—a geographical and political snapshot

Vuda New *tikina* includes the Old *tikina* of Vuda, Sabeto and Vitogo. The Old *tikina* of Vuda and Sabeto comprise the western part of Vuda New *tikina* and were covered in the course of my researches.

The main polities based in these Old *tikina* were, at the time of Cession in 1874, and are still recognised as follows:

Name of *vanua*	Leading *yavusa*	Title of paramount	No. of *yavusa*	Levels of hierarchy	No. of villages
(a) Vuda Old Tikina					
Vuda	Sabutoyatoya	Momo Levu or Tui Vuda	6	2	6
(b) Sabeto Old Tikina					
Sabeto	Conua	Momo or Tui Sabeto	7	2	4

Vuda Old *tikina*: the Vuda socio-political complex

I will now describe in more detail the origins and development of the *yavusa* which were based in the Old *tikina* of Vuda and which comprised the Vuda socio-political complex as it was at about the time of the 1871 Cakobau Government.

The following accounts of the origins and structure of each of the six *yavusa* of the Vuda polity emphasise the simple nature of the polity.

The Vuda vanua comprised the following elements:

(a)   three *yavusa*, based at the present village of Viseisei, including:

(i)   The leading *yavusa*, Sabutoyatoya, whose head is titled the Momo Levu of Vuda or, in eastern phraseology, Tui Vuda. Part of the Sabutoyatoya is based at Namara on the island of Waya Sewa.

(ii)   The two *yavusa* of Tububere and Cawanisa—the latter is now based on the island of Malolo in the province of Nadroga. Part of the Tububere is based at Lomolomo, living with the Vunativi people (apparently once a *yavusa*, but now of anomalous status).

(b)   the *yavusa* of Kai Vuda, based at the present village of Lauwaki, between Viseisei and the city of Lautoka. Part of the Kai Vuda is based at Tavakubu, formerly in the Old *tikina* of Vitogo.

(c)   the two *yavusa* of Navatulevu and Naviyagoisaukova, based at the present village of Abaca (was Nagwagwa). The latter *yavusa* is now almost extinct.

Myths of origin
General

According to the myths of origin of these people, the Sabutoyatoya and the Tububere are closely related by spiritual descent, and trace a common ancestry from Sagavulanavuda, son of Lutunasobasoba who was a member of the crew of the mythical ship, the *Kaunitoni*, which brought the original ancestors of the Fijians from the west to Fiji, where they landed at Vuda. These two *yavusa* claim a common mythical origin and maintain a close myth-based bond with the Cawanisa and the Kai Vuda, because the original ancestors of the Cawanisa and the Kai Vuda also arrived in Fiji on the *Kaunitoni*. The descendants of the four original ancestral spirits comprising these four *yavusa* were essentially coastal people and regarded themselves as the original inhabitants not only of Vuda but also of the whole of Fiji. In fact there are ideological parallels between the bonds uniting these shipmates on the *Kaunitoni* and the bonds which developed between indentured Indian labourers who came to Fiji from India on board the same ship and who created the relationship commonly referred to as *jehaji*. There was thus a close mythical and spiritual bond between the Sabutoyatoya, the Tububere, the Cawanisa and the Kai Vuda, based largely on the arrival of the ancestors aboard the *Kaunitoni* at Vuda. On the other hand, the Navatulevu and the Naviyagoisaukova came from the south side of the Tualeita range from the original settlement of Navatulevu and settled north of the range at Nagwagwa (whence came the ancestors of the Navatulevu *yavusa* of Nadi). They were essentially inland people and newcomers to Vuda territory. Their myths of origin before they were at Nagwagwa associate them with Vitogo.

The Kaunitoni myth

The telling of the myths of the origins and arrival in Fiji of a ship known as the *Kaunitoni* sailing from far to the west of Fiji and arriving at Vuda, and of the original ancestral spirits of the Vuda people and indeed of the Fijian people generally, has not been confined to the Vuda people. As Peter France (1966:107) so elegantly put it:

> This is the legend of the Kaunitoni migration; unlike most Fijian oral traditions, which relate to the exploits of local gods and heroes, it is told from one end of the group to the other. It has been given a place in authoritative books on Fijian history and custom, and has been used as corroborative evidence for the speculations of ethnographer and archaeologist in their reconstructions of Fijian history.

France went on to point out that the early missionaries (Williams, 1858; Carey, 1865 as noted in France 1966:109) or others (Heffernan in the 1880s as also noted in France 1966:109) who were interested in the traditions of the Fijians could find no such origin myth, although there were very early references to Degei and the Nakauvadra. I should add to France's evidence that of Richard Lyth, missionary, who wrote about Degei (1836–1844:87)[1] but nothing about the *Kaunitoni*. The first reference to the *Kaunitoni* myth appears to be that given to sometimes-imaginative Basil Thomson by his Fijian clerk in 1895. Since then the myth was related in detail by Osea Matakorovatu, the Sabutoyatoya representative before the 1914 Native Lands Commission (NLC), in response to questioning by investigators into the origins of the Fijian people.

---

1   (Editors' note) Parke gave the reference as 1844:87 and in the bibliography originally had this as *Buk Rotumah*. This 8-page primer, a copy is in the National Library of Australia in Canberra, seems an unlikely source and so we have substituted the more likely reference to his journals of 1836–1844.

France concluded (1966:112–113):

> So the Kaunitoni legend was born, of missionary parentage, and nurtured by the enquiries of the Native
> Lands Commission. Its general acceptance at the present time is one of the products of Fiji's transition
> from a geographical expression to a nation; it had the same socially cohesive qualities as the national coat
> of arms and the flag. But it is no more closely related to Fijian culture than they; it does not apparently
> antedate them.

Linguists may also point out that the name 'Kaunitoni' must be suspect as a Bauan invention,
because the initial element in the name, *kau*, is standard Fijian, whereas the western communalect
equivalent is *kai*. Vuda people refer to the name always as Kaunitoni, not Kainitoni which is
what they should say if the name is a genuine Vuda term. I can only say, in comparison, that the
Nakauvadra is always so pronounced in Rakiraki and in Vuda; that again the communalect form
of *kai* is the same in Rakiraki as it is in Vuda; and that no-one to my knowledge has suggested that
the Nakauvadra and its associated myths are Bauan inventions. I think that any such argument
to throw doubt on the *Kaunitoni* myth is but a linguistic quibble.

The explorations with which this part of the monograph is concerned relate to Vuda and its origins
and development as seen by the Vuda people. So the primary version of the myth which is related
here is the Vuda account given to me orally in 1995 by the late Ratu Epeli Vukinamoceyawa,
iTaukei Nakelo, the then recognised expert on the affairs of the Sabutoyatoya. He was born in
1910. This account was checked with him against, first, an account which he had written many
years before as part of a more general account of the affairs of the *yavusa* for future generations;
and, secondly, the 'official' account given by Osea, the Sabutoyatoya representative, as recorded
by the NLC in 1914.

The iTaukei Nakelo said that:

> Tura from Turkestan (Turakisitani, Esia) married Ranadi of Thebes (Cevi, Itipita), and they had two
> children, Lutunasobasoba and Kubunavanua. Tura's second wife was Naiovabasali, and their children were
> Degei, Waicalanavanua, Nakumilevu, Rokola and Erovu. They moved to Tanganyika.

> Three ships, the *Kaunitoni*, the *Kaunitera* and the *Duiyabaki*, later set out from Tanganyika and sailed
> east until they came to the Solomons. Lutunasobasoba was captain of the *Kaunitoni*, Kumilevu of the
> *Kaunitera* and Kubunavanua of the *Duiyabaki*. While at the Solomons, they quarrelled over a turtle the
> crew of the *Kaunitera* had eaten and not shared with the other crews. Kumilevu and his crew were left
> behind in the Solomons, and the other two ships left. The *Duiyabaki*, with Kubunavanua, went ahead and
> sailed to Lomaloma in the Lau group.

> The *Kaunitoni* followed, with many on board including Lutunasobasoba, Degei, Waicalanavanua, Rokola,
> Erovu and a number of women and children. The ship sailed on until they reached the land now known as
> Fiji. When they arrived, it was night and, as the moon was rising, they came opposite to a headland which
> they called Muainavula (Moon Point). They went on and struck the edge of the reef, and the canoe was
> holed (*lamu*), and so they called this edge of the reef Nalamu.

The 1914 NLC added that:

> when they passed through the passage in the reef which they called Lomoci, what is referred to as their *kato
> ni vola* fell overboard. It is said that this was a stone box in which there was an *ivola ni kawa* or account
> of the kin of Lutunasobasoba, engraved in stone. [iTaukei Nakelo referred to the box as a box of *tabua* or
> whales' teeth].

They sailed on and when they approached land they saw a place where coconuts were growing. Here they anchored, and the *Kaunitoni* was beached. The NLC said that the place where they landed was called Yavuni, and this is considered to be the very first place where the Fijians stayed, albeit briefly.

Ciba and his father, of the Kai Vuda at Lauwaki, told me that:

> Lutunasobasoba told the crew to go and pile up (*koronia* in communalect; *binia* in standard) some coconuts, and they called the place where they anchored Naikorokoro. When ashore, they sent Bulouniwasawasa to Rotuma.

This has an interesting parallel in a Rotuma myth (Parke 2001:43) that when the *Kaunitoni* passed by the island of Rotuma a woman was put ashore and became Hanitema'us, the wild woman of the woods and perhaps representing the earliest inhabitants of Rotuma. She tried to stop Raho (the first of the people from Tonga and Samoa who allegedly founded the Rotuman population) from breaking up the island. Rotuma, though culturally and linguistically different from Fiji, became part of the Crown Colony of Fiji in 1881, and such legends may have arisen as a pseudo-traditional connection to create some emotional relationship between these Government-created bedfellows.

iTaukei Nakelo went on to say that:

> they brought Lutunasobasoba ashore by carrying him in their arms (*kabe* in communalect; *keve* in standard), and they called the place Kabekokira (*kira* being the old communalect word for a man of high rank. [The NLC account said that Kira was a woman, and that it was she who was brought ashore in someone's arms]. They followed the coast southwards till they came to a river mouth. Lutunasobasoba was carried across on someone's back (*likoti* in local communalect; *dreketi* in standard Fijian). The place is now known as Dreketi, but iTaukei Nakelo said that it was formerly called Likoti. They then followed on along the coast until they came to a place where some *tabua* had been washed up after the box of *tabua* had fallen overboard at Lomoci. So they called the place Kasanatabua (the *tabua* drifted to shore). Then they all went to Vuda where they founded their settlement, and a house for Lutunasobasoba was built called Naciriyawa (to commemorate their long sea travel). Meanwhile the *Kaunitoni* was repaired on the beach at Yavuni.

> Lutunasobasoba was very upset about his box, and sent some of the crew to look for the box. They made two searches, once as far as the Yasawa (*sa yawa* means 'far') but failed to find it. Lutunasobasoba became angry and sent Degei and some of the crew to look for a place for themselves. So the place where they split up was called Viseisei (meaning 'split up'). Later Lutunasobasoba moved east and founded the village of Vuda. On the way, he rested at Naisasaro, a little islet in the mangroves south of the present village of Viseisei. He maintained his rage about the loss of his box; and his younger children including Rokomoutu and Rokomatu fled east to a place called Vatubabasaga, referring to the splitting up (*basaga*) of the chief's family.

The NLC added that:

> the second time the *Kaunitoni* had gone to look for the box, the wind had blown strongly and the ship had drifted away as far east as the island of Malake. Degei and Waicala and the others whom Lutunasobasoba had sent away to explore the countryside followed the coast to Tavua and then climbed up to the Nakauvadra Range from where they saw the *Kaunitoni* had arrived off Malake. They went down to await the *Kaunitoni* at Nacilaumomo Point, where they joined up with the crew. They discussed what they had found and agreed to tell Lutunasobasoba that they had discovered a good site for a settlement on the Nakauvadra. So the *Kaunitoni* returned to Vuda.

iTaukei Nakelo continued that:

when the message came that a good site for a village had been found on the Nakauvadra Range, Lutunasobasoba told them to go ahead and clear the land and build houses there. When all was ready there, someone should come back and tell those at Vuda who should then go on up there. So the site was cleared and the houses were built; and the Mata ni Vanua (ceremonial spokesman) was sent from Nakauvadra to inform Lutunasobasoba who was at his house called Naciriyawa.

When the message came that all was ready on the Nakauvadra, Lutunasobasoba's children at Vatubabasaga were brought back. The chief said that Sagavulunavuda (the eldest) and some others should continue to occupy the original house mound of Fiji at Vuda but that the others should go up to the Nakauvadra.

So began the chiefly journey to the Nakauvadra. The land party began by climbing the point at Edronu at the west end of the Tualeita Range and then followed the Range eastwards to the Nakauvadra Range. As they went, some went ahead breaking off (viti) the branches. They reached a hill where they rested, and the leader said that the land should be called Viti or Fiji. The hill where they rested was called Naisauniwaqa. From here the party moved on, until they came to a place where Lutunasobasoba called together his children and the other members of the party and told them that he was very weak. He bade farewell to his children and told them not to go to Degei. They should divide up and go and look for different places where they might settle. Then he died, and was buried. The place where he died was called Cibutanagodrodro or Magodro. The hill where he was buried was called Naweicavu in Magodro, and to this day no grass will grow on the traditional site of his grave.

So his children divided up. Buisavulu went to Bureta, Moturiki; Rokomoutu went to Verata; Tuinayau went to Batiki; Rokomatu went to Rewa; Daunisai went to Kabara. Of Lutunasobasoba's other children, Kaliova Revurevu had been born prematurely (lutudole) as the Kaunitoni passed the islet of Narokorokoyawa, to the south of the Yasawas, and here he stayed. Sagavulunavuda, the eldest son of Lutunasobasoba, remained at Vuda, and was regarded as the original ancestral spirit of the Sabutoyatoya yavusa.

The NLC, on the other hand, said that:

when the message had been received that a good site for a settlement had been found on the Nakauvadra Range, Lutunasobasoba said that Rokola and Waqabalabala should sail along the coast with his children (Buisavulu (fem), Rokomoutu, Vueti, Ratu and Daunisai); and that Degei and Waicala should go by land to Nakauvadra. So the Kaunitoni sailed off whilst Degei and Waicala climbed up from Edronu and followed the Tualeita (one of the spirit paths known as the Wakanivugayali) along the continuous ridge to Nakauvadra. Lutunasobasoba, Erovu and Sagavulu remained behind at Vuda.

When the Tunimata (communalect) or Matanivanua (standard) reported that the houses on the Nakauvadra had been completed, Lutunasobasoba said that Rokola (the original ancestor of the carpenters who settled at Narauyaba on the Nakauvadra) should make a wooden drum on the Nakauvadra as the lali ni vanua (drum for vanua messages to be sent from Nakauvadra to Vuda). The drum was called Rogorogo i Vuda (reporting to Vuda).

Lutunasobasoba remained at Vuda with his son, Sagavulunavuda, but as he became very weak, he thought a great deal about those on the Nakauvadra and planned to go there. He gathered together those who remained with him at Vuda, bade them farewell (Gifford [1952:349] said that a large rock fenced in at the present village of Lomolomo was the scene of this farewell, but this is nowadays denied at Lomolomo) and set off inland towards the Nakauvadra. When he was close to death on the Nakauvadra, he told his daughter Buisavulu (who was his eldest child on the Nakauvadra) that when he died, she and her brothers should not remain on Nakauvadra with Degei, because Degei was a hard (*kaukauwa*) man and always opposed to his elder brother's (Lutunasobasoba's) wishes. Then Lutunasobasoba died and was buried at Bua, Nakauvadra.

Buisavulu said to Rokola that they should all leave the Nakauvadra and go off in the *Kaunitoni*. So they went back on board with Rokola and Waqabalabala, to look for land. The *Kaunitoni* eventually reached Bureta. Degei and Waicala remained on the Nakauvadra.

Development of the Vuda *vanua*

The Vuda *vanua* as it developed was based on the descendants of those who remained behind. These descendants were:

- the spiritually related *yavusa* of Sabutoyatoya and Tububere descended from Lutunasobasoba's son Sagavulunavuda, who established the old village of Lomolomo;

- the anomalous *yavusa* of Vunativi, claiming descent from Sagavulunavuda through his son Draulunavua and his grandson Natuira but maintaining formal association with the Cawanisa at Naqoqa. They were first living at Lomolomo;

- the *yavusa* of Cawanisa descended from Sadidi, a member of the crew of the *Kaunitoni*, who were once living at Lomolomo with the descendants of Sagavulunavuda but who later established the old inland village of Naqoqa; and

- the *yavusa* of Kai Vuda descended from Erovu, half-brother of Lutunasobasoba, who established the village of Vuda below Korovatu crag.

In the course of time, while the Sabutoyatoya and the Tububere remained at Lomolomo, and the Kai Vuda stayed at Vuda (Korovatu), the Cawanisa moved inland to Naqoqa. The Navatulevu and the Naviyagoisaukova *yavusa* moved across the Tualeita Range from Navatulevu (near Navilawa, below Koroiyanitu peak) to the northern slopes, ending up at Nagwagwa. These *yavusa* heeded the authority of the Sabutoyatoya, as at that time the strongest polity in the area.

The NLC of 1914 said that:

> Sagavulunavuda, the eldest child of Lutunasobasoba and Naiobasali, came with his father and siblings on the *Kaunitoni*, and settled with his father at Vuda at Korovatu crag. He married Uqetenavanua, the daughter of Erovu (the original ancestral spirit of the Kai Vuda, whose *yavu*, Natamayawa, was also at Vuda), and they had three children, Uludranavanua, Naivilawasa and Qera.

> Sagavulunavuda remained at Vuda, but established at Lomolomo a settlement for Draulunavanua, whose house there was called Naturubasaga. Naivilawasa and Qera also went to stay at Lomolomo, together with the offspring of Sadidi, a member of the crew of the *Kaunitoni*, whose descendants were the Cawanisa *yavusa*. Later, Naivilawasa was sent by Sagavulunavuda to Rakiraki (the Rakiraki account was that Naivilawasa was a woman who came down from the Nakauvadra and, according to one account, married Waqabalabala, the original ancestor of the Navatu people); and Qera was sent to Nadroga where his descendants comprised the Leweiqera group.

> Draulunavanua married Nasaubuli (whom iTaukai Nakelo said was his mother), and they had two sons, Natuira and Natuilevu.

> Natuilevu went to Malolo. He married Lewatulekeleke of Vitogo, and their daughter was Sobu, (with a macron over the u). Their descendants at Solevu, Malolo, comprised the Kai Lawa (the leading group of the Malolo *yavusa*, whose paramount was titled Tui Lawa).

Natuira remained at Lomolomo, and married Munudranaqo, and they had a number of children, the descendants of the first five being the Sabutoyatoya *yavusa*. The descendants of the sixth, Vurabere, comprised the Tububere *yavusa*. Another *yavusa*, the Vunativi, also claimed to be descended from another son of Natuira, whom they said was the second eldest.

So far as the origins and development of each of the *yavusa* named earlier and of Vuda *vanua* generally, with their fission and fusion and their interrelationship between themselves and with polities outside Vuda are concerned, it matters little from this point of view whether Lutunasobasoba died on the Nakauvadra or in Magodro on his way up to the Nakauvadra. What is important is to remember the myths of origin of those *yavusa* which claimed descent from either Lutunasobasoba's son, Sagavulunavuda (that is, the Sabutoyatoya and the Tububere), or Erovu, Lutunasobasoba's half-brother (that is, the Kai Vuda) or Sadidi, who sailed on the *Kaunitoni* with the half-brothers, Lutunasobasoba and Erovu, (that is, the Cawanisa) who, according to the *Kaunitoni* myths as given above, landed together at Vuda.

Since the Sabutoyatoya were recorded by the 1914 NLC to be the leading *yavusa* at the time of Cession, it is their myth as given by the Commission and checked with the iTaukei Nakelo which will be given and discussed first. Not surprisingly, the early mythical genealogical evidence given by the NLC differs in detail from the account given by iTuakei Nakelo; but a general picture emerges as the basis for a useful discussion of how the Sabutoyatoya now understand or devise their mythical origins and the development of their *yavusa;* its position in the Vuda *vanua*; its relationship with other polities in the contexts of neighbours in the west and Fijian polities generally and indeed with the outside world.

Sabutoyatoya origin myth

iTaukei Nakelo agreed in discussion, that:

> Sagavulu was the son of Lutunasobasoba and Naiobasali. Although he had one written account that said that Sagavulunavuda had married Naiobasali, he claimed that this was wrong and that he had married Nasaubuli, and they had a son, Draulunavanua, who married Uqetenavanua, daughter of Erovu.

iTaukei Nakelo said that there were various accounts about the descendants of Draulunavuda. One was to the effect that he had five children—Tabutovatova, who stayed at Vuda and married Nadradra; Tuilevu who went to Malolo; Tutuvanua who went to Nadi; Qera who went to Nadroga; and Naivilawasa who went to Rakiraki. It was from these five brothers that the *matanitū ni Ra vakara* originated, that is, a western confederation stretching from Rakiraki to Nadroga and comprising the present coastal areas of the provinces of Ra, Ba and Nadroga. Within this overall confederation there was the so-called Ra ni (Y)Abola, comprising the *vanua* of Vuda, Sabeto, Vitogo, Malolo, Waya, Naviti, Viwa and Yakete; as well as Vaturu, Saunaka (the Kai Ua) and the Kovacaki. The leader of Ra ni (Y)Abola was the Vuda *vanua*. iTaukei Nakelo, following his preferred account, went on to say that:

> Draulunavuda and Uqetenavanua had two children—Natuira who married Munudranaqo and remained at Lomolomo and Natuilevu who married Lewatulekeleke of Vitogo and went to the island of Malolo (their daughter was Sobu, see below).

> The descendants of Natuira were the Sabutoyatoya *yavusa* of Vuda *vanua;* and the descendants of Natuilevu were the Leweilawa who became the leading *yavusa* in Malolo under the paramountcy of the Tui Lawa. Natuira had six children, all of whom were born at Lomolomo. The five eldest were the progenitors of five *mataqali* of the Sabutoyatoya *yavusa*. The eldest was called LeiSabutoyatoya and his descendants were the Elevuka *mataqali,* being the leading *mataqali* of the Sabutoyatoya *yavusa*. Lei is the old Vuda equivalent

of *taukei* or 'owner of'—in this case, the 'owner of Sabutoyatoya' or chiefly *yavu* of the Sabutoyatoya and thereby the chief of the Sabutoyatoya. As Natuira was on the point of death, his wife touched his arm and she became pregnant and duly gave birth to the sixth child, Vurabere (meaning 'appeared late'), whose descendants became the Tububere *yavusa*.

Leisabutoyatoya married, first, Savere, a woman of the Leweiwavuwavu of Sabeto, and, secondly Sobu, the daughter of Natuilevu who had gone to Malolo, and there were sons born from each wife. Rasilasila and Vuluma were sons of the first, and Bogisa and Uqeuqe were sons of the second.

The younger brother appointed leader: clouds on the horizon?

iTaukei Sawaieke went on to explain that:

> it was decided that a leader of the Sabutoyatoya should be appointed, and the descendants of Natuilevu from Malolo, the Kai Vuda and the Cawanisa came and carried out a ceremony for the installation of Bogisa, the son of the second wife of Leisabutoyatoya, in the presence of Rasilasila, the son of the first wife.

The iTaukei Nakelo, a ninth generation descendant of Bogisa, explained to me that it was sometimes the practice for the younger son to be installed so that he could be concerned with secular matters of the *yavusa*, while the eldest son was concerned with keeping in good communication with the spirit of the original ancestor and so maintaining the well-being and power of the *yavusa*, through his *sau* or *mana*. I have noted that in some other cases where the younger brother is appointed leader, the practice led to family arguments. However, in this case, the position may have been accepted during this generation, although the two second sons went to Sabeto, where Vuluma's descendants were the Naceru, and Uqeuqe's descendants were the Nasigatoka. It is not clear why they split away from their families at Lomolomo, but their departure may have reflected some underlying ill-feeling of jealousy developing from the installation of the younger half-brother as the leader of the Sabutoyatoya.

Bila, son of Bogisa, was next to be installed as leader of the Sabutoyatoya. iTaukei Nakelo said that he was installed at Lomolomo, presumably before the split up at Lomolomo discussed below.

The NLC recorded that Rasilasila had two sons, Natuwawa and Ledra'uwaqa; whereas another account I have been given by iTaukei Nakelo claimed that he had one son, Batimoko, whose sons were Natuwawa and Ledruwaqa; and a third account claimed that he had one son, Masibalavu, whose sons were Ledruwaqa and Batimoko. iTaukei Nakelo's preferred version was the second, and since it corresponds with the NLC account, except for the detail of the paternity of the two brothers, this is the version I record here.

Veibenu Vea—the breadfruit fight: serious trouble

The account given to me by iTaukei Nakelo claims that Bogisa had two sons, Bila, and Tuiweli, and also that Naereilagi was a son of Bogisa. It also says that Naereilagi was the son of Rasilasila. So what followed was a quarrel either between sons of the half-brothers, Rasilasila and Bogisa, or between two brothers. iTaukei Nakelo said that they were sons of the half-brothers, and it makes more sense to see the quarrel as between the sons of two half-brothers, the younger of whom, Bogisa, had been given the leadership of the Sabutoyatoya.

Be that as it may, iTaukei Nakelo said that:

> Following the deaths of Rasilasila and Bogisa, hatred arose between Ledruwaqa and Naereilagi, two of their sons, which erupted in the incident referred to widely in Vuda as the Veibenu Vea. These two made a mess of each other by smearing overripe breadfruit over each other's heads (*veibenu vea*). This was a terrible insult from two aspects. First, it was a serious matter for anyone to touch and even more so, to disturb the

head of a person of rank. [One reason that has been suggested as to why the Reverend Thomas Baker was killed and eaten, up in the mountainous interior of Viti Levu, in 1867 was that he had touched the head of the local chief]. Secondly, the *tabu kai* or sacred tree of these people was the breadfruit, the name of which could be hardly mentioned without serious consequences. The use of breadfruit for such a quarrel would have been unthinkable and could only have led to the gravest of trouble. Such an incident could well have been an outward manifestation of deep-seated jealousy being felt by the descendant of Rasilasila, the elder son who had apparently been passed over for leadership. The Sabutoyatoya *yavusa* split up, and scattered with the others living at Lomolomo.

The elder son of Rasilasila, Natuwawa, went to Naqoqa with the Cawanisa (descendants of Sadidi). His descendants were the Nadravua or Ketenatukani (descendants of the elder brother) and that is where they remained.

Ledruwaqa, the second son of Rasilasila, had married a woman from Vitogo, and he went to Vitogo together with Navunicagi, elder son of Bila (the eldest son of Bogisa). Ledruwaqa's descendants were the Nakuruyawa, and Navunicagi's descendants were the Navicaki sub-division of the Eluvuka *mataqali* of the Sabutoyatoya *yavusa*. The younger son of Bila, Tuiweli went to Votua, Ba. His descendants were the Nasalivakarua

Then the chief of the Kai Vuda at Korovatu, Vuda, said that those of the Sabutoyatoya who had scattered from Lomolomo should be brought to Vuda. So Ledruwaqa, Navunicagi and, apparently, Naereilagi went to Korovatu.

The NLC stated that:

> Bila as head of the Sabutoyatoya also went to Vuda. When his party came to Korovatu, they entered the *beto* or spirit house where a fan made of *masei* (symbol of paramountcy) was hanging. Bila was sweating, and the chief of the Kai Vuda said that the fan should be taken down and Bila should be fanned with it [I was told when Bila entered the *beto*, the question of paramountcy was being discussed by the Kai Vuda; and the fan which was hanging up turned and pointed in the direction of the Sabutoyatoya chief, indicating its sanction for his appointment as paramount].

Another account from the Kai Vuda to me said that Bila was already dead and that it was his son, Navunicagi, who was appointed paramount over the Kai Vuda. There is no way of reconciling these two accounts, and iTaukei Nakelo was ambivalent. It probably does not matter. What is important is that the Kai Vuda who, before, were probably the leading *yavusa*, now agreed to accept the Sabutoyatoya as paramounts.

Irrespective of the precise nature of the incident of the fan, the symbolic gesture either by the fan or by the chief of the Kai Vuda indicated recognition by the Kai Vuda that Bila (or Navunicagi) of the Sabutoyatoya should be made the paramount and that the Kai Vuda would heed his authority. Whatever the socio-political reasons may have been, the choice was hallowed by *mana* or *sau,* by the symbolism of paramountcy in the west, the *masei* fan. Whatever the accounts may be saying, there is still an underlying implication as well as occasional hints that the Kai Vuda were at one stage the paramounts in the area and that the Sabutoyatoya were either subservient to the Kai Vuda, or were peripheral to the Vuda heartland and became paramounts either through force of arms or through superior political ambition and ability. The current myths may well be hiding a military defeat of the Kai Vuda, and both the iTaukei Nakelo and the Kai Vuda people with whom I discussed the matter agreed that it was indeed a possibility.

Leadership challenge

To recap, Leisabutoyatoya had two wives, the elder son of the first being Bogisa, and the elder son of the second being Rasilasila. After the deaths of Bogisa's son, Bila, and his grandson, Navunicagi, both of whom had held the leadership of the Sabutoyatoya, the children of Navunicagi had met and agreed that the eldest, Natavuke, should succeed to the leadership. This was not acceptable to the Nakuruyawa, descendants of Ledruwaqa, the son of Rasilasila, and they challenged the appointment. The following account is based on that by the NLC and on lengthy discussions I held with the iTaukei Nakelo:

> The Tububere people had been growing coconuts, but it was noticed the nuts were being taken; so they asked Natavuke to put a *tabu* on the trees. Such a *tabu* was indicated by the placing of reeds by the trees. The Nakuruyawa removed the reeds and took them to Natavuke's younger brother, Nasorowale, in order to show their disagreement about the appointment of Natavuke and to indicate their preference for him. Natavuke was in Nadroga at the time, and when he came back to Vuda, he was told what had happened to the *tabu* he had imposed. The removal of the *tabu* represented a symbolic challenge to his appointment. He acceded to the challenge, and Nasorowale was installed as leader of the Sabutoyatoya, and paramount of the Vuda *vanua*. Another account said that Nasorowale was appointed successor to Navunicagi, and that his son, Natavukeniwailala, was accepted as 'probationary' (*wawa*) leader but was never confirmed. The appointment went instead to his son Ratu Josaia Natoko No.1, who was the first to be installed after Cession in 1874.

iTaukei Nakelo accepted the second account to the NLC. This account may well be more politically acceptable nowadays, when people like iTaukai Nakelo are trying so hard to give an impression of solidarity among the Sabutoyatoya, an impression which they saw as rudely negated by what they regarded as the treacherous behaviour of Dr. Timoci Bavadra in accepting in 1987 the post of Prime Minister of what they regarded as a pro-Indian and largely anti-Fijian Government. Bavadra was a member of the chiefly Eluvuka *mataqali,* and of Werevakaca sub-division, a group whose traditional responsibility was to protect the Momo Levu of Vuda. Bavadra died medically of cancer, or, as I was told, he got his just desserts through the revengeful powers of the insulted spirits of Vuda.

Interaction with other vanua: Sabeto, Bau and Nadi

Sabeto

The Sabutoyatoya *yavusa* was related to the Leweiwavuwavu (at an early time the leading *yavusa* of the Sabeto *vanua*), through the marriage between Leisabotoyatoya and Savere. Connections were furthered when the Naceru (descendants of Rasilasila's brother, Vuluma) and the Nasigatoka (descendants of Bogisa's brother, Uqeuqe) came to settle with the Sabautoyatoya. When Nayalobo, the son of Mataitoga, the paramount of Sabeto, plotted to kill his father, Mataitoga found out and Nayalobo took refuge with the Sabutoyatoya. Mataitoga sent *tabua* seeking the death of Nayalobo. Some wanted to protect him but others tricked him into going to Naqoqa. Nasorowale, leader of the Sabutoyatoya, ordered Sabori, a *qaqa* or strong man of the Werevakaca (the protectors of the Sabutoyatoya), to take a gun and shoot him in his house at Naqoqa. The shot hit his thigh and as Nayalobo rushed out of the house, he was struck dead by a spear. The Nasigatoka people came from Sabeto and collected the body and took it to Sabeto. Mataitoga wept.

Bau

Deryck Scarr (personal communication) tells me that there was a traditional path between Vuda and Bau, but I have not been able to determine its origin. Nevertheless this would explain how

Cakobau came to seek assistance once from Vuda. On this occasion, Cakobau was attacking the rebellious Lovoni people on the island of Ovalau. He tried again and again but could not achieve his aims. Sabori of Werevakaca, Sabutoyatoya, was renowned even in Bau as an exceptionally strong warrior, and Cakobau sent for Sabori to bring an army to help him. I was told by Ratu Vuki that Sabori went alone with his dog, and such was his repute than the people all fled. Sabori burned the village and killed one man with his gun and the dog sat in the blood. Cakobau would not believe his story until he brought the head of the man and the dog all covered with blood. Cakobau rewarded Sabori but never gave anything to the dog. In spite of the latter omission, from this time relations between Vuda and Bau were such that when Cakobau came to attack the west and especially Sabeto (see below), he apparently did not treat Vuda with anything but respect.

Nadi

Nakadrudru, a woman of the Nabati or leading group of Nadi, came to marry Wiliame Tuiwele, one of the highest-ranking chiefs of the Eluvuka *mataqali* and Sabutoyatoya. She lived with Tuiwele and duly became pregnant. However, in Tuiwele's absence on a visit to the Mamanuca islands, his elder brother, Ratu Jone Tavai, told the woman to marry him and not to marry Tuiwele. Tuiwele, on his return, was upset and told the woman to go back to Nadi and live with a certain man there. She went back and gave birth to Tevita Nawaqa. Later these two got married in Nadi.

Tuiwele and the Vuda people went to Nadi to *laki veikovaraki* or show their wishes that Tuiwele's son should come under the protection of the Nadi people. Tevita was never invited to return to Vuda, and he never participated in Vuda ceremonies. Thus Tevita Tavai came to be counted as a member of the Nakuruvarua chiefly group of the Navatulevu of Nadi, and not of the Nakelo (second most chiefly group of the Eluvuka of Sabutoyatoya); eventually he became the Momo Levu of Nadi.

Final movements

The Sabutoyatoya who were still at Vuda moved to a settlement at Basagarua, where the two rivers, the Varaqe and the Vuda meet. This became a war village at the time when Nayalobo was seeking refuge from Mataitoga of Sabeto. It then changed its name to Mereke, to commemorate, so the tradition goes, the arrival of an American ship in 1835, bringing Christianity and leaving a Bible with the Momo Levu. It was duly buried with him. Thus the Vuda people claim that Christianity came first to Vuda before the missionaries arrived from the east to settle in Lakeba later in the same year.

After Cession, the Sabutoyatoya moved back to the site claimed to be where the crew of the *Kaunitoni* split up (*viseisei*). The present village is known as Viseisei. At the time of the NLC in 1914, the Sabutoyatoya except those who had left long ago, were divided as follows:

- Rasilasila's descendants were split up, some at Naviyago (Vitogo), some remained at Viseisei and some at the new village of Lomolomo.
- Vuluma's descendants were still at Sabeto.
- Bogisa's descendants were at Viseisei.
- Uqeuqe's descendants were still at Sabeto.

The wanderings of the descendants of the other sons of Natuira

The Navocotia, now at Lomolomo

Leinavocotia, the second son of Natuira and brother of Leisabutoyatoya, had two sons, Ralevu and Naocoivalu, whose descendants were the Ruma and the Nailavanitawa respectively. At the time of the quarrels revolving round the Veibenu Vea incident at Lomolomo, the senior group, the Ruma, scattered and were settled at Vuda while the 'younger brothers', the Nainavanitawa, were sent by the Kai Vuda to live at Dreketi, a site in the mangroves at the coast. Here they lived with the Vuda people known as the Kai Kuruvalu and they were given planting land (*ivakova*). The behaviour of the Ruma was so arrogant that they were sent away to join the others at Dreketi. This behaviour continued and culminated when one of the Ruma made pregnant one of the wives of Nasorowale, the Momo Levu of the Sabutoyatoya *yavusa* and of Vuda *vanua*. Nasorowale burned Dreketi and the Ruma fled to Vitogo. Here they stayed until ceremonies of apology and reconciliation (*soro*) were performed, and the Ruma were brought back to Dreketi. From here they shifted inland to Nasauva, because of water shortages, and there they stayed until Cession. After Cession, they moved from Nasauva to the new village of Lomolomo, where they associated themselves (*kabi*) with the Vunativi.

The Naciriyawa, now at Viseisei

Leinawaka, the third son of Natuira, and his descendants lived in that part of the village of Lomolomo known as Nabalei. Following the Veibenu Vea incident, the descendants went to join the Kai Vuda at Vuda, where the *yavu* of the eldest son, Vuluma, was called Naciriyawa, reflecting the name of the *yavu* of Lutunasobasoba. Later they moved to Mereke and then to Viseisei

One of the most interesting features of the account of the Leinawaka is that it may help to solve an archaeological mystery. The NLC recorded that the third of the sons of Leinawaka was called Leinagaucia and that his *yavu* was named Naqaucia. Gifford (1951b: 202) who carried out excavations at Korovatu, Vuda, referred to a visit to 'the site of the temple of Nagathia, an oracular god represented by a stone 5 ft high and about 1½ ft in diameter'. In the 1990s we searched in vain for this stone, and those living in the area of old Lomolomo had never heard of it. Solomone, the *bete* or priest who lived at Lomolomo and was my chief guide, knew nothing of the stone or of Nagacia. It is quite likely that the names Nagacia and Naqaucia are in fact the same, and that the site which Gifford was shown was the *yavu* Naqaucia. The placing of a monolith on a *yavu* associated with ancestral spirits was a common practice, and while it may have existed on Nagaucia when Gifford saw it, the likely site of the *yavu* has been a cane-field for a long time, and the monolith may well have been buried or removed.

The Boutolu at Namara, Waya Sewa

The descendants of the fourth son of Natuira, Leiboutolu, were the Boutolu who are now mostly on the island of Waya Sewa, north of the island of Tokoriki and south of the island of Yasawa in the main Yasawa archipelago. Leiboutolu had one son, Tavutunawailala, who would keep on talking to his elders at Lomolomo until they sent him away. Seeing smoke there, he went to Navakai on Malolo, where his talkative manner persisted. The Malolo people asked the Vuda people to take him back but the Vuda people refused. So the Malolo people built him a village on the island of Mana, between the Malolo and the Mamanuca islands, and gave him the island on which to settle. Those on the nearby island of Tokoriki saw him and, as a member of the highly respected Sabutoyatoya *yavusa*, invited him to join them and be their chief. So he stayed at Tokoriki and married a local woman.

Following a split in the leadership among the Yabola people of Vuda, a group went to Waya Sewa where they settled. Not long after, two chiefly people of Solevu, Malolo went exploring and came to Waya Sewa. Having seen that the island was inhabited, one went back to Solevu, and the other stayed and was invited to join the Yabola (later known as the Waya Sewa) group. They divided the island between them. The Waya Sewa learnt that Tavutunawailala was on Tokoriki, and because he was a member of the paramount group at their place of origin at Vuda, invited (*lakovi*) him to come and be their chief. They presented him with some earth to indicate that both the people and the land were his. So he and his wife went there, and their descendants are still known as the Boutolu and were living in the village of Namara at the time of my main visits.

The Leweilomo, at Nabila, Nadroga

Very little is known in Vuda about the descendants of Tuisavere, the fifth son of Natuira, except that his two sons left Lomolomo and drifted south to Likuri where they were shipwrecked. They were found and taken to Malolo, having left Vuda for good. Their descendants, according to iTaukei Nakelo, now live at Nabila, Nadroga, where they are known as the Leweilomo.

The Vunativi, at Lomolomo

The surviving elements of the Vunativi are presently living in the village of Lomolomo, together with that part of the Tububere who are not living at Viseisei. It is problematic whether the Vunativi are descendants of Sadidi (and thus connected by descent with the Cawanisa, see below); or from Sagavulunavuda through his son, Natuira. Natuira had several sons from whom were descended the Sabutoyatoya *yavusa*, and the Vunativi may have been descended from the second son, Leivunativi.

The Vunativi at some stage seem to have had *yavusa* status, and were divided into three *mataqali*, the Kacowaqa (including a sub-group known as the Dele), Koronikalai and Tokoriki. When Gifford was working at Korovatu, he excavated a *yavu* known as Dele, which had been the mound of the house of Navoleone, who died in 1887 and was buried in Lomolomo cemetery (Gifford 1951b:199).

The NLC of Wilkinson in the 1890s recorded the original ancestor of the Vunativi as Sadidi. During the 1914 Commission investigations of Maxwell, the Vunativi explained to the Sabutoyatoya chief that their real original ancestor was not Sadidi but Sagavulunavuda, as claimed above. They presented a *tabua* of request to the Sabutoyatoya chief, asking that their true position as a *mataqali* of the Sabotoyatoya be not revealed. They wished to continue to be associated with the Cawanisa with whom they had been living for so long since leaving the rest of the Sabutoyatoya after the Veibenu Vea. The 1914 NLC confirmed the decision of Wilkinson that the original ancestor of the Vunativi was Sadidi but that they were a separate *yavusa* from the Cawanisa and not a mataqali of the Sabutoyatoya. Solomone of the Sabutoyatoya in Lomolomo, who was the *bete* or priest, told me that the current tradition is that the Vunativi were a separate *yavusa* descended from Sagavulunavuda and closely associated with the Sabutoyatoya, being descended from Leivunativi who was probably a son of Natuira. I have therefore discussed them here, following my discussion of the sons of Natuira, rather than after the discussion on the Cawanisa, in spite of what the NLC recorded. Officers working at present in the NLC are somewhat dubious about the accounts of the Vuda people, because they were recorded in circumstances of non-cooperation and refusal to answer questions. I therefore question their findings in respect of the Vunativi, and consider that Solomone's account may accord with what the Vuda people considered to be the position but which was hidden from the NLC.

I was given another account in Lomolomo to the effect the Vunativi were the first to settle at Naqoqa, inland from Lomolomo, followed by the Tububere who heeded the authority of the Vunativi. Finally the Cawanisa arrived to settle at Naqoqa, and they too heeded the authority of the Vunativi. It is probable that the origins and development of the Vunativi cannot be resolved with any degree of certainty. Unfortunately the iTaukei Vunativi, the head of the Vunativi, was too ill or unwilling to be able to discuss the matter with me, and no one else of the Vunativi was prepared to represent the group in discussions. The chiefly *yavu* of Vunativi is preserved in

Lomolomo, where, as in the case of the Kai Vuda, there are two installation stones lying on top of the *yavu*. They are half-covered with grass, and will probably soon become as completely obscured as will be the origins of the Vunativi themselves, the latter perhaps deliberately so.

The Tububere

The Tububere at present live in the villages of Viseisei and Lomolomo. iTaukei Sawaieke is the title of the head of the Tububere generally and of the Viseisei branch in particular. The head of the Lomolomo branch heeds the authority of the iTaukei Sawaieke, who in turn heeds the authority of the Momo Levu of Vuda. It should be noted that the paramount of the Naua people of Saunaka, south of Vuda and east of Nadi, is also titled iTaukei Sawaieke. Neither the Naua people nor the Tububere people could offer any explanation for any socio-political connection between the two *vanua* reflecting the similarity of title, nor indeed were they aware of any connection with Sawaieke on the island of Gau in the Lomaiviti group of islands.

The exact relationship between the Tububere and the Sabutoyatoya is not clear. As far as the Sabutoyatoya representatives at the NLC were concerned, Vurabere (the original ancestor, see below) was as much a descendant of Natuira as were the other five (or six, if Leitavui is included) sons, and therefore the Tububere were, by descent, part of the Sabutoyatoya *yavusa*. Nevertheless, in the event, the 1914 NLC registered the Tububere as a separate *yavusa,* for reasons which they did not record. It is possible that the symbolism of the account of the curious circumstances of the birth of Vurabere, recorded below, reflects an understanding by the informants to the Commission that the Tububere were not really descended from Natuira and that they were therefore a separate *yavusa* from the Sabutoyatoya. However, the informants probably wanted to ensure an intimate socio-political connection with the Tububere, whilst indicating their inferior status, by making them the descendants of the sixth son). Evidence that the Tububere and the Sabutoyatoya were at one level the same but at another level of descent they were different is provided by the symbols of unity and identification. The *vuti aca* of the Tububere were the *tovu lisilisi* (a kind of native sugar-cane), as the *kai* or tree; the *qoqi* (a kind of breadfruit) as the *magiti* or vegetable food; and the *miqa* or small river fish as the *ilava* or concomitant for the vegetable. On the other hand, those of the Sabutoyatoya were the *kulu du* or real breadfruit as the *kai*; and the *miqa* as the *ilava*. They did not have a separate *kai*. Instead they also had the *qoqi* as the symbol of the genital organs; and, being paramounts, the *dule* or trevally as the *ika ni sau* or chiefly fish. The differences were small but I think significant. iTaukei Nakelo thought that this was possible, but iTaukei Sawieke had no views on this interpretation of his origins, about which he was interested but not very knowledgeable. One line of future research on this matter could be to explore the possible connection between the occurrences of the name Sawaieke, whether the Naua and the Tububere had, at any rate in part, some common origin, and whether there is a connection with Gau.

Tububere origin myth

The original ancestral spirit of the Tububere was Vurabere who was born at Lomolomo. The 1914 NLC accounts recorded that Vurabere was the sixth son of Natuira, elder son of Draulunavuda (son of Sagavulunavuda and grandson of Lutunasobasoba). As Natuira was on the point of death, his wife just touched his arm and she became pregnant and duly gave birth to Vurabere (meaning 'late arrival'). Vurabere married a woman of the Cawanisa and they had three children, all of whom were born at Lomolomo.

Fission

At the time of the Veibenu Vea troubles, three groups representing the grandsons of Tububere and their relations scattered in two different directions. They did not go together in unified groups of descendants from each of the three sons, but some went to Naqoqa at the time when the Cawanisa were leaders of the settlement. They had the common name of Tububere, and heeded the immediate authority of the Vunativi. They later moved to the new village of Lomolomo where they are at present.

The others went to Vuda and also retained the common name of Tububere. Later they moved to Mereke and then to Viseisei. With those at Vuda were a separate *mataqali* of the Tububere known as the Navole, which in turn was divided into three. By the time of the NLC, the Navole had become almost extinct, and they were registered not as a separate *mataqali* but as a division of the senior *mataqali* of the Tububere. In this way, they maintained their traditional name, if not their status. As a result, their land was preserved for their use and, if they were to become extinct, for the surrogate parent *mataqali*. The implication of this decision is that if they were registered as *mataqali* and so a land-holding unit, their land would have reverted to the Crown if they were to become extinct. This is an interesting use of the practice of fission and fusion recognised traditionally, but used as a modern device for the benefit of the Tububere people, especially if they were faced with land-shortages.

The Kai Vuda

Kai Vuda origin myth

The 1914 NLC account said that Erovu was a member of the crew of the first vessel which came to Vuda. I was told that he was the half-brother of Lutunasobasoba and that their father was Tura who married firstly the mother of Lutunasobasoba, and secondly the mother of Erovu. Erovu came with his brother, Rainima, who was the original ancestral spirit of the people of Viwa, the westernmost island of the Yasawas lying 32 km to the west of Waya and Naviti. The NLC went on to say that Erovu settled at Vuda, at Korovatu. He married Ratu who also came on the canoe and they had two children, Leitavui and Uqetenavanua. The latter married Sagavulunavuda of Sabutoyatoya.

Leitavui married Kira who also came over on the canoe (I was told that her full name was Kiraelevu), and they had five children born at Vuda. Their descendants comprised the Kai Vuda *yavusa*. Their sons were Leivuda whose descendants are the *mataqali* (Na)Tabua; Naraviravi whose descendants are the Nakete; Sadranu whose descendants are the mataqali Sadranu; Tabakinavatu whose descendants are the Navitarutaru; and the youngest, Wakanimolikula, whose descendants are the Nanuku *mataqali* (see below). Leitavui may also have had a daughter called Nai who may have married Sadidi, who may have been the original ancestral spirit of the Cawanisa (see under the Cawanisa account).

Development of the Kai Vuda

Their first settlement was at Vuda, below the magnificent Korovatu crag. On top of the crag I have been shown the *yavu* of Erovu, the original ancestral spirit, as well as those of his *bete* and members of his household. These have been discussed earlier. The first to leave the Vuda site were the members of the Tabua *mataqali* for reasons unclear, whilst the rest remained at Vuda. Later, following a quarrel between the chiefs at Lomolomo, the Navocotia of Tububere (see under Tububere) and the Navibalawa group of the Eluvuka of Sabautoyatoya (see under Sabutoyatoya) scattered to Dreketi near Lauwaki and to Vuda respectively.

At the time of the NLC, the Kai Vuda were recorded as comprising the four *mataqali* of Vitarutaru, Nabasara, Natabua and Nakete. Traditions of the Kai Vuda provide good examples of fusion and of fission as factors in the mechanics of the development of a polity at the *yavusa* level.

Fusion. The Nakete Join up

The circumstances in which the Nakete became part of the Kai Vuda are not certain. Following discussions at Lauwaki with Ciba and his father, both interested in the origins and development of their *yavusa*, it is clear from my study of their respective *vuti yaca* or symbols of identity that the Nakete were of different origin from the Kai Vuda. The Kai Vuda had the *yabia* or arrowroot and the *dole* or trevally, whereas the Nakete had the *mami* or plantain, the *kumia* or tiny red prawn, and the *tola* or mangrove lobster. I was told by Ciba that the Nakete were originally part of the Vunativi, a nearly extinct group at Lomolomo.

Fission. The Nanuku Split away

The circumstances in which the Nanuku broke way from the Kai Vuda and became part of the Vidilo of Vitogo are clearer. They manifested their separation from the Kai Vuda by adopting separate *vuti yaca*. Instead of the *yabia* and the *dole*, they adopted the *tuwaci* or red cockle; the *ivi mali* or kind of edible chestnut; and the *bitu ni ema* or kind of bamboo.

The Kai Vuda obtained a *bokola* (body to be eaten) during a war. When the Kai Vuda came to eat it, the Nanuku had failed to bake it properly for them and they found that it was raw. So they were angry and chased away the Nanuku who fled to Saru. Later the Nanuku moved and established the village of Tavakubu just south of Lautoka, near where the Vitogo *vanua* had given them land for planting at an area then known as Natabua.

It is interesting that whenever I was at Tavakubu in the 1990s, and discussed their provenance, the Nanuku would smile enigmatically when I referred to the *bokola* incident, change the subject and explain instead that when the Kai Vuda were living at Odro, a small island south of the present village of Lawaki, two brothers of the Nanuku *mataqali* quarrelled about some *vudi* or plantains which were brought for one brother but the other brother wanted. So the latter chased his brother away. He went to Saru with his companions, and while living there associated with some Vidilo (Vitogo) people at Namoli, near Lautoka. The Vuda chief tried to get the Nanuku back but they preferred to *vakararavi* or depend on the Vidilo people. The Vidilo said that they should join them but form a separate group to be known as the Kai Saru. During the discussions with the NLC beginning in 1897 and ending in 1914, the Vidilo chief wanted to have one *yavusa*, the Vidilo, of which the Kai Saru (the Nanuku) would be a *mataqali*. The Kai Saru should be allowed to eat off the Vidilo land but should not be counted as owners. They should act as their own spokesmen before the NLC. When the moment came for them to come before the Commission, the Vidilo people presented a pig with a *tabua* in its stomach as a *ka vakatevoro* or magic to deceive the Commission. They made the Nanuku so drunk that they were unable to explain properly where they had come from. This was regarded as *vere vakaBau* or Bauan trickery, because the Vidilo chief was related to the Bauans through Ratu Jone Madraiwiwi (of the family of the spiritual chief of Bau, the Roko Tui Bau). In the event the true origin of the Nanuku was hidden, and the NLC recorded the Kai Saru as a *mataqali* of the Vidilo *yavusa*. They were divided into two parts, the Nanuku and the Nadakuvatu.

Fission. The Nanuku Split up

Later the Nanuku split up, because the Nadakuvatu part whose planting land was down stream from that of the Nanuku part were insulted when excreta from the Nanuku came floating down the steam to the Nadakavatu.

As a result of the split, many of the Nanuku dispersed to Waya (Yasawas), Nagado (where they formed the Nanuku of the Vaturu people), and to Lebaleba and Bemanu in inland Nadroga. Those who remained were known as the Moromoroilagi, meaning either 'white mucus under the foreskin' or a 'number of people'— perhaps it depended on who was using the term, the insulted Nadakuvatu part or other people.

Leadership and Changes in Leadership of the Kai Vuda

At first, the leadership of the Kai Vuda rested with the Natabua, the senior *mataqali* descended from the eldest son of Erovu. Later, while still at Vuda, the people chose to pass the leadership to the head of the descendants of the third son of Leitavui.

In course of time, the leadership of the Kai Vuda was passed to the iTaukei Vitarutaru, the head of the Vitarutaru, being the descendants of the fourth son of Erovu.

During the time of the 1871 Cakobau Government the Kai Vuda were moved from Vuda and nearby Tavanaki to the island of Odro. From there, after Cession they moved to the present village of Lauwaki because of a shortage of drinking water and of readily accessible planting land.

The Installation Stones

When the leader was installed (*veibuli*), he sat on a large stone and placed his feet on a smaller stone. These two stones were taken to Korovatu, Vuda, from a place called Sayake, at the river junction known as Basagarua (divided into two). The smaller stone is known as Sayake and the larger one as Dakuvatu. When the Vuda people moved to Odro they took the stones with them; and when the Nanuku were chased away from Odro to Saru they took the larger stone with them. The smaller stone remained at Odro and was later taken to Lauwaki where it rests beside the *yavu* of iTaukei Sayake, a Kai Vuda chief. The larger one remained at Saru when the Nanuku went to Tavakubu, Vitogo. Later two young men of Nanuku went with a lorry from Tavakubu and presented *yaqona* and a *tabua* to Sagavulunavuda, their ancestral spirit, to ask him for help in taking the stone to Tavakubu. When they came to lift the stone into the lorry, it was so light that they could carry it with ease and brought it back to Tavakubu where it lies at present beside the *yavu* of iTaukei Dakuvatu. It is a very heavy long stone, shaped like a shark and covered with man-made grooves. It is in two pieces, after it was broken by an Indian bulldozer driver. The bulldozer was damaged, and the driver was taken to hospital where he died.

Sabutoyatoya and Kai Vuda Relationships

The incident of the Veibenu Vea at Lomolomo had resulted in a split in the Sabutoyatoya *yavusa*, and the chief of the Kai Vuda had said that the Sabutoyatoya who had scattered should be brought to Vuda (see under Sabutoyatoya for the circumstances). Then the Kai Vuda agreed that they should acknowledge the authority of the leader of the Sabutoyatoya, and the latter was accordingly given a fan and a walking stick as symbols of paramountcy.

The Cawanisa

Cawanisa origin myth

The 1914 NLC account said that:

> Sadidi, a member of the crew of the *Kaunitoni*, had been at Vuda with Lutunasobasoba. He does not appear to be related to Lutunasobasoba or to any other of the main spiritual heroes who arrived in Fiji on board *Kaunitoni*. He went to Nacokoti near Korovatu, Vuda, and married Nai, daughter of Leitavui who was the eldest son of Erovu, the original ancestral spirit of the Kai Vuda. Sadidi's descendants were the Cawanisa *yavusa*.

> His son, Kalanasiga, married Dawai, a woman of Nabasara, the second group of the Kai Vuda and they had three children, whose descendants comprised the members of the three *mataqali* of the Cawanisa *yavusa*, the Namatua, Dovia and Yaubaba respectively.

> The elder son of Rasilasila, Natuwawa, went to Naqoqa with the Cawanisa (descendants of Sadidi). His descendants were the Nadravua or Ketenatukani (descendants of the elder brother) and they remained there.

> Splits and Movements

> Later, the senior *mataqali* of the Cawanisa, the Namatua, remained at Nacokoti, but the other two *mataqali* went to Naqoqa, inland from Lomolomo, where they established a settlement.

> It was at the time that, following the split at Lomolomo resulting from the incident of the Veibenu Vea involving Natuwawa, eldest son of Rasilasila (the elder brother who was not made leader of the Sabutoyatoya), that the descendants of Natuwawa, the Nadravua or Ketenatukani (descendants of the elder brother), joined with the Cawanisa at Naqoqa and here they remained.

> Also, following the Veibenu Vea, the Vunativi and part of the Tububere (descendants of the last son of Sagavulunavuda, who had settled at Lomolomo) came together with Natuwawa, and settled with the Cawanisa at Naqoqa. The Cawanisa gave them all permanent rights of usage of some of the Cawanisa land and they stayed together there until Cession.

At about the time of Cession in 1874 the Cawanisa moved to the present village of Lomolomo, where the Vunativi and part of the Tububere were already settled. The Vunativi and the Tububere there became known as the Lomolomo. Their lands lay between the point of Edronu and the point of Lomolomo—the Lomolomo land lying to seawards and the Cawanisa to landwards. Bukatavatava, chief of the Sabeto people, sold much of the Lomolomo land to European settlers, and presumably for this reason, most of the Cawanisa moved to the island of Malolo, though some moved to Nadarivatu in the interior of Viti Levu. I have not been able to obtain information directly from the Cawanisa. The iTaukei Sawaieke, chief of the Tububere at inland Viseisei, as well as the iTaukei Nakelo, spokesman of the Sabutoyatoya, told me that some Cawanisa (the Namatua who were the senior group) remained at Lomolomo. Here they have been fused with the Vunativi who are almost certainly, by descent, part of the Sabutoyatoya; although the NLC records the Namatua as part of the Cawanisa. I should record that none of the people with whom I discussed the NLC account disagreed with what was recorded there.

The Navatulevu and Viyagoisausova

Myths of origin

Labasara came from Vuda to Nase, Vitogo, near the coast, where he married a woman of the Tunuloa group of the Vitogo people. They had two sons, Lewaqamuqamu and Siganiera, who were the original ancestors of the Navatulevu and the Viyagoisaukova respectively. One account said that their sons, Lewaqamuqamu and Siganiera, were born at Nase, and that one day Lewaqamuqamu went looking for land in the interior until he came to Navatulevu, near the present villages of Navilawa and Nalotawa on the south side of the Tualeita range below the massive peak of Koroiyanitu. Here he built a house and married Lewatu, a woman of the Tunuloa group of Vitogo, and they had three children, Salaba, Sau and Yataninavatucili, all born at Navatulevu. His descendants were called the Navatulevu ('the big rock'), after a magical big rock where he built his house. This rock reputedly rises up high at night and sinks down low again at daybreak. I have not been able to visit it, as it is in an inaccessible position for me.

Another account said that Labasara went himself to Navatulevu, and that his sons were born there.

Siganiera married and had two children, Saukova and Yatanitoga. His descendants were the Viyagoisaukova, meaning the grandchildren of Saukova. They first lived at Navatulevu.

Fusion and fission

The families of the three sons of Lewaqamuqamu, who was said to have been the first of the two brothers to arrive from Vitogo to Navatulevu, had a dispute over *yaqona*. As a result, Wakanivukalou, son of Yatunivatucili, the youngest son of Lewaqamuqamu, fled to the island of Waya where he remained, and his descendants comprise the Vatucili. Those who remained agreed to recognise Koiluva who was the third son of Salaba, the eldest son of Lewaqamuqamu, as their leader. Koiluva's part of the village was called Natuvamasi.

However, those who claimed that the two sons were born at Nase said that it was at this time that Siganiera arrived. The settlement at Navatulevu was then divided into two: one part for Lewaqamuqamu which was called Navatulevu; and one part for Siganiera which was called Nasorovakatini.

Siganiera's elder son, Saukova, quarrelled with his younger brother, Yatanitoga, because the *yavu* or housemound of the latter was higher (a sign of arrogance and lack of respect). So Yatanitoga was chased away and he went first to his relations, the Nasara *yavusa* of Sabeto. Yatanitoga and his group of the Navatuleu then went to Nadi, where he had some relations, and was settled at Waqana, where he married Neileqe, a woman of rank of the Nabati people, then leaders of Nadi. Because these hill folk were recognised as strong and powerful people the Navatulevu were duly given the leadership of the Nadi *vanua* (referred to as the Nabati and the Yavusatini). The rest of the Viyagoisaukova, the descendants of Siganieri, remained at Navatulevu, and were later joined by the Yavoli of Ne (the inland people of the Sabeto valley) who went to settle with them at the Nasorovakatini part of Navatulevu.

Then news came that an army from Qalinabulu was arriving from the Colo, or mountainous inlands of Ba, with the intention of attacking the Navatulevu and the Viyagoisaukova who remained at Navatulevu together with the Yavoli people of Ne, Vitogo. So in order to avoid the strong Qalinabulu army, they left Navatulevu and crossed over the Tualeita Range and sheltered in Vuda territory at Nagwagwa on the north slopes of the range. Here they heeded the authority of the Momo Levu of Vuda. I was told at Abaca, the present village of these people, that they went first from Navatulevu to Naduguivalu below the mighty fastness of Navuivui (a prominent landmark inland from Lautoka), and then to Nagwagwa which was difficult of access and where there were caves in which to shelter. Naduguivalu may be the same as the place now known as Navatulevu near the road to Abaca from Lautoka

While at Nagwagwa, the Navatulevu split up because of a quarrel, and some went to settle in Vitogo and established a village at Yaukawa on Vitogo land at the head of the Vitawa River. Here they quarrelled over a pig, and the Nasau *mataqali* (being descendants of the Sau, second son of Lewaqamuqamu) of the Navatulevu fled to Namoli, Lautoka, while the rest fled back to Nagwagwa.

Some time after the Qalinabulu army had returned from the attack, the Navatulevu and the Viyagoisaukova went back to their original site at Navatulevu. After some local wanderings, they returned after Cession in 1874 to Nagwagwa where they remained until 1930 when the village was destroyed by a landslide.

Only three brothers survived, and they moved to the village of Abaca (named after the first three letters of the alphabet which, so the story goes, were found engraved on a rock at the old site). I discussed these matters with the son of the late iTaukei Navatulevu, Ratu Rupeni, who was one of the three surviving brothers who came down from the ruins of Nagwagwa.

One yavusa or two?

A criticism of the NLC has been that separate *yavusa* were created by the Commission which were not based on traditional groupings. This criticism is not entirely valid from the point of view of the reality of the situation with which the NLC was faced. In the case of the Navatulevu, it may be shown that those at Nadi and those at Nagwagwa were one descent group, having been based together at Navatulevu, (Navilawa, Nalotawa), and that they therefore comprised one major descent group, a *yavusa*. The reality of the situation was that they had split irrevocably, that they were associated with quite separate areas of land at Nadi and at Nagwagwa, that they had quite separate socio-political associations, and that it was simply common sense to register them as two separate *yavusa*. On the other hand, the Navatulevu and the Viyagoisaukova at Navatulevu (Navilawa) and Nagwagwa were registered as two separate *yavusa;* and though, on the symbolic level, the NLC recorded the manifestation of the original spirits of both groups as the *kuma* or a kind of moth, it distinguished between a white *kuma* for one *yavusa* and a black *kuma* for the other. The reasoning behind this decision to register two separate *yavusa* is not clear, as both groups appeared to have freely acknowledged descent from two brothers and a common grandfather; and recognised one group, the Wainile, as *bete* or common priests. The representative of the Navatulevu before the NLC claimed that they were one group and that their ancestors used to have formal connections by *lakovi* (adoption). However the other representative, descended from the younger brother, said that, though they were both descended from Labasara, at the next level they had different ancestors and that they were two groups and did not have a common chief. This may have been a case of the younger brother's descendants not wishing to be liable to meeting the demands of the other, senior group, whose authority they did not wish to heed. They were typical of the independent mountaineers.

Sabeto Old tikina: the Sabeto socio-political complex

The Old *tikina* of Sabeto lies to the south of the Old *tikina* of Vuda, from which it is geographically divided by the Tualeita range. The western end of the Tualeita is not far from the coastline and is marked by a rocky headland at Edronu, a mysterious site of considerable significance both mythically and archaeologically. To the east, it finally ends at the Nakauvadra Range with which it is mythically connected as a spirit path, referred to as the Wakanivugayali. This is similar, first to the mythical spirit path from the Nakauvadra to Verata also referred to as the Wakanivugayali (see account of Verata); and secondly to the path across the sea to Bua, to the headland called

Naicobocobo (the jumping-off place of the spirits of Vanua Levu on their way to the Nakauvadra). To the west lies the sea. The southern boundary marches with that of the lands of the Nadi *tikina*, including the Naua people of Vagadra (whose present village is Saunaka). To the east, in the uplands, is the territory of the Old *tikina* of Vaturu (Nawaka). To the north-east are the mountains of Magodro.

The Old *tikina* of Sabeto is of particular interest for three reasons. First, it illustrates typical simple federations and a series of independent *yavusa* similar to those characterising the socio-political situation described for the *tikina* of Nawaka. Secondly, the Conua *yavusa* which became the leading *yavusa,* had a quite different origin geographically, politically and mythically from that of the other *yavusa*—both the piedmont *yavusa* of the Sabeto heartland, and the group of independent upland *yavusa* at the top of the Sabeto valley. Thirdly, the myths of origin of the Fijian people as accepted by the various *yavusa* other than the 'stranger' *yavusa,* the Conua, were different in interesting detail from that accepted not only by the Vuda people but also (*pace* Peter France), for whatever the reason, much more generally in many parts of Fiji. I will first record the Sabeto myths of origin, symbolised, as in the case of the *Kaunitoni* myth, by the arrival of the first vessel.

A canoe first came to Nasoso at the mouth of the Sabeto River and sailed up the river as far as NeiSosovu, which lay on the right bank of the river (travelling upstream). Here they came ashore—the name meaning 'the place where the *vu* (original ancestral spirits) came ashore' (*soso* is the communalect equivalent of *sobu* or 'come ashore'). Opposite this site there are two sites called Leleti Levu and Leleti Sewa, where feasts were then prepared, the Levu (big) for the chiefs and the Sewa (little) for the people. *Leleti* means *tatavu* or 'broil'. The chiefs and crew members of the vessel went with Degei to settle first at Edronu, where there are two caves, the Qwara ni Yau which was Degei's, and the Qwara ni Masumasu, which was that of a spirit called Balawakula. *Balawa* is a communalect word for *vadra* or screwpine/pandanus. There used to be a *balawakula* tree on the flat area outside the cave, to which people would go to seek favours or good fortune. First they had to present offerings at the tree which hid the path to the cave. If the offerings were acceptable, the tree would reveal where the path to the cave lay. If not, it hid the path. Similarly, people would present offerings at Degei's cave, the Qwara ni Yau, and would typically place a club in the cave and leave it for blessing before going to war or to a *meke*. The last people on record as having gone to the caves for *sau* or *mana* (spiritual strength) were members of the Fiji Military Forces before they left for the Solomons campaign during the Second World War. Under the influence of the Methodist Church, the local chiefs have said that no more ceremonies should be performed at the caves. The *balawakula* was cut down at the same time, ostensibly to allow for the construction of some public works.

From Edronu the ancestors spread to Vuda, including Sagavulunavuda whose residence at Edronu was evidenced by a petroglyph pointed out as representing his genital organs. Degei remained until someone stole his *dalo*, and he was so upset that he left for the Nakauvadra. As for the rest, they and their descendants in course of time occupied all the south side of the Tualeita as far as Ulu i Conua, far up in the interior.

I will now describe in more detail the origins and development of the *yavusa* found in the Old *tikina* of Sabeto. These included, first, the four *yavusa* which comprised the Sabeto socio-political complex as it was at about the time of the Cakobau Government; and secondly, the three (there were originally six) independent upland *yavusa* known generally as the Ne. The following accounts, based on the myths and traditions given to me, relate to the origins and structure of each of these seven *yavusa* (the other three are discussed elsewhere). They emphasise the uncomplicated nature of the socio-political situation in the Sabeto valley and the independence of the *yavusa* in the uplands.

The Sabeto socio-political complex or vanua includes the following elements:

(a)   the three *yavusa*, based on the present villages of Koroiyaca/Narokorokoyawa (nowadays referred to collectively as the village of Koroiyaca or loosely as Sabeto), including:

- the leading *yavusa*, Conua, the chief of which has the title of iTaukei Erenavula. That person is also given, as the paramount of the Sabeto *vanua*, the title of Momo Levu of Sabeto or, in eastern phraseology, Tui Sabeto. Part of the Conua is based in the present sub-village of Naboutini, up the Sabeto valley.

- the two *yavusa* of Leweiwavuwavu and Nasara, whose heads hold the titles of iTaukei Navakalolo and iTaukei Nasara respectively.

(b)   the *yavusa* of Waruta, based in the present village of Natalau, the chief of which has the title of iTau Nacekwaya.

The Leweiwavawavu, the Nasara and the Waruta are so closely related that they are referred to collectively as *Na Yavusa Balavu* or The Extended *Yavusa*.

The Ne group of independent yavusa formerly included the following yavusa:

(a)   the three *yavusa* of Ne, Leweidrasa and Leweikoro, presently based in the village of Korobebe (formerly Nadele) and now known collectively as the Ne. The Rarawaqa *yavusa* formerly associated with the Ne group, before going to Vaturu. I cannot trace its present whereabouts (see under Vaturu, Nawaka).

(b)   the two *yavusa* of Navatulevu and Viyagoisaukova, now based in the village of Abaca (formerly Nagwagwa) and included in the socio-political federation of Vuda (see under Vuda Old *tikina*).

The Sabeto vanua

I spent much time, especially in the 1990s, first with Ratu Kaliova, the Momo of Sabeto and other members of the Conua *yavusa*; secondly, with Timoci Saukuru, the grand old man of the Leweiwavuwavu; thirdly, with Paula, a former policeman representing the iTaukei Nasara whom I was only able to farewell as he lay on his deathbed; and fourthly, with Apisai (Mohammed) Tora and representatives of the Waruta. What I record here is what they told me while I compared their personal knowledge with the accounts recorded by the 1914 NLC, which I would read to them. They all agreed on the myths of origin, though sometimes differing on details which did not alter significantly the main picture.

Myths of origin: Vuniqele and Raiqelo

> Among those who landed in the first canoe at NeiSosovu and went on to settle with Degei at Edronu were Vuniqele and his younger brother, Raiqelo (recorded as Nauci by the NLC). Raiqelo's *yavu* or housemound was called Yavukoso.

> The two brothers later went to Betoraurau, beside the Waruta stream in the Sabeto Valley. It was there that Raiqelo went and stole Degei's *dalo* at Edronu—an incident which resulted in Degei leaving in anger for the Nakauvadra (see above).

Betoraurau is now the ceremonial name for Sabeto land, though the actual settlement was pointed out to me to be on the slopes of the Tualeita. Its name means 'leafy or shaded spirit house', referring to the first spirit house on the tree-covered slopes. It is interesting that in 1840 the United States Exploring Expedition under Wilkes (1845: 261) 'anchored under Vitilevu shore, off the point called Viti-rau-rau, where we lay until 2 A.M.' before proceeding to the island of Malolo. This place name is surely the same as Betoraurau, and either the latter term has been changed from Vitiraurau (meaning 'breaking off branches') over the century and a half, or, as is more likely, Wilkes misheard it or miswrote it. Those who have been concerned with the origins of the meaning of the name of Fiji (Tongan for Viti) which in Standard Fijian could mean 'breaking off' may well have picked on this reference in Wilkes' narrative, and elaborated the myth of Degei and his party going along the Tualeita to Nakauvadra, claiming that they broke off branches as they journeyed along. This could well be a suitable *ex post facto* explanation. Be that as it may, the myth continues.

First Settlements:

Descendants of Vuniqele, the Elder Brother

Vuniqele, at Betoraurau, married a woman of Vitogo, and they had two sons, Varorairiba and Varonaqai. The descendants of the elder were the Leweiwavuwavu, and those of the younger were the Nasara. These two brothers went and settled at the mouth of the Sabeto river at Navakalolo where they were until the flood (see below). The descendants of Varorairiba, the elder brother, remained at Navakalolo, but those of the younger brother later went to Drakoro, where they settled until the flood.

Some time later, at the time of the Nadi war known as the Volo Levu (see under Nadi), the Naua people (of Vagadra, now at Saunaka) were attacked and some scattered to Drakoro where they were given planting land (*vakovu*) by the descendants of Varonaqai, the younger brother.

Leadership. Descendants of Vuniqele

At Navakalolo, the third son of Varorairiba, elder son of Vuniqele, was made their leader by the descendants of both sons of Vuniqele, and was installed on a specially made mound of earth, and given *yaqona* to drink.

Descendants of Raiqelo, the Younger Brother

Raiqelo, younger brother of Vuniqele, married a woman of the Cawanisa (descendants of Sadidi, who came on the *Kaunitoni* to Vuda and settled first at Lomolomo before going to Naqoqa). Their descendants were the Waruta, also known as the Tacini (younger brothers, because of their progenitor). They had two sons, the elder going to Waruta nearby, and the younger remaining at Betoraurau.

Later both groups joined up at Raracici in the mangroves, where most of them were until the flood. Some split off, either because of drought or from an angry quarrel over a woman; and they went to Qaru. From here, they went to Dramata were they were until the flood.

The Conua. Origin Myth and Arrival at Sabeto

Ravuravu came from the Nakauvadra to Yauyau, Ba. He had two sons, and one day these two went to work in the gardens. When they returned, the elder, Tawake, ate all the *oco* or food provided for them both, and the younger, Nagilolevu, was very angry. Tawake was ashamed, and kept moving away from Ba until he could see it no more. Then he settled in the hills at Conua at the top of the Sabeto valley, where he married Lauvatu, one of the descendants of Varonaqai (the younger son of Vuniqele), who were living at Drakoro. They had a son, Ratu, who as *vasu* to the Leweiwavuwavu and the Nasara, was sometimes looked after by them.

The *Yavusa* Balavu, being those two *yavusa* and the Waruta, were so impressed with their *vasu*, Ratu, that they *lakovi* or ceremonially invited him to come and live with them. He and his followers were settled at Luvuni near where the descendants of Varonaqai lived. Ratu's descendants were known as the Conua, bringing the name from their settlement in the hills.

Installation of First Momo Levu

The *Yavusa* Balavu invited the people of the uplands, the Ne, to come and participate in the installation of Ratu as the paramount chief, with the title of Momo Levu, of the Sabeto socio-political federation or *vanua* of the four *yavusa,* Leweiwavuwavu, Nasara, Waruta and Conua. Two round stones were brought from Drakoro where Ratu's mother lived. One was used for Ratu to sit on (the *vatu ni vibuli)* and one was the *vatu ni vitataunaki* which, when given to Ratu to hold, symbolised the handing over to him of the control of the land and of the people of Sabeto. These stones appeared to have gone missing, but I eventually found them secreted behind a curtain in the chiefly house on Erenavula *yavu*; at least they were said by Ratu Kaliova, the present Momo Levu, to be the same as the original ones. *Credant qui velint.*

Ratu had three sons, and the two elder agreed that Leiluvuni, the youngest, should be installed as paramount chief. So it came about that the group of the descendants of the youngest son, known as the Luvuni, became the leading group and obtained and retained the position of Momo Levu of the Sabeto polity. The Conua were at Luvuni until the flood.

The Great Flood and all Move to Sabeto

A great flood destroyed the villages of Navakalolo, Drakoro, Raracici, Dramata and Luvuni; and most of the people went to a new village site at Sabeto (closer to the Sabeto River than the present village. Some Conua people went to relations in Vaturu and in Vagadra (the Naua); and the Nabau group of the Conua went to Koronisau.

Wars

The Conua were involved in three remembered local wars with which the neighbouring polity of Nadi (to the south of Sabeto) were concerned. These were known as the Cebuwalu (eight anuses), the Volo Levu and the Tola (the *mana* or mangrove lobster). In the Tola, the then-leaders of Nadi, the Navatulevu, were driven away from Nadi as being too arrogant. They sought refuge with the Sabeto people, sending messages to the Nadroga people with requests for assistance.

The Navatulevu were settled at Lomolomo under the protection of Mataitoga, the Sabeto war chief, while the Navatulevu chief, Rokomatu, stayed with Mataitoga at Sabeto. Mataitoga was at that stage under the authority of Nasolo, the spiritual chief of Sabeto. He and Rokomatu plotted and Rokomatu's warrior companions, the Bolaciri, chased Naloto away to the Colo (the mountainous interior) and burned his village.

Rokomatu, as a chief of the powerful Navatulevu neighbours, then regularised Mataitoga's position as leader in place of the absent Naloto, and installed him as spiritual paramount chief of the Sabeto, before returning to Nadi. Mataitoga was the first to have the spiritual and secular power as well as the ambition and competence to forge the Sabeto groups into a locally strong and stable socio-political complex. At his installation, the Leweiwavuwavu/ Nasara, as the original inhabitants of the valley, carried out the installation ceremonies, preparing the *yaqona* and offering it to him to drink. A house for the purpose had been built by the upland Ne groups, using timber supplied by the Waruta.

Mataitoga further established his position through judicious marriage with his powerful neighbours at Vuda. He married first a woman of Tububere and secondly Natukula, a woman of rank from the Sabutoyatoya. The Oi group from the Eluvuka *mataqali* of the Sabutoyatoya came to look after Natukula, their relation. They were given land for planting by the Waruta and came under their protection until they were later included among the Luvuni *mataqali* of the Conua.

> After the Nadroga army had driven away the upstart Yakuilau from Nadi, and successfully prepared for the return of the Navatulevu to a position of paramountcy in Nadi, Rokomatu returned to Nadi, with most of the Navatulevu. Meanwhile some of the Yakuilau had taken advantage of their relationships in Sabeto, and had settled for a while with the Conua until peace returned to Nadi and most of them were later brought back.

This is discussed further under the Nadi account, but it is interesting to see how relationships had developed and were built up between these coastal polities to the extent that they could seek refuge with each other, and request and give military aid from and to each other when the occasion demanded or when they saw it to their advantage. Such mutual assistance was perhaps ephemeral, but it could give rise to a situation of considerable obligation on the part of the assisted, especially if the assisted polity failed to thank the assisting polity to the extent that was expected.

> Mataitoga's power was such that he was in a position to unite the Leweiwavuwavu/Nasara, the Waruta and some Ne and (because of his marital relationships) to invite some Vuda people to go and attack and burn Vitogo. This was in order to avenge an insult occasioned when his son, Yalobo, had asked the Vitogo people for a chiefly necklace of *sovui* shells and his request had been refused. In due course, Mataitoga showed his power and chiefly behaviour further, when not only did he arrange for the houses in Vitogo to be rebuilt and for the people to be brought back, but also at the time when he had accepted Christianity, he made a presentation of a *malo* or chiefly loincloth to *buluta na dra* or bury the blood as reparations for the burning of Vitogo.

It must have been soon after this that Yalobo plotted against his father. When Mataitoga learnt of the plot, Yalobo fled to the Vuda people and was given refuge at Mereke. He was betrayed by the Sabutoyatoya people and taken to Naqoqa where he was killed (see the Vuda account of the killing and its aftermath of Mataitoga's grief). Mataitoga must have been a very arrogant, even if successful, leader because he was subjected to a series of plots apart from Yalobo's plot.

> The chief of the Taladrau (a sub-group of the Luvuni *mataqali* of the Conua *yavusa*) stood up to Mataitoga who ordered his death. He was killed and the Taladrau people fled to Dramata where they established a village of their own. Another plot was devised by a chief of the Naduruvatu group of the Conua in order to reduce (*tabaka sobu*) his power. Mataitoga again ordered his death and he fled but was killed. The Nadurumata fled to Koronisau where they established a village.

> On another occasion, the Waruta planned to kill Mataitoga, in order to become leaders of the Sabeto polity. The Waruta were regarded as especially dangerous people, specialising in *caka sausau/mana*, or sorcery, and the practices of the *luveniwai* cult, concerned with the little people of the sea. When Mataitoga went to visit the Waruta, he went with a chief of the Oi who had come from Vuda with his second wife, Natukula, and had been looked after by the Waruta. The Waruta hid by the roadside in order to club Mataitoga. When they came to club him, his *sau/mana* was so strong that the clubs simply struck without doing any damage. The Oi chief, out of gratitude for the Waruta's protection of his people, sought to save the Waruta from revenge, and because Mataitoga was related to the Oi through his wife, he could not refuse this request.

There seems to have been perpetual rivalry between the Waruta, perhaps regarding themselves as spiritually powerful local inhabitants and guardians of Betoraurau (aided by the spiritual guardian of Sabeto, Bituwewe, with whom they were in close association), and the Conua whom the Waruta perhaps regarded as arrogant strangers. Be that as it may, another incident between the Waruta and the Conua took place when the Waruta who were living next to the Momo Levu of Sabeto, stole his daughter, Adi Waqa. They were told to go away. They moved to the Leweiwavuwavu/Nasara, but the Momo could still see them. So they moved to Koroisue, to Nasara lands where the Natova sector office of the Sugar Company is now situated. The Momo could still hear their voices, so they moved on to Natalau where they are at present. I was told that this took place before the arrival in Sabeto of the Cakobau army in 1873.

I was very aware of this feeling of near-hostility between the two *yavusa*, when I was there in the 1990s, and found that Natalau was a village with a mysterious atmosphere of its own. This atmosphere was manifested by the very neat appearance of the village and its cemetery (perhaps due to the great influence of Apisai Tora who was then traditional head of the Waruta). There was notably a great quietness that prevailed especially near the house of Tora and the traditional *beto* or spirit house which was used for special meetings and into which I was eventually permitted to enter. Speaking in it except at a whisper is not allowed. It stood on a *yavu*, at the corner of which was a monolith brought from original settlement of the Waruta at Yavukoso, as a memorial imbued with *mana* from the original ancestral spirits. The Waruta are a much-feared group even now, closely associated with the spirit centre at Edronu. I do not think this is due to Tora himself, but it appears likely that Tora has assumed the mantle of the magical powers of the Waruta in order to foster his own ambitions in politics.

The Cakobau attack

Although the Sabeto had accepted Christianity at an early period, Mataitoga later quarrelled with the *ivakavuvuli* or lay preacher who had been assigned to Sabeto. So he then rejected Christianity. One result of this was that although some Sabeto people continued to accept Christianity and later sided with the Cakobau Government, others joined with the Karawa pagans in the Colo of Ba (see below). They aided the Karawa people when, in February 1873, they murdered a family of European settlers, the Burns, who lived in a most precarious place at Vunisamaloa, some distance up the river from Ba.

The European settlers then called on Cakobau, leader of the 1871 Cakobau Government which some of them had insisted should be established as a focus point to whom they could address their complaints and as a power to look after their own interests and problems with lesser Fijian chiefs. They wrongly thought that Cakobau's traditional powers extended over all Fiji and so he was given the title of Tui Viti. Cakobau rejoiced in such a concept, being especially aware that his neighbour King George the First was King over all Tonga. So Cakobau sent his army to Ba, in what proved to be a test of strength. This was vital if he was to justify his position of Tui Viti and Cakobau Rex, especially after his purposely delayed (he quite rightly doubted his own powers) and eventually unsuccessful attempts in 1868 to avenge the 1865 murder of the Reverend Baker in the interior of Viti Levu. By the early 1870s many Europeans doubted his claims (albeit partly European-generated) of omnipotence. Indeed in the west, the Europeans including the self-named Nadi Swells had no faith in him and in fact openly opposed him, preferring to rely on their own strengths to deal with the recalcitrant locals, especially as he had refused to take punitive action after the murder of Spiers and Macintosh in the Ba area in 1871. He had lost face, especially when some virtually insignificant but nevertheless overt form of revenge was finally attempted not by his troops but by the local Europeans who took the law into their own hands against the advice of the British Consul, and with the aid of some warriors of Tui Ba stormed the hill-folk, achieving little and burning the wrong village.

When the Burns family was murdered in 1873, Cakobau took action and sent his army to Ba, only to find that the Europeans had assembled themselves and on the basis of past experience had no faith in the Cakobau army which they were prepared to resist with firearms. To avoid such a clash, the government troops under Major Fitzgerald re-embarked and headed back to Levuka, the seat of the Cakobau Government.

Fortune favoured Cakobau. At Drauniivi (see Ra account under Vatukaloko), news came of the murder of a Bauan by the Kalokolevu people. The army went ashore and took revenge at the battle of Korowaiwai in early 1873. Flush with success at last, the Cakobau Government army returned to Ba and proceeded to attack with some success the murderers of the Burns family. They burned the village of the murderers at Karawa who duly returned with a huge pig, *tabua* and *yaqona* as their *soro* or apology. Having achieved their objective of vengeance for the murder, the army pressed on, no longer as a punitive force but intent on bringing the independent and wild hillfolk under the control of the Government. This may well have been the official reason, but the coastal chiefs were aiding the army and they had their own ambitions and interests to pursue in the Colo.

Having achieved some success in the Colo of Ba, the Cakobau Government army was ordered to go to Sabeto. It had been discovered that some Sabeto had been involved in the murder and the defence of Karawa. In February, the people of Nubutautau, Magodro, Sabeto and Vaturu had met in the Vaturu villages of Natawa and Namagimagi on the banks of the Nadi River at the Vaturu gorge, and had bound themselves to resist any encroachment on their domains by the Cakobau Government. Then they were to continue from Sabeto up into the Colo with the same intent as during the attack from Ba.

So the Government army left Ba and, going along the coast past Vuda, went inland to the Sabeto piedmont. Here they attacked and burned the villages of Sabeto, Dramata and Koronisau where the Conua, the Leweiwavuwavu/Nasara, and the Waruta were living. Some scattered to their relations at Vuda, some were taken prisoner and sent to Bau where Cakobau could sell them as labour to Europeans and thus recoup part of the cost of the war, while others were sent to Nakelo (with which polity the Sabeto retain a close association). Mataitoga was publicly executed as an example for all to witness, especially those who thought to continue to oppose the Cakobau Government. His son, Bukatavatava, and the rest of the Sabeto people were deported to the island of Koro. These included those who protested (and, as they made quite clear to me, they are still protesting against such treatment) on the grounds that they had supported Cakobau by showing his army the way to the hills, when the Cakobau army went on to attack the Colo, including at first the independent group of *yavusa* known collectively as the Ne.

During a council of war, it was decided that once the Sabeto people had been all brought in or had surrendered and had been deported, there should be no re-occupation of the Sabeto lands except under direct order of the government. A discussion of their return from Koro would be held later at the same time as the return of the Ne who, in the event, suffered the same fate as the Sabeto.

The later attack of the Ne will be discussed when I describe and discuss these people (see below). Meanwhile the Cakobau army established Sabeto as a base for a drive into the interior and as a place where auxiliary contingents of volunteers from the neighbouring districts could assemble. For instance, Navula, the war leader from Nadi, and Ratu Kini, the Kwa Levu from Nadroga, came to join the Cakobau army, not necessarily or totally out of loyalty to Christianity and Cakobau. These coastal chiefs could see material gains for themselves, as well as chances to cut down to size the impudent hill folk who for too long had shown little respect for these chiefs.

The Ne group of independent yavusa

The Ne lived well up the Sabeto valley under the shadow of their fortress on the mighty peak of UluiNe. When I first knew these people in the early 1950s, they were living in the village of Nadele which was destroyed by Hurricane Bebe in the early 1970s. When I returned in the late 1990s to discuss their origins and development with the remaining people of Ne, they were living at the new village of Korobebe. The village was so named by Sir Robert Foster, the last Governor of Fiji and the first Governor-General; and the people were not slow to point out to me that the village of Koroiyaca (Arthur's village) where they were first settled on their return from exile (see below) was so named by the first Governor, Sir Arthur Gordon. The Sabeto valley was proud of its first and last gubernatorial connections; and they were eagerly awaiting the formal opening of their electricity scheme to which I was invited. Unfortunately I was no longer in the area when what must have been an amazing occasion for these formerly wild and independent mountaineers. For ease of reference, I repeat the summary of the Ne yavusa which I stated earlier:

(a)   the three yavusa of Ne, Leweidrasa and Leweikoro, presently based in the village of Korobebe (formerly at Nadele). The Rarawaqa yavusa was formerly associated with the Ne group, before going to Vaturu. Its present whereabouts are unknown to me (see under Vaturu, Nawaka).

(b)   the two yavusa of Navatulevu and Viyagoisaukova, now based in the village of Abaca (formerly at Nagwagwa) and included in the socio-political federation of Vuda (see under Vuda Old tikina).

I was told at Korobebe that the people now living there represent two groupings: the Ne grouping (divided by the NLC into the three yavusa of Ne, Leweidrasa and Rarawaqa); and the Leweikoro. Here I will discuss only these four yavusa. The other two yavusa, the Navatulevu and the Viyagoisaukova, used to live in the vicinity of UluiNe but now live at Abaca, Vuda. They are discussed under Vuda, and mythically their origins from the other side of the Tualeita from Vitogo, are different from those of the other four yavusa which are from Edronu. The myths and traditions of the four yavusa were told to me at Korobebe, and differ in detail from those recorded by the NLC.

Myths of origin

Among those who came by vessel to the mouth of the Sabeto River, sailed up the river and landed at NeiSosovu were three brothers, Momoriqwa, Leva or Lave (recorded by the NLC as the son of Nayau), and Navakayau, as well as Matabiau who was no relation to the brothers. These four first settled with Degei at Edronu at the west end of the Tualeita. Then they all went inland up the Sabeto valley to land lying below the south slopes of the Tualeita in the region of the peak of UluiNe.

Momoriqwa went to Ne and married a woman of Vunamaoli, and they had four sons. The fourth son was Riqwa who went to Nawaka where he became the progenitor of the Senibua yavusa (see the Nawaka account). The remaining sons chose the middle one to be leader. Momoriqwa's descendants were the Ne yavusa.

Leva or Lave went to Koromaka and also married a woman of Vunamaoli, and they had two children, the younger of whom was recognised by the elder as leader and settled in that part of the village of Koromaka called Drasa. Leva's descendants were the Leweidrasa.

Navakayau (whom the NLC recorded as coming from the Nakauvadra) settled nearby at Rarawaqa. His elder brothers quarrelled with him about the size of his *yavu* (the relative height of a person's *yavu* was symbolic of his status in a hierarchy—in this case a hierarchy based on the relative age of brothers), and Navakayau ran away to where he could not see his brothers. The NLC, however, recorded that while still at Rarawaqa, an old man of Rarawaqa had manhandled and chased away a woman of the Leweidrasa who had come to steal some of his *dalo*. She complained to her people and they attacked and drove away those at Rarawaqa. Whatever the reason, Navakayau and his people left his brothers and settled in Vaturu, and his descendants were known as the Rarawaqa *yavusa* (see under Vaturu account).

The *vuti yaca* or symbols of identity and unification were the same for both the Ne and the Leweidrasa, indicating that they were once a single group. This supports what I was told, that the NLC had separated the Ne people into different *yavusa*. Unfortunately my informants knew as little about the *vuti yaca* of the Rarawaqa as they did about their present whereabouts. The *vuti yaca* of the Leweikoro were different from those of the Ne and Leweidrasa, as might be expected since they were different descent groups as the following account claims.

Matabiau came separately from the three brothers of whom he was no relation, only a shipmate. He followed the Tualeita and then climbed down and settled on the slopes at Raraikoro. He married a woman of Vitogo and they had three children. The children agreed among themselves that the middle son should be leader. The youngest built a *yavu* which was higher that that of the other two. This was *viavialevu* (presumptuous and arrogant), and so they chased him away. Matabiau's descendants were the Leweikoro, named after the last element in the name of the place where they first settled.

Leadership

Once the Ne, Leweidrasa, Leweikoro, Navatulevu and Viyagoisaukova were settled around UluiNe, they agreed that while remaining independent of each other, they should recognise the head of the Ne *yavusa* to be their leader. This would be for the purposes of any communal activities, such as the installation of the Momo Levu of Sabeto, in which they would be involved. Although they would respect the head of the Ne *yavusa*, and indeed, the Momo Levu, they would not heed the authority of these chiefs.

Apart from such quarrels as I have referred to, these groups do not appear to have been involved greatly in local warfare. Perhaps their neighbours were aware of their almost impregnable positions of defence on the Tualeita; and when, for instance, the Qalinabulu from the Ba Colo attacked, the Ne groups went first to their war villages on the slopes and then to their fortress on the peak of UluiNe. From here they repelled the Qalinabulu. Meanwhile, the Navatulevu and the Viyagoisaukova had avoided the Qalinabulu by crossing the Tualeita and settling on the north side at Nagwagwa, not far inland from Vitogo whence they had first come.

The Cakobau attack continued

As was the case following the punitive attack on the Karawa people who had murdered the Burns family at Ba, the Cakobau army did not stop after punishing the Sabeto. For the same reasons as before, the army was determined to show its power in support of Cakobau, and to convince the people of the Colo that they must accept the supremacy of Cakobau and his, to them, alien form of government, with perhaps the implied acceptance of the associated religion of Christianity. Further it was reported that the people of Nubutautau had caused the murder of Spiers and Macintosh, and here was a chance to take revenge.

So when the Cakobau army had overcome the Sabeto people, they followed up the valley and at first successfully attacked the Ne, Leweidrasa and Leweikoro. There was at first a spirited defence of a Ne village, before the villagers burned it and retired to their almost inaccessible stronghold at the peak of KoroiNe. The Ne defenders used slings and hurled stones with great force and wounded some attackers. Next day, on 20 June 1873, the government army scaled the heights only to find that the defenders had escaped during the night, perhaps aided by the Vuda contingent. Some of these were later captured. Of those captured, some went to Vuda, some as prisoners to work for the Nadi people and the rest were deported to the island of Koro. As in the case of the Sabeto deportees, it was agreed that the Ne people should not be allowed to return and occupy their lands without the direct order of the government.

The Sabeto and the Ne return from Koro

Those of the Sabeto and the Ne groups who were deported by the Cakobau Government to Koro remained there until after Cession which had taken place on 10 October 1874. In due course, the Governor, Sir Arthur Gordon, established the new village which he named after himself as Koroiyaca. He then authorised the return of these people from Koro and settled them all together under Mataitoga's son, Bukatavatava, at Koroiyaca. From this time, the Ne agreed to heed the authority of the Momo of Sabeto, and the Old *tikina* of Sabeto was created under the first Buli Sabeto who was Bukatavatava. So he had traditional and official authority over the returned people.

Bukatavatava duly settled the Conua at Koroiyaca; the Leweiwavuwavu/Nasara at Narokorokoyawa (immediately adjacent to where the Conua were); the Waruta at Nakoroiyaca where they remained for a while until at their request they were allowed to return to Natalau; the Naduruvatu (who had plotted against Mataitoga, see above) at Naboutini; and the Ne groups at Nalesutale. Because of certain deaths there, the Ne later left Nalesutale and were settled at Nadele by Nemani Driu, the great Nadi leader (see under Nadi) who became the first local chief to be RokoTui Ba.

The Sabeto people are still very proud and independent. This is manifested in their myths of origin (no *Kaunitoni* landing at Vuda for them, but instead a first arrival together with Degei, no less, at the Sabeto River mouth, and a first spiritual settlement at Edronu, not Vuda). It is also manifested in Erenavula, their magnificent Were Levu or ceremonial house, which is equal to, if not bigger than, Vunisei, and the Were Levu of the Sabutoyatoya of Vuda.

The Ne people are equally proud because of their very independence and the struggles they put up against the Cakobau army. They successfully resisted the army and managed to escape defeat by the very acceptable traditional practice of trickery (*vere*) through their honourable escape at night, even if they were captured eventually.

10

Polities of Nadi *Tikina*

The New *tikina* of Nadi is bounded on the north by the Milika River which divides the Sabeto part of the New *tikina* of Vuda (see Chapter 9) from Vuda. To the east and the south, Nadi is bounded by the New *tikina* of Nawaka (see Chapter 11) and the province of Nadroga, of which the Old *tikina* of Vaturu lies along the eastern part; the Old *tikina* of Nawaka bounds the south-eastern part; and the hills of the Old *tikina* of Rukuruku as well as the New *tikina* of Malomalo in the province of Nadroga border the southern part. The sea and the mangrove swamps of the extensive Nadi River delta form the western mainland part of Nadi. Also within the boundaries of Nadi *tikina* are several islands, including Yakuilau, Yavulo and Sonaisali. The terrain is mostly easy for communication. The highest spot in the presently inhabited coastal area is 37 m at Rasusuva, and in the whole region is 117 m at the spiritual centre of Namarasa to the south and 176 m at Nagado to the north.

Nadi New *tikina* comprises the Old *tikina* of Nadi and Sikituru. The administrative area which later became the Old *tikina* of Nadi included at Cession in 1874 the Old *tikina* of Nadi and the Old *tikina* of Buduka.

Three groups who became the three *yavusa*, the Tukani, Noi Naiqoro and Botiluvuka, known together as the Kovacaki, were the first to settle in the Nadi area. The collective name for these three and the fourth, the Vucunisai, was Vanua o Nadi. Other groups arrived later and developed socio-politically to form the basis of three other *yavusa*, the Navatulevu, Yakuilau (Nabati) and the Sila. The term Nadi then included these newcomers and their leader achieved paramountcy of all these *yavusa*. The paramount, titled the Momo Levu of Nadi, was from the Nakuruvarua family (from Nadroga) of the Navatulevu *yavusa*. Much later, thanks to the energy of Navula, the war chief of Navatulevu, the polity of Nadi was considerably expanded to include the other neighbouring polities commented on in this chapter. My main sources for this chapter are the accounts of the 1913 Native Lands Commission (NLC) investigations, and more particularly my own investigations in the area since I first lived there as District Officer in 1971, and which continued until 2003. My explorations involved extensive discussions with members of all the groups, visits to all sites except the evasive and most sacred site of Nasaumomo (an account of my unsuccessful endeavours would fill a separate chapter), and some limited excavations.

A study of the origins and development of descent and socio-political complexes which duly came to be registered as *yavusa* by the NLC under the Nadi area, together with the various explanations for different reasons given at various times, is a completely absorbing exercise which could be continued *ad infinitum* without final and omni-satisfying conclusions. This situation is sometimes deliberately involved, in order to support conflicting arguments about leadership; and also, particularly nowadays, in order to confuse the Native Land Trust Board and the Fijian Administration concerning the allocation of moneys derived from land rents or from other income derived from the very extensive tourism continuing to develop in the area.

The situation is also very involved and open to close investigation, using every technique available to anthropologists, linguists and archaeologists, to determine the overt and often covert origins of the various groups who make up in fact what are by myth and legend nicely compact *yavusa*. Finally, the Nadi area is ideal for exploring the bases of relationships between neighbouring polities, especially by marriage or spiritual connections; and also between polities without such connections but using such diplomatic devices as the *calevu ni matamataraki* or diplomatic channel of communication.

A feature which distinguishes Nadi from other areas in the Yasayasa vakaRa in the west is the fact that many of the polities are either simple *yavusa* or groups of a few *yavusa*. We are dealing with mini-socio-political situations compared with those in the extreme cases in the east or the intermediate cases in Rakiraki. But they are every bit as fascinating, and also, at least geographically, more easy to cover completely and in great detail in the time available.

The main polities: Nadi *tikina*—a snapshot of structure

The main polities in the area covered in the course of my research project in Nadi New *tikina* comprising the Old *tikina* of Nadi (including the original Old *tikina* of Buduka) and Sikituru, are currently recognised as follows:

Name of *polity*	Leading *yavusa*	Title of paramount	No. of levels	No. of *yavusa*	No. of villages
Nadi Old *tikina* (including Buduka)					
(i) Nadi *vanua*					
Nadi	Navatulevu	Momo Levu	2	3	2

The Momo Levu (now commonly referred to as the Tui Nadi) is paramount chief of the major polity of Nadi, which includes the following six dependent and associated polities.

(ii) Nakovacaki, formerly Buduka Old *tikina* later amalgamated with the Old *tikina* of Nadi					
Nakovacaki	Tukani	No paramount	1	4	2

The three *yavusa* comprising the polity known as the Nakovacaki regard themselves as equal. These three individual *yavusa* now heed the authority of the Momo Levu of Navatulevu, Nadi. Their ancestors were evidently among the first people to settle in the Nadi area, but the paramountcy was given to the Navatulevu who came later from the hill country. The original position of the Nakovacaki was acknowledged after Cession in 1874, when they were recognised as comprising the Old *tikina* of Buduka. The *yavusa* Vucunisai was once associated with the Kovacaki but is now dispersed.

(iii) The Naua independent *yavusa*					
Naua	Naua	Momo Levu Naua or iTaukei Sawaieke	1	1	1

The Momo Levu of Naua now respects the Momo Levu of Navatulevu, Nadi.

Name of polity	Leading *yavusa*	Title of paramount	No. of levels	No. of *yavusa*	No. of villages
The Sikituru Old *tikina*					
(i) The Saunivalu independent *yavusa*					
Saunivalu	Saunivalu	No paramount	1	1	1

Formerly associated with the following two *yavusa* (now extinct or dispersed): Kai Loa (extinct); and Vucunisai (dispersed, see under Kovacaki). The Saunivalu now heed the authority of the Momo Levu of Navatulevu, Nadi.

(ii) The Ketenavunivalu *vanua*

Ketenavunivalu	Ketenavunivalu	iTaukei Naqwaranivualiku	2	3	1

The three *yavusa* of Natutale, Sauvana and Nacaqaru comprise the *vanua* of Ketenavunivalu. Formerly an independent *vanua* and heeding the paramountcy of the iTaukei Naqwaranivualiku, they now show respect to the Momo Levu of Navatulevu, Nadi.

iii) The Yavusania *vanua*

Yavusania	Noi Vulani	iTaukei Nakauvadra	2	5	1

The two *yavusa* of Noi Vulani and Neilavutu comprise the *vanua* of Yavusania. Formerly an independent *vanua* and heeding the authority of the head of the Noi Vulani, they now show respect to the Momo Levu of Navatulevu, Nadi.

(iv) The Noi Navo *vanua*

Noi Navo	Noi Yaro	iTaukei Nakauvadra	2	5	1

The five *yavusa* of Navo, Digilo, Noi Yaro, Noi Takuci and Eloto comprise the *vanua* of Noi Navo. They are an independent *vanua* and heed the authority of the iTaukei Nakauvadra, now of the Noi Yaro *yavusa*. They currently show respect to the Momo Levu of Navatulevu, Nadi.

Kovacaki (Vanua o Nadi)

The Kovacaki, now comprising the three *yavusa* of Tukani, Noi Naiqoro and Botiluvuka, live at present in the villages of Namotomoto and Navoci on the north side of the Nadi River just to the north of the main urban area of Nadi town. The fourth *yavusa* of Vucunisai live at present in the Mamanuca islands and the Yasawa islands of Waya and Viwa.

Myths of origin and first settlements

The NLC of 1913 recorded that these four *yavusa* were each descended from children of Tutuvanua, whose full name according to what I was told by the Vucunisai and some Noi Naiqoro representatives, was Waicalanavanua Lutumailagi Tutuvanua. The NLC account of the myths of origin stated that:

> Tutuvanua lived at Nasaumomo, sited in the middle of the mangroves at the mouth of the Nadi River near Vunatoca beach. He was living there before the arrival of the *Kaunitoni*, the canoe which according to the myth of the Vuda people brought the progenitors of the Fijians from somewhere to the west of Fiji. [Modern accretions to what could well be a myth of considerable antiquity place the origins in Tanganyika and before then in Turkestan (see Chapter 9).] When the *Kaunitoni* arrived off Nadi, the crew saw smoke rising from the mangroves and decided to sail on to Viseisei. Tutuvanua married a woman of the Leweiwavuwavu, the original inhabitants of Betoraurau, the Sabeto lands; and they had three sons who settled and who had descendants as follows:
>
> - Ulinadi at Nasau, and his descendants were the Tukani;
> - Masiwale at Naiqoro near the river, and his descendants were the Noi Naiqoro;
> - Leawerenalagi at Dra opposite the present village of Narewa, and his descendants were the Botiluvuka.

The Botiluvuka spokesman told me quite a different myth of origin of the Botiluvuka. He said that Tutuvanua had married a woman of Nawaka, called Leawerenalagi, and that they had a son, Ulinadi, whose sons were the progenitors of the Botiluvuka. This was agreed to by the senior member of the Tukani, although others of the Tukani said that Ulinadi was their progenitor. The Botiluvuka spokesman also claimed that the Botiluvuka people came from Malolo, and were settled by the Tukani in an area in between the Tukani and the Noi Naiqoro. Therefore they became known as the Eluvuka, the people in the *luvuka* or middle.

The NLC myth of origin went on to claim that:

> Tutuvanua also had a daughter called Lewaturatjeke. Her descendants first lived at Dra with the Botiluvuka and then moved to Maqalevu which was divided into three parts, one for the descendants of each of the sons of Lewaturatjeke who were at first known collectively as the KawaiLewatu or the Nadi. Later they were known as the Vucunisai, as will be explained below.

This is similar to the myth of origin of the Vucunisai which was given to me by their representative who claimed, however, that the Vucunisai were descended from Tutuvanua through a son whose name was forgotten, but that Lewatu was their war spirit.

There are other myths of origin of the Vucunisai which were recorded by the NLC. One claimed that the Vucunisai were part of the Botiluvuka *yavusa*, and that though they were descended from Lewatu, Lewatu was not a child of Tutuvanua. As one account claims that the Botiluvuka and the Vucunisai came from Malolo, it is interesting to speculate whether this Lewatu was the same as Lewatulekeleke who went from Vitogo to Vuda where she married Tuilevu. They then went on to Malolo, and Tuilevu became the original ancestor of the LeweiLawa people of Malolo, whose paramount had the title of Tui Lawa.

Another account amplified this connection with the Botiluvuka. It claimed that the Vucunisai, the Botiluvuka and the Kai Loa, another *yavusa,* now extinct but once associated with the Saunivalu of Sikituru (see under Sikituru), were *vu vata* or of the same origin, but not descended from Tutuvanua and that they came to Nadi from Malolo. They moved together from Malolo to Denarau, at the mouth of the Nadi River. From here the Vucunisai went to settle at their first Viti Levu settlement, at Maqalevu.

The Tukani: the Naobekwa, Weilulu, Nadakia and Vuralosi mataqali

I was told by the Tukani people that the only Tukani *dul dina* or true Tukani descended from Tutuvanua through his son, Ulinadi, were the *mataqali* known as the Naobekwa. The Weilulu were originally a part of the Nabau people who lived in the Nausori highlands. The Nadakia came from Nawaka, probably from the Vunatoto *yavusa* with whom they have a common *kai* or tree symbol of unity. The Vuralosi are regarded as strangers but I could not find out their origins. Although the whole *yavusa* has a common *kai*, the *titi* or mangrove (*Bruguiera rheedii*, Rhizoporaceae), each *mataqali* has, as well, its own *kai*. This supports the account that the Tukani are a composite polity rather than a descent group.

While the Botiluvuka were at Dra, they put a *tabu* on the land in the Nadi area. The Vucunisai attacked the Tukani, and though a number were killed, the rest escaped. The Naobekwa remained on the coast at Vunatirikoturase, but the rest of the Tukani took fright and occupied land called Buduka near the present village of Narewa. After a long time they moved to Lotoiqere, near the mangroves seaward from Buduka. Here they were joined by the Naobekwa.

On one occasion the paramount Navatulevu chiefs of Nadi became arrogant and oppressive, and the Yakuilau (see later) refused to heed their authority and drove them away from Nadi.

Rokomatu, the Navatulevu chief and *vasu* of the Noi Naiqoro (see below) and the Navatulevu went and joined with the Tukani at Lotoiqere. Here they stayed with the Tukani until Mataitoga, chief of the Sabeto, came and took them to Koroiqawa, being Sabeto territory on the banks of the Milika River (the boundary of Sabeto/Vuda lands). The Tukani remained at Lotoiqere.

After a number of years, the Yakuilau who had become paramounts of Nadi proved to be as arrogant as the Navatulevu had been. Rokomatu and the Navatulevu saw their opportunity to return and asked the Nadroga chiefs to send an army to suppress the Yakuilau. The army, known as the Tola (or mangrove lobster, *mana* in Standard Fijian), arrived, and defeated and scattered the Yakuilau at Koroiqawa. Their supporters, the Tukani, fled from Lotoiqere; and some went to Sabeto, while others took refuge in the Nabau defended site at Naqwavula, below the present village of Nausori.

When Rokomatu came back from Sabeto territory and was installed in Nadi as paramount, he brought back the Tukani from Sabeto and Naqwavula and settled them in Lotoiqere. They remained here until floods drove them to Korokoro. After a hurricane had destroyed Korokoro, they moved to Buduka where they stayed until they moved to Namotomoto.

The Noi Naiqoro

The Noi Naiqoro representatives told me that their first settlement was at Naiqoro, on the banks of the Nadi River. The elder son of Masiwale (son of Tutuvanua) gave the leadership to his younger brother, Wetula, who was duly installed as Momo.

On one occasion the Saunivalu people of Navosa (the Colo part of Nadroga/Navosa) quarrelled about a pig; and a group of them under Qio came down to the coast and were invited by the Noi Naiqoro to join them at Naiqoro. The Voreivaga (*vore* means pig in the communalect) as they became known were strong warriors and helped the Noi Naiqoro in two battles. Out of gratitude the Noi Naiqoro gave Qio a high-ranking woman as his wife, and gave the Voreivaga land at Sikituru and made them independent. The Kai Loa (now extinct), the Vucunisai and the Voreivaga were settled together at Sikituru and they installed Qio as Momo.

The Noi Naiqoro then moved the Vucunisai to Naiqoro, to settle with the Botiluvuka. However, the Vucunisai became arrogant, building their *yavu* higher than those of the Noi Naiqoro, and putting a *tabu* on the gardens of the neighbouring Navo people (see below). The Navo removed the fences put up by the Vucunisai and complained to the Noi Naiqoro. The Navo killed a number of the Vucunisai who scattered to Yanuya in the Mamanucas, and to Waya and Viwa in the Yasawa group. The Noi Naiqoro and the Botiluvuka were afraid of the rage of the Navo, and scattered to various places in the mangroves. The leading *mataqali* of the Noi Naiqoro went to Vunamasei and the others to Nasavusavu. They were proposing to install the daughter of Wetula as Momo, but the leading chiefs of Nadi asked for her to go to them, so she married the Navatulevu chief and bore a son, Rokomatu. Her younger brother, Veqa, was installed as Momo in her place.

Taking advantage of this marriage relationship, the Navatulevu asked that Limasa, the Noi Naiqoro war spirit, should be sent to the Navatulevu as their war spirit. In the event, Limasa's son, Rukuse, was sent to the Navatulevu, together with Votuku as his mouthpiece and the Natogo as his protectors.

After a long time the Noi Naiqoro moved to join the Tukani at Lotoiqere. When the Yakuilau, the arrogant Navatulevu and their chief Rokomatu were driven away from Nadi, Rokomatu went to Sabeto territory at Lotoiqere to the Noi Naiqoro as his *vasu*. Lotoiqere became overcrowded, and the Noi Naiqoro returned under Veqa to Vunamasei.

The Botiluvuka quarrelled with the Navo and asked Veqa for help. The Botiluvuka, the Noi Naiqoro, the Tukani and the Vucunisai attacked and burned Navo and the Navo fled to Korolevu (Rukuruku, see below) in the hills between Nadi and the Sigatoka River. On the occasion when the Tola arrived at Nadi, these four groups scattered, and went to the defended site in the hills at Naqwavula.

When Rokomatu returned from Sabeto to Nadi, he recalled the Noi Naiqoro and settled them at Vunamasei. Some Botiluvuka and some Tukani went back to Nadi with the Noi Naiqoro, and were settled at Duiyata/Vunaividamu and at Lotoiqere respectively, and others went to Sabeto. The Vucunisai went with the Noi Naiqoro.

Before they had all gone to Naqwavula, the Tukani were the leaders. On their return, after the Vucunisai had gone from Nadi (as explained above), Rokomatu gave the paramountcy of the Kovacaki to Lewavai, son of Veqa, of the Noi Naiqoro. Meanwhile Rokomatu himself was installed as paramount of the three Nadi *yavusa* (the Navatulevu, the Yakuilau and the Sila), as well as the three Kovacaki *yavusa* (the Tukani, Botiluvuka and Noi Naiqoro).

The Navatulevu and the Yakuilau quarrelled again because the Yakuilau tried to take over the leadership. The Yakuilau asked the Tukani to join them, and Rokomatu asked the Noi Naiqoro who persuaded the Tukani to change sides. The war village of the Yakuilau at Nadroumai was burned, and they scattered to Yavulo, and to Malolo.

Following the introduction of Christianity, the establishment of the 1871 Cakobau Government and presumably the spreading of the fame of the French Emperor (or one of his descendants), the younger son of Rokomatu, Navoleone Ragiagia, was installed as the Momo Levu of Nadi in succession to his elder brother Naigaga. On behalf of the Kovacaki, as original landowners, Lewavai acknowledged Ragiagia's paramountcy and presented him with baskets of earth, and the chiefs of all the associated groups swore allegiance to Navoleone on the Bible. On the death of Lewavai, Ravetale took his place as leader of the Kovacaki. After Cession in 1874, the Noi Naiqoro went to Kovaci land at Buduka to join the Tukani; and out of respect for the Kovacaki as the original Nadi landowners their traditional territory was referred to under the Colonial administration as the *tikina* of Buduka under Buli Buduka. Later the Noi Naiqoro went from Buduka to their present village of Navoci; and following the 1945 amalgamation of *tikina*, the Old *tikina* of Buduka became part of the present *tikina* of Nadi.

The Botiluvuka

The NLC recorded the first settlement of the Botiluvuka, being the descendants of Leawerenalagi (third son of Tutunavanua) as at Dra, opposite the present village of Narewa. Here the Botiluvuka were later joined by the Vucunisai. I was told (see above) that the Botiluvuka came originally from Malolo, and were settled between (*luvuka*) the Tukani, then living at Buduka, and the Noi Naiqoro, then living at Dra. They settled there together with the Vucunisai; and one account said that the Vucunisai were in fact part of the Botiluvuka. The Botiluvuka name was originally Nadi, but was changed to Botiluvuka at the time of the Commission in 1913, presumably out of recognition that the Navatulevu were by then paramounts in Nadi and it would have been inappropriate for the Botiluvuka to retain the toponym.

After the Vucunisai had moved to Bilaki (later Nakavu), they became arrogant towards the Noi Naiqoro, and also put a *tabu* on Nadi land. The Noi Naiqoro asked for help and an army came from Namosi and smote the Vucunisai, killing many – the rest fled to Malolo. The Botiluvuka became frightened and took refuge in the mangroves at Duiyata and Vunavutu.

On the later occasion when the Yakuilau rebelled against the arrogance of the paramount Navatulevu and drove them away from Nadi, the Navatulevu asked the Nadroga people for assistance. The Tola, the Nadroga army, came and burned the Botiluvuka villages, and the Botiluvuka scattered to Naqwavula and to Vuda. Some of the Botiluvuka had previously fled to Sabeto, having stolen some women to whom they were not entitled.

When Christianity came and Navoleone was installed as Momo Levu of Nadi, Lewavai of the Noi Naiqoro brought the Botiluvuka back and settled them in Buduka and Dra, though some remained at Vuda and their descendants are still living at Viseisei as members of the Sabutoyatoya *yavusa*. The Botiluvuka, together with the rest of the Kovacaki, agreed that Lewavai of Noi Naiqoro should be recognised as their leader, and he heeded the authority of the Momo Levu, Navoleone Ragiagia of the Navatulevu (see above).

The Botiluvuka moved from Dra and Buduka at the time of the Cakobau Government, and settled in the present village of Namotomoto.

The Vucunisai

Whatever their origin and relationship (be it by common mythical descent with, or as part of, the Botiluvuka, or indeed if any), it seems to be generally agreed that the Vucunisai and the Botiluvuka were at first together at Dra, and that the Vucunisai then moved to Maqalevu. Here they may have been known at first by the descriptive name of Kawa i Lewatu (Lewatu's family) or perhaps by the name of Nadi (meaning, in the communalect, 'mature' as of oysters or crabs). It is equally likely that the common name for the Vucunisai and the Botiluvuka was LeweiLewatu. It is, however, still problematic whether the name Nadi was originally used to cover all four (or three, if the Vucunisai were then simply part of the Botiluvuka *yavusa*), so forming the Vanua o Nadi or Federation of Nadi; or whether the Vucunisai alone were the Nadi and the other three are the Kovacaki; or whether the Vucunisai and the Botiluvuka were one, known as the Nadi, and the Tukani and Noi Naiqoro were the original Kovacaki, later to be joined by the Botiluvuka; or whether the Vucunisai and the Botiluvuka were one grouping, perhaps known by the common name of Nadi, and the others were known as the Tukani and the Noi Naiqoro respectively. It was only later that the term Vanua o Nadi (comprising the four, later three *yavusa*) was replaced by the term Kovacaki. This term may have been introduced to refer to the three remaining groups after the departure of the Vucunisai; or even after the arrival of the Navatulevu and the Yakuilau, when the Navatulevu were recognised as paramount and it would have been inappropriate to refer to the three original *yavusa* alone as the Nadi.

Be that as it may, the traditional responsibilities of the Kawa i Lewatu, the Vucunisai, were to act as *bai ni valu* or war fence for the protection of the Kovacaki in Buduka or in the war village of Nadroumai. They acted with powers given them by Limasa, the very powerful war spirit, through the mediation of the *bete* or priest who was a member of the Noi Naiqoro.

Perhaps because of their special warrior status and their special relationship with Limasa, the war spirit, the Kawa i Lewatu became very arrogant towards the Noi Naiqoro, and also marked out the Nadi gardens as *tabu* (implying for their control only). The Vucunisai representative went on to tell me that:

> The Noi Naiqoro sent a large *tabua* to the Sabeto people asking for help against the Vucunisai who at the time were living at Bilaki (Nakavu) and three other adjacent sites. The *tabua* was passed on to the Nawaka, the Nadroga, the Navosa and finally to the Namosi people who accepted it and sent an army which smote the Kawa i Lewatu at their four settlements. After their defeat, they buried their weapons (*voco ni sai* means 'burying the spears' in the communalect) and so became known as the Vucunisai. Having taken handfuls of

earth which they left piled as a memorial at Dela i Bua (at Bilaki, now Nakavu), they then went to Denarau (*dei na raurau* means 'the leaves were thrown away' in the communalect) where they threw away the leaf baskets used for the food for their last meal together. Here Ratu ni Yawe, the chief of the Vucunisai, died. One of his daughters went to marry the Kwa Levu of Nadroga, and the other daughter went to Kadavu and named an area there Yawe in memory of her father. When the Vucunisai left their land at Maqalevu, it was given to the Noi Sikituru (presumably the Voreivaga referred to above).

From Denarau, the Vucunisai returned to their place of origin on Malolo. From here they split up and some went to Yanuya (Mamanucas), some to Viwa, some to Waya and some to Natubasa on Yasawa Island. Others went to Vanua Levu, to Nadivakarua (Kubulau Point), to Nacavanadi (Savusavu) and Vuinadi (Natewa Bay). Wherever they settled they heeded the authority of the local chiefs.

It is interesting to speculate whether they were forced to leave Malolo because they maintained their arrogant behaviour. Indeed it may have been this unfortunate trait which forced them to leave Malolo in the first place.

Nowadays the Vucunisai at Yanuya, Viwa and Waya foregather at Bilaki for special ceremonial occasions requiring their joint presence. This may be for sentimental reasons—indeed I was told that they would like to return to the land at Maqalevu which they still regard as their own. Alternatively, they may consider that if they foregathered at Malolo, they would not be regarded as *personae gratae* by the Malolo people; or it may simply be more convenient and simpler for all concerned to travel to Nadi.

The newcomers (Vanua o Nadi)

Three *yavusa*, the Navatulevu, the Yakuilau (Nabati) and the Sila, were newcomers to Nadi. They are based at present in the villages of Narewa, near to the town of Nadi, and Nakavu. On the road to Lautoka at least two groups of people arrived in succession and the first group were given land by the Noi Naiqoro. They were the first of the newcomers to arrive, and they became the Navatulevu. Then several other groups came in succession and the first of them was given land by the Tukani. They became the Yakuilau, having first been known as the Nabati. Finally came the Sila who settled between the other two. In course of time and in spite of continuous inter- and intra-*yavusa* quarrelling, the leader of the Navatulevu became recognised as the paramount of these three *yavusa* and of the Kovacaki. The polity continued to be known as the Vanua o Nadi. The paramount was installed with the title of Momo Levu of Nadi, and was a member of the Nakuruvarua family of the Navatulevu *yavusa*. Much later, thanks to the energy of Navula, the war chief of Navatulevu, the polity of Nadi was considerably expanded to include neighbouring polities.

This account is based on what I was told in the 1990s by the people concerned, and the details differ appreciably from the NLC accounts. Perhaps I should record that the head of the present NLC office told me that the NLC accounts were confusing and suspect and asked me to see if I could shed some light on what the local traditional authorities on the affairs of Nadi could throw on the situation. Alas, almost anything to do with Nadi affairs and leadership is controversial, especially now that there is so much tourist development on Nadi lands and the chiefly share of rent money and other income flowing from dealings with hoteliers is very significant. There was a dispute about who should succeed to the position of Momo Levu, when Ratu Dawai the then-paramount died during the course of my investigations, and the Assistant Roko Tui Ba who had responsibilities for Nadi affairs asked me to restrict my enquiries to non-controversial matters. The dispute, revolving round the question of what was the traditionally acceptable basis of succession, was taken to the High Court which did not consider it appropriate to adjudicate on the matter. In 2003, I heard that a successor had been formally installed as Momo Levu, but I was also told that the installation was not recognised by all the Navatulevu chiefs or by all the *vanua* of Nadi.

Myths of origin and first settlements

The NLC recorded different myths of origin for the Navatulevu, whose progenitor was Duwaka, and for the Yakuilau (progenitor, Tanitaniulu) and Sila (progenitor, Tunaqai), especially as to possible relationships and associations between the respective progenitors. The Navatulevu myths include reference to Tutuvanua, the progenitor of the Kovacaki people, but exclude reference to Tanitaniulu, progenitor of the Yakuilau. The accounts also said that there may have been a fourth relative or associate, Lewatu(tjeke), who was the original ancestral spirit of the somewhat elusive Vucunisai; some of whom are nowadays on Malolo Island. The NLC accounts of the myths of origin for the Navatulevu and the Sila claimed that:

> Du(w)aka and some others went from the Nakauvadra mountains to Nadi on Vanua Levu where he stayed with Tunaqai as well as with two other spirits, Tutuvanua and Lewatu. Later all four left Nadi and sailed west to the Liwaliwa reefs near the Mamanucas. They separated at sea, and Duwaka and Tunaqai landed at Nasaumomo at a time when, the Navatulevu claimed, all Nadi was unoccupied.

The Navatulevu claim differs from that of the Kovacaki people who say that the Nadi area had been occupied by Tutuvanua, their progenitor who had settled at Nasaumomo before the arrival of the mythical first vessel, the *Kaunitoni* (see the Kovacaki account).

> Duwaka married a woman of the Natuvulevu group of the Naua people, now at Saunaka (see separate account). They had two children who became human and went to settle at Navatulevu.
>
> The elder son had two sons, whose descendants were the Navatulevu and the Valemagimagi *mataqali* respectively. The elder of these two sons had five children including Raisiko (the eldest) and Raimoqe. They all lived at Navatulevu.
>
> Duwaka's younger son, Kubu, settled at Nadurumai, and married Turuva, a woman of the Botiluvuka (Kovacaki). His descendants were known as the Nadurumai.

Nasaumomo is a site in the mangrove swamp opposite to Yakuilau Island. It is visible as a group of coconut palms, but despite my best endeavours I have not been allowed to visit this very *tabu* place. Navatulevu and Valemagimagi were the names of the two original *yavu* situated near to each other inland to the left of the road to Denarau and which have been identified to me. Navatulevu is a very impressive and elaborate mound. Three areas known as Navatulevu, Valemagimagi and Nadurumai formed what was described to me as a *rara balavu* or long village, of which the three integral parts were divided from each other by ditches. Separate from these three areas was that of Nakinimai, the settlement of the *bete* or priests of Duaka.

The NLC accounts of the myths of origin for the Yakuilau claim that:

> Tanitaniulu, together with Duaka and Tunaqai, went from the Nakauvadra to Nadi, but they separated at sea. Duaka and Tunaqai went to Nasaumomo. Tanitaniulu landed at Yakuilau where he stayed for a while before going on to Nasaumomo and married Neileqe, daughter of Tutuvanua, the Kovacaki progenitor. One account, later corrected, said that he married Nabure, the eldest child of Tunaqai. It is not known how many children they had, but they are said to have had four grandchildren, the second of whom was called Tuitoga.

Tanitaniulu having settled at Nasaumomo, Tunaqai left Nasaumomo and went to settle at Naqaya. He married Lewanicugitu, and they had one daughter and one son. The son in turn had four children, and they all lived at Naqaya.

These myths of origin given to the NLC are interesting in providing the basis of a spiritual relationship between the three groups which they wanted to maintain in order to demonstrate their sense of unity to what they regarded as an interfering outside Government organisation set on registering them in groups of landowners in accordance with principles they claimed did not accord with their local traditional practices. Not only that, they gave me every impression that they were united, at any rate as far as other federations were concerned, and that their local strength was based on this ideology of unity. The concept of unity and the confidence and comfort derived from it far outweighed the fraternal and internal bickering and rivalries which may perhaps be regarded as perfectly normal in any family or association, however close the bonds may be. As evidenced by my study of their symbols of unity and identification such as the *kai* or tree, a different account of the origins of these people emerged from my explorations. Local representatives of all three *yavusa* told me in the course of discussions in the 1990s that:

> The first elements of the group now known as the Navatulevu came from the islands of Yasawa and Naviti, and they formed the Valemagimagi sub-group which include divisions named Sawailau and Natubusa. These two names are reflected in the place name of Sawailau, an islet off the south-east tip of Yasawa Island; and the kinship group name of Natubusa found presently in the village of Tamasua, Yasawa. These Valemagimagi came to Nadi and were given land by the Tukani who claim to have been in the area before the arrival of the first canoe. At some stage some people came over, probably from Naviti, and their origin is reflected in the name Suelevu by which the Navatulevu were first known. Suelevu is a kinship group on Naviti, and the word *sue* is a word in the Naviti communalect meaning 'house', whereas the Nadi word for house is *were*.

> The next to arrive were some of the Navatulevu from Nagwagwa on the northern slopes of the Tualeita range. They had left their original settlement at Navatulevu on the southern slopes of the Tualeita and crossed the range after attack by an army from Bulu, a mountainous inland part of Ba. The Valemagimagi recognised the strength of these hill people and invited them to settle with them on land near to that already inhabited by the Yakuilau (then known as the Nabati after their land) and the Sila, and be their leaders. The overall name of the Valemagimagi and the Navatulevu then, as a matter of courtesy, became Navatulevu, though it was still being referred to sometimes as Suelevu when the NLC were carrying out their investigations.

> The exact origins of the breakaway Naduruniu are not clear.

> Later came some members of the chiefly family of Nakuruvarua from Nadroga, and they were invited to stay and were made leaders of the Navatulevu. The Momo Levu of Nadi is still appointed from the Nakuruvarua, although there are still bitter arguments about the succession, reflecting the quarrels and rivalries that occurred throughout the recorded period of development of the three *yavusa,* or rather of the Navatulevu and the Yakuilau.

There is evidence that these newcomers to Nadi proceeded to validate and strengthen their position of leadership in two spiritual ways. First, they claimed Duaka as their *nitu* or originating spirit. Duaka is also known as the sea sibling of three inland siblings associated with the interior of Nawaka (see account of the Le Va, the four sibling spirits in the account of the Nine *Yavusa*). Duaka manifested as a *dadakulaci* or sea snake which acted as the defender (*sasabai*) of the entrance through the reef at Momi, with its head at Malolo Sewa Island and its tail at Beqa Island. It was regarded as a *nitu* of great strength and with an extensive personal sphere of influence and close blood relations with the strong folk of the interior.

Secondly, they requested from the Noi Naiqoro of Kovacaki that the powers of their very strong war spirit, Limasa, be made available to the Navatulevu. The Noi Naiqoro sent the son of Limasa, Rukuse, to the Navatulevu people, together with a man of special power of communication with Rukuse and a group called the Natoga to go and look after his requirements. Later they apparently sent Limasa as the war spirit for the Navatulevu and the federation of Nadi.

The development of the Nadi yavusa

A characteristic of the development of so many Fijian polities and federations throughout Fiji is the extent to which continual jealousy (*vuvu*) and rivalry (*veiqati*) within and between descent groups led to quarrels and fighting. This in turn led to socio-political fission from, and fusion with, existing polities or to the creation of new groups. Such quarrels were often concerned with the position of a leader who might have been a member of the group involved or might have been a stranger to the group invited to lead or accepted as leader. They are also concerned with the reaction of subordinates if the paramount behaves in an un-chiefly manner, especially in being overbearing or dominating with unreasonable demands on the goods and services of the subordinates. The traditional accounts may ascribe quarrels to some breach of etiquette in a *yaqona* ceremony or in the distribution of particular pieces of a pig or a fish at a feast. It is often apparent that, underlying such breaches, feelings of rivalry or jealousy are the root causes of quarrels.

The development of the Nadi *yavusa* reveals this situation as prevailing to perhaps a greater extent than elsewhere, especially in my study areas. For this reason in particular, a detailed investigation of Nadi is important for the understanding of the procedures and mechanics of the development of Fijian polities generally. An exploration of the development of Nadi is really a determination of the relationships within and between the Navatulevu and the Yakuilau *yavusa*, and their relationships with the Kovacaki and the neighbouring polities such as Vuda, Sabeto, Nawaka, Naua, Navo, and Sikituru (these polities are described elsewhere).

The development of the Nadi yavusa: Navatulevu

The NLC accounts of even the earliest stages of the development of Navatulevu reveal internal quarrels within the Naduruniu part of the Navatulevu *yavusa*. These were manifested in a quarrel over an area of sugar cane (*tovu*, which had ceremonial value apparently approximating that, later, of *yaqona*), and resulted in some of the Naduruniu going to join with the Yakuilau while the rest remained loyal to the Navatulevu.

It is not clear from the available NLC accounts or from what I learnt myself whether the quarrels involved rivalry over leadership. However, the following quarrel between Raisiko and Raimoqe (see above) as recorded by the NLC made the situation much clearer:

> Duaka was the progenitor of the Navatulevu and the eldest of the progenitor siblings (Duaka, Tanitaniulu and Tunaqai). At first the Navatulevu as descendants of the Duaka, the eldest of the progenitor siblings, were the leaders of the Yakuilau and Sila, being descendants of the younger siblings. Duaka had two sons. The eldest had two sons, Raisiko and Riamoqe whose descendants became the Navatulevu and Valemagimagi *mataqali* respectively. The descendants of Duaka's second son, Kubu, became the Naduruniu *mataqali*. Of the Navatulevu *yavusa*, the recognised leader was Raisiko, being the elder brother. Raimoqe was ambitious to take the leadership from Raisiko, and he went to join the *bete* (the priests) at Nakinimai. This was presumably to gain their spiritual support for his plans. He asked Lomanikaya, an old man of

Tavarua (Rukuruku, see above), for a *buli leka,* a cowry shell symbolising the high rank which Raimoqe wished to achieve. The request was refused, the Tavarua were attacked and burned, and Lomanilaya fled and was killed. The *buli leka* was taken to Raimoqe, and he was brought back to Navatulevu by the Naduruniu and installed as Momo Levu in the presence of the Navatulevu, the Yakuilau and Sila as well as the Kovacaki and other neighbouring polities including the defeated Tavarua. Raisiko was angry and went to join the Yakuilau.

Two generations later the Yakuilau planned to take away the leadership from the Navatulevu *mataqali* of the Navatulevu *yavusa* and give it to the junior branch, the Naduruniu. The NLC recorded that:

> Mudunatua, chief of the Yakuilau, planned that Nawairabe of the Raralevu part of the Naduruniu should be acknowledged as leader. He built an installation house, but Rokomatu, the grandson of Raimoqe, burned it. In revenge, the Yakuilau killed an old man of Navatulevu, and a split between the Yakauilau and the Navatulevu followed. Rokomatu and the Navatulevu took fright and fled to the Tukani (Kovacaki) village of Lotoiqere, where they sheltered with the Noi Naiqoro and some Sikituru people. Mataitoga, a warrior chief of Sabeto heeding Naloto, the paramount of Sabeto, came and took Rokomatu and his Navatulevu followers (known as the Bolaciri) to Sabeto. Mataitoga had ambitions of leadership, and he and Rokomatu chased Naloto away to the Colo and burned his village. With the flight of the Navatulevu, the Yakuilau became paramount in Nadi, and the remaining part of the Navatulevu, together with the Kovacaki, Yavusania, Sikituru, Naua and Vunatoto (Nawaka), heeded the authority of the Yakuilau chief, Mudunatua.

> In course of time, the Yakuilau became arrogant and oppressive (*voravora*) to the other Nadi groups. The Navatulevu in Sabeto met with the Navo, the Utiloaloa (see under Nawaka) and the Ketenavu of Moala, in order to plan a return to Nadi.

What followed is an interesting example of how Fijians would use a network of traditional diplomatic paths (known as *calevu* in the communalect), to make a request through the medium of a *tabua.* The *tabua* would be passed from polity to polity along these 'paths' until some power accepted the *tabua,* thereby becoming bound to meet the request. The ceremonial procedures leading to the killing of the Reverend Thomas Baker were similar. The Navatulevu procedures were as follows:

- The Navatulevu passed the *tabua* along the Calevu ni Valu to the Ketenavu of Moala.
- The Ketenavu passed the *tabua* along the Calevu ni Nukuvou to the Nakaria of Yako.
- The Nakaria who were being harassed by the Noi Yasawa people in the interior, passed on to Nabekasiga, the Kwa Levu or paramount chief of Nadroga, not only this *tabua* but also added one of their own with a request for help against the Noi Yasawa.

Nabekasiga accepted the *tabua* and summoned an army from Serua and Namosi as well as from various Nadroga polities. The war which followed was known as the War of the Tola (communalect for the mangrove lobster—see above). The Tola army, which had the advantage of guns, set off for Nadi from Cuvu and on the way defeated the Noi Yasawa on behalf of the Nakaria. The Sabeto sided with the Navatulevu in their endeavours to return to Nadi, but the Ketenavunivalu (the Moala, Navo and Vunataqwa of the Utiloaloa) did not participate and simply hid. The Yakuilau had never had firearms, and when the Tola started to fire their guns, the Nadi thought it was *nitu* or spirits attacking them. They fled with their supporters to Naqwavula, the fastness inland below Nausori, and their lands fell into the hands of Rokomatu who had returned from Sabeto to Narewa where Nabekasiga, the Kwa Levu, had had houses built for the returning Navatulevu. Nabekasiga and those who had come from so far to join the Tola army were duly thanked, and they returned home. A Naua chief, Naloku, had also returned to Naua from Sabeto where he had sought refuge. His return had been facilitated by his relation, Rokomatu; and because of this relationship and out of gratitude for Rokomatu's assistance Naloku, now paramount of the Naua, was willing to heed the authority of Rokomatu and the Navatulevu.

Rokomatu then recalled those groups who had scattered to Naqwavula and elsewhere, and settled them back in their own lands. Through this obligation, these other groups heeded the authority of Rokomatu, as did the defeated Yakuilau. Rokomatu thus became paramount of the Nadi polities. He was succeeded by his son Koroigaga.

Following Koroigaga's death, the Yakuilau again strove for the leadership and planned to install one of their own as paramount, preparing a ceremonial compound for the purpose. When their candidate was about to enter the compound for installation, the leading warrior Navula threatened him and told him to go away. The Yakuilau who had assembled for the installation were chased away. After trying to defend themselves, they were overcome by Navula; and they fled to the Yavusania on the island of Yavulo where again they were overcome. The Yakuilau and the Yavusania fled to Navo but Navula burned them out. The Navo and the Yavusania fled to Yako on the Nadroga boundary; and the Yakuilau escaped to Malolo. Some of the Navo lands were sold to Europeans in 1867. In due course, Navula recalled the Navo, the Yavusania and the Yakuilau and resettled them at Navo, Yavulo and Nabati respectively. Navula had been too young to fight in the war of the Tola, but because of his proven military ability, he became leader of the Navatulevu, though he refused to accede to the wishes of the Navatulevu and be installed as Momo Levu, the spiritual paramount.

After the arrival of Christianity in Nadi, the Navatulevu installed Navoleone Raigigia, younger brother of Naigaga, as Momo Levu in the presence of the Yakuilau, the Kovacaki, the Naua, the Vunatoto (Nawaka), the Navo and the Sikituru. They all swore on the Bible to heed the authority of Navoleone. When the Cakobau Government was established in 1871, Ratu Peniani Vukinamualevu was appointed Governor of the *yasana* of Ba which included the *tikina* of Nadi. When it became evident that the Cakobau Government could not assert its authority over all of Fiji, a meeting was held on Bau at which Navula was present, and this was followed by Cession in 1874. Under the Colonial Government, Ratu Vuki was made Roko Tui Ba and Yasawas, and Navula was made Buli Nadi. When Navula retired, Nadi was divided up, and Sailosi Dawai, Navula's elder brother, was made Buli Buduka (covering the Tukani and Noi Naiqoro, the Naua and the Noi Tubai in Vaturu). Luke, Navula's son, was made Buli Nadi (for the Navatulevu and Yakuilau, the Sikituru, the Ketenavu, Navo, and the Rukuruku hillfolk). The Naduruniu, because of age-old differences going back to the quarrels about sugar cane, had always lived separately from the rest of the Navatulevu *yavusa* and they had some ambitious members who wanted to break away completely from the rest of the Navatulevu. They had now gone to Nakavu which was some distance from the Navatulevu centre at Narewa; and Nemani Driu (of the Naduruniu) was made Buli Nawaka (for the Vunatoto, the Utiloaloa and the inland members of the Nine *Yavusa*—see Nawaka). Ratu Vuki, though he had had relations in Ba, was a man of rank on Bau (Scarr 1980:116). He served in Ba until the Province turned against him perhaps mainly because of his heavy handedness but also because he was a stranger. He was duly dismissed; and in 1884, Nemani became the first local Roko Tui Ba. He maintained the Naduruniu separation from the rest of the Navatulevu, continuing to live at Nakavu and refusing to be buried in the Navatulevu cemetery. He had bought land on the island of Waya; and though he never lived there, he was buried on Waya in the 1890s.

The development of the Nadi yavusa: Yakuilau

I have given the Navatulevu accounts in some detail for the reasons stated in the introduction to them: so much rivalry and quarrelling involved a struggle for primacy between the Navatulevu and the Yakuilau, and reaction to the oppressive nature of whichever *yavusa* was in power at the time. To complement these accounts, I will give accounts, though less detailed, of the development of the Yakuilau and their version of their interaction with the Navatulevu. The accounts also fill out some of the gaps in the Navatulevu accounts. The 1913 NLC accounts of the Yakuilau said that:

> At first the Navatulevu had authority over the three *yavusa* of Navatulevu, Yakuilau and Sila. Then the Yakuilau determined to gain paramountcy, and they agreed to install Tuitoga, the second of four sibling grandchildren of the original ancestor, Tanitaniulu, to be paramount over the Navatulevu. The installation house was made by the Sikituru, and the ceremony was attended by some Navatulevu, the Sila, all the Kovacaki and the Vucunisai, and the Yavusania.

> Later, the sons of Tuitoga quarrelled and war followed in which the younger brother chased away the elder brother who went to Vuda. Here he gathered an army from Vuda and Sabeto, and attacked the Yakuilau and re-occupied Nabati. After further splits in the Nasaru sub-group of the Yakuilau, all who had fled were brought back and peace was resumed.

> When the Navatulevu increased in numbers, the Yakuilau under Mudunatua feared for their position and planned to exterminate them. They murdered Taleqwailagi, a Navatulevu chief; and Rokomatu and the Navatulevu fled to Lotoiqere. The Yakuilau attacked them here, and Mataitoga brought them to Sabeto, where Mudunatua was murdered, as related in the Navutulevu account.

> When the Tola army arrived from Nadroga, the Yakuilau and their associated groups fled to Naqwavula in the hills. Some of the Yakuilau had gone to join relations at Moala, Sabeto, Vitogo, Malolo, and Waya and Viwa in the Yasawas. Those at Naqwavula stayed there until Rokomatu returned to Narewa in Nadi. He recalled Nakilivaturubu, the Yakuilau chief, and settled the Yakuilau at Narewa. Some who had gone far away to other places did not return. At Narewa, they came under the authority of Navatulevu, and Rokomatu could keep a close watch on their activities and their plots. His suspicions were well founded, because Turaga, the Yakuilau chief, invited the Yavusania to come and partake of some sugar cane (I explained earlier that the sugar cane was evidently used ceremonially in the same way as *yaqona* was later used when seeking some favour). They plotted to kill Navula of Navatulevu. They put up defences and killed Matalulu, an old man of Navatulevu. Navula sent *tabua* to the Noi Naiqoro, the Naua, the Vunatoto (Nawaka), the Sikituru and the Raviravi of Yako. They attacked the Yakuilau who scattered, some to Sabeto and some to Malolo. While on Malolo, the Yakuilau lands fell into the hands of the Navatulevu. Some had gone to join the Moala on the island of Yavulo, but they were attacked here and driven away. In course of time, the Yakuilau on Malolo prepared pigs and *iyau* or valuables such as bark cloth, coconut sinnet and clay pots, as made on Malolo. These were presented to Navula as *isoro* or apology with a request that the Yakuilau be allowed to return to Nadi. In course of time, Navula called the Yakuilau back, and the Yakuilau presented *vudi* or plantains mixed with *yabia* or arrowroot as their *matamatanisali* or formal request to persons by strangers to be allowed to stay with them. This indicated that the Yakuilau were not at all certain what reception they would receive from the Navatulevu. However, Navula settled them at their old territory at Nabati, and peace was resumed.

> The Yakuilau acknowledged the Navatulevu as paramounts, and were present at the installation of Navoleone Raigigia as Momo Levu. At this ceremony, Lewavai, chief of the Tukani, presented the soil at the ceremony (symbolising the handing over of the land and the people to come under the authority of the

installed Momo Levu). This he did in view of the antiquity of his ancestors in the area.

When the Cakobau army attacked Sabeto, some of the Yakuilau were still there, and Navula brought them back to stay at the Navatulevu village of Waqana (on the opposite side of the road to Narewa but a little closer to Denarau). Here they remained in Navula's service for some twenty years until Navula agreed to release them from their obligations and allowed them to join the others at Nabati. The Yakuilau are at present in their own part of the modern village of Narewa.

Although my informants agreed generally with this account, they also told me that, before the arrival of the Navatulevu from the hills, the people who became known as the Yakuilau were the first to settle among the Kovacaki, followed by the Sila. They said that:

The first of these people settled in the area on land at Nabati given to them by the Noi Naiqoro. When Tanitaniulu, the original ancestor of the Yakuilau, married Neileqe, the daughter of Tutuvanua, the progenitor of the Tukani, the Tukani gave the Nabati the island of Yakuilau as *lea i bolo na likoliko* or land provided by the woman's relations for her use when she marries a stranger. When a group of the Tuilawa people came over from Malolo, they rested on Yakuilau which was vacant at the time. The Nabati saw them there and invited them to come and join them. The Nabati saw that the Malolo were very clever people and made them leaders of the combined group which then became known as the Yakuilau.

These accounts show the development of the Yakuilau *yavusa* from local and stranger groups of arrivals, and the changes of leadership by agreement. When the Navatulevu came down from the hills, the Yakuilau and the Sila recognised the strength of the Navatulevu hill folk and acknowledged them as the leaders of all the three groups, that is, the Navatulevu, the Yakuilau and the Sila. The Yakuilau currently occupy their own part of the modern village of Narewa, next to those of the Navatulevu and the Sila.

The development of the Nadi yavusa: Sila

The Sila currently occupy their own part of the village of Narewa. The 1913 NLC records about the Sila are relatively scanty, and I had difficulty in finding out much from the senior members of the *yavusa* who were somewhat diffident in discussing their background, although they were perfectly ready to talk about any other matters. The NLC account said that:

Tunaqai's son was called Naibaubau and he had one son, Vasu, and four grandsons. The four grandsons lived together at first at Naqaya, Tunaqai's place, and then they became arrogant, and they quarrelled and split up. The youngest remained at Naqaya, but the others established their own places (which were separate but adjacent to each other, lying, as I was shown, to the left of the road to Denarau). As their numbers increased, they joined up and moved to the mangroves at Korosamiti.

When the Navatulevu and the Yakuilau quarrelled, the descendants of the eldest grandson of Tunaqai, because their original ancestral spirits were siblings, went with one other group and joined with the Navatulevu. Presumably reflecting their earlier quarrel, the descendants of the other two grandsons went and joined the Yakuilau at Nabati. The duties of the Sila at Nabati were to prepare food for the Yakuilau; but they were not, however, given any planting land by the Yakuilau.

Following this quarrel, some of the Sila fled with the Navatulevu, but the others remained with the Yakuilau. When the Tola army came from Nadroga to assist in the return of the Navatulevu, those members of the Sila who had been with the Yakuilau went with the Yakuilau to Naqwavula. The others remained with the Navatulevu. After peace resumed, Rokomatu, chief of the Navatulevu, brought the Sila back with the Navatulevu and placed them in the compound of Navula. The Sila were in Navula's compound at the time of Cession in 1874. The others were brought back from Naqwavula, and Navula joined all the Sila together and settled them at Korosewa, a part of the village of Waqana. Rokomatu gave them planting land, and the Sila performed the ceremony of *matamatanisali* (performed when taking up residence with a different *yavusa*) at Waqana and promised to fill Rokomatu's yam house with produce from their gardens.

The Sila and others in Narewa with whom I discussed the affairs of the Sila told me that these people came from Nadroga from a place called Sila at Tau in Malomalo *tikina* inland from Momi Bay. There was a split but I could not determine whether it was due to an internal quarrel or due to external threat. The nearby Karia people at Yako had suffered from attack by the Noi Yasawa from Rukuruku (and were duly helped by the Tola army – see above), and there may well have been continuing pressure from the hill people on those living near the coast. Whatever the cause, some of the Sila went to Sanasana on the coast, some 20 km south of Tau; others went to the island of Naloma (near Denarau marina); and others went to Nadi where they were settled by the Navatulevu between the Navatulevu settlement and Nabati, the settlement of the Yakuilau. The Sila made ceremonial presentations (*cobo*) to the Momo Levu of Navatulevu, thus acknowledging his paramountcy, and indeed one division (*beto*) of the Sila is known as the Nacobo, symbolising this position of inferiority of the Sila – a position which is reflected in the NLC account. Though traditionally providers of food for the chiefs, the Sila may not have been particularly successful in this role, and there is a place known as Namaru in memory of an occasion when they left the food so long that it smelt bad (*maru,* in the communalect). When the Navatulevu moved from Waqana to Narewa *makawa*, the Sila went and occupied some small islands in the mangroves in the Nadi River delta. When the Navatulevu moved to the present village of Narewa, the Sila moved to be near them.

As we have seen, the myths of origin claimed that Duwaka, Tanitaniuli and Tunaqai, progenitors of the Navatulevu, the Yakuiilau and the Sila respectively (and Lewatu of the Vucunisai) were siblings, although Navatulevu associated Duwaka with Tunaqai in particular, perhaps reflecting the intimate connections claimed between the Sila, as their providers of food and the Navatulevu paramounts. Since the Navatulevu ignored Tanitaniulu, they may have done so deliberately in order to keep themselves separate from the Yakuilau with whom they had been on bad terms for so long. It is tempting to accept this explanation based on consistency of inter-*yavusa* relationships rather than the more prosaic explanation of a scribe's error, especially as in theory all NLC accounts were supposed to have been read back to the representatives for endorsement.

The Saunivalu

(a) Saunivalu yavusa

The Saunivalu *yavusa* based at present in the village of Sikituru, is an independent part of the strong and influential Saunivalu people at present living in the village of Keiyasi far up the Sigatoka River in the Old *tikina* of Namataku in the province of Nadroga. Their original ancestral spirit, Naqilolevu, came from the Nakauvadra; and having sailed round the coast to the mouth of the Nadi River, he walked inland to Namoli and finally settled at Korovutia.

On an occasion of the ceremonial presentation of a pig, Qilolevu's two grandsons, Qio and Vavoka, were upset about the way the pig was distributed, and they left the village. In the course of their travels, Qio married a woman of Bemanu, in inland Nawaka; and they finally reached Naqereqere near Nadi Bridge. Here the brothers were seen by the Noi Naiqoro who took them to Naiqoro, and Vatuka was given a woman of Noi Naiqoro to be his wife.

Later, the Noi Naiqoro engaged the Sabeto in a great battle at Vauroka (Mount St Mary's, on the road from Nadi to Sabeto). The two brothers came to their assistance in this battle and also in another battle. Because the brothers had done so well in battle, the Noi Naiqoro, the Kai Loa and the Vucunisai gave them land; and the Kai Loa and the Vucunisai agreed that Qio should be installed as Momo of the three, the Saunivalu, the Kai Loa and the Vucunisai. Before the installation, the Saunivalu had been living at Naiqoro and heeding the authority of the Noi Naiqoro. Afterwards the Noi Naiqoro agreed that the Saunivalu should be independent, and they left Naiqoro and went to settle at Sikituru with the Vucunisai and Kai Loa.

The Saunivalu split up and lived separately following two quarrels, one resulting from excessive *yaqona* drinking and the other from fraternal disagreement. One of their villages was called Nasonini. At the time of the Tola, the Saunivalu because of their association with the Yakuilau were burned, and they scattered, some to Sabeto and some to Naqwavula in the hills. They were later brought back and settled at Vunatawarau by the Navatulevu war chief, Navula, who also introduced them to Christianity. Later, Navula agreed that the Saunivalu should return to their village of Nasonini, and finally they went back to Sikituru, where they are at present.

They were formally reconciled with the Saunivalu at Keiyasi in 1993 in the course of a tearful ceremony, with pigs being carefully presented in correct manner. The descendants of Vavoka, the younger brother, have the responsibility for the burial of the Momo Levu of Nadi, in the event that the Navatulevu decide that the *vasu* (relations of the mother of the deceased) should not carry out these usual traditional responsibilities of the *vasu*. This group of the Saunivalu is referred to as the iTutu or Bekwa. In the 1990s, I witnessed the carrying out of these responsibilities by the iTutu, one of whom wore a high pyramid-shaped hat and sat beside the coffin on the bier as it was carried from the Great House to the Church and from the Church to the chiefly burial-ground. Sitting on the same level as the corpse and wearing a hat in the chiefly presence, normally unheard of, were symbols of the great respect felt by the Nadi people for the iTutu group of the Saunivalu.

(b) Associated yavusa: Kai Loa and Vucunisai

The Kai Loa are now extinct and it was difficult to find any independent information to add to that recorded by the 1913 NLC, and anyone who was prepared to discuss the matter indicated their agreement with the NLC records. Tavitaviqalau, the original ancestral spirit of the Kai Loa, came from the Nakauvadra and followed the coast to the island of Vunamoli. From here, he went on to Gaganamoli near Korovuto where he settled. When the two Saunivalu brothers came down from Namataku and helped in the Noi Naiqoro wars, the Kai Loa joined the Noi Naiqoro and Vucunisai in giving the brothers land at Sikituru; and they joined the Vucunisai in installing Qio of the Saunivalu as leader of the three groups. The Kai Loa then moved and settled with the other two groups at Sikituru. It is not known whether the Kai Loa became extinct through war or disease; and there was no survivor at the time I was conducting the research.

The Vucunisai (see above under Kovacaki) are now scattered to Yanuya in the Mamanuca Group, to Waya and Viwa in the Yasawa Group, and to Vanua Levu. Their original ancestral spirit was Lewatu, expanded by some to 'Lewatutjeke', the daughter of Tutuvanua (progenitor of the Kovacaki). Others said that Lewatu was not connected with Tutuvanua. As suggested earlier, she may have been the Lewatu(lekeleke) who married Tuilevu of the Sabutoyatoya (see under Vuda), and went to Malolo where he was the original ancestral spirit of the Tuilawa chiefly group of Malolo. The origins of the Vucunisai are obscure; and they may have come from Malolo to Nadi, perhaps with, or as part of, the Botiluvuka. They may have first settled with the Botiluvuka at Dra, having landed at Denarau. Their first independent settlement appears to have been on Noi Naiqoro land at Maqalevu where they had three settlements. They were known collectively as the Lewe i Lewatu or the Nadi, and their duties were to protect the Kovacaki. The term Nadi then covered the three *yavusa* of the Kovacaki, and later included not only the Kovacaki but also the three newcomer *yavusa* of Navatulevu, Yakuilau and Sila (see above). All these together duly comprised the federation or *vanua* of Nadi, under the paramountcy of the Momo Levu of Nadi.

In course of time the Vucunisai became overpoweringly arrogant, especially towards the Noi Naiqoro, until, at the request of the Noi Naiqoro, the Namosi people came from the interior and smote the Vucunisai who left Nadi and went back to Malolo. The land of the Vucunisai was given to the Saunivalu. It may well have been the arrogant behaviour of the Vucunisai that led to them being chased away from Malolo in the first place. It may also have been that such behaviour resulted in the Vucunisai, in course of time, having to leave Malolo once more. From Malolo, the Vucunisai moved on to the islands of Yanuya, Waya and Viwa, and perhaps to Vanua Levu, carrying their old name of 'Nadi' with them. This, they claim, accounts for the occurrence of the name of Nadi in several areas on Vanua Levu. In the province of Bua, the name occurs as the village of Nadivakarua, and in the *vanua* of Nadi, of which the leading chief is traditionally titled Buli Nadi, (whence the origin of the title of Buli as that of the Fiji Administration official in charge of a *tikina*).

The Ketenavunivalu

The three *yavusa* of Natutale, Sauvana and Nacaqaru had associations with, or came originally from, various parts of Nadroga, according to what the iTaukei Naqwaraivualiku, their paramount, told me. They are known collectively as the Ketenavunivalu (a term which may have at one time included the Navo and Utiloaloa). They are referred to light-heartedly as the Ralete—*lete* meaning 'baked' in the communalect; and they regard themselves as very jolly (*viwali*) and say that they work well together now, even if there was some internal jealousy at one time.

The three *yavusa* settled in the Nadi general area in various places but after Cession lived together at Moala. The Sauvana, who may have come first to the area, are now extinct. The myths of origin are particularly interesting, especially in relation to the Natutale who claim ultimate original mythical connections with the once powerful eastern confederation of Verata. The three *yavusa* do not claim to be related either by descent or by spiritual connection. It is difficult to determine the basis of the bond between them which became strong in course of time, except that all three were neighbours and newcomers from possibly the same general area of the inland hills of Nadroga. It is interesting to see how the three newcomer *yavusa* settled down in the Nadi general area. Here they split up and then joined together again, became interrelated with the Nadi chiefs and other neighbours, and then seemed to validate their status and outside connections through myths of origin based on the Nakauvadra Mountains and the travels of their ancestral spirits. The myths as I record them took into account those given by the 1913 NLC; and during the 1990s I discussed them at length with the well-educated and interested iTaukei Naqwaranivualiku or paramount chief of the Ketenavunivalu people, and with the knowledgeable *bete* or traditional priest of the Ketenavunivalu, as follows below.

Myths of origin

The Natutale

The myths of origin of the Natutale related how Rokomoutu came from the Nakauvadra and drifted to Verata from the island of Koro. Here he married and had several sons, one of whom was Kurukuruivanuakula who sailed away to Dama, Vanua Levu. He then sailed to Vanuakula, Tavua, on the north Viti Levu coast, and from there to the island of Vomo (the holiday island of the Momo Levu of Vuda). He then went on to Tube at the mouth of the Nadi River, and then up a little creek in the mangroves at the north of

Natutale island to Vanuakula. He built a house on Natutale called Bau and married a woman of the Nabati (Yakuilau). They had four children.

Three of the children went to Tiliva and then to Dama, down the river from Moala; whilst the fourth went to the Noikoro at Korolevu, Namosi.

The Sauvana

Lekeninasau came from Nakauvadra and followed the Tualeita (the spirit path along the mountain range ending at Edromu, near the sea between the Vuda and the Sabeto people). He came eventually to Nasau near Korovuto where he married a woman of the Leivunaniu. They had two sons, the elder of whom married a woman of Nalevaka (Yavusania). Hence the Sauvana are *vasu* to the Yavusania.

The families of the two brothers quarrelled, when the elder son and his family were not invited to drink *yaqona* which had been prepared for both of them. So the younger son was chased away and went to the inland area of Waicoba where he settled at Sauvana. His brother later called him back and they all went to settle at Vusama; and they were here when the Noi Nakurusiga came from Nokonoko, Nadroga, looking for land and were brought by the Sauvana to settle with them at Vusama.

The Nacagaru

Vuyavuya came from the Nakauvadra and went first to Vuya on Vanua Levu which was occupied. So he sailed to Nalamu (where the *Kaunitoni* hit the reef off Viseisei) and then to Malolo which was already occupied. He sailed on to the island of Nacova (then called Nacava) near Moala, where he settled on vacant land now called Vuya, and married a woman of the Nabati (Yakuilau) who were then at Waqana. They had two sons. Vuya was subject to flooding, and so the sons moved to Nacagaru which was unoccupied.

The Ketenavunivalu and other polities

The quarrels resulting in fission and fusion intra- and inter-*yavusa* which characterise the development of these three *yavusa* are typical of polity development in the west. In this part of the west, until about the time of the 1871 Cakobau Government, no strong and ambitious leader had emerged who was in a socio-political position backed up by military power to achieve any significant degree of federation. Even today, the power bases of the leading western polities such as Vuda, Sabeto, Nawaka or Nadi are relatively minor and unstable, as witnessed by recent disagreements about leadership succession. Far more typical are the independent *yavusa* such as the Naua (see below) or the minor groupings of *yavusa* such as the Ketenavunivalu or the Navo (see below). What is more interesting than the exploration of unity and minor federation of western polities is the identification of formal lines of diplomatic communication between these independent polities and the background to their establishment. This will be discussed separately from the exploration of origins and development.

The development of all three *yavusa* will be discussed together, and the following narrative and commentary are based on accounts given to me by the iTaukei Naqwaranivualiku and the *bete* of the Ketenavunivalu, as well as those taken from the results of the 1913 NLC investigations checked by me with these two leaders of the Ketenavunivalu federation.

The development of the Ketenavunivalu

The descendants of the three sons of the original ancestral spirit, Kurukuruivanuakula, were at Dama upstream from Moala when they saw that the island of Natutale was vacant. So they went and settled there. They agreed that the descendant of the second son should be made leader, described as Tseitseimata ni Tara Were ('Leader of the Housebuilders'), and his yavu was called Naqwaranivualiku.

The son of this person was in due course formally installed as their Momo by the Natutale, the Sauvana and the Nacagaru, known collectively as the Ketenavunivalu. The installation symbolising the federation of these three neighbouring *yavusa* was carried out on the installation mound on Natutale, and known as Bau. The Momo was seated on a stone and given a stone to hold, symbolising the handing to him of responsibility for the land and the people of the three *yavusa*.[1] At this time, the Natutale were living on Natutale, the Sauvana were at Vusama, and the Nacagaru were at Nacagaru.

After the installation of the first Momo, his son was installed and he became very arrogant and oppressive. As an example, he gave away three women for a gun. Then later the Ketenavunivalu became generally oppressive in the Nadi area and arrogant towards the Navatulevu chiefs. For instance, the Sauvana went without permission and picked some *vudi* or plantains and *kulu* or breadfruit belonging to the Navatulevu. Because of their behaviour, the Ketenavunivalu were duly smitten by a chief of the Navatulevu, Sorovakatini, and the Natutale and the Sauvana scattered to the island of Malolo. The Nacaqaru went to Yako on the Nadroga boundary where they remained for a long time. Later they were all brought back by the Navatulevu and settled in their old villages.

Bad relations between the Ketenavunivalu and the Navatulevu continued. Then the Navatulevu became themselves so oppressive to the Nadi people that they were chased away by the Yakuilau aided by the Ketenavunivalu. However, when the Nadroga army, the Tola, came at the request of the Navatulevu in exile to drive away the Yakuilau and enable the Navatulevu to return to Nadi, the Ketenavunivalu joined with the Navo and Utiloaloa, and did not oppose the Tola. Indeed, the Natutale fed the Tola and carried messages for the Navatulevu. Presumably in acknowledgement of this support, the Navatulevu asked that the villages of the Ketenavunivalu not be burned, although one account said that Nacaqaru was burned as a mark of respect for the visiting army.

Nevertheless, after the departure of the Tola, relations between the Ketenavunivalu and the Navatulevu continued to be bad, and the Ketenavunivalu still displayed arrogant behaviour towards the Navatulevu. For instance, the Natutale killed a pig belonging to Ratu Isireli Turelau Naulia Namulo, chief of the Navatulevu. The Navatulevu took immediate revenge by killing the animals of the Natutale, before taking more widespread military action against them.

The Navatulevu army was under the command of Navula, the ambitious war leader of the Navatulevu. He now saw his chance to prove his worth, and he called on various polities near Nadi and also in the hills of Namataku and Magodro to come and attack the Ketenavunivalu. He burned the villages of Natutale, Vusama and Nacaqaru. The lives of the Natutale were spared at the request of Namulo's wife who was of Natutale, and the Natutale were taken first to Waqana to be under the Navatulevu, and later to Malolo. At this time there arose much jealousy (*vuvu*) among the Sauvana and the Nacaqaru against the leading *yavusa*, the Natutale, and the Natutale at Waqana had asked Navula to burn Vusama especially. When Vusama was burned, the Sauvana went to Yako where they spent eight years before being taken back by Navula and settled in the Nadi area at Raviravi. The Nacaqaru were taken by the neighbouring Yavusania and were given refuge on the island of Yavulo, where for a third time they were attacked by the Navatulevu. They scattered, some to Malolo with the Natutale, some to the mountainous interior (the Colo), and some to Yako with the Sauvana.

---

1   On the island of Natutale, I saw the mounds of Bau and Naqwaranivualiku as well as the installation stones carefully hidden in a growth of cevuga or tall ginger plants.

The Ketenavunivalu were all still away at Cession in 1874, and Navula, war chief of the Navatulevu, brought most of them back over a period of time, and settled them eventually at Moala. Some Natutale remained on Malolo, where they still live. While they were away, the Ketenavunivalu lands came into the hands of Navula who sold some to European settlers in 1867. When they were brought back and settled at Moala, the Ketenavunivalu performed appropriate ceremonies of apology to Navula.

After Navula had, over a period of time, brought back these three and those other *yavusa* which at various times had scattered from in and around the Nadi area to the Colo, Malolo and elsewhere, he was recognised as the leader in the area. All those who had come in answer to his call for help against the Ketenavunivalu as well as the defeated Ketenavunivalu began to make ceremonial presentations to him, thereby acknowledging his paramountcy. This was out of recognition that it was he who had either brought them together as an army under his control, or had consented to bring back those who had scattered after his successful attacks on their villages. The Natutale also gave Navula a holiday place on an island near Moala where he planted a lemon tree that died not long before my visits in 1995 and 1996.

The surviving Ketenavunivalu nowadays maintain their formal independence from the Momo Levu, but continue to make presentations to the Navatulevu on appropriate occasions and to show respect to the Momo Levu of Nadi.

The Yavusania

The two *yavusa* currently known as the NoiVulani (sometimes but incorrectly referred to as the LeweiVulani) and the Neilavutu are known collectively as the Yavusania. The NoiVulani live in the villages of Yavusania and Korovuto. Their war spirit is Lewatu. The Neilavutu live in the village of Korovuto. As in the case of the Saunivalu, the Noivulani came from the mountainous interior of Nadroga and originated through a split from the parent group (known as the Leweivunaniu). They appear to be a unified descent group. On the other hand, the Neilavatu are a composite group, originating partly from the island of Ovalau, where Levuka, the old capital of Fiji, is situated, and partly from the Navatulevu people of Nagwagwa (see under Vuda).

The Yavusania territory lies between the western boundaries of Nadi town and the present north-western boundaries of the Old *tikina* of Momi in the New *tikina* of Malomalo in the province of Nadroga. To the north-west lie the polities of Ketenavunivalu based on the village of Moala, and the Saunivalu based on the village of Sikituru. To the north-east lie the polities of the Navo based on the village of Dratabu (and previously on the village of Vunayasi), the Vunatoto or Nawaka based on the village of Nawaka, and the Utiloaloa based on the village of Vatutu. These were all small, not particularly powerful polities by themselves. They would, however, periodically gain in importance especially when, from time to time, they aligned themselves with each other or opposed each other, in association with or opposition to, either the Yakuilau or the Navatulevu.

As in the case of the Ketenavunivalu, the Yavusania *yavusa* are of great interest in an exploration of fission and fusion in polities. They demonstrate, in particular, first, how minor polities in the west maintained their independence and their individuality; and secondly, how they refused to sacrifice their independence by confederating permanently with such relatively major polities as Nadi, either in order to seek protection or to symbolise their defeats in the course of their many quarrels and disputes. On the other hand, though they may have maintained their political independence, they also developed an elaborate socio-political network with other polities through a fascinating system of political pathways of communication.

The two *yavusa*, the NoiVulani and the Neilavutu, probably have based their socio-political association on mutual convenience and expediency. As in the case of the Saunivalu, they validated this association spiritually through myths of origin linking them with the Nakauvadra, claiming their respective progenitors both came down from the Nakauvadra and followed the Sigatoka River and climbed up from Waicoba before proceeding to their respective first places. The myths of origin and the accounts of the development of these two *yavusa* and their relationships with their neighbours were based on what I was told by leaders of the two *yavusa* who were interested and knowledgeable in such matters, and on accounts recorded by the NLC and checked with the present *yavusa* representatives. The myths of origin and accounts of development are as follows.

Myths of origin

The NoiVulani

The progenitor, Sarekwa, came down from the Nakauvadra Mountains and walked along the banks of the Sigatoka River until he came to Waicoba where he climbed inland and settled at Vunaniu, Nasaucoko. He married a woman of the NoiVatuma, from the village of Nawaqadamu in the hills of Rukuruku (see Nawaka); and they had four children. When they were together at Vunaniu, they were known collectively as the LeweiVunaniu (a name by which they were sometimes known when they came down to Yavusania).

There was a family quarrel, and the two youngest sons left Vunaniu and went down towards the coast, looking for land. They finally found vacant land at Yavusania, and here they settled. The elder brother made the younger brother to be leader. Their descendants were known first as the LeweiYavusania and later as the NoiVulani.

The Neilavutu

The progenitor, Senivesi, came down from the Nakauvadra Mountains and walked along the banks of the Sigatoka River until he came to Waicoba. From here he climbed up inland and having slept at Nabuasa, he went down to the coast to Emua, between Yako and the island of Sonaisali in the province of Nadroga. Here he stayed and married a woman of the Naqavui people of Momi, and they had two children. These two children later left Emua and went to look for land. Eventually they came to Yavusania, where there was some vacant land which was given to them by the NoiVulani. Here they stayed, and their descendants were known as the Neilavutu. The rest of the family remained at Nasaucoko, where their descendants still live.

The development of the two yavusa: the Yavusania

The NoiVulani claim to have originated at Nasaucoko in the mountains of Nadroga/Navosa. They followed the Sigatoka River down to the coast, stopping at the villages of Lawai, Yavulo, Sigatoka and Yadua, and up to the inland Nawaka village of Rukurukulevu. At this stage they were known as the LeweiVunaniu. While still at the coast, they were preparing to install Neibuli, their most senior member, to be leader, when some women out fishing found a man hiding in a tree on the island of Yanuca. They took him to the Leweivuniu who noted that he was a person of great beauty and was fair-skinned whereas Neibuli was dark-skinned. They decided to install him instead as their leader. He had drifted over from Tonga, and he was given a woman of Leweivunaniu to be his wife. His children tended to have fairish skin and to resemble Tongans. During my visits to the village of Yavusania, a member of the Leweivunaniu in the village was pointed out to me as having what were regarded as Tongan physical characteristics.

In time, the Leweivunaniu split up, some remaining in the Sigatoka area, others going north first to the LeweiVagadra at Bavu and Tau in Nadroga, and then going on to Yako on the Nadroga/ Nadi boundary. From here they went on north until they came to the island of Yavulo (presumably bringing the name with them from Sigatoka) and finally establishing the village of Viivi, a short distance from the present village of Yavusania. Here there was a grove of *ivi* or native chestnut trees. From there they went to the site of the present village of Korovuto which was dry and where there were only *qaro* or casuarina trees. They wanted also to have easy access to the fruits of the sea and the mangroves of the Nadi River delta, and so some moved back to Viivi while the rest remained at Korovuto. At this stage they became known as the NoiVulani. My informants did not know why they took this name except that it may have been derived from that of an island, Vulani, on the Sabeto border. There was an old village site on Vulani at the time of my visits in the 1990s (since destroyed by developers) and the Sabeto people told me that the NoiVulani had occupied the island at one time. The Leweiwavuwavu of Sabeto owned Vulani, before the Sabeto chiefs sold it to Europeans in 1870.

When the two *yavusa* from the two villages gather together, any formal address to them is '*ki Yavusania*' or 'to Yavusania', being the collective name for both *yavusa*. If the gathering is at the village of Yavusania, the form of address was '*ki Rukunaivi*' or 'to below the *ivi* trees', referring to the trees under which the first village of Viivi was situated. If the gathering is at Korovuto, the address is '*ki Rukunaqaro*' or 'to below the casuarina trees', referring to the trees around the village of Korovuto.

While the NoiVulani were settled at Yavusania, they were joined by first, a group of people from Lovoni, Ovalau, who came after the Lovoni people had been defeated by Cakobau in June 1871 (Derrick 1950: 201 but disputed), and who then became known as the Lovonakoto; and secondly, by a group of people who had come from the hill village of Navatulevu on the south side of the Tualeita Range overlooking the north side of the Sabeto valley, and who then became known as the Keteisaba.

It is not clear whether the Keteisaba had come direct from Navatulevu or from the later village of Nagwagwa on the north side of the Range, from which the Navatulevu of Nadi had directly originated. Whatever their origin, they were of the same stock as the Navatulevu people of Nagwagwa and later of Nadi; the Nakuruvarua chiefs of Navatulevu who had come late to Nadi from Nadroga refer to these Keteisaba as Na Qase or Old Men, and call them Tai or Grandfather.

These two groups, the Lovonakoto and the Keteisaba became known as the Neilavutu. The Neilavutu did not formally heed the authority of the NoiVulani but the land which was given to them by the NoiVulani served to confirm a bond of cooperation between the two *yavusa*. The name of Neilavutu refers to this association between them and to the position of the Neilavutu as the *bai kei Yavusania* or defenders of Yavusania, the joint name of the two *yavusa*. *Lavutu* means 'to challenge by striking the handle of a club on the ground' (Capell 1941:135). However, in course of time, the Neilavutu, as newcomers to the territory of the NoiVulani, respected the latter and jointly installed a member of the Nalevaka *mataqali* of the NoiVulani to be the leader of the Yavusania. The installation took place at the old village site of Viivi, where I saw half of the *vatu ni veibuli* or installation stone under an *ivi* (*Inocarpus edulis*) tree next to a mound said to be that of the *bito* or spirit house. This surviving half has a smoothed area in which there were some long grooves. The whereabouts of the other half of the stone is unknown. The stone I saw is said to have been brought from Nasaucoko, the original place of the NoiVulani, and perhaps the other half is still up there.

In the early days when they first joined up together, the two *yavusa* of NoiVulani and Neilavutu heeded the authority of the Yakuilau (Nabati) who were then the paramounts of Nadi.

There is also a close connection between the Senibua of Nawaka and the Lovonakoto of the Neilavutu. Momoriqwa, the progenitor of the Senibua, had a descendant named Lewavore. This man of high rank among the Senibua married a woman of the Neilavutu, and they had a son, Leakui. Before the arrival of the Tola army at Nawaka, the woman took her son for safety to Yavusania, where she had a younger sister married to a member of the Lovonakoto. Lewakui and his relatives *tiko vakararavi* or became dependent on the Lovonakoto. When he grew up, he heeded the authority of the Yavusania chiefs, not the Nawaka chiefs, and there is a recognised Senibua group among the Lovonakoto people of Yavusania.

When they were first at Yavusania, the NoiVulani were associated with the Vucunisai, although they did not share villages. The NoiVulani were leaders in this association, and were looked after (*qaravi*) by the Vucunisai. The Vucunisai, who were associated with the Kai Loa, were then living in three villages: at Wala, where they heeded the authority of the Nabati (Yakuilau); at Yasawa, heeding the Saunivalu at Sikituru; and at Nadua. The Vucunisai and the Kai Loa were both under the general protection of the Yakuilau.

Then, as explained earlier, the Vucunisai became arrogant, claiming the Nadi food gardens as theirs. They were duly smitten by the Naua on the instructions of Raimoqe of Navatulevu, and the Vucunisai fled to the Mamanuca group. The Navatulevu army under Raimoqe also attacked the NoiVulani at Yavusania, presumably because of their connections with the Yakuilau, and the NoiVulani scattered to the unoccupied island of Yavulo where the Yakuilau protected them. The Neilavutu remained at Yavusania.

The NoiVulani were on Yavulo and the Neilavutu were at Yavusania when the Tola army arrived at the request of the Navatulevu. As said above, the Navatulevu had been chased away from Nadi because of their arrogant behaviour, and they were sheltering with the Sabeto people under Mataitoga when they asked the Nadroga people for help in getting them back to Nadi.

Both the NoiVulani and the Neilavutu sided with the Yakuilau, as did the Noi Naiqoro, the Kovacaki and the Naua, under the leadership of Ravato of Yakuilau. The Tola on behalf of the Navatulevu attacked the Neilavutu and burned the village of Yavusania; and the NoiVulani and the Neilavutu scattered with the Yakuilau to Naqwavula in the hills behind Nawaka. Their land fell into the hands of Navula, war chief of the Navatulevu. Navula brought the Neilavutu and the NoiVulani back from Naqwavula and re-settled them on Yavulo, and from that time they heeded the authority of the Kuruvarua family of the Navatulevu, Ravato having *soro* or apologised to Navula. The power of the Yakuilau and the independence of the Yavusania group came to an end.

All went well until some young men of the NoiVulani group stripped naked in front of Navula. Because of this disrespectful behaviour (*valavala vakasausa*), Navula, with his army the Nasanini, attacked the NoiVulani, burned the village of Yavulo and took the people to Nadi. However the Kai Navo came to the rescue and with the agreement of Navula took over the responsibility for the NoiVulani and settled them at Navo. Later, under instructions from Navula, the Navo together with the NoiVulani attacked the Nawaka people. The Nawaka assisted by the Noi Naiqoro, Naua and Utiloaloa repelled the attackers and burned the village of Navo. The Navo and the NoiVulani scattered to Yako until Navula brought them back and settled the NoiVulani at Yavulo. Here they remained until after the time of the Cakobau Government, when they went to Yavusania. At the time of Cession, the NoiVulani divided. Some remained at Yavusania and some went to Korovuto, where the Neivaluti were already living.

The Noi Navo

The territory of the Noi Navo lies immediately to the west of the Nawaka and the Utiloaloa people; to the east of the Saunivalu at Sikituru, and the Yavusania at Yavusania and Korovuto; and to the south of the Old *tikina* of Nadi. To the south of the Noi Navo are the Karia people at Yako on the boundary of the Old *tikina* of Momi in the province of Nadroga. Most of the land is fairly flat with modest hills, rising to wooded hill country around the rocky prominence of the spirit site of Namarasa, where there are also old village sites.

The five *yavusa* of Navo, Digilo, Noi Yaro, Noi Takuci and Eloto, known collectively as the Noi Navo were, when I first started my investigations, based in the village of Vunayasi. They later moved to Dratabu after a hurricane. Their *nitu ni valu* or war spirit is Namama, son of Limasa, the war spirit of the Kovacaki, and brother of Rukuse, the war spirit of the Navatulevu before Limasa himself was recognised as the war spirit for Nadi generally. The paramount of the Noi Navo holds the title of iTaukei Nakauvadra and is currently of the *yavusa* of Noi Yaro (see below about leadership). Except for the hill site of Namarasa, most of the sites associated with the spirits of the Noi Navo are near Dratabu and Vunayasi.

The myths of origin and the accounts of the development of these five *yavusa* and their relationships with their neighbours were based on what I was told by leaders of each *yavusa*, and on accounts recorded by the NLC and checked with the present *yavusa* representatives. The Turaga ni Koro or village headman of Dratabu took a great interest in my research and was particularly helpful. The myths of origin and accounts of development, so recorded, are as follows.

Myths of origin

The five progenitors of the five Noi Navo *yavusa* all came originally from Nakauvadra. Two of them came along the north coast of Viti Levu, and two came across country. The progress of the fifth is not known. They settled in places not far apart and around the site of Navo. One representative said that they all lived together at Navo and only later after a flood did their descendants settle apart.

Nakutavi followed the coast to Vatia Point, between the towns of Ba and Lautoka, from where he went on to the Nadi area which was already occupied by the Tukani, Noi Naiqoro and Botiluvuka (the Kovacaki), the Vucunisai and the Kai Loa. He went on to Navo, then unoccupied. Here he settled and married a woman of the Noi Naiqoro and they had two children. His descendants are the Navo *yavusa*.

Waselo came and settled at Digilo. No one could remember how he came there from Nakauvadra, or who his wife was. He had three children. His descendants are the Digilo *yavusa*.

Waqavere followed the coast to Lautoka then occupied by the Vidilo. He moved on to Navo where Nakutavi and Waselo had already settled. They gave him land and he settled at Yaro where he married a woman of the Noi Naiqoro, and they had two children. His descendants are the Noi Yaro.

Nabala followed the spirit path of the Tualeita Range across the middle of Viti Levu, and came to Namarasa. From there he moved towards the coast and came to Navo where he was given land at Navulai. He married a woman of the Vucunisai, and they had two children. His descendants are the Takuci.

The name of Takuci is said to symbolise Nabala's arrival after the others. *Takucia* means 'follow' in the local communalect. Although Navulai is regarded as the first settlement of Nabala, the place where he is respected and communicated with is at Namarasa, the spirit site in the hills. There was a cave among some big rocks which used to contain bones of bats and humans, where the *bete* would go and communicate with Nabala. When I visited the place with the permission of the current *bete* who was head of the Vunasaqalo *mataqali*, the rocks had been disturbed perhaps by an earthquake and the entrance to the cave had been covered up with fallen rocks.

> Leka came along the Tualeita Range to Magodro. He then went on along the spirit path and came to Navo where he was given land at Digidigi. He married and had two children. The descendants of the elder son are the Ekubu, and those of the younger are the Viyagoitora. The collective name is sometimes referred to as Viyagoitora, but the *yavusa* was registered by the NLC as Ekubu.

The origins of the Ekubu are unclear. A representative of the Kovacaki told the 1913 NLC that the Ekubu were a part of the Kovacaki *yavusa* of Noi Naiqoro, and that they had come to Navo before the Tola. He did not know the name of Ekubu but said that they were generally known as the Kausa (the spear holders). They were the *bete* of Namama, the war spirit of Navo who was the son of Limasa, the Kovacaki war spirit. A representative of the Ekubu said that the Ekubu were Navo people, not Noi Naiqoro, but that they were related to the Noi Naiqoro because Salele, a woman of the Kovacaki *yavusa* of Tukani, had married Leka, their progenitor.

When I discussed this with the Navo people, and particularly with the heads of the Takuci and the Ekubu, I was told that when Leka settled at Digidigi he married Salele, a daughter of Tutuvanua, the progenitor of the Tukani and father of Masiwale, the progenitor of the Noi Naiqoro. This would have created a *vasu* relationship between the Noi Navo and the Kovacaki. When Salele came to marry Leka, the Kovacaki sent Namama, son of the Kovacaki war spirit Limasa, to accompany her and to remain at Digidigi in order to protect her and Leka. Namama's manifestation was a *bebe* or butterfly which accompanied Salele and her escort, landing first at Toaleka near what is now the Hindu temple at the west end of Nadi town. Namama and Salele stayed together with Leka at Digidigi, and their present place is a deep pool in the stream at Digidigi. Namama became the war spirit for all the Noi Navo, acting as their *ba ni valu* or war fence.

It is entirely reasonable that when a high-ranking woman of the Kovacaki (whose status was exalted by the myth that she was the daughter of the progenitor) came to marry a leader chief of the Noi Navo, the Kovacaki sent not only a group of Kovacaki to escort Salele as her secular protection but also a son of their war spirit, Limasa, to provide spiritual strength. In the same way, the Kovacaki had provided Rukuse, another son of Limasa, to be the war spirit of the Navatulevu of Nadi. Such a group of Kovacaki warriors, known as the Kausa or spear bearers, could well have been adopted into the Noi Navo and either joined with an already existing group or been given formal recognition with *yavusa* status, with the name of Viyagoitora (grandchildren of Tora). To further enhance their status, they may later have been given the name of Ekubu, reflecting that of Kubuna, the paramount *yavusa* of the Cakobau Government. Ekubu is the local communalect form of the eastern Kubuna. By the time of the NLC, it would have been most impolite and impolitic to acknowledge Salele's escort as anything but Noi Navo, irrespective of their actual origins.

The flood and the installation

> The Navo representative told the NLC that some time after the descendants of the five progenitors had increased in numbers at the five settlements referred to above, the rivers flooded and swamped the settlements, and all went to Nakutavi's settlement at Navo which was on the highest ground. There they held discussions that a leader should be installed; and they duly installed Naovasi of the Takuci, to be leader with the title of Kalevu, with authority over all five *yavusa*.

The Takuci representative disagreed in detail with this account. He told the NLC that all five families were living together at Navo, when the flood came. The Navo scattered to Navo i yata on the hill, the Digilo went to Lovaravara, the Noi Yaro stayed at Yaro, the Takuci went to Raralevu and the Viyagoitora went to Digidigi. They then all went to Navo i yata for the installation of Naovasi as Momo.

The Noi Yaro representative said that the first to be installed as chief of the Noi Navo was Nagicuvaravara, of the Nakauvadra subdivision of the second senior *mataqali* of the Noi Yaro. Then Naovasi of the Vunavau subdivision was appointed in his place. Nagicuvaravara went off to the Navatulevu and asked them to burn the house of installation of Naovasi, which they did.

The Navo representative had said that Naovasi was chief of the Takuci. However, at the time of his installation, Naovasi was recognised as a member of the Noi Yaro. The accounts above indicate that there was not unity in the choice of the paramount, and that the first choice was overthrown in spite of outside interference from the Navatulevu who at that time had no authority over the affairs of the Noi Navo. Such leadership quarrels were by no means uncommon in the west nor indeed in the east.

The Noi Yaro continued to be the leaders of the Noi Navo from the time of Naovasi's installation until the first NLC. At that time, the Takuci were becoming small in numbers, and the Commission transferred the Vunavau, Naovasi's *beto* or sub-division, from the Noi Yaro to the Takuci. So at the time of the later enquiries, the Vunavau were regarded by the Takuci as their leading sub-division, and the Navo representative was correct in that respect to say that Naovasi was a chief of the Takuci. This transfer gave the Takuci apparent paramountcy, but nowadays the paramount is generally recognised to be the iTaukei Nakauvadra, chief of the Noi Yaro. I attended some discussions at which the iTaukei Nakauvadra was present. On such occasions he was the centre of ceremonial attention and people would heed his words and speak when he indicated that they should. Nevertheless, considerable respect was paid to the head of the Takuci, and the atmosphere was very interesting and charged with undertones.

It probably does not matter very much which account was correct, but both reflect what I was told. The progenitors settled in various places which I was able to visit. A natural disaster brought them together at Navo, the site of Nakutavi, the first to arrive. Although the Takuci came late to Navo, the Noi Navo agreed to appoint Naovasi of the Takuci (but who was possibly of the Noi Yaro and transferred to the Takuci by the NLC) to be their paramount chief with the Nadroga title of Kalevu (nowadays, the Nadi title of Momo). They may well have gone to separate settlements but they signified their desire for unity by voluntarily establishing a joint leadership formalised through this installation of Naovasi. Nevertheless, the period following the installation was characterised by almost continuous internal quarrelling and fighting with nearby polities.

Troubles with neighbours

The Vucunisai and Kai Loa: the first burning

The Noi Navo quarrelled with their neighbours, after they had gone to weed their yam gardens and had cut some *vudi* or plantains belonging to the Vucunisai and the Kai Loa. Next morning they returned to their weeding, but the Vucunisai and Kai Loa were waiting for them fully armed and suddenly attacked them. The Noi Navo only had their digging sticks and were worsted and chased away back to Navo. An old man of the Digilo who was related to the attackers tried to halt the attack and so to allow the women and children to escape. However, Navo was burned by the two *yavusa*, and the Noi Navo, after unsuccessfully trying to defend themselves in two places, finally scattered to Korolevu near Vatutu, to the Utiloaloa. The Karia were also at Korolevu, having been chased away from their village at Yako by the Noi Yasawa people who had come down from the hills of Rukuruku. The Vucunisai and the Kai Loa attacked Korolevu; and the Noi Navo, the Utiloaloa and the Karia all went to the Utiloaloa village of Vatuma in the hilly interior.

The Tola Army from Nadroga take action

The Noi Navo wanted to return, and asked the Utiloaloa and the Karia to help them to do so. After discussion, these two *yavusa* agreed to ask Nabekasiga, the Kwa Levu of Nadroga, for assistance. The Navo account recorded that it was proposed that five persons from each of the five Navo *yavusa* and from the Utiloaloa and from the Karia should follow the traditional path to Nadroga, known as the Calevu ni Kamoa; and should take a *yaqona* root from Vatuma, together with *tabua*, decorated *masi* or bark cloth, and roast *kamoa* or edible creeper; and should make a request to the Kwa Levu for help. This proposal was agreed to and the request was duly made and acceded to. Those making the presentations then returned to Vatuma. Later the Namakatu people of the Nausori highlands brought an enormous *yaqona* root from Naqwavula; and this was taken to the Kwa Levu to speed up the assistance. The presentation was accepted, and the army from Nadroga was promised in eight days. The number 'eight' in such a context is notional, as in the expression 'bogiwalu' for a medium period strong wind. The Takuci account said that it was only representatives of the Karia who took the presentations and followed their traditional Calevu ni Vuse to the Kwa Levu. The huge root of *yaqona* referred to above was taken later with some *tabua*, only by the Karia chief as a warmer (*ivakatakata*) of the other presentations, and the army was promised when the yams first sprouted.

On their way to Nadi, the Tola, the Nadroga army, had burned Nabila, a village of the Noi Yasawa of Rukuruku, Nawaka. This was at the request of the Karia who had been attacked and driven away from Yako by the Noi Yasawa. In anticipation of the arrival of the army, the Noi Navo had taken food and built shelters for them at Koroloa, and moved from Vatuma to their old village of Namarasa. From here, they went to present to the army the food that they had brought for them. The army including warriors from Serua moved north to Tube near the present Ketenavunivalu village of Moala at the mouth of the Nadi River. They burned two of the Ketenavunivalu villages, Natutale and Nacaqaru, but at the request of the Karia chief who had a relation living there, did not burn the third village of Vusama. The Tola army then prepared to attack the Nadi villages at the request of the Yakuilau, as described earlier. When the Nadi people heard the sound of the guns of the Nadroga army, they fled first to the mangroves and then to Sabeto, Vuda and Naqwavula. The Tola destroyed the Nadi villages except for Nawaka which was preserved as a base for Nabekasiga, the Kwa Levu of Nadroga.

The next two or three years were a period of interesting socio-political activity and ceremony. First, the Tola army had to be suitably thanked, and secondly the Kwa Levu of Nadroga who held authority over Nadi by virtue of conquest had to arrange for suitable local powers to resume authority.

The Noi Navo, the Karia and the Utiloaloa gathered at Nawaka, and Nabekasiga said that he was returning to Nadroga, leaving Naovasi of the Noi Yaro (later Takuci, see above) with authority over the people and lands of all the Noi Navo and all the Nadi *yavusa*. Nabekasiga then went to Navo for ceremonies of farewell. The Noi Navo promised certain goods in return for help in the war, which they would send when they had been prepared. Nabekasiga then returned to Nadroga. The Noi Navo rebuilt their houses and re-occupied the village.

Some time later, Nabekasiga came back and said that the houses of the Navatulevu should be rebuilt at Narewa and that all the *yavusa* should return. This was his decision and not that of the Noi Navo.

When the various absent *yavusa* were still away, their lands were in the hands first of Nabekasiga and then of Naovasi. When they had all returned, certain ceremonies had to be performed, at which those who had lost their lands could request these lands to be made available to them once more. At this stage, the position was not as aggravated as it was later on when the conquerors were wont to sell to Europeans some of the land over which they had obtained *de facto* authority through conquest. For instance, the Tukani and the Noi Naiqoro asked Naovasi for the return of their Bilainadi (rich river flats) land; and the Navatulevu asked for their land of Tukutuku. The ceremony requesting the return of land, known as *ivakalutu ni qele,* was duly performed and the return of their lands was acceded to by Naovasi.

Some two years later, the last chapter in the incident of the Tola was completed. The Noi Navo went to the Kwa Levu at Cuvu, Nadroga, taking cloth, salt, kerosene, boxes, a kind of bark cloth known as *qativa* and special black bark cloth (*kulabasaga*) in order to meet the promises made earlier to Nabekasiga at the time the Kwa Levu was being thanked for his assistance in the wars.

The Noi Navo become arrogant: first burning by Nawaka

During a quarrel between the Yakuilau and the Navatulevu, the Takuci of the Noi Navo went and took up defences with the Yavusania who sided with the former; and the rest of the Noi Navo sided with the latter. Yavusania was burned, and the Takuci fled back to Navo, together with the Yavusania, but were not pursued by the Navatulevu. When all the Noi Navo had joined up again at Navo, they became arrogant and despised all the Nadi *yavusa* but respected the Nawaka. However, they plotted to burn all the Nadi villages and also Nawaka. They left the Yavusania at Navo and went to attack Nawaka. The Nawaka people drove them back and burned Navo. The Navo people scattered to the Karia at Yako where they spent eight years.

Then the news of the death of Nayalobu, son of Mataitoga of Sabeto, (see under Sabeto), reached the Noi Navo at Yako. He was their *vasu,* and they went by night to Yavusania where they performed the *reguregu,* the mourning ceremony. From there, they went to Nawaka where they presented eight *tabua* to Nabati, chief of the Vunatoto, requesting that they be allowed to return to Navo. After discussing this request with Navula, the war chief of the Navatulevu, it was agreed that the Noi Navo should rebuild their houses at Navo, and Navula sent a message to Yako to say that the Noi Navo could return to their own village. So the Noi Navo went back from Nawaka to Yako, and having performed the ceremony of *Takadravu,* seeking permission from their hosts, the Karia, to leave the village, they returned to Navo, rebuilt their houses and re-occupied the village.

The Noi Navo refuse Christianity: second burning by Nawaka

A long time after the Tola incident, Christianity came to Nadi, and Navula brought the *sulu* or cloth which was the symbol of acceptance of Christianity, to Navo about the time of the 1871 Cakobau Government. Although the Takuci had accepted Christianity, the rest of the Noi Navo had refused it. So Navula planned to destroy all the Navo *yavusa.* Under instructions from Navula, the Nawaka people attacked and burned the Naua at Vagadra and the Noi Navo at Navo. The Navo *yavusa* and, according to the Takuci representative, the Takuci scattered to Vunatawarau, Sikituru, some of the Ekubu fled to Maqalau in the Colo and the rest were taken as prisoners of Navula to Nawaka village. Their lands were in the hands of Navula.

The Noi Navo return to Navo territory and are finally re-united

Navula then sent instructions to Ramagimagi, the chief of Sikituru, to bring back the Navo and Takuci to Navo. He also instructed that the rest of the Noi Navo should be brought back from Maqalau and from Nawaka. Navula had been holding their lands, but on their return, the Navo re-occupied these lands on the instructions of the Momo Levu of Nadi, Navoleone Dawai. Because of this, the Navo always took food to Navatulevu out of respect, though claiming formal independence. The Takuci and the Ekubu were settled at Nasoso, and the rest at Nalua. These two villages were swamped by a tidal wave, and the people scattered to Dratabu and Bulolo. At this time the Noi Yaro were still leaders of the Noi Navo.

All the Noi Navo accepted Christianity and later in the time of the 1871 Cakobau Government they were re-united and were settled together at Dratabu. They were still at Dratabu at the time of Cession and of the measles epidemic after Cession. At the time of Cession, Nakairukua of the Noi Yaro was the paramount. Food for formal presentations was taken to Nakairukua in the first place, and from him some was still taken to the Momo Levu of Nadi.

The Noi Navo later moved from Dratabu to Vunayasi where they were during my visits in the 1950s; but the village was destroyed by a hurricane in the 1980s and the people moved back to the old village site at Dratabu where they were during my 1990s visits.

Commentary

The Noi Navo provide a fascinating study of a number of *yavusa*, their interactions with each other and with other polities, both neighbouring and distant. This is a classic example of fission and fusion on a small scale and also on a larger scale (typifying the western socio-political situation), but not as politically dramatic as in the cases of highly complex confederations in the east. As well as fraternal quarrels, ambitions and jealousy, and small-scale socio-political squabbles (often, it is true, involving burning and fighting), a non-traditional feature which later split the Noi Navo *yavusa* was the forceful attempt of Navula of the Navatulevu to introduce Christianity to the Noi Navo at the time of the 1871 Cakobau Government. Sometimes the Navo sided with a neighbouring polity and later changed their affiliations and opposed that same polity. Such fighting, resulting in Navo being burned at least three times, illustrates the formal procedures of how the defeated can be brought back by the conquerors, and how the status of a polity vis-a-vis another polity can change as a result of such procedures, and independence can be lost for a period of time or indefinitely. The accounts also show how these relatively small polities created and used traditional pathways of communication in order to seek assistance from powerful but more distant polities, and how they met their obligations. The elaborate system of such diplomatic pathways which was the basis of communication between polities who could not always rely on the communication network based on relationship, particularly the *vasu* relationship created by external marriage, is well illustrated by the systems of the five *yavusa* of the Noi Navo. The Noi Navo also showed how a weaker polity could fortify its independence and unity by a judicious marriage whereby a powerful war spirit was brought as protector of the bride: when Leka of the Viyagoitora/Ekubu, married Salele of the Tukani, Kovacaki, Namama, son of Limasa, the Kovacaki war spirit, was sent to protect her and, so, the Noi Navo. As many of these paths as I could identify by discussion are referred to at the end of this chapter.

It is not stated in their records why the NLC, at the time of the 1913 Commission enquiries in Nadi, made the Takuci the senior *yavusa* of the five Navo *yavusa*. The Takuci were then a very small *yavusa*, and the Vunavau, the sub-division of the Noi Yaro of which Naovasi, paramount of the Noi Navo, had been a member, was transferred to the Takuci. As suggested earlier, perhaps the NLC considered that with the transfer of the Vunavau to the Takuci, the position of paramountcy was transferred at the same time, and so it was only right that the Takuci should become the senior *yavusa* of the Noi Navo. This situation causes some grumblings at present, but for the sake of maintaining the unity of the Noi Navo, these grumblings have remained *kudrukudru i Ra Mo* or subdued and internal to the polity.

The Naua polity

The independent polity of Naua is based at present in the village of Saunaka, north of the town of Nadi. Naua territory stretched originally from the Wai Milika River, bordering on Sabeto, to the north; to the boundaries of the Old *tikina* of Nawaka, to the south; to the boundaries of the Old *tikina* of Vaturu, to the east; and the sea to the west. The Nadi River bisects the region providing rich *bila* or alluvial flats; and the region is generally flat, with hillocks such as the spirit place of Taqainasolo (98 m) and rising in the north-east corner to the rounded hill of Nagado (176 m).

What was recognised and registered by the 1913 NLC as the single, simple descent group or *yavusa* of Naua emerges, from my explorations of the Naua polity, as a socio-political complex, the groups of which had leaders such as the iTaukei Sawaieke or the iTaukei Natauvesi. It was evidently not long, once the groups had settled fairly close to each other, that the only practical way for them to conduct their political and social business to their best advantage was to have a paramount leader or Momo Levu. This they proceeded to do and continued to do, although the basis of the leadership changed between groups and between divisions of a group. Naua is a wonderful example of the small, independent polities which are characteristic of the west.

I obtained a great deal of information about Naua, first, from the 1913 NLC accounts; and secondly, and especially, from my own lengthy and detailed checking of these accounts and in pursuing further lines of original investigation with not only Ratu Josateki Savou, the iTaukei Sawaieke, who has since been installed as the present paramount or Momo Levu of Naua, but also others whom the Momo Levu suggested, particularly Apakuki Tuitavua of the Vatuburu group, with whom I spent many hours in discussion and site exploration. Under the circumstances, I allotted as much time as possible to the exploration of the origins and development of this fascinating little polity and its relations, first, with neighbouring polities; and secondly, with polities from further afield, especially those with which Naua had traditional lines of communication through agnatic and descent relationships or, to a certain extent, through *calevu ni matamataraki* or established diplomatic pathways. This account is therefore more detailed than those of other polities in the general area.

Myths of origin: NLC account

Tevita Navu, one of the Naua representatives, told the 1913 NLC that Korowabu, the original ancestral spirit of the Naua, came from the Nakauvadra Range and followed the north coast of Viti Levu firstly to Tavua and next to Narogoua, Sabeto, where he spent a long time. He then went on to Taqainasolo, inland from Saunaka, where he stayed and married a woman of Ne, a polity inland from Sabeto. His descendants became known as the Naua *yavusa*.

Korowabu had six sons named, in order of birth, Leweinabua, Vidirinasau, Vasukiwavuwavu, Raweya, Tabaravu, and Nakia. Their descendants became known as the Vunamaoli, Vunaivi, Natuvulevu, Ketenatacini, Yavusasivo and Vatuburu *mataqali* respectively.

Korowabu and his six sons later moved with their families to Nabua. When they increased in numbers, Tabaravu moved seawards to Namo, and Nakia moved to Natauvesi. The others remained at Nabua.

Origins of the Vatuburu: present account

Apakuki Tuitavua, a member of the Vatuburu who lived at Saravi, told me that the progenitor of the Vatuburu was known as Keteketewalu. His place was called Natauvesi, near Saravi. The Buduka people of Kovaki, Nadi, invited him to come and stay with them, and he was given land later called Saravi. The Vatuburu were the first of the Naua people to settle in the area.

Later they went to the island of Malolo, because the second wife of Keteketewalu was from the village of Yaro. After some time they planned to return to Saravi but a *tokavuki* or hurricane blew them off course to the mouth of the Sabeto River. Here they established the settlement of Nasoso on an island in the estuary, though others told me that they landed at Nasoso and moved up river to the junction with the Malika River and established their settlement at Koroiqava. Be that as it may, people at Buduka saw smoke rising from Nasoso; and having found out who the people were, they invited them as relations (*vakaveiwekani*) to come back and live on the land which they had previously occupied and which was then vacant—'*Muju ravi koto mei ki Buduka*', 'Come and be in a dependent relationship with Buduka'. Because Keteketewalu's family thereby became dependent on (*ravi*) the Buduka, the land was called Saravi. The Vatuburu were told that they would, however, be politically independent; and a member of the Vatuburu was (and still is), anointed (*lumuti*) as iTaukei Natauvesi or chief of the Vatuburu group.

To symbolise this relationship, they cut two palm trees and laid the trunks across the Vunaburu River as a bridge between Buduka and Saravi. Two coconuts were then taken and tied by creeper, one on one side of the river and the other on the other side. The *bukutia* (or tying) of these two coconuts was the basis of the traditional path from the Naua to the Kovacaki, known as the Calevu ni Niubukurua or Path of the Two Coconuts Tied Together.

The Development of the Naua Polity

According to this account, Keteketewalu of Natauvesi and his descendants who came to be known as the Vatuburu (or Navatu, for short) were the first of the groups in this area who later developed into the Naua *yavusa*. There is still at Saravi a *yavu* or housemound with reddish stones in its side, known as Natauvesi; and this name had been carried over to the present village of Saunaka where there is a chiefly *yavu* of the same name. The others whose descendants, together with the Vatuburu, eventually formed the Naua *yavusa*, came from various nearby areas of Vuda, Sabeto, Toko near Naqwavula, and Batiri, Nadroga, some by land and some by sea. Their reasons for coming are not remembered. On the other hand, iTaukei Sawaieke and his advisers told me that originally six people came down from Ne, up the Sabeto valley, and settled at Drakanabou on the Wai Mailika River which separates Sabeto territory from Naua territory. From here they and their families went to Nakorowai (now inside the boundaries of Nadi Airport at Namaka) and thence inland to Taqainasolo. From here, they went seawards to Kou and finally to the coast at Saravi. Their descendants came to be known collectively as the Naua.

The Vunamaoli group came from Vuda, where they had been part of the Tububere, the second senior *yavusa*; and they settled on Lele, an area of high ground on what was then the mainland to the east of Saravi Island. The senior division of the Vunamaoli is the Yavulagi.

The Vunaivi group came from Sabeto, where they had been part of the Conua *yavusa;* and they settled near the Vunamaoli, at Navola, part of the area of Lele. The senior division of the Vunaivi is also called the Vunaivi and a more junior one is Nadrau.

Collectively those at Lele were referred to as the Mataqali Levu or Main *Yavusa*.

The Natuvulevu came from Toko, a settlement of the Nabau people from Nausori, Namataku, Navosa, across the river from Naqwavula. They settled on the island of Koroua at a place called Natuvulevu on the boundaries of Naua and Kovacaki territories.

The Vunamaoli, Vunaivi and Natuvulevu were closely associated and were known collectively as the Senau. There is an area of land known as Senautari (*senau* or *menemenei* means 'being looked after'), and this land was for the use of these three groups, the Senau. Currently the *yavu* or mound of the house of the Methodist Minister at Saunaka is called Senautari, and the Minister is accorded the ceremonial title of iTaukei Senautari.

The Ketenacini or Neidiri, originally from Neidiri, Batiri, Nadroga, had split after they had moved from Neidiri to Korowaiwai, Votualevu. On this occasion, they quarrelled over the distribution of *yaqona*, and some returned to Batiri. Later those who remained settled at Nawaimalua on what was then the mainland near the island of Saravi. They were associated with the Vatuburu and with the original landowners, the Tukani of Kovacaki. The traditional path between the Ketenatacini and the Tukani was known as the *Calevu ni Qai* or 'Path of the *Qai/Vasili* or Cordyline Tree'. Later on there were quarrels between the descendants of Raweya and his younger brother Tabaravu; these were recognised at the time of the 1913 NLC, when Tabaravu's descendants who had previously formed a division of the Ketenatacini group were recorded as a separate *mataqali* from that of the Ketenaticini *mataqali*.

The installation of head of the Vunamaoli as Momo

When the families who became the Vunamaoli, Vunaivi, Natuvulevu, Ketenatacini and Vatuburu groups had increased in numbers, the family of Leweinabua (the Vunamaoli) who had gone to Namo, and the family of Nakia (the Vatuburu) who were settled at Natauvesi (see above) gathered together the other groups who had remained at Nabua. All the descendants of Korowabu, father of the six sons whose families became the groups, were present.

They discussed whether one of them should be recognised as paramount, and agreed to appoint Raseru of the Vunamaoli and *vasu* to the family of Vasukiwavuwavu (the Natuvulevu) to be installed as Momo. The family of Leweiwavuwavu piled up the earth for the mound of installation; the family of Nakia provided the *lauvatu* or stone surrounding for the mound; the family of Qoro, the second son of Raweya (the Nakasamai division of the Ketenatacini) prepared the *yaqona* for the installation ceremony; and all the family of Raweya (the Ketenatacini) provided timber for the house of installation. Raseru was duly installed on the mound known as Betobalavu (which has survived and which I have visited) at Nabua.

Quarrels and wars: influence on social development

The development of the *yavusa* was characterised by sometimes-fearsome internal quarrels based on breaches of protocol, arrogant behaviour and jealousy, as well as on voluntary or involuntary involvement in wars between neighbouring polities.

Near extinction of arrogant Vatuburu

The earliest internal quarrel of which I could find an account nearly resulted in the extinction of the Vatuburu group who were the first in the area, followed by the other groups. They settled near to each other, but as time passed, some of the Ketenatacini who were settled at Nawaimalua considered that the Vatuburu were behaving arrogantly towards them. The newcomers became jealous of the Vatuburu because they considered themselves superior in everything (*cecere e na veika kece* or *sila* in the local communalect). To this end, many plotted (*buki druadrua* or *vere*) for the Vatuburu to be killed; and several unsuccessful attempts were made to kill them. The Vunaivi people then asked (*vatadumata*) the people of Sabeto and Nawaka to come and help to kill the Vatuburu.

A message was sent to the iTaukei Tauvesi, the head of the Vatuburu, at his chiefly *yavu* called Wasina (the *yavu* is still visible near to the railway track where it crosses the river), to say that a discussion was to be held near Wasina, to which the Vatuburu were invited to come. This was but a trick because the real purpose of the invitation was for them to come and be killed because they were so arrogant (*sila*) in their behaviour. Meanwhile, a large gathering had assembled on the opposite side of the river to the chiefly *yavu* of Wasina. It was attended by many including Saqe, the *qaqa* or strong man of the Vunaivi who were at the forefront of the plot. The Vatuburu were surprised when they found out the true intention of the invitation, and they shouted out, 'U! U! U! This should be a discussion, not a plot.' The name of the land where this took place is now Na U.

Those who had been in hiding came out and killed all the Vatuburu including Tuwawa, the iTaukei Tauvesi. The place where the killing took place is now called Koro i Tuwawa (in the area now known as Maigania). There was only one survivor whose name is not remembered, and he escaped to those of the Ketenatacini group who were at Saravi and had not been involved in the plot. This sole survivor had hidden under a *diva ni quto* or pile of firewood. The Vunaivi put the bodies of the Vatuburu on rafts made of *madolo/ tolo ni jaina* (banana stems), and floated them downstream to Nubu ni Vunayasi, a pool near the present village of Saunaka. The bodies were taken ashore from Koro i Tuwawa and left to rot. They smelt badly (*bona* or *ilo* in the local communalect), and the place is called Vailo. The bodies were buried between the present villages of Saunaka and Nakavu in the area of the cemetery called Bulubulu Koro i Saravi or Saravi Village Cemetery, still used by the Vatuburu who had formerly occupied Saravi.

When peace was resumed, the sole survivor of the plot was given a woman of the Ketenatacini to be his wife. Eventually the Vatuburu increased in numbers, and the Ketenatacini then called the Vatuburu, 'Na Luve ni Yalewa' or 'The Children of the Woman', as a memory of the woman.

Later the Vatuburu moved from Saravi to join the other groups at Vagadra, near Saunaka, because the site was safer and the water supply was better. Then the Vatuburu left Vagadra and returned to Saravi where they remained. Before Cession in 1874 the other groups went from Vagadra to establish, the village of Saunaka nearby, while the Vatuburu remained at Saravi. After they duly moved to Saunaka, all the groups were based at Saunaka; and when they had all joined up at Saunaka, they were known collectively as the Naua polity and later were registered by the 1913 NLC as the Naua *yavusa*.

When the Vatuburu settled finally at Saunaka, the rest of the Naua were determined not to let the Vatuburu be arrogant again towards them. For instance, the Vatuburu were then told to settle on the low ground beside the river and were told, '*Kua ni cecere/sila*' or 'Don't be arrogant'. This was as a punishment for being arrogant in the old days. So Saunaka is now divided in two: Saunaka on the high ground, for those other than the Vatuburu; and Sila on the low ground below the church, for the Vatuburu.

The war of the Na Vololevu

The earliest war of which I have accounts took place after the installation of Raseru of Vunamaoli as Momo (see above). The war was known as Na Vololevu. I was unable to discover the reason for this name meaning 'Big Lemon'. Accounts of the war were recorded by the NLC from both Naua and Navatulevu, Nadi, sources. Both accounts emphasise the critical involvement of at least the Tavarua people, from among those of the Rukuruku polity who lived in the uplands between Nawaka/Nadi and the Nadroga boundaries. The Rukuruku accounts (see under Nawaka) make no mention of the war, although reference is made to the name of the protagonist, Lomanikaya. There are important similarities in the accounts, but also there are significant differences. It is not possible today to obtain further traditions which might confirm either of these accounts. However, the purpose of my explorations was not to discover which was the 'correct account' but to document the various traditions and to analyse the way that they represent relationships, first, within and between groups existing at the time covered by my explorations; and, secondly, between groups and the various sites where they settled. The Naua account served to explain how the six groups that later formed the Naua were living at Nabua and nearby, and how they came to leave this inland part of the Naua territory and go and live nearer the coast.

The Naua Account

Lomanikaya, a chief of Tavarua, Rukurukulevu (in the hills between Nawaka and Nadroga), had in his possession a *bulileka* or small white cowry shell which was a symbol of chiefliness, which Nacobi, chief of the neighbouring Noi Yasawa, requested from him. When Lomanikaya refused to give it to him, Nacobi declared war on him and Lomanikaya fled to the Noi Sesevia at Vatuma. Nacobi followed him to Vatuma, and Lomanikaya left the Noi Sesevia and went to the village of Nabua. The Noi Sesevia changed sides and joined with the Noi Yasawa, and the joint army known as the Vololevu went and burned Nabua.

After the village of Nabua had been burned by the Vololevu, those descendants of Korowabu, the Natuvulevu, who were still living there as well as those who had earlier left to settle at Namo and Natauvesi, went and established their villages near the coast. The Vunamaoli and the Vunaivi went and settled at Lele. The Natuvulevu settled at Natuvulevu. The Ketenatacini split and some, including the Neidiri, went to settle at Nawaimalua and others went to Nakasamai. The Vatuburu settled at Saravi.

The Navatulevu, Nadi, account relates that Raimoqe, warrior head of the Navatulevu, wanted Lomanikaya's *bulileka* but that Lomanikaya refused to give it to him. At that time, Yakuilau had authority over the Navatulevu. One day, after Lomanikaya had refused to give the *bulileka* to Raimoqe, Raimoqe and Bekebeke, the chief of the Noi Yakuilau, were bathing together. Raimoqe dived down and threw a *tabua* between Bekebeke's legs. Bekebeke made enquires as to the meaning of the *tabua*, and Raimoqe explained that it was a request for help in fighting the Noi Tavarua, because Lomanikaya had refused to give him the *bulileka*. So Bekebeke took the army and burned the Noi Tavarua and the neighbouring Noi Yasawa. The Naua played no part in this campaign. Lomanikaya swallowed the *bulileka* and was later killed. The *bulileka* was taken to Raimoqe who was then installed as the Momo Levu of Nadi. The Naua were among those attending the installation.

The war of Lutia na Qo

Breaches of protocol and personal insults were sometimes the cause of quarrels. The order of drinking *yaqona* is symbolic of the relative status of those participating. If a person drinks out of order, this could be regarded simply as an unfortunate breach of protocol or it could be that the person drinking out of order wishes to indicate his socio-political ambitions for leadership. For instance, in the case of the *yaqona* drinking by the Neidiri sub-division of the Ketenatacini referred to above, some felt so insulted that they left and went back to Batiri. Personal insults could be so grave that violence could develop into widespread warfare. As an example, there was the insult leading to the war known as the War of Lutia na Qo, of which the following accounts were recorded by the 1913 NLC and checked by me with the iTaukei Sawaieke and his advisers. I was told that *lutia na qo* means 'spearing a pig (*qo*) and lifting it up on the end of the spear.'

This war is interesting not only as an example of socio-political fission following personal insult but also in showing how an ambitious person could take advantage of such a situation in order to further his own ambitions for leadership. In this case, Nalokubalavu of the Vunaivi succeeded in taking the leadership of the Naua from Raseru of the Vunamaoli, and so created a change in the recognised order of hierarchy of the component *mataqali*.

The Naua people had been living in the coastal villages for some time, when Raseru, the Momo of Naua who came from the Vunamaoli *mataqali,* put a *tabu* on pigs, forbidding that pigs should be killed or taken away. Then one day he lifted the *tabu* and went to catch some pigs owned by the Natuvulevu people. The owners were very upset and touched Raseru's hair and ruffled it. The serious nature of this insult reflects that of the occasion when, according to a rather unlikely account (Gravelle 1979:10), the Reverend Thomas Baker removed his comb from the head of the chief Nawawabalavu in upland Namosi and was murdered and eaten for the offence in 1867.

When they realised the seriousness of what they had done, they took fright and fled to their *vasu* relations at Sabeto. Nalokulevu, a member of the Vunaivi sub-division of the Vunaivi *mataqali,* went with them as their leader. One account said that Raseru had been so angry with the Natuvulevu that he went to his *vasu,* the Navatulevu of Nadi, and asked Raimoqe, the Momo Levu of Nadi, for help. Raimoqe passed a message to the Yakuilau and they burned the village of the Natuvulevu. The miscreants fled to Sabeto, and the rest stayed at Lele, the village of the Vunaivi, under the Navatulevu. Another account said that because of their arrogant behaviour, the Navatulevu had already been driven away from Nadi by the Yakuilau at the time of the incident and that they were at Lotoiqere on Buduka land.

Be that as it may, all are agreed that the Natuvulevu miscreants, together with Naloku (as he is usually referred to) had fled to his *vasu* at Sabeto and been settled at Koroiqava, by which time the Navatulevu had left Nadi and gone to Lotoiqere. Naloku discussed with Mataitoga, a powerful chief, but not yet the Momo or leading chief of Sabeto, about approaching the Navatulevu and inviting them to join him. As recorded, under Sabeto, Mataitoga was striving to obtain the leadership of the Sabeto people and he would have welcomed help to drive out the then-Momo of Sabeto. Mataitoga agreed that Naloku should go to Lotoiqere and bring the Navatulevu to Koroiqava in Sabeto territory. Naloku was afraid that the *katikati,* the women and old men, would be killed on the way by the Yakuilau army that by this time had appeared in order to oppose the escape of the Navatulevu. He pleaded that they should be protected; and Mataitoga said to Naloku that they should exchange fans. Mataitoga said that Naloku should take his chiefly fan (*masei*) as a symbol of the authority he had given Naloku to protect the *katikati*; and that Naloku should take the *katikati* to Koroiqava, where they would join the Natuvulevu refugees previously settled there by Mataitoga.

When the Navatulevu and the Natuvulevu refugees were safely settled at Koroiqava, Naloku went to stay with Mataitoga at Sabeto. By now, Mataitoga had succeeded, presumably with the help of the Natuvulevu and the Navatulevu, in driving away the Momo and taking the position of paramount for himself. Then the Yakuilau kept sending messages to the Naua, asking them to kill Naloku. Naloku told Mataitoga about these requests for his death, and Mataitoga brought the Navatulevu closer to Sabeto.

When the Yakuilau saw Naloku's influence on Mataitoga with respect to the Navatulevu people, they sent a *tabua* to request that the Sabeto people should kill Naloku. Mataitoga showed his appreciation of Naloku's assistance in obtaining the paramountcy, and did not heed this request. Later he showed his appreciation even more when, after the War of the Tola (see below), he took Naloku of Vunaivi back to the Naua and had him made the paramount of Naua. Thus the Vunaivi took precedence over the Vunamaoli who were the previous leading *mataqali* of the Naua, and Naloku's ambitions for the paramountcy of the Naua came to fruition. This shows how socio-political change can come about in a polity, through secular power. There is, however, no evidence that this change was ever validated by seeking spiritual endorsement and, as will be seen, Naloku duly got what those who were in communication with the spirit world would have understood to be his just desserts.

The war of the Tola

After the Natuvulevu refugees from the wrath of Raseru (the Momo of Naua and a man of the Vunamaoli) and Naloku (of the Vunaivi *mataqali* of the Naua) had been together for some time at Koroiqawa, Sabeto, the army of the Tola from Nadroga came to assist the Navatulevu to return to Nadi. Because they had sided with the Yakuilau, the rest of the Naua scattered to Naqwavula, in the hills, together with the Yakuilau and other supporters.

At this time, the Naua lands came into the hands of Mataitoga, because of the *vasu* relationship. Naua was geographically in an unfortunate position, being between the polities of Nadi and Sabeto. Whenever there was war, the Naua found themselves subject to attack and burning, and to consequent loss of their land to the hands of the victors. Before the arrival of European planters in the area, it was usual for the conquerors to call back the defeated and resettle them in their old village sites and for the traditional landowners to obtain formal permission from the conquerors to get back possession of their lands (*ivakalutu ni qele*). With the arrival of planters in the 1860s, however, they found that they could obtain such land from the chiefs of Nadi or Sabeto who protected their possession to some extent, irrespective of the feelings of the traditional owners. At first, such arrangements were made informally, and the chiefs understood that they retained ultimate authority over the land. Later, arrangements were formalised by written document and this was understood by the 1871 Cakobau Government to mean alienation.

When the Tola returned to Nadroga, Rokomatu, grandson of Raimoqe (chief of the Navatulevu in exile at Sabeto) and Naloku (*vasu* to Mataitoga and therefore able to make special requests to the Momo Levu of Sabeto) were together in Sabeto. Rokomatu wanted to return to Nadi, and Naloku was intent upon gaining the position of Momo of the Naua. Rokomatu said to Naloku that if Naloku could obtain leave from Mataitoga for them both to return to Nadi, he would reward Naloku with pigs, but Naloku said that he wanted to be rewarded with *wa sasala* (a creeper to symbolise that he was to be chief). Naloku asked Mataitoga for permission for them both to return, and Mataitoga agreed.

Mataitoga gave Naloku a housepost called Duru ni Degei or Degei's Housepost which he took to Vagadra and used for building his house. When all the houses at Vagadra were ready, Naloku called the Naua to come back from Naqwavula and they settled there. Not all the Naua at Sabeto returned with Naloku but some remained there. Mataitoga also gave Naloku a stone as his *vunau*, meaning that he used his authority to make Naloku paramount of the Naua at Vagadra. In this way, the Vunaivi achieved seniority over the Vunamaoli as the leading *mataqali* of the Naua *yavusa*. Naloku heeded the authority of Rokomatu of the Navatulevu.

The case of Naua is an excellent example of the development and leadership problems of a single *yavusa* polity. A detailed study of the polity indicates well the machinations of an ambitious person who was not qualified by birth for leadership but who acquired the position by cunningly working his way to the paramountcy by imposing obligations on powerful neighbours with whom he had *vasu* relationships.

The war of the Cebu Walu

The *vasu* relationship by itself was not always enough to commit the person requested to provide some goods or service to meet the request. The War of the Cebu Walu is important in illustrating further the relationships between two polities, the Sabeto and the Naua, where the *vasu* relationship was the basis of the bond between them, especially where there are conflicting interests. In this instance, some Naua were still at Sabeto while most of them had been resettled at Vagadra. In both cases, there was a *vasu* relationship between the Naua at Sabeto and the Sabeto people, and also between the Naua at Vagadra and the Sabeto people.

At the start of my exploration of the socio-political implications of the War of the Cebu Walu, I was intrigued by the significance of the name itself. With some linguistic knowledge aforethought, I had asked for the meaning and, as I expected, the people told me with a wan smile that it meant 'the War of the Eight Anuses'—*cebu* meaning 'anus' in the local communalect. When they realised that I was recording what they said for posterity, they came up with another, more polite, possible interpretation. The name was perhaps based on the understanding that the war had scattered about (*ceburaki*) over eight years. I simply record both interpretations.

As for the war itself, the Naua had put a *tabu* on some sugar cane growing at Legalega where Senikase, a man of Namataku, Nausori and a *vasu* to the Naua, had his house. Some children of the Naua who were living at Sabeto came and picked some of the cane; and Senikase was very angry with them. The fathers of the children came from Sabeto and killed Senikase. Naloku made a request to Mataitoga that those responsible for the murder should be killed, but Mataitoga would not agree to this request. Naloku then summoned an army from as far afield as the Wainimala River, Nadrau and Batiwai (Serua).

Apakuki Tuitavua explained to me that the connection between Naua and Batiwai was based on the origins of the Ketenatacini who came from Neidiri, Batiri, and Nadroga. There were in turn relationships between the Neidiri and the people of Batiwai. Equally intriguing was the explanation of the connection between the Naua and the people of the Wainimala and Nadrau. This was based on a tradition that a man was living on the island of Narokorokoyawa between the Mamanuca group and the Yasawa group. This island is of great importance in the Fijian spiritual landscape because the ultimate destination of many of the spirits of the dead is beside this island. It was here that the *Rogovoka*, one of the first mythical canoes which, like the *Kaunitoni*, came to Fiji from the west, had stopped on the way, in order to allow a woman on board to come ashore and give birth to Tui Revurevu. He is regarded as the *itaukei* or guardian owner of the island and the surrounding area where the spirits of the dead dive into the sea. The man living there became fed up with hearing the sound of the splash as the spirits *vila* or plunged into the sea. He moved to the mainland where there is the village of Narokorokoyawa in Sabeto. Then he moved through Naua territory to Yavuna inland from Vatutu (see under Nawaka) but he could still hear the sound of spirits plunging into the sea. So he went on into the interior to Nadrau and the Wainimala area, where he could no longer hear the sound. Here he established the village of Narokorokoyawa which is still there. These connections between the west and the interior are similar to those between Nadroga and the interior, which proved significant when the Kwa Levu of Nadroga was collecting the army of the Tola to attack the Yakuilau at Nadi. There may have been generally grave suspicions between the coastal polities and the independent folk of the interior. Nevertheless these *calevu ni matamataraki* or formal lines of communication were maintained and proved to be invaluable when circumstances of necessity overcame local prejudice and feelings of independence.

When the army had assembled, it besieged Sabeto for a period of eight years. As I suggested earlier, the number 'eight' need not be taken literally but often occurs with the implications of approximation, as in *bogi walu* which refers to a storm lasting about eight nights, or as in Cagawalu (the name of the war spirit of Bau who was said to have had a forehead eight finger-spans wide). In the course of the war, 250 of those on Mataitoga's side were killed and Mataitoga was upset and planned to take revenge on Naloku. He passed a *tabua* to the Noi Vunatoto of Nawaka with a request that they should kill Naloku. They were unsuccessful and so they returned the *tabua* which was then passed on to the Noi Navo. They were equally unsuccessful. Finally the *tabua*, together with a pig, was taken to some of the Vunamaoli *mataqali* of the Naua who were living at Narukuniivi, Yavusania. They had previously had the leadership of the Naua until Mataitoga gave the leadership to Naloku of the more junior *mataqali* of Vunaivi. So they would have regarded Naloku for what he was, an ambitious upstart, and they went secretly at night and killed Naloku while he was sleeping at Saravi. As I described earlier, the appointment of Naloku had been achieved through Mataitoga and was not in accordance within the traditional pattern of choice of leader by order of birth and formal installation. It had not therefore been validated by the spirits of Naua; and it is not at all unexpected that Naloku should have been killed by those who were upset by the manner in which he achieved the leadership of Naua.

The traditional site of the killing at Saravi is marked by a broken monolith lying near a *yavu* on the edge of which are other stones in interesting array suggestive of some ceremonial or burial site. There is no body there at present, as far as I could determine by limited excavation. The monolith is referred to as Naloku's *kali* or pillow. One account which Apakuki knew but doubted was to the effect that Naloku had been buried here at Saravi but his body was later disinterred and taken to Saunaka where a memorial has been erected to his memory. Another account preferred by Apakuki was that the Naua who had killed Naloku at the request of Mataitoga of Sabeto were taking his body to Sabeto, having sounded the *lali* or drum to publicise the killing. The Naua at Vagadra heard the drum beat and realised what had happened. So they went and intercepted those taking the body to Sabeto and snatched the body and took it for burial at Vagadra. The actual burial place is unknown, although it is tempting to suggest that where I excavated in Saravi was either his temporary grave or some form of cenotaph. Only further excavation may provide some more clues, but I fear that Naloku's final resting-place will forever remain a mystery.

The war of Christianity

The introduction of Christianity to the west and in particular to the Nadi region in the 1860s provided an external element in the development of relations between polities. Some accepted it either because they saw its advantages as a potential source of European goods, or because they associated it with the powerful polities of the east, especially Bau, and were afraid to refuse the *sulu*, or European cloth used for the loin cloth, which served to symbolise Christianity. The Navatulevu, the Noi Yakuilau, the Tukani, the Noi Naiqoro, the Noi Navo, the Yavausania, the Saunivalu at Sikituru and the Naua proceeded to accept Christianity when it was introduced to Nadi. Others refused to adopt Christianity, perhaps because they saw its acceptance as tantamount to acknowledging the overlordship of Cakobau, especially when the Kingdom of Bau was established in 1867. Perhaps more importantly, they foresaw that the acceptance of Christianity and the new practices they would be expected to adopt, and, more particularly, the old practices they would be forced to reject, would bring dire retribution from the *nitu* (the western term for ancestral spirits) which the Wesleyan adherents referred to as *tevoro* or *timoni*—devils or demons.

This situation led to war. Isireli Namulo Rokomatu, son of Koroigaga and grandson of the Rokomatu who had been leader of the Navatulevu in exile in Sabeto, quarrelled with Navoleone Raigigia, son of Nasorovakatini who was the younger brother of Koroigaga. Navoleone was a great womaniser (*dau caka yalewa*), and his behaviour was hardly acceptable to a Christian chief. In his anger, Navoleone told the Vunatoto at Nawaka not to accept Christianity and to attack the Christianised villages. Nawaka was still pagan, and the Vunatoto of Nawaka sent messages to the hills and collected an army comprising the Utiloaloa, the Noi Sesevia, the Noi Yasawa, the Noi Tavarua, the Yamisa, the Yawada, the Leinamataku and the Noi Tubai. This army assembled, and burned the Naua village of Vagadra, on a Sunday, and later the Noi Navo village of Navo. The Naua went to seek refuge with the Navatulevu at Waqana. Having burned these two Christian villages, the Nawaka army then went to Waqana. When the army reached Waqana, Navula was there but Navoleone was kept in a hut at Tutunavokai near Saravi because it was known that he was the cause of the war. He was duly freed and, ever the opportunist, he forgot his anger with Navula. He went to Nasorowale, chief of Vuda, and to Mataitoga, chief of Sabeto, and enlisted their aid in repelling the Nawaka army. This attack by the Nawaka and their allies can be dated to about 1868, from evidence given to the Lands Claims Commission (LCC) set up under the Lands Claims Ordinance (No. XXV of 1879) to investigate claims to land by Europeans. Claimants were required 'to give satisfactory evidence of the transactions with the natives on which they rely as establishing their title; and, if the land appears to have been acquired fairly, and at a fair price,' Crown grants were to be issued.

When the Nawaka army attacked Waqana, they were chased away by Navula and the Navatulevu and their allies who followed them and burned Nawaka. Presumably Navoleone's part in starting this war was forgiven on the basis of the help that he had obtained for the Navatulevu from Vuda and Sabeto, because he was duly installed as Momo Levu after Navula had refused the title which was offered to him. This was traditionally correct, because Navoleone was the son of the elder brother and Navula was son of the younger brother. Those who had scattered after being burned by the Nawaka army were brought back, and the Navatulevu built a village for the Naua at Korokoro near Natuvulevu (Saravi).

Attempts to murder Navula

Relationships within and between groups within the polity of Naua and relationships between Naua and strong neighbours such as Nadi were bedevilled with quarrels, jealousy, plots and counterplots that must have frustrated attempts by even the most responsible leaders to establish a powerful and stable confederacy. An outstanding figure to emerge from this situation of instability was Navula, who had been very successful as head of the Navatulevu army in the course of those wars referred to above in which he had participated.

As Navula became more powerful, there were among the Nadi people those who objected to what they considered to be the arrogant behaviour of a social upstart, especially as they had ambitions to be leaders themselves. So they went with some Noi Naiqoro people of the Kovacaki to Naboutini in Sabeto, where they proposed to make a *solevu* or ceremonial presentation with the intention of asking the Sabeto people to return with them to Nadi and to murder Navula. This plan came to the notice of Navula who sent a Sabeto man to Mataitoga, requesting that those who had gone to Sabeto with such intentions should be killed.

As those at Naboutini were dressing up in preparation for the *solevu*, the Sabeto people were assembling at Sabeto. When Mataitoga said 'Buli Waqa', which was the name of his house at Naboutini where he used to go and relax, those assembled understood this to be a signal for the execution of his instructions that they should go to Naboutini and kill those gathering for the *solevu*. They duly went and killed all those at Naboutini who had come to plan for the killing of Navula. Among those who took part in the killing were some Vunamaoli and Vatuburu people of the Naua who were staying at Sabeto, though they were not part of the plot planned by Navula and Mataitoga. All were killed except for Nemani Dreu of the Naduruniu *mataqali* of the Navatulevu. He returned to Nadi but did not settle with the Navatulevu at Narewa. He took the Naduruniu still surviving and established the separate village of Nakavu. A ceremony of *soro* or apology brought an end to the plot and its consequences.

External influences affecting Naua: the Cakobau attack

The Cakobau army arrived in Sabeto in 1873 in order to attack Sabeto. This was part of a campaign with the immediate object of avenging the murder of the Burns family at Vunisamaloa, Ba, and also to subdue the mountaineers who showed few signs of recognising the Government. Navula brought those of the Naua people then settled at Narukuniivi, Yavusania, to stay with him at Waqana as members of his household. When the Cakobau army attacked Sabeto, all the chiefs there, including those of the Naua who were settled at Sabeto, were taken prisoner. Navula asked for the release of the Naua people whom he took with him back from Sabeto, and they also remained at Waqana with Navula.

External influences affecting Naua: European settlers

The first Europeans to settle in the Nadi area were A. Campbell and C. Irvine who settled in 1867 first at Tiliva and then at Nasusuva i Nadi between the Naua of Vagadra, the Vunatoto of Nawaka and Navula at Waqana. The village of Navo was nearby. When war broke out in 1868, the Nawaka, having burned Vagadra and Navo, went and burned the Campbell and Irvine property at Nasusuva i Nadi. The numbers of Europeans in the area increased modestly, but the so-called Nadi Swells were ever in fear of being burned out without much hope of protection from the local chiefs or from the far-away Cakobau Government.

Before the Naua took refuge with the Navatulevu, they had, in April 1868, sold some of their land to Herman Luks and George B. Ridsdale. After the Naua went to seek refuge with Navula at Waqana or with Mataitoga at Sabeto, they had come under the authority of the Navatulevu and Sabeto chiefs who thus had control of the Naua lands. The Nadi and Sabeto chiefs took advantage of Naua people in refuge with them and sold much of their land to Europeans, keeping the goods traded for their own use and not sharing them with the traditional owners.

External influences affecting Naua: the 'Dido' incident

As the number of British settlers increased in Fiji generally, the British Government through the Royal Navy developed an increasing concern for the well being of British subjects in their relationships with the Fijians. The corollary of this concern was the action that should or could be taken in the event of what the British considered to be a travesty of law and justice. Before the Cakobau army attacked Sabeto in 1873 as part of the campaign to avenge the murder of European planters in the Ba area, a European had been killed in the Denarau area on the coast of Nadi. HMS *Dido* came with the Commodore and Ratu Cakobau, as Head of the 1871 Government, to investigate the death and to hear the case against the Fijian suspect. William Berwick interpreted, and after the case was heard, Navula as strong leader of the Nadi people, was found ultimately responsible for the death. He was fined an area of land and 100 turtles. The turtles could not be caught, but the land given was the Navatulevu land at Nabuabua, and the Naua/Naiqoro land of Wailoaloa. Wailoaloa comprised the Naua land of Solowaro ('*solowaro*' means 'collecting shells from the sea' as opposed to *qeicara* or 'collecting shells from the river'), and the Naiqoro land of Enamanu.

The Naua united at Natuvulevu

This has been a detailed exploration of first, the changing loyalties involving socio-politically so much fission and fusion in the case of both the various social divisions and groups of the Naua polity; and secondly, their interrelationships with the Sabeto, Navatulevu and other polities in the general area. Finally it touches on external influences such as Christianity, Cakobau, European settlers and the British Government. It confirms that Naua is an excellent microcosm in which to study and analyse the origins and development of a simple western polity. I now investigate some of the mechanics of the procedures whereby Naua attained and maintains its present outward and visible appearance of unity, whilst still retaining a covert undercurrent of private but manageable disagreement.

Before the attack by the Cakobau army on Sabeto, some Naua had been living at Sabeto and some at Waqana with the Navatulevu. After the attack, they all came together to *soro* or formally apologise to Navula, because, in the course of the War of the Cebu Walu, they had killed so many of the Navatulevu of Nadi living with Mataitoga at Sabeto. Then after some time, those

Naua people living in the village of Natuvulevu, where Navula had settled them, brought a request (*lakovi*) to Navula for the Naua at Waqana to return to Naua territory. Navula released the latter group from their obligations (*sereki*) to their hosts at Waqana, and the Naua at Waqana performed the ceremony of *matamatanisali*. This ceremony symbolises a *matamata* or gate for those who had *sali* in the local communalect or *tiko vakararavi* (been in a position of dependence on some polity) to go back through and return home. The Naua people at Waqana ended the formalities with another *solevu* to express thanks to Navula. Then the Naua people all joined up at Natuvulevu, near Saravi, on traditional Naua territory. At that time, Naunu of the senior Vunaivi division of the Vunaivi *mataqali* had held the position of Momo or paramount of the Naua people, following on from the time when he had been appointed to that position through the authority of Rokomatu of Navatulevu on the return of the Naua from Sabeto. Previously, the paramount had been appointed from the Vunamaoli *mataqali*. From Natuvulevu, the Naua people went to Saravi, their former settlement homeland, at about the time of Cession in 1874. Naunu gave the position of Momo of Naua to Ratu Taito Nalukuya No.1 of the more junior Nadrau division of the Vunativi *mataqali*.

When Nemani Dreu of the Naduruniu breakaway group of the Navatulevu *yavusa* was appointed to be Roko Tui Ba in the Colonial Fijian Administration, the Naua left Saravi and were settled at their present village of Saunaka. The leadership of the Naua continued to be held by members of rank, both men and women, in the Nadrau division of the Vunativi *mataqali*, except on one occasion when a member of the Vunaivi division was appointed leader but not installed. The leader on appointment had the title of iTaukei Sawaieke, referring to the chiefly house mound of Sawaieke. After Ratu Taito had been called from Sabeto by Navula to be installed as the first of the Nadrau subdivision to be Momo, there followed three leaders of the Naua who were not formally installed. The first two were the son (Ratu Josateki) and the daughter of Ratu Taito, and the third was Ratu Taito No. 2, son of Ratu Josateki. Then followed two granddaughters of Ratu Josateki. Finally Ratu Josateki Natuigalugalu, son of Ratu Taito No. 2, and iTaukei Sawaieke, was installed with great ceremony as Momo Levu iTaukei Naua in 1997.

This may have been due partly to internal dissent based on the change of the senior division of the Vunativi from Vunaivi to Nadrau. It may also have reflected disagreements about the change of leadership from the Vunamaoli *mataqali* to the Vunaivi *mataqali* at the time when Naloku was made leader by Rokomatu of Nadi. The present Momo, Ratu Josateki Sovau, is the great-grandson of Ratu Taito; and he was the first to be formally installed as Momo Levu iTaukei Naua after 117 years. The installation took place before important chiefs of western and eastern Fijian society, represented by the two Tui Ba or paramounts of Ba (recalling an old split in the polity of Ba); the iTaukei Vidilo from Namoli, Lautoka; the Kwa Levu or paramount of Nadroga; and the Ratu mai Verata or paramount of the ancient and revered eastern polity of Verata. Other invited guests included the wife of the Prime Minister and the Head of the Wesleyan Church of Fiji and Rotuma. Nadi was not represented because of a current disagreement about the appointment of a Momo Levu for Nadi.

This installation ceremony probably symbolised a deliberate attempt on the part of the Naua people to decide once and for all on the division and group of the Naua from which the Momo Levu was to be appointed and installed; to put aside a long history of leadership changes and consequent demurrals and quarrels; and to present Naua as a firmly united polity with connections with important polities in both the west and east of Fiji. These ceremonies were carried out in the most open, solemn and binding manner possible as traditionally recognised by Fijian society.

Naua: a descent group or a socio-political complex?

The Naua people who had sought refuge with Navula at Waqana after the attacks by Nawaka, found themselves short of land when they eventually returned to their own territory, and there was nothing they could do about the situation. The Naua polity was socio-politically very much a nut between the crackers of the increasingly more powerful and stable neighbouring polities of Sabeto and Nadi. This situation may have been due partly to the relative socio-political and military weakness of the Naua; partly to their constant quarrels and disagreements resulting in fission and instability; and partly to the socio-political fact that they were not a single descent group, but a collection of descent groups who had joined together for mutual protection and convenience but found they had no powerful united spirit world to support them against the bickering of the secular leaders.

The chiefs of Naua (especially Ratu Josateki Savou, then iTaukei Sawaieke and now Momo Levu iTaukei Naua, and Apakuki Tuitavua, former Government veterinary officer and international football player) told me, in the course of lengthy discussions, about many current traditional accounts of the origins and development of the people comprising the various groups which became the recognised *mataqali* of the Naua *yavusa*. In these traditional accounts, five different socio-political groups are said to have settled at different times in what is now regarded as the Naua area. That they were different socio-political groups is evidenced from an exploration of those features which generally distinguish one such group from another.

The Vatuburu, the first arrivals, came originally from Sabeto (said iTaukei Sawaieke), or from Buduka and later went to, and came back from, the island of Malolo (said Apakuki). Their ancestral spirit was Keteketewalu (not Nakia), referred to as Tai or Grandfather, whose manifestation was a *manupusi* or mongoose. His place is at Natauvesi, in the Nubu i Tauvesi or Tauvesi Pool in the river near Natauvesi. Their *vuti yaca* are the *vesi ni waitui* or kind of *Afzelia bijuga*, being their *kai* or tree; the *vudi waiwai* or kind of plantain; and the *bibi* or kind of sea shellfish.

The Vunamaoli came next from the Tububere people of Vuda. Their ancestral spirit was Korowabu whose manifestation was a *vevewa* or owl but who sometimes appeared as a *gwata* or snake. His place is on the inland rocky hillock of Taqainasolo. Their *vuti yaca* are the *dravo* or reed, the *ba sousou* or kind of plantain, and the *yadrava* or kind of river fish. The *wior* (*Spondias dulcis*) is their *kai*, and is their symbol of both the male and female genital organs.

The Vunaivi came from the Conua people of Sabeto. Their ancestral spirit was Tai Udu (Grandfather Udu, whose full name was Mudunalagi), son of Vidirinasau who was a son of Korowabu. His manifestation was a *gwata lekeleke* or kind of snake. His place is at Bonunaqwele on the raised ground overlooking the beach at Nadi Airport. He is referred to as iTaukei Bonunaqwele. His *tobu* or *qwara ni sisili* (swimming pool or cave) is in the Vonovono stream below Bonunaqwele. Their *vuti yaca* are the *ivi selala* or kind of native chestnut (*Inocarpus edulis*), as *kai*, the *ba sousou* or kind of plantain, and the *yadrava* or kind of river fish. The *kai* is therefore different from that of the Vunamaoli, though the *magiti* and the *ilava* are the same. Perhaps this reflects recognition that their progenitors were related.

The Natuvulevu came originally from Toko, near Naqwavula, far up in the hills and below the present Navosa village of Nausori. Their ancestral spirit was Tai Ulurua (Grandfather with Two Heads), whose manifestation was a two-headed snake. His place is at Labe Edromu, just below what is now the McDonald's eatery on the Nadi/Nanaka road hard by the Saunaka junction. He is said to have appeared before a member of the staff, showing some anger, when McDonald's was built and his peace was being disturbed by the customers. He was suitably appeased with a *yaqona* ceremony of apology. Their *vuti yaca* is the *sevai* or kind of plantain. They have no *magiti* or *ilava*.

Associated with the Natuvulevu are Na Lewa Soro, two female spirits whose place is in a pool known as Nubu i Vunayasi in a stream which flows through the land of Lawa (once that of the Ferrier-Watsons) near Saunaka. They can be compared with two female spirits at Nasinu 4 Miles on the Suva/Nausori road; and with two other female spirits associated with a monolith known as Ledru Nono na Lewa Rua ('The Place of two Female Spirits') inland from Nagado, up the Sabeto valley. When I saw it, it had been defaced by miners exploring the area known as Vatutu.

The progenitor of the Ketenatacini was, I was told, Duaka, whose manifestation was a *gwata* or snake. This is particularly interesting because this Duaka appears to be the same Duaka who was progenitor of the Navatulevu of Nadi. He may also be the same as the Duaka who is one of the four Le Va spirits connecting the inland villages of Vatutu, Namulomulo and Yavuna with the coast (see Nawaka). Duaka's place is at the entrance to the reef at Momi, and his manifestation is a *dadakulaci* or sea snake with its tail at Beqa and its head around Malolo. The NLC-created *yavusa* of Yavusasivo symbolises its separateness from the parent group of Ketenatacini by claiming its own spirit, Tabaravu, whose manifestation is a *gwata lewa* or female snake and who may appear as an old woman. The NLC recorded the progenitor as Tabaravu. This snake's place is at Kou, the swimming place near Namo and inland from Saunaka. Those people who became the Ketenatacini/Yavusasivo came from Batiri, Nadroga, and they have the same *vuti yaca*, a *vai* or stingray, but no *kai* or *magiti*. This confirms that they were of the same stock. The *bete* or priest for Vasukine, the *nitu ni valu* or war spirit of the Naua polity, was from the Somulo division of the Ketenatacini.

Each group then had a different place of origin. Each had different and, except in one case, unrelated ancestral spirits who settled in different places and had different manifestations (*waqawaqa* or, in the communalect, *tolatola*). Each had different sets of *vuti yaca* or symbols of unity and identity (*kai* or trees, *magiti* or staple food, and *ilava* or concomitant for the *magiti*). There was no overall original ancestral spirit, and there is no overall *vuti yaca* for the polity now registered as the Naua *yavusa*. Although the Education Department listed the *vasili* as the *kai* or tree for the Naua *yavusa* generally, this was denied to me. A feature the *yavusa* may have in common is the *ivilavila ni yalo* or jumping-off place of the spirits of the dead, but this is by no means clear-cut. I was told that it may be at Bonunaqwele and that from here, the spirits of the dead go to the spiritually significant islet of Narokorokoyawa. Narokorokoyawa is the home of Tui Revurevu who was born there when his mother had to come ashore, in order to give birth, from the mythical vessel, the *Rogovoka*, one of those coming from the west with the first of the ancestral spirits to settle in Fiji. At Bonunaqwele, the spirits of the Naua people plunge into the sea, as indeed do spirits from many other places and socio-political groups. These accounts present a significantly different picture from that of the 1913 NLC.

The 1913 NLC accounts record myths of origin which present a picture of spiritual and social unity. There was a progenitor spirit, Korowabu, with an impeccable Nakauvadra background who had six spirit sons. The progenitor was associated as a unifying spiritual force for the totality of his Naua descendants. The sons were in turn original ancestral spirits of the six *mataqali*, and were the particular spiritual guardians for their respective descendants. The progenitor was married to a woman of Ne, and the *nitu ni valu* or war spirit was known as VasukiNe. This name reflects a *vasu* relationship between the hill folk of Ne (see under Sabeto), and indeed suggests that when the woman from Ne came down from the hills to marry Korowabu, the coastal progenitor, she came with the war spirit as her guardian and escort. The situation is parallel with that at Navo, when Salele, a woman of the Kovacaki, recorded as the daughter of the progenitor, Tutuvanua, came to marry the progenitor of the Ekubu *yavusa* of the Navo polity. She was accompanied by Namama, son of Limasa, the Kovacaki war spirit, who was sent as her escort. Korowabu and Salele settled at first inland at Taqainasolo and moved westward to Nabua, where the families of their sons became too numerous to be supported by the available land there, and two of the families separated and went towards the coast. Later they all moved towards the coast, presumably to have ready access to salt and seafood.

The traditional accounts of the historical origins of the Naua groups that I recorded are significantly different from the mythical origins. The latter suggest a unity and cohesion of the groups which the Naua *yavusa* would like to be the true position in the face of the quarrels and disagreements which characterise most of their powerful and not so powerful neighbours and also, though they would probably not admit it publicly, themselves. Many of these western polities such as Naua had found it difficult enough to assimilate with the outside influences of Christianity, the 1871 Cakobau Government, and often with European settlers. As I have suggested, the recent installation ceremony, the first for 117 years, may have symbolised the realisation on the part of the Naua *yavusa* generally, of the necessity to unite overtly and lay aside past internal quarrels and jealousies if they are to maintain any significant degree of the traditional way of life which so many to whom I spoke in Saunaka deemed to be the best buttress for them in this changing world of foreign spiritual beliefs, interracial politics and new forms of government. The myths of origin visualise a unified spiritual basis for the *yavusa,* in the face of disturbing new factors. The ceremony could be interpreted as a symbol of mature socio-political unity, reflecting the meaning of *nadi* (mature) in the local communalect.

Calevu ni Matamataraki and other bases for inter-polity relationships in the west

The narratives and analyses expounded in this chapter show that the present Fijian Administration *tikina* of Nadi comprising the Old *tikina* of Nadi and Sikituru (and formerly Buduka) is an area characterised by small, somewhat unstable, independent polities. Such polities, however independent they may have been socio-politically, nevertheless often found themselves in a position where they were oppressed by neighbours or subject to internal quarrels based on arrogance, jealousy, ambition or breach of etiquette. In either situation, they found that they might be forced to develop relationships with other polities, or take advantage of those already established. In the case of external oppression, they might have had to seek military assistance from another polity to drive away the attackers; or they may have been burned out and been forced to flee and seek refuge with another polity. In the case of internal quarrels, one party to the quarrel might have found it more amenable to leave for pastures new; or might have been driven away. In either of these typical situations, if no alternative vacant land was available for refuge or resettlement, association with another polity was inevitable.

Relationships with other polities in the west were frequently based on marriages from which *vasu* or *itutu* (the equivalent in the local communalect) relationships were derived. For instance, Conua, Sabeto had *vasu* relations with Nawaka. Vuda and Vitogo were closely related because Lewatulekeleke of Vitogo had married Natuilevu, son of Sagavula, the Sabutoyatoya progenitor. Relationships were also based on common descent from spiritual relations (the spiritual progenitors of the polities were siblings) from which *tauvu* or, as referred to in the communalect, *vitabani* relationships were derived. For instance, Vuda and Viwa, the furthest west of the Yasawa group, were *vitabani* on the basis that Erovu, the spiritual progenitor of the Kai Vuda, and Rainima, the spiritual progenitor of the Viwa people, were brothers.

Relationships could also be established and maintained through a system of *mata* or socio-political representatives. For instance, Vuda and Nakuruvarua, Nadroga, maintained diplomatic relationships through the Mata i Vuda stationed at Nadroga, and the Mata i Nakuruvarua stationed at Vuda. Perhaps because of Vuda being one of the most respected and stable polities in the west, there was considerable diplomatic traffic between Vuda and other polities. For ease of communication and in order to spread the responsibilities of receiving and providing accommodation for visiting missions, the burden was divided as follows:

The Naciriyawa *mataqali* of Vuda was responsible for Nawaka, Sabeto and Ba.

The Nasalivakarua *mataqali* was responsible for Rewa and Nadroga.

The Navicaki *mataqali* was responsible for Vitogo.

Sabeto maintained relationships with Nadroga, Vuda and Vitogo (and also with the associated but somewhat independent *yavusa* of Waruta) through representatives titled Mata i Naboutini. The Vuda representative is also referred to as the Matainaciriyawa. The names refer to certain important *yavu*.

Relationships could also be maintained along what are referred to in the western communalects as *calevu ni matamataraki* or diplomatic paths of communication. The nature and significance of these paths has not been explored before, and they do not have many features in common with what Sayes (1984) refers to as 'paths of the land'. Sayes identifies these paths as *sala volivoli* or tribute paths. They were evidently established at the time when the major complex eastern polity of Verata had extended its sphere of influence along the north and south coasts of Vanua Levu. Considerable administrative ability was required to ensure that tribute was brought to Verata from her 'colonies' on Vanua Levu. This resulted in the establishment of these paths as lines of communication along which the tribute was brought to centres of collection. One path came from Udu Point along the north coast as far as Labasa and thence across Vanua Levu to Wailevu. The other path came along the south coast to Wailevu. Labasa and Wailevu were regarded as tribute collecting centres, and tribute was eventually taken from Wailevu to Verata.

The places connected by *calevu* which I was able to record in the course of my explorations into the development of single *yavusa* polities as well as federated or associated polities in my study areas in Vuda, Sabeto, Nawaka and Nadi were as follows:

Vuda: Connected with Nadroga, Navo, Sikituru and Narewa (the Navatuevu). They said that there was no need for other *calevu* because they were connected by marriage with so many places.

Sabeto: Connected with Nadroga and Navo.

Ne: None recorded.

Nawaka: Connected with Sila. As in the case of Vuda, they said that there was no need for other *calevu* because they were connected by marriage with so many places.

Utiloaloa: The four component *yavusa* are connected with ten other peripheral polities.

There are also *calevu* between closely related places, as in the cases of the Yako, Navo and Korotabu, and of Vatutu, Yako and Navo.

Yamisa: None recorded.

Inland Le Va: None recorded.

Rukuruku: None recorded.

Vaturu: None recorded.

Nadi: Connected with Ketenavu, Yako (Nadroga), Vunatoto (Nawaka), Nabau (Namataku, Navosa), Momi (Nadroga) and Tukani (Kovacaki).

Kovacaki: Connected with Yakuilau, Navatulevu, Naua, Takuci, Nabau, Sikituru and Moala.

Ketenavu: Connected with Malolo and Navatulevu.

Navo: The five component *yavusa* were connected with thirty polities throughout the study areas and Nadroga.

Sikituru (Saunivalu): Connected with the Kovacaki, the Yavusania, Moala and Yaro (Navo).

Yavusania: The two *yavusa* were connected with eighteen polities in the Yasawa group, Nawaka, Rukuruku, the neighbouring polities and some in northern coastal Nadroga.

Naua: No overall connection, but the Ketenatacini *mataqali* was connected to the Tukavi (Kovacaki), and the Vatuburu with the Kovacaki at Buduka. This reflects the absence of overall homogeneity in the Naua *yavusa*, and supports the proposition that the *yavusa* is in reality a complex of generally unrelated groups.

If a polity wanted to make a request to another polity with which it had no connection by relationship or *calevu,* it would go, in the first place, to a polity with which it had such connections, and would ask that polity to make that request on its behalf. For instance, at the time of the Tola when Navatulevu chiefs of Nadi were seeking military assistance from Nadroga, Navatulevu followed the *Calevu ni Valu* to the Ketenavu of Moala. The Ketenavu followed the *Calevu ni Nukuvou* to Yako on the Nadroga boundary. Yako went to Nadroga, and the Kwa Levu of Nadroga sent out messages of request along his own lines of communication to Serua, Namosi, Deuba, Batiwai, the Djavutjukia people (in the hills of Nadroga) and the Conua (in Nadroga to the east of the Sigatoka River). In each case the request would be accompanied by *tabua.*

It seems from the evidence I have gathered, that the hill folk may not have had such an elaborate system of communication as was developed among the coastal polities. This may, however, be due simply to a gap in the evidence or a lack of traditional knowledge of my informants. Be that as it may, it does seem that the smaller polities such as the Navo or the Yavusania had a more developed system than the bigger ones who claimed that there was no need for *calevu* when they could connect with other polities on the basis of marriage relationships. Perhaps the Navo and the Yavusania were not able to develop connections by marriage, because, as wife producers, they were not considered sufficiently important socially, politically or militarily, to be approached by neighbours for the formal establishment of a *calevu.* Similarly as wife seekers, they might not generally have been considered particularly worthy of attention, although there was a sufficiently important marriage between a woman of the Kovacaki and a man of the Navo to justify the need for a war spirit, Namama, to be sent as her escort. More explorations into these *calevu* are necessary before answers to these questions can be satisfactorily given in respect of the details of the system. For the purpose of this monograph, it is sufficient to draw attention to the general system as providing a basis of communication between polities not connected by marriage or myths of related spiritual progenitors.

11

Polities of Nawaka *Tikina*

General background

The present Fijian Administration *tikina* of Nawaka is part of the *yasana* or province of Ba. Nawaka lies in the middle of the west side of the island of Viti Levu, separated from the western coastline by the *tikina* of Nadi. To the north, Nawaka borders the *tikina* of Magodro in the mountainous interior of Ba. To the east lie the Nausori Highlands and the area known as Namataku in the mountainous territory of Navosa, which forms part of the present province of Nadroga/Navosa. To the south, that part of Nawaka known as Rukuruku borders on the *tikina* of Malomalo and of Sigatoka (the latter being the heartland of the powerful polity of the Kwa Levu of Nakuruvarua, the present paramount of Nadroga, which through marriage has close traditional connections with Rewa and mythical connections with Tonga). Associated with Nawaka are thirty-one *yavusa*, the origins, development and grouping of which will be discussed in this chapter. These include mainly independent groups, many of which lived in the interior of Viti Levu where the rugged terrain made communication difficult, but the steep slopes, rocky peaks and, in certain parts, thick bush, provided natural features for defence.

Nawaka is important as an area of research for the purposes of my hypothesis that the more distant a polity is from the east, the less it will be affected by the east from the point of view not only of communalect and spirituality but especially of socio-political complexity. In Nawaka with its mountainous terrain, distance from the east may not be the only factor, but I suggest that it is probably the most significant. As the following accounts will show, Nawaka has socio-political (including linguistic), geographical and spiritual features significantly different not only from those of the major polities of the east but also from those of the polities of Rakiraki, which, I suggest, are intermediately situated geographically and also intermediately developed in terms of socio-political complexity, between the polities of the east and the west. The further west one goes from the highly developed socio-political complexes of the east, the less evident will be the tendency towards stable forms of federation and political hierarchy. In the present *tikina* of Nawaka, there is a great variety of differing geographical features. The western part of Old Nawaka *tikina* which borders with Nadi is relatively flat, but further inland the terrain gets increasingly hilly and bush-covered, with a backdrop of mountainous territory overlooked by the mighty peak of Koroba (1075 m). Rukuruku is mountainous with peaks up to 511 m, as is Vaturu with peaks up to 645 m and overlooked by dividing ranges of up to 981 m. Many areas of mountainous crags and dense bush are difficult to access even nowadays and these are features which in the past provided natural defences. Socio-politically Nawaka was characterised by a number of small and independent groups, being either single *yavusa* or loose confederacies of a few *yavusa* or part-*yavusa*. For socio-political purposes many of these groups recognised marital or spiritual connections within themselves or with other groups, and as they developed they accepted a form of group leadership by mutual consent. Nevertheless, the accounts of Nawaka polities show how choice of leadership by mutual consent can be overridden by ambition which led to jealousy (*vuvu*) and discontent (*veiqati*), two emotions which occurred frequently in the affairs of a polity and bedevilled the ideology of unity of a group. Generally these groups did not, however, formally acknowledge the imposed higher authority of either one of themselves or of outside polities in the coastal region or from the east.

Perhaps the most powerful neighbours were the strong warriors of Nadroga or, to be more precise, of the polity based on the Nakuruvarua group of which the Kwa Levu was the paramount. The Nadroga polity in turn had connections through marriage with Rewa and also with Tonga. By tradition, as we have seen, a fair-skinned Tongan was found hiding up a tree by some fisherwomen. Nadroga at the time was seeking an appropriate leader, and they chose this Tongan stranger named Wakanimolikula. During the 18th or early 19th century, Tongans adventuring along the south coast of Viti Levu attacked Beqa and moved on to Nadroga. Here they landed in the area known as Korotogo, and moved inland, establishing themselves near Tavuni hill fort on the lower reaches of the Sigatoka River. Their descendants still live in the villages of Narata, Nawamagi and Nadrala.

Nawaka itself is an independent polity of particular interest because its later development was inevitably associated with involvement in the post-1855 Christian wars and the wars of the Cakobau Government in the early 1870s. Cakobau was attempting to impose Christianity and the force of his rule on those in the west and the interior of Viti Levu who did not consider that they came within his traditional sphere of influence. These wars caused many quarrels among the western polities. They however eventually provided, on a basis of force on the one hand and the need for mutual co-operation on the other, for a situation which led to the establishment of medium socio-political polities, comprising a number of smaller polities and an increase in the number of levels of hierarchical complexity. The heartland of the polity based on the village of Nawaka was renowned as a place of experts whose powers of assistance or destruction were derived from their association with the Fijian spirit world. Independent Nawaka (especially those with these arcane powers) were therefore naturally hostile to the attempts of the Church Militant of the Cakobau Government to extend their powers of influence over Nawaka, either directly or through the polity of Nadi.

Nadi, which played a large part in the forceful attempts to Christianise Nawaka in the course of the wars known as Na iValu ni Lotu or 'the Wars of Christianity', had earlier accepted Christianity and the authority of Cakobau. Their reasons for this acceptance may have been either because they knew that the military power of Cakobau was too great to be resisted, or because they saw an opportunity to extend, under the guise of helping Cakobau, their own sphere of influence over Nawaka and the other inland polities which had the same attitude to Cakobau as had Nawaka. The situation provides interesting evidence for the mechanics and emotions of polities being subjected to influence from forces, both political and spiritual, outside their own customary world. Later, this spirit of independence and a stern refusal to accept the authority of outsiders, especially the Christian warlords of Bau at the time of the Cakobau Government, led to attacks on these groups including Nawaka, by armies of polities such as Nadi who realised the strength of Cakobau and were seeking allegiance with Bau. Similar sentiments also led to attacks on their neighbours up the Sabeto valley by the troops of the Cakobau Government, which resulted in their deportation to Koro (see Sabeto account). After Cession, these people were brought back and resettled on their lands.

Though far from Bau, Nawaka became subject administratively to Bau's influence when Ba (of which Nawaka was a part) became a province under the pre-Cession Cakobau Government. Although Sigatoka and Nadi had accepted Christianity and the military might of Christian Cakobau earlier on, those polities sympathetic with, or subject to, the powers of Bau and the associated Church Militant and those polities opposed to Christianity and Cakobau's Government (which they considered to be one and the same) became involved in struggles that tended at first to confirm old socio-political alignments. Later the military might of the forces of Cakobau brought about new confederations by compelling or persuading the recalcitrant Nawaka people to accept the new religion and to heed the authority of those paramounts who had bowed earlier to what they saw to be the inevitable. These paramounts had, under the guise of accepting Christianity, found favour with the Cakobau Government and had gained its support for their ambitions to extend their spheres of influence over the defeated pagans.

Nawaka is important linguistically too because it is furthest geographically from the east and should be expected to have the fewest connections linguistically with the communalects of the east. People of Nawaka who wished to show how, traditionally, they had so little in common with the polities of Bau and the east, could point out how different their communalects were in the spheres of phonetics, grammar and vocabulary. Their communalects were certainly mutually incomprehensible. Language was very much a symbol of unity and differentiation within and between polities.

Nawaka is also important spiritually because it is furthest geographically from the Nakauvadra Range and the pan-Fijian culture heroes associated in myth with the Range. One set of origin myths current in the west of Fiji related to these culture heroes arriving in the Vuda area, where some remained. It is interesting to explore whether the original ancestral spirits of Nawaka are associated more with the Nakauvadra, or with those who remained behind at Vuda, or with other original ancestors who may have come from the southern interior of Viti Levu or from the southwest coastal areas of Nadroga with their Tongan associations. In particular, I shall question whether the Nawaka polities considered the Nakauvadra Range to be important as a basis of the spiritual unification of Fijian society, or whether the Nawaka and others in the west were not so much concerned with the concept of a pan-Fijian society as with their own unity against the increasing influence of those major polities of the east, especially Bau, with whom they had no traditional socio-political association of confederacy. It is a popular notion nowadays to regard 19th century Fiji as two societies, the east and the west, and to believe that there is no real basis for the concept of a monolithic society, but the dichotomy of Fiji into east and west is certainly at best an oversimplification and at the worst is simply not true. The case of Nadroga to which I have referred shows that there were patterns of association between the western Nadroga and the eastern Rewa. I suggest that, to pursue the geological analogy, Fijian society has features in common with conglomerate or pudding stone, with an overall matrix made up with a quantity of pebbles of different size and quality; although in the case of Fiji it is not a random mix.

Socio-politically, linguistically and spiritually, Nawaka itself is among the western areas least affected by the polities of the east. This is largely because of its distance to the west, but also because of its determination to remain independent of eastern socio-political and ideological influences. Thirdly, the mountainous and, in some parts, the thickly-vegetated nature of the terrain of upland Nawaka meant that distant association and difficult communication mitigated against the easy development of a closely knit complex polity. But I suggest that the overriding factor in the development of Nawaka was its distance from the east and from the expansionist policies and ambitions of powerful and able eastern chiefs for whom the Tonga semi-monarchical influence was so much stronger than were the relatively minor incursions and settlements for the polities of Nadroga. Even so, in far-away Nadroga, the respect by Fijians for Tongans was so strong that they accepted Wakanimolikula as a 'stranger king'. Nawaka itself may be regarded as typical of an area in which the pre-Christian independent polities were of a relatively simple nature from being least influenced by the complexities of the eastern polities and with communalects and spirituality similarly least affected by the east. The traditional accounts of these western polities feature the basis and development of the polity and its leadership, internal quarrels as much as quarrels with neighbours, internal disputes about leadership, and social fusion and fission. Such features are found frequently in the accounts of the major eastern polities, and give rise to treachery and open combat often on a mighty scale. In the west, by contrast, they have more the flavour of family squabbles arising from what were seen to be personal insults, such as the presentation of the wrong part of a pig or subtle variations in the procedures for *yaqona* drinking. The implications of the latter are important generally, but especially so in the circumstances of minor western polities.

One such case involved the presentation of *yaqona* to two different brothers in what they considered to be either in the wrong order or in a manner inappropriate to their respective status. This was superficially a matter of personal insult, but it may have reflected an underlying feeling of ill-will between the two brothers, or it may have been a manifestation of the ambitions of the younger brother to supersede the elder brother. It may indeed have been a sign on the part of the people preparing the *yaqona* by which they wished to indicate that they preferred that the younger brother should be the leader, either because he was a more competent leader or was one more kindly disposed towards and more considerate of his people.

Minor independent groups occurred in the far west of Viti Levu and were least susceptible to the influences of Tonga. They are therefore of particular interest because they provide examples of the least developed forms of polity, typifying one end of a continuum of forms of polity in late pre-historic and early historic Fijian society. The other end of the continuum is typified by the highly complex polities of Bau and Rewa.

There are actually several uses of the term Nawaka other than that of the New *tikina* which is the one used here. The literal meaning of the word, Nawaka, could be 'the root' (based on *na waka*), but I could find out no satisfactory explanation for such a meaning. Some said in Nawaka village that it referred symbolically to the place where the Nawaka people first took root. I suspect that this was an *ex post facto* reconstruction. The basis of this problematic explanation will become apparent when I discuss the mythical origins of the Nawaka people.

Nawaka then, is a name with several referents, such as:

(a)   The general name for the mythical place of settlement of the four original ancestral spirits of the four descent groups which currently comprise the Nawaka socio-political complex;

(b)   After Cession, the Old Fijian Administration *tikina* of Nawaka, which comprised the area between the Old *tikina* of:

    (i)   Namataku (to the east, now part of the Colo or mountainous interior of the province of Nadroga/Navosa),

    (ii)   Rukuruku (to the south, see below),

    (iii)   Nadi (to the west, see below),

    (iv)   Vaturu (to the north);

(c)   After the enactment of the 1945 Fijian Affairs Ordinance, the New Fijian Administration *tikina* of Nawaka, comprising the three Old *tikina* of Rukuruku, Nawaka and Vaturu;

(d)   Nowadays, commonly used to refer to the main socio-political complex in Nawaka *tikina*, otherwise referred to as Vunatoto, after the name of the leading *yavusa*, or as Nalagi, after the name of the currently leading *mataqali*;

(e)   The present village (Nawaka) and the old village (distinguished, when necessary, by the use of the modifier *makawa* or 'old', as Nawaka Makawa).

The main polities: Nawaka *tikina*—a geographical and political snapshot

Nawaka New *tikina* comprises the Old *tikina* of Nawaka, Rukuruku and Varutu. These are the Old *tikina* which I covered in the course of my research project in Nawaka *tikina*.

The main polities based in these Old *tikina* were at the time of Cession and are still recognised as follows:

Nawaka Old tikina

Name of *vanua*	Leading *yavusa*	Title of paramount	No. of *yavusa*	Levels of hierarchy	No. of villages
Nawaka	Vunatoto	Momo or Tui Nawaka	4	2	1

Since the wars of Christianity, the Momo of Vunatoto (now referred to by the eastern title of Tui Nawaka) had heeded the authority of the Momo Levu of Navatulevu, Nadi. Before this, the Momo of Vunatoto was independent.

Na *Yavusa* Ciwa (The Nine *Yavusa*), as follows:

Utiloaloa	Korolevu	Momo or Vunataqwa	4	2	1

The term Utiloaloa also covers the Noi Vatuma or the Navo (accounts differ).

Yamisa	Nasevaravara	No title	3	2	1

Before the wars of Christianity, each *yavusa* was independent.

Three (one now extinct) equal *yavusa*			3(2)	2	1

After the wars of Christianity, the three *yavusa* of the Yamisa group and the heads of the three (now two) individual *yavusa* heeded the authority of the Momo of Korolevu, head of the Utiloaloa, who in turn heeded the authority of the Momo of Vunatoto, Nawaka.

The Rukuruku Old tikina, which includes:

Noi Sesevia	Nawaqesara	Tui Sesevia	6	2	3
Noi ni Yasawa	Naqalitala	Tui Rukuruku	6	2	3

These were two independent complex polities, the paramounts of which heeded no higher authority.

The Vaturu Old tikina, which includes:

Viyagoiranitu	Viyagoiranitu	Momo	1	1	1

This *yavusa* was evidently associated at some time and in some way with the Rarawaqa group.

Noitubai	Noitubai	Momo	1	1	1
Nanuku	Nanuku	N/A	1	1	1
Nasau	Nasau	Momolevu	1	1	1

These three *yavusa* were previously recognised as separate and politically independent. They were regarded as forming a loose social unity, known collectively as the Nadua. Nowadays the Nanuku and the Nasau are regarded as sub-groups of the Noitubai.

Yalatina	Yalatina	N/A	1	1	1

This *yavusa* has a spirit-based connection with the Nanuku group referred to above.

The accounts which follow will show the origins and development of the structure of these polities up to the time of Cession. Since Nawaka polities do not extend across Old *tikina* boundaries, I am not producing separate tables for the geographical and the political structures. It should be noted that some Old *tikina* include more than one *vanua* (for instance, Rukuruku includes both the Noi Sesevia and the Noi ni Yasawa *vanua*). Similarly one *tikina* may include not only one or more *vanua* but also one or more independent *yavusa*.

The main polities: Nawaka *tikina*—details of structure

Nawaka Old tikina: the Nawaka socio-political complex

In more detail, the origins and development of the polities which were found in the Old *tikina* of Nawaka and which comprised the Nawaka socio-political complex as it was at about the time of the Cakobau Government are found in the following accounts to emphasise the simple nature of the polities and their determination to remain politically independent of outside authority. The accounts show how the individual *yavusa* or loosely federated groups of *yavusa* reacted to pressures from physical attack, and to intrigues by ambitious leaders. Such attacks and intrigues involved not only neighbours whose behaviour they understood but also eventually involved military and ideological forces far removed from the spheres of communication and interaction with which the westerners were familiar. Attacks and intrigues came about either directly from the eastern military might of the Cakobau government, or indirectly through neighbours who had accepted the new regime. They may have done so themselves under pressure. They may equally have accepted the regime voluntarily, probably hoping for some socio-political advantage or military aid in their local struggles and in forwarding their own local ambitions.

Nawaka Old *tikina* includes the following elements:

(a)   *The Nawaka polity*, which comprises the following four *yavusa*, based on the present village of Nawaka:

    (i)   The leading *yavusa*, Vunatoto, whose head is titled the Momo of Vunatoto or, in eastern phraseology, Tui Nawaka;

    (ii)   The three *yavusa* of Nawaka, Bemanu and Senibua.

Myths of origin state how four original ancestral spirits came down separately from the spiritual centre on the Nakauvadra Range in Ra and headed in a westerly direction. These four took different routes but arrived eventually in the lowland area known generally as Nawaka where they settled together. As each successive spirit arrived, he was welcomed by those already there and he married one of the women associated with the other spirits. By common consent, each newcomer was recognised as the leader. These four spirits became the original ancestors of the four *yavusa* which comprise the polity of Nawaka. The last to arrive was the original ancestor of the Vunatoto *yavusa*. He in turn was recognised as leader, being presented with *yaqona* (kava) to drink ceremonially. He was endowed with *mana* or spiritual power and Vunatoto became recognised as the leading *yavusa* of the polity of Nawaka which is of particular interest in showing how a number of descent groups can combine into a relatively small and simple socio-political complex polity on the basis of their mutual feelings for each other and a feeling of spiritual unity. This feeling was derived from the myth that their respective original spiritual ancestors came from the same place of origin, settled together in harmony and reached agreement on leadership.

> The original ancestral spirit of the Vunatoto had two sons. One day those living at Nawaka planted a garden for the elder son who duly prepared *yaqona* to thank (*oco*) the workers. The younger son arrived to find that all the *yaqona* had been drunk. He was so upset by what he regarded as a serious insult that he left Nawaka and went east to the mountainous interior where he stayed at Natauva.

His descendants formed the Korolevu *yavusa* and refused to go back to Nawaka and rejoin their confreres, the Vunatoto. Instead they remained a *yavusa* separate geographically and socio-politically from the Vunatoto and the polity of Nawaka. They later went and settled at Vatutu, with the Utiloaloa polity (see below).

> The elder brother arriving at Nawaka had two sons, who were the progenitors of the two *mataqali* of Vunatoto and Nalagi. These two sub-groups came to hate each other, starting from the younger brother's arrogance towards his elder brother. This led to warfare in which the Korolevu, remembering their old quarrels with the Vunatoto, came to assist the Nalagi. There was continuing hatred and jealousy between the brothers, and rivalry between the Vunatoto and Nalagi persisted and was manifested in warfare in which neighbouring groups became involved through bonds of relationship. Nawaka became involved in warfare with the neighbouring polity of Navo, based on insult when a man of Navo offered raw *vudi* or plantains to some visiting Nawaka people. The then head of the Nalagi, Nabatuiteci, was so successful in taking revenge on the Navo that the chiefly Vunatoto *mataqali* offered the leadership to Nabati. From this time, the leadership of the Vunatoto *yavusa* and of the Nawaka polity remained with the Nalagi.

The rest of the descendants of the four original ancestors remained together and established the village of Nawaka Makawa which was divided into four. When Nawaka was attacked by Nadi during the wars of Christianity, all four *yavusa* scattered to the hills and took refuge with groups with whom they had marital relations. After the wars, they were brought back on the orders of the Nadi chiefs, with whom they formed a loose affiliation while remaining socio-politically independent. All four *yavusa* are currently associated with the present village of Nawaka.

So it came about that the paramount of the four groups came and still comes from the Nalagi sub-group of the Vunatoto, and is installed with the title of Momo or Tui Nawaka. The Nalagi was not originally the senior sub-group, but a change of recognised seniority came about through internal rivalry and resentment, based on the arrogant behaviour of the leader and quarrels. A covert but deeply felt feeling that Nalagi is an upstart became more apparent to me as over the years I became more attuned to the nuances of the internal affairs of this polity. Leadership was first achieved by mutual consent, but this amiable atmosphere of consent which was the basis of the initial development of the polity was countered by the rise of rival ambitions for leadership. This led to internal struggles, a change in the hierarchical structure of the *yavusa* of Vunatoto and to feelings of discontent which still prevail. This was a slightly different situation from that leading to fission within the *yavusa* of Vunatoto that resulted in members of the *yavusa* leaving their relations and the emerging polity of Nawaka and going away to form a separate *yavusa* in a different geographical area and in association with a different polity—the Utiloaloa of Vatutu (see immediately below). This fission however affected the internal rivalries of the remainder of the Vunatoto because the Korolevu (descended from the younger brother) came to the support of the Nalagi (the junior *mataqali*) against the senior Vunatoto *mataqali*.

(b) Na Yavusa Ciwa (The Nine Yavusa) comprise the following nine *yavusa*, the survivors of which are based on the present inland villages of Vatutu and Namulomulo, and the further interior and upland villages of Yavuna and Tubenasolo.

The features of these simple western polities were very different from those of the highly complex polities of the east in late prehistoric and early historic Fijian society.

Although they had some connections based on spiritual associations, it was not until the wars of Christianity and of Cakobau that they developed into a more elaborate confederation. As a case study for the development and structure of simple polities in the far western coast and interior of Viti Levu, a consideration will be given in some detail to the Nine *Yavusa* and their associates, as follows:

(i)   The four *yavusa* of Vunataqwa, Korolevu, Korotogo (Toga), and Yaumali, based on Vatutu, about 3km south-east of Nawaka—known collectively as the Utiloaloa (Black Penises).

The original ancestral spirit of the Vunataqwa came from Nakauvadra Range and followed the coast westerly and southerly. He came to Nawaka which was already occupied. So he went on inland to Vunataqwa, and his descendants formed the *yavusa* of Vunataqwa. He married a woman of Nadi and had two children, and they and their descendants formed the leading *mataqali* or sub-group. He also had an affair with a female spirit, Lewatu, his penis extending to the black sands of Wailoaloa beach. Lewatu's children and their descendants were the *mataqali* Nagaga.

The exact significance of this myth is not clear. On close investigation, it appears that the *vuti aca* (symbols of identification and unification of descent groups) of the two sub-groups are different. These are generally symbols of unity and identification of a single descent group. The evidence of two sets of symbols suggests that instead of being a single descent group, the Vunataqwa are a construct of two separate groups or part-groups of different origins. This may be reflected in the myth that one *mataqali* are the descendants of the ancestor and his recognised wife, whereas the other are descendants resulting from an extra-marital adventure and therefore not of quite the same background.

The original spirit of the Korolevu came from Nawaka after a fraternal quarrel already referred to in the Nawaka account. On the invitation of the Vunataqwa spirit, he settled at Vunataqwa and then moved inland, leaving his descendants at Korolevu, near Vunataqwa. They formed the *yavusa* of Korolevu.

The Korolevu remembered the insult to their original spirit when at Nawaka he was not given a share of the *yaqona* to drink after he had helped his brother preparing a garden. They were preparing to attack Nawaka to avenge this old insult, when Nawaka learned of the pending attack and instead attacked the Korolevu and the Vunataqwa who scattered to the hills between Nawaka and the Nasigatoka River. Seeking refuge with the Vatuma people, they were joined by the Korotogo people and the Yaumali people. At Vatuma, a strong man of the Korolevu, was recognised as the leader of the four *yavusa*.

The Korotogo are a part of the descendants of a canoeload of Tongans who came under their leader, Maile, from Niua in Tonga to Rewa, thence to Serua and finally to south-east Nadroga. Some remained here and their descendants who live in villages by the lower reaches of the Nasigatoka River still maintain their connections with Tonga. Others went up the river and then west into the hills between the river and Nawaka where they joined the local Vatuma and the refugee Korolevu.

The village of the Korotogo in the hills was burned in the course of local warfare, and the villagers took refuge with the Korolevu who by now were back at Vunataqwa. After further attacks, they settled with the Korolevu, the Vunataqwa and the Yaumali.

One account which is now denied by the Yaumali, says that the Yaumali were of Tongan origin. They were part of the Korotogo people, being descendants of the youngest son of Moala.

All other accounts including those given to me in 1953 and 1995 indicate rather a spiritual origin with the Nakauvadra Range, an origin which is the spiritual basis for the association between three of the Nine *Yavusa* and also a connection with the coastal polities of Nadi. There is no independent evidence of which I am aware to confirm or discredit these two irreconcilable accounts. For the purposes of exploring the origins and development of the Nine *Yavusa* and particularly their connections with each other and with the western coastal polities, it is tempting to emphasise the Nakauvadra accounts, bearing in mind that these could be *ex post facto* explanations.

I will give an account of the myths of origin from Nakauvadra, which will also refer to the *yavusa* involved other than those of the four at Vatutu.

> Two spirits came from Nakauvadra to Koroba, the mighty mountain overlooking the south-western part of the *tikina* of Nawaka and in particular the hilly periphery of Rukuruku (see below). They had four children, referred to as Oitou na Le Va or 'The Four'. The eldest was the original ancestral spirit of the Nakorovau people (one of the Nine *Yavusa*) at Tubenasolo, far into the mountainous interior of Nawaka *tikina*. The second was the ancestor of the Yaumali. The third was the ancestral spirit of the Koroba people, one of the Nine *Yavusa* living at Yavuna, in the interior between Vatutu and Tubenasolo. These three were land spirits. The fourth was a very powerful sea spirit guarding the entrance through the reef and the general reef line from the island of Malolo to the island of Beqa, who came to be regarded as the original ancestral spirit of the Navatulevu people, the paramount group of Nadi.

> The brother who became the ancestral spirit of the Yaumali was at Koroba when he was told to go and draw water. He was very annoyed at being given such a menial task and he left and went towards the coast where he settled. The original spirit of the Korolevu came to visit the place where the spirit of the Yaumali had settled and was given some yams to eat. The yams were so small that the Korolevu spirit was angry and the hosts planned to kill him. However the Yaumali spirit successfully pleaded for his life, and they became friends.

This was the spiritual basis for the later association between the Yaumali and the Korolevu when the former went to join the Korolevu (together with the Vunataqwa and the Korotogo) at Vunataqwa. This was before the coming of Christianity. Later they were burned by the Nawaka people in the course of the wars of Christianity and again they scattered to the hills. At this time the person who was accepted as the leader of the four *yavusa* was a man of Vunataqwa, because he had a gun. In due course, the leader of the Nadi people who was the champion of Christianity in the area ordered the four *yavusa* to return to their own territory and so they settled in the craggy area of Korotabu, where it was that the ancestral spirit of the Vunataqwa had had his extra-marital experience with the spirit Lewatu. These four *yavusa*, the Vunataqwa, the Korolevu, the Korotogo and the Yaumali, together with their former hosts in the hills, the Vatuma, are referred to informally (*kacakacivaki*) as the Utiloaloa, the Black Penises, perhaps reflecting the myth of the ancestral spirit of Vunataqwa whose penis extended to the black sand beach of Wailoaloa.

Because of these past changes of recognised leadership, a current problem is whether the Vunataqwa or the Korolevu should be recognised as the head of what was once a loose polity but after the wars of the Cakobau Government had become more formalised through the development of the polity of Nadi and its associations with neighbouring polities such as Nawaka. This affected the position of the four *yavusa* in the overall federation of the Nine *Yavusa* which then acknowledged the authority of the paramount of Nawaka, the Momo of Nalagi/Tui Nawaka, who in turn acknowledged the authority of the paramount of Nadi. At Vatutu, I was told by the Vunataqwa that they were the original inhabitants and should be recognised as senior. The Korolevu were, however, recognised by the other *yavusa* as the senior *yavusa*. Nowadays such rivalry for seniority is a feature of Fijian society, either because larger sums of rent money go to the paramount or simply because social and political ambition has increased among non-paramounts.

The varied *yavusa* origins and socio-political factors affecting the affiliations and developments of the Utiloaloa are against a background of:

- the frequent wars (based at first on local matters such as insults and personal slights and, later, on the coming of Christianity and the expanding influences of the Cakobau Government, at first through Nadi and later by direct intervention); and

- the changes in leadership by consent (based on achievement rather than inheritance) which make the Utiloaloa an interesting polity to study.

These *yavusa* are also of interest because their communalect is significantly different from that of Nawaka, and shows features more characteristic of the Nadroga communalects, such as a change in the word for 'pig'. The Nine Yavusa starting from the village of Vatutu used the same word as was used in Nadroga—that is, *vore*; whereas the Nawaka *yavusa* in the village of Nawaka used the same word as was used in the chain of communalects in areas stretching north and north-east from Nawaka as far as Rakiraki—that is, *qo*. The eastern word for 'pig' is *vuaka* (with phonetic variations such as *puaka* or *pua'a*).

(ii)   The two yavusa of Saumata and Leweinaqwali (now extinct), based on Namulomulo, four miles inland from Vatutu.

The original ancestral spirit of the Saumata came from Nakauvadra Range and followed the coast westerly and southerly to Nadroga, and then turned inland to settle in the area known broadly as Rukuruku, now the southernmost part of Nawaka tikina on the Nadroga border. This became the first settlement of the Saumata.

The original spirit of the Leweinaqali also came from Nakauvadra and settled in the general area where the spirit of the Saumata had settled and established the first village of the yavusa.

Later, caught in the course of fighting between local groups, the Saumata and the Leweinaqali scattered and together took refuge with the Noi Nabau, a group at Naqwavula below Nausori, who gave them a village in their territory in the very interior of eastern Nawaka. The Saumata and the Leweinaqali were both independent polities, each owing some customary allegiance to their 'landlords'. Then they were attacked by Nawaka at the time of the wars of Christianity and they once more scattered until the Nadi leader brought them back and settled them on land belonging to the Bolabola (see below). From here they moved to Namulomulo.

These *yavusa*, their origins and development in a background of local warfare are typical of the simplest forms of polity settled by refugees far from their ancestral acres. Though the Leweinaqali became extinct, the Saumata are still at Namulomulo, and though independent before the wars of Christianity, afterwards heeded the authority of the Momo of Korolevu of Vatutu who in turn heeded the authority of the Momo or Tui Nawaka of the Nawaka polity. This line of authority arose after the wars of Christianity and the Cakobau Government before Cession which saw the development of more complex forms of polity. This was due partly to the expansive ambitions of Navula, the powerful and able leader in Nadi, and partly to the influence of Cakobau's government which had been established as pan-Fijian and therefore needed to demonstrate its authority especially in the independent west.

(iii) The three *yavusa* of Koroba, Nasevaravara and Bolabola, based in the upland village of Yavuna, four miles inland from Namulomulo—known collectively as the Yamisa.

The original ancestral spirits of the Koroba and the Nasevaravara came from the Nakauvadra, but the original ancestor of the Bolabola came from the opposite direction from the Djavutjukia people inland from Sigatoka, Nadroga.

The ancestor of the Koroba who was one of four siblings (known as Na Le Va or 'The Four') who were the basis of a spiritual unity between the inland *yavusa* of the Koroba, the Yaumali of Yavuna, and the Nakorovau of Tubenasolo as well as with the coastal polity of Nadi.

Each of the three spirits arrived in that order in the mountainous area overlooked by Koroba peak and settled there in harmony. Although the three groups maintained their political independence, they agreed to accept the leadership of the Nasevaravara for the purposes of communal duties and responsibilities and for mutual protection.

The importance of the Yamisa is that three groups came together from different areas of spiritual or actual origin, settled together and agreed on changes of leadership. These three *yavusa* suffered similar fates to the others already described. They became threatened by local wars and scattered and took refuge with other *yavusa* in the interior or even with the Naua people (now of Saunaka) in the coastal plain near Nadi. Different *mataqali* went to different people with whom they could claim some connection such as by marriage. Following the wars of Christianity, the three *yavusa* were brought back by those under the authority of Nadi and Nawaka, and were finally settled together at Yavuna.

These three *yavusa* had a loose social association based on the myth that their respective ancestral spirits, though not related, had lived together in harmony. Nevertheless, like those based on Namulomulo, they were politically independent of higher authority in the times before the wars of Christianity. After these wars, they formally recognised the Nasevaravara as the leading *yavusa*, and the head of the Nasevaravara heeded the authority of the Momo of Korolevu (Vatutu) who in turn heeded the authority of the Momo or Tui Nawaka.

(iv) The single *yavusa* of Nakorovau, based in Tubenasolo, which lies among craggy mountains 13 km inland from the village of Namulomulo.

Tubenasolo is even now inaccessible save on foot or horseback, and when I visited the village, it was still surrounded by thick bush. It and the village of Natawa in the Old *tikina* of Vaturu (to which I shall refer later) are the most isolated upland villages in my project areas.

The original ancestral spirit of the Nakorovau people came from the Nakauvadra Range. He was a brother of the original ancestors of the Yaumali of Vatutu; and of the Koroba of Yavuna; and of the coastal spirit who was the original ancestor of the Navatulevu of Nadi. With his parents and siblings, he lived first at Koroba, and then moved south-east to the general area known as Rukuruku (see below) on the Nadroga border.

His descendants were chased away by local groups, and they moved to the Nabau people at Naqwavula (see above). Here they were attacked by the Magodro people from the interior, and they scattered to Tubenasolo, which was then owned by the Nasevaravara people. They took refuge here and provided services (*vakalala*) for the Nasevaravara, the Bolabola and the Koroba (the Yamisa), but their hosts turned on them and attacked them and they fled to Nawaka. They remained under the authority of the Nawaka people who settled them nearby until after the wars of Christianity, when they went back to Tubenasolo.

In spite of their isolation and their determined spirit of political independence, the Nakorovau had, through the sibling relationship between the various original ancestors, recognised spiritually-based social connections with other interior and coastal polities. The Nakorovau, Yaumali and Koroba were regarded as *vitacini* or brothers, because of these spiritual connections. It was through these spiritual connections that those living at Tubenasolo (the Nakorovau), those at Yavuna (the Koroba) and those at Vatutu (the Yaumali) maintained a social connection and, after the wars, a socio-political connection not only with each other but also with Nadi through the sister of the spirits of the three groups named here.

After the wars of Christianity, the Nakorovau became part of the recognised association now referred to the *Yavusa Ciwa* (The Nine *Yavusa*). The head of the Nakorovau heeded the authority of the Momo of Korolevu (Vatutu), who in turn heeded the authority of the Momo or Tui Nawaka. In this way the *yavusa* of Nakorovau became an element of the Nawaka polity.

Rukuruku Old tikina: two separate socio-political complexes

The two polities recorded as associated with the Rukuruku Old *tikina* were independent of each other and of any other polity at the time of Cession. Indeed the twelve *yavusa* of Rukuruku never seem to have developed into a single socio-political complex with a recognised paramount leader. Instead six of the *yavusa* comprised the socio-political complex known as the Noi Sesevia and based on the three adjacent villages of Nawaqadamu, Uto and Vunamoli. The other six *yavusa* comprised the socio-political complex known as the Noi ni Yasawa and based on the three villages of Tore, Rararua and Narata which lie to the east of the Noi Sesevia villages.

As the result of provincial boundary changes, Narata now falls outside the boundary of Rukuruku Old *tikina* (and the administrative province of Ba) and lies within the boundary of the administrative province of Nadroga/Navosa.

The twelve Rukuruku *yavusa* were almost constantly involved in local fighting resulting from or leading to the fission and fusion of the *yavusa* within and between the Rukuruku polities and their neighbours. This local fighting was similar in nature to what occurred in the socio-political environment of polities described in other areas in the New *tikina* of Nawaka.

These Rukuruku *yavusa* were also affected by the wars of Christianity and the wars of the Cakobau Government. At first, under the guise of spreading Bau's traditional sphere of authority, Cakobau attempted forcefully to impose Christianity on the pagan west and especially the hillfolk. Later, his government attempted to assert itself outside the traditional sphere of authority of Bau and again found itself at odds with the many polities of the west. On the Ba/Nadroga boundaries, the Kwa Levu of Nadroga and the government's armies attacked those in the mountainous interior who were traditionally opposed to the Kwa Levu and had come to be highly suspicious and hostile of the intents and personal ambitions of Cakobau and the eastern chiefdoms with whom they associated the forceful spreading of Christianity to what they saw to be the detriment of their own spiritual power base. The attacks affected many polities in Nawaka *tikina*, and the Noi Sesevia and the Noi ni Yasawa especially became either directly or peripherally involved. These polities suffered in battle, were split up and joined others as refugees, or eventually accepted Christianity and paid lip-service to the Cakobau Government, at any rate so long as his armies were in the neighbourhood. After Cession, many in the mountainous interior initially refused to accept the Colonial Government, because they said that they were not represented at discussions agreeing to Cession, nor did any recognised representative sign the Deed of Cession. The Governor Sir Arthur Gordon's 'Little War' against those who did not recognise the Colonial Government did not affect other parts of Nawaka. At Cession the Rukuruku lands became administratively the Old *tikina* of Rukuruku in the Fijian Administration of the Colonial Government. After the amalgamation of *tikina* in 1945, Rukuruku became part of Nawaka, under Buli Nawaka.

Rukuruku was recognised as including, at Cession, the two socio-political complexes, as follows:

(a) The Noi Sesevia polity, which comprised the following six *yavusa*:

(i) The leading *yavusa*, Reiwaqa (or Raiwaqa in Standard Fijian), whose head was titled the Tui Sesevia. Tui Sesevia, who was independent of higher authority, lived at Nawaqadamu, although most of the *yavusa* was based at the village of Uto with the Noi Rukuruku.

The origin myths differ about the name and immediate origin of the original ancestor, though an ultimate origin in the Nakauvadra Range is generally agreed upon.

> The Reiwaqa had first settled at Vunamoli with the Rukuruku people until they were attacked by a neighbouring group and both groups scattered to take refuge with the Vatuma. During the time of the Cakobau Government, the Reiwaqa left the Vatuma, some going to Nawaqadamu and others going to Uto where they heeded the authority of the Rukuruku people.

> Those at Nawaqadamu claimed one spirit as the original ancestor of the Reiwaqa, whereas those at Uto claimed another. Each claimed to be the leading group.

This probably reflects a split in the group. The position of the Tui Sesevia was certainly the subject of disagreement between the Reiwaqa of Nawaqadamu and those of Uto on the occasions that I visited those two villages.

Disputes about leadership within a *yavusa* are typified by this situation within the Reiwaqa. Such evidence for ambition-driven or quarrel-based rivalry within the *yavusa* is in contrast to the ideology of unity which is associated with the official model of a descent group.

(ii) The two *yavusa* of the Nawaqesara and the Noi Vatuma, based at the village of Nawaqadamu, together with some of the Reiwaqa *yavusa*.

> The original spirit of the Nawaqesara came from Nakauvadra with the original spirit of the Noi Tualeka and they settled at Waicoba on the Nasigatoka River. The Nawaqesara had split up earlier, when two brothers became jealous because one of them had a tall *masei* (chiefly palm tree) shading his part of their house whereas the other had only a little *digi* or fern. The Nawaqesara and the Noi Tualeka split up, and the former went eventually to Nawaqadamu and settled with the Reiwaqa who were there.

> The original spirit of the Noi Vatuma came from Nakauvadra and settled at Uto. His descendants split because of a quarrel based on one person drinking all the *yaqona*, but later came together again until news of attack by the Noi Yasawa and Tavarua people caused them to split up and take refuge with four different groups with whom they had relationships. After the wars, they re-united and joined the Nawaqesara. More fighting ensued and then the Nadi war-leader, Navula, began to forcefully impose Christianity on the hill-folk. After peace returned, the village of Nawaqadamu was established for the Noi Vatuma.

(iii) The single *yavusa* of Rukuruku, based on the village of Uto.

> The original spirit of the Rukuruku came from Nakauvadra and settled at Vunamoli. The Reiwaqa arrived at Vunamoli and settled under the authority of the Rukuruku people. The Rukuruku were attacked by neighbours and fled to be with the Noi Goro at Uto on land made available by the Noi Vatuma who were living at Nawaqadamu. While the Noi Rukuruku were living on the land made available to them by the

Noi Vatuma, they presented food to the Noi Vatuma by way of *Ne itau ni qwele* or traditional form of rent, but they did not heed their authority.

All three *yavusa* were equal in the socio-political hierarchy, but all three heeded the authority of the Tui Sesevia at Nawaqadamu.

(iv) The two *yavusa* of the Noi Naboro and the Noi Tualeka, originally from Nadroga and later based on the Rukuruku village of Vunamoli.

The original spirits of the Noi Goro, the Noi Tualeka and the Nawaqesara came from the Nakauvadra, and they and their descendants settled on the upper reaches of the Nasigatoka River.

The Noi Naboro later went lower down the river to Nadroga. From there they went to the Rukuruku area and attacked the Rukuruku and Reiwaqa *yavusa* and burned their villages at and near Vunamoli, and drove them away. The Noi Naboro then settled at Vunamoli themselves.

The Noi Tualeka who had first settled together with the Nawaqesara were attacked and driven away by their neighbours and settled with some Nadroga people. Later when the Noi Tualeka in Nadroga were trying to escape from the measles epidemic which was devastating Fiji just after Cession, the Noi Naboro invited them to come and settle with them in the village of Vunamoli.

The Noi Tualeka heeded the authority of the Noi Naboro, and the Noi Naboro heeded the authority of the Tui Sesevia of Nawaqadamu.

The origins, wanderings, disputes and periodic co-residence of these six *yavusa* which comprised the Noi Sesevia socio-political complex were typical of the circumstances in which polities developed in these upland western areas at these times. The Noi Sesevia polities, though more complex than the simple polities of the Nine *Yavusa* and of Vaturu, tended to remain relatively less complex than those of Rakiraki and very much less complex than those of the east.

During all the disputes and quarrels among the Noi Sesevia polity, no one leader emerged who had a sufficiently strong character to conciliate when internal disputes split a *yavusa*, or who was astute enough or sufficiently powerful or politically acceptable to prevent the various *yavusa* from quarrelling among themselves and thereby making themselves vulnerable to outside attack. During all the outside attacks on Rukuruku, no one leader emerged to combine all or many of the *yavusa* into an alliance strong enough to resist the outsiders who persistently attacked them.

(b) The Noi ni Yasawa polity, which comprised the following six *yavusa*:

(i) The leading *yavusa*, Noi Yasawa, whose head was titled the Tui Rukuruku. Tui Rukuruku, who was independent of higher authority, lived at the village of Rararua.

The original ancestral spirit came from Nakauvadra Range and went to Vuda and then to Nadroga, where the first settlement was established.

This is particularly interesting, because the Noi Yasawa thus connect themselves spiritually with the main Fijian culture heroes of the Nakauvadra Range They also connect themselves with those of the original culture heroes who sailed to Fiji from the west and settled in the general area now known as Vuda (see above under Vuda *tikina*). The other culture heroes then went on to the Nakauvadra.

So it was that the Noi Yasawa had spiritual connections with both Nakauvadra and Vuda. These connections were important as spiritual symbols of validation for the Noi Yasawa to adopt a leading position in a hierarchical socio-political complex. The Noi Yasawa also connected themselves historically with those mighty Nadroga people on the Nasigatoka river whose leader was a 'stranger king' from Tonga. This Nadroga/Tongan connection was important as a secular symbol of validation for the Noi Yasawa to establish themselves as leaders.

The Noi Yasawa's spiritual and secular background was thus impeccable. All they lacked was the military might, the negotiating powers and ability, and the overweening ambitions which characterised the leaders in the east, and brought about the conditions under which the widespread and multi-hierarchical polities of the east were able to develop successfully.

> Little is known about the early movements of the Noi Yasawa who later established the Rukuruku village of Rararua. Here they were attacked by a pagan army from the interior which was avenging the incursions of the Nadroga armies when, backed by Cakobau, they were forcefully imposing Christianity on their traditional enemies, the mountaineers. They took refuge with Navula, the Nadi war leader, who later re-settled them on their own lands back in Rukuruku.

It was at this time that the two paramounts, the Kwa Levu of Nadroga and the Momo Levu of Nadi, on behalf of the Cakobau Government fixed the boundaries of Ba and Nadroga. The Rukuruku village of Narata was included in Nadroga.

(ii) The two *yavusa* of Tavarua and Werelevu, who lived with the Noi Yasawa in the village of Rararua.

> The original ancestral spirits of these two *yavusa* as well as the ancestral spirit of the Noi Yasawa came together from Nakauvadra to Vuda and then to the Nasigatoka River, and at first they all three settled together.

Reflecting the spiritual bond between their respective original ancestors, these two *yavusa* are closely associated with each other and with the Noi Yasawa.

> The spirit of the Tavarua was female, and became pregnant through drops of rain. Her son was called Waituruturu, meaning 'raindrops'.

This is the only case which I have recorded of such a birth, and may suggest that the spiritual origins of the Tavarua were not only associated with the lofty ranges of Nakauvadra but with an even loftier and more mysterious element, *na lagi* or the sky.

> Both *yavusa* were split internally in the course of local wars, some sub-groups siding with one side while others sided with the other. A major split occurred among the Tavarua following the presentation of *yaqona* to two different brothers in what they considered to be either in the wrong order or in a manner inappropriate to their respective status. This split resulted in one group seeking their neighbours to attack the other group, and each group settling separately.

Each group of the Tavarua and the Werelevu were involved in constant warring not only with neighbours but also with the forces of Christianity, the pagans of the mountainous interior and the army of Cakobau.

> Eventually, the Cakobau Government gathered together and settled the Tavarua, partly in Narata, partly in Rararua and partly in Tore; and the Werelevu in Rararua.

Both *yavusa* were equal and independent of each other, but both acknowledged the authority of the Tui Rukuruku. Both these *yavusa* and the Noi Yasawa *yavusa* were socially connected, having a spiritual bond based on the mythical symbiosis of their original ancestors.

(iii) The three *yavusa* of Ketenatukani, Naqalitala/Vodawa and Sawene, of which the first two lived in the village of Tore, and the Ketenatukani lived in the village of Narata.

The original ancestral spirits of these three *yavusa* came down separately from Nakauvadra Range and following different routes (two following the coast through Vuda, and one following the Rewa River and coming across land), they settled on the upper reaches of the Nasigatoka River. As the name indicates, the original ancestral spirit of the Ketenatukani (The Band of Elder Brothers) was the first to arrive, and he married a woman of the Noi Yasawa who had already settled there.

Next to arrive was the ancestor of the Tavarua who married a woman of the Ketenatukani; and he was followed by the ancestor of the Naqalitala/Vodawa who married a woman of the Ketenatukani (the name of the group varies, but I think that the group name was Naqalitala, and their first settlement was Vodawa). He was followed by the original ancestor of the Sawene who married a woman of the Noi Yasawa.

The socio-political relationship that developed between these three *yavusa* and the *yavusa* of Noi Yasawa was based not only on the spiritual symbiosis of the original ancestral spirits but on intermarriage. The latter feature enforced the bond which formed the ideological basis for the socio-political relationship not only between these *yavusa* but ultimately between all of the six *yavusa* of the Kai ni Yasawa polity of Rukuruku.

The consequent histories of the Ketenatukani, the Naqalitala/Vodawa and the Werelevu relate to squabbles, fissions, movements and involvement in local warfare similar to those already described in accounts of the other *yavusa* in Rukuruku. Further, these three groups which bordered on Nadroga were particularly involved in the wars of Christianity and the Cakobau Government, in which the Kwa Levu or paramount chief of Nadroga sided with the Christians and the might of the Government armies and took advantage of this situation to legitimise attack on his old enemies of the mountainous interior. Even after Cession, there were internal security problems for the Colonial Government which led to Gordon's 'Little War' which peripherally affected the Kai ni Yasawa. In spite of this continuing saga of warfare, fission and fusion, the *yavusa* of both the Kai ni Yasawa and the Noi Sesevia became united into the two minor socio-political complexes described. The Colonial Administration fossilised the situation and made it a lasting reality.

It is the very flexibility and fluidity of the situation as it developed in place and time in the Old *tikina* of Rukuruku which show why a study of these back-blocks polities are so pertinent and interesting from the point of view of exploring the development of socio-political complexes in late Fijian society in the west. The contrast between the structures of these polities in the back-blocks of the west, and of the structures of ambition-driven polities in the Tongan-influenced east is highly significant.

Vaturu Old tikina: some loose socio-spiritual associations

The five *yavusa* of Vaturu never seem to have developed into any one recognised socio-political complex with an acknowledged paramount leader. It was made quite clear to me in 1953 and again in 1996 when I visited the area that in the past as well as nowadays each *yavusa* regarded itself as independent, and did not heed the authority of any hierarchically superior group. The groups however appear to have fallen into three recognised associations, the Viyagoiranitu (Grandsons of the Original Ancestral Spirit); the Noi Tubai (Those within the War fence), now a single *yavusa* but at the time of Cession three *yavusa* known collectively as the Nadua; and the Yalatina (Those on the Boundary). There is record of a sixth *yavusa*, the Rarawaqa.

These five or six *yavusa* have similar features and are similar in origin and development to the independents *yavusa* of the Nine *Yavusa* described and commented on above. The main difference between them is probably their experiences with Cakobau's military forces. Apart from internal quarrels and neighbourly disputes resulting in temporary fission and resulting fusion with neighbours with whom they were related spiritually or by marriage, the Vaturu *yavusa* like many others encountered the violent hostility of the Cakobau army which, on behalf of the Cakobau Government, was marching from the coast to the interior, ostensibly avenging the murder of some European planters in the Ba district. In reality, the army was determined to expand by force the sphere of influence of Bau over territories that had traditionally not acknowledged its supremacy, as well as to demonstrate and enforce the powers of the Cakobau Government as a newly established pan-Fiji authority. Some of the Vaturu people sided with the Cakobau army, but those who opposed the army were deported to the island of Koro in the eastern Lomaiviti group. After Cession they were brought back; and after a probationary period either with the Fijian Administration official, Roko Tui Ba, or with the Sabeto people who were recognised as Cakobau-philes, they were resettled on their own lands. These lands became administratively the Old *tikina* of Vaturu in the Colonial Government.

The five *yavusa* forming the three socio-spiritual groupings of the Old *tikina* of Vaturu are now described in more detail.

(i) Viyagoiranitu, an independent single *yavusa*, based on the village of Nagado, about seven miles inland from Sabeto and at the east end of the Sabeto valley.

> The original ancestral spirit came along the Tualeita, the spirit path following the mountain ranges from Nakauvadra to the west coast at Edromu just south of Vuda. He settled in the area known as Vaturu, where it is overlooked by the Tualeita range, and married a woman of the Noi Tubai (see below) living in another part of Vaturu.

This spiritual marriage was the basis of a close bond between the Viyagoiranitu and the Noi Tubai.

> When the Noi Tubai later quarrelled among themselves, some went to join the Viyagoiranitu. The rest of the Noi Tubai attacked the dissident Noi Tubai sheltering with the Viyagoiranitu. The Viyagoiranitu scattered and heeded the authority of the victorious Noi Tubai until the latter were successfully attacked by the army of the Government of Cakobau.

> The Viyagoiranitu thus regained their independence from the Noi Tubai. However they had not accepted Christianity nor the Government of Cakobau, and so they were attacked in turn by the Cakobau Christian army. They were deported to the island of Koro.

On their return to Vaturu, various sub-groups were settled in various places, but, in due course, they came together again. It says much for the strength of the spiritual bonds uniting the *yavusa* that in spite of all these tribulations and wanderings, together or separate, the Viyagoiranitu still regarded themselves, and were recognised by others, as an independent unity.

(ii) Noi Tubai, Nanuku and Nasau, three separate and independent *yavusa* known collectively as the Nadua, based in the village of Nagado.

> The original ancestral spirit of the Nanuku came first from the Nakauvadra Range and settled at Nadua, in Vaturu; and he was followed from there by the spirit of the Nasau who also settled at Nadua. Then came the spirit of the Noi Tubai, though myths differ as to whether he came himself direct from Nakauvadra or whether he settled elsewhere on an islet of the Malolo group and his children went to Nadua.

The co-residence of the ancestral spirits at Nadua, albeit for a short time, formed the mythical basis for a loose socio-spiritual association between their descendants; and an ideological basis for the feeling of unity between members of the three *yavusa*. This feeling is said by them to account for and be reflected in the overall name of Nadua (The Unity). Nadua is also the name of the place first settled, but it is not clear whether the place was named after the unity of grouping or the unity of grouping was named after the settlement where the spirits had first been in one (*dua*) place. This may be an *ex post facto* explanation, because although the word for "one" in eastern Fijian is '*dua*', the equivalent in the local communalect is '*lia*'.

> Because of the prior arrival of their original ancestor at Vaturu before those of the Noi Tubai or the Nasau, the Nanuku had the status of Na Ulumatua (First-born or Eldest) of the three *yavusa* of the Nadua. Reflecting the friendly relationship between their ancestral spirits, the Nasau had the status of Na Tokani (Companions or Partners) with the Noi Tubai.

This association between the three *yavusa* continued to be very close, not only during the times of internal squabbles (at one stage the Nasau were split over a case of adultery) and local fighting, but also in the face of the 'invasion' by the Cakobau army. It continued after the deportation to Koro and return to Vaturu. Thus no objection was raised when their numbers were so diminished that it was considered inappropriate to continue to regard Nanuku and the Nasau as two separate *yavusa* and they were made out to be *mataqali* of the numerically greater *yavusa* of Noi Tubai.

(iii) Yalatina, an independent single *yavusa*, based in village of Natawa, 14 km east of Nagado, and situated in the mountains on the very eastern boundary of the Old *tikina* of Vaturu.

> The original ancestral spirit came from Nakauvadra to Vaturu and settled there; and later the ancestral spirit of the Nasau group arrived and settled alongside him. This created a spiritual bond which was the basis of the close but independent association between the Yalatina and the Nasau of Nagado.

> The Yalatina became peripherally involved in an incident of adultery which split the Nasau people and led to fighting. The Yalatina sided with one of the parties to the quarrel and were worsted. So they fled north to the Vuda people and sought refuge with them. When the armies of Cakobau arrived, the Yalatina were with the Vuda people who were prepared to acknowledge, albeit not very enthusiastically, the new Government and the new religion. Vuda was not attacked, but the Cakobau army proceeded to sweep up the Sabeto valley and through Vaturu, bringing death and destruction and eventually deportation, to Koro, for many of those who opposed the Cakobau Government forces.

The Yalatina did not suffer the indignity of being deported to Koro which most of their neighbours suffered. This was not because of any regard they had for Cakobau or for Christianity, but because they chanced to be under the protection of Vuda at the time of the wars.

After Cession the Yalatina were taken back to Vaturu where they remained independent of any group, but acknowledging the authority of the Colonial Government and the Fijian Administration, and acquiescing to the authority of the Buli Vaturu, administrative head of the Fijian Administration Old *tikina* of Vaturu.

(iv) The Rarawaqa were once recognised as a sixth separate independent *yavusa* living on Vaturu land, but information about this group is sadly lacking.

> Their original ancestral spirit had come from Nakauvadra to Vaturu, and settled at Rarawaqa where they were independent. An old man of Rarawaqa manhandled and chased away a woman from a nearby group who had come and stolen some *dalo* (taro). She reported this incident and the Rarawaqa were attacked and driven away to another place where they were until attacked by the Cakobau army and scattered. They were captured and deported to Koro. On their return, they heeded the authority of the Viyagoiranitu.

The whereabouts of the Rarawaqa, or indeed their very existence, is at present a mystery to me and to all in Vaturu with whom I have discussed the matter. It was suggested to me that they are now extinct, and I have no reason to disagree. I simply include them in order to show that there may well have been other *yavusa* in the late prehistoric or proto-historic times for which no account survives.

Overview of Chapters 12–13
Polities of the Natu Yasawa: The Yasawa Group

Including the outlier of Viwa and excluding the island of Wayasewa which falls within the territory of the Sabutoyatoya *yavusa* of Vuda, the Yasawa Group comprises seven permanently inhabited islands and many small islands. The main group stretches over a distance of about 80 km in a north-north-easterly direction from Waya in the south to Yasawa in the north. About 23 km to the north-east of Yasawa lies the uninhabited rocky islet of Alewa Kalou, or Round Island, with inaccessible slopes rising to a height of 152 m. These islands stand within the shallow seas to the east of the Great Sea Reef. Within these seas there is a maze of barrier reefs and isolated coral patches with the Ethel Reefs among them. The only safe passage is between Yasawa and Round Island, the passage used by Captain Bligh in May 1789 in the course of his epic journey by ship's launch from near Tofua, Tonga, to Koepang, Timor, after the mutiny by the crew of the *Bounty*.

Except for the coral cay of Viwa and the elevated limestone islet of Sawa-i-lau off the south-east tip of Yasawa, the islands are volcanic in origin. They are generally long and narrow, and the major islands are high, with peaks rising to 610 m above sea level. Their main ridges follow closely to the west coasts, the west slopes being steep and drained by short water courses flowing through deep valleys, while the east slopes are more gradual and drained by longer streams often ending in mangrove swamps and lagoons. The surface of the islands is rugged and broken, and the area of land suitable for planting is limited. At the mouths of streams there are areas of flat land up to 16 ha in extent, often with light sandy soil. The peaks and high ridges are wooded, especially on the windward side, but otherwise the slopes are grassy and mostly bare of trees due to cultivation and fires. The dry climate and the soil have been favourable for the production of copra; and during a limited period in the 1870s when there was a world-wide shortage following the American Civil War, cotton was grown on some of the islands by and for Europeans. The climate was also favourable for the production of fibre for the making of sail mats, which attracted attention from people from Bua and Bau, from Tongans and, probably, from Samoans.

At the time of my visits in the 1950s, there were four villages on Waya, three on Viwa, seven on Naviti, one on Yaqweta, two on Matacawalevu, four on Nacula and six on Yasawa, with a total population of about 4000, compared with the 1891 Census figure of 3166. The latter figure is low because of the dire effects of the 1875 epidemic of measles.

The Yasawa Group and outside influences

The present people of the Yasawa Group are largely descended from bands of dissidents, renegades and refugees who came from along the north coast of Viti Levu, especially from Vitogo, Votua, Ba and Rakiraki. (My findings generally support Wilkes 1845:260). They settled in small groups which increased or decreased in number both through natural causes but especially through amalgamation with new bands from Viti Levu or local fission and fusion. They appointed their own separate leaders either from the original band or from new bands who proved themselves to be more energetic and acceptable. They did not have paramount leaders, certainly not from outside their polities and islands. They were renowned to be very independent, quarrelsome and dangerous if offended, but welcoming to those who came with good will. They were probably as suspicious of early European visitors as these visitors were of them.

Bligh had received some information about Fijians from Captain Cook, so when passing through Fiji waters on his way to Timor after the *Bounty* mutiny, he must have been apprehensive of his possible reception when, after spotting tall, rocky, partly-wooded islands which are presumed to have been the Yasawa group, he was 'chased by two large canoes'. He did not wait to find out what his reception might have been but proceeded with all speed through Round Island Passage.

The first to record first-hand information about the behaviour of the people of the Yasawa group was Commodore Charles Wilkes who spent part of 1840 in Fiji with his squadron of four vessels comprising the United States Exploring Expedition. The Expedition spent three months surveying the more important islands and reefs and gathering material for a new chart of the Group. Wilkes landed on Round Island but could not climb to the summit. The party then went on to the island of Yasawa and climbed to the top of the major peak of Taucake. They landed with 'a strong party, well armed, as we knew the natives were particularly savage.' (Wilkes 1845:256). However, the 'natives appeared friendly and were powerless from the late depredations'— by Gigi, chief of Galoa, an island off Macuata, who earlier in the year had led a raid to the Yasawa Group and devastated gardens and villages. Wilkes recorded (1845:232) that Gigi was 'remarkable for the energy of his character, and his savage disposition when offended.' Wilkes then went on to an islet south of Naviti where he landed for observations, being acutely conscious that his activities were the subject of observation by the inhabitants of Naviti. He then climbed the peak on Wayasewa i yata, keeping guard constantly against attack. The Waya islanders were said to be quite independent of any authority and any attempts to subjugate them were unsuccessful. They kept themselves secure within their own defences and only went forth when making an incursion against defenceless villages of other islands. They had a reputation among their neighbours for cruel conduct and savagery. I consider it remarkable that no clash occured during the survey of the Yasawa Group, as it did in Malolo when two ship's officers, including Wilkes' nephew, were killed after an indiscretion on the part of the visitors. In revenge, Wilkes landed parties on Malolo, destroyed the food gardens and the two villages and killed fifty-seven Fijians without loss to themselves (Wilkes 1845:281). The Malolo people then abjectedly surrendered. Wilkes, somewhat smugly but perhaps as justification for the punishment of the people of Malolo, claimed (Wilkes 1845:285) that 'Such has been the effect on the people of Malolo, that they have since been found the most civil, harmless, and well-disposed natives of the group.' Wilkes was accused of murder when he returned home to the United States, and he defended his actions by saying that Fijians could not expect to behave as they did without punishment. It is difficult to judge Wilkes' actions outside the context of the times, but it should be noted that similar action by Fijians sometimes resulted in harsh treatment at the hands of other visiting naval vessels.

Some twenty years later, a boat belonging to the Reverend J. Binner, Wesleyan missionary and trader, had gone to Waya to trade for coconut oil and beche de mer, carrying a crew of an Englishman, an American and some natives. The natives of Waya captured the boat, ate the crew and took the merchandise. The US corvette *Vandalia* arrived at Levuka and, at the request of the American Consul, the commander, Captain Sinclair, sent a party of fifty to Waya to demand the murderers and obtain indemnity. The Waya people numbering some 500 men defied the party and were attacked by the Americans in their fort on the summit of a hill about 244 m high. Some twenty of the Wayans were killed, as many wounded, and their village and fort were burned at a cost of five Americans wounded (Pritchard 1866:212–13). Presumably this was the same incident to which Mrs Smythe referred (Smythe 1864:93) though she said that the crew was one American, one German and a coloured man who leaped overboard and was probably eaten by sharks. The other two were eaten by humans. This was said to be in revenge for 'a very shameful piece of dishonesty practised on them by some white men a short time before.' Evidently she had discussed the matter with Tui Vuda, who said that he was often at war with the Waya people. She said that she had been told that the American operations had been so unskilfully conducted that the Wayans claimed a victory. Pritchard, who had just taken over the position of British Consul, and Mr Binner are probably more reliable, and were in touch with the commander of the *Vandalia*. Nevertheless, Mrs Smythe may well have been right about the Wayan claims. They were very proud people.

Relations between the people of the Yasawa group and other Fijian polities are intricate and of the greatest interest in providing evidence of how such relationships originated and developed. To place them in perspective, it is first necessary to understand the then socio-political situation of these other polities. The people of the Yasawa Group, when quarrelling among themselves in the mid-19th century, would come to be involved in the affairs of major eastern polities especially those of Bau, Bua and Macuata, as well as Tonga. Before that, it seems, there had been periodic visits between the people of these places and those of the Yasawa group, presumably based on requirements for the sail mats for which the Yasawa people were famous, and some intermarriage had taken place. In the 19th century however, Bau and Bua were vying for dominance over the group, and this rivalry manifested itself particularly in the islands to the north. Latterly Ma'afu and his lieutenants also had some considerable involvement in the affairs of the Group.

The Lands Claims Commission (LCC) in 1881 considered twenty claims for land in the Yasawa Group. Before considering individual applications, the Commission heard general evidence about the polities in the group from Navatuorooro, native magistrate of Matacawalevu, and John Stark, a trader who lived in the group from 1864 to 1875; and from Ratu Epeli Nailatikau, eldest son of Cakobau, then the Roko Tui Tailevu, who in his younger days was in the habit of visiting the Group, especially Nacula and Yasawairara, where he was welcomed in a manner befitting a high chief of Bau. Indeed the people of Naviti, whose chief had a Tongan mother and were tending towards the Tongan-influenced Bua, presented him with a basket of earth by way of *soro qele*. This in the old days implied that the people conferred rights over the land and especially the fruits of the land in order to recognise the establishment of a *qali* or tributary relationship. After the arrival of Europeans, some considered it appropriate to confer the right to sell land irrespective of the wishes of the traditional landowners. This was hotly argued against, and the Governor in Council, when considering land claims based in such sales, would not accept that a paramount could sell land without evidence of the endorsement of the traditional landowners.

In considering this evidence, the LCC noted that the islands received occasional visits from Bua chiefs, and from Nayagodamu, a high Bau chief and brother of Cakobau. Probably reflecting an old quarrel when they were all living on the island of Nacula, Nacula was quarrelling with the Vanuakula people of Matacawalevu; and Nacula seemed to favour a connection with Bua after the introduction of Christianity by Bua and Tonga, when the group was placed within the Bua circuit. Matacawalevu inclined towards Bau especially after a visit from Nayagodamu. Yasawa was apparently divided by internal quarrels between Teci and Yasawairara, and Teci sought the help of Macuata. However, up to the time of Cakobau's coronation as Tui Viti in 1867, the various island polities were independent of each other and of outside political authority, although Tui Bua took Ma'afu's lieutenant, Wainiqolo, along the islands in an attempt to induce them to come to Bua. There was no paramount chief, and the polities quarrelled both internally and with each other. The first attempt to unify the group for the purposes of government was in 1866 when the British Consul, Jones, met with the chiefs of the group, and Roko Dinono, a chief of Yasawairara, was appointed by Bua to be magistrate for the group. He had previously exercised magisterial functions, having been appointed apparently by the Tongans. After the coronation of Cakobau in 1867, Sovatabua of Nacula was appointed Lieutenant Governor of the group under Bau, but his powers were limited to matters of general politics relating to Cakobau as King, and did not extend to local matters.

To understand the situation in the Yasawa Group, then, it is necessary to have some understanding of the situation developing in the eastern polities of Bau, Bua and Macuata, a situation overseen by the *eminence grise* of Ma'afu. At that time Bua had been involved in internal warring between two high chiefs, Ra Masima, the Tui Bua, and his cousin Tui Muru which continued until Tui Bua asked Bau for help in return for his daughter. Fighting was indecisive until 1845 when Tui Muru accepted Christianity and made peace with Tui Bua. Macuata was associated with Bau, though the exact relationship is not clear. Bau probably considered Macuata as *qali* or tributary, whereas Macuata was ambivalent about the relationship, viewing it more as an association among equals. Macuata leadership was the subject of violent rivalry with intervention from Bau which wanted to maintain what it saw to be its position in the region and protect it from Ma'afu and the Tongans with their expansionist ends. The Tongan high-ranking chief, Ma'afu, and his lieutenants Semisi Fifita and Wainiqolo (Vainikolo in Tongan) at Vanua Balavu, were using their considerable force of men under the guise of spreading Christianity. Ma'afu was expanding Tongan influence westward over Fiji and presumably had pan-Fijian ambitions. In Macuata and Bua, Ma'afu took advantage of the quarrelling by playing one side off against the other and made his presence felt in the Yasawas too.

In a case which was investigated in Levuka in September 1861 by Captain Leveque of the French corvette *Cornélie*, the head of the French Roman Catholic mission in Fiji, Père Bréheret, complained that Ma'afu's lieutenant Semisi had flogged some Roman Catholic natives at Yasawa. Captain Leveque sent for Cakobau, the 'acknowledged supreme chief of Fiji in treaty with France', and for Ma'afu as the representative in Fiji of the King of Tonga. Cakobau, under the terms of the treaty, was asked to send for Semisi, and because he did not comply with this request as promptly as the Captain thought he should, he was detained on board the *Cornélie* until Semisi appeared. Not unnaturally, Cakobau was upset about his detention and when he later saw the British Consul, Pritchard, 'he was writhing under the effects of his detention' and anxious to restore his own prestige among the Fijians (Pritchard 1866:282). The case was heard on board the *Cornélie* in the presence of Cakobau and Ma'afu, and Ma'afu admitted that Semisi had flogged the natives but not because they were Roman Catholics. Père Bréheret was able to satisfy Captain Leveque that their religion was the cause of the flogging and the latter deported Semisi, taking him to New Caledonia because he thought that Cakobau would not punish a Tongan of Semisi's rank and influence. It is not known what happened when he reached New Caledonia.

Togitogi, chief of Nacula and one of those flogged, told Pritchard (1866:304) about the circumstances leading up to this deportation of Semisi. Before the Christian religion came to the Yasawa Group, there had always been jealousy between Togitogi and Sovatabua, also of Nacula. When Christianity arrived, Sovatabua became a Wesleyan in order to get the help of the Tongans against Togitogi and to make him chief instead. Togitogi became a Roman Catholic, saying that he did not want the Tongans to come. He wanted his lands to be ceded to the Queen of Great Britain with Bau and all Fiji. Tongans bringing Christianity to Yasawa left the Wesleyan teacher Maika at Yasawa i rara, but Togitogi would not follow Maika's teachings, because he represented the Tongans who were siding with Sovatabua. Sovatabua went to Maika at Yasawa i rara and told him that Togitogi and others were Roman Catholics and were making the land bad. Maika said that he would bring the Tongans to make the Roman Catholics give up their religion, and to get sail mats for Ma'afu and Semisi. Maika had already complained about Togitogi not giving him food when he went to preach at Nacula and not sending him enough fish and yams to Yasawa i rara.

Semisi himself had then come to Tamasua, Yasawa, and sent for Togitogi who went there with some other minor chiefs of Nacula. Semisi, the Tui Bua and Maika who was also from Bua together with many other Tongans were waiting for them. Semisi asked Togitogi why he did not follow Maika and Tui Bua, and said he was a bad man and must be flogged. Togitogi was flogged, kicked in the ribs and the head and struck in the eye. He was told that he must give the Yasawa islands to Tonga and give up the Roman Catholic religion. At this stage, an English trader, Hicks, who happened to be at Yasawa at the time, intervened. Tui Bua had said that the Tongans were strong and the white men were weak, and the people from Nacula were making the land bad and divided. However, Semisi stopped the flogging. He said that he was returning to Ma'afu who would send Wainiqolo, his other lieutenant, down and he would make the land bad and would continue the flogging unless they gave their land to Tonga. Semisi then sent his men down to Nacula, and they took everything away from Togitogi's part of the village and many things from Sovatabua's part. Semisi also sent for two men of Waya who had become Roman Catholic and told them that if they did not follow Maika, he would send Wainiqolo to make the land bad for them. He threatened that what the Americans had done on Waya was nothing to what the Tongans had the strength to do. They promised to do what they were told to do, but it was doubtful whether the Tongans would have attacked such a difficult island as Waya. It was sufficient for their purposes if they could take control of Waya by making the local chiefs jealous with each other and by helping one of the chiefs and so gain political control. The chief of Naviti escaped the cruelty of the Tongans because his mother was a Tongan and Semisi could not ignore his claims on the Tongans. But for this relationship, the Naviti chief would have been deposed by the Tongans in favour of someone who would have been their ready tool because his position and power would have depended on them. The Naviti chief was not concerned about Maika, because he had his own Wesleyan teachers from Rewa. They were good men and did not interfere in local politics. Before going, Semisi had said that Roko Dinono was to be chief over all the Yasawa Group, assisted by Raitona, and that the Yasawa Group now belonged to Tonga, Roko Dinono, Raitona, Sovatabua and Maika having signed a paper to this effect.

This illustrates how Ma'afu, through his lieutenants and the assistance of Tui Bua whose mother was Tongan, attempted to extend his authority to the Yasawa Group by imposing the Tongan Wesleyan religion on the people and meeting any opposition with brute force. He also used his cunning to divide the loyalties of local chiefs, seeking out existing jealousies and turning them to his advantage. The account also shows how Bau and Tonga continued their machinations to develop their respective power over territory which did not owe them traditional loyalty. The Yasawa Group was a valuable source of sail mats which both Bau and Ma'afu needed for their war canoes, and it may be that it was a need to control this source which diverted the attention of these two major eastern powers to what appears at first sight to be an out-of-the-way and otherwise unimportant string of islands, of little value for their natural resources and their potential manpower.

The polities of the Yasawa Group are included in the present *tikina* of Naviti and Yasawa.

12

The *Tikina* of Naviti

The island of Waya

Except for the inhabited island of Waya Sewa and the garden island of Kuata which are included in the territory of the *vanua* of Vuda, the southernmost island of the Yasawa group is the island of Waya. Waya lies about 40 km north-west of Lautoka and about 25 km from the Great Sea Reef forming the western edge of the shallows within which the islands of the Yasawa Group form a chain. Waya is about 6 km from north to south, and about 4 km from east to west. It has an area of 22 square km. There are wide bays on the north and south coasts. It is the highest and most broken island in the Yasawa Group, with sharp peaks at the north-east corner (571 m) and at the south-west corner (500 m), dropping sheer to the shore. It is well-watered and densely wooded in parts, and there are at present two coastal villages at the north end and two at the south end. There is a population of about 600.

The myth of Tunaiau and the Samoan connection

Tunaiau is regarded as the *ivakatawa* or guardian, or *itaukei du* or true owner of Waya. He did not come from Vuda or Nakauvadra or from anywhere else. Tunaiau's place is on top of the south peak, known as Ulu i Tunaiau, where the Lomati people cut the grass because Tunaiau dislikes long grass.

As indicated in the following lines which I recorded in 1953, Tunaiau is said to be autochthonous and was created at the same time as Waya was created:

> Buli ko Rotuma, buli ko Waya,
>
> Buli vata kei na kena ivakatawa.
>
> Rotuma was created, Waya was created,
>
> At the same time as its guardian was created.

Tunaiau took some *yaqona* to Samoa and brought back a girl but they had no children. Other Samoans accompanied the girl, and they lived on a *yavu* known as Samoa. There was a *yavu* called Samoa at the village of Yalobi when I visited the place. The Waya people told me that they thought that their communalect had features similar to Samoan, citing the word *laka* or go. In fairness, there is a Samoan cognate, *la'a*; but Andrew Pawley, who has investigated the communalect extensively, is not aware of any other similarities (personal communication). However he told me that there are two groups at Yalobi who claim a Samoan lineage. Recently I checked that there are people there who claim descent from Samoans. The Samoan connection is of some importance to the people of Waya and especially to those in Yalobi. The origin of the myth may well be seen as a rationalisation of some admixture of Wayan and Samoan blood, following some occasion(s) when Samoans came as far west as the Yawasa Group, perhaps to obtain the sail mats for which the Group was famous. From early times there was known communication between Fijians, Tongans and Samoans, and within this area there was exchange of crafts and a mingling of the people themselves.

Origins of the four yavusa

Waya is said to have been unoccupied until the arrival of certain individuals or small groups whose descendants formed the core of the four Waya *yavusa* registered by the Native Lands Commission (NLC) and currently recognised by the people of Waya. These arrivals and their descendants were as follows:

(a)   A man from Rakiraki and a man from Votua, Ba, followed the coast west from Ba to Saru, Lautoka, and thence sailed first to the island of Vomo and then to Waya. After landing at Vuai, their party established a settlement on the slopes at Yaketi which they called Lomati in memory of the home of the man from Rakiraki. They appointed the eldest son of the man from Rakiraki as leader and installed him with the title of Takala i Waya.

Their descendants developed into the *yavusa* of Lomati. There is a division of the Lomati mataqali called Rakiraki, and the descendants of the man from Votua are the mataqali of Narewa.

The origins of these two progenitors are reflected in the chants used in the course of a *yaqona* ceremony on Waya, where the *meke ni yaqona* or chant while the *yaqona* is being prepared is the same as that used at Votua, Ba, and the *meke ni tu yaqona* or chant while the *yaqona* is being offered is the same as that used at Rakiraki.

(b)   After a long time, some Lauvatu people from Nalotawa, Ba came and were settled in Lomati but lower down the slope from the first settlers. The first settlers were then known as the Lomati i Yata and the Lauvatu as the Lomati i Ra (the upper and lower Lomati respectively).

Currently the Lomati i Yata are known simply as the Lomati; and the Lomati i Ra are known as the Lauvatu.

(c)   Not long afterwards some Kai Yaukuve from Navatucili, Nagwagwa, Vuda, arrived and were settled between the other two groups. Their descendants developed into the *yavusa* of Yaukuve.

The three groups duly met and appointed the head of the Yaukuve as the paramount and installed him with the title of Nasau or Saumalumu; and then the Lauvatu installed the head of their group with the title of Roko.

(d)   Not long after, some Vunavau people of Ketenasau, Vitogo landed at Vuai and sheltered under a large *vunabuevu* or *buevu* tree. The Lomati settled them beside the Lomati village, and the settlement was known as Vunabuevu in memory of the tree under which they had sheltered when they first landed. Their descendants developed into the yavusa of Vunabuevu.

They were given the heavy work of the village, and everything they undertook they carried our energetically, including the building of a house for the Takala i Waya. The other groups realised how energetic and useful the Vunabuevu were; and following general agreement, the Lomati and the Lauvatu people installed a man of Vunabuevu as paramount of all four groups, giving him the title of Saubuli. The stone on which the installation was carried out has survived until the present day.

Then the Lomati installed this man as leader of the Vunabuevu, giving him the title of Ratu.

The Yaukuve did not attend the ceremony because they were looking for other land on which to settle. When they returned, they were upset that they had not been present at the installation, especially as they had previously been given the status of paramountcy. So they moved, first to establish a village at Navatucili, and then to settle at Nalauwaki.

There is an anomalous group known as the Vunasalamaca. It is not at all clear where they came from. The only evidence which I could discover was that they have some spiritual association with Viwa (see *ivilavila ni yalo*). The NLC registered them as a *mataqali* of the Lauvatu *yavusa*, but I recorded them on one occasion as once a separate group but now associated with the Vunabuevu. I also recorded them as once part of the Vunabuevu, with whom they had the responsibilities of *dau vakasaqa* or people responsible for cooking for the Vunabuevu. On one occasion, they were preparing *lolo ni qalu*, a kind of pudding, but they let the water dry up and spoilt the pudding. They were no longer regarded as part of the Vunabuevu and were called Vunasalamaca because they had let the water dry up (*maca*).

The jumping-off place of the spirits of the dead of the Vunasalamaca is different from that of the Vunabuevu; and their features of identity (*vuti yaca*) are not exactly the same. The *kai* of the Vunabuevu is the *tawa* tree, whereas that of the Vunasalamaca is the *raro*, although they also respect the *tawa*. So they may have once been one group but after a quarrel symbolised by the spoiling of the pudding, they may have separated; and the NLC may have been asked to record the Vunasalama as of the Lauvatu, not of the Vunabuevu because of this quarrel. On the basis of different *ivilavila ni yalo* and different *kai*, it is more likely that they were groups of different origin and that the Vunasalamaca were late arrivals who associated with the Vunabuevu as servants but later quarrelled and separated.

Later arrivals

From time to time more individuals or small groups arrived from Viti Levu or from other neighbouring islands and settled on Waya, joining the already established groups, as follows:

(a)

    (i)   Some people came from Vuda and joined the Vunabuevu *yavusa*, forming the *mataqali* of Nalotu;

    (ii)   Some people came from the island of Malolo and joined the Vunabuevu *yavusa*, forming, I was told in 1953, the *mataqali* of Werelevu;

(b)   A woman of high rank from Batiri, in Nadroga, came with her attendants to marry the Ratu of Vunabuevu. The descendants of the attendants formed the *mataqali* of Vunawi of the *yavusa* of Vunabuevu, with the status of house servants;

(c)   Some Nanuku people of the Kai Vuda came from Saru, Lautoka, and joined the Yaukuve, forming the *mataqali* of Nanuku. They were almost extinct in 1953. The Nanuku people had been chased away from Vuda and had fled to Saru. Some then went to Waya and others to Tavakubu (see Vuda); and

(d)   When the Suelevu of Muaira, Naviti, split up, two groups came and settled at Ravouvou, Wayalevu, and were given land by the Lauvatu. They were included as a *mataqali* of the Lauvatu.

Installation of the Saubuli

At the time of the NLC, the paramount chief of all Waya was still installed with the title of Saubuli. He was chosen by the Lomati, as the original inhabitants of the island, from among the Vunabuevu. They would then discuss their choice with the Vunabuevu and the Yaukuve as the chiefly *yavusa*. When they reached agreement on who should be installed, the person chosen was duly installed on the installation stone.

Later the title of Saubuli was easternised to that of Tui Waya. More recently, as the result of a split among the Vunabuevu people, there have been two people holding the title of Tui Waya, one from the Nalotu division living at Nalauwaki on the north side of the island, and the other from the Vunakura division living at Yalobi on the south side of Waya. Andrew Pawley (1981) recorded that in order to solve this dichotomy of paramountcy, the people agreed that the title of Saubuli should alternate between the Vunabuevu and the Yaukuve. The problem was solved, albeit temporarily, after I had last met up with the Waya people at Lautoka in 1996: one of the two Tui Waya died.

The spirits of Waya

The main *anitu* or spirit of Waya is Tunaiau, the autochthonous *itaukei du* or *ivakatawa* from whom no-one on Waya claimed descent. All the groups on Waya claim descent not from a spirit coming to Waya, but from an individual or group coming from groups on other neighbouring islands or from Viti Levu. It is interesting to consider, under these circumstances, the nature of the spirit world on Waya, particularly in the case of late arrivals who joined established original groups.

The Lauvatu *mataqali* of the Lauvatu *yavusa* and the Vunasalamaca respect Tunaiau as their *anitu* or spirit with whom the *bete* or priest communicates at his *mata ni sava* or place of spiritual communication. During my 1953 visit, the *bete*, who was also a *daurairai* or person who foresaw the future, lived at Natawa. However, the Suelevu *mataqali* of the Lauvatu *yavusa* who came from Muaira, Naviti, respect Maravulevu as their spirit.

The Lomati who are closely associated with Tunaiau and have traditional responsibility for cutting the grass at his place on Ulu i Tunaiau, respect the spirit of their progenitor who came over as a person from Rakiraki.

The Vunabuevu respect a spirit called Ranadi whose place was in the middle of the village of Natawa. Andrew Pawley (1981) recorded that she was sent by the Yaukuve to the Vunabuevu who arrived without a spirit. She was famous for stealing. There is no evidence whether the late arrivals from Vuda and Malolo brought their own spirits. However, the Vunawi *mataqali* of the Vunabuevu who came from Nadroga respect Levui, whose place is in Nadroga. She is sometimes referred to simply by the female term of respect, Lewatu.

The Yaukuve respect Vureibulu whose place and *mata ni sava* are at Nalauwaki, where Andrew Pawley (1981) recorded a second spirit called Mudu. She is the spirit of the unborn daughter of a Yaukuve woman who died before the child was born. There is no evidence that the Nanuku, the late arrivals from Saru, brought a Vuda spirit.

Each of the original four groupings whose descendants formed a recognised *yavusa* respects a separate *anitu*. The later arrivals respected their own *anitu*, which in the case of the Nadroga people was their spirit in Nadroga. In the other cases, the information is not available.

iVilavila ni Yalo

Except for the Vunasalamaca, the spirits of the dead of all the Waya people go first to Nacilau point near Nalauwaki. Then they fly round Waya before returning to Nacilau. From here they jump with their belongings into a pool beside a flat rock called Waqa (canoe) ni Senio. The sound of two thuds is heard, representing the sound of the spirit and its belongings as they fall into the pool. Then they go by the rock canoe to Narokorokoyawa for which, see below.

However, the spirits of the dead of the Vunasalamaca jump from a rock on Narara Island to Koroua where they eat plantain and crab for the journey. The spirits of the dead go from Narara to Kavua on Viwa Island before finally going to Narokorokoyawa. If the spirit is that of an unmarried man, there is at Kavua a spirit called Limalimanidawai who will strike the spirit of the bachelor (*dawai*) with a club.

The island of Narara is at present the southernmost of four islets which are associated with the island of Naviti. It is, however, closer to Waya than to Naviti, and may once have been associated with Waya. The procedure followed by the spirits of the dead of the Vunasalamaca is so different from that followed by the other spirits of the dead on Waya that it suggests that the Vunasalamaca were different in origin from the rest of the Waya people, and may indeed have come from Viwa.

Settlements

At the time of the NLC, the villages of Yalobi, Nalauwaki, Wayalevu and Nasau were occupied, and the recognised order of seniority of the *yavusa* was Vunabuevu, Yaukuve, Lauvatu and Lomati (i Yata). When I visited Waya in 1953, Nasau had been abandoned and the village of Natawa had been established. The *yavusa* of Vunabuevu and Yaukuve had groups in all four villages.

Waya and the neighbours

The women of Waya used to make pottery such as *saqa ni wai* or water jars and *dare* or flat dishes used for food or for *yaqona* bowls. They used resin which they obtained from the mainland. Women used to go to Malolo to teach the women there how to make pottery.

Waya and outside influences

In 1881 the Lands Claims Commission (LCC) considered and allowed a claim (1,059) for the purchase by Messrs Villa, Webb and Tyreman in 1871 of two areas on Waya, known as Naseva and Vita. They planted 7 acres of cotton at Vita and a total of about 60–70 acres in both places. After the end of cotton, they had planted the same total of acreage of coconuts by 1881.

The island of Viwa

The westernmost island of the Yawasa group and indeed of the whole of the Fiji group is the lonely island of Viwa. Viwa lies about 30 km north-west of Waya and is situated on the edge of the Great Sea Reef. It is a cay of sand and coral debris, about 80 ha in extent, and lies in a lagoon. The highest point is only about 2 m above sea level, and the island is just visible from the heights of Waya. It is covered with coconut palms but there is no natural water supply on the island. The only natural fresh water comes bubbling up in the lagoon from a spring under the sea. Drinking water comes either from cement tanks or from rainwater collected from holes scooped in the sloping trunks of palms. In times of drought, water has to be brought by boat from Waya. There are at present three villages on the island, with a population of about 200.

The myth of Rainima and the Kaunitoni connection

Tunaiau is regarded as the *ivakatawa* or guardian, or *itaukei du* or true owner of Waya. He was a member of the crew of the first canoe, the *Kaunitoni*, and a brother of Erovu, the progenitor of the Kai Vuda. He first landed at Vuda and then went to Waya where he met Rainima. They quarrelled and Tunaiau sent Rainima to a reef which Tunaiau could see from the heights of Ulu i Tunaiau. As a punishment for the quarrel, Tunaiau told Rainima to bail (*nima*) the water from inside the reef. This he did, and so he formed the island of Viwa. He went to settle on the land that he had formed. As there was no fresh water on the island, Tunaiau brought over some in a *dalo* leaf. Rainima poked his finger into the leaf, and the water fell into the sea and formed the fresh water pool in the channel at Kavua.

Rainima's place is a *yavu* at Natogo, in the middle of the island, which serves as his *mata ni sava* or place of communication. He had a son called Rabaraba whose *yavu* is at Balenatuivi near Yakani.

Origins and development of the three yavusa

Viwa is said to have been unoccupied until the arrival of certain individuals or small groups whose descendants formed the core of the three Viwa *yavusa* registered by the NLC and currently recognised by the people of Viwa.

The initial occupation of Viwa came about because three men from Waya happened to see the reef at Viwa and went to explore. They were:

(a)   Two brothers from the Ketenasau division of the Yaukuve *yavusa*; and

(b)   a man from the Kai Lauvatu *yavusa*.

They formed a settlement at Nakovu and divided the island into two parts, one for the Ketenasau (Yaukuve) and one for the Lauvatu.

They then returned to Waya and the chiefs of the two groups agreed that some from each group should go and settle on Viwa. When they returned, the Lauvatu installed one of the Ketenasau as paramount with the title of Sau, presumably because on Waya the Yaukuve were senior to the Lauvatu. They then separated and went to their respective sides of the island as follows.

(a) Descendants of the Ketenasau

The Ketenasau remained at Nakovu, and were later joined by another group of Ketenasau who were very energetic and their leader was installed as Sau. From here, they moved first to Nabogikolo and finally to Nasoso facing Yakani beach where they built a ceremonial house for their leader that was called Namatoka. At Yakani, some split off and went to settle at Cobocobo. They had not been long at Yakani when they were struck by a hurricane and a tidal wave. After this disaster, they still remained at Yakani.

The descendants of those who remained at Yakani became the Namatoka or Yakani *yavusa*.

The Ketenasau who had gone to Cobocobo were joined by some Leweivawa from the island of Naviti who settled next to them at Bakubaku. The Leweivawa were very energetic in the work for their settlement, and the Ketenasau agreed to give the Leweivawa the leadership of both groups. They installed one of them and gave him the title of Ratu.

Later, a second group of Leweivawa and some Kai Koro from Marou, Naviti came and landed at Natia. They were given land called Taganikula beside Cobocobo and Bakubaku, and all joined to form one settlement. Here they were struck by the hurricane and tidal wave; some food was brought from Waya and Naviti, but it was not enough and some of the Ketenasau went to Nadroga. The Leweivawa and the rest of the Ketenasau remained at Cobocobo.

When the first group of Leweivawa at Bakubaku saw how energetic the second group of Leweivawa at Taginakula were, they gave them overall authority and installed one of them as leader with the title of Ratu.

Later, those of the Ketenasau who had remained at Cobocobo changed their attitude towards the Leweivawa and began shouting in the middle of the village and being arrogant before the chiefs. Eventually the Leweivawa chiefs could stand the bad behaviour no longer and the Ketenasau were killed.

The Ketenasau at Yakani determined to avenge the killing of the Ketenasau at Cobocobo, and plotted the death of the Leweivawa at Taginakula, inviting them to a feast at Nakovu. When the Taginakula were returning from the feast, they were attacked by the Ketenasau. Those who survived wanted to return to Naviti, but were induced to stay.

The name of the joint village became known as Natia, and the people living there form the *yavusa* of Natia. The title of the leader is Ratu who is independent.

At the time of my visits, all but five of the Yakani had died. It was explained to me that a member of the Yakani had gone to Koro in Lomaiviti where he had joined a group to *vuli meke* or learn chants from a *dau ni vucu* or poet inspired by a spirit. He had not thanked the spirit. On his return to Viwa, he had taught the young men the *meke* he had learnt. They performed the *meke* at meetings not only in the Yasawa islands but also at Vitogo. Then the people of Waya wanted them to perform the *meke* on the main *darata* or ceremonial green on the island. After the performance, the man who had learned the *meke* at Koro as well as the young men who had performed on the *darata* died. People on Viwa considered that these deaths had been caused through the anger of the *anitu* or spirit on Koro who had not been thanked for the *meke* which he had taught through the *dau ni vucu*. The spirit may have been Dakuwaqa, the shark spirit, because it was common for descendants of the *meke* group to be bitten by sharks.

This is a very good example of a situation and associated belief I frequently encountered in the course of my explorations into the interaction of spirits with people. A spirit which is not thanked or is not given due respect will react against not only the perpetrator of the discourtesy but will also continue to react against relations and associates, causing sickness or death until or unless appropriate apologies are made to *vakasavasavataka* or clean up the situation.

(b) Descendants of the Lauvatu

The Lauvatu people left Nakovu and went to the other side of the island and settled first at Pacai and then at Ra where they were joined by some more Lauvatu (the Vunatoto) and some Leweivawa from Naviti. The Vunatoto were very energetic and one of them was made leader.

They were joined by Tongans who had come ashore at Nakauveve. Basil Thomson (1908) claimed that they were castaways, and like the Samoans at Waya may have been in the area looking for sail mats. The Lauvatu made one of them leader with the title of Navatanitawake, and the Tongans and their descendants were known as the Veruku.

After the hurricane and tidal wave, the Lauvatu and Tongans at Ra were joined by people from Nadi and Momi; and their descendants became the Ra *yavusa*.

The Tongan descendants retained the leadership; and the line of authority at present is that the Navatanitawake of Ra heeds the authority of the Ratu of Natia who in turn heeds the Sau of the Yakani.

All three *yavusa* are closely connected and have the same *kai*, the *tawa* tree (*Pometia pinnata*) and the same *ika* or fish, the *cumu* or trigger fish (*Balistes* sp.) Only the Veruku (those of Tongan descent) have different *vuti yaca*, the *damudamu* as their *kai*, and the *sokisoki* or porcupine fish (*Tetrodon* sp.) as their *ika*.

The spirits of Viwa

The main spirits of Viwa are Rainima and his son, Rabaraba. No-one claims to be descended from either of these two, although all three *yavusa* on the island respect Rainima. The Yakani and the Ra also respect Rainima's son, Rabaraba. I could find no evidence that any of the groups or their component *mataqali* brought any spirits with them, or that they respected spirits in the places whence their progenitors came.

The only other spirit about which I could obtain any information was a female spirit or *anitu* called Lewatu ni Nuku, whose place is on a little islet called Nuku near Kavua. It is called Nukunuku, and is a rock shaped like a vagina. Lewatuninuku is a bad spirit and I was told in 1953 that she often appeared at Naibalebale, near the point of Kavua. If people want to go fishing at Nuku, they must first make a presentation of *yaqona*, coconuts or pawpaws to Lewatuninuku.

iVilavila ni Yalo

The spirits of the dead of the Yakani and the Natia *yavusa* go to Rainima's place at Natogo and eat *yabia* or arrowroot (which is the plant presented to Rainima as *isevu* or first-fruit offering). Then they go to the reef at Navovokulu and from there to the spirit centre at Naicobocobo, at the west end of Vanua Levu.

The spirits of the dead of the Lauvatu/Ra *yavusa* go to Natogo, Rainima's place, where they too eat *yabia*. Then they go to Kavua, the point near Naibalebale, from which they plunge into the sea, and from there they go to Naicobocobo.

Viwa and the neighbours

The Viwa people were regarded as very strong, and the island was never attacked. However, if there was external or internal trouble affecting their neighbours in the Yasawa group, the Viwa people were willing to go to their assistance. They had a large outrigger canoe called the *Lialiabula* and a wooden *lali* or drum called Duguirevo that they would take with them on board. When they neared the place they were visiting they would beat it, as a signal to let the people know so that they could prepare a *revo* or earth oven for the feast with which to greet the visitors. Some of their victories were as follows:

- The people of Macuata, Vanua Levu, came over to join the people of Teci in attacking the people of Yasawairara at the north end of Yasawa Island. The Viwa people went to Yasawairara to help the group of the paramount with whom they were related; and assisted in defeating the Macuata and Teci people, and in saving the Tui Yasawa.
- The Drola people of Nacula Island were engaged in internal struggles, and one group asked the people in the neighbouring island of Matacawalevu for help. The request was passed on to the Yaqweta people and thence to the Viwa people through a woman of Viwa who was married to a man of Yaqweta. The Viwa people went to Nacula and slaughtered the dissenting party in their war village.

After these two victories, the Viwa people became accepted as the *ivakayadra* or watchmen of the Yasawa and Malolo groups. As they sailed about, people learned of their victories and recognised their strength.

- Yaravoro, the Kwa Levu or paramount of Nadroga, was preparing to attack Malolo and the Malolo chiefs sent a request for help to their relations on Viwa. The Viwa people went to Malolo and boasted that they would challenge the Nadroga people on the island of Tavarua where they were preparing for the attack. They landed on Tavarua and clubbed Yaravoro and the Nadroga people.
- Tui Sabeto came to the island of Naviti to weaken the people of the island. When the Viwa people heard about this, they went by canoe to Naviti where they went ashore at Somosomo. Tui Sabeto took the empty canoe, and when the Viwa people saw what had happened, they went and clubbed the Sabeto people who were in the canoe. Also in the canoe was Ratu Taito, the head of the Naua people of Saunaka. He was shot in the arm by an arrow, but was allowed to live and return home.

Later he returned to Viwa to thank the people and to show them where he had been shot in the arm. The person who gave me this account was on Viwa when Ratu Taito returned.

- At the time when the Yaqweta people from Ba had accepted Christianity but Ba had not, a war party came over from Ba to Yaqweta to attack them for accepting Christianity. The Ba people came with their faces blackened (*qumuloa*) as for war, and dressed in *masi* or bark cloth up to their nipples as only important chiefs could do. The Ba people were sitting in their canoes, when the Viwa people arrived to help the Yaqweta people with whom they were related. At the time, a church service was in progress.

Viwa and outside influences

The Viwa people pulled up plantain suckers and struck the Ba people on the forehead, so that the juice flowed down their faces and mixed with the blacking, and they had difficulty in seeing. The Viwa people then seized their testicles and told them that their *masi* must come down to the level of their loins, like ordinary people. So the Ba people were chased away and they returned to Ba.

I was told that the Vunivalu of Bau brought an army to introduce Christianity to Yasawa, Naviti and Viwa. He told the people of Viwa that he had brought them *sulu* or cloth symbolising Christianity. He loaded his gun and asked the Viwa people whether they accepted the *sulu* or would prefer war. They accepted the *sulu*, and all the people of Viwa assembled at Natia and put on the *sulu,* and the Vunivalu went away.

The LCC in 1881 investigated two claims relating to the purchase of land on Viwa (1057 and 1058). From the evidence given, it appears that the first to purchase land on the island was Duncan Murray who in 1869 bought a strip of land in the middle of the island from Ratu Semi, the chief of the island, for eight guns. A witness to the 1869 deed was Peter Danford, who happened to be on Viwa in search of labour. Danford is presumably of the family of 'Harry the Jew' Danford who came to Fiji from England in 1826 and lived in Namosi. His family was still living in the Navua area in the 1960s.

Murray was living in Nadroga at the time. Then he heard that F.R.Evans had bought the whole island from Ratu Epeli, son of Cakobau, for 1000 dollars. So Murray went over promptly to take possession of his land. While a house was being built for him, Evans turned up with Veli, a member of the household of Ratu Epeli, who said that Ratu Epeli had sold the island to Evans and that if Evans could not occupy the island at once, it would be depopulated. Veli told the people to build a house for Evans. Evans went away, leaving some of his belongings which the people promptly removed to another house. Evans returned with Veli and left more of his belongings in Murray's house. They quarrelled and Murray told the people that Evans had taken over his house. Evans sailed off and the Viwa people removed his belongings from Murray's house and overtook Evans' canoe and put his belongings on board. Veli accused them of defiance, and later Evans returned with Alexander Eastgate, Major Harding and some soldiers to collect taxes for the Cakobau Government. Evans left with the soldiers, having told the people to build his house. The young men were taken away to work for their taxes, and the elders built the house. When the young men returned, they threw the house into the sea. When Evans came back, he saw what had happened and went away, never to return. Meanwhile five houses were built for Murray, who took a local woman to live with him. He planted 30–40 acres of cotton and coconuts and lived permanently on the island from 1872 to 1878 before going to live on Kadavu. He was taken before the Supreme Court by Evans over his land claim, but I have found no record of the outcome.

The Viwa people showed great courage in defying the threats of Ratu Epeli and the power of Bau and the Cakobau Government. To my knowledge, this defiance was never avenged. Perhaps mighty Bau thought that the tiny, worthless, far-off island of Viwa was beneath contempt.

Perhaps they had heard of the valour of Viwa as evidenced above and thought that discretion should be exercised in this case. It was perhaps fortunate for Viwa that David was never brought to the physical test against Goliath.

The islands of Naviti and Yaq(w)eta

The island of Naviti

The island of Naviti lies about 13 km north-north east of Waya. In between these two islands are four small and uninhabited islets. Irregular in shape, Naviti is nearly 15 km from north to south, and varies in width from nearly 5 km to about 700 m. It has an area of over 34 square km, and is the largest and most populated island in the Yasawa group. As are the other islands except Viwa, Naviti is volcanic in origin with a steep, rugged ridge following the west coast. The highest point, Vaturualewa (388 m), is in the middle of the island, and sends out four spurs. The surface is broken and there is little flat land. The north coast has a large, wide bay comprising three smaller bays. At the south, Soso Bay is narrower but extends about 3 km into the land. There are many streams rising from the central slopes. There are at present seven villages on the island, with a population of about 1000. Of these, two villages are on the shores of the northern bay, four grouped along the windward, eastern coast, and one at the head of the southern bay.

Naviti is a very interesting island because the polities are composed of a series of *yavusa* based, first, on the descendants of two spiritual progenitors, Tunaqaia and Botabota, who came there from the Nakauvadra and settled first at Somosomo and Kese; and secondly, on groups or parts of groups of people who came over from Viti Levu. These were those from Vitogo who settled at first at Kese and became known as the Leweivawa; those from Votua, Ba, who settled at first at Somosomo and became the Kai Nadua; and others from Votua who settled at first at Suelevu and became the Kai Koro. These newcomers were included as *mataqali* in their host *yavusa*, and just as the original *yavusa* of Somosomo split and sought to establish new settlements and formed new *yavusa* based on the new settlements, so the groups of newcomers also split up and parts of the groups joined the newly formed *yavusa*. In some cases the newcomers became recognised as the leaders, and the host *yavusa* would install one of the newcomers as paramount chief with a given title.

Naviti is also interesting as a case study of the spirit world of *yavusa* which includes elements of groups descended from local spiritual progenitors as well as from spirits from Vitogo and Ba. The newcomers would also have been associated with other sorts of spirits at least in the areas from which they came. It is interesting to try to explore whether the newcomers brought their old spirits with them to a new area, or at least whether they continued to respect and communicate with the old spirits; or whether they respected spirits of the areas where they came to settle. Equally interesting is an attempt to explore what happened to the spirits of the dead of the newcomers. Did they acquire a new jumping-off place, and if so what was the basis of such an acquisition? Did they go eventually to the same place as that to which the spirits of the dead went when a person died in Vitogo or Votua?

The myths of Ravuravu and of the progenitor nitu/spirits

Ravuravu

Ravuravu is a *nitu* or spirit, regarded as the *ivakatawa* or guardian, or *itaukei du* or true owner of Naviti.

Progenitor nitu/spirits: Tunaqaia and Botabota

(a) Tunaqaia at Somosomo

I was told in 1953 that the first progenitor spirits to arrive on Naviti, which was then unoccupied, were Lekenidavule and his wife who appeared mysteriously at Nasau on the north coast, where Tunaqaia was born. They went and settled in a cave at Davule, where Tunaqaia married a woman of Vuda and they had two sons who were men. The NLC recorded that Tunaqaia came from the Nakauvadra and settled at Davule, a narrow strip of land between the hills and the sea. His descendants became known as the *yavusa* of Somosomo.

Davule became too cramped and so they went to settle on a wider area of land at Somosomo, divided from Davule by a stream. The elder son had three sons.

(b) Botabota at Kese

I was told in 1953 that after Tunaqaia came to Somosomo the next progenitor spirit to arrive on Naviti was Botabota, who came from the Nakauvadra and stayed at Vatunitu on the beach at Kese where the Church now stands. I could not find out whether this was a deliberate juxtapositioning of church and spirit stone. From there, he moved to the centre (*luvuka*) of Naviti and settled at a place called Vanua. Here he had six children. They later moved to the coast at Kese. Tunaqaia's descendants became known as the *yavusa* of Kai Luvuka.

Settlements and development of *yavusa*

(a) Tunaqaia's descendants (the Somosomo yavusa) and their four settlements

The first settlement of the descendants of Tunaqaia was at Somosomo, and the people were known as the *yavusa* of Somosomo. From there a hunting party found a suitable site for a second village they established at Gunu. Not long after, the settlement at Somosomo was faring badly because the eldest son kept on hitting people. So he was chased away and went to establish a settlement at Nasoqo/Liku. Finally the youngest of the three sons was taken by the other brothers to establish a new settlement at Suelevu.

Later some of those at Suelevu went and established the villages of Marou and Malevu.

The settlement at Somosomo and later arrivals: development of Somosomo yavusa

After the quarrels, the Somosomo people retained their status of seniority and in order to make the position quite clear, they held an installation ceremony, at which they installed their leader and gave him the title of Sau.

Later two groups arrived from Vitogo in search of the two daughters of the chief of Vitogo who had been so upset over an insult to their father (a piece of *kawai* or yam-like tuber had been thrown at him) that they left Vitogo. The girls eventually reached Naviti and were hospitably received at Somosomo. One of them, Lewatulekeleke, went to Malolo where she married the Tui Lawa. The other, Lewatubalavu, went around the Yasawa group and then to Lomaiviti, and finally she settled on Bau. The two groups from Vitogo remained at Somosomo, and were included by the NLC as two divisions of the chiefly *mataqali* of Natula in the *yavusa* of Somosomo.

On another occasion the young men of Somosomo gave an old man the tail of a *saqa* or trevally to eat, and he was so upset and dissatisfied with his share that he went to Kese and asked the Kai Koro, Leweivawa and Suelevu people living there to come and attack Somosomo. A representative of the Somosomo people went to Votua, Ba, and asked the Nadua people for help. The groups from Kese came and, as a gesture, burned the outskirts of the village of Somosomo but left the village intact. These Nadua people remained at Somosomo, and were included by the NLC as a separate *mataqali* in the Somosomo *yavusa*. This connection provided the basis for an occasion which led to the gift of the island of Yaqweta by the chief of the Somosomo people to the family from Votua, Ba, and to its being populated by the Nadua people of Votua.

The Somosomo people claimed to be very strong and warlike, going to the other side of Naviti and filling the cooking pots of the villagers with excrement and the water jars with urine. They were often attacked but the only time they failed to repel the enemy was when the people came from Kese, as related above.

At the time of the first NLC, the position of the chief of Somosomo was recognised as superior to that of the other chiefs of the island. However, the Tui Marou later approached the Sau of Somosomo with *tabua*, *iyau* or valuables and with food, and asked him to give up his position as senior chief. He agreed to do so, and at the second NLC, Tui Marou was recognised to be senior. The Somosomo chief later bitterly regretted that he had accepted the gifts of Tui Marou and had given up the position of senior chief of the island.

Spirits

The Somosomo respect Ravuravu as the *itaukei du* or *vakatawa* of Naviti as well as Tunaqaia as their own *nitu* or spirit. Tunaqaia's ceremonial site is at Nasau, and when I visited in 1953, the *bete* or priest in communication with Tunaqaia was Isimeli.

The *nitu* of the Leweivawa was Nakia (see under Kese).

Also at Somosomo, there is a female *nitu* called Lewatu or Lewatuturaga who is respected not only at Somosomo but also by the people of Malolo and the Naciriyawa of Vuda. The communalect word for chief is *momo*, and it is possible that this Lewatuturaga should properly be called Lewatumomo, the name of a famous female spirit in the Ba area. The Somosomo spirit may be a local borrowing from the Ba spirit, perhaps brought over by the Nadua people as their protector.

iVilavila ni Yalo

I was told that the spirits of the dead go to a stone at Vatunikasami on the lee side of Naviti, where a spirit will wait for its spouse. Then it goes to Ori, an islet off the northeast coast of Naviti. Here it eats *vudi* or plantain (the *magiti* symbol of unity and identification or *vuti yaca*). Then it goes to a little headland and plunges into the sea.

The Somosomo settlement at Gunu and later arrivals: development of Kai Gunu

The Somosomo people at Gunu and Nasoqo heeded the authority of the Somosomo people at Somosomo settlement.

Then two groups of Leweivawa people (originally from Vitogo) came to Gunu, one from Kese and one from Soso. Their leader was Vuki from Kese, and they were settled at Gunu by the Somosomo and given land at Nabebe. When Ro Seru became leader on the death of Vuki, his father, he was installed as chief by the Leweivawa. However, there was disagreement as to whether he was to be chief of the Leweivawa or paramount over the Somosomo as well. So the Somosomo installed Tokalaulevu as their own leader. Ro Seru was most upset about this second installation, and gathered a force of Leweivawa from those Leweivawa living at Kese, Soso and Marou. They attacked and killed Tokalaulevu and the rest were taken to Yaqweta. Ro Seru duly brought them back, and was installed as paramount of the Leweivawa and the Somosomo at Gunu and Nasoqo, being given the title of Ratu.

These people were duly registered as the *yavusa* of Kai Gunu, and their different origins were recognised not only in the three component *mataqali* of Leweivawa (chiefs), Somosomo and Nasoqo, but also in their symbols of unity. The Leweivawa had the *niu* or coconut and the *vai* or stingray; whereas the Somosomo had the *bausomo* tree and the *vai*.

Spirits

The *nitu* for the Leweivawa was Nakia (see under Kese)

For the *nitu* for the Suelevu, see under Somosomo.

iVilavila ni Yalo

Not recorded.

Somosomo, Gunu, Nasoqo and outside influences

The 1881 LCC investigated claims in respect of purchases of land at Somosomo (1051), Gunu (1055) and Nasoqo (1052) at the north end of the island of Naviti. The purchase, by J. Harman, of 400 acres at Somosomo in 1865 is the earliest sale of land in the Yasawa Group to a European of which I have a record. From 1865 to 1868 Thompson traded there for cotton grown by the local people and by Harman's tenants. One tenant grew 105 acres of cotton and another grew about 85 acres. Other Europeans traded from 1868 to 1875. The property was abandoned in 1875. J. Stark purchased about 80 acres at Nasoqo in 1868. He planted some 25–30 acres of cotton, and the locals also planted on the land. These two blocks and also the block at Gunu were adjacent.

The Commission also considered but disallowed a claim (1063) for the purchase by J. Harman of the five islands of Nanuya, Vunivau Balavu, Sesaro, Bule and Nakara (Narara?) off the east coast.

The settlements at Suelevu, Muaira, Soso and Marou

Origin and development of Suelevu yavusa

The youngest of three grandsons of Tunaqai was taken by his brothers to establish a new settlement at Suelevu. After a long time, the people at Suelevu increased in numbers and two groups were sent off to find other land on which to settle. One group established the village of Muaira, and the other group established the village of Soso. After that, some from Muaira and, later, some from Soso went and settled on the island of Waya. Of those remaining at Suelevu, some went off and established a village at Marou. The descendants of the youngest grandson as well as some later arrivals from Suelevu, Muaira and Soso, as described below including the Kai Koro from Ba and the Leweivawa, originally from Vitogo, comprised the *yavusa* Suelevu.

Village of Suelevu: later arrivals

A party of people from Ba, known as the Kai Koro, arrived at Suelevu, and the Suelevu people gave them a place to stay.

The Suelevu then established the villages of Marou and Malevu (see below).

After the Kai Koro had been with the Suelevu for some time, the Suelevu agreed to appoint the chief of the Kai Koro as the paramount over the Suelevu, and gave him the title of Sau. The NLC included the Kai Koro as part of the *yavusa* of Suelevu.

Spirits of the Suelevu

The *nitu* of the Suelevu was Dolonisakau.

iVilavila ni Yalo

Not recorded by me.

Village of Muaira: later arrivals

The site of Muaira where the Suelevu from the village of Suelevu first settled is a different site from that of the present village. The first site is between Kese and Soso, near the site of the Vatu ni Vula (see below).

Not long after the Suelevu had settled at Muaira, a party of people from Vitogo came to Naviti and settled with the Suelevu at Muaira who gave them a place to settle at Vawa. So these people from Vitogo became known as the Leweivawa. They later accepted an invitation from the Luvuka people of Kese to go and settle with them at Nabouvatu (see below under Kai Kese).

After the party from Muaira had gone to Waya, the remaining Suelevu at Muaira installed one of their own as leader with the title of Ravouvou.

Spirits of the Suelevu

The *nitu* of the Suelevu was Dolonisakaui.

iVilavila ni Yalo

Not recorded by me.

Vatu ni Vula

On the path from Muaira to Soso, I was shown twelve stones, known as the Vatu ni Vula or 'Stones of the Moon/Months'. At each new moon, the villagers of Muaira used to move one of these stones, and this form of calendar served to indicate the planting season.

Village of Soso: later arrivals. The yavusa of Kai Naviti (or Yavusa Ratu)

Not long after the Suelevu had settled at Soso, the Leweivawa at Nabouvatu split of their own accord, and a party went to join the Suelevu at Soso, who gave them land at Mavoca. The Suelevu, as landowners, remained leaders until they saw how energetic the Leweivawa were in carrying out their responsibilities in the settlement. So they agreed to install one of the Leweivawa as paramount at Soso, giving him the title of Ratu. There is an installation stone (*vatu ni vibuli*) at Soso, and I was also shown a stone seating arragement where the elders used to sit on formal occasions, to discuss such matters as installation. The paramount now has the eastern title of Tui Soso or Tui Naviti.

The Suelevu as landowners at Soso and the Leweivawa as chiefs were registered by the NLC as a single *yavusa* under the name of Kai Naviti (I was told that the present name is *Yavusa* Ratu). I was told that the Leweivawa were included in the *yavusa* of *Yavusa* Ratu as the two *mataqali* of Leweivawa and Nabuya.

Ratu Apenisa of the Leweivawa was renowned as a chief of aggressive and challenging nature. He involved the Kai Soso in a number of warlike visits from the mainland, as on the following occasions:

- He sent a pig with a *tabua* in its stomach as a challenge to Vuda to come and fight. The Vuda people, however, attacked Yalobi on Waya and Ratu Apenisa was sent an invitation to go and witness how strong the Vuda people were. He went and showed his own strength by stopping the attack, saying that some of the survivors should go to Naviti and make pottery there (The Waya women were famous for their pottery). The Vuda people went home and Ratu Apenisa went back to Naviti.

- At the invitation of Ratu Apenisa, some people of Vitogo, Nadi and Sabeto came and anchored in Cavu Bay and landed but did not go to Soso. They went and attacked Kese, Muaira and Malevu, which villages had been quarrelling with Soso. They did not go and attack Gunu and Somosomo, because Soso, Gunu and Somosomo were *to vata* or associates through the common relationship between the Suelevu people and the Somosomo people based on descent from Tunaqaia.
- People from Vitogo came to help Ratu Apenisa when he attacked Nalauwaki on Waya. As a result of this attack, some land on Waya between Wayalevu and Natawa and known as Namotu became Soso territory.

Spirits of Soso

The *nitu* of the Suelevu was Dolonisakau.

The *nitu* of the Leweivawa was Nakia (see under Kese).

Nitu ni Valu: connecting Soso, Naviti, and Soso, Kadavu

Soso on Naviti and Soso on Kadavu have a *tauvu* relationship, based on a spiritual connection of common origin.

I was told that the people of Naceva, Kadavu, were looking for a *nitu ni valu qwaqwa* or strong war spirit. They came to Viti Levu and followed the Nadroga coast, asking where such a spirit could be found. They were told to look for an island with a double rock, and so they moved north to Vuda, Vitogo and Votua and finally across to Waya. Here they were told of a bay in Naviti where such a rock could be found. So they went to Soso, where there was a double rock where the *nitu* was supposed to be. Its name was Rokonakana and it communicated through a man called Betekece.

They explained to Betekece what they had come for, and Betekece said that they should wait for five nights. If during that period, the lightning split an *ivi* tree beside Rokonakana's *yavu* or mound, the spirit would be theirs. This is what happened, and so the Kadavu people acquired Rokonakana as their *nitu ni valu*. His house was a short stick, so the people took the stick and the *bete* Betekece on board their canoe. They sailed off, having picked up a rock called Navatunicaginiwaidroka ('the rock of the fresh-water wind') at the islet of Nabawaqa. They came to Nacilaumomo on the Ra coast and here the stick fell into the sea. They went back to look for it and it was erect in the water. They retrieved the stick and sailed on down the eastern coast of Viti Levu. Betekece was a weak old man and said that he wanted to be buried on Kadavu. If that was not possible, the place where he was buried would always be revered in the future. They reached Bureibau on the southeast corner of Ra. Here the old man died and the place was called Soso in memory of the occasion. The people remembered the old man's wishes to be buried in Kadavu and took the body on with them to Namara where the body rested (*mara* is a place where a body being taken on a long journey for burial is set down to rest). The body was smelling badly but the people pressed on until they came to Bau, where the body was smelling so badly that they landed there and buried the body at Soso. The words of the *bete* foretold the future importance of Bau. The canoe sailed on with the *nitu* in the stick and the rock until they came to Kadavu. They kept the stick and the rock at Nasosoceva, where the rock can be seen. The stick has disappeared.

To show their gratitude to their *tauvu* on Naviti, the Soso people of Kadavu brought a rock from Kadavu and presented it to the people of Soso, Naviti. I have seen it, lying on the *yavu* of the *Were Levu* or main ceremonial house of the chief, now known as Tui Soso or, during my visit, Tui Naviti. When called upon to do so by the *bete*, the rock would produce a favourable wind for travellers. The Bauans call the Soso people Na Qase or the Old Ones, because of the connection through the burial there of the *bete* Betekece and his prophesy.

iVilalavila ni Yalo

When a member of the Kai Naviti (both Suelevu and Leweivawa) dies, the *yalo* or spirit goes to a rock at Vawa, on the path between Soso and Muaira. It jumps from the rock into a pool among some *ivi* trees. As it jumps, there is a sound of thunder, which had been heard by my informants, the Tui Naviti and Paula. It goes to a rock in the pool which represents a canoe in which the *yalo* sails away to an unknown destination, taking its possessions with it.

Soso and outside influences

The 1881 LCC investigated a claim (1053) for the purchase by George Evans of about 300 acres of land known as Sa or Esa on the southwestern peninsula of Soso on the island of Naviti. The deed, dated June 1869, was signed by Ratu Apenisa Nayatu, the Tui Soso, of the Leweivawa people, by Sovatabua, the Governor of Yasawa under the Cakobau Government, and by others; and witnessed by Thomas James Morton (brother-in-law of George), then living at Somosomo and trading in the Yasawa Group. After trading here for twelve years, he went to live at Korotubu, Ra.

Ratu Apenisa had previously offered the land to John Stark, then living at Nasoqo, who did not want it and arranged for the sale to George Evans, at the time living at Matacawalevu. The land was in fact owned by the Suelevu people of Soso, and although Ratu Apenisa, a strong socio-political figure in Soso, may have been the paramount chief of Soso who by virtue of this position took the lead in local politics, he was not in charge of the land of the Suelevu and therefore had no powers to approve the purchase without the agreement of the leaders of the Suelevu. Also Sovatabua, not even a chief of high rank in his own island of Nacula, might, as Governor under the Government of Bau, have had political power over the Yasawa group, but he certainly had no traditional power over the administration of land in Soso. The landowners did not at first realise the true situation about the sale of their land by Ratu Apenisa, but when they did, they indicated their displeasure. Fifteen guns were given for the land but were left with Ratu Apenisa and the Suelevu people were told by the Turaga ni Koro or Village Headman not to touch them. They were kept by the Leweivawa until Major Harding and soldiers who had come to collect outstanding taxes arrived with Robert Evans, seized the guns, and burned the village of Soso. Some people were taken by the military to Saivou, Ra. A suggestion was raised by the LCC that the people were taken to Saivou because of an anti-Government plot. The people also showed their anger with Ratu Apenisa in customary manner and *buturaki* or stamped on him and expelled him from Soso, sending him to relations in Vitogo where the Leweivawa had come from.

Francis Richard Evans occupied the land under lease from his brother George until his brother Robert came to Fiji in 1871 and went to occupy the land at Soso, living with his brother Louis, until the lease was transferred to Robert. John Gaggin occupied the land for a short time in 1872/3, when George demised the land to Francis Richard. In April 1874, the lease was transferred to brother Robert, who gathered nuts from 1874 until 1879 when he abandoned the property and went to live in the Fiji capital at Levuka.

The LCC also considered a claim (1064) for the purchase by T.R. Shute of four islands off the south end of Naviti, being Naukucavu, Nanuyabalavu, Nakara (Narara?) and Nadredre (Drawaqa?). These had not been occupied and the claim was disallowed.

Villages of Marou and Malevu: later arrivals, Yavusa of Kai Marou

After some of the Suelevu people living at the village of Suelevu had gone off and established the village of Marou, there remained a close connection between the two villages of Suelevu and Marou. There was a series of later arrivals, as follows:

- After the village of Marou had been established, those of the Leweivawa (originally from Vitogo) who had been settled by the Luvuka at Nabouvatu quarrelled and came to stay with the Suelevu at Kese. The Leweivawa when they had first come from Vitogo to Naviti had settled at Vawa on land given them by the Suelevu living at Muaira. So they were rejoining their original hosts, the Suelevu.

- Then following a split at Votua, Ba, a group of Kai Koro came over to Naviti and anchored at Marou. The Suelevu brought them ashore and they settled together at Marou. The Kai Koro heeded the authority of the Suelevu at Marou, and the Suelevu at Marou heeded the authority of the Ravouvou or chief of the Suelevu at Muaira.

- After the Suelevu, Leweivawa and Kai Koro were firmly established together at Marou, a second group of Leweivawa came from Muaira, following a split.

By this time, the village of Suelevu had been abandoned; the Suelevu had moved from Suelevu and established a new village of Malevu between Marou and Kese. All those living at Marou and Malevu, irrespective of origin, were registered by the NLC as the *yavusa* of Kai Marou.

Shortly after the arrival of the Kai Koro at Marou, the Suelevu had discussed the installation of a Kai Koro as paramount of all the groups in the two villages of Marou and Malevu. They duly installed the chief of the Kai Koro and gave him the title of Sau. I was told that formerly a chief used to be installed on a *vatu ni vibuli* or installation stone at Nasivi, when there was no *yaqona* ceremony; but nowadays he is installed in Marou village.

The Kai Koro were upset because the younger brother had been installed, not the firstborn. So they split, and some went to Malevu and others went to the Luvuka at Kese.

The Sau of Marou is now commonly referred to by the eastern title of Tui Marou. As already related, he approached the Sau of Somosomo who had been recognised by the first NLC as the senior chief on Naviti, and made him presentations and asked him to give him the status of senior chief. This was agreed to and confirmed at the second NLC, to the later regret of the Sau of Somosomo who had accepted the presents and had agreed to this arrangement.

Spirits

The *nitu* or spirit of the Suelevu at Muaira was Dolonisakau.

The *nitu* of the Kai Koro (now Nasukamoce) was Batisekaseka.

The *nitu* of the Luvuka was Naqovuloa (see under Kese).

The *nitu* of the Leweivawa was Nakia (see under Kese).

The Kai Koro at Votua, Ba, have their *nitu*, Vulakanawa (female) and Tui Vaturua (male) who had a place near Nailaga called Nadikilagi.

There are at Marou two female spirits, Tinaidrekedreke vina and Tinaidreke cakaca, the first one being of good disposition and the second one being evil unless well appeased.

The two rocks, Vaturualewa and Vaturuatagane which dominate Naviti are said to be the places of *nitu*.

iVilavila ni Yalo

The spirits of the dead of the Kai Koro go to a hill on a headland called Dovu near Soso. From here they plunge into the sea. The spirits of the chiefs of the Kai Koro go to Viwa and jump from there. The *ivilavila ni yalo* of the Suelevu and Leweivawa have already been discussed.

(b) Botabota's descendants (the Kai Luvuka yavusa) and the settlement of Kese

Origins and development of Kese settlement and Kai Kese: late arrivals

The descendants of the six sons of Botabota settled at Kese. There were later arrivals, as follows:

(i)   A group of people had come over from Vitogo and had settled with the Suelevu at Muaira where they were given land at Vawa. So they were known as the Leweivawa. The Luvuka at Kese agreed to invite the Leweivawa to join them at Kese, and passed a message to this effect to the Suelevu at Mauaira. The Suelevu agreed to the proposal and so the Leweivawa left the Suelevu and Muaira and went to join the Kai Kese at Kese, where they were given land at Nabouvatu. The Leweivawa agreed among themselves to install their chief with the title of Ratu, but they heeded the authority of the Luvuka as the original landowners.

The person installed was an elder brother. Then it became known that the younger brother would obstruct the leadership of the Ratu. So the Leweivawa split up and some went to Soso which was occupied at the time by some Suelevu who had gone there from Muaira.

(ii)   Not long after this split in the Leweivawa at Kese, there was a split in the Kai Koro (from Votua, Ba) who were living at Marou. They had been living there with the Suelevu (who had established the village) and some Leweivawa (who had gone there following the split at Nabouvatu). Following this split at Marou, some of the Kai Koro came to settle with the Luvuka at Kese who gave them land at Nasukamoce. They were later registered by the NLC as the Nasukamoce division of the Luvuka *mataqali* of the *yavusa* of Kai Kese, which comprised the Suelevu, Leweivawa and Kai Koro living at Kese.

The Kai Koro were firmly established with the Luvuka at Kese, when the Luvuka agreed to appoint the Kai Koro leader as paramount and gave him the title of Rokotakala. The paramount leadership of the Kai Kese remained with the Kai Koro up to the present time.

The LCC were told that Kese and Soso were constantly at war in the old days, but I could find no oral traditions to this effect still surviving in the 1950s.

Symbols of identity

Each element in the Kai Kese *yavusa* retained its own *kai* or tree, and its own *ika* or fish, as follows:

The Luvuka have the *baka* or fig tree and the *ika bula/vonu* or turtle.

The Kai Koro have the *vesi* (*Afzelia bijiga*) and the *vai* or stingray.

The Leweivawa have the *niu* or coconut and the *vai*.

Spirits

The *nitu* or spirit of the Luvuka is Naqovuloa.

The *nitu* of the Kai Koro (now Nasukamoce) was Batisekaseka.

The *nitu* of the Leweivawa (while they were at Vitogo and later on Naviti) was Nakia, who came down from the Nakauvadra. His first-born son, Ratu Vuki, came to Naviti as a man, and his *yavu* at Kese is called Nabouvatu. His spirit is communicated with here. Nakia is also respected and communicated with here as well as at Vitogo.

iVilavila ni Yalo

Not recorded.

The island of Naviti, less Soso Peninsula, Nasoqo and Gunu, and outside influences

The 1881 LCC investigated a claim for the purchase in 1870 by F.R. Evans for the whole of the island of Naviti, about 4000 acres, less Soso peninsula (1054), Nasoqo (1052) and Gunu (1055), from Ratu Epeli and his brother Ratu Timoci, sons of Cakobau, Ratu Apenisa (Tui Soso), Ratu Isireli Wainiqeqe (chief of Gunu, with Tongan mother), and others.

Before the execution of the deed, George Evans had gone to Marou with John Stark to see Meli, the chief of Marou, with the object of purchasing some land at Yaro for Evans. Meli said that they were short of land and that his people would rather die than sell the land. Evans said that they were slaves and he would go to Bau to get the land.

Not long afterwards, Evans returned to Somosomo where Morton, his brother-in-law lived. He came with Veli, a personal follower of Ratu Epeli's but having no official connection with the Yasawa Group, and Sovatabua, the Governor. They gathered the leading people of Naviti together, including Ratu Esekia of Marou, Noa of Kese, Isireli Wainiqeqe of Gunu, and Ratu Apenisa of Soso; and Sovatabua told the people that they had come from Bau and that Ratu Epeli had ordered that they should make sail mats. Veli displayed twenty guns, ten axes and other trade goods, and said that Ratu Epeli had sold Naviti and the trade goods were theirs to divide up. It was not the purchase price but a present from Ratu Epeli. He told them not to despise or disobey Ratu Epeli lest some great wrath or evil should fall upon them. In Ratu Epeli's anger, they may be driven away or clubbed or shot. The people were dumbfounded and strongly objected to the sale. They set up a very strong opposition until Veli said that if they did not sign, a vessel would soon come from Bau and remove them. So, all except Isireli signed under protest. Isireli ran away and hid but was found by Veli and brought back and threatened with deportation. He too signed. They were also forced to take away the trade goods which had been divided up for the villages of Soso, Kese, Marou, Malevu, and Gunu, but later the shares for Gunu, Marou and Soso were returned to Somosomo and left with the people there.

The Evans brothers then occupied Naviti between 1870, when the deed was executed, and the 1874 hurricane when they were ruined, and then for some years after. They had cotton plantations at Marou, Kese, Malevu and Soso. They sold some land to Eastgate at Gunu, and leased to him some land at Yaro. The occupation of the Yaro land was only effected after desperate resistance by the people of Marou and Malevu who threw his house timbers into the sea at his first attempt to land. Heffernan then went to Bau, and with the assistance of Sovatabu and Bau messengers, threatened to remove the people to Bau and insisted that they build Eastgate's house for him.

Disputes between Evans and the locals occurred so frequently that a meeting was held in Levuka in 1872, attended by G.A. Woods, the premier, Evans and the Naviti chiefs, at which Evans tried to induce the Government to remove the people entirely from the island. A compromise was reached, in which it was agreed that, except for the people of Gunu, they should move to the *likuliku* or lee side of the island. However, the people persistently resisted the occupation by the Evans brothers and their lessees. Not only did they not want to leave their own land which they regarded as still theirs in spite of deeds and threats from Bauans and their appointees like Sovatabua, but the leeward side was arid, hot and infertile and, on inspection, the Deputy Warden Blyth agreed that the Soso people should remain. Later they were forcibly removed by Major Harding with Government troops and driven to the *likuliku*. The people of Marou and Malevu were taken to Somosomo; and after a month, they were taken by Sovatabua to Nacula. They were uncomfortable there and preferred to go to other Yasawa islands or to the mainland rather than go the *likuliku*. Those who went to the *likuliku* but continued to go to the *yaro* or windward side to pick from the fruit trees and coconuts, were threatened by Sovatabua and flogged or imprisoned for trespassing. The people of Kese were determined to stay but Deputy

Warden Blyth came and arrested the elders who were sent to Somosomo. The rest were told that the elders would remain in gaol for the rest of their lives, if they persisted in their obstinacy. They left for the *likuliku* and the leaders were released. However, their condition was so miserable that they preferred to work as labourers for Evans rather than stay on the lee side. Evans may have permitted the people to return and plant on the *yaro* side; but it is highly likely that the supply of labour was obtained only by intimidation and threats under arrangements whereby they supplied twenty men to fish for bêche de mer. In spite of this evacuation of the population to make room for unfettered plantations, it appears that only a total of 150 acres was planted with cotton and perhaps 200 acres with coconuts. Agricultural development by Europeans on Naviti appears to have been somewhat exaggerated by the planters.

It was agreed that the Kese, Marou and Malevu people should return in 1878 without being molested by Evans, and Robert left the Yasawa Group in 1879.

The island of Yaq(w)eta

The island of Yaqeta, or Yaqweta in the local communalect, lies about 3 km north of Naviti. It is a volcanic island, 8 km long, from north to south, and about 1.5 km across at its widest part; and has a ridge running the length of the island with its highest point at the south end. It is nearly 8 square km in area, and has one village, Matayalevu, with a population of about 350 people. I was told in 1953 that it was originally owned by the Somosomo people of Naviti but was not inhabited until proto-historic times when, as I noted in the Somosomo account, it was given by a chief of Somosomo to a family from Votua, Ba.

Myths of origin

I was told that the island had no particular guardian spirit or *nitu*.

The populating of Yaqeta: the yavusa Nadua

A man of Votua was married to a woman of Somosomo and, because their position at Votua was uncomfortable, they came over together with their two sons to stay with the woman's relations at Somosomo, Naviti. The woman later gave birth to a third son, Kava; and at the request of the father who collected some valuables for the purpose, the wife went to ask her brother, Dudulevu, the chief of the Somosomo for the island of Yaqeta so that the family could go and settle there and gather *sici* or trochus to eat. The chief gave the island to Kava who was his *vasu*. The family went and settled at Tabana, the first village on Yaqeta.

The other two sons had gone to stay at Soso, Naviti and were asked by their father to come over to Yaqeta. They settled at Donomai, and they all formed the *mataqali* of Nadua. Others from Votua followed and formed the *mataqali* of Votua. Collectively they formed the *yavusa* of Yadua, as registered by the NLC. One of these was installed as leader with the title of Ratu, and he was independent, heeding no other authority. At the time of my visit there were disputes about the leadership and ownership of the island.

The people of Nacula used to attack the Nadua people on Yaqeta, who would retire and take refuge in a cave at Koro. A large snake is said to live in the cave and sometimes appear in the village. It is not clear whether the snake is regarded as the *waqawaqa* or manifestation of a spirit, perhaps the guardian spirit, Devu. It used to eat the bats in the cave which is full of bat bones.

Spirits

The present inhabitants, the Nadua people from Votua, regard their guardian spirit at Yaqeta to be Devu, their guardian spirit at Votua.

iVilavila ni Yalo

At Votua.

Yaqweta and outside influences

The LCC considered in 1881 and allowed a claim (1076) for the purchase in 1870 by Messrs Milligan and Williamson of two areas of the island of Yaqweta. 30 acres of cotton were destroyed by the 1871 hurricane. In 1872, 15 acres of cotton had been replanted, and then another 15. All were destroyed by the 1874 hurricane. J. Vernor was then in occupation. By 1881,100 acres of coconuts had been planted and there were 350 goats on the island. Leslie was then in occupation and he planted about 10 acres of cotton.

iVilavila ni Yalo

At Votua.

13

The *Tikina* of Yasawa

The islands of Nacula and Matacawalevu

The island of Nacula lies about 2 km south of the island of Yasawa and 8 km north of the island of Matacawalevu. It is nearly 10 km long from north to south, and 3 km across at the widest part. It had a total area of about 22 square km. The coastline is indented on both sides. The main ridge roughly follows the west coast, and the highest part is the peak of Korobeka (251 m) towards the north end. There are two other peaks, 237 m and 221m high towards the south end. Near the centre, a transverse ridge rises to 153 m. Along the west coast, streams flow into the sea through flats and mangrove swamps. There is a wide bay in the middle of the west coast. There are at present four villages, two at the north and south extremes of the east (windward) coast, and two to leeward in the western bay, with a total population of over 500.

About 1.5 km to the west of the southern end of Nacula is the freehold island of Tavewa with an area of about 160 ha.

The island of Matacawalevu is about 5 km long from north to south, and over 2 km across at the widest part. It has a total area of about 9 square km. The highest peak is Uluikorolevu (300 m) towards the southern end of the island. Along the windward, eastern coast, streams flow into the sea through mangrove swamps or lagoons. There are at present two villages, Matacawalevu at the north of the windward coast, and Vuake in Nasomo Bay which lies in the middle of the east coast, with a total population of about 200.

These accounts are based on the records of the Native Lands Commission (NLC), checked and supplemented by my own explorations in 1951 and 1953, and on the records of the Lands Claims Commission (LCC) hearings in 1881.

The island of Nacula and part of Matacawalevu

Myths of the Qotuqotu

Ron Gatty, writing in the *Canberra Times* of 30 July, 1996, said that he had heard from Ratu Dovi Tavutavuvanua, a Nacula chief, that the earliest known inhabitants of Nacula were the Qotuqotu, a very fair-skinned people who had settled directly from the West. Ratu Dovi believed that these ancient people were absorbed, or perhaps mostly killed off. They are remembered as a pre-Fijian priestly, religious people who composed music. Their singing or chanting is still heard occasionally, and the people, mostly women, are still sometimes seen in the countryside, outside the village. They disappear when approached. He discussed this with me but I had not heard of these people.

The myths of Revo and of the progenitor nitu/spirits

Revo

Revo is a *nitu* or spirit, regarded as the *ivakatawa* or guardian spirit of the island of Nacula and of that part of the island of Matacawalevu occupied by the Vanuakula people.

Progenitors: Tavutavuvanua and Leka

(a) Tavutavuvanua at Drola

The NLC recorded that the original ancestor of the Kai Drola people was Tavutavuvanua who came from the Nakauvadra and established a village at Drola on the windward side of the island of Nacula facing Viti Levu. He had four sons, who agreed among themselves that the second son should be the leader.

Tavutavuvanua's descendants became known as the *yavusa* of Kai Drola, divided into five *mataqali*.

(b) Leka at Vanuakula

The NLC recorded that the original ancestor of the Vanuakula people was Leka who came from the Nakauvadra and settled at Vanuakula on the island of Matacawalevu. He had two sons.

His descendants became known as the *yavusa* of Vanuakula, divided into two *mataqali*, Vanuakula and Nabuya.

Tavutavuvanua's descendants (the Kai Drola yavusa) and their settlements

Malakati and Nacula

Because of water problems, the descendants of Tavutavuvanua all moved from Drola to Malakati. Later the second son, the leader, decided that he should stay at Malakati and the others should go and establish other settlements.

So the other three moved to three sites near the present village of Nacula, and then joined together at Nacula where they installed the son of the firstborn to be chief with the title of Masibuli

Meanwhile the second son, the leader at Malakati, had died and his son was installed as chief with the title of Ratu Mai Drola.

The Kai Drola at Nacula: new settlements

The NLC said that after the Kai Drola at Malakati had been there for a long time, two groups left to occupy new land. One group went to Cobe and the other to Navotua, and both continued to heed the authority of the Masibuli of Nacula. I was told that the first group were descendants of the firstborn son of the progenitor and the second group were descendants of the youngest son.

Origins of different groups comprising the Kai Drola

The NLC registered the Kai Drola as a *yavusa*, divided into the *mataqali* of:

- The *Yavusa* Ratu and Vunikavika who lived at Malakati. I was told in 1953 that the *Yavusa* Ratu came from Verata, and the Vunikavika came from the island of Malake, Rakiraki.
- Those divisions of the Vatia who lived at Nacula included the Nabuya, the Rakiraki and the Lasakau. I was told that the Nabuya (of whom Leka was the progenitor) were the original inhabitants of Nacula. The inclusion of a division called Lasakau (the name of a *yavusa* on Bau) is interesting and will be considered later when I discuss the overall origins and development of the polities of the islands of Nacula and Matacawalevu, and outside influences on these polities.

- Those divisions of the Vatia who lived at Cobe, including the Cobe and the Navatu. I was told that the Cobe came from Rakiraki, and that the Navatu came from Ra (presumably from Navatu, west of Rakiraki).

- The Navitabua, most of whom lived at Nacula, though some lived at Cobe. I was told that some now live at Navotua. I was also told that the Navitabua all came from Rakiraki.

- The Nacokobasaga, some of whom were living at Nacula. I was told that the rest were living at Navotua. I was also told that the Nacokobasaga all came from Ba, except for the Qelema, the division of the *bete* or priests, who came from the island of Vatulele, Nadroga. These different places of origin for the Qelema and the rest of the Nacokobasaga are reflected in their *icavu* described below.

Attack by Roko Dinono

The NLC recorded that the Kai Drola and the Vanuakula people kept killing each other, and the latter asked the Yasawa people for assistance. Roko Dinono, chief of Yasawa i rara, brought an army of Yasawa and Nadroga warriors to attack Nacula, and the Kai Drola left Nacula and sought refuge on Naviti.

Later the Kai Drola returned and settled in their old villages, where they were at Cession. By the time of my visit in 1953, the village of Cobe had been abandoned and the people had moved to Nasisili.

Kai Drola: development of chieftainship

At first, the Kai Drola had two chiefs, the Masibuli at Nacula who was descended from the second son of the progenitor, and the Ratu Mai Drola at Malakati who was descended from the firstborn son of the progenitor. They were both regarded as of the same seniority and were independent of each other.

Later the chiefs of Malakati and Nacula agreed among themselves that they should all follow the leadership of Sovatabua, a descendant of the original Masibuli, and they installed him as paramount of all the Kai Drola with the title of Tui Drola. He must have been an exceptionally strong and energetic leader; he was later appointed to be the Governor of the Yasawa group under the Cakobau Government and is generally referred to as Ko Koya Na Kovana. Later, the Tui Drola were appointed, apparently in turn, from the descendants of the sons of the progenitors, though it may simply have been that the most appropriate person was appointed irrespective of his ancestry.

At present, no one has been installed as Tui Drola and the two groups based on Malakati and Nacula take joint decisions.

iCavu

Both the Kai Drola of Malakati and those of Nacula have the same *kai* or tree, the *yabia* or arrowroot. This is the same for the Vanuakula people on Matacawalevu. This may indicate that at an early stage they were one group. Their later differences may have been manifested in different *ika* or fish, the *salala* or mackerel (described as the *ika ni tobu mai Malakati)* for the Kai Drola at Malakati; the *sulua/kuita* or octopus for the Kai Drola at Nacula; and the *warua* or *kikio* for the Vanuakula.

Although the Kai Drola at Nacula have as overall *icavu* the *yabia* and the *sulua* as symbols of unification and identity, some of the component *mataqali* or divisions of *mataqali* have also their individual *icavu* which they respect. For instance, the Nacokobasaga, except for the Qelema division, have the *vadra* as their *kai*, whereas the Qelema have the *vudi* or plantain as their *kai* as well as the *lewamatua* or *kasewa*, the stonefish, as their *ilava* or concomitant. The Koroinamoli division of the Nacokobasaga have the *dalo* as their *kai* as well as the *tave* or *kai*, a kind of bivalve, as the *ilava*; and this suggests that they may had an origin different from that of the Nacokobasaga other than the Qelema. The Navitabua have the *yega* or *yaga* as their *ilava*. The retention of these individual and different *icavu* in addition to the acceptance of overall ones recognised by the Kai Drola generally at Nacula reflect their different places of origin and their desire to retain some symbolic linkage to indicate their individuality as well as their unity, symbolised by the common *icavu* shared by all the Kai Drola at Nacula. A close and detailed exploration of *icavu* can tell much about the origins and development of a *yavusa*, and the evidence can usefully complement that of oral traditions and also serve as a check on such traditions.

Spirits

I was told that if the people were troubled by shortages of food or by threats of war, they would go to the Qelema, as *bete*, and the *bete* would seek help from Vanavana, the *nitu ni bete* or spirit of the priest who was a spirit of the Kai Drola. His place, called Vale ni Siga, is on the island of Tavewa; and his *waqawaqa* or manifestation is the *moko vulavula* or white lizard.

I was also told that a *nitu* called Rokoolu has a place called Baloui at Malakati, the village of the *Yavusa* Ratu. I was told that these people came from Verata, and that they associate Rokoolu with Rokomoutu, the progenitor of Verata. Indeed they say that Rokoolu is another name by which Rokomoutu is known. This may reflect the claimed connection between the *Yavusa* Ratu and the people of Verata.

Ron Gatty (personal communication) was told that people of Nacula recount that in the bush, usually by a stream, they had seen very small non-Fijian spirit women with long hair carrying babies. They are called *yalewa soro* because they beg to retain their freedom. Another name for them is *na nitu mata qwa*. These are not apparently connected with the Qotuqotu referred to at the beginning of this account of Nacula, its people and spirits.

iVilavila ni Yalo

Not recorded.

Yasawa and outside influences

The LCC investigated a claim (1056) for the purchase in 1869 of Tavewa island by W. Doughty who planted cotton there. He had planted about 60 acres of coconuts on the island by the time of the Commission enquiries in 1881. The island is still held under a freehold title. It remains to be determined whether there is still an association with the *nitu ni bete*, or whether Vanavana has left the island.

Leka's descendants (the Vanuakula yavusa) and their settlements

The settlements at Vanuakula and Matacawalevu

The NLC recorded that when the Vanuakula people comprising the *mataqali* of Vanuakula and Nabuya, were at Vanuakula, they chose as their leader a person from the Vanuakula *mataqali* and installed him with the title of Ratu. I was told that the Ratu of Vanuakula heeds the authority of the Tui Drola of Nacula. After the Vanuakula people had been at Vanuakula for a long time, there was not enough planting land for their increasing numbers and they moved to the present village of Matacawalevu.

I was told that the Kai Nabuya were the original inhabitants of the island of Nacula. Though most of them live at present at Matacawalevu, some still live at Nacula as part of the *mataqali* of Vatia.

iCavu

According to the NLC, the *kai* or tree of the Vanuakula is the *yabia* or arrowroot, and the *ika* or fish is the *wakua* or *kikio*.

iVilavila ni Yalo

Not recorded.

The Vanuakula and outside influences

The LCC considered two claims (1060 and 1062) based on purchase in 1869 by the firm of Evans and Sandiman of areas of land known as Nakeli (or Melbourne Plantation, about 150 acres) and Navunigalaka (about 1 acre) from chiefs other than Ratu Semi, chief of the Vanuakula.

Evans and Sandiman wanted to buy the land of Nakeli, but the owners were only prepared to lease it. A house was built for them and they started to plant cotton. Evans then asked Ratu Epeli for the lease to be converted to purchase. Ratu Epeli sailed to Matacawalevu and when Ratu Semi resisted the sales and defied Evans and Ratu Epeli, he was seized by the crew, put in the hold, and told that if he tried to escape he would be shot. He was held on board Ratu Epeli's boat while Ratu Epeli forced the other chiefs to sign. Ratu Semi was then taken ashore and was told that the land had been sold and he was not to interfere. Ratu Semi may eventually have signed under such duress, but the original documents were lost at sea when Sandiman disappeared between Matacawalevu and Levuka, while taking them to be registered.

At the same time as they purchased Nakeli as a cotton plantation, Evans and Sandiman also purchased a nearby coastal area of about 1 acre where they erected a large store, a ginning house for the cotton, an engine and a windmill. The position was favourable for the landing of goods for the store and the taking away of ginned cotton. It served as a landing place near Nakeli known as Navunigalaka. Ratu Epeli had evidently told Ratu Semi that the cotton was to be planted in one place and was to be shipped at another which he was to indicate to the purchasers. This was after Ratu Semi had been released from the hold of the vessel. Ratu Semi as the authority over the land had evidently signed the deed after he had suffered violence in the hands of Ratu Epeli and had been subjected to further threats. The original 1869 document was lost at sea, but the 1871 deed was signed by Ratu Semi. As in the case of the purchase of Nakeli, Ratu Semi had evidently signed the deed under duress.

Evans and Sandiman planted about 75 acres of cotton, cutting down breadfruit trees to the fury of the locals who asked Evans to plant up to the trees and not cut them down. Evans told them not to interfere since the land had been sold to him by Ratu Epeli, and he flogged some of them. His overseer, Cowper or Cooper, was a drunkard and kept firing into the village so that, as a result of his behaviour, the people were in a state of constant terror. The cotton crop was destroyed in the 1871 hurricane and the store and ginning machinery were destroyed by the accompanying tidal wave. The estate eventually fell into financial difficulties and James Hillyard was sent by the creditors to look after it. Hillyard left in 1873. A smaller store had been erected but was destroyed in the 1874 hurricane. The estate was abandoned, partly because of financial difficulties incurred but also because of the general state of violence prevailing and the atmosphere of terrorism induced by Evans and Cooper.

Ratu Epeli may have been influenced in his treatment of Ratu Semi by the fact that Ratu Semi was one of the leaders of the movement by which it was intended to bring the Yasawa Group under the influence of Bua and not under Bau. This account is relevant to an exploration of the interesting and perhaps unexpected relationships that were developing between these little western islands and the mighty polities of the east, including the Tongans. This will be discussed elsewhere.

The LCC also considered and allowed two claims (1065 and 1066) by John James Frew and G.J.P. Gore Martin separately for the islands of Nanuyalevu and Nanuyalailai respectively. Nanuyalevu had been occupied by Frew between 1871 and 1881. About 60 acres of cotton had been grown until the complete destruction of the plantation by the 1874 hurricane. After that 70 acres of nuts were planted in the small bays. The island of Nanuyalailai was bought in 1869, and after the 1871 hurricane perhaps 35 acres of cotton had been planted. After the 1874 hurricane, coconuts were planted and there were 50 acres of nuts in 1881.

Part of the island of Matacawalevu: Ketekete

The myth of Ravokavoka

The NLC recorded that the *nitu* or ancestral spirit of the people of Ketekete who occupy part of the island of Matacawalevu is Ravokavoka who had two sons. The NLC did not record where he came from and I have no independent information about the origins of the Ketekete people.

Development of the Ketekete yavusa

Ravokavoka's descendants became the *yavusa* of Ketekete, which was divided into two *mataqali* of which the chiefly *mataqali* was the Nasivitu.

The leader was installed with the title of Ratu, and he was independent.

After a long time, the Ketekete people left Ketekete because of a shortage of water and moved to Vuaki. Here they stayed until Cession and were still there at the time of my visit in 1953.

iCavu

Part of the Nasivitu *mataqali* was the Bau division or *kausivi*. They may be people of different origin from that of the rest of the *yavusa*, because the *kai* or tree of the Bau people is the *vurai*, a kind of yam, whereas that of the rest of the Ketekete is the *tiri tabua* or kind of mangrove, *Rhizophora mucronata*; and the *ilava* or concomitant of the Bau is the *tave* or *kai*, a kind of bivalve, but that of the rest of the Ketekete is the *ogo* or barracuda. The implications of this matter will be considered later when discussing the overall origins and development of the polities of the islands of Nacula and Matacawalevu, and outside influences on these polities.

iVilavila ni Yalo

Not recorded.

Vuaki and outside influences

The 1881 LCC considered one claim (1061) based on the purchase in 1869 by the firm of Evans and Sandiman of two lots of land at Vuaki from the Turaga ni Koro and others at Vuaki for five guns each. Then they leased the lots to Marsh and Barnett for ten years, and the latter planted cotton which was destroyed by the hurricane in 1871. They moved to Yaqeta from where they continued to manage the land which was occupied by James Vernor, one of the firm. He planted about 75 acres of cotton which was destroyed by the 1874 hurricane. He continued to live there, planting and gathering a few nuts and making a little copra. What rights he had are not clear because the ten-year lease had expired and the original document was lost at sea together with Sandiman who was taking it and other documents to Levuka for registration.

The Commission also considered a claim (1068) for the islands of Kubulau and Nanuyaiyata which had been purchased by J. Bennet, and was told of a number of goats on Nanuyaiyata. Kubulau was not occupied.

The islands of Yasawa and Sawa i Lau

The island of Yasawa is the northernmost of the inhabited islands which from the chain of the Yasawa Group, the Natu Yasawa. It is about 22 km long from north to south, and 1.5 km across at its widest part. It has a total area of 28 square km. A volcanic island, it has a main ridge running for three-quarters of its length close to the west coast, with the highest summit of Taucake (230 m) at the south end. The western slopes are generally steep, whereas the eastern slopes are longer and gentler. Another summit, 194 m high, rises above the present village of Bukama. From this summit, the ridge veers towards the east coast and ends on the island of Yawini which lies just off the north-west end of Yasawa. In this northern part, the eastern slopes of the ridge are steep and the western slopes are gentler. The present six villages of Yasawairara, Bukama, Teci, Dalomo, Tamasua and Nabukeru are on the coast below the gentler slopes of the ridge and have a total population of about 700.

The uninhabited island of Sawa i Lau, with the islet of Nanuya, lie immediately south of the village of Nabukeru. Sawa i Lau is the only limestone island in the Yasawa group and has sheer rock faces rising above steep slopes covered with dense bush. There are caves there with their entrances on the western side of the island.

The island of Yasawa

The yavusa of Rara, Yasawa, Tamasua and Natubasa: minor socio-political complex

The four *yavusa* of Rara and Yasawa (based in the village of Yasawairara), and Tamasua and Natubasa (based in the villages of Tamasua and Nabukeru) formed a minor socio-political complex, of which the paramount holds the title of Tui Yasawa. In each case, the original ancestor came from the Nakauvadra to the island of Yasawa. The first to come was the progenitor of the Rara people who settled at Rara. He was followed by those of the Tamasua and the Yasawa people who were brothers and settled at Tamasua and Yasawa respectively, and by the original ancestor of the Natubasa who came from Nakauvadra together with the two brothers and who settled at Natubasa.

Myths of origin

According to the NLC, Raiboto was the first to come from the Nakauvadra to Yasawa, and he settled at Yasawa at the north end of the island. Later the two brothers, Tabusua and Sawa, and Momo arrived together on the island. The two brothers went to Tamasua on the south-west end of the island, and Momo went to Natubasa just down the coast from Tamasua, at the south-east end of the island. Tabusua remained at Tamasua, and he sent his younger brother Sawa to the north end where he settled at Sawa, next to Raiboto at Yasawa. Sawa had a son, Momonibawaqa or Chief of the Bawaqa. There is a stone on the beach near the present village of Yasawairara called Bawaqa or Canoe Fence which, having the *sau* or spiritual power of Momonibawaqa, is regarded as the *ilati* or defence screen for the village

The myth as related to me was that Tabusua and Wasayawa were two brothers who came from Nakauvadra and rode on a shark to the north end of the island of Yasawa where they built a house at Manuqila on the east coast. One day they noticed the hill called Iesue on the west coast, and they went there and built a house. One day the people went fishing when the tide was out. By the time they were ready to go back, the tide was so high that they could not do so. So some went to Nacula, some to Waya and some to other islands. When they failed to come back, Tabusua told his younger brother to wait at Iesue, and he would go and look for them. He followed the west coast to Taucake near the present village of Tamasua. He saw smoke rising from the neighbouring islands and realised that the fisherfolk must have gone to stay there. He went back to Iesue and told Wasayawa to remain there, and he would go and settle at Tamasua. He remained at Tamasua with his two sons, Ratu and Momo. Momo then went to Natubasa to settle, whilst Ratu remained at Tamasua.

The two myths differ in detail especially about the connection between Momo and the brothers, and about their places of first settlement. However, there are no significant discrepancies in the myths, which serve to account for the origins of and connections between the four *yavusa*.

Development of settlements and yavusa: Yasawa and Rara

The descendants of Raiboto (the Yasawa *yavusa*) lived separately from but adjacent to the descendants of Wasayawa/Sawa (the Rara *yavusa*) at Yasawa and Rara respectively. However, in the time of the chieftainship (*sau*) of Rokomatanivai, the great-grandson of Momonibawaqa, the Yasawa people decided to join with the Rara people, to establish a joint village called Yasawairara, to heed the authority of the Rara people and to install the head of the Rara as their paramount with the title of Tui Yasawa.

At a later stage, these two *yavusa* formed an association with the *yavusa* of Bukama, but only during the *sau* or chieftainship of Savutini, a particularly strong chief of the Bukama, who was installed as Tui Yasawa (see under Bukama).

Development of settlements and yavusa: Tamasua and Natubasa

The descendants of the elder brother, Tabusua, became the *yavusa* of Tamasua and lived at Tamasua village; and the descendants of Momo became the *yavusa* of Natubasa and lived at Natubasa.

I was told that the head of the Tamasua was chosen in consultation with both *yavusa* who gathered to discuss the matter at the *mata ni sava* or ceremonial site at Namoli. On reaching agreement, they would inform a rock at Namoli which would indicate to those who had the power to hear if it approved of the choice. If the groups could not agree on an appointment, they would consult the stone at Namoli, which would indicate to those who could hear how to determine the new appointment. The new appointment was installed with the title of Tina Levu.

The head of the Natubasa was installed with the title of Ratu who heeded the authority of the Tina Levu who in turn heeded the authority of the Tui Yasawa.

The main settlement remained at Tamasua until the time of the wars. Then those at Tamasua and at Natubasa went to Nadela. After peace was resumed, most of the people went to Tamasua, although some went and settled at Nabukeru, where they were during my visits in the 1950s.

Spirits

Each of the four *yavusa* respects the spirits of their respective progenitors. For instance, the Tamasua people respect the spirit of Tabusua whose place is at Taucake near Tamasua, and whose *mata ni sava* or ceremonial centre is at Namoli where there is the consultation rock and the *yavu* of his spirit house.

In addition, each *yavusa* has its own *nitu* or guardian spirit: Sesetia for the Rara people; Nauleti for the Yasawa people; Naika for the Tamasua people; and Nataleqailagi for the Natubasa people. Each has its own form of manifestation whereas the spirits of the progenitors do not appear to have such manifestations.

It was not clear at the time of my visits in the 1950s and 1990s who was the spirit of the rock of Bawaqa, though it may be that of Momonibawaqa. It is likely that the spirit of the rock at Namoli is that of Tabusua.

iVilavila ni Yalo

I have not recorded the *ivilavila ni yalo* of the Yasawa or the Rara people. That of the Tamasua and the Natubasa people is on the island of Vawa, to the north-west of Tamasua. The spirit of the deceased goes first to the beach at Liku near Tamasua where it leaves a footprint in the sand. Liku is the *ivodovodo ni waqa* or embarkation place, where the spirit embarks on a canoe, represented by a rock or *vatu waqa*, and then sails to Vawa to Vai i Savasava. It climbs a hill and from there plunges over a cliff into the sea.

iCavu

At the north of the island of Yasawa, the two *yavusa* do not have a *kai* or tree, but both have *ika* or fishes. The Rara people have the *ika ni vatu* or stonefish; and the Yasawa have the *vai* or stingray.

At the south end of the island, both *yavusa* have a tree and a fish. The Tamasua have the *moli/ wi* or *Spondias dulcis*, and the *moci* or *urau*, the shrimp or prawn (the NLC recorded the former, I recorded the latter). The Natubasa have the *ivi* or *niu*, the *Inocarpus edulis* or the coconut (the NLC recorded the former and I recorded the latter), and the *tuace* or *kai koso*, a saltwater bivalve. These are symbols of the male and female genital organs respectively.

Yasawa and outside influences

In 1881 the LCC considered and allowed a claim by the Wesleyan Mission for an area of land at Muana which was occupied by the Mission at the time of the Commission.

The independant yavusa of Bukama

The *yavusa* of Bukama formed an independent polity consisting of the single *yavusa*. The original ancestor, Tuiwedre, came from the Nakauvadra to settle at Vanuakula, beside the present village of Bukama. He had three sons, and the eldest was installed as leader with the title of Ratu.

The descendants of Tuiwedre established the village of Bukama, but they kept giving their land away to people from elsewhere. It is presumed that these strangers were absorbed into the *yavusa* of Bukama but I have not recorded this.

The great-grandson of Tuiwedre, Savutini, was a strong and energetic leader. When he was installed as Ratu, he united the Bukama, the Yasawa and the Rara people into a single *vanua* or polity, and was also installed as the Tui Yasawa. After his death, this association came to an end and Bukama became once more an independent polity consisting of the single *yavusa*.

The *yavusa* of Bukama remained at Bukama and were there at the time of my visits in the 1950s.

Spirits

Apart from the spirit of Tuiwedre whose ceremonial place or *mata ni sava* is at Vanuakula where he first settled on coming from Nakauvadra, the Bukama have a *nitu* or guardian spirit called Momodro whose place is at Nakorodamu on the peak near the village of Bukama.

iVilavila ni Yalo

Not recorded.

iCavu

The Bukama have the *dovu* or sugar cane as their *kai* or tree, and the *balolo* or sea-worm/annelid and the *daniva* or sardine-like fish as their *ika*. The inclusion of two kinds of *ika* suggests that the *yavusa* includes more than one group of people.

The independent yavusa of Bouwaqa

The *yavusa* of Bouwaqa formed an independent polity consisting of the single *yavusa*. The original ancestor, Savase, came from the Nakauvadra to settle at Korokoro, Vivau, near the present village of Teci. From there he moved to Bouwaqa on the edge of Teci. He had three sons, of whom the two eldest remained at Bouwaqa and the youngest went to establish a new settlement at Dalomo. They then installed the great-grandson of Savase as leader with the title of Tui Teci. He was independent and did not heed the authority of any one else.

As they increased in number at Bouwaqa, they spread out to Teci where they were joined by some from Dalomo. As strangers arrived, they were given land by the Bouwaqa people and presumably included in the *yavusa*. Two of the leading chiefs of the Bouwaqa married women from Bila, Tavua, and this suggests that there was some established connection with Tavua, perhaps through the arrival of some Tavua people who settled at Teci. Also one of the divisions of one of the *mataqali* was called Nadua, suggesting an origin either from Yaqeta or from Votua, Ba.

On one occasion that I was told about, the people of Macuata came over to Yasawa to help the people at Teci to fight the people at Yasawairara. The people of Viwa came to assist Joni Cakautavatava, the Tui Yasawa, with whom they were related. He was Tui Yasawa at the time of the NLC. The Macuata and Teci people were defeated.

The Bouwaqa people remained at Teci and Dalomo where they were at the time of my visit in the 1950s.

Spirits

Apart from the spirit of Savase, the Bouwaqa had a *nitu* or guardian spirit called Mateanitani whose place was at Nakorodamu on the peak overlooking Bukama and Teci. This was also the place of the *nitu* of the Bukama people.

iVilavila ni Yalo

Not recorded.

iCavu

The *kai* or tree was the *balawa*, either the screwpine or the wild pineapple. The *ika* or fish was the *galau* or *kawakawa,* the grouper.

Yasawa, Teci, Nacula and Matacawalevu interrelationships and outside influences

I referred earlier to quarrels between Teci and Yasawa i rara. Teci had evidently sent messages to Macuata, seeking assistance, at about the same time as Yasawa i rara had sought help from Tui Bua. The Macuata party (presumably that led by Gigi of Galoa referred to above) while on its way to Teci, was passing the Naivaka peninsula just west of the island of Galoa, towards the west end of Vanua Levu, when they met up with and drove away the Tui Bua's party on its way to Yasawa. However both parties reached their destinations and Tui Bua was able to warn the Yasawa people that the Macuata party was approaching and that they should put up their defences.

The Teci and Macuata people advanced on Yasawa i rara and laid siege to the village. Meanwhile Tui Bua, who was in the village, sent a party of five to Bua to say that in the event of his death his wives were not to be strangled. On their return, the messengers were caught at sea by the besiegers and were killed. The siege lasted for six months, after which Tui Bua went home. From this time forward, the people of Yasawa i Rara used to visit the people of Bua and became connected with them through intermarriage. They never had a *qali* or tributary relationship with Bua.

Three months later, Tui Bua returned to Yasawa i rara for the *magiti ni valu* or feast of thanks for his military assistance. At that time a war was going on between Matacawalevu and Nacula. The Matacawalevu people sent *tabua* and *madrai vudi* or fermented bread made of plantain to the Yasawairara village of Tamasua and asked the Yasawa people for help against Nacula. Meanwhile the Nacula people had gone to Teci to seek help. Teci was still quarrelling with Yasawairara. On the way, they met the people of Tamasua who were going with Tui Bua and the Matacawalevu people to attack Nacula. They fought and the Teci people were worsted and eight were killed. They then went on to Nacula, and Tui Bua and the Matacawalevu people burned the houses of Nacula outside its ditches. They then all went home.

Sometime after this, Nayagodamu of Bau visited Yasawairara and Teci, where the people asked for his assistance in getting back the bodies of the eight people slain by Tui Bua and the Matacawalevu people. Nayagodamu passed Nacula and went on Matacawalevu where through a trick, he succeeded in killing two of the Matacawalevu people and took their bodies to Nacula. He returned with the Nacula people to Matacawalevu and attacked the village. One Bauan was killed, and Nayagodamu went back to Bau taking one woman and two men. The Matacawalevu and the Nacula people continued their quarrels, and eventually the Matacawalevu burned Nacula. The people fled to the island of Naviti and took refuge in the various villages there.

When Nayagodamu next visited the Yasawa group, he went to Naviti where the Nacula people were. They made a feast for him at Kese, asking for his assistance in attacking Matacawalevu. They went off but when they reached Matacawalevu, they found that the warriors were with their associates at Teci, and only old men and women and children were left behind. So they killed the old men, but the women and children escaped. One lad brought the news of the attack to the warriors at Teci. By night, the Matacawalevu returned to their village, put up their defences and gathered together the fugitives. Then they waited for the attack but Nayagodamu never came because he had returned to Bau. Some time later he returned to Nacula with Ratu Epeli, son of Cakobau, to receive the *magiti ni valu*. The war was over and peace was restored. After the death of Nayagodamu, Ratu Epeli used to visit the Yasawa group, mainly going to Nacula, but he did not assist in any wars.

It was only later in the time of the Cakobau Government that the Yasawa group became administratively integrated under Sovatabua, a Nacula man who happened to be at Bau at the time of Cakobau's coronation and who was made lieutenant governor. He had no high rank and no authority over local affairs. The Yasawa group continued up to the present time to comprise a number of independent polities without a paramount chief. Indeed, as in so many parts of Fiji, the existing polities in the case of Tui Waya were internally divided and continued to be divided on the question of leadership and loyalty. They tend to disguise such differences, especially in front of strangers, but undercurrents of feelings of jealousy and rivalry continue to throb through this beautiful string of islands. The spiritual element does not appear to be so significant in these communities of varying origins that it can be regarded as a binding force stronger than the divisive secular forces of rivalry and jealousy. This may reflect the very tough imposition of Tongan Wesleyanism and the equally tough determination to accept Roman Catholicism as symbolic of opposition to Bua and Tonga.

The island of Sawa i Lau

The island of Sawa i Lau is owned by the people of Nabukeru. It is currently uninhabited and there is no evidence from oral tradition or from my own explorations on the island that it has ever been permanently inhabited. It is, however, an island of great importance for its associated myths which relate to connections between features and spirits associated with the caves on the island and with other places in Fiji which are distant from Sawa i Lau. One of the main myths is centred round the activities and fate of a *manulevu* or eaglehawk, and another relates to the fate of a female *nitu* or spirit who once lived there. It is also important for the archaeological remains in one of the caves, the origins and significance of which are still debatable. I am aware of three series of caves that occur at various levels in the western face of the island.

Na Qwara ni Manulevu

The uppermost of the cave series is known as the Qwara ni Manulevu or Cave of the Eaglehawk, and may be approached by a fairly difficult climb up the cliff face. This is an extensive complex of passages and caverns, in which there are some impressive stalagmites. The entrance is shaded by a *baka* or fig tree usually associated with spirits. Curei, a *manulevu* from Vasilele (Vatulele, Nadroga), used to live in the cave, living on turtle and porpoises and on men; and used to go out far and wide to seek them and take them back to the cave. One day the women of Naicobocobo, a spiritually important headland in Bua from which the spirits of the dead used to jump into the sea at the west end of Vanua Levu, were out fishing. Curei appeared and seized one of the women and took her back to his cave. The other women went back to Naicobocobo and told the husband what had happened. The husband and Rokoua, one of the chief spirits of the area, went to look for the woman. Reaching the island of Yasawa, they went to Dalomo and were told that the *manulevu* came from Sawa i Lau. Taking a roundabout route so as not to be seen by the bird, they sailed towards the cave and anchored nearby. They climbed up into the cave, carrying one spear, and found it empty, though they saw an arm in the cave with certain tattoo marks (*qia*). They recognised the *qia* as those of the missing woman and so realised that the *manulevu* living in the cave was the one that had seized her. They were hiding inside the cave when the *manulevu* came back with turtle and porpoises which it started to eat. Rokoua told the husband to spear the bird, but he had urinated in his barkcloth and was afraid. So he asked Rokoua to spear the *manulevu*, chanting:

> O na coka lau, daru sa toki; (Spear and hit, and we will leave;)
>
> O na coka cala, daru sa mate. (Spear and miss, and we will die.)

Rokoua prayed for a wind, and the wind blew the tail feathers of the *manulevu* up around its head. Rokoua then struck its windpipe and killed it and threw it into the pool down below. It made such a big splash that the resulting wave divided Votua in Ba, and Tamasua which until then had been connected. On the wall of the cave there is a wet patch indicating where the husband had urinated, and those who know what to look for can still see the bones of the *manulevu* lying at the bottom of the pool called Tobukabuasali.

This myth may reflect connections between the people of Tamasua/Nabukeru and Bua, Vatulele and Votua, and also between the Teci people of Dalomo and Bua.

In part of the cave complex there is a narrow passage known as Oso na Bukete. If a woman in the village tries to deny her pregnancy, she may be taken to this passage for testing. If she is at any stage of pregnancy, she will not be able to pass through this passage. When I went I was accompanied by, *inter alia*, the local doctor who was famous for the size of his stomach. His attempts at the passage were watched with considerable interest.

Na Qwara ni Sisili

The lowest of the series of caves is known as the Qwara ni Sisili or Cave of the Bathing Pool. It is divided into two chambers connected by an underwater passage. The outer chamber may be approached on foot directly from the beach and is easy of access.

The outer chamber is full of water, and in the deep pool there are a *gwadru* or small shark and a *damu* or red fish. These are said to be the *waqawaqa* or manifestations of *nitu* or spirits. Also in the chamber are what are described as yams turned to stone. There is a series of steps carved into the side of the chamber which lead up to a small cavity in the wall in which a person can sit and overlook the pool.

On the walls of the chamber approach there are many petroglyphs of unknown prehistoric origin and significance, although they are referred to as the *ivakatakilakila* or signs of Lewaqoroqoro. Lewaqoroqoro was a female *nitu* or spirit who lived on Sawa i Lau. People claimed to hear her singing *meke* or chants until one day when she was heard no more. On that day she was standing on the rocks (her footprints can still be seen on the rocks) while she urinated. Tutusilo of Malolo smelt this and his penis stretched and stretched until it reached Sawa i Lau. It then penetrated Lewaqoroqoro and lifted her up and carried her off to Malolo. She never returned to Sawa i Lau and her singing has not been heard since.

The approach to the inner chamber is along a short passage below sealevel. In the inner chamber there is said to be a shoal of *uruuru* fish, the significance of which was not known to my guides. Derrick (1950:219) recorded a legend that a young chief used the cave as a hiding place for his intended wife, a woman of rank whom the elders wanted to marry to someone else, until the two were able to escape to friends on another island.

Lewaqoroqoro is a spirit famous in the west, and I find the myth interesting as reflecting a possible socio-political connection between Malolo and Yasawa islands. It is very difficult at this stage to comment on the petroglyphs. Petroglyphs in large numbers have been found engraved on a large rock at Dakuniba, south Vanua Levu, and on a large rock and a series of nearby smaller ones found by me in 1996 at the spiritual centre at Edronu, at the west end of the Tualeita near the coast bordering Sabeto and Vuda (see Vuda and Sabeto). There is no obvious resemblance in the design between those at Edronu and those at Sawa i Lau, but there are similarities between the Sawa i lau petroglyphs and those at Dakuniba.

The middle cave has not yet been explored, to my knowledge, and the people of Tamasua and Nabukeru know nothing about it. I simply record its existence for posterity.

Northern Mamanuca group

Islands of Eori/Ori, Navadra and Narokorokoyawa

The island group of the Mamanuca lies between the island of Malolo and the southern islands of the Yasawa group and Waya Sewa/Kuata. The group is divided into Mamanuca i ra or Leeward Mamanuca and, to the south, Mamanuca i cake/yata or Windward Mamanuca. Of the Mamanuca i ra islands, only Tavua and Yanuya are inhabited, with a total population of about 275 people. The most northern of the Mamanuca i ra and those closest to Waya Sewa/Kuata are Eori/Ori, Navadra and Narokorokoyawa which belong to the people of Tavua. Whilst they may be uninhabited, they are nevertheless of importance in the spirit world. The first two are of local spiritual significance, and the third island, that of Narokorokoyawa, is well-known and of wider significance in the Fiji spirit world, especially in the west.

Eori is an islet with a raised rocky interior and an area of flat land to the west now planted with coconut palms. The spiritual owner or caretaker of Eori and the adjacent sea is Mudumudu, who can be approached for assistance through suitable ceremonial presentations made on the flat land. In the grove there is said to be an old *lali* or wooden drum and a village site associated with Mudumudu. His actual settlement is known as Tukunamanulava and is situated under the sea near the island of Navadra.

Navadra is a much bigger island with several groves of coconut palms near the sandy beaches. No information has yet been recorded about sites on Navadra.

Narokorokoyawa lies about 45 km west of north-west Viti Levu, Fiji. It is one of the most well-known and spiritually significant sites of Fiji. By its very geographical position, it has been difficult to access; and because of its spiritual significance, it is not easy to obtain permission to visit, and Fijians are generally too frightened to go there anyhow.

The island is also known as Ra, Vanua Levu and Vanuasagasaga. Just over 1 km in length, the island has a white sand beach with rocks, a steep-sided rocky interior and a flat area between the beach and the interior. It is steep sided and more or less covered with bush, and is home to a few goats. There are coconut plantations, and areas of *vudi* or plantains and bananas have been planted for those who come to cut the copra. To the west, the beach extends as a tombolo to a separate rocky islet. Nearby lie the other islets known as Eori, Navadra and Tavuriba.

Over the years I have managed to record some accounts, albeit tantalisingly inadequate, of the myths and beliefs associated with this and nearby islands. Fortunately one of those who could help me was a *bete* or priest, now deceased, who though he was a man of Vuda (one of my research areas on the mainland opposite to the island) was related to the traditional owners of the island and had a developed interest in the place. Two series of myths are associated with Narokorokoyawa and the nearby rocks. The first are associated with the *Rogovoka*, described to me as *nodra waqa na vu* or the canoe which brought the first spirits; and the second with the *Kaunitoni*, described to me as *nodra waqa na turaga* or the canoe which brought the first ancestors. Myths well-known throughout Fiji relate how these canoes came to Fiji from far away to the west.

Associated with the *Rogovoka*, the rocky islet joined by a tombolo to the west of the island is called Na iRaviravi ni Karikari ni Rqgovoka or 'The Support for the Spars of the Rogovoka'; and there is another rock out at sea called Na iMusimusi ni Karikari ni Rogovoka or 'The Refitting of the Spars of the Rogovoka', where the *Rogovoka* anchored at times to get its spars refitted. There is no hard wood on the island but sometimes people find *demanu* or hardwood leaves on the rocks. *Demanu* is a kind of hardwood favoured for spars. Between the islands of Monu and Yanuya which lie to the south there is a rock which is said to be the ashes from the *miqa* or fireplace on the *Rogovoka*.

When the *Kaunitoni* anchored here, Tuirevurevu's mother came ashore, and he was born and slipped into the sand where he was partially buried. His place is a pool called Nubunimoala, after which a burial ground at Viseisei, Vuda, and the *yavu* or housemound of the present Momo Levu or paramount chief of Vuda are said to be named. No one should remain upright on the island, out of respect to Tui Revurevu who is a spirit held in great awe in the Mamanuca group.

Narokorokoyawa is also of particular importance as the ultimate place to which spirits of the dead from many places in Fiji are said to go. The name is the same as that of villages in Sabeto and in the middle of Viti Levu, all connected through the myth of a person who journeyed from place to place, starting from the island.

So the island is spiritually significant, first, as the initial place visited by canoes with original spirits and mythical progenitors of many descent groups throughout Fiji, and secondly as the last place visited by the spirits of the dead. From this originates its name of Narokorokoyawa or 'The Place of Reverencing from Afar'.

If a vessel from Nadroga or Yasawa wants to visit the island, it should go first to the rocky islet of Yavuriba where spiritual sentinels are stationed. It waits here and the crew *tama* or respectfully call out to Narokorokoyawa. If the reply is favourable, the vessel proceeds to Narokorokoyawa.

If a person wishes to go fishing in the area or wants a boat of the enemy to capsize, he should first make an *isevusevu* or formal presentation of *yaqona* to Tuirevurevu at the *mata ni sava*.

Also on the island are *yalewa wedewede* or sirens known as Na Yalewa Sekula who try to seduce fishermen.

My first opportunity to visit the island was in 1954 when I was in the area as District Officer looking for shipwrecked victims and small craft reported missing after a hurricane. I was warned that if I should ever go ashore at Narokorokoyawa, I must keep my head lowered out of respect for Tuirevurevu, the spiritual caretaker of the island. Following this warning, I was most careful to keep my head down, and I covered most of the island without incident. Maybe I was getting a neck ache or just becoming sceptical, but I then raised my head and walked straight into a hornet nest.

In 2004, I had an opportunity to return to the island, remembering only too well my first painful visit. After *yaqona* or *kava* had first been presented to Tuirevurevu to seek his permission, my wife and I went ashore where the sandy beach was overlooked by a large rock. Here was the present *mata ni sava* or site where offerings or *isevu* of *yaqona* are now made to Tuirevurevu, asking for his permission to visit the island or seeking his assistance in any particular venture. The site comprises two parallel lines of stones, starting from two terminal monoliths of beach sandstone and leading to a dolmen-like structure with a capstone of sandstone resting on clamshells, and a wooden 'roof' on which clam shells and a large trochus shell had been placed. Our offering of *yaqona* lay on the capstone. In the large rock overlooking the *mata ni sava* is Tuirevurevu's rock shelter known as Qwaranitubunitoga.

Proceeding inland across the flat area to the rocky interior, and keeping my head well lowered, I visited a series of rock shelters facing the sea. Some were faced with stone walling which had been constructed on the flat area. These, as well as the beach shelter, appeared to have a considerable depth of sand or soil. In the flat area itself had been constructed a rectangular feature, about ten paces by fifteen paces, comprised of two rows of stones leading in one case, from a terminal monolith, to a length of low free-stone stone walling. The opposite side of the rectangle was delineated by a row of scattered stones. This was probably the old *mata ni sava* before the construction of the one on the beach. A few sherds of typically late period Fijian pottery and a white *ovulum*-type shell with side-piercing were found on the surface. Time constraints, alas, prevented further exploration of the island, but I was fortunate to have had this opportunity to revisit the island, a visit from which this time I escaped unscathed.

I believe that this little group of islets, the Mamanuca i ra and especially Narokorokoyawa, are indeed an ethnology-inclined archaeologist's dream. A fascinating project awaits someone who is prepared to locate and survey the sites and to record the myths and oral history associated with this group, and to relate them to those of the neighbouring small islands and the mainland of Viti Levu, whither the two canoes are said to have sailed after leaving Narokorokoyawa. Formal permission for such a project would have to be sought not only from the Fiji Museum authorities but, naturally, from the iTaukei Motu, the chief of the area which includes the group. He lives on the island of Yanuya. Either he or the *bete* or priest, if there is one, or whoever is regarded as the expert on the traditions of the islands should be invited to accompany the researchers, and to help locate the sites and explain the myths and traditions associated with them. Excavation in the rock shelters, if permitted, could be very worth-while, especially as Lapita pottery has recently been found on Waya, to the north of the group.

14

Conclusion

In order to assist in my investigations of the origins and development of various polities in pre-Colonial times, current oral accounts were recorded in the course of discussions with representatives of all the polities in my three study areas comprising Rakiraki in north-eastern Viti Levu; Nadi/Nawaka/Vuda in Western Viti Levu; and the western archipelago of the Yasawa Group. For comparative purposes, the project took into account polities in areas other than the study areas. In the course of the project a record was made of the current oral accounts of Fijian myths, traditions, histories and symbols associated with eighty-seven *yavusa* in the Nadi/Nawaka/Vuda and Yasawa areas, and with thirty-six *yavusa* in the Rakiraki area. These accounts were recorded by me, first as District Officer in the areas in the early 1950s (see Preface), and later as a researcher at The Australian National University in the 1990s. These were all the *yavusa* currently recognised in my areas.

Common features and themes for polities

The term 'polity' refers to both *yavusa*, or descent groups, and socio-political constructs or federations, such as *vanua*. An analysis of the current oral accounts recorded indicated how the Fijians with whom the matter was discussed understand and explain:

- the origins, structure and dynamics of polities in pre-Colonial times;
- the basis of pre-Colonial socio-political and military leadership;
- pre-Colonial intra- and inter-*yavusa* relationships; and
- the internal and external influences that brought about and affected such relationships.

From these accounts and from accounts of polities in other parts of Fiji, features and themes emerged as common to the pre-Colonial polities studied. These accounts indicate that:

(a)   each *yavusa* had myths of origin and ancestral spirits;

(b)   each *yavusa* exhibited certain symbols of group unity and identification;

(c)   each *yavusa* had a pattern of social hierarchy and a recognised basis for leadership;

(d)   a number of *yavusa* often joined together and formed a socio-political federation referred to as a *vanua*;

(e)   a number of *vanua* sometimes joined together and formed a socio-political confederation referred to as a *matanitū*;

(f)   there were patterns of linkage and bonding between polities at all levels;

(g)   there were recognised channels of communication between certain polities at *yavusa or vanua* level; and

(h)   the spirit world of ancestral and other spirits, such as war spirits and defending spirits, was important in:

    (i)   achieving and maintaining unity and 'proper behaviour',

(ii)   validating group activities and appointments to chiefly office of leadership, and

(iii)   maintaining some degree of stability in a society faced with outside influences from Tonga, Christianity, and European visitors and settlers.

Common themes

Two common themes emerging from the accounts of pre-Colonial polities in the study areas were the following contrasting sets of ideologies and realities:

(a)

(i)   the ideology of social unity and integrity, and

(ii)   the realities of social fusion and fission; and

(b)

(i)   the ideology of allocation of power based on the concept of inherited *mana* or spiritual   power, and

(ii)   the realities of achieved secular power, leadership disputes and external leadership, based on the war club and the spear.

A key focus of the research has been to assess the linking of and synthesis between these two contrasting sets of ideologies and realities.

Social unity, fusion and fission

The current oral accounts may reflect an ideology of social unity and integrity at the *yavusa* level, but they also indicate how a *yavusa* was seen to develop not only on the basis of natural increase but also on the realities of social fusion and fission. The latter occurred not only internally through factors of ambition and jealousy, but also on the development of good and bad relationships with other polities.

Current accounts of the past are also important to a *yavusa* as symbols of its unity and identification. They recount its supposed victories and successes that are a matter of pride, and its supposed defeats. The victories and successes are recounted in order to explain how a *yavusa* became the paramount of a polity consisting of a number of *yavusa,* either by defeating its neighbours or by associating with weaker *yavusa* which came to it for protection or by forming military alliances with other *yavusa*. The defeats could have been included as an explanation for the *yavusa*'s formal association with the strong, respected polity that defeated it and brought it under its authority. Currently the *yavusa* may well take pride in this association, however it may have developed in reality. In this way, the accounts can turn successes and defeats to the advantage of a *yavusa* in its position in current Fijian society.

Spiritual and secular power

The current accounts also indicate an underlying ideology of allocation of power based on the concept of maximum *mana* inherited through the most direct male line of descent from the original ancestral spirit. They also indicate how leadership may have been based not only on inherited *mana* and descent but also on the realities of internal leadership changes or disputes, as well as the acceptance (forced or voluntary) of external leaders.

Such themes are relevant to the understanding of Fijian society past and present, and also, to a limited extent, to an exploration of Fijian society in the wider context of neighbouring Tonga, Rotuma and even Samoa as forming a quadrilateral interaction zone in late prehistoric and proto-historic times. There is archaeological evidence of such interaction before the period covered by this monograph. In Chapter 2, the forms of structure and leadership of Fijian polities were considered synchronically and diachronically in the general perspective of neighbouring Oceanic polities. The study was placed in the context of an overview of relevant literature relating to Fijian polities, places and spirits.

Factors affecting variation in polities

An analysis of available evidence based on current accounts has indicated that during the earliest periods to which these accounts relate, the simplest form of polity, the independent *yavusa*, or descent group, was, generally, the earliest form of polity recognised in these accounts. More complex forms of polity, such as *vanua* based on a federation of *yavusa*, were usually a later development. However polities developed in the pre-Colonial period, they retained certain common features and themes as already described.

Whether or not there had ever been a golden age of homogeneity, an analysis of current Fijian understandings of the structure and dynamics of pre-Colonial polities indicates a considerable variation in the degree of complexity of these polities. Variation was manifested in such factors as socio-political unity, and structure and dynamics, including leadership, especially as socio-political federations developed, at any rate towards the end of the pre-Colonial period. An analysis of the factors affecting the variation between polities can be undertaken from the point of view as to whether they were internal or external to the system of polities being studied. Internal factors are those which can be considered within the parameters of the three elements of the ideological concept of *vanua;* that is, people, places and spirits. This ideological concept of *vanua* permeated all forms of polity, including the *yavusa*, or descent group, and such socio-political constructs or federations referred to as *vanua* or *matanitū*.

Internal factors

People and places

Variations in pre-Colonial socio-political unity and structure, in fusion and fission, and in federation and confederation, may have been due in part to internal factors, such as ease of geographical access between polities, availability of planting land in the areas involved, insults and quarrels, and ambitious and able leaders with military and naval powers, such as Cakobau.

Spirits

Another significant factor affecting the variations in the unity, structure and dynamics of polities is the extent to which they were connected with important centres of the spirit world, often based on dramatic natural features. For instance, the settlements of the various *yavusa* of the polities in the Rakiraki area lay just below the glowering Nakauvadra range and one of the most respected of Fijian spirit centres on the peak of Uluda. Those of the various *yavusa* of the polities in the Vuda area were adjacent to the spirit path along the dramatic Tualeita Range and a most respected spirit centre based on caves at Edronu at the west end of the Range. Uluda was associated with the spirit Degei and the other spirits who settled there with him and later spread throughout Fiji as progenitors of many *yavusa*. Edronu was associated with the first mythical arrivals in Fiji, many of whom went on and settled on the Nakauvadra range. The Rakiraki and Vuda *yavusa* had close traditional connections with these places. They gained considerable spiritual and political prestige from their close association with these spirit centres and from their spiritual connections with other *yavusa* whose progenitors had spread from these centres to other parts of Fiji.

External factors

Variation between polities may also have been due to factors external to the polities being studied, such as:

- the influences of Tongan ideologies of paramountcy and eventual monarchy on ambitious and able Fijian chiefs, especially Cakobau of Bau. They were fully aware of Tongan monarchical ambitions as reflected in the patterns of political, military and religious rivalries between the leaders of the three major groups in Tonga during the early 19th century. These culminated in the uniting of Tonga under King George Taufa'ahau in 1845. He became Tupou I, the first King of Tonga. There had been for many years considerable social intercourse between Bauan chiefs and Tongans, and Cakobau aspired to follow the example of Taufa'ahau in Tonga, and achieve the position of monarch in Fiji;

- Tongan expansionist ambitions in Fiji, culminating with the arrival of Ma'afu in 1848;

- the introduction of Christianity, accelerated through the arrival of the first European Wesleyan missionaries in 1835, and Roman Catholics in 1844;

- the demands of European settlers for land and security to conduct their agricultural and trading activities, culminating in their meaningless crowning of Cakobau as King of Bau, in 1867, and their proclamation of him as King of Fiji, in 1871, in the hope that he would protect their interests; and

- the need for the Cakobau Government launched by certain Europeans at Levuka in 1871, to assert its authority on a pan-Fijian basis, especially in the independent west.

West-east continuum of varieties of polities

Immediately preceding Cession in 1874 the polities in the Yasawa Group, the west and north-east of Viti Levu, and eastern Fiji, especially Bau, Rewa and Cakaudrove, had developed with different degrees of socio-political complexity and internal stability, of which the simplest were generally in the west and the most complex and stable were in the east.

The simplest polity was an independent *yavusa,* a group which claimed descent from a single original ancestral spirit and which maintained its internal unity and its independence from any external authority.

The most complex form of major polity was a stable *matanitū* or confederation of several *vanua,* or federations of *yavusa,* with a leading *yavusa* and a recognised paramount chief. Such a confederation included a number of *bati* or military allies, and of *qali* or tributaries, being minor federations of *yavusa* (or *vanua),* or of single *yavusa,* which might have been conquered or have sought protection from hostile neighbours or have simply recognised the socio-political advantages of a formal association with a strong and respected leading group and a powerful and generous paramount chief.

In between these extremes, analysis showed that there were forms which manifested varying quantitative degrees of federation of *yavusa* or parts of *yavusa* or of groups of *yavusa,* experiencing varying qualitative degrees of stability.

The monograph has considered the extent to which such differences can be explained historically or whether oral accounts as now recorded are driven by current concerns for prestige or by more mundane issues such as access to a higher share of money derived from rents of native land or of money derived from tourism. The key factors in the emergence of differences between polities as they developed were:

(a)   local ambitions and quarrels within the *yavusa,* leading to fission and fusion with other *yavusa* or to the establishment of a separate *yavusa;*

(b)   recognition by a *yavusa* that another *yavusa* was particularly strong and worthy of respect and subservience;

(c)   regional pressures from other *yavusa* with ambitious leaders wishing to expand their sphere of influence through the development of socio-political relationships or through warfare;

(d)   external pressures from expansionist Tongans in Fiji, Christianity and the missionaries, Cakobau, the European-crowned King, and later the Cakobau Government established with the connivance of some European settlers;

(e)   the ideology of Tongan authority and eventual monarchy, of which ambitious Eastern chiefs especially of Bau, had had first hand experience during visits to Tonga;

(f)   proximity to spiritual central places such as the Nakauvadra or Edronu, and the interplay between the spiritual unifying force derived from a common place of origin of ancestral spirits, and the secular sense of security derived from association with a strong and protective paramount;

(g)   the degree of availability and loyalty of allied military and naval forces which could enable an ambitious leader to expand his traditional sphere of influence and to maintain his position of paramountcy in the face of internal dissidents and external hostility; and

(h)   the realities of *kaukauwa or* secular power as symbolised by the war club and the spear, and the ideology of *mana* or spiritual power as a legitimising force.

As far as the east is concerned, the most important and significant factors in the dynamics of polities were the highly ambitious and remarkably able chiefs, the external influences of Tongan ideology of paramountcy, Tongan military power and expansion ambitions, and the acceptance of Christianity (partly in return for Tongan military assistance).

As far as the central regions are concerned, the most important factors were:

- the proximity to the main spiritual centre of the Nakauvadra as a unifying force;
- warfare to the south of Nakauvadra resulting in people being forced over the range to take refuge with the polities on the north side; and
- quarrels between ambitious leaders who gathered people together to assist them in their warfare.

As far as the west and the islands are concerned, the polities were noteworthy for the spirit of independence and local pride that prevailed, especially as regards the east. This spirit was symbolised by the myths of origin of several groups which relate not to the Nakauvadra but to the central spirit place at Edronu near the traditional first landing, where those who did not go on up to the Nakauvadra remained. Edronu was regarded as more important than the Nakauvadra because it was an earlier and therefore more respected site. The factors listed had a minimum effect on the west, until the time of Cakobau and the forced introduction of Christianity, which was regarded as a device of Cakobau and of the eastern polities. These outside influences were regarded with grave suspicion in the west, as likely to affect their independence, except perhaps in those areas in Vuda which regarded themselves as having become Christian before the east.

This monograph is particularly concerned with this variation between polities following a general geographical pattern. This pattern represents a broad continuum of polities of differing degrees of complexity, with the simplest in the western areas of Fiji, and the most complex in the east. Previous studies (Schütz 1962; Pawley and Sayaba 1971; and Geraghty 1983a, 1983b) have contrasted the east and the west in terms of linguistics and mutual intelligibility of communalects. They have indicated a broad dichotomy between an eastern group of communalects and a western group, whilst pointing out that within each group there is a chain of communalects of differing degrees of mutual intelligibility. No explanation has been put forward which accounts satisfactorily for the dichotomy between the linguistic groups or the continuum of communalects within each group. This study puts forward an explanation for a pan-Fiji continuum of differing degrees of complexity and stability of polities taking into account the various internal and external factors as well as the patterning of communalects.

Such factors variably affected different polities at different times, depending on local circumstances which were liable to vary from time to time. Such differences could sometimes be explained by recourse to the current oral accounts. Other differences, especially those involving outside pressures from Tonga, could be explained by recourse to sources other than the current accounts and also by taking into account the proximity of the polity to the source of the pressure.

Appendix A

Details of the four main matanitū referred to in Chapter 7

Appendix A (i) The *matanitū* of Bau: *Lei, ko Bau na Yanuyanu*

Material for this account of the development and structure of the *matanitū* of Bau is taken from the Native Lands Commission (NLC) records; Deve Toganivalu's (n.d.) early 20th century 'History of Bau'; and my own enquiries when I was Deputy Secretary of Fijian Affairs, and when, on behalf of the Fiji Museum, I was carrying out excavations on Bau in the main spirit mound of Navatanitawake (Parke n.d.- b, 1993, 1998).

The present leading polity of Bau is the registered *yavusa* of Kubuna. Kubuna had its origins in three groups, two of which originated at Verata, which was described by Sayes (1984:8) as 'the most important power centre in this area prior to Bau'; and one from the Nakauvadra range, an important spiritual centre associated with so many of the myths of origin of Fijian society. This is explained in the following account:

> The first of these groups, the Vusa Ratu, came from Verata. This group travelled to Ovalau and Moturiki before settling at Kubuna, a place on the mainland of Viti Levu opposite to the island of Bau. Their leader held the title of RokoTui Bau.

> Another group also came from Verata and travelled to Moala and Totoya. Some went on to Tonga and then returned to Moala and Verata. From here some went to Nayau on the Wainibuka river, and thence to Viria and finally to Kaba where they became known as the Tui Kaba. Their leader had the title of Tui Kaba, using a version of the Tongan title of Tu'i. They moved to Oveya opposite to Bau, where they met up with a group from Nakauvadra whose leader was the Vunivalu. They joined together under a paramount leader, with the complex title of Vunivalu Tui Kaba.

Although there are other oral accounts of the origins and development of the Kubuna, this is the account which is generally accepted by the Kubuna themselves. Marshall Sahlins, who has carried out considerable research into the history of Bau told me that he was aware of several versions of the origins of Kubuna but he was not prepared to give credence to any one particular account (personal communication). I agree that there is really no evidence except that of oral tradition to account for those wanderings which are said to have resulted in the Kubuna. Archaeology is not helpful in this case. For present purposes, the account which gives the details of the origins and meanderings of the protagonists is not important. Although the details of accounts may differ, all traditions of origin agree that the Kubuna are of mixed origin. On the other hand, it is the details of the following account of the development of the groups of the *matanitū* of Bau that are more important from my point of view, and Sahlins, to whom I showed it, regarded this as a reasonable and generally acceptable version of the fortunes of Kubuna and Bau. The account goes as follows:

> At the time that the Vusa Ratu were living at Kubuna on the mainland, the fisherfolk of the offshore islet now known as Bau were subservient to the Vusa Ratu. The islet was then known as Korolevu, according to NLC records; or perhaps Ulu ni Vuaka (Pig's Head), according to Waterhouse (1866), a mid-19th century missionary in Fiji. On one occasion, however, the fisherfolk were derelict in their duties and refused to send, as tribute to Kubuna, a *sakula* (a large deep-sea fish) that they had caught. This angered

the Kubuna, and the fisherfolk fled, fearing that they would be killed. The Butoni went to the island of Koro in Lomaiviti, where they are still living in the village of Namuca. The Levuka fled to Tui Nayau at Lakeba and then settled in Levuka, Ovalau, where they still live. Both groups still retain their connections with Bau. The Butoni have responsibilities in the installation of the Vunivalu who is now paramount of Kubuna. The Levuka have responsibilities connected with the installation of the Adi Levuka, the wife of the Vunivalu. After the incident over the *sakula*, the Vusa Ratu together with the Vunivalu and Tui Kaba groups decided to move to the islet and establish a power base from which to expand politically. These three groups decided to join and form one group, the Kubuna, named after the mainland settlement of the Vusa Ratu. They re-named the islet Bau after a *yavu* or mound at Ucunivanua, Verata. This was the mound associated with Vueti, who according to myth was the original ancestral spirit of both the Verata people and the Kubuna people.

Lest it be thought that this account of the origin of the name of Bau is an *ex post facto* reconstruction, a more likely explanation is that the Kubuna people were following a common practice when moving to a new place. Not only the name, but also the general pattern of the new village, was based on that of the earlier settlement, and frequently the names of the new *yavu* or housemounds were the same as those of the old mounds. Previously people used to be buried in their *yavu*, and by bringing the names of the *yavu*, the villagers were also bringing symbols of association with the ancestors. Sometimes they brought stones, especially those associated with the ancestors, from the old site to the new. For instance, the Wasavulu people of Labasa, Vanua Levu, brought from their ancestral area on the south side of the mountain range the biggest monolith known to me in Fiji (Parke 1971:265). It would be quite natural for the Kubuna to call their new island home after the name of the mound associated with their original ancestral spirit, especially as a symbol of their connection with venerable and then powerful Verata. The account continues:

> There were then two chiefs, the Roko Tui Bau, who came from the senior *mataqali* of the Vusa Ratu group; and the Vunivalu Tui Kaba, the recognised joint chief of the Vunivalu and the Tui Kaba groups, who came from the Tui Kaba group. When the three groups decided to join together to form the group to be known as Kubuna, the Roko Tui Bau was acknowledged as paramount by the other two groups which were only partial *yavusa* – for instance, they did not have their own *bete* (priest), nor a *matanivanua* (official spokesman/master of ceremony). The *bete* of the Vusa Ratu who came from the second senior *mataqali* of the Vusa Ratu group, became the *bete* for the Kubuna group; and the *matanivanua* of the Vusa Ratu who came from the third senior *mataqali* of the Vusa Ratu group, became the *matanivanua* for the Kubuna group.

So it came about by agreement that the Roko Tui Bau was regarded as the sacred and paramount chief of Kubuna. Whereas the chief of the Tui Kaba and the Vunivalu was acknowledged as the second senior chief, the secular chief, of the Kubuna. At first, Kubuna's territory of influence was restricted to the islet of Bau and a modest area of land on the mainland (the *tailevu*) of Viti Levu. This territory lay between the powerful and longer-established polities of Verata and of Burebasaga (Rewa).

Kubuna had established itself firmly on the islet of Bau. The stage was now set for the ambitious chiefs of Kubuna to expand their sphere of socio-political influence over their neighbours by marriage, by alliance for mutual convenience, by offering protection or by war – acting with the assistance of their associated spirits, of whom the most important were known as Ratu Mai Bulu and Cagawalu. In expanding their spheres of influence or imposing their powers of leadership, they had to beware lest they show undue arrogance. They also had to beware of the jealousies of rival relations, exercised either physically by assassination, or spiritually through *draunikau* or witchcraft. These sorts of general factors are relevant to the consideration of the development of any of the major polities. The account continues:

Typical of these early diplomatic marriages was that between Ratu Raiwalui, the Roko Tui Bau and Adi Salauca, a high-born woman of Cakaudrove. Later a canoe from Rewa which was going to Verata for a woman who was to marry a chief of Rewa, sheltered off Bau. The Rewans were invited to come ashore and take a Bau woman instead. So it came about that there was a marriage between a lady of Bau and a chief of Rewa, and in exchange the Rewans sent a woman of Rewa to Bau.

Archaeological evidence can be integrated with that of the oral accounts. When Banuve was the secular chief of Kubuna (traditionally towards the end of the 18th century), Bau islet was increased by reclamation; and from this time, canoe docks were built. Further, the population of Bau increased when fishermen from the island of Beqa (part of the Rewa federation), and craftsmen from Soso, Kadavu (also allied to Rewa) who had been brought over to assist in the developments of Bau, were settled there in the villages of Lasakau and Soso respectively. Indeed, as the improvements to Bau were carried out, so the prestige of the secular chief, the Vunivalu, increased. The account continues:

> As his prestige increased, so did the ambitions of the Vunivalu. Matters came to a head when the chiefs of Cakaudrove came to Bau for a *solevu* or ceremonial exchange of gifts. These chiefs had earlier murdered the brother of Adi Salauca, the Cakaudrove wife of the Roko Tui Bau. Her children planned to kill the visitors out of revenge. The Vunivalu's sons heard of the plot and sided with the Cakaudrove chiefs. This led to a violent quarrel between the Vusa Ratu (the Roko Tui Bau's group) and the Tui Kaba (the Vunivalu's group). The Vusa Ratu fled, but were pursued by the Vunivalu, and the Roko Tui Bau was killed. As a result of this tour de force and the political ambitions of a more junior chief, the paramountcy of Kubuna was transferred from the sacred chief, the Roko Tui Bau, to the secular chief the Vunivalu.

Symbolic evidence for such a transfer of paramount power comes from two sources, archaeological and ceremonial. One of the main structures on Bau was the spirit house of Navatanitawake. At first this was the spirit house of the Kubuna's sacred ancestral spirit, Ratu mai Bulu. When the paramountcy was transferred to the Vunivalu, Navatanitawake was increased in size and magnificence, and became the spirit house of Cagawalu, the secular war-spirit. Archaeological investigations into Navatanitawake showed that the mound was indeed built in two phases. Further, this transfer of power was symbolised through the *yaqona* or kava-drinking ceremony which had earlier been a method of communication between the *bete* or priest on behalf of the sacred paramount and the spirit, Ratu mai Bulu, but which then became a socio-political ceremony aimed at proclaiming and maintaining the person holding the secular title of Vunivalu, as the paramount leader of the Kubuna group. The account continues:

> In this case, the leader of a polity, the Kubuna, was deposed and replaced by a strong and ambitious leader from a group other than the traditional dynasty of sacred leaders. His power base was dependent not only on his secular strength but also on his spiritual power flowing from the war-spirit Cagawalu. His leadership continued to be acceptable. In another case, the Vunivalu, Ratu Naulivou, showed himself to be tyrannical towards the Kubuna, and some conspired to kill him. The plot was discovered, and the conspirators fled to Verata, a centre of power and so already a target of the Vunivalu's ambitions. As a haven for the conspirators, Verata now became a target of the Vunivalu's wrath. This led to war between the two polities.

It is important to note that the early development of Kubuna was indeed characterised and influenced by almost incessant warfare waged between this polity and one or other of the neighbouring federations of Verata and Burebasaga. When it was observed that Bau and Verata were about to indulge in warfare, a number of independent chiefs and of towns allied to Bau joined Verata. This was presumably because they considered that it was safer from their own point of view to support the polity that in the past had been so powerful. Bau had not yet proved itself in such a contest of strength. The development of a major polity was characterised by an interplay of loyalty and expediency. The account continues:

> Bau then attacked Verata, with the aid of 'the Vunivalu's white man', Charlie Savage. He used his musket to good effect (its novelty value and the noise of its explosions may have been as effective as his shooting) and the Verata warriors panicked and fled. An attack on neighbouring Nakelo, also with the aid of Charlie Savage, was equally effective. Later on, Verata became preoccupied with the outliers of her sphere of influence, especially on the island of Vanua Levu, and came into conflict with Cakaudrove as the increasingly ambitious chiefs of the AiSokula acted to extend their sphere of influence. Kubuna (Bau) took advantage of this situation, and destroyed the supremacy of Verata. In this way, additional territory including the island of Viwa came to be included in Kubuna's sphere of influence. During these campaigns, Burebasaga (Rewa) came to the assistance of Kubuna, because of the so-called *vasu* relationship which had been forged through the chiefly intermarriages to which I referred earlier.

Relations had been generally good between Bau and neighbouring Rewa. This state of affairs had been cemented by judicious intermarriage, ceremonial exchanges and, for instance, the presentation to the Vunivalu by the Roko Tui Dreketi of Rewa of thirty-nine canoes which became the nucleus of the Bau navy. Once, however, Bau had defeated the erstwhile paramount power to the north, Verata, the Bau *matanitū* was now in a strong enough military and political position to devote its expansionist ambitions to facing its greatest rival for power, Rewa. It so happened that during the first part of the 19th century there were signs that the power of Rewa, based on its internal unity and its developed socio-political relationships with its neighbours, was on the wane. The account continues:

> The chiefs of Narusa, the family of the Roko Tui Dreketi, fell out among themselves, and Burebasaga was internally divided. As Burebasaga became divided, so its allies and tributaries became divided in their loyalty. The ambitious Vunivalu of Bau took advantage of this situation, and in the course of a decade, fought and defeated or won over a series of Rewa supporting polities and especially the *bati* or allies of Tokatoka and Nakelo. Nakelo was won over by a promise by the Vunivalu that he would give his sister to the Tui Nakelo in marriage—a promise which was never kept. A bitter and bloody struggle lasted on and off for more than a decade from 1843 to 1855. During this time, Bau could take full advantage of the fleet which ironically Rewa had given to the Vunivalu as a gift of good-will. Finally, Bau burned the Rewa capital and Rewa villages including Noco. The Roko Tui Dreketi was killed, and the power of Rewa was broken. At the same time, the Vunivalu of Bau had overcome his internal problems which had come near to overcoming him, when his warriors defeated the rebels with the help of the Tongans at the battle of Kaba.

Bau in the early 1850s was at the height of its power. With its determined and able leaders, its army and its extensive fleet, Bau had absorbed the Lomaiviti islands which were referred to as *Qali vakaBau* or tributary to Bau. Bau was also disputing with Tongan immigrants the suzerainty over the Lau group. On the northeast coast of Viti Levu, the influence of Bau was felt in the eastern parts of Ra, where the polities of the Gonesau, the Ratu ni Natauya and the Ratu ni Natokea came under her sphere of influence. Bau exercised political influence over the chiefs of AiSokula at Somosomo, Cakaudrove; and they received tribute from the island of Vanua Levu, especially Macuata, from Taveuni and from Northern Lau, although the ties were loose and relationships were unstable. This position was achieved in spite of internal problems and rebellion on Bau due mainly to dissatisfaction on the part of minor chiefs and jealousy between sons of different mothers of the senior chiefs. These internal problems were, however, becoming very serious and threatened the very being of the *matanitū*.

Particularly interesting was the interrelationship between Bau and Tonga. Tonga came close to conquering much of Fiji, and was threatening the paramountcy of Bau. After a semi-threatening diplomatic exchange between Cakobau and the King of Tonga, Cakobau had virtually been ordered by the King of Tonga to accept Christianity in exchange for military assistance against his internal rivals. Indeed Bauans only succeeded in overcoming their internal difficulties when they were forced by circumstance to accept the help of the King of Tonga in exchange for promises to adopt Christianity, and the Tongan and Fijian forces jointly defeated dissidents and rebels at the Battle of Kaba in April 1855. The Tongans eventually ceased their military expansion over Fiji but remained a significant element of the eastern Lau archipelago where they settled. There are still Tongan settlements in Lau, which is in fact closer to Tonga than it is to Viti Levu. The Vunivalu of Bau, by virtue of his defeat of Verata and Rewa and having forced his own house to come to order, now considered his position to be paramount in these areas. Following Cession, the Vunivalu of Bau was regarded, at any rate by the Government, as *primus inter pares* among the paramounts of the three major polities at the time—Bau, Rewa and Cakaudrove.

At the time of Bau's greatest development as a socio-political complex, the major socio-political complex of the *matanitū* could be analysed into what I refer to as the core groups and the periphery. The core groups were based on the islet of Bau itself and included the Kubuna *yavusa*, based on three groups, of which two originated from Nakauvadra and two from Verata. Associated with the Kubuna were the Vunivalu, the war leader who was currently paramount; the Roko Tui Bau or sacred chief; the Masau or personal *matanivanua* of the paramount chief; the Tunitoga or *matanivanua* of the Vusa Ratu generally; the Takala, responsible for maintaining law and order; the Tui Rara, responsible for helping the *matanivanua* to divide up feasts presented to the paramount chief; the Naitaka, who was principal *bete* or priest of the war-spirit, Cagawalu; and the Bouta, who were the personal servants of the paramount chief. The other core groups on Bau were the specialist craftsmen, the Lasakau fishermen (whose duties included the providing of *bakola* or victims for the cannibal ovens) and the Soso craftsmen, who had come originally from Beqa and Kadavu.

The periphery included the specialists such as carpenters and potters, the allies (the *bati*), the tributaries (the *qali*), and the weak and insignificant neighbours sometimes referred to as the *kaisi* or persons of very low rank. The specialists included the *bete* or priests of Daku, the potters of Waikete, the craftsmen of Matainoco, and the canoe maintainers of Kaba. The allies (the *bati*) included the Namata and Namuka (to the north), the Dravuni just opposite on the mainland, and the Navuloa at the base of the Kaba peninsula. They also included the Viwa islanders under Tui Viwa, the Waimaro under Tui Waimaro, and the eastern Ra groups known as the Gonesau, the Natauya and the Nasese. These *bati* were groups who would come to the help of Kubuna in times of war, provided that they were properly treated with appropriate presentations in order to retain their alliance. If not, they were liable to change their alliance to a chief who would pay them proper respect for their services. The tributaries or *qali* included those people of Lomaiviti who were referred go as the Qali vakaBau, the people of Macuata, the people of Lau, and the people of Cakaudrove. These were people of significance in their own immediate neighbourhood who either sought protection by Bau from ambitious nearby major polities, or who had been conquered by Bau. In exchange for such protection or in recognition of being conquered, these people were required to provide tribute regularly to the Vunivalu of Bau. If they failed to do so, they were liable to suffer retribution at the hands of the warriors of Bau. The tributaries of Cautata and Daku had a special relationship with Bau. Renowned for their loyalty, they provided both military assistance by way of large and strong warriors and also spiritual assistance by way of powerful and respected *bete*. Finally there were the *kaisi*, neighbours who were people of little account. They had been forced, as groups who were very weak, to come under the protection of Bau and rely on Bau for their very survival, or they had been conquered by Bau and perhaps rendered landless. They included the Buretu, the Namena and the Kaba people. The *kaisi* were subservient to the will of the Vunivalu in whatever menial task he might impose on them. Indeed they could well provide for the basic needs of the cannibal ovens, if the fruits of war or of the hunting expeditions of the Lasakau people were not forthcoming.

The overwhelming of the Verata *matanitū*, the killing of the Roko Tui Dreketi and the collapse of the Rewa *matanitū*, and the defeat of the Bauan rebels at the battle at Kaba, resulted in the *matanitū* of Bau attaining a position of paramountcy, at any rate in the areas described earlier. What happened next illustrates what I have found to be a characteristic of Fijian polities. This is the potential element of instability that can be activated by internal jealousy or external ambition even in what appears to be the most stable of Fijian polities, be it a descent group or a socio-political construct. I emphasise this point because the nub of my study of the structure and development of Fijian society may be interpreted narrowly as assuming that development refers to an increase in complexity of a polity. Development can however be interpreted more widely to refer to any change in the structure of a polity, including the fragmentation of the unity of the component building blocks. A development within this wider meaning is what happened in the case of Bau and a description and analysis of the salient points of what happened is therefore relevant to any study of the structure and development of Fijian society, as being illustrative of the processes and principles at work.

In considering the development of Bau in this wider sense, it is necessary to realise that for some time fresh winds of external influence had been blowing over the islands of Fiji, especially in the Natu i Cake (the Eastern Parts)—particularly through visits and, later, settlement by Samoans, Tongans and Europeans including Christian missionaries. This led to the realisation by Fijians that Fiji, for better or worse, had a position in a much wider world than its interaction zone of Tonga and Samoa (and, though perhaps to a lesser extent, Rotuma and Uvea/Futuna). Traditions and archaeology suggest that there had been interaction between Fiji and Tonga for perhaps a thousand years. By the 1840s, there were said to have been about 1000 Tongans in Fiji, ambitious to spread Tongan influence beyond their immediate settlements in the Lau group. This they proceeded to do under the guise of 'spreading the true religion'. The Tongan Church militant fell upon parts of Lomaiviti, Vanua Levu and Kadavu, under the leadership of, at first, Lausike of the Ulukalala house of Tonga. Later Siaosi Taufa'ahau of the rival house of Tu'i Kanakopolu, who became King George I of Tonga, appointed Ma'afu'atuitoga to be governor of the Tongans in Fiji. Ma'afu consolidated his position in Fiji, and continued to spread the influence of Tonga, together with the teachings of Christianity. He became so strong and powerful that Lau and Cakaudrove tended to associate with him rather than with the Vunivalu of Bau who was relatively far away. The position of Kubuna was being gradually but forcibly undermined by the Tongans, and Cakobau, as Vunivalu, realised this.

On the other hand, some European settlers with an eye to their own ambitions and fortunes tried to convince Cakobau that he had paramount powers over all the polities of the islands of Fiji and that he qualified for the spurious title of Tui Viti. This they followed up with a coronation at which he was crowned King of Fiji, Cakobau Rex. In symbolic recognition of this new royal status, postage stamps were issued bearing his head together with the letters CR. There were, however, insufficient traditional grounds to validate such a position, because Fiji, unlike Tonga, had never been a socio-political unity. Not all Europeans could see the advantage of a king who was unable to solve their problems, including ones involving murder or landholdings which arose in relation to their Fijian neighbours. With the spread of the influence of the Tongans over Fijians hitherto allied to Bau and the growing realisation that Bau was not as omnipotent as was once thought, chiefs of other polities challenged the position of Bau.

All was not well in the lands of Fiji, and some Europeans realised it, and sought the formal protection of the United States or Great Britian. Perhaps influenced by the views of those Europeans whom they relied upon or respected, some powerful chiefs also saw that not all was well. They however realised that the solutions to the problems lay not in the judicious use of clubs (or muskets) or of internal diplomacy as heretofore. A number of chiefs agreed, allegedly willingly and wittingly, to resort to taking a traditional step along quite unfamiliar lines and to heed the authority of a paramount chieftainess across the water. They signed the Deed of Cession, ceding Fiji to Queen Victoria. Only in 1874, at Cession, did Fiji become an administrative unity as a British Crown Colony. In recognition, however, of his conclusive victories over Verata and Rewa, the Vunivalu of Bau and the *matanitū* of Bau were recognised as *primi inter pares* among the chiefs and polities of Fiji. In situations involving seniority among leaders of recognised *matanitū*, the Vunivalu was recognised as the senior chief. For instance, he was presented with the first bowl of *yaqona* at *yaqona* ceremonies, as an outward and visible symbol of such recognition. How much of this situation was due to what was acceptable to the Fijian chiefs as according with traditional processes and principles, and how much was due to the influence of the first substantive Governor, Sir Arthur Gordon, who is often reckoned to have regarded himself as an expert on such matters, is not clear.

Appendix A(ii) The *matanitū* of Rewa: *Se ni Misimisi mai Rewa*

This account of the development and structure of the *matanitū* of Rewa is based mainly on the works of Thomson (1908) and Routledge (1985) as well as my own lengthy discussions with the then Vunivalu of Rewa, Ratu Etuate Namocea, and, after his death, with his knowledgeable and interested daughter, Ro Rejieli.

The present leading polity of Rewa is the registered *yavusa* of Burebasaga, which had close traditional associations with Verata and indeed probably originated from there, as a separate polity, following a political split. The main sphere of influence of Burebasaga was based on the vast Rewa Delta. An account of the origins and development of the groups of the *matanitū* of Burebasaga is that:

> Both Burebasaga and Verata recognised the same original ancestor, Vueti, who came from the Nakauvadra Mountains; and had spirit houses dedicated to the same spirit.

The very name of the *yavusa*, Burebasaga or split spirit-house, may be indicative of its origin from a political split. The name is multi-faceted. It has the social meaning of the overall name for the descent group or *yavusa* comprised of the descendants of the original ancestor, Rokoratu, who came from Verata to the Rewa delta. It has a political meaning as the ceremonial name for the socio-political complex of Rewa, of which the Roko Tui Dreketi, the chief of the Burebasaga, was the paramount. It also has the geographical meaning as the name for the first main settlement of the Burebasaga descent group.

Thomson (1908) recorded the tradition that the first settlers in the delta came from higher up the Rewa River, having been driven down 'by internal commotion among the tribes that inhabited the mountains'. Present tradition does not record who these first settlers were, but there seems to be no doubt that the delta was already inhabited either by these people or others (whose names are recorded and will be discussed later), before the arrival of the ancestors of the Burebasaga chiefs. Indeed Jackson (1853) who lived in the area in the first half of the 19th century indicated that 'the proper Rewa king and chiefs' were still alive, including, so he said, the Vunivalu of Rewa. Routledge (1985) referred to present traditions about the arrival in Rewa of Ro Melanisiga, also known as Rokoratu. He sailed down the coast from Verata in his canoe, the *Namako* (meaning 'the shark'?) and settled at Dreketi. Routledge said that Dreketi was on the south-west coast of the delta, whereas Parry (1977), with whom my own informants agree, indicated that it was on the south-east side. The title of the paramount chief of Rewa is Roko Tui Dreketi, presumably derived from the name of this first settlement and its inhabitants. The Dreketi people had, by John Jackson's time, been relegated to what he described (Jackson 1853) as a position 'of low status and kept for human sacrifices and for food upon any public occasion'.

The early inhabitants of the delta may not always have been so treated. For instance the Vanualevu people who provided a feast at the installation of the son of Rokoratu as Roko Tui Dreketi were referred to as the Qalitabu, the sacred tribe, according to Thomson (1908). They had special responsibilities for the *yaqona* ceremony in later installation ceremonies. Thomson considered that their special status was dependent on their being descended from the same ancestor as the chiefs and perhaps from a senior branch. They lost their right to lead because of some internal disturbances, but they maintained recognition of their previous status by being closely involved in the installation ceremonies. Equally the Vanualevu people may have been earlier inhabitants of the delta, whose position was respected by the newcomers. After their initial stay at Dreketi, the group from Verata moved to the east side of the delta, to their first main settlement, Burebasaga, on the banks of the Rewa river. Here they were surrounded by those subservient to them, as reflected in the settlement pattern. Later they moved to the new site of Rewa and through an application of military force and judicious marriage, Rewa expended its sphere of influence to the island of Beqa, the northern part of the island of Kadavu, and the south coast of Nadroga (south-east Viti Levu).

At the time of its greatest development and expansion, the core groups in the major socio-political complex of Rewa were based at first on the senior settlement of Burebasaga and then at the main settlement of Rewa just south of the Nasali creek. The main settlement is at Lomanikoro, near the junction of the main Rewa River and the Nasali creek. The core groups included the Burebasaga *yavusa*, of which there were two leading families, the Narusa and the Nukunitabua. The holder of the title of Roko Tui Dreketi, the sacred or spiritual chief, was a member of the senior family, the Narusa. The holder of the title of Vunivalu, the secular or temporal chief, was a member of the second most senior family, the Nukunitabua. The supreme power (both the *mana* or spiritual power, and the *kaukaua* or physical power) of the polity was vested in the holders of these two titles. The traditional head was the spiritual chief, the Roko Tui Dreketi. Below these two ruling sub-groups of the Burebasaga *yavusa* were six sub-groups known collectively as the Sauturaga. Their responsibilities and functions were limited to those of leading the army into battle and of providing *matanivanua*. They owed no other service to the chiefs, nor did they provide them with produce. They were the landowners and received rent (*covacaki*) from their tenants. Included among the core groups were three groups known collectively as the Kaso (descendants of junior wives of chiefs or of junior sons of chiefs). The senior of these were the Kai Nalea from whom were appointed the hereditary priests. The next were the Kai Buli, and they had the Kai Nalea as tenants. Reference has already been made to the Kai Vanualevu known as the Qalitabu, who were either descendants of earlier inhabitants of the delta or were members of a junior branch of the descendants of Rokoratu. They played a special role in the installation ceremonies of the Roko Tui Dreketi. Among core groups again were the specialist craftsmen who owed service to the chiefs by exercising their crafts in return for grants of land. These included the fishermen of Nukui and Nasilai, the potters of Vutia, the carpenters of Nadorokavu, and the Tongan sailors of Nabua and Sigatoka. Finally, the Kai Batikeri (a collective name for the Kai Nadoi, and the villagers of Nakuru, Drekena and Veiniu), the Muainasau, the Qalivakawai (a collective name for the those whose lands were in the mangrove swamps, namely the Kai Narocivo, Kai Tavuya and Kai Nateni), and the virtually landless Kai Lokia and Kai Nadoria were also regarded as elements in the core of the Burebasaga polity. The nature of their services and responsibilities was not recorded. These groups were regarded as *vakarorogo,* or owing direct allegiance to Burebasaga, and the settlement pattern of these groups is roughly elliptical with the main settlement of Rewa on the northern focus.

The periphery included those who were tributary (*qali*) to Burebasaga, and those who were allies (*bati*). Among those with a tributary relationship were three *vanua*-level polities of the island of Beqa. These were the *vanua* of Raviravi comprised of four *yavusa* under the paramountcy of the Tui Raviravi: the *vanua* of Sawau comprising three *yavusa* under the paramountcy of the Tui Sawau; and the *vanua* of Rukua comprised of the single *yavusa* of Rukua. These people paid tribute and provided services on demand to the Roko Tui Dreketi, and suffered if they failed to heed the command of the chief. Not all the island was tributary to Rewa, and one small group living at Naceva on the south-west coast heeded the authority of the Vunivalu of Serua whose *matanitū* was based on the islet of Serua off the south coast of Viti Levu to the west of Navua.

Also on the periphery were those groups who were allied (*bati*) to Burebasaga. These included the important *vanua* polities of Tokatoka and Nakelo. Tokatoka had seven associated settlements which formed a more or less equidistant pattern on the levée between the Wainibokasi River and the Nasoata swamps. Except on the south-east where it merged with the lands of the settlement of Burebasaga, Tokatoka had natural boundaries. The leader was originally the Roko Tui Tokatoka; but following later migrations, a Vunivalu was appointed, apparently by Rewa, to take over leadership of Tokatoka, in recognition of its status as *bati* to Rewa. The Vunivalu replaced the Roko Tui Tokatoka as head of the *vanua* and the Roko Tui Tokatoka took the lesser title of Malo Sivi. The *vanua* of Nakelo lay on the north side of the Wainibokasi River. It had twelve settlements, all of which were larger than those of Tokatoka. Its leader held the title of Tui Nakelo. Also regarded as *bati* to Rewa, though subject to Nakelo, were the people of Kuku. They came from an independent polity in the interior of Viti Levu, having been 'forced towards the sea-board through intertribal wars' (Waterhouse 1866:148). These *bati*, as explained, would come to the assistance of the paramount chief on request. They would continue to do so until they considered that they were not properly rewarded for their services, or until they were made greater offers of reward for their services, or until they considered that it was against their own interests and safety not to continue to do so. Then they would not hesitate to change their allegiance to the paramount of the polity against whose warriors they had previously been fighting.

Rewa is of particular interest as a polity which reached its peak not only with demonstrations of strength with the aid of tame Europeans, but also through judicious marriage between the Roko Tui Rewa and the daughter of the Vunivalu of Bau, thus achieving the most vital social link of *vasu.* At any rate in theory the Bauan paramount family could not now refuse any request except for land by the Rewan family. By the 1820s, the Roko Tui Dreketi, Tabaiwalu, had governed firmly and fairly, and Rewa was at its zenith. However, his sons by two women of Bau each strove for power, and this led to a lengthy and bloody struggle, in the course of which Tabaiwalu was murdered. Rewa came then to be ruled by three sons of Tabaiwalu: Banuve, described by Jackson (1853) as 'fat, lazy and rendered effeminate by luxurious living'; Qaraniqio, a fearsome warrior; and Cokonauto, who was well-known to Europeans. There was, under these circumstances of division, envy, and jealousy, little hope of decisive or cohesive action in the face of external threat from an expanding and ambitious Bau. This culminated in the Bau-Rewa war of 1843–1855 and the realisation that Rewa, so divided and at enmity within itself, would have little chance of survival against Bau, once Bau had beaten its rebel elements at the great Battle of Kaba on 7 April 1855 and become solidly unified under the Bau Vunivalu, Ratu Cakobau and his fleet and troops. The case of Rewa is of such interest because it is a study of how a once mighty *matanitū* under a firm and undisputed paramount such as Tabaiwalu could become permanently weakened until *Pax Fijiana* after Cession. Much of this was due to the curse which so often affected Fijian polities —internal rivalries between sons of the paramount spurred on by jealous wives of differing ranks.

Appendix A (iii) The *matanitū* of Cakaudrove: *Na Se ni Makosoi mai Vuna*

Evidence for the development and structure of the *matanitū* of Cakaudrove is taken from the NLC records, from Sayes' investigations and from my own enquiries into individual accounts on and off over a period of two years when I was Commissioner Northern. The origins and development of the *matanitū* of Cakaudrove are described in detail by Sayes (1982, 1984), and my own findings and conclusions generally accord with her description and analysis of Cakaudrove.

The present leading polity of Cakaudrove is the registered *yavusa* of Cakaudrove. Close examination of the account shows that this *yavusa* is not a single descent group in origin but rather is a political construct of several groups who migrated from time to time to the area now known as Cakaudrove. They were held together by political allegiance to the Tui Cakau, the paramount of the *matanitū* of Cakaudrove. The development of these various groups into a recognised *yavusa* is characterised by a series of power takeovers. The ranking of these various groups within the *yavusa* changed from time to time as the result of internal rivalries, although the basic structure of the *yavusa* remained the same. The *matanitū* of Cakaudrove provides an excellent example of the constant changing of the structure of Fijian society. An account of the origins and development of the groups comprising the *matanitū* of Cakaudrove is as follows:

> The earliest known inhabitants of Cakaudrove were the Nakorovou people. They consider themselves to be the original *itaukei*, or owners of the land, and do not (purposely or otherwise) remember if they came originally from elsewhere. A sub-group of the Nakorovou known as the Mataikadavu claim, however, that their original ancestor, Mai Nukusemanu, came from the west. He travelled from Bau to Nakorovou, through Vunilagi to Vunisavisavi on the east bank of the Cakaudrove River on the south coast of Vanua Levu. The Nakorovou accepted the leader of the Mataikadavu to be their leader. He was duly installed as the overall leader of the people living in Cakaudrove, and held the title of Tui Cakaudrove. It is still debatable whether the Mataikadavu were migrants who became accepted as leaders by the possibly autochthonous Nakorovou, or whether they all came together from the west.

> The next to arrive in the area were the Mataikoro people who claimed to come from Tiliva, Bua. This was evidently part of a more general eastern migration from Bua, which included the Wailevu and in due course the AiSokula. The Wailevu remained on the borders of the present provinces of Bua and Cakaudrove, while the Mataikoro headed on east until they came to the west bank of the Cakaudrove River. They settled there on some land which they had obtained, by conquest or subordination, from those already there. Their leader had the title of Vunivalu—a title of significance suggesting eventual connection with Nakauvadra, because descent groups (such as one of the components of the Bauan *yavusa* Kubuna) whose original ancestors can be traced back to these mountains are often associated with the title of Vunivalu. The leader of the Mataikoro became leader of all those who had settled on both sides of the river, including the Nakorovou and Mataikadavu. He became the new paramount of Cakaudrove and was installed with the title of Mai Nakamakama.

To the east of the Mataikoro lands were the Korocau people whose chief was the Ratu of Korocau. They owed allegiance to the Mataikoro people and were responsible for building the house of installation for Mai Nakamakama. Korocau bordered on Natewa, and the Ratu's strength was increased when two Natewa groups known as the Nabuco and Nadaraga people joined with the Korocau as subordinates.

The next group to arrive in Cakaudrove were the AiSokula people who came from Bua and earlier from Rakiraki, Ra. (See the Rakiraki account on the origins of the AiSokula.) On reaching Cakaudrove, the AiSokula settled by the Sawaimosoi swamps up the Wakavu River.

At this time the *matanitū* of Verata was influential in the area, but the Mataikoro people who were becoming increasing powerful and ambitious, were planning a rebellion against Verata's representatives there. The Mataikoro invited the AiSokula for help in this rebellion against Verata's representatives and hence against Verata itself. At this stage, the AiSokula were acknowledged as the leaders of Cakaudrove; and the head of the Mataikoro, titled Mai Nakamakama, lost the leadership of Cakaudrove to Rokevu, the head of the AiSokula. The latter was duly installed as leader of Cakaudrove, and was given the title of Tui Cakau.

Rokevu was installed by the Mai Kavula people whose origin is uncertain. The reference in the name to Kavula suggests some connection with the Gonesau people of Nabukadra, Ra, where Kavula is a place name. They may have arrived at the same time as the more general migration of the Gonesau who came from Nabukadra to Cakaudrove at the direction of their chief, Naboutuiloma.

The Wailevu people to whom reference was made earlier claimed a common origin with the AiSokula and were content to help them as the western borderers of the Cakaudrove sphere of influence. A number had also accompanied the AiSokula to Cakaudrove and they became a *mataqali* in the Cakaudrove *yavusa*.

So it was that oral accounts explained how the structure of the Cakaudrove *yavusa* was developed. The most recent newcomers to the area were accepted as leaders on the basis of their reputation of strength and their assistance in the rebellion against Verata. In the leading chiefly *mataqali* of Vale Levu, the AiSokula were given pride of senior place as the sacred chiefs.

The Nakorovou were the *mataqali sauturaga* (the chief executive officers of the Tui Cakau, and his secular chiefs). The Mataikoro were the *bati* or warriors responsible for the personal safety of the Tui Cakau.

The Mai Kavula who installed the Tui Cakau became the *mataqali mata ni vanua* with the name of Cakaudrove. There were three main *mata ni vanua* for Cakaudrove, namely Mai Kavula (the most senior), Mai Nanukurua (the personal attendants of Tui Cakau), and Mai Nayala (the Tui Rara with ceremonial responsibilities for the division of feasts presented to Tui Cakau). Each was installed at the same time as the Tui Cakau.

Finally, two other *mataqali* were duly included in the *yavusa* of Cakaudrove. These were the Welitoa and the Mataitoga, Samoans and Tongans who were especially welcomed by the Tui Cakau because of their skills as craftsmen and carpenters.

Such outsiders would usually be absorbed into an already existing *mataqali*, but their status as *vulagi* or *kai tani* would be remembered and drawn to their attention if they became too arrogant or spoke about matters which really only concerned the true members of the descent group. The status of the Samoans and the Tongans as members of their own two separate *mataqali* indicates the special regard with which they were held by the Cakaudrove people. The inclusion of these people in the *yavusa* as separate *mataqali* may also reflect the wishful thinking, embodied in an origin myth which is sometimes related, that the AiSokula were really descended from high-born Tongans and not from relatively low-born people of Rakiraki.

So the *yavusa* Cakaudrove came to be composed of the following *mataqali*:

- Vale Levu, of which AiSokula was the senior element;
- Nakorovou;

- Mataikoro;
- Cakaudrove;
- Wailevu;
- Welitoa; and
- Mataitoga.

The cohesion of the *yavusa* Cakaudrove was derived not from common descent from a single recognised original ancestor, but through a close loyal subordination to a common head, the Tui Cakau. The ranking of the *mataqali* reflects not genealogical hierarchy but power seniority. It is also noteworthy that the three main ancestral spirits of the Cakaudrove polity, Natavasara, Koroiruve and Veidole, are associated with early Tui Cakau. Perhaps deliberately, these three are not associated by current myth with the Nakauvadra Mountains of Ra from where so many of the original ancestors of Fijian polities are said by myth to have originated either directly or indirectly. This again may be an attempt to conceal the relatively humble origins of the mighty AiSokula, but it may at the same time be an attempt to equate the status of a dead chief of Cakaudrove with the same status and powers of the culture heroes from those mountains. In course of time, the chiefs of AiSokula split up. Some remained on Vanua Levu and others moved across the straits to the island of Taveuni. By 1820 all the chiefs had moved to Taveuni, leaving some *lewe ni vanua*, or commoners, on Vanua Levu. Most of the commoners, however, accompanied the chiefs to Taveuni, which now became, and remains to this day, the headquarters of the Cakaudrove *matanitū*.

The development of the *yavusa* Cakaudrove shows how the introduction of new groups within the *yavusa* is related to the constant changing of political and military power balances. The change in leadership from the Mataikoro to the newcomers, the AiSokula, at the invitation of the former, should not be seen by the purist proponents of the socio-political model to be an irreverent upsetting of an immemorial principle of leadership based on order of rank. Nor should Cakaudrove's expansionist activities be seen as contrary to recognised, acceptable and time-honoured practices.

At the time when Cakaudrove's sphere of influence was confined to a relatively small area around the Cakaudrove River, the sphere of the *matanitū* of Verata included southern Vanua Levu. This influence waned and indeed ceased following, first, a rebellion by the locals against Malodani, the Verata representative in the area; and secondly, Bau's successful aggression against the Verata homeland, whereby Bau eclipsed the power of the more venerable *matanitū*. Cakaudrove took advantage of this situation to extend its own sphere of influence by filling the local socio-political vacuum that resulted from Verata's withdrawal from southern Vanua Levu. Then Loaloa, son of Rokevu, the first Tui Cakau, was sent to Tunuloa, a strong independent *vanua* in southeast Vanua Levu, to marry the daughter of the chief of Tunuloa. Their son became the chief of Tunuloa and an ally of Cakaudrove through his father's blood. Cakaudrove went on to extend its martial and diplomatic tentacles up to Udu Point at the eastern tip of Vanua Levu, and here came to clash with the northern Vanua Levu *matanitū* of Macuata.

The development of the *matanitū* of Cakaudrove has features that can again be regarded as generally characteristic of the development of major highly complex eastern polities. One feature was the alliance based on judicious marriage. Much of the political power of the *matanitū* of Cakaudrove was based not only on strength of arms but also on alliances brought about by polygamy, involving marriages between the Tui Cakau and daughters of powerful neighbouring chiefs. There were, however, fearful struggles for leadership among the members of the AiSokula family itself, and jealous and ambitious rivals relied for support on their relationships through their mothers with Bau or other powers such as Vuna, at the south end of Taveuni. Jealousy and ambition may indeed have been stirred by the respective mothers wishing to assert their own status in relation to their roots of origin. A Bauan mother would consider herself superior to a Vuna mother, even if the Bauan were the junior wife in order of marriage.

Another feature of the development of polities was the use of *vere*—cunning, plotting or treachery. The expression '*vere vakaBau*', or plotting in Bauan style, is illustrated in the case of Cakaudrove when Cakobau, the Vunivalu of Bau, heeded with concern the ever-increasing expansion and political influence of Cakaudrove. He proceeded to resort to cunning strategies in coming to help Cakaudrove against Natewa, which had earlier revolted against the Tui Cakau. He thereby succeeded indirectly in crippling Cakaudrove, which incurred severe losses at the hands of Natewa in the war of suppression. At the same time he gained an ally in the Cakaudrove heartland at Natewa, which transferred its allegiance from Cakaudrove to Bau.

A third feature of the development of polities as illustrated by the case of Cakaudrove was interaction with other polities to mutual advantage, either by exchange of goods or services. Cakaudrove interacted with the Tongans, who by the beginning of the 19th century had established themselves in the Lau group and were seeking to expand their sphere of influence westwards. Indeed, tradition and increasing archaeological evidence provided by Frost (1974, 1979) and Best (1984) indicate that people had been coming from Tonga to eastern Fiji for perhaps a millennium. Later, Cakaudrove had experience with Tongan craftsmen who came to the area to build canoes because the necessary timber was not available in Tonga. Tongans also came to Taveuni to obtain red feathers, which were then traded to the Samoans for use with their ceremonial attire in exchange for fine mats. Perhaps in exchange for such feathers, Tongan artefacts such as whale tooth figurines and breastplates appeared and were spread around from Cakaudrove, possibly as objects of appreciation for services rendered in times of war.

A fourth feature of the development of polities as illustrated by Cakaudrove was the instability which could be introduced into a powerful polity under a strong paramount, if a relation such as a brother or half-brother himself had ambitions for the paramountcy. Although the Tongans and the Cakaudrove fought against each other, this reflected not only the expansionist ambitions of the Tongans but also leadership struggles between the Tui Cakau and his ambitious younger brother, Ratu Kuila. These struggles ended at the battle of Wairiki in 1862, when the Tongan leader, Wainiqolo, who had supported Ratu Kuila, was killed by Tui Cakau's youngest brother. Peace between the Tongans and the Cakaudrove chiefs was restored, and relations improved within the AiSokula family.

A fifth feature of the development of major eastern polities as illustrated by the case of Cakaudrove was the very respectful relationships that developed between the polity and the Tongans. Samoan and Tongan craftsmen were formally included as an integral part of the Cakaudrove *yavusa* by being given *mataqali* status as the Welitoa and the Mataitoga. Further, a myth duly evolved to the effect that the Tui Cakau was of Tongan origin, implying that Tongan origin was as important a form of legitimisation of leadership and a basis of secular power as was association with the culture heroes of Nakauvadra as a basis for spiritual power.

Appendix A (iv) The *matanitū* of Verata: *All except her sun is set?*

This account of the development and structure of the *matanitū* of Verata relies on Derrick (1950), Sayes' (1982, 1984) investigations and my own enquiries on and off when I was based in Suva, more especially when I was District Officer Ra, and later when I served as Deputy Secretary for Fijian Affairs.

Verata in eastern Viti Levu is described by Sayes as 'the most important power centre in this area prior to Bau'. Verata is of particular interest because of its strong mythical links with the spiritual centre on Nakauvadra range as well as with the polities of Rewa, Cakaudrove and part of Ra. The present leading *yavusa* is the registered *yavusa* Vunivalu, the head of which has the title of Ratu of Verata.

The *matanitū* of Verata provides an excellent example of the origins, expansion and decline of a polity which once had a major highly complex socio-political sphere of influence over a wide geographical area. The decline may have started when Verata over-extended its lines of communication on Vanua Levu and failed to maintain an adequate administrative infrastructure in its outposts there. No polity could afford to do this, especially in the face of the ambitions of powerful neighbours such as the upstart Bau that was determined itself to expand. An account of the origins, expansion and decline of the groups comprising the *matanitū* of Verata is as follows:

> The original ancestor of Verata was known as Rokomoutu. A migration from the Nakauvadra range followed the east coast of Viti Levu to Verata. The origin myths of Verata and of Rewa record that one of Rokomoutu's sons, Vueti, went to Rewa and became the original ancestor of the Rewa chiefly *yavusa*, Burebasaga; and another son, Manumanu ni Valu, went north to the eastern Ra coast and became the original ancestor of the Gonesau people. Rokomoutu's eldest son, Buatavatava, quarrelled with his father and was sent to Vanua Levu. He first went to Setura, in Bua, and then moved on to Nasavusavu Bay.

The first known settlement of Verata, known as Old Verata (Verata Makawa), is at the base of the Ucunivanua peninsula in the present district (*tikina*) of Verata in the province of Tailevu. In the present chiefly village of Ucunivanua at the top of the peninsula, the Wakanivugayali, the roots of the myrtle tree, symbolise the spirit path linking the spiritual centre on the Nakauvadra range in Ra with Verata. The path ends in a cliff, where I was shown what were described as the roots of the mythical *vuga* tree which appeared as markings in the cliff. Such myths of origin symbolise Verata's attempts to validate her claims: first, to a close connection with Nakauvadra, from where came the spirits of origin of so many of the Fijian polities and secondly, to a close paternal (hence superior) connection with Rewa, Vanua Levu and Ra. These myths need not be regarded as historical accounts, nor need Buatavatava be taken as a historical figure but rather as a culture hero symbolising Verata and her expansionist ambitions and activities. He and his companions may represent Verata's expansion to and settlement in Vanua Levu perhaps over an extended period of time. Coupled with these myths of origin are what purport to be historical traditions of how the people of Verata divided up.

> One group went on to Burebasaga in the Rewa delta, and founded the ruling family of Rewa. Another group went to the island of Moturiki in the Lomaiviti group and a third to the Yasayasa Moala, which now form part of the province of Lau. This third group settled first on the island of Totoya and thence spread to the other islands. Of this group, some went on to Nayau in the Lau archipelago and were founders of the Lauan chiefly *yavusa* of Vuanirewa. From here, some went on to Tonga where they settled for a while. They then returned [it is not clear whether some stayed in Tonga, where Fijians had been living for many years] to Viti Levu. Here they joined up with the descendants of the Moturiki group and formed the Bauan chiefly *yavusa* of Kubuna.

These myths and traditions are put forward by people at present in Verata to show how the chiefs of Verata are related to the chiefs of Rewa, Lau and Bau, and had some affiliations with Tonga. The traditional accounts of many of the groups living along the south coast of Vanua Levu claim that these groups are descended from Buatavatava and his companions.

Thomson (1908) commented that before Bau came to power, Verata, Rewa and Cakaudrove seem to have been the only powers that wielded influence beyond their boundaries. Routledge (1985) recorded that Verata possessed some control northwards towards the Ra coast and southwards to the Rewa delta, as my inquiries in the 1950s had shown. It extended its hegemony to the island of Viwa, and the Roko Tui Viwa heeded the authority of the Ratu of Verata. It maintained a tributary network throughout Vanua Levu, where chiefly families, as in Lomaiviti, acknowledge a Verata origin.

> Oral tradition explains how Verata established control over her places of initial contact in Vanua Levu by sending tributary expeditions, and by sending emigrants from Verata and from her spheres of influence in Ra to Vanua Levu in order to found colonies. Because of these traditional ties between Verata and Nakorotubu, Ra, an army under Naboutuiloma, war leader of the Gonesau people of Nakorotubu, went in support of Verata to Vanua Levu to collect tribute and to display the power of Verata. It divided into two parts. One followed the north coast and one followed the south coast. As the army progressed, it left settlers behind or arranged for other settlers to come out to Vanua Levu. Malodani, a chief of Navatu people living on the eastern Ra coast, came out to Natewa Bay in order to settle as Verata's representative and to protect the settlers. Matawalu, another Navatu chief, came out and expanded the Verata sphere of influence by leaving settlers among the local population along the south coast from Natewa Bay to Udu Point, at the east end of Vanua Levu. At its zenith, Verata's area of influence extended east of Vanua Levu to the island of Laucala, whose people claim to be descended from Buatavatava, and to the islands of northern Lau as well as the islands of Naqelelevu and Cikobia which were subject to Laucala.

The traditions of the overseas development of the *matanitū* of Verata provide a good illustration of how an expanding polity with long lines of communication to tributary polities could be organised administratively. Organisation was essential if demands were to be passed down from the paramount to the tributaries and tribute brought eventually to the paramount. My enquiries support Sayes (1984), who recorded that tribute was brought to Verata from Vanua Levu along traditional *sala volivoli* or tribute paths. One path started from Udu Point at the east tip of Vanua Levu and went along the north coast as far as Labasa. Thence it crossed the dividing range to Wailevu. A second path went along the south coast of Vanua Levu also to Wailevu. Labasa and Wailevu were regarded as tribute collecting centres, and tribute was taken eventually to Verata. It is possible that the island of Laucala was also a collecting centre for northern Lau and other islands subject to Laucala.

Verata's power was based on its military strength, spiritually legitimised through Rokomoutu and Vueti and their myths of origin in the Nakauvadra Mountains. It maintained its military expansion through a system of settling people from Verata, as well as its relations in Ra, as colonists with chiefs such as Malodani as representatives. Oral accounts up to this point in time indicate how the *matanitū* of Verata developed into a major polity, of considerable geographical size and of considerable socio-political complexity. Verata's powers, however, then began to decline; and it may have experienced administrative difficulties in maintaining long lines of communication in Vanua Levu that led in part to the weakening of Verata.

> Oral tradition records that there was a successful rebellion by southern Vanua Levu people against Malodani, the Verata representative; and finally Verata's paramount position in Vanua Levu was negated by superior Bauan military power.

> The *matanitū* of Bau and of Cakaudrove proceeded to dominate the areas previously subject to Verata. From time to time Verata tried to reassert itself, but without success. For instance, on one occasion, Bau was preparing to assist its ally Vuna on Taveuni in a struggle with Cakaudrove, because this would have

been an opportunity to reduce the power of Cakaudrove as a potential rival. Verata tried to take advantage of the occasion to attack Bau but was beaten off.

Eventually the power of Verata was so reduced in the politics of Fiji that the Ratu of Verata was not even invited to join the recognised paramounts and sign the Deed of Cession in 1874. By the end of the century Thomson (1908) commented that Verata then controlled less than ten miles of coastline. Nevertheless, Verata is still highly respected as a polity, and hers is by no means a case similar to that of Greece where, as Byron mourned, 'All except her sun is set'.

Appendix B

Details of three intermediate political constructs referred to in Chapter 7

The Navua Delta polities: Korolevu/Dravuni/Nabukebuke

These accounts are based on NLC records, Geddes' (1945) study of Deuba, Parry's (1982) study of ring ditches in the Navua Delta, and my own enquiries as District Officer, Suva/Navua, with an area of responsibility which included the provinces of Namosi and Serua. I visited all the villages at least once and was able to make widespread enquiries

In and around the extensive delta of the Navua River, there were three main polities, each with its associated sphere of influence. The Dravuni polity, of which the paramount chief was the Tui Dravuni, comprised two recognised *yavusa*, the Dravuni and the Deuba. It was based at the mouth of the Navua River. To the west of the Dravuni was the Korolevu or Serua polity based on the offshore islet of Serua, which was the seat of the paramount chief, the Vunivalu of Serua. The Korolevu sphere of influence merged with the Komave people who now form the south-eastern borderers of the province of Nadroga/Navosa, and included the island of Yanuca.

To the east of the Dravuni, and up the Navua River towards the mountainous interior was the Nabukelevu or Namosi polity based at the village of Namosi where I have stayed. The paramount chief of the Namosi polity was the Tui Namosi. Namosi village was, and still is, situated on the other side of the mountain range dividing the headwaters of the Navua/Wainikoroiluva River from those of the Waidina River which flows east into the Rewa River. The district of Namosi borders to the east with the Waimaro people. The Nabukelevu/Namosi sphere of influence extended over the areas now included in the district of Veivatuloa bordering to the east with the Suva people of Rewa; and the district of Wainikoroiluva bordering to the west with the Baravi people of Nadroga and to the north-west with the Navosa people. The Nabukelevu established a military stronghold for the paramount chief, the Tui Namosi, at Delainavua, some three miles up from the mouth of the Navua River, and also at a major settlement on the coast at Veivatuloa.

Appendix B (i) The Dravuni polity

The myths and traditions of the two *yavusa*, Deuba and Dravuni, which comprise the polity of Dravuni, paint a complicated picture of the peopling of the mouth of the Navua River. The Deuba people are said to have been fisherfolk who lived on their boats at the mouth of the river. There are now only two *mataqali* recognised, and only a few members of each were surviving during my time.

> The Dravuni represent a socio-political construct of several groups (now recognised as different *mataqali*) who came down from the interior. Two of those *mataqali*, the Vuanisaqiwa and the Dravuni, claim to be descended from the same original ancestor, Gusuidelana, who came from Nakauvadra. His distinguishing feature, his mouth being at the top of his head, gave rise to his name, 'Mouth on Top'. The original settlement of the ancestors of these two *mataqali* was at Wainivalau, near the present village of Namosi. They then moved down the Navua River to a knoll known as Vakabalea, about 11 km up from the mouth of the Navua River. With them from Wainivalau came the Seniyale who had a different original ancestor and must have been a different descent group when they lived in the interior. However they are

now recognised as a *mataqali* within the *yavusa* of Dravuni. Later they moved on down the Navua River and settled at the mouth of the river. The Deuba fisherfolk joined the Dravuni and settled permanently on land at the site then called Dravuni. Here they were joined by the Nasoki, who had been oppressed by the Namosi and were forced to leave their village of Namelimeli, about five miles east of the present urban area of Navua. The last group to join the Dravuni were the Nasamita who lived near Namosi. Many of them were killed by the Namosi, and because a woman of the Nasamita had married a man of Deuba, the Nasamita were invited to come and settle at Dravuni. Both the Nasoki and the Nasamita were duly recognised as separate *mataqali* of the Dravuni *yavusa*. For some time after this, the Deuba and the Dravuni (then comprised of the five *mataqali*) lived together at the mouth of the Navua River, at peace and intermarrying. The two Deuba *mataqali* continued in their customary role as fishermen, while the Dravuni people were cultivators. It appears that the five Dravuni *mataqali* did not each have separate recognised roles. One, however, was recognised as the *mataqali turaga*, or chiefly *mataqali*, of which the Tui Dravuni was the chief. Two others were known as *mataqali sauturaga*, or *mataqali* of secondary chiefs. One of these was the group for the *mata ni vanua* and the *bete* (the ceremonial officials and the priests). The other provided emissaries to the Korolevu (Serua) chiefs. They all heeded the authority of Tui Dravuni, as paramount of the *vanua* of Dravuni.

Appendix B (ii) The Nabukebuke (Namosi) polity

The myths of origin of the Nabukebuke people claim that:

> The original ancestor of the Nabukebuke people, Veredrau, came from Nakauvadra. He went to Naituvutuvu near Lutu in the district of Matailobau just north of Vunidawa. Here he married Radi ni Waikalotu. They went to the Wainimala River and then followed the Wailase creek to Nabukebuke near Nakorobalavu. Here they established the settlement of Nabukebuke which gave its name to their descendants who formed the chiefly *yavusa* of Namosi, Nabukebuke. Nabukebuke is regarded as the original settlement of the *yavusa*. Veredrau and his wife had nine children; and the names of their *yavu* or housemounds became the names of nine *mataqali* descended from the nine children.

These are the nine *mataqali* which are recognised as comprising the Nabukebuke *yavusa*. Capell and Lester (1941:331) recorded the special roles of the various *mataqali* below that of the chief, the Tui Namosi. They included the roles of *mata ni vanua*, chief's grave diggers; those responsible for putting on the chief's *malo*, or girdle; those responsible for presenting *tabua* at *veibuli*, or installation ceremonies; the chief's personal workers and the so-called 'foundations of the spirit house' who presumably served as priests.

While the descendants of Veredrau were at Nabukebuke, they were attacked by the neighbouring Waimaro people, under their leader the Roko Tui Waimaro. Some of them moved south and were again attacked. They moved on until they came to the site of Namosi where they settled. The Vunivalu of Namosi, Qereqeretabua, quarrelled with his son about some coconuts, and told him to go away to his mother's village. The son went and collected an army, and told his father to vacate Namosi so that he could burn it. It was to be a *buka vakaturaga*, or chiefly burning without bloodshed. His father's supporters scattered down to the south coast, where some settled with the Dravuni people. The rest were recalled by the son, to reconstruct Namosi. At Namosi, there were continual family quarrels about the leadership, and one of the chiefs, Kuruduadua, went south to Navua. Another group went southwest to Korolevu territory in Serua where they were given land at Rewalau. Kuruduadua quarrelled with a brother about a woman, and asked Dravuni for help. Kuruduadua also sent a *tabua* to the Korolevu, requesting their assistance. The Korolevu agreed to come and help, and Kuruduadua's brother with whom he had quarrelled was killed.

The Namosi people were then based at two centres, at Namosi in the mountains, and at Delainavua (a hill, where in my time the Namosi Hotel had been built) near the coast. The Tui Namosi, Kuruduadua, made the knoll at Delainavua into a stronghold on the slopes of which his supporters were settled. Later there was a third centre on the coast at Veivatuloa, where Kuruduadua's son, Ro Matanitobua, went to live. Here he made his headquarters, and here he lived when later he was appointed to be governor of Namosi at the time of the Cakobau government shortly before Cession.

Appendix B (iii) The Korolevu (Serua) polity

Those members of the present polity (including the renowned Dr Ratu Mara who was Vunivalu at the time) were not able to tell me much about the origins of the Korolevu people of Serua, except that their progenitors came down from the interior. Council Paper No. 27 of 1914 recording investigations by the NLC declared that the Korolevu were a fragment of the Noikoro *yavusa* in the heart of the interior of Viti Levu. Brewster (1922) recorded in *Hill Tribes of Fiji* that the land of the Noikoro was 'in the central part of the hill country of western Viti Levu, on the upper reaches of the Wai Levu or Great River, of Sigatoka.'

> Their original ancestor was called Nagoneva, and he was sent forth by Degei on the Nakauvadra. He wandered until he came to Noikoro where he stayed with some people already there, and was made their leader.

> The people of Noikoro were building a house one day, when a stranger appeared. He said that he came originally from an island a considerable distance away in a north-easterly direction and that he had been brought to where he landed on the back of a friendly shark. He was 'a well-favoured young man, with a fair skin, light brown, and not dark like the natives of Tholo in general' [apparently a Tongan]. He was invited to remain in the village and was given the daughter of the chief in marriage.

The Noikoro thus associated themselves with Nakauvadra, thereby claiming a basis for *mana* or spiritual power; and with what is presumed to be Tonga, thereby claiming a basis for *kaukaua* or secular power. From this intriguing beginning a group, which came to be known as the Korolevu after their original settlement, split from the Noikoro; though neither Brewster nor my own informants were able to give any reason as to why they broke away.

> They fought their way down to the coast; and eventually through its prowess in war the group attained its position of political importance in the area of what is now the province of Serua. The paramount of the polity of Serua holds the title of Vunivalu. The Korolevu first settled in the area near the islet of Serua, but they were to be subjected to incessant attacks by their neighbours who resented their intrusion. Living with the Korolevu were a group of people known as the Qaloqalo who accompanied a Dravuni woman marrying a Korolevu chief. The Qaloqalo were formerly part of the Dravuni *yavusa* living at the mouth of the Navua River to the east of Korolevu territory. Eventually the Korolevu sent a Qaloqalo man to the Dravuni, asking if they could settle in Deuba. This was agreed to by the Dravuni, on condition that the Korolevu acted as labourers in their banana plantations; and the Korolevu then moved to Deuba in large numbers.

Appendix B (iv) The Korolevu/Namosi wars

The course of the wars that followed neatly illustrates how independent polities interacted, alternately attacking each other and forming alliances with each other against the third polity. Ambitions waxed and waned, victory alternated with defeat, polities continually got stronger or weaker, and fear from attack by a third group drove previous enemies together. It also illustrates how polities involved in quarrels with their neighbours might seek assistance from polities outside their own immediate sphere of influence but connected to them by bonds of marriage or of some distant relationship, historical or spiritual.

> After the Korolevu moved to Deuba, they willingly met their obligations to their hosts at first. Then they either became resentful at having to labour in the gardens of their hosts, or they had ambitions to dominate the Deuba/Dravuni people. Either they finally became so arrogant and rude, or they became sufficiently strong, that they forced the locals to leave. The Dravuni and some Deuba went east along the coast to Mau, and the rest of the Deuba went to the Rewa island of Beqa and the village of Suvavou on the western edge of Suva city. From Mau, the Dravuni sent a message to the Namosi people with whom they were related, asking for help against the Korolevu. The Tui Namosi came with an army including warriors from Naitasiri, and they mounted a joint attack on Nasasa where the Korolevu were living. The rest of the Korolevu came to the rescue of their co-*yavusa* members, and there was much fighting. The son of the Vunivalu of Serua was killed [and was buried in a cave on the island of Yanuca, where I saw his skeleton lying on a wooden structure]; and the Korolevu left Deuba and their other settlements near Navua, and returned to Serua. The Dravuni/Deuba returned to their villages which had been evacuated by the Korolevu.

> The Dravuni people then presented a big feast with *masi*, *tabua*, and mats to the Tui Namosi at his headquarters at Delainavua, to thank him for his assistance against the Korolevu. Tui Namosi did not then return home to Namosi village but remained at Delainavua. From there he took advantage of his position as their saviour and began to demand tribute each day from the Dravuni. Out of gratitude for the assistance of the Namosi for driving off the arrogant Korolevu, the Dravuni initially supplied land crabs, fish or *dalo* pudding with good grace. However, these demands by the Namosi went on so long and became so excessive that the Dravuni found themselves virtually as slaves (*kaisi*) of the Namosi. Finally the Tui Namosi was demanding not only food but also women and *bokola* (bodies for cannibal feasts). Next to Dravuni and Deuba a village was established called Vunibau.

I was told that Vunibau was known as Tui Namosi's chicken coop, where people were kept against his demands for *bokola*. When wanted, the bodies would be taken to a nearby area now called Naitata, the chopping place, and the pieces would be taken to an area near a stream, now called Naitonitoni, the place where bodies were *toni* or steeped in water, before being taken to Delainavua. The present government station is at Naitonitoni, and in the 1950s, when I stayed there, many who lived there were afraid of the spirits associated with the place. When I revisited the place in 1995, I was told that appropriate ceremonies of exorcism had been performed.

Oppressed by the ever-increasing and increasingly unreasonable demands on the Dravuni by the Tui Namosi, the Dravuni became resentful and determined to drive the Namosi away from the Navua area. As in the earlier case of the Serua people, who asked the Dravuni people for shelter from the oppression of their neighbours, this stage of the wars illustrates how a polity can make a request to a neighbour and so put itself under an obligation when the request is granted. Both situations indicate how a polity under such an obligation would go so far in meeting its obligations but once the obligation went beyond what was seen to be reasonable, that polity would turn hostile. The later situation was then resolved not by diplomacy but by force. Unfortunately for Dravuni, it was not a great military power itself.

> Tui Namosi showed himself to have become so powerful that he threatened to dominate not only the Dravuni but also the Korolevu. The latter were as anxious to overcome the potential dominance of the Tui Namosi as were the former. So when the Dravuni sent a message to the Korolevu to say that they were about to attack the Tui Namosi, and to ask for assistance, the Korolevu told the Dravuni to repair their

village fortifications. When the work was almost complete, a message came from Tui Namosi, demanding the usual tribute. Three times he came and three times the messenger was told that the Dravuni were too busy repairing their pig-fence. Tui Namosi was angry and sent some spies to assess the situation. Three of them were slain and the survivors fled back to Delainavua and reported what the Dravuni were doing. As a token of good faith and a present for the Vunivalu of Serua, the three bodies were sent to Serua. A Korolevu army then came to Dravuni, to assist the Dravuni against the anticipated attack by the infuriated Tui Namosi. When, at the same time, the Namosi people attacked the Korolevu at Serua, the Dravuni sent warriors to help the Serua.

The Tui Namosi attacked the Dravuni at night but was repelled after considerable losses on both sides. Then the Dravuni attacked Delainavua, but they too were driven back. The war continued for a number of years, until the Namosi were ambushed and the son of Kuruduadua was killed together with a large number of Namosi. After this defeat and with pressure from both Dravuni and Korolevu, Tui Namosi and the Namosi army abandoned Delainavua and retreated to the west to Lobau and Veivatuloa, and finally the majority was forced to go back across the mountains to Namosi.

During the latter stages of this tri-partite war, the Dravuni and the Korolevu had been helping each other against the powerful and arrogant Tui Namosi. After the war, the Vunivalu of Serua, Nagagabokola, prepared a *solevu*, or ceremonial exchange of goods and food, to show appreciation to the Dravuni people for their assistance in the war; and the Dravuni did the same for the Korolevu people. Good relations between these two polities were further sealed by intermarriage, and some Korolevu were given land at Vunibau, at the alleged site of the Tui Namosi's former chicken coop near Navua.

War therefore was an integral part of the life of the three polities in the Navua delta, namely Dravuni, Namosi and Serua, with Dravuni situated geographically between the other two. None of them however seems to have been able to accumulate for any length of time sufficient resources such as warriors or goods to enable it to exercise military or diplomatic power over the other two. Success on the part of one polity would be countered by a union of the other two. The two would aim at jointly minimising those effects of the success of the third which might reduce their own status and independence. The short-time conqueror soon found himself more concerned with self-preservation. A state of balance was maintained, and no one polity was able to induce the other two to form a single socio-political complex.

I have described and discussed only one particular situation to show how intermediate polities can develop, interact with other polities, disintegrate and form new polities, but there are many varieties of polity which fall in the socio-political continuum between the extremes of the simple descent group and the stable, highly developed socio-political complex or *matanitū*. What characterises these intermediate polities is instability caused by the fluidity of the federation of component groups or the looseness of the bond between them which may have been created simply in order to meet the needs of a certain situation. Such an ephemeral bond may be broken and the federation may simply break up either when the needs leading to the federation have disappeared, or when a party to the federation decides that it is more beneficial or prestigious to join another polity, or is forced to join another in the face of superior military strength. A federation can also collapse if senior members of the leading polity, especially ambitious and jealous half-brothers, fall to quarrelling over leadership.

This pattern of fusion and fission, which appears frequently in the development and decline in less complex polities such as Dravuni, Namosi and Serua, has parallels in the development and decline in even highly complex major polities such as Rewa and Verata, as I have shown in Appendix A.

My analysis of the stability, development and decline of polities at either end of the socio-political continuum and of those polities which fall between the extremes suggests that the procedures did not involve different kinds of patterns. Rather, it was differences in the geographical size and socio-political complexity of the arena in which fusion and fission occurred that frequently affected the stability of a polity, along with the very different external factors so prominent in Fiji since the early 1800s.

Bibliography

Cited in the text

Anderson, A., S. Bedford, G. Clark, I. Lilley, C. Sand, G. Summerhayes and R. Torrence 2001 'A List of Lapita Sites Containing Dentate-stamped Pottery' in G.R Clark, A.J. Anderson and T. Vunidilo (eds) *The Archaeology of Lapita Dispersal in Oceania*, pp. 1–13, Terra Australis 17, Pandanus Press, Canberra.

Best, S. 1984 Lakeba: A Prehistory of a Fijian island, Unpublished PhD thesis. Department of Anthropology, University of Auckland.

Blust, R. 1987 'Lexical Reconstruction and Semantic Reconstruction: The Case of Austronesian "House" Words', *Diachronica* 4(1/2):79–106.

Brewster, A.B. 1922 *The Hill Tribes of Fiji*, J.B. Lippincott, Philadelphia.

Burns, A. 1960 *A Report of the Commission of Enquiry into the Natural Resources and Population Trends of the Colony of Fiji, 1959*. Report No. 1, Government of Fiji, Suva.

Capell, A. 1941 *A New Fijian Dictionary*, Australasian Medical Publishing Co., Sydney.

Capell, A. and R.H. Lester 1941 'Local Divisions and Movements in Fiji (part 1)', *Oceania* 11:313–341.

Capell, A. and R.H. Lester 1941 'Local Divisions and Movements in Fiji (part 2)', *Oceania* 12:21–48.

Carnarvon. 1875 Despatch from Earl Carnarvon to Sir A.H. Gordon, dated 4 March 1875, 'On the policy to be planned in future Government of Fiji'. Section V, 'Title of Land'.

Churchward, C. M. 1940 *Rotuman Grammar and Dictionary*, Australasian Medical Publishing Co., Sydney.

Clark, G. 2000 Post-Lapita Fiji: Cultural Transformation in the Mid-Sequence. Unpublished PhD thesis, The Australian National University, Canberra.

Clark, G. and A. Anderson 2001 'The Pattern of Lapita Settlement in Fiji', *Archaeology in Oceania* 36(3):77–88.

Derrick, R.A. 1946 *A History of Fiji*, Government Printing and Office, Suva, Fiji.

Derrick, R.A. 1950 *A History of Fiji*, Vol. 1, 2nd ed. Printing and Stationery Department, Suva, Fiji.

Derrick, R.A. 1951 *The Fiji Islands, A Geographic Handbook*, (2nd revised edition, 1965), Government Press, Suva.

Fiji Legislative Council, 1907–1970 Legislative Council Debates, 1917:176, Government Press, Fiji, Suva.

Fiji Legislative Council, 1949 Council Paper, No. 29, Government Press, Suva.

France, P. 1966 'The Kaunitoni Migration: Notes on the Genesis of a Fijian Tradition', *Journal of Pacific History* 1:107–113.

France, P. 1969 *The Charter of the Land: Custom and Colonization in Fiji*, Oxford University Press, Melbourne.

Frost, E.L. 1974 *Archaeological Excavations of Fortified Sites on Taveuni, Fiji*, Asian and Pacific Archaeology Series, No. 6, Social Science Research Institute, University of Hawaii, Honolulu.

Frost, E.L. 1979 'Fiji' in J.D. Jennings (ed.) *The Prehistory of Polynesia*, pp. 61–81, ANU Press, Canberra.

Geddes, W.R. 1945 *Deuba: A Study of a Fijian Village*, The Polynesian Society, Wellington.

Geraghty, P.A. 1977 'How a Myth is Born: the Story of the Kaunitoni Story', *Mana* 2:25–29.

Geraghty, P.A. 1983a 'Pulotu, Polynesian Homeland', *Journal of the Polynesian Society* 102(4):343–384.

Geraghty, P.A. 1983b *The History of the Fijian Language*, University of Hawaii Press, Honolulu.

Gifford, E.W. 1951a 'Fijian Mythology, Legends and Archaeology' in *Semitic and Oriental Studies*, University of California, Publications in Semitic Philology 11:167–177.

Gifford, E.W. 1951b 'Archaeological Excavations in Fiji', *University of California Anthropological Records* 13:189–288.

Gifford, E.W. 1952 'Tribes of Viti Levu and their Origin Places', *University of California Anthropological Records* 13:5, University of California Press, Berkeley.

Gravelle, K. 1979 'A History of Fiji in Three Parts', *Fiji Times*, Suva, Fiji.

Green, R. and A. Pawley 1999 'Early Oceanic Architectural Forms and Settlement Patterns: Linguistic, Archaeological and Ethnological Perspectives' in R. Blench and M. Spriggs (eds) *Archaeology and Language*, Vol. 3, pp. 31–89, Routledge, London.

Jackson, J. 1853 'Jackson's Narrative' in J.E. Erskine, *Journal of a Cruise among the Islands of the Western Pacific Including the Feejees and others Inhabited by the Polynesian Negro Races, in Her Majesty's Ship Havannah*, pp. 411–477, John Murray, London.

Kaplan, M. 1988 Land and Sea and the new White Men: A Reconsideration of the Fijian *Tuka* Movement. Unpublished PhD thesis, University of Chicago, Chicago.

Kaplan, M. and M. Rosenthal 1993 'Battlements, Temples and the Landscape of *Tuka*: the Archaeological Record of a Cultural Transformation in 19th-Century Fiji', *Journal of the Polynesian Society* 102(2):121–146.

Katz, R. 1993 *The Straight Path*, Addison-Wesley, Reading, Mass.

Koto, S. n.d. *A iTovo Vakaviti*, 45 pp. (This is an account of Fijian customs.)

Lasaqa, I. 1984 *The Fijian People before and after Independence*, ANU Press, Canberra.

Lyth, R.B. 1836–1844 Journal of Richard Burdsall Lyth 1836–1844, Manuscript, Mitchell Library, Sydney.

MacNaught, T. 1971 Subjugation of the Highlands of Viti Levu, Fiji. Unpublished BA Hons thesis, Macquarie University, Sydney.

MacNaught, T. 1982 *The Fijian Colonial Experience: A Study of the Neotraditional Order under British Colonial Rule prior to World War II*, Pacific Research Monograph 7, ANU Press, Canberra.

Markham, G.H.W. 1869–74 The Diary of G.H.W. Markham, 1869–1874. Manuscript, Mitchell Library, Sydney.

Nayacakalou, R.R. 1975 *Leadership in Fiji*, Oxford University Press, Melbourne.

Nayacakalou, R. R. 1978 *Tradition and Change in the Fijian Village*, Fiji Times and Herald Ltd, Suva.

NLC [Native Lands Commission] Legislative Council Paper No. 27 of 1914, paras. 3–11. Proceedings of Native Lands Commission dated 6 June 1914.

NLC [Native Lands Commission] Legislative Council Paper No. 94 of 1927, paras. 36–45. Proceedings of the Native Lands Commission dated 4 October 1927.

NLC [Native Lands Commission] n.d. Notes taken from Ao i Tukutuku Raraba, for *yavusa* in the Yasawa Group, the Nadi/Lautoka area, and N.E. Viti Levu (Ra).

Palmer, J.B. 1969 'Ring-ditch Fortifications on Windward Viti Levu', *Archaeology and Physical Anthropology in Oceania* 4:181–187.

Parke, A.L. 1971 'Some Prehistoric Fijian Ceremonial Sites on the Island of Vanua Levu, Fiji (part 1)', *Archaeology and Physical Anthropology in Oceania* 6:243–267.

Parke, A.L. 1993 'Investigations at Vatanitawake: a Ceremonial Mound on the Island of Bau, Fiji', *Bulletin of the Indo-Pacific Prehistory Association* 13:94–115.

Parke, A.L. 1998 'Navatanitawake Ceremonial Burial Mound, Bau, Fiji: Some results of 1970 investigations', *Archaeology in Oceania* 33(1):20–27.

Parke, A.L. 2000 'The Monolith and the Cross: The Wesleyan Assault on Fijian Customs and Beliefs' in T. Denham and S. Blau (eds) *Proceedings of the Second National Archaeology Students' Conference* (01/09/1999), pp. 13–18, School of Archaeology and Anthropology, The Australian National University, Canberra.

Parke, A.L. 2001 *Seksek e Hatana: Strolling on Hatana*, Institute of Pacific Studies, University of the South Pacific, Suva.

Parke, A.L. n.d. –a. *Navatu Origins and Dialect*, 109 pp.

Parke, A.L. n.d. –b. *Vatanitawake, Bau: The 1970 Investigations,* 72 pp.

Parry, J.T. 1977 *Ring-ditch Fortifications in the Rewa Delta, Fiji: Air Photo Interpretation and Analysis*, Bulletin of the Fiji Museum 3, Oceania Printers, Suva.

Parry, J.T. 1982 *Ring-ditch Fortifications in the Navua Delta. Fiji: Air Photo Interpretation and Analysis.* Bulletin of the Fiji Museum 7, Oceania Printers, Suva.

Pawley, A.K. and T. Sayaba 1971 'Fijian Dialect Divisions: Eastern and Western Fiji', *Journal of the Polynesian Society* 80:405–436.

Pawley, A.K. 1981 'Melanesian Diversity and Polynesian Homogeneity: a Unified Explanation for Language' in J. Hollyman and A. Pawley (eds) *Studies in Pacific Languages and Cultures in Honour of Bruce Biggs,* pp. 269–309, Linguistic Society of New Zealand, Auckland.

Pritchard, W.T. 1866 *Polynesia Reminiscences: Life in the South Pacific Islands*, Chapman and Hall, London.

Raven-Hart, R. 1953 'A Dialect of Yasawa Island (Fiji)', *Journal of the Polynesian Society* 62(1):33–56.

Ravuvu, A. 1983 *Vaka i Taukei, The Fijian Way of Life*, Institute of Pacific Studies, The University of the South Pacific, Suva.

Ravuvu, A. 1987 *The Fijian Ethos*, Institute of Pacific Studies, Suva.

Rosenthal, M. 1991 *Realms and Rituals: the Form and Rise of Civitas and Urbs in Southeastern Viti Levu, Fiji.* PhD Thesis, University of Chicago, University Microfilms, Ann Arbor.

Roth, G.K. 1953 'Some Chiefly Fijian Customs', *Transactions and Proceedings of the Fiji Society of Science and Industry* 2:155–163.

Routledge, D. 1985 *Matanitu: The Struggle for Power in Early Fiji*, University of the South Pacific, Fiji Times Ltd., Suva.

Sahlins, M.D. 1963 'Poor Man, Rich Man, Big Man, Chief: Political Types in Melanesia and Polynesia', *Comparative Studies in Society and History* 5(3):285–303.

Sahlins, M.D. 1968 *Tribesmen*, Prentice-Hall, Englewood Cliffs, New Jersey.

Sahlins, M.D. 1981 'The Stranger-King or Dumezil among the Fijians', *Journal of Pacific History* 16:107–132.

Sayes, S.A. 1982 Cakaudrove: Idea and Reality in a Fijian Confederation, Unpublished PhD Thesis, The Australian National University, Canberra.

Sayes, S.A. 1984 'The Paths of the Land: Early Political Hierarchies in Cakaudrove, Fiji', *Journal of Pacific History* 19:3–20.

Scarr, D. 1980 *Viceroy of the Pacific. The Majesty of Colour: A Life of Sir John Bates Thurston,* Vol. 2, ANU Press, Canberra.

Scarr, D. 1984 *Fiji, a Short History*, Allen and Unwin, Sydney.

Schütz, A.J. 1962 A Dialect Survey of Viti Levu. Unpublished PhD Thesis, Cornell University, New York.

Seemann, E.G. 1862 *Viti: An Account of a Government Mission to the Vitian or Fijian Islands in the Years 1860–61*, Macmillan and Company, Cambridge.

Seymour-Smith, C. 1986 *Dictionary of Anthropology*, Palgrave, London.

Smythe, S.M.B. 1864 *Ten Months in the Fiji Islands*, J.H. and J. Parker, Oxford.

Spate, O.H.K. 1959 *The Fijian People: Economic Problems and Prospects, a report*, Government Press, Suva.

Thomas, N. 1986 *Planets Around the Sun: Dynamics and Contradictions of the Fijian Matanitu*, Oceania Monographs No. 31. University of Sydney, Sydney.

Thomson, B. 1908 *The Fijians: A Study of the Decay of Custom*, Dawsons, London.

Toganivalu, D. n.d. A History of Bau, Typescript in National Archives of Fiji, F62/247.

Toren, C. 1995 'Seeing the Ancestral Sites: Transformations in Fijian Notions of Land' in E. Hirsch and M. O'Hanlon (eds) *The Anthropology of Landscape*, pp. 163–183, Oxford University Press, Oxford.

Triffitt, G. 2000 'The Dialects of the Yasawa Islands of Fiji' in B. Palmer and P. Geraghty (eds) *SICOL: Proceedings of the Second International Conference on Oceanic Linguistics, Vol. 2: Historical and Descriptive Studies*, pp. 315–327, Pacific Linguistics 505, ANU Press, Canberra.

Ward, R.A. 1965 *Land Use and Population in Fiji: A Geographical Study*, Her Majesty's Stationery Office, London.

Waterhouse, J. 1866 *The King and the People of Fiji*, Wesleyan Conference Office, London.

Wilkes, C. 1845 *Narrative of the United States Exploring Expedition (during years 1838, 1839, 1840, 1842)*, Vol. 3, 1985 reprint, Fiji Museum, Suva.

Williams, T. 1858 *Fiji and the Fijians*. Vol. 1, *The Islands and Their Inhabitants*, Alexander Heylin, London.

Other references on Fijian history and archaeology consulted by Aubrey Parke

Anderson, A. and G. Clark 1999 'The Age of Lapita Settlement in Fiji', *Archaeology in Oceania* 34:31–39.

Best, S. 1981 Excavations at Site VL 21/5 Naigani Island, Fiji, a preliminary report, Department of Anthropology, University of Auckland.

Bigay, J. and F. Rajotte (eds) 1981 *Beqa, Island of Firewalkers*, Institute of Pacific Studies, University of South Pacific, Suva.

Birks, L. 1973 *Archaeological Excavations at Sigatoka Dune Site, Fiji, Bulletin of the Fiji Museum*, No. 1, Suva.

Burley, D.V. 1998 'Tongan Archaeology and the Tongan Past, 2850–150 B.P', *Journal of World Archaeology* 12(3):337–392.

Churchward, C.M. 1941 *A New Fijian Grammar*, Government of Fiji, Australasian Medical Publishing Co., Sydney.

Clark, G. and G. Hope 2001 'Archaeological and Palaeoenvironmental Investigations on Yacata Island, northern Lau, Fiji', *Domodomo* 13(2):29–47.

Clark, G., A. Anderson and S. Matararaba 2001 'The Lapita Site at Votua, Northern Lau', *Archaeology in Oceania* 36 (3):134–145.

Clark, G.R. and G. Hope 1997 Preliminary Report on Archaeological and Palaeoenvironmental Investigations in Northern Lau (Mago, Yacata-Kaibu and Vatuvara), Report to the Fiji Museum, Suva.

Clark, J.T. and T. Cole 1997 Environmental Change and Human Prehistory in the Central Pacific: Archaeological and Palynological Investigations on Totoya Island, Fiji, Unpublished report to the Fiji Museum, Suva.

Clunie, F. 1977 *Fijian Weapons and Warfare*, Fiji Museum Bulletin 2, Fiji Museum, Suva.

Clunie, F. 1986 *Yalo i Viti, Shades of Fiji*, Fiji Museum, Suva.

Crocombe, R. (ed.) 1987 *Land Tenure in the Pacific*, 3rd ed., University of the South Pacific, Suva.

Crocombe, R. and M. Meleisea (eds) 1994 *Land Issues in the Pacific*, Macmillan Brown Centre for Pacific Studies, Christchurch, New Zealand.

Derrick, R.A. 1953 'Fijian Warfare', *Transactions and Proceedings of the Fiji Society of Science and Industry* 2:137–146.

Derrick, R.A. 1959 '1875–Fiji's Darkest Hour–An Account of the Measles Epidemic of 1875', *Transactions and Proceedings of the Fiji Society* 6:3–16.

Duperrey, L.I. 1826 *Voyage autour du Monde executé par Ordre du Roi sur la Corvette de sa Majésté 'La Coquille', pendant les années 1822–1825*, Bertrand, Paris.

Fison, L. 1880 'Notes on Fijian Burial Customs', *Journal of the Royal Anthropological Institute* 10:137–149.

Fison, L. 1882 'On Fijian Riddles', *Journal of the Royal Anthropological Institute* 11:406–410.

Flower, U.H. 1881 'On the Cranial Characteristics of the Natives of the Fiji Islands', *Journal of the Royal Anthropological Institute* 10:153–174.

Garvey, R. 1959 'The Chiefly Island of Bau', *Transactions and Proceedings of the Fiji Society* 6:157–167.

Gifford, E.W. 1955 'Six Fijian Radiocarbon Dates', *Journal of the Polynesian Society* 64:240.

Green, R.C. 1963 'A Suggested Revision of the Fijian Sequence', *Journal of the Polynesian Society* 72:235–253.

Green, R.C. 1986 'Some Basic Components of the Ancestral Polynesian Settlement Scheme: Building Blocks for more Complex Polynesian Societies' in P.V. Kirch (ed.) *Island Societies: Archaeological Approaches to Evolution and Transformation,* pp. 315–327, Cambridge University Press, Cambridge.

Henderson, G.C. 1931 *Fiji and the Fijians, 1835–1856*, Angus and Robertson, Sydney.

Hocart, A.M. 1929 *Lau Islands, Fiji*, Bernice P. Bishop Museum Bulletin No. 62, Honolulu.

Hocart, A.M 1952 *The Northern States of Fiji*, Occasional Papers No. 11. The Royal Anthropological Institute of Great Britain and Ireland, London.

Hunt, T.L. 1980 Towards Fiji's Past: Archaeological Research on Southwestern Viti Levu. Unpublished MA Thesis, University of Auckland, Auckland.

Hunt, T.L. 1986 'Conceptual and Substantive Issues in Fijian Prehistory' in P.V. Kirch (ed.) *Island Societies: Archaeological Approaches to Evolution and Transformation*, pp. 6–32, Cambridge University Press, Cambridge.

Jennings, J.D. (ed.) 1979 *The Prehistory of Polynesia*, ANU Press, Canberra.

Kamikamica, J.N. 1987 'Fiji: Making Native Land Productive' in Crocombe R. (ed.) *Land Tenure in the Pacific*, University of the South Pacific, Suva.

Kirch, P.V. 1984 *The Evolution of the Polynesian Chiefdoms*, Cambridge University Press, Cambridge.

Kirch, P.V. (ed.) 1986 *Island Societies: Archaeological Approaches to Evolution and Transformation*, Cambridge University Press, Cambridge.

Kirch, P.V. and T.L. Hunt 1988 'The spatial and temporal bounds of Lapita' in P.V. Kirch and T.L. Hunt (eds) *Archaeology of the Lapita Cultural Complex: A Critical Review*, pp. 9–31, Thomas Burke Memorial Washington State Museum Research Report No. 5, Seattle.

Lesson, R.P. 1839 *Voyage autour du Monde enterpris par Ordre du Gouvernment sur la Corvette 'La Coquille'*, Pourrat Freres, Paris.

Lester, R.H. 1941 'Kava Drinking in Viti Levu, Fiji', *Oceania* 12:97–121, 226–254.

Lester, R.H. 1953 'Secret Societies in Viti Levu', *Transactions and Proceedings of the Fiji Society* 2:117–134.

MacLachlan, R.R.C. 1938 'The Native Pottery of the Fiji Islands', *Journal of the Polynesian Society* 49:243–271.

Mead, S.M. 1975 'The Decorative System of the Lapita Potters of Sigatoka, Fiji' in S. Mead, H. Birks, L. Birks and E. Shaw (eds) *The Lapita Style of Fiji and its Associations*, pp. 19–43, Polynesian Society Memoir, Wellington.

Milner, G.B. 1971 'Fijian and Rotuman' in T.E. Sebeok (ed.), *Current Trends in Linguistics* 8:397–425. Mouton, The Hague and Paris.

Milner, G. B. 1972 *Fijian Grammar*, 3rd ed., Government Press, Suva.

Nadalo, I. 1959 'Old Wars of Western Fiji', *Transactions and Proceedings of the Fiji Society* 6:5157.

Nunn, P. 1999 'Lapita pottery from Moturiki Island, Central Fiji', *Archaeology in New Zealand* 42:309–313.

Nunn, P. and S. Matararaba 2000 'New Finds of Lapita Pottery in Northeast Fiji', *Archaeology in Oceania* 35:116–119.

Oliver, J. and W.G. Dix 1848 *Wreck of the Glide*, Wiley and Putnam, New York.

Overton, J. 1994 'Land Tenure and Cash Cropping in Fiji' in Crocombe, R. and M. Meleisea (eds), *Land Issues in the Pacific*, pp. 117–132, University of the South Pacific, Suva.

Palmer, J.B. 1965 'Excavations at Karobo, Fiji', *New Zealand Archaeological Association Newsletter*, 8:26–34.

Palmer, J.B. 1967a 'Sigatoka Research Project-Preliminary Report', *New Zealand Archaeological Association Newsletter* 10:2–15.

Palmer, J.B. 1967b *Archaeological Sites of Wakaya Island*, Records of the Fiji Museum, 1:2.

Palmer, J.B. 1968a 'Caves and Shelter Sites at Vatukoula, Fiji', *New Zealand Archaeological Association Newsletter* 11:150–4.

Palmer, J.B. 1968b 'Recent Results from the Sigatoka Archaeological Program' in I.Yawata and Y.H. Sinoto (eds) *Prehistoric Culture in Oceania: A Symposium*, pp. 19–27, Bishop Museum Press, Honolulu.

Palmer, J.B. 1971a *Sigatoka Research Project. Miscellaneous Papers: Naga Ceremonial Sites in Navosa Upper Sigatoka Valley*, final report No.1, Records of the Fiji Museum 1(5):92–106.

Palmer, J.B. 1971b 'Fijian Pottery Technologies: Their Relevance to Certain Problems of Southwest Pacific Prehistory' in R.C. Green and M. Kelly (eds) *Studies in Oceanic Prehistory* Vol. 2. Pacific Anthropological Records 12, pp. 77–103, Department of Anthropology, Bernice P. Bishop Museum, Honolulu, Hawaii.

Parke, A.L. 1965 'Archaeology in Fiji', *Transactions and Proceedings of the Fiji Society* 8:10–42.

Parke, A.L. 1972 'Some Prehistoric Fijian Ceremonial Sites on the Island of Vanua Levu, Fiji (part 2)', *Archaeology and Physical Anthropology in Oceania* 7:56–78.

Parke, A.L. 1995 'The Qawa Incident in 1968 and Other Cases of "Spirit Possession", Religious Syncretism in Fiji', *The Journal of Pacific History* 30(2):210–226.

Parke, A.L. 1997 'The Waimaro Carved Human Figures: Various Aspects of Symbolism of Unity and Identification of Fijian Polities', *The Journal of Pacific History* 32(2):209–216.

Parke, A.L. 2000 'Coastal and Inland Lapita Sites in Vanua Levu, Fiji', *Archaeology in Oceania* 35(3):116–119.

Parke, A.L. 2001 'Phallus-shaped and other Ceramic Handles of Vanua Levu. Fiji' in G.R. Clark, A.J. Anderson and T. Vunidilo (eds) *The Archaeology of Lapita dispersal in Oceania*, pp. 141–149, Pandanus Books, Canberra.

Parke, A.L. 2003 'Late Lapita Site on Yacata, Fiji' in C. Sand (ed.) *Pacific Archaeology: Assessments and Prospects. Proceedings of theInternational Conference for the 50th anniversary of the first Lapita excavation, Koné-Nouméa 2002*, pp. 187–190, Le Cahier de L'Archéologie en Nouvelle-Calédonie 15, Nouméa.

Parry, J.T. 1984 'Air Photo Interpretation of Fortified Sites: Ring-Ditch Fortifications in Southern Viti Levu, Fiji', *New Zealand Journal of Archaeology* 6:71–93.

Phillips, W.J. 1953(a) 'Breast Plates of Fiji', *Transactions and Proceedings of the Fiji Society* 4:52–53.

Phillips, W.J. 1953(b) 'Hillmen Armlets, Oldman Collection', *Transactions and Proceedings of the Fiji Society* 4:70.

Phillips, W.J. 1958 'Tabua in the Oldman Collection', *Transactions and Proceedings of the Fiji Society* 5:22–25.

Poignant, R. 1967 *Oceanic Mythology*, The Paul Hamlyn Publishing Group Ltd., London.

Quain, B.H. 1948 *Fijian Village*, University of Chicago Press, Chicago.

Raven-Hart, R. 1956 'A Village in the Yasawas (Fiji)', *Journal of the Polynesian Society* 65:95–154.

Reid, A.C. 1977 'The Fruit of the Rewa: Oral Traditions and the Growth of the Pre-Christian Lakeba State', *Journal of Pacific History* 12:2–24.

Roth, G.K. 1973 *Fijian Way of Life*, 2nd ed., Oxford University Press, Melbourne.

Roth, G.K. and P.A. Snow, (eds) 1944 *Extracts from Sources describing Fijian Customs for the Use of Candidates for the Lower Standard Examination in Fijian Customs*, Government Press, Suva.

Sahlins, M.D. 1962 *Moala: Culture and Nature on a Fijian Island*, The University of Michigan Press, Ann Arbor.

Sand, C. and F. Valentin 1997 'Cikobia et Naqelelevu: Programme archéologique et anthropologique sur deux iles de Fidji. Resultats préliminaires de la mission', Department Archéologie, Service des Musées et Patrimoine, Nouméa, Nouvelle Calédonie.

Sand, C., F. Valentin and T. Sorovi-Vunidilo 2000 'At the border of Polynesia: Archaeological research in the East-Fijian islands of Cikobia and Naqelelevu' in P. Bellwood, D. Bowdery, J. Allen, E. Bacus and G. Summerhayes (eds), *Indo-Pacific Prehistory: The Melaka Papers* Vol. 4, Bulletin of the Indo-Pacific Prehistory Association 20:107–123, ANU Press, Canberra.

Sand, C., F. Valentin, T. Sorovi-Vunidilo, J. Bole, A. Ouetcho, S. Matararaba, F. Naucubalavu, Baret et L. D. Lagarde 1999 *Cikobia-i-ra. Archéologie d'une ile fidgienne*. Département Archéologie, Service des Musées et Patrimoine, Nouméa, Nouvelle Calédonie.

Smart, C.D. 1965 'An Outline of Kabara Prehistory', *New Zealand Archaeological Association Newsletter* 8:43–52.

Surridge, M.N. 1944 'Decoration of Fiji Water-jars', *Journal of the Polynesian Society* 53:17–36.

Thompson, L. 1938a 'Adzes from the Lau Islands, Fiji', *Journal of the Polynesian Society* 47:97–108.

Thompson, L. 1938b 'The Pottery of the Lau Islands, Fiji', *Journal of the Polynesian Society*, 47: 109–113.

Thompson, L. 1940 *Southern Lau, Fiji: An Ethnography*, Bernice P. Bishop Museum Bulletin No.162, Honolulu.

Thomson, B. 1894 *Diversions of a Prime Minister*, Dawsons, London.

Tippett, A.R. 1958 'The Nature and Social Function of Fijian War', *Transactions and Proceedings of the Fiji Society* 5:137–155.

Tippett, A.R. 1959 'The Survival of an Ancient Custom Relative to the Pig's Head, Bau, Fiji', *Transactions and Proceedings of the Fiji Society* 6:30–39.

Tippett, A.R. 1968 *Fijian Material Culture: A Study of the Cultural Content, Function and Change*, Bernice P. Bishop Museum Bulletin No. 232, Honolulu.

Tui Nawaka. *Yavusa ko Vunatoto*, 29 pp. (This is an account written in about 1919 by the chief of the Nawaka polity.)

Unknown. *Ko Viti Makawa*, 17 pp. (An account of the traditional origins of the Fijians.)

Unknown. *Ai Tukutuku Makawa kei Viti: A i Tekivu ni Kawa ni Kai Viti*, 7 pp. (An account of the traditional origins of the Fijians.)

Wilson, J. 1799 *A Missionary Voyage to the Southern Pacific Ocean*, Chapman, London.

www.ingramcontent.com/pod-product-compliance
Lightning Source LLC
Chambersburg PA
CBHW061306270326
41935CB00032B/1848